The Super '70s

Memories from Pro Football's Greatest Era

By

Tom Danyluk

The Super '70s
Published through Mad Uke Publishing

ISBN 0-9770383-0-0

Table of Contents

Acknowledgements

To the Good Lord, for motivation and helping me to find the right word.

To my father, for teaching the game to me. There's no better complement than hearing you say, "That's good stuff!"

To my mother, for understanding why all those Sunday afternoons were so important.

To Paul Najjar – "Jiggs" – who walked along for the entire journey and reminded me that "You gotta put the crib in the crib."

To AJR, for being a friend and opening some very important doors.

To Dr. Z, pro football's greatest writer, for inspiration.

To Steve Sabol, the game's invaluable historian, for keeping the past alive.

To Pete Rozelle, who always felt the game was more important than the dollar sign.

And finally, to my wife Melinda, for everything.

Foreword

On the first day of freshman football practice at Stanford in September 1949, our coach, Chuck Taylor, who would later coach a Rose Bowl team and become Director of Athletics, gave us the straight talk on the battle for positions.

"Everything is wide open," he said, echoing a sentiment I've heard, oh, maybe 500 times since then. "There will be competition at every spot."

Then he lined up his first unit, consisting of the guys who had been the most highly recruited. During the course of our season that lineup changed by exactly one position, and that was caused by injury. So much for competition.

This was one of the early lessons I got in what I came to call Coaches' Bullshit. You know, the same old jazz they feed the media: "Well, on offense we've got to make a positive gain on first down to stay out of third and long situations, and on defense we've got to mix things up and give 'em different looks, and...blah blah blah..." My wife once recited the whole shpiel for me, verbatim, and if there would have been any reporters around, they'd have dutifully written it all down.

Only back in '49 those were his own guys that Chuck Taylor was bullshitting. It's just that this is so deeply ingrained in the fabric of the sport that it's impossible to avoid, the coaches' bullshit being only a microcosm of its deeper manifestation, which permeates what you constantly hear on TV (call it Hype) and read in the papers, etc. We are so regularly bombarded with this stuff that we don't even notice it anymore. It's like waves washing on a beach.

Therefore it comes as a bit of a shock and a distinct pleasure to run across something that cuts through the layers of fluff, that seeks the truth beneath the clichés, that actually tries to bring across observations that have not been already repeated ad infinitum. That's Tom Danyluk's *Super '70s*, a book that has given me tremendous enjoyment, which is not easy for me to say about any sports book.

OK, I can hear the cynics out there. Danyluk praises Z in Chapter Three; Z returns the favor in the foreword. One hand washes the other, and away we go in a journalistic hall of mirrors. C'mon now. It's not all praise, is it? The guy called me an arrogant prick, did he not? My wife cried when she read that. She cried because she was laughing so hard.

"Really nailed you, didn't he?" she said. Yeah, nailed me, and nailed a lot of other people, too, in this eyes-wide-open look at a tremendously important era in the history of the game. As they say in those book review digests --- "*Highly Recommended*."

Paul Zimmerman
June 2005

Introduction

It was an age of giants. David and the Goliaths, only in these times the Goliaths roamed the earth unopposed, raising havoc in the villages while David hid under a blanket in the corner. In this version of the story, David didn't have much of a say in anything.

It was pro football, and these terrors were called Steelers and Raiders, Cowboys and Vikings. Some took on names of the animal gods, like Rams and Dolphins. Not much is remembered about the factions that rose to challenge them – teams from places like Atlanta, Detroit, Philadelphia or St. Louis. And those challenges, mostly futile, were also few.

As the National Football League moved out of the turbulent 1960s, it carried along memories of a Green Bay Packer dynasty that blanketed nearly an entire decade, as well as the satisfaction that its war with an emerging AFL had ended efficaciously.

In 1970 a new football league had been forged. The merger of two former adversaries now combined the rugged defense and ground attack mentality of the NFL with the bold, quick-strike progressiveness of the American Football League. The mixture was a dynamic one, and what emerged became the modern face of America's sporting passion. It was now the NFC versus the AFC, and that chemistry produced what many now call the golden age of pro football.

It was The Super '70s.

The decade was marked by a handful of elite teams and the thunder of their head-on collisions. There were multiple-Super Bowl winners such as the Miami Dolphins, Pittsburgh Steelers and Dallas Cowboys. There were powerhouses like the Oakland Raiders, Los Angeles Rams and Minnesota Vikings, which made frequent appearances in their conference title games. The rest of the league could only stare on in envy.

The 1970s revealed timeless moments, like Roger Staubach's "Hail Mary" heave, the Steelers' Immaculate Reception and O.J. Simpson cracking the 2,000-yard mark in frozen Shea Stadium.

The decade gave us tremendous feats and milestones, like the St. Louis Cardinals allowing just eight quarterback sacks in all of 1975, or Baltimore's Bert Jones completing 17 straight passes against the New York Jets. 73,000 fans watched the Rams' Lawrence McCutcheon erupt for 202 rushing yards in a playoff at the L.A. Coliseum.

This book is a collection of interviews with some of the individuals who made pro football of that era memorable. Winning coaches like Chuck Fairbanks and Bum Phillips. Electrifying players like Cliff Harris and Archie Manning. Hall of Fame broadcasters like Curt Gowdy and Charlie Jones.

Not all the names are as well known or as celebrated, but their stories are equally as engaging. Pittsburgh's Mike Wagner, an eleventh-round draft pick, started at safety on all four Steelers Super Bowl teams. Cedric Hardman anchored a raging defensive line in San Francisco that once sacked a quarterback 10 times in a game. Jack Patera took a bunch of expansion rejects called the Seattle Seahawks and turned them into the most entertaining sideshow in football.

The questions posed to these individuals were meant to be stimulating, to avoid cliché. I wanted to know about their relationships and separations in football, about their great successes and painful failures. The intent was to provoke thought, to hear that short pause before a response. I wanted to hear emotion in their voices.

There's one further point I'd like to address, and that's regarding the disparity between white and black subjects in this book. The mix is way out of proportion. 15 of the interviewees are white and only three are black – Larry Little, Hardman and McCutcheon. Meanwhile, nearly 50% of the NFL players during that decade were black.

That's troublesome. It bothers me that this could be interpreted as some form of racial slant, that the reader could view this imbalance as some sort of underlying bias.

Is it possible that I intentionally minimized or ignored the contributions of black athletes to the NFL? Or that I simply *didn't* want to hear their stories? Of course not.

In selecting interviewees for this book, only two criteria had to be met. First, the individual must have played a significant role in professional football during the 1970s – coaches, players, media members, whoever. Identifying people that met this requirement was the easy part.

The second criterion was simply finding those who'd *agree* to participate. That's where the balance started to tilt.

For the record, the following individuals either politely declined or chose to ignore my request for their time: Drew Pearson, Robert Newhouse, Lynn Swann, Earl Campbell, Harold Carmichael, Matt Blair, Chuck Foreman and John Jefferson. All are African-American.

On the other hand, Bill Walsh, Don Shula, John Madden and Pat Summerall also refused. So did Terry Bradshaw, Joe Theismann, Dan Fouts and John Riggins. All of them are white.

The truth is that the men featured in this book were simply the ones who said, "*Yes, count me in. Let's have a conversation.*" Black or white wasn't an issue, and that's a point of clarity I felt obligated to make.

Moving on, the NFL of the 1970s is much different than the one we see in 2005. Today's players are larger, faster and richer. They train for a job that is now a year-round commitment.

But the game itself still mattered back then. "Football was still something *sacred*," says Hardman. Big money hadn't poisoned it yet. The action on the field was what counted most.

Today, marketing is king, and hype is its henchman. Overexpansion has helped erode the overall caliber of play in the NFL, while 49ers head coach Mike Nolan can't wear a suit on the sideline because it's not "officially licensed." Lawyers are everywhere. For today's league, pro football is no longer a game. It's "the product." The whole thing has gone corporate.

Show me the money.

"You can argue that pro football reached its apex during the 1970s," says Steve Sabol, president of NFL Films. "We'll never see another era like it. So much passion and intensity and tradition. It wasn't overexposed. Each Sunday was still an event. It's unfortunate that writers and historians haven't done more to promote what happened during those years."

In *The Super '70s*, I present an honest attempt.

— 1 —
Art Rooney, Jr., Director of Player Personnel
Pittsburgh Steelers (1964-1986)
July 19, 2002

•

"I am a choreographer. A choreographer is a poet. I do not create. God creates. I assemble, and I will steal from everywhere to do it."
- George Balanchine, former director, New York City Ballet

"You can lose with good football players, but you can never, ever win without them."
- Art Rooney, Jr.

• •

From a hill overlooking downtown Pittsburgh known as Mount Washington, you get a very clear look of what used to be.

"Right down there," said Steelers Vice President Art Rooney, Jr., staring out from his window seat in a bustling restaurant. "That's where it all happened."

"Where" is the plot of ground on which Three Rivers Stadium once stood, the former domain of the Pittsburgh Steelers. An arena of concrete that housed a team of steel, and the words etched into its tempered metal read: "Abandon All Hope, Ye Who Enter Here."

A place where champions and heroes once dwelled. Cars and buses now park there.

"I watched the stadium implode on TV that day," he said. "They showed it over and over. The first seven or eight times, it didn't really faze me. Then after the ninth time, something hit me. I began to think of all the players and coaches and the workouts and the great games. I spent so much time down there, trying to build something good, and then it was gone. I needed a moment, I really did.

"It's funny. I go down to Heinz Field, where the team plays now, and nobody there knows me anymore."

But, oh man, do people still remember those fearsome, conquering Steeler units that Rooney helped construct during the early 1970s. "Probably the greatest collection of football talent ever assembled," proclaimed George Young, the late general manager of the New York Giants. "A team with no weakness."

He started out simply as a member of a pro football family, son of team owner Art Rooney, a man they called "The Chief." That, in Art Junior's mind, is where the football privileges ended.

"People think that if you were a Rooney you automatically could work for the Steelers," he says. "That wasn't true. You had to really show some genuine interest and dedication. Going through school, I had interests in history and acting, but I really wanted to be a part of that football team. My mom finally got me a job selling tickets. Hey, it was a start."

By the mid-1960s, Art Jr. had worked his way into the world of college scouting and was given the title of Director of Player Personnel. The Steelers had always been a Jenga-type operation in the way it collected and secured its young talent – bring in the players, erect the foundation while at the same time pulling out

1

key parts and throwing away gobs of valuable draft choices. Coaches came and went, but inevitably by each season's end the inspectors would come by and hammer up condemned signs on the teetering structure.

One thing was consistent in Pittsburgh – it was always a good time to rebuild. Same old Steelers.

From 1958 through 1967, the Steelers owned 70 choices in the top seven rounds of the NFL draft. They used only 26 of them and frivoled away the rest. It was frustrating to Art Jr., who had finally seen enough.

"Ridiculous," he remembers. "We were always trading away our future and getting players other teams didn't want. That had to stop or we were never going to get better. I don't think we had more than one complete draft between 1958 and 1970."

The bleeding finally ended in 1969 in the form of a raging obstruction from North Texas State named Mean Joe Greene and his rookie head coach, Chuck Noll, who'd been given final say over the team's draft decision. The Steelers were to be built on defense, around their new, prized defensive tackle. Pittsburghers scratched their heads. The papers asked, "Joe Who?"

"They'll find out who he is," answered Noll.

The Steelers had their first significant draft in years that winter, adding defensive end L.C. Greenwood and tackle Jon Kolb. It had begun. The first bolts had slammed into the frame of a coming juggernaut. Pro football shuddered as an ominous roll call continued to ring out through the Steel City:

Terry Bradshaw and Mel Blount in 1970.

Jack Ham, Dwight White and Mike Wagner in '71.

Franco Harris in '72, J.T. Thomas in '73.

1974 brought Lynn Swann, Jack Lambert, John Stallworth, Mike Webster and Donnie Shell, who they called "Torpedo." Then Noll looked around and saw that all his men were ready, and the march of champions commenced.

It began that season as the Steelers won their first-ever championship, stopping Minnesota in Super Bowl IX. It ended on the grass of the Rose Bowl five years later, as Art Sr. held up his team's fourth Lombardi trophy.

"My dad loved that football team, and I wanted to do the best job for him I could," says Rooney. "My goal was to give the coaches *too* many great football players. I wanted them to lose sleep at night thinking about who they had to get rid of because our talent was so deep. No easy cuts."

Roy McHugh, the former sports editor of *The Pittsburgh Press*, feels he understands the key to Rooney's success.

"Hard work, that's how. Art was extremely devoted to his job, almost obsessed by it. He didn't want any player that could help the Steelers to slip by him. People who knew Art outside of his job always saw a friendly, personable man. But when he was working, he was a completely different character – intense and very driven."

Nine of those men Rooney helped collect now have busts in the Hall of Fame. Noll is a member, too. "The Chief" was inducted in 1964. There are those that feel Junior and his eye for talent belong in there with them.

"I've campaigned for years to get Art elected," says *Sports Illustrated*'s Paul Zimmerman, a member of the Hall's selection board. "I don't vote for owners and administrators very often. They should have their own wing, separate from the players. But Art Jr. would get my vote in a heartbeat. Look at all the talent he helped assemble. His '74 draft is the greatest in NFL history."

"I'd be honored even if they just considered me," admits Rooney. "But I'm getting old now, and people are starting to forget. Besides, there are still some Steeler players that belong in there ahead of me."

Society often builds monuments to its great men and their glorious achievements. I've passed by this proud, neglected statue of a soldier in Chicago's North Side for years. Most people ignore it, but one day I stopped to take a look. It was General Phillip Sheridan, a Civil War hero, the man who cut off Lee's retreating forces at Appomattox. He helped rebuild the city of Chicago after its great fire. The statue was done by the same artist who chiseled the faces at Mount Rushmore, Gutzon Borglum.

A nod to history here, but nobody really knows of these men anymore. Time has marched on for too long.

In the world of pro football, those great men were the Pittsburgh Steelers of the 1970s. Chuck Noll was their leader. Art Rooney, Jr. was the artist.

And then they tore his monument down.

• • •

What was the path that led you from the Steelers ticket window to becoming the man behind the team's legendary drafts of the 1970s?

AJR: Scouting was something that always interested me. When I joined the scouting department in '64, Buddy Parker was the head coach and we didn't have any draft choices. He traded them all away! No firsts or seconds or thirds. It was awful. The team was always starting over, so when I started there was nothing for me to screw up! Parker was a great guy, a real character. He wanted his scouts to take pictures of the top prospects because he didn't want any stupid-looking players. He once said, "If I knew how ugly that Bob Ferguson from Ohio State [first-round choice in 1962] was, I never would have drafted him!"

I felt the scouting department was the one place where I could really make a difference, to do something good for the team. Working for the Steelers was a family thing, so it quickly became a passion. To me, it was an honor and a privilege just to be involved. Eventually, I asked my dad for a job in the scouting department.

Later I remember talking to one of my father's friends, an older gentleman who was very successful himself. He said, "You don't want to get into that scouting business. You're a family man, Art. You're going to be away from them all the time." He was right. I was never home. Man, I put a lot of time on the road, but I didn't care. I was willing to make the sacrifices. My wife really should've kicked me out. People talk about having priorities. Well, my priority was that fucking football team. Football was like a narcotic to me, and I got addicted. My family really wasn't a priority. It should've been.

Who were your most valuable teachers in learning how to evaluate pro football talent in those early days?

AJR: Two scouts named Will Walls and Jack Butler come to mind first. They started taking me around the country with them to watch players. Butler was once a top Steelers defensive back. He started out in the seminary, then went to college at St. Bonaventure. My Dad's brother, Dan, was the athletic director there, so he put a fix in for Butler to get a football uniform. Jack became a fine player and eventually signed as a free agent with the Steelers in 1950. Then he hurt his knee real bad and became a Steelers coach. He was a good coach but he kept getting run over all the time in practice by the players. I could relate to that. I could be run over on a wide sweep, too. Jack's problem was a gimpy knee, but mine was being a fat-ass without any lateral movement. Finally Coach Parker told Dad to get Butler off the field before he got killed. Lucky for me, Butler became a Steelers scout and really helped me. We traveled a lot together, talking about what made good prospects and good organizations.

Tell me about Will Walls.

AJR: A big, good-looking guy – part Indian, part Texan. That was until after JFK was shot in Dallas. Then he'd tell me, "Ya know, Arty, I'm really from Arkansas." Will was Sammy Baugh's top target at TCU, then he played for the Giants. He went to Hollywood and had a few parts, even turned down a screen test for *Gunsmoke*.

As a scout, Will logged more miles than a professional truck driver. He had a big ol' car loaded with things like hot plates, coffee makers, projectors and a sill camera, so much stuff that he crushed the damn springs. He always carried light bulbs because the motels skimped on them back then and he couldn't read at night without them. He also took a great big bar of soap because the motels had those little bars for "skinny-assed folks." And, of course, his .38 pistol.

Walls was forever putting the cart before the horse. His priorities were all mixed up. Ken Stilley, our head scout at the time, said that if Will was a stable boy, he'd spend more time cleaning up the little clump of horseshit in the corner than the big pile in the middle of the stable. He spent more time taking pictures of players for Parker than evaluating them, but he did log the miles and cover the schools.

I ran into him once at Colorado U. He came into the film room and watched a reel of a top prospect with me. "Artie," he said, "did ya see that fella flinch there?" He ran the picture back ten times in a row. "Remember, Artie – once a flincher, always a flincher."

Later, I asked him where he was headed next. "I'm movin' on, going to Utah," he said. "Then the Northwest."

I said, "That's a lot of driving, Willie."

"Yep," he said, "but I gotta cover these fellas."

Willie was very well loved by a lot of top people in the game. I liked him a lot, too, but I learned to discount his reports a bit. In terms of sophistication, they were comparable to the old World War I barn stormer or a two-winger. Don't ask him for the details about why a guy can play – he just felt it. Walls worked with BLESTO [Bears Lions Eagles Steelers Talent Organization] until he retired. He passed away when he was about 75. As the scouts would say, "He died with his boots off."

In becoming a scout, were you a quick learner?

AJR: I'd say so. I never stopped asking questions about what to look for. It was always, "Why? Why? Why?" I was probably a pain in the ass to a lot of people, but I made all the stops.

All those old scouts were terrific to me. They taught me everything from not forgetting foul weather gear to how to run a film projector. Stilley told me to make sure I was always invited back to a college the next year. He said, "Never be an asshole like that guy out west. What's his name? The guy from The Citadel... *Al Davis, that's it.* Stay away from Davis, Artie. And always send the coaches a postcard saying, 'Thanks for being so nice.'" He stressed how the small things were important.

What were some of your first observations in scouting football talent?

AJR: All football players are good athletes, but I had to learn to make distinctions in quickness, control, playing strength and playing speed. Then there are the intangibles – football intelligence and football character, which are important.

Take, for instance, a guy like Bobby Layne. Maybe he wasn't the greatest Christian in the world, but Layne had football character. He was never late for practice. He was always there early and stayed late. After the season was over, I sat down and added up all Layne's extra practice time. I couldn't believe it! Layne had practiced an entire month longer than the rest of the team! Now *that's* football character.

I believe in good citizenship, but you can't have too many cherubs on your team. Players have to be tough guys because football is a violent, emotional game. The intelligence part? They still give that Wunderlick test to players, but does that translate to how they think and react on the field? Not always.

As I became more involved, I saw that changes had to be made in our organization. We still didn't have any significant draft picks until around 1968 or '69, but we had started to run our scouting department like we did. My attitude was to bring in so many good players that the coaches couldn't fuck up the team. That might've been an immature approach, but that's exactly how I felt. Trading away our draft picks had really hurt us over the years, so I became a terror on insisting we build through the draft. In 1970, we were offered a bundle for the pick we used on Terry Bradshaw but we turned it down. In the old days we might have made that deal.

Did you seek advice from scouts or personnel men from other teams in the league?

AJR: Occasionally I would. One summer my dad sent me over to see Wellington Mara of the Giants. He was a serious draft guru in those days. One bit of advice he suggested was to have a big spring meeting to get the college prospects slotted in order. He told me, "Most of the players will remain the way you rated them in the spring, so that will become your map once the season starts. Barring any injuries, the good players should still be good." The Steelers had never done that, so that meeting with Wellington Mara became one of the stepping-stones we used to help mold our scouting department.

Eventually we learned that still wasn't good enough, that our system still needed refining. Butler suggested ranking players by their skill on the football field, regardless of position, and draft them accordingly. The idea was not to draft out of need. We developed a preferred 200-player list that would become our guideline during the draft. Mel Kiper and those TV draft gurus all do it now, but it wasn't common back in the '60s. The school of thought is, even if you need a tackle and the best one available is rated 15th best overall, you shouldn't pass up a cornerback or a receiver who is rated higher overall. You're leaving too much on the table. You're giving up the chance to draft a great player in order to take a good one, to fill a need. That's not the way to build a team.

I learned an early lesson, too. Occasionally I'd run into scouts who'd brag about all their draft picks who made the team. I was equally as bad until one of our assistant coaches, Jim Doran, straightened me out real quick. Once he said to me when I was boasting, "It's not only who made the team, Art, but what kind of a contribution did the players make? Did they become starters that the team could win with?" I never forgot that. You don't want to draft stiffs who come in and replace the stiffs you already have.

In the early 1960s, the Steelers began scouting many of the small, black colleges around the country – unknown, mysterious places like Bethune-Cookman and Florida A&M and Jackson State. That practice eventually yielded huge benefits to the team. How did the Steelers get directed toward that untapped talent pool?

AJR: I had been on the road since 1964 and eventually had developed some confidence in my ability to spot talent. The one thing that I saw was the great number of athletes at these black schools. I mean, you wanna talk about athletic bodies! These guys had great movement and skills and willingness, and they were just begging for the league to give them tryouts and jobs. The old white scouts would agree that these guys had ability, but they kept coming up with excuses as to why they couldn't play.

"They can't be quarterbacks, they can't be centers." All this *can't, can't, can't.* It was bullshit! I never fell for that. The black coaches and kids kept saying, "We can play! All we need is a chance." Well, the league is now 70-percent black. They were right. They could play!

Bill Nunn was the scout who really opened us up to the black schools. He is black, too. Nunn either scouted or signed seven guys who started on a Steelers Super Bowl team: Donnie Shell, Mel Blount, 'Fats' Holmes, L.C. Greenwood, Frank Lewis, Glen Edwards, John Stallworth and Sam Davis. Not bad work for an ex-sports writer. Maybe we could have done that without him, but I wouldn't bet on it.

How did Nunn join the Steelers organization?

AJR: My dad had a friend who was a writer for *The Pittsburgh Courier.* He talked Dad into hiring Nunn, who was the paper's sports editor, as a part-time talent scout for the Steelers. I was pissed purple. I knew we needed a scout, and I had come to realize how important the black schools were going to be for us, but I wanted to hire the scouts. Bill had been covering the black schools for the papers and visited them all the time. He had outstanding contacts. He even named the Black College All-Star football team for *The Courier*, but he was not my "A" guy.

One evening Dad got us both together. Nunn seemed like a nice guy who wanted to do well. He wasn't a bullshitter. So I gave Dad a qualified "okay," not that it made a difference. Well, Nunn quickly became very important to me. At first it was just his contacts, then it was his insight, then his dry humor. Before long he became a fine scout of all players. His agenda matured. He had to win, no matter if the prospect was black, white, blue or green. He even consented to toss Dad an Irishman now and then, but that's another story.

A token Irishman?

AJR: [Laughing] A player like Tyrone McGriff. What a great Irish name! Except he was from Florida A&M, an all-black school. I was a big pain in the ass as far as wasting draft picks, even if they were used late on Irishmen or relatives of Dad's friends or politicians. Free agents, maybe, but not draft picks. You only had twelve of them and I didn't want to waste a single one. Nunn would say, "C'mon, it's a late pick, Artie. And besides, 'The Chief' owns the team!" Dick Haley, another important scout for us, would say, "Yeah, lighten up a little with 'The Chief,' will ya?"

After the draft Dad said to me, "You said it was going to be an Irish kid in the 11th round. *McGriff's not even white!*" I said, "Well, Dad, you know the South – those black kids with Irish names. The kid probably had an Irish ancestor." He seemed to understand.

The next year he got me and said, "Look, I agree with what you said about those black Irish kids, but this year could you please get a *white* Irisher on a late round?"

Anyway, Nunn was insightful in his eye for football, but he also understood people and their ways, the human condition. For instance, John McMakin was a southern kid who lasted three years with us. He was a tough tight end, a slug-it-out type who made a nice contribution while we were still building the team. Near the end of his time as a Steeler he walked into our camp office. Nunn was the camp manager at the time. McMakin's hair was longer and he had a stylish bag over his shoulder, almost like a purse. A number of younger men were carrying them in those days. Nunn checked him in. He was very nice to the kid, but after he left Bill said to me, "McMakin is finished here – done."

I said, "We haven't even seen him on the field yet! Why would you say that?"

He replied, "McMakin's a biter and scratcher. Did you see that bag he's carrying? That's not his style. He was a fighter and now he's lost his edge. Without it he won't make the team." Well, Nunn was right again. He didn't make it.

Who Was That Moustached Man?

I was at a football banquet in New York with my Dad back in 1972. It was springtime. Toward the end of the evening, some guy with a big, handlebar moustache came over and handed him a piece of paper. I didn't know who he was. "The Chief" took a look at it and said, "Oh, that's very nice. Thank you, thank you…" then handed it to me. It was a drawing of my Dad, a quick sketch. I just folded it up and put it in the pocket of my sport coat and forgot about it.

About a year or so later, I was out at Yonkers Racetrack in New York, watching a few of our horses run. Walter Sullivan was there. Walter was in the printing business and a relative of Billy Sullivan, the Patriots owner. He did a lot of programs for the racetracks. We were standing there talking, and for some reason I reached into the pocket of my sport coat. There was a piece of paper in it. I pulled it out, thinking, "What the hell is this?" and I opened it up.

"Whatcha got there, Art?" Walter asked me.

"Oh, just a sketch some guy did of my Dad. I must've been wearing the same sport coat the night he gave it to him." He asked to see it then took a look at the drawing. It was a picture of my Dad in a tux, puffing on one of his cigars. He stared at it for a moment.

"Where did you get this again?"

"At a dinner in New York, maybe a year ago. Jeez, I'm lucky I didn't send this coat to the cleaners with that in my pocket."

"You're right about that," he said. "I'm sure there aren't very many Art Rooney sketches like this one around.

"At least not ones done by Leroy Neiman."

— **Art Rooney, Jr.**

Let's talk about the events that led to the Steelers hiring Chuck Noll as head coach in 1969?

AJR: Bill Austin was our coach at the time and his teams weren't doing very well. We were 2-11-1 in his last year and it was obvious we needed to look for somebody else. My dad had me asking people I met on the road the question, "Who are the best three people available that would make a good NFL head coach." This Baltimore assistant coach named Chuck Noll was always being mentioned. Not always as the top guy, but still in the group of three. Our friend Upton Bell was with the Colts and mentioned Noll's name to us more than a few times. He said Noll was Don Shula's right-hand man. Dad finally called Shula, and Shula said he was real high on Noll so they brought him in for an interview.

Were you directly involved in the hiring process?

AJR: My brother Dan and Dad were the ones who really handled the interviews with coaches. I had a lot of ideas about who we should bring in, but they handled it. One day I stopped by our offices at the old Roosevelt Hotel in downtown Pittsburgh. It was a character place, like something out of Damon Runyan. We had real crummy offices there, but we were waiting for Three Rivers Stadium to be built to get our new quarters. I was told that Chuck Noll was in the hotel restaurant being interviewed by Dad and Dan. I wasn't invited but I sorta elbowed my way in. They were at the big front table where Dad held a lot of his conferences. I was introduced to Chuck and sat down and listened. Dad and Dan were very much the proper gentlemen, and all the proper business questions were being asked. It wasn't a lively event at all.

Well, I had my own agenda that day. I wanted to talk about committing to build the team through the draft. I wanted to talk about the Negro players. Did Noll have a quota system in mind? I think I made a statement that you couldn't win that way. Although Dad and Dan didn't say so, they gave me the impression that I was horning in on their party. The looks, the glares and the body language told me, "Hey rube, know your place and shut up." I got it all but a kick under the table.

Noll was this intelligent, mild, soft-spoken guy, but then all of a sudden he came to life on the subject. With a forceful tone he said, "I don't care what color my players are. I want great athletes, not good athletes. I want good people, and I want smart people. I will not make decisions based on race or the school the player attended. You find good players where they are." He was adamant in his position, and I absolutely agreed.

Was there a strong indication that Noll was going to want a large role in personnel decisions, decisions that would've crossed into your area of responsibility? You remember Bill Parcells' famous quote about "having to cook the dinner but not being allowed to buy the groceries."

AJR: I got that impression right away. Noll said he was a teacher, and that his players had to be teachable. They had to be decent men. He wanted nothing to do with troublemakers. He was saying exactly what I wanted to hear.

But then he started saying words I didn't want to hear. He said he needed the final say on draft picks, and that his coaches had to be involved in a big way. He also said he would be making all trades. I started to debate these points vehemently with him. I wanted to get right into it with Noll. Dad finally put me in my place and shut me up. Then as fast as it became a real meeting, things returned to being quiet and proper. It soon ended, and I kinda felt that I had queered the whole thing.

I wanted to have the last say in the draft. I told my Dad afterwards, "I'm doing all the work out there, so I want all the responsibility." I was still at the age where I had these noble ideas.

Dad wouldn't go for it. He said, "You're in charge of the scouting department, the book-keeping on players. The coach is the one who's going to get fired if he doesn't win, so he should be the one making decisions on his players."

So I was given the job of collecting, organizing and interpreting the information. I would follow Dad's orders, but I didn't intend on being a flunky. I made my opinions very clear. Sometimes I would get into it with the assistant coaches.

In what kind of situations?

AJR: Usually over personnel issues. What kind of players we were looking for, which guys we wanted to keep. Not so much with Noll as with his assistants. The assistant coaches helped me in a lot of ways but they were always so inconsistent. Also, they answered to the head coach, not to me, so I'm sure some of them thought I was just getting in the way. That friction existed up until my end times with the team.

Some of the coaches were very good judges of talent, some were okay, and others didn't give a damn. They wanted to spend all of their time coaching. Now and then you'd get one who was a mischief-maker, who put in no work at all and waited till the day before the draft to call Bo Schembechler or Woody Hayes and get the scoop. Then they'd push that player real hard. Hey, it was okay to talk to the college coaches, but be timely about it. Give us a chance to check those sources out.

How long into Noll's tenure did you recognize that he had become an asset to your scouting department?

AJR: Not long at all. Hey, I'll never deny that Noll was the man. When Noll arrived, we became great drafters. Before him we weren't. Our methodology was in place, but he was the balance that made the difference. He was very difficult to work with because he was so exacting. He'd come in after practice at St. Vincent's and talk to the scouts for an hour and a half. He liked working with the scouts. Do that four nights a week during camp, year after year, and that's a lot of hours spent with the coach. So we knew exactly what Noll was looking for.

Chuck Noll really had brass balls. Once he told me that's what was needed to run a successful football team. There wasn't a bit of phony in him. The Rooneys were all "people" people. Noll was like General George Marshall, and that was what we needed. Eventually Dan took on some of Noll's tough characteristics in running the team. Me? I was more like my mother. I was always afraid of being an asshole.

Noll was hired the night before the 1969 draft. You two quickly became acquainted.

AJR: We sure did. Noll arrived in Pittsburgh and we went right to our draft boards. All that was listed was the player's name, rating, height, weight, speed and school. Without a note, I stood there and talked about every one of them. Afterward, Dan told me it was my finest hour. "How could you recall all that stuff?" he asked. I didn't make anything up either. There was immediate agreement over whom to take in the first round. It was Joe Greene, who became the cornerstone of our defense.

The Steelers went 1-13 in that first year under Noll. The reward came in the form of a coin toss with the Chicago Bears over the right to draft a Louisiana quarterback named Terry Bradshaw. Bradshaw was widely regarded as the top collegiate talent in the 1970 draft. Were you convinced he was the right man for the Steelers?

AJR: Absolutely. We heard all the talk about him being a "dumb quarterback," but that was way overblown. He was a real talent. We had a lot of scouting reports on him, even the IQ test. Terry's score was okay. Not M.I.T. stuff, but okay.

Actually, Noll wanted to test the waters on a trade for Terry's rights, which bothered me. I had preached like St. John the Baptist about building the team through the draft and now we might look to trade him? Jack Butler told me that there wouldn't be another player like Bradshaw around for 10 or more years. I felt the same way. But Dad was thinking like Noll, leaning toward trading that pick to acquire some depth for the team.

If you trade that pick for, say, seven players, here's what you'd get – a couple of good players, a couple of injured guys, a troublemaker or two and another gingerbread they're trying to unload. So in adding this so-called "depth" to your team, at best you're buying respectability, not a championship. I really got into it with Dad once. We were in the car with my brother John, and I was almost crazed, really yelling at Dad. John had to calm me down. But I knew we absolutely had to take Bradshaw.

Had you lost that coin toss, the Steelers history might have been dramatically altered. What was Plan B?

AJR: That's an interesting question. 1970 wasn't a great year for overall talent in the draft, so there weren't a lot of other names that stood out for us. We looked at Mike Phipps of Purdue, another highly rated quarterback. He ended up going early, but we didn't think Phipps would ever be a great pro. The guy who actually was picked second was a defensive tackle from Notre Dame named Mike McCoy. Chuck wasn't too high on him. I recall McCoy having back problems so we shied away.

We thought a lot of a Penn Stater named Mike Reid, who ended up with the Bengals, but we didn't really need any more help on the defensive line. Then there was Duane Thomas, a very talented running back from West Texas State, but he had some personality issues that we weren't willing to deal with. My guess is if we had lost the coin toss, we would've traded the number two pick and moved down. That's exactly what the Bears did. They traded the pick to Green Bay.

Let's talk about the Noll-Bradshaw relationship that developed in the early '70s. Bradshaw has always claimed to be very bitter about the way Noll treated him during their years in Pittsburgh. He resented Noll's aloofness and lack of warmth. Do you feel that Noll should have handled Bradshaw differently?

AJR: Think of the toughest professor you ever had in college. They have their own sense of humor, their own agenda, maybe a little eccentric. To get through the course you had to get into their groove. That's the way it was with Chuck Noll.

Bradshaw was a real southern kid that came up to Pittsburgh with all this raw talent. He had never been exposed to a guy like Noll, an intellectual who'd say "We're gonna do things the right way. We're gonna take care of the little things, which helps take care of the big things." Basically, Terry couldn't relate to him.

Then the whole thing started about Bradshaw not being an intelligent guy, and that really hurt him. I guess Chuck didn't do much to help that situation. But remember what I said about football intelligence? Noll once told me, "Terry's not a dumbbell at all. He's smart enough to learn the plays. He's just a flighty guy." Noll wasn't being mean or cruel. He was commenting more on Terry's personality than his intelligence. But Bradshaw never looked beyond it and that wasn't going to change.

My dad was very concerned about Bradshaw in those early years. He'd take him home for dinner sometimes and say, "Terry, I'm an old man now, but I've been around the great ones – Babe Ruth, Jack Dempsey, Billy Conn, Man O' War. You're right in there with those guys. You're like Man O' War. You're like Babe Ruth."

Can you imagine having to tell Babe Ruth or Ty Cobb or Jimmy Brown that they were great? *They already knew it!* Well, Terry needed to hear that stuff but he wasn't going to get it from Chuck Noll. What Chuck eventually gave him was stability. He didn't screw him up on the field. It really was like a father-son relationship in many ways.

Do you recall a point when Bradshaw, in terms of his overall confidence, hit bottom?

AJR: It was probably back at the start of the '74 season. Chuck had given up on Terry a number of times, and he did again that year. Joe Gilliam was going to be Noll's man. Terry Hanratty was moved up to second-string and Terry was demoted to third. Noll was confident that Gilliam would develop. He had a great setup, a quick release and terrific vision. Babe Parilli once told me that out of those three, Gilliam had the best football mind.

After his demotion, the first thing Terry did was grow a beard. Then he started the old Johnny Unitas routine with us, coming into the stadium early and throwing the ball to whomever was around – the grounds crew, office guys, ball boys. "Just run as far as you can," he'd tell them, then he'd throw it and the ball would end up bouncing off their heads.

Terry was out there working his ass off. He spent a lot of time talking to "The Chief." He also turned to the Lord and started reading the Bible a lot. Then the breaks started to go his way. The next stops were the championships and Hall of Fame. I really admired the way he worked himself out of that low point in his life.

The 1971 draft was a jackpot, producing future stars like Dwight White, Jack Ham and Mike Wagner. Frank Lewis, a wide receiver from Grambling, was the Steelers' first-round choice that year.

AJR: We all really liked Lewis. We were in desperate need of offensive weapons to give Bradshaw some help. Lewis was poetry in motion, a beautiful athlete, but he was a very mild guy. Not flashy or aggressive like Lynn Swann and John Stallworth.

I remember one time we were playing the Houston Oilers. Their coaches box was on the same floor as the press box. I'm sitting there and this guy comes rushing past me, yelling, "He's in the game! He's in the game!" Everybody looked around to see what the hell was going on. This guy was alerting the other Houston coaches that Lewis was going in. They were scared to death of him. "Back those [secondary] guys up!" he yelled. "Get those bastards to drop back!"

You know, everybody talks about the great draft of 1974, with all the Hall-of-Famers, but look at some of the other names we got in '71: Ham, tackle Gerry Mullins, Dwight White, Ernie Holmes, Mike Wagner, Larry Brown. That draft gave us seven Super Bowl starters. It's a very underrated draft!

I'll tell you a funny story. After that draft was over, I was talking to Uppie Bell, who had become the GM of the Patriots. He was looking over the names of the players we had picked and giving me his opinion on them. He started right at the top.

"Frank Lewis – good player. I like the pick."

"Jack Ham? He's not strong enough to play linebacker in the pros."

"Mullins- don't know much about him"

"Dwight White? Who's Dwight White?"

His overall opinion was, *"Who the hell are these guys?"* Talk about feeling your heart sink. Here's a real good friend of mine, a very solid personnel guy, looking over my players and basically just shaking his head. At the time I thought, "Boy, I really screwed this one up."

1971 didn't offer a bumper crop of college linebackers, but the Steelers were thin at the position and needed help. The choice in the second round was between Penn State's Ham and Phil Villapiano of Bowling Green. Why Ham?

AJR: The scouting department loved Jack, but our assistant coaches wanted Villapiano. I blew my cork over this one. I said, "Ham is one of the top-rated players in the country, and you want us to take a guy who's no better than a second-rounder?!" The assistants were all good guys, but they were wrong on this one. Villapiano became a great player. He played a lot of years, but he was no Jack Ham.

I still joke about this story: After the draft we brought all the kids in for a physical and a brief team indoctrination. We had them in a suite at the Pittsburgh Hilton. They were all big, solid kids. Strong-looking, athletic types. Then I heard this knock on the door of the suite and I went over to answer it. There was a guy standing there in blue slacks, a white golf shirt and a windbreaker. Very meekly he says, "Is this the Steelers room?" I said yeah.

He said, "I'm looking for Mr. Rooney."

I said, "That's me. Why? Do you have a message for me?" Maybe I was a little curt because I thought he was a bellboy.

He said, "They told me to come up here. I'm Jack Ham."

I couldn't believe it! I had no idea who he was! I scouted Ham a lot in college but I'd never seen him in the lockerroom or out of his uniform! He didn't have the great, athletic body by any means. This future Hall of Famer is standing right in front of me, and I thought he was delivering a message or bringing up the urine sample bottles.

The next day we had all the players down at Three Rivers for a brief workout. Ham was standing there in a pair of shorts. He had no chest at all. No arms either. Skinny! Ham is an example of how Chuck Noll's weight-lifting program paid off. It built his upper body strength. He went from about 215 to 222, all muscle, and held it for most of his career.

Jack Ham became a tremendous player. The whole league was impressed by the way he played football, even the best players. One year he was playing in the Pro Bowl and Noll was coaching the AFC team. One of our scouts was in the elevator with a bunch of AFC defensive players. Some of them were bitching about having to learn Noll's defensive scheme for the game. "That damn Noll! We can't play this kind of defense. It's impossible to do some of this stuff!"

One of the other players spoke up and said, "It'll work."

They piped back, "What do ya mean it'll work? How's it gonna work?"

He looked at them and simply said, "Ham."

They paused for a moment. "Yeah, it'll work…"

The Steelers' Future? All They Saw Were Stars

The basement of the Pro Football Hall of Fame is, in many ways, a shelter, a place where the old days look for solace when they've been forgotten and left behind.

Treasures abound. Rare AFL media guides and old wool warm-ups. Cleats worn on famous days. Rows and rows of worn, beaten helmets sit on shelves with stories to tell. Legendary eyes peered from behind the facemasks.

Here is O.J. Simpson's Bills headgear, the paint still very white and clean. That's because you couldn't catch him. An ancient Raiders helmet sits without a number like an unmarked grave. The scrapes on the facemask say it probably belonged to a lineman. Maybe Art Shell or Jim Otto. An angry, black scuff remains after an attack from a Pittsburgh Steeler.

And nearby, off in a lonely corner, sits a large collection of books. Stacks of files in brown bindings, all piled hurriedly on top of each other. Some are water damaged. All of them are old, neglected.

Those books also have stories to tell. They speak of scouts' days on hot, sweaty practice fields and nights in front of clicking projectors. They were written by tired, frozen hands or in a dimmed motel room on a lonely wayside. Within those pages, friends, one can find the magic formula that produced one of pro football's most tyrannical reigns – the college scouting reports of the 1970s Pittsburgh Steelers.

I spent some time in that Canton basement one summer, sifting through pages and pages of profiles. Oh, the names! Joe Greene, Terry Bradshaw, Lynn Swann, Jack Lambert… Could those scouts have really conceived the greatness they were watching?

"All that work, all those hours traveling to places we'd never heard of," says former Steelers scouting director Art Rooney, Jr. "And now those reports are sitting in big, forgotten piles…Well, I guess it paid off, didn't it?"

I'd like to share a bit of what I found in that basement.

● ● ●

Mel Blount, cornerback, Southern University (6'3", 201): Perfect size and speed…Very tall and rangy, but still moves feet well…Comes up to hit good in drills…Covered man-to-man well and they have some fast kids here…Quick, but seems to lose something when receiver makes a break. I don't know if it's a lack of acceleration or a coaching point…I would like to get more of a line on his hitting ability…His coaches say he hits and I saw him crack a kid in practice…I think he could help us at free safety…I'd like to say for sure he could be a cornerback but I don't know how he would do with a guy like [Roy] Jefferson all the way deep…Maybe I am too cautious about this. **Projection: *Potential starter, 2nd round pick***

Jack Ham, linebacker, Penn State (6'2", 220): Pittsburgh area boy who is a top player…I think he would be playing regular for us by the middle of his first year…A middle backer at school but would be an OLB for us. However, he improved so much each game at MLB that I feel he'd play there for us with a little more weight and strength...He has the frame to get bigger and stronger...Does a good job of pursuing and getting to the wide plays...Plays off blockers well and fills holes good...Shows toughness in use of arms...Pass coverage is impressive...Good hands on interceptions...Much better than Ray May of the Colts at the same stage...I think he is the type of kid we need. **Projection: *Potential starter first year, 1st/ 2nd round pick***

Lynn Swann, flanker, USC (5'10½", 173): Fine quick athlete who reminds me of [Steelers WR] Jon Staggers...Good body control and quickness...Makes use of the talent he has, which is not great but good...Good field vision as a punt return man. Has a burst and a smooth gait...Hands are good...Can adjust or catch in noise...Can make the over shoulder catch of the bomb...Routes are disciplined but not mechanical...A fair blocker but on the semi-tough side...I don't feel he is a starter but he can make it and contribute. **Projection: *Potential starter, 4th/ 5th round pick***

Jack Lambert, linebacker, Kent State (6'4½", 206): Narrowly built guy but has gotten stronger since last spring...Looks like a smart and great effort player...Seems to play with reckless abandon at times...Flexibility and quickness in his pass drop...With his height he is a big obstacle to the passer...Good blitz...Uses hands and arms to play off blockers...At times gets his legs tied up but his balance is good and clears his feet good for the most part...Must get a bit more buck and develop some strength...I feel he will make it and develop into an NFL starter. **Projection: *Potential starter, 2nd/ 3rd round pick***

Dwight White, defensive end, East Texas State (6'3", 234): Good athlete who plays very inconsistently...Looked good against every type of play and then looked just as bad...Effort was ok...In fact he worked hard in practice and didn't seem to be a "hot dog" but he blew a lot of plays and the coach yelled at him a bit...They told me he wasn't a dumb kid and took coaching well, but I wonder what kind of smarts he has...Not a coward...Gets off with the ball very well, but did not show a burst of speed in pursuit. However, his lateral moves are good and he did chase a runner down once...His balance is good in as much as he is never on his rear end...Has the talent to make a club and develop into a good starter...Reminds me a little of Joe Jones of the Browns. **Projection: *Make roster and improve, 4th/ 5th round pick***

Mike Wagner, safety, Western Illinois (6'1½", 196): Has size, effort and pretty good movement. However, backpeddle is a little labored...Seems to keep good position on the receivers...More of a chest catcher than a hand catcher...I was impressed with the way he comes up to hit. However, he had some of his tackles broken. It seemed to be due to lack of strength and technique rather than guts...Has frame to get a bit stronger...I think he has the tools to merit a good look. **Projection: *Good prospect, 13th/ 14th round pick***

Franco Harris, fullback, Penn State (6'2", 225): Top physical prospect...The type of kid we're looking for...Breaks down like a 5'11', 190 guy only he's bigger...Fine body control and quickness...Slides and picks well...Does a good job of running pass patterns...Only a fair blocker but shows the tools to develop into a good blocker as a pro...Has strength and speed to be a big threat outside or in open field. However, I feel he doesn't use his strength to break tackles as much as he should...Not a straight line runner...Lots of movement and wiggle...Would give us a big gun in the backfield...I question his competitiveness...Has the talent to be a star, but I don't know if he will be...Worth the gamble. **Projection: *Potential starter first year, 1st round pick***

Moving on to the 1972 draft. More weapons were needed to boost the Steelers offense. Overall there's a weak array of college running backs available, but your man was Penn State's Franco Harris.

AJR: He was, but not without debate. Overall our running back position needed upgrading. Our backs at the time were Frenchy Fuqua and Preston Pearson. Noll loved Pearson, but he was a fumbler. Every fifth time he touched the football he put it on the ground. He wouldn't block either. At least Fuqua blocked like hell.

Franco was a big, strong guy with moves like a tailback. He had tremendous sophomore and junior years at Penn State, but his senior year wasn't as productive. That may have bothered some teams. They acted like he fell off tremendously, but that worked to our benefit. We had an offensive line coach named Dan Radakovich, who'd been at Penn State with Harris. He convinced us this drop-off wasn't a big deal. The rap on Franco was that he was a moody, emotional guy…sensitive, that his feelings got hurt easily. Radakovich said it was a bum rap. He said he knew Harris was a good person.

Who were the anti-Harris factions before the draft?

AJR: Our scouting department really liked him, but Noll wasn't crazy about him. He was finding reasons to be negative about Harris while we were finding reasons to be positive. I remember talking on the phone to George Young, who at the time was a scout for the Baltimore Colts. George loved Noll but he knew how he could be. He said, "What's the matter, Art? You sound really down. Is Chuck giving you a hard time again?"

I said, "Yeah, he keeps telling me that [University of Houston FB] Bobby Newhouse is better than Franco." George couldn't believe it!

He said, "You tell Chuck this debate was settled 2,000 years ago, when Socrates said, 'A good big man is worth more than a good little man any day.'" And of course, Franco ended up being Rookie of the Year in 1972.

Years later, we were watching films of a running back from Miami (FL) named Ottis Anderson. He was another good, big runner. During the discussion Noll said he didn't like Anderson, for whatever reasons. But then he added, "I could be wrong, like I was wrong about another big fullback that came here. I won't mention his name." Then he got up and walked out of the damn room. Woody Widenhofer, our linebacker coach, shut the projector off and turned on the lights.

I said, "Woody, what the hell was that all about?" He said, "That, Art, was as close as you're gonna get to Chuck admitting that you were right and he was wrong about Franco Harris."

Quarterback Joe Gilliam was an eleventh-round pick in '72, a real long shot to make the team. What kind of chances did you give this kid to ever beat out the great Terry Bradshaw, which Gilliam eventually did in 1974?

AJR: None! I didn't envision Gilliam even making the damn team! He was a Bill Nunn guy. According to my ratings Joe was a worthy draft choice, but he was an 11th rounder for a reason. Gilliam was both talented and tragic. He wasn't a dumbbell but he had little common sense. We had one of the all-time great defenses and a Hall of Fame runner in Franco Harris, but all Joe wanted to do was toss the ball. He got the defense in trouble a lot. Bradshaw worked his way back into the starting lineup by listening to Noll, by playing to the team's strengths. Joey was too impatient to do that. He was all downfield, a mad bomber.

At those lower depths like the 11th round you're really just throwing darts anyway, right?

AJR: Oh, no, no, no! We never threw darts! [Irritated] Who are you talking to? We *never* threw darts! We worked our asses off creating that list of 200 players! Hey, we didn't come up with guys like Donnie Shell and Randy Grossman by throwing darts. You *never* tell a personnel guy that he's throwing darts!

Wrong choice of words…

AJR: Yeah, it sure was. But that's not to say we didn't make mistakes. I remember running into Don Shula at a banquet years later. He said, "Sit down here and talk to me. Before you hired Chuck, you guys were all set to draft Terry Hanratty with the number one pick, weren't you?" He was poking fun a little bit, but we actually did consider taking Hanratty in the first round of the '69 draft. He was a local kid and a Notre Damer. Heck, we ended up taking him in the second round when he should've gone in the fourth. Taking him in the first round would've been a disaster.

The Pittsburgh Steelers' crown jewel was the famous draft of 1974. The names read Swann and Lambert, Stallworth and Webster. We could spend hours here.

AJR: We could, and I'd enjoy every minute.

First, Lynn Swann. According to the BLESTO scouting reports, he was highly regarded but had some flaws.

AJR: It was his speed that concerned people. I visited USC the fall of Lynn's senior year. Coach [John] McKay drove me around on his golf cart telling me about all his senior NFL prospects. USC was the Mecca of prospects back then, complete heaven for scouts. He drove me by each player. Wow! There were a lot of good ones. Then he showed me Lynn, who he said was his best. Too small and too slow, however, was the word from the scouts.

Swann was truly a great, competitive athlete who made big plays in the big games consistently. Physically he moved like the greatest Olympic gymnast you ever saw on TV. The only difference was when the floor exercise ended for the gymnast he wouldn't get belted in the teeth by a defensive back. Well, Swann could take that hit and hang onto the ball. We all liked him, but that 4.6/40 was a killer for the first round.

Noll wanted an offensive weapon on Round 1. Swann was quick, could jump like a gazelle, had great hands and concentration, but he was too slow to draft that high. It was something we couldn't look past. I went through the same kind of thing when we scouted Doug Flutie of Boston College, but in his case he was too short. The discussions were heavy at our draft preparation meetings, and we finally set Swann aside because of his poor height and speed. We were going to try and get him later, but I doubted he'd be available.

Stallworth was pushed into our top spot by Noll. Stallworth was a great talent and the scouts loved him but not as a first rounder. We felt we could get him in the third. Noll didn't care. He didn't want to chance losing him.

Then luck hit again. Jack Butler got a tip that that [New England scouting director] Bucko Kilroy had arranged for another speed timing of Swann. BLESTO somehow got their West Coast scout in to watch it and Swann ran a 4.5/40. The argument was over. Swann was our man.

Here's a funny story about Swann and Stallworth. Stallworth had true 4.5 speed. Lynn, when he ran alone, typically was around 4.59 or 4.60 in the forty. But when he raced against Stallworth in camp Lynn would almost beat him. And if Stallworth stumbled even a little, Lynn *would* beat him. Swann was such a true competitor. McKay said about him, "Remember the Sundance Kid shooting targets? He couldn't hit a darn one until it got competitive. Then he never missed." *That* was Lynn Swann.

Stallworth was a little known talent from Alabama A&M. Another Bill Nunn discovery?

AJR: Pretty much. BLESTO's Joe Bushofski had a real good report on Stallworth, which gave us an initial heads up, but Nunn always had extensive talks with the coaches at those places. He came up with the game film of a great game showcasing John. We got a copy of it and watched it over and over again. Stallworth was unbelievable, a real player.

Eventually I told Haley to send the film back to Alabama A&M, that their coach was calling for it. The next week I got another call – *Where's that film?* I told Haley again to send it. The next week came, another complaint – no film. By that time I knew Dick was up to something. He probably didn't want any other teams to see it. I confronted him and he finally said, "I'll send it out at the end of the week, promise." So it went out a month late.

In the Senior Bowl they played Stallworth at defensive back for some reason, so he wasn't showcased at his natural position. That was the luckiest thing that ever happened to us. Without that film it was just word-of-mouth about how great Stallworth could be. He was still available in the fourth, and we got him.

Let's talk about Jack Lambert, a skinny, undersized linebacker who was a surprise pick in the second round. Eight linebackers were taken before him, from muscle schools like Penn State, Ohio State and UCLA. Lambert came out of Kent State.

AJR: We were looking at another kid from UCLA named Cal Peterson, who we had graded about even with Lambert. One of our assistant coaches, Woody Widenhofer, said, "Peterson will be all right, a good player, but Lambert will make a strong contribution on special teams right away, while he's still learning the position." That shifted the balance toward Jack. My cousin Tim Rooney saw him take a penalty drill with the starting quarterback the week of a very important game. The quarterback had to finish the drill to play, so Lambert did it with him to make sure he finished. Lambert was tough, all business.

Let me rewind the story on Lambert back a few years. In the early '60s, I was at the University of Minnesota watching a game, taking notes. I was sitting next to an elderly lady who was obviously a big football fan. She asked me what I was doing, and I told her I was a scout for the Steelers. She said, "Well, watch this lineman Carl Eller. He's only a junior, but he's a pretty good player." Everyone could see how good Eller was, even this old lady. Well, Eller went on to be a first-round pick a year later and a great pro for the Vikings. That's where I got the expression "This guy's so good your grandmother could scout him." I told a lot of newspaper guys that story over the years.

Fast forward to early in the '74 camp. We were running our Oklahoma drills, a four-man exercise where a linebacker or lineman tries to stop a running back while fighting off a center. Lambert was going up against another rookie, a center we picked in the fifth round. First set of plays – Bam! Lambert gets knocked right back on his ass. They lined up again, and Wham! This center knocked Lambert down again, really belted him. Phil Musick, a writer for *The Pittsburgh Press*, was watching and gave me a little dig, saying, "Hey, Art, what little old lady told you about this Lambert guy?"

Lambert went on to become a Pro Bowl and Hall of Fame linebacker, but the center in camp that day was a guy named Mike Webster, who turned out to be a pretty good player himself. Who would've figured the first cracks in camp that year would come between a Hall of Fame linebacker and Hall of Fame center?

Mike Kruczek was Bradshaw's backup at quarterback from 1976-79. He was steady but unspectacular, playing sparingly except for several key starts during his rookie season. Did you push for having a better player at that position, or was Noll comfortable with Kruczek, who never threw a single touchdown pass as a Steeler?

AJR: Kruczek was a smart guy. Big and strong, very dedicated. The way he played during his starts in '76 was something else. He did a fine job for us, and we beat Cincinnati, Miami and a few other teams with him. Kruczek was basically programmed by Noll to not get the defense in trouble. No turnovers! We only scored a few points in each of the games he played, but Kruczek did what Noll wanted. That was also part of his problem – he was way too mechanical. Defenses could lock onto him. I'm not sure he would've gotten much better had we kept him around.

In 1977 we drafted Cliff Stoudt to eventually replace Kruczek. The coaches fell in love with that guy. Stoudt had a great arm, but I never thought he had the touch or the accuracy. I remember seeing Paul Zimmerman from *Sports Illustrated* before our '83 playoff against the Raiders. Bradshaw was hurt and Stoudt was going to start the game. He said, "You know, Art, Stoudt is the worst quarterback in football." The worst part of it was I agreed with him. Stoudt was terrible, although I couldn't admit it to Zimmerman since I was the Steelers' personnel guy. I think we would've been better off keeping Kruczek over Stoudt.

How much consideration did you give to Notre Dame's Joe Montana, who was available in the '79 draft? He was a local kid who had an exciting career in college for the Irish.

AJR: Not very much. We had him slotted as a third-rounder, and that's right where he went. Haley liked Montana a lot, but I wasn't as high on him. He wasn't a big player, and he tossed a soft ball, one that was easy to catch or intercept. Overall we were more interested in bigger, stronger quarterbacks like Bradshaw. Stoudt, Kruczek and Mark Malone were all big guys, too.

And now we move to the turbulent point of the interview, those disastrous Steelers drafts of the late 1970s and early '80s. Miscues were everywhere, like Willie Fry (#2, 1978), Greg Hawthorne (#1,

1979), Bob Kohrs (#2, 1980) and Keith Gary (#1, 1981). From 1975-86, Pittsburgh drafted 182 players; only five of them ever made the Pro Bowl with the Steelers. What happened?

AJR: Well, in that 182 you're also counting low-round draft choices, who by nature have very little chance of making the team, let alone the Pro Bowl. But obviously those were very disappointing years for us. Success had spoiled us in a sense, and by the mid-1970s we started getting into trouble with our drafting philosophy. We outsmarted ourselves by thinking we could put heart and consistency into great athletes who had showed occasional production and toughness. As "Bear" Bryant would say, we were trying to make chicken salad out of chicken shit.

We began to draft great athletes who were flashy but lacked consistency, those who had shown occasional flashes of greatness. That was the old Will Walls philosophy – if a guy does it once, he can be taught to do it all the time. That obviously was too simplistic an approach and it finally caught up with us. With all the success we had, I think we developed a certain amount of arrogance – that our weightlifting program was the best, that our coaching was the best, etc. We believed we could coach consistency into these great athletes. Bullshit! There's no way you can teach consistency. We thought that's what we had done with Franco Harris, but in reality that wasn't true. Franco was already a consistent player. We just started using him differently, which made him even more productive.

Our first real mistake in drafting on flash came in 1975 with a guy named Bob Barber, a defensive end from Grambling. We took him in the second round. In college he had all the statistics and would make beautiful plays, but when he got to camp he was terribly inconsistent. He didn't even make the team. Barber was an indicator of things to come. Hawthorne, a running back from Baylor, was another one. We took him first in '79 on his potential, but again there was no consistency.

Now keep in mind when you're drafting in the later rounds, you *need* to have that philosophy. For example, L.C. Greenwood was a flashy player in college. He played in spurts. L.C. was inconsistent, so we didn't take him in until the 10th round. At that level you can afford to gamble and make mistakes. You can't do that with your high picks. Jack Butler would occasionally pull me aside and say, "Art, you gotta get guys that are productive, ones that make more than two plays a game. The Steelers don't need any more guys who leave it all on the college field."

Who was the biggest heartbreaker of all your draft choices?

AJR: It was a guy who actually *made* the team – Frank Lewis. Not because he didn't turn out to be a great player, but because he didn't turn out to be a great player for the Steelers. Getting playing time with Swann and Stallworth around was a tough chore. Frank didn't truly develop until he went to the Bills in '78. That was the year they put in the five-yard chuck rule, and I believe that really helped his game. He had some trouble getting off the line and past the defenders under the old rule.

Who was your favorite long-shot success story?

AJR: A real favorite of mine was Loren Toews, a linebacker from Cal-Berkeley that we took in the 8th round in '73. Cal's stadium is huge, and I was sitting way up near the top by myself. All of a sudden a bunch of Boy Scouts came up and sat next to me. They were having a little picnic in the stands and they noticed I was scouting the game. The leader pointed to one of his scouts and said, "This kid's brother is the best player around here. His name is Loren Toews. If you have time, watch him." I had him way down on my list and didn't expect to be impressed.

As the game went on, I saw all the characteristics in Toews that Noll was looking for in a linebacker – smart, aggressive, even had a little bit of Jack Ham in him. Toews had some pretty damn good days in camp his rookie year and made the team. He ended up starting in our first Super Bowl. Toews was never a Pro Bowl guy, but he became one of my favorite success stories.

Randy Grossman is another one, an undrafted free agent. Our rating system for pass receivers went 0, 1, 2, 3…the lower the number, the better the hands. Grossman could get some separation from a defender, but he wasn't a big guy. What he did have was 0 hands, the best. With Bradshaw at quarterback, you didn't feed him some free agent with just "nice hands," a guy who rated a 2. Terry threw the ball so hard that the receiver had to be a 1 or a 0, which Grossman was. He caught whatever was near him.

Do you recall your biggest argument with Chuck Noll over drafting a player? I once asked Noll this question, and he dodged it. He said there were never arguments, only disagreements.

AJR: [Laughing] That sounds like something Chuck would say. If you had credibility with him, he'd go along with you on certain things but he still had the final say. At times there was a lot of tension between Noll and me. I had some battles with him. I once called him a "know-it-all." He looked back at me with an expression like, "You rich-kid jerk."

[Assistant coach] George Perles heard me say it. He told me that if my dad didn't own the team Chuck would have knocked me on my ass. I told Perles to take a walk. Actually, all of us were right: Noll was a know-it-all, but the best coach and a great man, Perles was a big mouth, and I was an obstinate rich kid whose dad owned the team.

The drafting of Franco Harris was probably the biggest battle we ever had. It got heated. I thought we should take Franco but Chuck wasn't sold on him. Well, it turned out like the Battle of Midway in World War II. Before Midway the U.S. Navy never won a battle; after Midway we never lost one. Before Franco the Steelers couldn't get a winning season; after Franco arrived, we went 13 years without a losing one.

...And Stars the Steelers Watched Go By

More from the Steelers' scouting reports of the 1970s:

Dave Casper, offensive tackle/tight end, Notre Dame (6'3", 248): Has the talent to do a lot of things as a blocker but doesn't, at least not consistently...Has strength, blocking quickness and balance, but if he is not directly involved in the play he is just a stand-around...They say he sort of walks like a farmer plugging through a plowed field but he sure runs with fluidness...As a TE he got open short and caught the ball...I don't think he can contribute as a pro TE...Can be good but will tax the best of coaches. **Projection:** *Make Roster and Improve, 4th/5th round pick* **(Result: 2ⁿᵈ round by Oakland in 1974)**

Brian Sipe, quarterback, San Diego State (6'1", 195): An exciting player at times but plagued with a scatter-arm...Short on passing talent...Moves well in pocket and can scramble but has trouble finding second receiver...Can get it close enough to make you think it is the receiver's fault on an incompletion...Can get the ball deep...Had some big games in college, but not any better than a camp player. **Projection:** *Questionable Prospect, 17th round pick/free agent* **(Result: 13ᵗʰ round by Cleveland in 1972)**

Duane Thomas, fullback, West Texas State (6'2", 213): Has all the equipment to be a great one...Intangibles are questionable...[West Texas] Coach Harris says he's a fine kid who has some small character flaws like running up credit card bills, not showing up for practice, poor school work, walking off the field, and not playing with pain...He also has a black militant for a brother, but the brother isn't supposed to get to him...He isn't a fine practice player but didn't "dog it." In fact, he showed flashes of brilliance in practice...Big, strong and fast, can explode through a hole...Hard for one tackler to bring him down...Durable, even if the coach said he didn't like pain...Does a good job of picking his way through traffic and running over people in the open field...Would be a fine screen pass runner...If his character would hold up, I think he would be a terrific offensive weapon as a pro...Let someone else motivate him. **Projection:** *Potential starter, 1st round pick* **(Result: 1ˢᵗ round by Dallas in 1970)**

Cliff Branch, flanker, Colorado (5'10 ¾", 169): [scouted during '72 Hula Bowl] Still feel the same way about Branch, although he did catch the ball in practice a little better than I thought he could but not much...He's a little bigger than I thought he was...Don't believe this boy is very tough...The footing wasn't the best but he fell down too many times...A couple of times I got the impression he was hunting for a place to lay down. Could be wrong on this...I still feel this is a very dangerous football player but it's going to take a far better passer than these QBs to hit him cause I don't think he is going to catch the off-thrown ball well...There is also no doubt that with his great speed he can kill a club. **Projection: *Make roster and improve, 4th/5th round pick*** (**Result: 4th round by Oakland in 1972**)

Dan Dierdorf, offensive tackle, Michigan (6'3", 255): A squatty built guy...Looks like if he got any heavier he would be a fatso...Strong kid with a good pop but inconsistent sustain and follow-through...Not a real quick in-line blocker...Did not pull for sweeps or traps but from his pre-game workout and the way he covered punts I'd say he'd have difficulty in those techniques. Effort is ok. I wasn't impressed with his foot movement or his potential to be a good pass protector as a pro. Did show good one-on-one strength and pop on a goal line drive. Perhaps he would have some defensive possibilities. **Projection: *Good prospect, 12th/13th round pick*** (**Result: 2nd round by St. Louis in 1971**)

Jack Youngblood, defensive tackle, Florida (6'4", 242): [from junior year] I feel Jack is a sure thing to make our club. However, I don't feel he's a sure thing to help us...Doesn't dominate his teammates in scrimmages...Showed good lateral pursuit, not stiff at all...I felt his pass rush was ordinary...Low blocks tie him up but he won't have that problem with us...The best I saw him was a little OT he played in a drill. Blocked strongly, so might be an OT prospect...Very raw and would have to be taught an awful lot to help us...I was starting to question his meanness until he handled a fellow pretty well in a fight during a scrimmage. **Projection: *Make roster and contribute, 5th/6th round pick***

[from Youngblood's senior year] Very strong...Lateral move, pursuit and agility are good...Gets off with ball okay...Has a mean streak (at times I felt he was a cheap-shotter)...Hard to run at him...Good pass rush...Showed good rate of improvement over last spring...Not a finished product but the way he's going I think he'll start in NFL and be a winner...I rate him above Bill Stanfill of Georgia at the same stage...Not great but has chance to be real good. **Projection: *Potential starter, 1st round pick*** (**Result: 1st round by L.A. Rams in 1971**)

The biggest criticism of Steelers management was that its Super Bowl stars, the veterans of all the great teams of the 1970s, were kept way past their prime. Do you agree with that criticism?

AJR: I can agree, but that's what happens when you put together a great team. Those players performed for you and brought you championships, so it's easy to get emotional about them. You wouldn't think that Noll would get emotional over players. He was a straight-laced, hard-nosed guy that didn't let his feelings get in the way of progress. But Noll did get sentimental, just not in front of the camera. He kept some guys on longer than he should have. He wasn't able to find room for younger guys like [DL] Dwaine Board or [TE] Brent Jones, and that obviously hurt us. I'm not criticizing him for it. It would've been very hard to just throw away those guys who had done so much for your team.

Looking back, are there any players that you regret not drafting?

AJR: In the scouting game, you shouldn't look back at the other cards in the game that could've been played. You'd constantly be second-guessing yourself and drive yourself crazy. I can't really think of anybody, to be honest. The thing I always fought for was sticking to the preferred list of 200 players. And I was always pretty satisfied we did that.

What about Noll? Were there any players that he regretted passing over?

AJR: I know one guy Noll kicked himself over was Dan Marino. He loved Marino with a passion. 1983 was a strange time for quarterbacks in Pittsburgh. Bradshaw was hurt and ended up missing most of the season. Stoudt was going to be the starter because the coaches loved him, and Mark Malone was the backup. But Noll had identified Marino was being his top choice. We had chased down all the rumors that Marino was into drugs and found they weren't exactly true. Marino wasn't a horrible person in that respect, but he was a smart ass. I guess one drawback to scouting Pitt players was that we got to know them a little too well. They were local kids so we heard all the rumors.

We were drafting 21st that year and had identified three players we wanted to take – Dave Rimington, a center from Nebraska; Gabe Rivera, a defensive tackle from Texas Tech, and Marino. Rimington had knee problems and we backed away from him, so it came down to either Rivera or Marino. Noll was all for Marino.

Then he had a sudden change of heart. He said, "Let's start rebuilding this team the way we did back in '69 – with a great defensive lineman." He was referring to us drafting Joe Greene years earlier. Well, why not? It seemed like a good idea again. Rivera played pretty well for us, but then he broke his back in a car wreck six weeks into the season. We never really had a chance to fail with the guy. It wasn't necessarily a bad draft pick, and it was unfortunate what happened to him. Still, "The Chief" used to always growl, "You should've taken Marino!" Right up till the day he died he'd give us a little dig on it.

You must have been devastated by Rivera's accident.

AJR: It was such a sad, difficult thing. I believe he would've been a solid player for us. But let me give you a quick story about Rivera. After his accident, we looked back over his personal files and we saw that he had something like 32 traffic tickets. I brought that up to one of the scouts. The scout said, "Well, Tony Dorsett also had 32 traffic tickets in college. Would we have passed on him, too?" In terms of driving, Rivera had no regard for the law. Maybe somebody in the scouting staff who was a little more astute might have said, "This guy could be trouble," but we weren't smart enough to see that.

The failure rate on your first- or second-round picks is pretty high because of the intangibles. Maybe the guy has an attitude problem or a drinking problem or a drug problem. It's a big jigsaw puzzle you're trying to put together. For example, Gabe was supposed to go on a diet, to eat a lot of tuna. Well, he was eating *25 cans of tuna a day!* It was something you sorta laughed at. Then we brought in a psychologist to give us a lecture about the qualities of a winning personality. He pointed out that the tuna thing, along with all the speeding tickets, were red flags. But heck, we didn't know. We weren't psychologists.

You talked about the feelings you had as you watched Three Rivers Stadium being destroyed. Yet the Steelers dynasty had long been over and the stadium was past its prime. It was symbolic in a way, like the great naval battleships that had won the wars then were banished to the scrap yards. How does it feel today when taking a long look back at that tremendous Steel Curtain era?

AJR: The glory days were so long ago, and now nobody around the team really knows who I am anymore. It reminds me of a story. Once I took my family to an NFL meeting that was being held in Hawaii. Joe Foss, the former governor of South Dakota, was there. As a former Marine reservist, I knew all about Foss and wanted to meet him. He was a great marine aviator in World War II, a war ace. He shot down more Japs than [Cleveland DE Joe] "Turkey" Jones had sacks. I went over to him and said, "Governor, I'm Art Rooney, Jr. of the Steelers. I just wanted to say hello and thank you for what you've done for our country." He was real nice to me, and I could see that he loved our game.

The next day I was with my son, Mike, who was around 13 years old. We saw Joe Foss standing around a reception room by himself, so I felt it was a good time to introduce the great ace to the kid, something for the lad to remember. So I walked over and said, "Governor Foss, I'd like you to meet my son. Mike, this is Governor Joe Foss. He's a friend of your grandfather." We were all smiling, shaking hands. I told Mike, "Governor Foss was a great Marine aviator, a top ace."

Mike, who didn't know anything about Foss' career, asked him, "Oh, where did you fly your airplane?"

Foss looked at him and, in a somewhat proud but sincere manner, answered, "A little west of here, son…a little west of here."

Years later, when the Steelers played the last game at Three Rivers Stadium, we hosted a big party. Most of the great players of the '70s were in attendance, all the stars. Mike, now a grown man, introduced me to a friend of his who was on Bill Cowher's coaching staff. It was quite obvious that his friend didn't know about me, or really even care, but he was nice. To him, I was Mike's old dad and a Rooney, so this fellow went out of his way to make a little conversation.

The young coach asked me what I'd done with the Steelers. I said, "Well, I was a scout."

"Oh!" he said. "Who did you scout?"

I looked around me and saw those old Steelers – Lambert and Swann and Larry Brown and the others – standing nearby. For a moment I thought of Governor Foss' reply to my son years before. I didn't know how to put it into my own words, so I just kept it to myself.

"A little west of here, son… a little west of here."

— 2 —
"Bum" Phillips, Head Coach/General Manager

Houston Oilers (1975-1980); New Orleans Saints (1981-85)
October 15, 1998

It's unfortunate that coaches who are blessed with a quick wit and snappy comebacks are more often remembered for what they say rather than for what their teams achieve on the field. John McKay won 127 games and three undisputed national championships at Southern Cal, then miraculously guided a ragtag group known as the Tampa Bay Buccaneers to the 1979 NFC Championship game after only the team's fourth year in existence. Yet McKay is generally remembered today as being a hilarious, off-the-cuff quipster. ("The offense's execution today? I'm all for it.")

Ara Parseghian and Dan Devine are lauded for the great battles and national championships they won at Notre Dame, but Lou Holtz, who also captured a title for the Irish in 1988, is somehow the wacky guy who dreamt up proverbs like *The man who complains about how the ball bounces is likely the one who dropped it."*

I can still see that hungry, pleading, please-say-something-funny look in faces of the media horde that crowded around Houston Oilers coach Jerry Glanville after games in the late 1980s. I never got the impression that they were there to hear him describe his corner blitz strategy or why he liked using his big-footed tailback Lorenzo White in bad weather. I got the feeling that most of them were there to hear Glanville's goofy stuff – Whom did he leave tickets for this week, Pope Pius VI or Sitting Bull? Or to hear his jabs at Steelers coach Chuck Noll. They all came ready to laugh. And Glanville rarely disappointed with his answers.

Then there was Bum Phillips, pro football's best-known "funny" coach in the 1970s – part one-liner, part two-a-day workout. Once after passing a physical he announced, "If I drop dead tomorrow, at least I'll know I died in good health." In reference to his wife he once said, "I take her everywhere I go because she's too ugly to kiss good-bye."

But what was no joke was Phillips' ability to coach the game of football and motivate the men who played for him. "My idea of discipline," he once said, "is not *making* guys do something; it's *getting* them to do it. There's a difference between bitching and coaching."

His relaxed, honky-tonk approach to coaching, paired with a humble, caring demeanor made him extremely popular with his players. "The only discipline that lasts is self-discipline," he said in 1980. "A long time ago I gave up this philosophy of not getting close to players...I'm around these guys seven months, seven days a week. I laugh with them. Cry with them. I know them. I want them to understand my fondness. I want us to be close. I think it helps them play better."

Phillips' pro coaching career began in 1967 with the San Diego Chargers, where he held the defensive coordinator position under Sid Gillman for four seasons. "I knew my defense had better be prepared on Sunday," said Phillips. "Sid had that offense scoring so damn fast that it seemed we were always back on the field."

After a brief return to the college ranks, he rejoined Gillman's Houston Oilers staff as defensive coordinator in 1974, then was named head coach the following season, guiding a roster loaded with question marks to a startling 10-4 record. It was the team's first winning season since 1967. Over the next four years, Phillips' Oilers rattled the cage of an AFC almost exclusively dominated by Pittsburgh, Miami and Oakland.

By the end of 1980, he had guided his team to three straight playoff appearances and became the winningest head coach in Oilers history with a 59-38 record. But it was an embarrassing 27-7 loss to the Oakland Raiders in the 1980 AFC wild card game that triggered his emotional eviction from the team.

"Bum was very well liked in the Oilers organization, and he took more of the blame for that playoff loss than he should have," says a former Oilers executive who was close to the situation but requested anonymity. "Our quarterback, Kenny Stabler, was coming back to play in Oakland, and he was supposedly out late with some of his buddies the night before the game and really wasn't in the best shape to play. That had a lot to do with the offense stinking so badly in the Oakland game.

"The firing of Bum Phillips was a very touchy situation around here for a long time. The word that got out publicly was that he wouldn't hire an offensive coordinator, but there was more to it than that."

The "more to it," according to Phillips, involved an internal power struggle with Ladd Herzeg, the team's chief administrative officer, particularly in the area of personnel decisions.

"Ladd wanted to run the doggone team," Phillips told *The Houston Chronicle* in 1990. "He wanted to make the decisions on who to draft, trade and waive. Basically, he wanted to decide who played... I don't think for a second that [Oilers owner] Bud Adams really cared if I hired an offensive coordinator. I think Ladd *convinced* him of it."

Phillips lost the battle in Houston and was dismissed from his job for the first time in his career. But five months later he resurfaced as head coach of the New Orleans Saints, hired by owner Tom Benson.

The Oilers, however, actually worsened their fortunes by releasing Phillips. The team went into an immediate free fall, winning only 14 of its next 63 games, and didn't capture another winning season until 1987. During our conversation, the tone in Phillips' voice suggested that his dismissal was a subject he still wasn't comfortable recalling or discussing.

It would have been easy to bait Bum Phillips into dropping more of his witty one-liners with questions about the Clinton White House improprieties or his solution to the Y2k problem, but I wanted to stay away from the Comedy Central stuff. Phillips was too important of a character during the 1970s to turn it into one of those "Say Something Funny" interviews. I wanted solid stuff. I wanted to hear his thoughts on overworking his punishing tailback, Earl Campbell; on playing on that concrete Astrodome floor; on trading Dante Pastorini and waiving a rookie named Steve Largent.

It was Phillips who helped orchestrate (is there anything *orchestral* about fellas who wear dress denims and drive pick-up trucks and cattle?) one of the NFL's great playoff upsets when his battered, limping Oilers ambushed heavily favored San Diego in the 1979 playoffs.

His undermanned Oilers reached two AFC title games, losing twice to the mighty Pittsburgh Steelers in 1978 and '79. "Bum's teams always came to play, always ready for a collision," said former Steelers defensive lineman John Banaszak. "If it's worth anything, they were probably the second best team in pro football during those years."

So I'm content in leaving the epigrams on the sidelines and will focus on the nuts and bolts. Here's what the ringleader of the "Luv Ya Blue" hysteria has to say about football and the first true glory days of the Houston Oilers.

• • •

First topic, and in terms of pro football history, I think it's an underrated one: How were you able to take that badly injured wreck of an Oilers team to San Diego and stop the explosive Chargers in the 1979 playoffs? San Diego was a solid 8-point favorite in that game, but your team came out of there with a stunning 17-14 win.

BP: The biggest thing I remember was we didn't have [QB] Dan Pastorini or Earl Campbell or [WR] Kenny Burrough. Those were our key guys! But then our free safety Vernon Perry, who wasn't a widely known player, intercepted four passes and blocked a field goal. That was the contribution of one guy! That was the thing that amazed me the most that day. You don't see one guy do that very many times in football. Vernon was a free agent who had played some Canadian ball. He was in the right place at the right time against San Diego. I think he got a tipped ball or two that helped him with the interceptions. But it was amazing that we could come back and beat the Chargers. Overall, San Diego was a better football team than we were, but not that day.

What kind of odds were you giving your team at the start of that game?

BP: I don't know. I thought we'd win. I'm stupid, like most coaches are. I always thought we were going to win them all.

To make the situation even worse, Rob Carpenter, Campbell's backup, had tripped over a blocking dummy in practice and sprained his ankle. He was still on crutches heading to the stadium that day but left them on the bus so the Chargers couldn't see. I remember Carpenter being gang-tackled after catching a pass during that game, then literally pulling himself to the sidelines with his arms, like a man with two broken legs.

BP: Rob just sucked it up and played. He played well. A sprained ankle is not that bad other than pain, and he was tough enough to stand the pain. There's a difference between pain and injury. Rob gave a great effort in that game, but that was the way he always played. He was a hard-nosed football player.

The previous time you faced the Chargers – on the last weekend of the 1978 season – they scored 45 points on your defense. In fact, San Diego's offense had been held under 20 points only seven times in its last 32 games prior to your playoff meeting. Yet your team intercepted five Dan Fouts passes and held them to two touchdowns. What kind of voodoo did your coaching staff come up with to defuse Fouts and that incendiary offense?

BP: We didn't really come up with anything special. Being fair, I think the Chargers were a little bit over-confident and didn't think they were going to have to play hard. You see that all the time on weekends, when good football teams don't get themselves mentally ready to play. But you can be sure their opponents are mentally ready because it's a challenge for them. It's like being the Super Bowl champion – every team on your schedule the next year will play their best game against you.

I don't remember a whole lot about the San Diego gameplan, but I remember we needed to rush Fouts up the middle and try to block his passes, rather than rush him from the outside. He was too good at sitting in the pocket and getting the ball off. We put a strong rush up the middle with the front three linemen we had, and tried to force his line back into his face. Evidently, he couldn't see very good because he made some bad throws that day.

The book on Fouts was to beat him with gut pressure, taking away his pocket, knocking him down and hurrying his throws. It seems your team had a similar scheme that afternoon.

BP: We didn't know if we'd knock him down, but we wanted to look him in the eye and rush straight on. If we couldn't get to him, we insisted our players get their hands up and try to block the ball. We did block some passes, and we forced Fouts to throw some with too much loft on them. That made it tougher on his receivers.

In pass defense we played our regular zone coverage on them. Some man-to-man, but very little. We felt like we could get to the ball, maybe knock it loose or get an interception. You get way more interceptions with zone than you do with man-to-man. Their receivers were too good for us to turn both corners loose on them, to put a strong safety out there on [TE] Kellen Winslow. God, we didn't have anybody that could cover them man-to-man. They would have destroyed us had we tried to do that.

Was that afternoon in San Diego your greatest win as a head football coach?

BP: It was everybody on the team's greatest win because we did it without a lot of players that were important to us. It had to be the best game we ever won. We were playing away from home and the Chargers had a great football team, a Super Bowl caliber team. Like I said, I think they took us too lightly because we were so banged up. But whatever the reason, I'm happy we did it.

You were introduced to pro football by a legend named Sid Gillman. He first hired you to join his Chargers coaching staff in 1967, then later asked you to become his defensive coordinator with the Houston Oilers. Describe your relationship with Gillman.

BP: Sid Gillman was a great football coach, maybe the best offensive mind of anybody who ever coached the game. He was really a genius. I had a good relationship with him. Sid would get along with everybody. Put it this way: If you liked football, he liked you. If you didn't like football, Sid had no use for you.

What impressed you most about Gillman's coaching style and philosophy?

BP: I'd say his ability to adapt his offense to whatever talent he had on the team. Sid wasn't a guy who said, "We're going to run the West Coast offense, or the Midwest offense or the East Coast offense." He was a guy that said, "Here's what we got: we've got this kind of receiver and that kind of quarterback and this kind of running back." Then he adapted his offense to whatever he had. That's why he was so good for a number of years, because he could adapt. The year that he coached in Houston, 1974, he had nothing as far as talent. We were really bad. We had just come off two 1-13 seasons, then he took those same players and made them into a 7-7 team. Now, *that* is utilizing your personnel.

What did you learn from Gillman that helped you become a better coach?

BP: Sid was also the Oilers' general manager, so I'd say handling and judging people was his biggest asset. Sid was really good at judging the type of people you'd want on your football team. He was the kind of guy that could just talk to a player and know whether he wanted him on his team. He could tell which guys would contribute and help the team. He was a great offensive football coach, but he was also a good defensive football coach. If you know something about offense, you also know something about the defense that stops it. Obviously, when you work for a guy for six years, you pick up his ideas all the way through. He definitely taught me something.

Memories of the 'Luv Ya Blue' Days

"I'll never forget Bum's words on the phone. He asked me if I'd like to come down and play a little ball. He sounded like an old farmer trying to get a game going out in the pasture. Bum blew my mind. I came out to the field on a bus and asked when practice was. I guess it was when everybody got there. I couldn't believe it. Here were guys sitting on helmets and shinning up goalposts. There were stray dogs running across the field. No whistles. Everybody did his own calisthenics. Guys were wearing different outfits, T-shirts, hats."

– Andy Dorris, Houston Oilers DE, 1977-81

The Good Ol' Boy family atmosphere on the Oilers is not a myth. In search of the perfect chord, Phillips has fine-penciled the waiver lists to bring in every reject, castoff and renegade this side of Jesse James to help the Oilers. At different times he has hired on a fireman, a softball player and a cement-mixer truck driver. This year's return man, Carl Roaches, was driving an ice-cream truck last year... Phillips' 1978 team, which went to the AFC title game, included 21 free agents. Andy Dorris, the defensive left end, calls the Oilers "football's melting pot."

Recently a 5'9", 230-pound Mexican-American named James Juarez turned up on the Oilers' doorstep wanting to know if – "Don't laugh, Amigo," he said – he could help at linebacker. Juarez said he hadn't played football in a couple of years but that he'd been working out at a health club. A trainer told Juarez that Bum would get back to him. That was the whole ball of wax, don't you see. The reason Bum Phillips has captured the imagination of all football is not so much the hats and the boots and the twanged-out jokes in between the tobacco juice flying into his makeshift spittoons. Why, this fat old red-neck truck driver has turned a disheveled, downtrodden NFL franchise into a Salvation Army Sunday-afternoon sandlot pickup crew, the same kind we see celebrating a W in all those TV beer commercials every week. Luv Ya Blue is nothing but buzz language for "Kick ass, blue collars." Come on down, James Juarez.

– Curry Kirkpatrick, *Sports Illustrated*, September 27, 1980.
Reprinted with permission.

Upon your arrival the Oilers changed from a 4-3 base defense to a 3-4, a radical departure from the way defense had been played in the NFL. Did you initially receive much resistance from your players?

BP: Yeah, from our defensive ends! They didn't like it because they had to go head-up on a tackle, which affected their outside rush. It was a move we had to make because of the depth on our team. We could find four good linebackers – even if we had to use free agents. But you can't find many really good defensive linemen, and we only had two. And if you only have two, you'd better play a 3-4 rather than a 4-3. If you're stubborn and stick with the 4-3, then you're in trouble.

Plus, in a 4-3 you need a real hoss at middle linebacker. We didn't have that kind of guy, just a bunch of good linebackers. The players we had dictated what kind of defense we could play. Robert Brazile, one of our best linebackers, liked the 3-4 because he got to rush the passer a lot. He got a lot of sacks. Robert was the guy who made the 3-4 popular for sending an outside linebacker. The Giants' Lawrence Taylor got all the credit for it, but Robert was really the guy that got it started.

You worked under Gillman in Houston for only one season (1974) before he gave up the coaching duties and named you head coach for 1975. Your contract with the Oilers gave you control over team policies and personnel decisions, but one of those "fine print" clauses still gave Gillman final approval on your decisions. Considering that you would ultimately be held responsible for the success of the team, did that clause bother you?

BP: When Sid asked me if I wanted to be head coach, the only thing I told him was that I wanted to make the decisions. And he said, "Certainly, no problem there." We never had an argument about that.

But there's a story that you went to team owner Bud Adams and demanded that the clause be removed. Then three weeks later Gillman was fired. Did you have any hand in his dismissal?

BP: No, of course not! I had nothing to do with Sid leaving. I respected him enough as a football man that if he didn't want to do something, I wouldn't do it. He knew more about running a team than I did.

Looking back on the 1974 roster you inherited, in which areas did you feel the team required the most upgrading?

BP: It was more an issue of attitude. We needed some more winners. Aside from [DE] Elvin Bethea and [DT] Curley Culp, all my talented players were young guys. We had Dan Pastorini, Ken Burrough, Billy Johnson and [LB] Ted Washington, but we needed more leadership. I knew that to improve the team we needed to acquire some veterans. My first step was trading for [C] Carl Mauck from San Diego. Carl is the kind of guy that everybody needs on their football team, a real winner. He's somebody that says, "Hey, we're gonna do it – I don't care what happens." We needed three or four more like Carl. We brought in [DL] Bubba Smith from the Raiders. In '76 we picked up John Hadl to give us some experience at quarterback.

What were your impressions of the Oilers' quarterback situation, particularly the battle between Dan Pastorini and Lynn Dickey? At that time, did you believe that either of the two quarterbacks had the talent to lead the Oilers to a championship?

BP: We couldn't afford to keep two quarterbacks that good. I just made my mind up to go with Dan, so we traded Lynn. I believe either one of them had the talent to win for us, but I felt after watching them both play in '74 I feel I made the right decision. Dan was just better for the style of ball we were trying to play.

How so?

BP: I don't remember what the deciding factors were. It was just a decision you make. If you make it wrong, you're wrong. If you make it right, then everything is okay. In 1975 Lynn was hurt. Dan, despite getting hit really bad, held up physically so he played. We knew what we were getting with Dan, and he could also punt. I'll just say this – my instincts told me to go with Pastorini.

What are your memories of Dan Pastorini?

BP: Pastorini was a great quarterback. He called almost all of the plays from the line of scrimmage. We'd send in a play, but he had the right to check it off. That system was working good. Then one day he said to me, "Bum, why can't I just take a look at the defense and call some plays at the line?" I said sure. He'd go into the huddle and say "check-with-me." That was it. The players would stand in the huddle a little bit, then go to the line of scrimmage and Dan would call the play. He could see the splits and the spacing, and whether their defensive end was head-up on our tackle or on the outside shoulder. Dan could see things that we couldn't see from the sidelines. It got to the point where we let him audible everything, and he was real good at it. He'd call "check-with-me" about 90-percent of the time.

What was Pastorini's biggest strength as a quarterback?

BP: Deep ball throwin'. Dan could do one thing that we really liked, and that was throw the bomb. He had a great knack of putting enough air on the ball so somebody could run under it. He could hit Kenny Burrough going full stride, either down-in or down-out. He was the best long-ball passer that I've ever seen. Daryle Lamonica was a good one, but I believe Dan was better.

How could Pastorini have improved his game?

BP: It would probably be thinking more sharp in short-yardage situations. Dan was always a guy who wanted to go for the bomb, no matter the down and distance. I would've liked for him to think a little more "short-yardage" when we were in things like 3rd-and-4, 3rd-and-5. He'd still look for the bomb, regardless of the situation. He'd look deep first then work his way back up the field.

Do you remember a specific game or moment that defined Pastorini's emergence as the leader of the Oilers?

BP: I'd say the time we went down to Miami in 1978 and he played a playoff game with two broke ribs. Dan was in a tremendous amount of pain, but got a flak jacket and led the football team to a victory. I don't know how he did it. I was almost certain we'd have to use [backup QB] Gifford Nielsen in that game, that Dan wouldn't be able to make it. But he went out there and threw for over 300 yards in all that pain. I think that really gained him the respect of our players. You have to be one tough man to do something like that.

The Oilers continued to improve under your watch and were a very respectable 10-4 in 1975, beating every team on the schedule except Pittsburgh and Cincinnati. But in '76 the Oilers were a flop, winning only five games and finishing last in the AFC Central. Why the collapse?

BP: Honestly, I think we slipped up on a few people in '75, surprised a few teams. Maybe we weren't as good as our record that year. We played a good 3-4 defense, and nobody except New England knew anything about it. Nobody knew how to block it, so it gave teams some trouble.

We started off good in '76, winning four of our first five games. But then all of our wide receivers got hurt. In football, when you start getting injuries at one position it seems to disintegrate. People have to play longer and play hurt, so the quality of the position drops off. We weren't as much of a threat to throw the ball, so teams could try to stop our run. I think Tampa Bay rushed for more yards than we did and they were an expansion team!

The Oilers rebounded in 1977, finishing 8-6, but again missed the playoffs. Then came the '78 draft.

BP: And we got Earl Campbell! You don't win all of them with one player, and one player usually can't make that much difference. But Earl Campbell made that much difference to us.

Prior to Campbell joining the Oilers, you said that on each Sunday Pastorini was headed into a sword fight armed with just a pocketknife. Campbell gave him something to fight with.

BP: *I mean* he had something to fight with! We finally had somebody we could depend upon in the fourth quarter. I'll say this – Earl Campbell was the greatest fourth-quarter football player I've ever seen. Everybody griped about how much he carried the ball, that I overused him, but he always played better in the fourth quarter than he did in the first. You can check this. I don't know how he did it. He just had great stamina. He was a guy that could carry the ball 30 times before the fourth quarter, then carry it 12 or 14 more times during the fourth quarter. We played Miami one Monday night and he ran for an 80-yard touchdown at the end of the game to win it. He had already run for 130 or so that night, then he breaks off a run like that. It was almost superhuman.

What were your thoughts when you first watched Earl Campbell play in person?

BP: It was in practice. We'd do these agility drills where you'd run around the cones and put your hand on the ground and turn to the right, and go around to the next one and go backwards. You're checking to see if a guy has any balance or agility, and Earl couldn't do them, not at all. [Offensive backs coach] Andy Bourgeois came to me and said, "Coach, I don't know about Campbell. I'm not too impressed. He can't run backwards in those drills at all. Every time he runs backwards he falls down." I said, "Hell, Andy, we didn't get him to run *backwards*! Don't worry about it!" And Earl never did run backwards. He ran forward, and he took a bunch of people with him.

Building Up a Mean Head of Steam

Did Earl Campbell really become a stronger, more-effective runner as the game wore on? Bum Phillips thinks so. And after dissecting Campbell's game-by-game numbers, it appears that the old Oilers coach wasn't telling tall tales from Texas.

> During Earl's first three years in the NFL (1978-80), the thunderous tailback averaged 4.6 yards/carry in the first half of games. Against tiring, second-half defenses, that average surged to 5.1.
>
> "I can't really explain that," says Campbell. "Part of it was conditioning, and part of it was just getting the engine warmed up."
>
> Campbell was never more of a gathering force than in 1980, when he averaged almost 6.0 yards/carry in the second half of games. Here is the breakdown of his rushing production by half during those first few rampaging years in Houston (in carries-yards-average):
>
> | | **1st Half** | **2nd Half** |
> |---|---|---|
> | **1978 (15 games played)** | 162 – 715 – 4.4 | 140 – 735 – 5.3 |
> | **1979 (16 games played)** | 198 – 986 – 5.0 | 170 – 711 – 4.2 |
> | **1980 (15 games played)** | 182 – 805 – 4.4 | 191 – 1129 – 5.9 |

Describe your favorite Earl Campbell moment, one that left you shaking your head in disbelief on the sidelines.

BP: There was probably one play every ball game. The one that really got me was a short touchdown run against Washington in 1979. I don't believe it was longer than 10 yards, but I swear about seven people hit him on the play. He just kept going, spinning off one player, bounding into another, knocking another one down. It was the best run he made in the whole time he played for me.

Campbell was the NFL's most feared rushing force from 1978 through 1980, pilling up 5,081 yards while averaging nearly 5.0 yards per carry with his battering-ram style. But by 1981, his average had dropped to 3.8; it never again rose above 4.0.

BP: I think I know where you're going with this. After 1980, Earl was playing on football teams that didn't win. My opinion is that the number of times he carried the ball for me had nothing to do with any drop-off in his numbers. It's just that he didn't have as good a football team around him, and defenses had an easier time stopping him.

Paul Brown once said about coaching Jim Brown, "When you have the big gun, you pull the trigger." But there is also a school of thought that says you shouldn't fire a cannon like a machine gun. Campbell averaged nearly 23 carries per game in your offense. In retrospect, was that too much work for a power runner like Campbell?

BP: I don't know. I always thought that you tried to win the game you were playing. If we used Earl enough to win the game we were playing, then I think that's the only thing that counts. And I'm sure that's what he thought. If he had to carry thirty times or forty times to help us in the game, he would. I'm sure his attitude was, "Hey, let's win this game and worry about next week when we get to it."

Were you ever concerned that Campbell's running style would shorten his career?

BP: It shortened a helluva lot more people's careers than it did Earl's. I'm telling you now, when he broke through that line of scrimmage and those little 180-, 190-pound defensive backs tried to hit him going twenty-five, thirty miles an hour, who was hurtin' more the next day?

The Pittsburgh Steelers, from 1978-80, did the best job of slowing Campbell, holding him to an average of 70 yards per game for the regular season and 39 yards/game in the playoffs.

BP: Hell, they did a damn good job against everybody! Who in the hell else ever played good against Pittsburgh? They had an ability to play at whatever level they wanted, and that's why they won so many Super Bowls! That's why we could only beat them once a year. They'd always beat us in the playoffs because they were a better football team. They had more defensive players that are Hall-of-Famers than any other football team. And there are some who aren't Hall-of-Famers that should be.

What other teams defensively did a good job of containing Campbell?

BP: None. We played against some people that would do a good job against him for a quarter or two, but nobody could stop him except the Pittsburgh Steelers.

"When I got to Houston, I asked Bum what he expected from me. He said, 'I don't want you to fumble. And every yard you move the ball toward the goal line, that's one less yard that Earl won't have to get by himself.'"

- Richard Ellender, Houston Oilers WR/KR, 1979

Let's talk about those memorable battles with the Steelers in the late 1970s. You once said after a regular season meeting in 1978, a bloody 13-3 loss at the Astrodome, that, "In my 31 years of coaching, I've never seen a game that was as hammer and tong as this one."

BP: [Laughing] All of them were. They needed an ambulance on the sideline for those Pittsburgh games.

Was the rivalry a mean-spirited one, like the great Pittsburgh-Oakland or Kansas City-Oakland wars of that era?

BP: No, our players got along good with Pittsburgh's. Everyone respected the Steelers, even our fans, and the Steelers liked and respected our guys. It was just good, hard football, that's all. Part of the reason it became a great rivalry was that we knew we had to beat them to get to the Super Bowl. The road went through Pittsburgh in those days. When we beat them, they were gracious losers and gave us the credit for winning. They'd say we won fair-and-square and move on with no excuses. Whenever they beat us, they'd still give us credit for playing hard. You have to respect a team that does that.

Describe your memories of "Luv Ya Blue," the city of Houston's love affair with the Oilers during the last part of the decade. The blue and white pompoms...the Oilers fight song blaring over the Astrodome speakers... the huge crowds at the airport when the team landed.

BP: Those people were lined up the whole way from the airport to the Dome after both those championship games! They knew the route the buses were taking. I'm not exaggerating when I say there were at least 50,000 people along the way – standing in the medians, in their cars, on top of their cars the whole way. They lined the streets of Houston. It was just a special time, one where everything fit together. The western craze was going across the country about that time. I'm kind of a western guy. It just all fit in good.

The people of Houston loved our players. They liked Earl. They liked Dan and Carl Mauck and Billy "White Shoes" because they were easy to like. Our players always put on a good show. They tried. I had *never* seen that bunch not try. The Oilers have had good players since I was there. Jack Pardee's teams had a lot of good players, and they were probably good kids but the people didn't know it. Those players weren't as close to the fans as ours were. They were a little more distant, but I guess when they got rich they felt they didn't need anybody.

Your teams played on that notoriously hard surface of the Astrodome. Do you feel that artificial turf tears up a football team much worse than grass does?

BP: No, definitely not. Because at least on Astroturf – even in the wet, stormy rainy weather – no matter now many times you run up and down the field, when you put your foot down it was gonna hit where it was supposed to hit. On a mud field or a grass field, there are always dug out spots that can injure an ankle or leg. I say it's harder to run on a wet grass field than a wet artificial field. Defensive backs have no chance at all on a wet, muddy field because they have to wait till the receiver makes his cut before they can react. Then they have to chase him down the field.

I liked playing at the Dome. While I was coaching at the University of Houston in 1966 we opened the Astrodome. To be honest, the turf at that time was not good. It didn't even have a pad under it. It was just laid on top of hard ground. But by 1968 it was much better. They developed a pad to go under it, and from that time on it was good.

Nowadays players and agents use turf as an excuse in negotiations, trying to tell everybody that it's bad. Well, Dallas still plays on it and they've won a bunch of championships. Pittsburgh plays on it and practices on it, and they've got a bunch of championships. I just can't believe that it's bad.

Steeler Black and Oiler Blue

Bum Phillips called 'em "hammer and tong" games, those AFC Central clashes between Pittsburgh and Houston that highlighted NFL action towards end of the 1970s. Wide-eyed, head-on collisions that left both sides wobbly and bracing for the next roundhouse. More aesthetically pleasing football had been displayed in the league – the teams combined for 12 turnovers on a dry field in '77, 14 on a slushy turf the next year– but few matched Steelers-Oilers in terms of raw emotion and punishing exhibits of might.

"There are football games, and there are 'extra-tape games,' when you wrap your people just a little bit tighter," says former Steelers trainer Ralph Berlin. "Houston-Pittsburgh was always an 'extra tape' game.

"I was on the sidelines for every Steelers game from 1968 to '93, and one of the hardest shots I've ever seen came in the Astrodome. It was 1978. The place was all wound up, and Earl Campbell was averaging five or six yards every time he carried the ball. Then [S] Donnie Shell slammed into his mid-section on a play and put an end to all that. We had to break two of Campbell's ribs to get him out of there."

From 1977 through 1980, the Steelers and Oilers played 10 times, splitting all four regular season pairings. However, Pittsburgh captured both keynote games – the '78 and '79 AFC Championships – to advance to the Super Bowl, a place Phillips and his Oilers never got to visit.

"There's no doubt we were the second-best team in the NFL by '78," says Phillips. "Had we gotten into the Super Bowl we could've handled Dallas. We could've handled the Rams. Look at the success we had against the rest of the league. We just had the bad luck of being in the same division as the best football team ever."

The numbers are displayed below, a statistical comparison – Bum's Oilers versus the NFL, then Oilers versus the Pittsburgh Steelers. They tell a story. Like trying to crack the Top Ten with a really cool record but The Beatles were still around. Like the unknown Phil Price finishing 10-under par and losing. By eleven strokes. To Tiger Woods.

Phillips recognized his unconquerable challenge shortly into his rookie season as head coach. It was a Monday nighter in 1975. He had just watched his team fall 32-9 on the home field.

"FDR said the only thing we have to fear is fear itself," he told the press afterwards. "Well, the Steelers *are* fear itself."

	vs. rest of NFL (1977-80)	vs. Pittsburgh (1977-80)
Games Played	59 (including playoffs)	10 (including playoffs)
Record	40-19	4-6
Winning Percentage	.678	.400
Points Scored/gm	20.5	13.2
Points Allowed/gm	17.4	21.4
Rushing Yards/gm	163.0	102.0
Rushing Yards Allowed/gm	118.1	141.4
Passing Yards/gm	169.3	137.5
Passing Yards Allowed/gm	182.7	200.7
Turnovers/gm	2.7	3.9

You developed a reputation as being a great judge of hidden talent. For example, there were 21 free agents on your 1978 team, which reached the AFC Championship game. It was easy to spot the greatness of an Earl Campbell or a Robert Brazile, but you also got mileage out of free agent throwaways like DE Andy Dorris, LB Steve Kiner and kicker Toni Fritsch. What specific qualities or intangibles did you look for in a player?

BP: I wanted a guy that was like the guys I already had. I didn't want anybody that wouldn't be happy on our team. If I thought a player had the wrong attitude or didn't have strong work habits or didn't put the team first, then I didn't want him.

Players had to have a certain amount of ability, of course. Attitude alone won't beat anybody. But those overachiever types can help you win. They don't necessarily have to be starters. They can be good special teamers. They can be good men off the field. They can be leaders. They can pay careful attention in practice.

Take Guido Merkins. He played wide receiver and backup quarterback for us. He punted, held for all extra points, and covered every punt and kickoff in the eleven years he played for me. He even started at strong safety once when we needed him. Jerrell Wilson, the old Kansas City punter, was a scout for us. Before the '78 season he told me, "Coach, I played softball this summer with a guy that I think would be a good football prospect. His name is Guido Merkins."

I said, "What did he play?"

He said, "He played quarterback at Sam Houston, but he's a heckuva athlete, and he's a good kid."

I said, "Well, tell him to come on down here."

So we brought Guido on down there and he made the team and played every doggone year. He was probably the best athlete out of all the kids I've ever had on my teams. He did everything that a guy can do for a football team. He wasn't a good enough player to start at any one position, but he was a good enough player at a lot of positions to help you win.

Who was the toughest training camp cut you had to make, and why?

BP: [Pause] John Hadl, probably. We picked him up in a trade with the Packers to be a veteran backup for Pastorini. We had him for two years. I knew John back from when I coached in San Diego. It was like cutting an old friend. In 1978 we drafted a kid named Gifford Nielsen that we felt was smart and good enough to play behind Dan. We couldn't afford to keep three quarterbacks, so we gambled and kept Gifford. We thought Gifford would eventually replace Pastorini down the road, but that didn't work out. There were other tough cuts, but releasing John Hadl was the toughest.

In 1976, you drafted a wide receiver out of Tulsa named Steve Largent. Largent couldn't beat out names like Jim Beirne or Earl Thomas or Mel Baker for a spot on the Oilers roster, but he was good enough to be voted into the Hall of Fame. What did or didn't you see in Largent that prompted you to trade him to Seattle during training camp?

BP: I thought Steve was an excellent player and I didn't want to cut him. I felt we needed a good possession receiver on the Oilers. I don't want to sound like it was somebody else's fault but it was. Largent didn't fit what our receivers coach [Fran Polsfoot] wanted at the time. He didn't think Largent had the breakaway speed to catch the deep ball. He wanted guys who could outrun everybody. He said, "If cornerbacks play bump-and-run on this guy he'll never get off the line of scrimmage." He talked me into it. Of course, it turned out to be a terrible mistake, but it's not the only one I've ever made.

Also, you gotta remember that players don't always perform at their highest level. Then, after a guy's cut or traded and his back is against the wall, he does really good because he's got more incentive. He wants to prove his old team wrong. Regardless, Largent was a great one and I sure messed up letting him get away.

Everybody remembers your brazen Super Bowl prediction after the 1979 AFC Title game – "Last year we knocked on the door. This year we beat on it. Next year we're gonna kick the sonofabitch in." That door, however, never opened for you in Houston. Did you really believe you had enough talent on the Oilers to win the Super Bowl?

BP: I can't even answer that question because no matter how I answer, it ain't going to come out right. 1980 was gonna be our year. We added Kenny Stabler and Jack Tatum from the Raiders and had a big season. We finally beat out Pittsburgh for the AFC Central championship. We were good enough to win the Super Bowl and thought we would. But we just didn't play good against the Raiders in the playoffs and they beat us. That made it three years in a row, the team that beat us in the playoffs went on to win the Super Bowl.

Did you feel that Stabler, a 10-year veteran unwanted by Oakland, still had enough in his tank to lead the Oilers to the Super Bowl? A lot of people, including Al Davis, felt his career was in decline by the late '70s.

BP: Sure I did. He had plenty left. Kenny wasn't the same player he was four or five years earlier, but I saw him walk out on the practice field and, in a 7-on-7 practice drill, throw eighteen straight passes and complete every one of them. That was the first time he worked out with the Oilers. He didn't know any of our receivers and had never thrown a pass to one of 'em. He just walked out there and completed 18 in a row. That was against a defense, too – linebackers and secondary. Kenny was a phenomenal thrower.

To acquire Stabler, the Oilers had to part with their longtime veteran starter, Dan Pastorini. How difficult of a decision was it to let Pastorini go, considering the progress the team had made under his direction?

BP: It was *his* decision.

It was Pastorini's decision? The story fed to the public was that it was management's decision to make the move, that Pastorini had taken the team as far as he could. Not true?

BP: No. Dan came to talk to me after the season was over and said, "I want a trade. They've never liked me here, and I want to leave."

I told him, "Dan, that's not right!"

He said, "Well, that's what I want. You told me when you first came to Houston, standing in front of the team, that when somebody didn't want to be here, all they had to do was ask. You didn't want anybody on the team that didn't want to be here. I'm telling you right now – I want to be traded." I knew he'd been upset at the fans. They had booed him when he was injured and being taken off the field on a stretcher. He took it real personal and never let it go.

I told him, "I don't even want to discuss it. Go on home and think about it." He came back the next week and told me he still wanted to go. I said, "This is a bad decision, and you're gonna regret it the rest of your life." Then we made the deal for Stabler.

Did you suspect that Pastorini had been unhappy playing for Houston?

BP: I can't answer that. The fans got a little upset with him once in a while, but Christ, they got upset with me too. Fans get upset with anybody when you don't win. You just take that with a grain of salt and move on. You gotta learn to do it that way. Dan evidently couldn't.

The story goes that Davis was looking for a stronger arm to jump-start his deep passing game. Stabler's arm apparently wasn't getting the ball downfield far enough for the Raiders.

BP: Yeah, that's true. No doubt about it that Davis wanted Dan because he could throw it deep.

Unfortunately, Dan broke his knee very early on when he was in Oakland, and he physically never got over that.

After the trade you commented, "We weren't looking for a better passer than Dan. We were looking for a different type of passer, a more consistent, intermediate guy that would fit into a ball-control offense." Was that a damage control PR statement, or was Stabler really an appealing addition to your offense?

BP: I had to say something. When Kenny came to play for us, I didn't really know him that well or what he was still able to do on the field. We had him running an offense that had been built for Dan. Had I been there another year, I think we would have changed some things around and utilized him better.

From 1978-80, your Oilers had a 32-16 record and made three straight playoff appearances, but shortly after that playoff loss to the Raiders you were fired by Bud Adams. Was that a shocking moment for you, or had there been some friction building with management?

BP: It surprised me. But at the same time, it's Bud's team. He's the owner, and if he thinks he can do better without you, he can let you go. If he's wrong, well, you'll just have to go somewhere else and prove he was wrong. But if you can't get another job, then he was probably right to fire you.

I never had a cross word with him, even on the day he fired me. When Bud hired me, I thanked him and told him, "Someday you'll probably fire me. On that day I'll shake your hand again and say Thank You."

But it surprised me. I was disappointed to leave Houston because I had everything there. Everything was going good. If I had been allowed to stay another year, we might have gotten to the Super Bowl. Instead, Cincinnati made it from the AFC (in 1981), and we had beat them twice in 1980. We just didn't play good at Oakland. I don't know how to explain it. We just didn't play good.

What circumstances do you think led to Adams' decision?

BP: You'd have to ask him. I have no idea. All I know is the Oilers went from being a good, competitive football team to nothing in less than a year and a half. He called me down to his office and told me he wanted me to hire an offensive coordinator. I told him I wasn't going to do it. Somebody had convinced him the offense would've done better if we had one.

I said, "Look, Mr. Adams, we only have but seven coaches on our staff, and three of them run the offense. I don't believe I'm going to hire somebody from outside, bring him in, and say, 'These three guys have been to the playoffs for three straight years, but now they're gonna work for you. They're gonna do what you tell them to do.' It won't work. I won't hire a coordinator."

It was like the criticism I received when we didn't make a whole lot of yards rushing. People would say, "You only have one guy back there – Earl Campbell – and everybody watches him. Everybody knows he's going to get the ball. You have to change your offense."

Well, everybody knew Walter Payton was gonna get the ball and he gained a lot of yards. Everybody knew Eric Dickerson was gonna get the ball. In the Rams offense, he was the only guy in the backfield too! He made 2,100 yards in one season playing like that. If you win, people are happy. If you get beat, people are gonna find things to gripe about. Like I told Dan Pastorini, you just take it with a grain of salt and go on.

Emotionally, how hard did you take the firing?

BP: It was very hard. I had never been fired before. The last time I talked to Bud about my job was to discuss a contract extension, then all of a sudden I'm no longer the coach. What hurt the most was leaving a team that was still on the verge of being great. I had a group of guys I really, really loved. I knew them all good, and we had a lot of great times together. But I knew I still wanted to coach, and to do that I knew I had to leave Houston.

You were back on your feet shortly thereafter, as the New Orleans Saints offered you their head coaching position. New players, new challenges, a new dome. Can you recall the last thing you said to yourself as you were packing up and leaving Houston?

BP: One more year. All I needed was one more year.

— 3 —
Paul Zimmerman, Senior Football Writer
Sports Illustrated
March 6, 1998

It was a frameable June afternoon in midtown Manhattan. Stunning, sunglassed women taking their lunch break strolls. Sidewalk café seats filled with touristas and lounging students. Lots of bright sunshine, a super view from the tip-top of the Empire State Building, and there I sat, buried in a sweaty corner of the New York Public Library, scrolling through roll after roll of blotchy, scratched microfilm. Next to me was some nutty professor type – complete with the sweater and matted hair, gnarled teeth and low-cut black Chuck Taylor's – researching Louisiana Republican primaries from the 1880s.

My search? The Zimmerman Archives. Great pro football tales from the past. I'd read nearly everything Paul Zimmerman has written since he was hired by *Sports Illustrated* in 1979, and now it was time to dig back even further, into this author's forgotten days with *The New York Post*.

Here's an attention grabber from January 1977. The day's top story was a review of Super Bowl XI between Minnesota and Oakland. "Dr. Z," as he is also known, was irritated by another losing Vikings' effort in the championship game, their fourth of such kind. A "gang of zombies," he called them this time.

"Another year, another Super Bowl, same old Vikings. In four tries, they have yet to score a point in the first half. They have yet to offer any kind of competition at this level. The halftime show was Walt Disney's 'It's a Small World.' It was aimed at the Vikings. A great Mickey Mouse emblem was unfurled. That was the Vikings yesterday. Hundreds of balloons were sent into the air – in honor of [QB Fran] Tarkenton's passes. Pigeons were released. Yesterday the Vikings were the biggest pigeons of all."

Yep, this was the stuff I was looking for, and these microfilms are loaded with it. Here's a column blasting the bungled officiating in the '76 Patriots-Raiders playoff game. A January 1973 article takes a quirky trip down memory lane with the expansion Miami Dolphins of '66. A lot of the material is a chore to read because of the film's condition, so I'm squinting my way through a lot of the photocopies. The dozing volunteer behind the counter is getting cranky with all my refund requests...

An interview with Paul Zimmerman is included in this book because he is arguably pro football's greatest chronicler; the project wouldn't be complete without a good dose of him. I remember hearing the old 49ers coach Bill Walsh talk about the refining and tweaking and polishing of his offense until "It got to the point where it became something of an art form." Zimmerman's writing on football exists on a similar level – as its own art form, a thing of literary beauty. The game's details, the memories, the quotes and strategy, the drama – it's all there, woven together. It belongs in a museum for words.

As an offensive lineman at Stanford and Columbia, Zimmerman learned the game from the inside out before moving into his career in journalism. After stints at the now-defunct *New York Journal-American* and *New York World-Telegram & Sun*, he spent 13 years on the sports desk of *The New York Post*, covering the Jets and pro football while also contributing a popular wine column. He joined *Sports Illustrated* in 1979 as its senior football writer.

Zimmerman is a well-known statistics freak. He compiles his own set of annual numbers and compares them to what the NFL publishes, a compulsion that actually paid off for one quarterback back in 1972. That year, Zimmerman discovered the NFL had mistakenly omitted an entire quarter of Fran Tarkenton's passing stats. The correction stripped Tarkenton of the league passing title and gave it to the Giants' Norm Snead.

For as much as he loves the game, Dr. Z equally detests the mass media's overwhelming obsession with human-interest stories and fluff items, which nearly overwhelms the intricacies of the game itself. Consider this sophomoric insight by Michael Silver – the writer who eventually replaced Zimmerman as *Sports Illustrated*'s top NFL feature man – in his story on Denver's win over Green Bay in Super Bowl XXXII:

"Sex before competition is not the [John] Elway way. Not in our family, it's not,' Janet [Elway] said. 'But if he wins, I'm sure he'll deserve any favor he wants.' That may explain the huge smile that was plastered on John's face as he hoisted the Lombardi trophy over his head on the victory podium."

That's cute, Mikey. What a brilliant angle. The great John Elway finally wins a championship in the fading days of a fabulous career, and your focus is on whether or not the guy is getting laid. Next time, please submit that kind of garbage to *Maxim* or *FHM* or any of those juvenile magazines targeted at the twenty-something, "Man Show" crowd. Guys in the backwards baseball caps will love it.

The question is, What about the game? What about the action on the field? In most publications and newspapers, it's now a secondary item, taking a disturbing backseat to hype and triviality. And once the hype becomes more important than the event itself, it's never long before the whole institution sits on the verge of collapse. The masses, the fans, steadily begin to lose interest, and they'll never really come back.

Recent *SI* covers include a photo of a heavily tattooed Kenyon Martin, screaming in rage as he tears his Nets jersey in half. The next week, the psychotic Mike Tyson is snarling on the cover, despite the fact that the thuggish boxer hadn't won an important fight in over a decade? These are today's top stories? Can you see the "condemned" signs plastered on the face of modern sports writing? After 18 years, I cancelled my subscription.

To his credit, Zimmerman refuses to contribute to its demise, although the ranks on his side continue to shrink.

"I'm an analyst," he says. "I make my living at analyzing games. I'm intrigued by the game itself, solving the many puzzles that present themselves over a three-hour period each Sunday. Or as one gentleman in England, a rare fan of American football, so aptly put it some years ago: 'A chessboard constantly coming to life.' I love the ebb and flow of strategy and counter strategy, defense trying to catch up with offense and then vice versa, the trends of the game, the techniques, all played out in an arena of intelligence and pain, courage and high emotion. To me, at least, there is nothing like it."

There is a potentially serious drawback, however, to pursuing an interview with the good Doctor. Despite the wealth of dynamite information and insight he can provide, spending an hour with him on the telephone is like zipping a unicycle through a Cambodian minefield. Say something with which he disagrees, utter a partial truth, offer a historical inaccuracy, and Wham! Z might rip into you without warning, in a tone that screams, "*Why am I wasting my time with this yuck-a-puck!*"

Condescending? If he senses you're uninformed. Intimidating? At times. Worth the trouble? Absolutely, but I'll also admit there were several points during our conversations that I wanted to tell him to fuck off and slam the phone down and forget the whole deal. I omitted some of his rips from the text simply because they were embarrassing. They read like some old grump trying to pick a fight with the paperboy on the front porch.

Example: I opened the entire interview by asking for his thoughts on the Jets reviving their retro, 1960s-style uniforms, the kind that was worn during Zimmerman's years as the team's beat writer. Bad move.

"No comment," he snapped back at me. "Don't give a fuck. I don't really care about the glitzing of the game and the selling of the game. I don't care about that shit. That's for Nike and the guys selling t-shirts. To me, that's not anything. Bullshit presentation is not football. I don't care about it."

Uh, okay…got it.

I've spoken with several of Zimmerman's peers from the world of sports media, and their opinions of him were rather consistent. "He's a smart guy," one told me, "probably the most knowledgeable football writer in the business. But he treats everyone else like they're second-class, like they're stupid and don't understand what they're watching on the field. C'mon, football is a simple game."

"Zimmerman played in college," another said, "though I don't think he was very good. He knows the X's and O's better than writers who never played, which is the majority of them. That gives him a big edge, and he uses it exceptionally well in his work. But there's an arrogance that turns everybody off. He'll bark at you. People tend to steer clear of him." Several others concurred.

After reviewing a copy of the raw text of our interview, Zimmerman responded to me with a quick note. *"In reading the transcript,"* he wrote, *"I seem to come off as a kind of an arrogant prick. I don't think I'd like the person who gave you that interview. 'Arrogant, a bit nuts, with an occasional warm spot,' was the way my wife described it. So be it. That's me, folks."*

Right, so be it. You take the good with the bad. Enjoy the Halloween apple but watch out for the roofing tacks. A number of former Packers have always maintained they hated playing for Vince Lombardi, but they respected him and gathered their championships along the way. More than a few of the Italian patriciate would have liked to have seen the irritable Michelangelo drop off his Sistine Chapel scaffolding, yet his work is still incomparable.

Is Zimmerman the greatest football writer in history? I haven't found one better. Every art has its masters, and this art belongs to him. He owns it.

Rudyard Kipling, once describing how he found his lines, stated, "I keep serving six honest men (They taught me all I know); their names are What and Why and When and How and Where and Who."

When it comes to the words that describe and chronicle professional football, America's true sporting passion, Paul Zimmerman is the game's seventh honest man. And away we go....

● ● ●

How has pro football most changed since you first started covering games in the mid-1960s?

PZ: It was a white game, now it's a black game.

You mean at the skill positions?

PZ: I didn't say that. I'm saying it used to be a white game, now it's a black game. It used to be a strength game, now it's a speed game.

Well, white cornerbacks have pretty much disappeared. You have to go all the way back to...

PZ: [Interrupting] What about the Giants' Jason Sehorn? Last time I looked he was white. It sounds like you didn't do your homework for this. It sounds like you're not very well prepared.

I meant prior to today's rosters. You have to go back to the late 1980s to find the last white cornerback, Brian Davis of the Redskins. Back to the question: Is professional football a better game today than it was thirty years ago?

PZ: More skill now, but not at all positions. Some techniques were better then. People knew how to play the run better than they do now. Run-blocking techniques on the offensive line were better then. Linebackers could play the run better then. But the athletes are much faster today. You can teach these players to do things, but you can't teach them to run fast.

You covered the New York Jets from 1966-76, which, other than the few years prior to their victory in Super Bowl III, was a rather bleak stretch. Did the team's continuously dismal performance ever become a drain on the creativity of your work?

PZ: No. If anything, covering a losing team makes you work harder, and probably makes you do better work. The best work you do is when everybody is mad at you and they're not talking to you, because then you can't lean on the quotes and you have to go on your own opinion. You come up with different, sometimes better angles. You think of things that the average "master of the obvious" reporter would never come up with, although they might end up stealing it later.

What, in your mind, was the main reason for the Jets' long, downward slide through the 1970s? Poor drafting? Inferior coaching? Weak management decisions?

PZ: Absentee ownership hurt the Jets terribly. But they had absentee ownership when they won the Super Bowl, as well, so I guess it's not a good argument. The Jets never were strong in the ownership division, going right down through this current era. That's been a real problem with the team, ever since Sonny Werblin owned it. They were cheap. I don't want to knock [former head coach] Weeb Ewbank because he is a friend and I wrote a book with him. You could say that the organization in general would not spend top dollar. And in those days, it wasn't the free agent system where everyone spent the same and it just depended on how you juggled it around. If you really spent a lot of money you could somehow figure out a way to win and get better players – free agents, trade for a guy who is demanding a lot of money. The Jets were never at the forefront when it came to money.

Their personnel department? Uh, pretty good. I think one big thing that set them back was they absolutely stayed too long with Namath. They could not believe he was on the decline when he was obviously not effective. There were a lot of things at work that led to the decline of the Jets.

When did you first sense that the skills of Joe Namath, New York's franchise quarterback, were deteriorating? Was there a specific moment in the press box that you remember saying to yourself, "Namath is finished."

PZ: It's very difficult to pinpoint it because when you watched him every day in practice, he still threw as well as he ever did. I saw him in one game in Cincinnati in '73. Cincinnati's secondary had been dominating. Namath came off the bench because he had been hurt and within one minute he had the Bengals completely fucked up. I mean, his throws were just so quick and he ran that two-minute offense so well that he just turned them upside down. New York lost at the end on some bad calls, but he was dynamic.

The thing was that you couldn't project that into an entire game because there was no rush on him. Right up until the end he could set his feet and throw with no rush and be very accurate, still put a lot on the ball. His decline came with the team's inability to protect him as well as it used to. Then it became glaring. He really looked like he was slipping around '74. That's when he started showing real decline.

In '75, I wrote an article saying they ought to get rid of him, that the Jets were kidding themselves. I got ripped royally for that one. I wrote a wine column for *The New York Post* as well, and Sal Marciano at ABC said I'd been hitting the grape too much for writing something like that. The guys at *The Post* told me, "That's libel! You should go after him!" and all that bullshit.

I said, "I've got a better idea: I'll buy him a good bottle of wine." So I gave Marciano a bottle of wine. But I was writing in '75 that the Jets ought to get rid of Namath while they could still get something for him, that there were still suckers out there.

So when the Rams acquired him up in 1977, all they really were gaining was publicity?

PZ: [Former Rams GM] Don Klosterman called me up and said, "What do you think of how Namath is playing?"

I said, "Don, he can't play. *He can't play.*"

He said, "Well, we've had guys at practice, and they say he can still throw as well as..."

And I said, "Yeah, he can throw in practice. He can't face a rush. Stay away from him, Don."

He said, "Thanks for your help."

Twenty minutes later the Rams pick Namath up, and he lasts half the season. I covered his first game with L.A. against Atlanta and he couldn't face the blitz. They threw a big blitz against him that day. Usually he was very good against the blitz, but Atlanta could see he'd never be able to handle it. He'd get it to his hot receiver pretty quick, dump off the short passes to avoid the sack, but in running a complete offensive package he couldn't function anymore.

The Jets drafted Alabama's Richard Todd in 1976 to succeed Namath. Do you think the pressure of replacing a legend and playing in New York City was too much on Todd early in his career, that it impeded his development as a quarterback?

PZ: No. Todd's biggest problem was reading defenses. He wasn't very good at it. His arm strength wasn't a problem. I just think he would get confused back there and throw a lot of bad balls. As for playing in New York, the press in New York isn't that tough. It really isn't. Too much is made out of that. The New York press is whiny. They love to whine and complain, but that's because they want to see the local teams do well. The New York press isn't nearly as tough as it is in, say, Boston or Philadelphia. In those cities, the media almost wants the teams to do badly, just so they have something to bitch about in the papers.

I don't think the pressure of New York got to Todd at all. He had Namath working with him during his first year in New York – two Alabama boys. Namath helped him out quite a bit that first year, although it was his last year with the Jets. Dan Henning was his quarterback coach, and he was a good one. So Todd came into a pretty good situation. He just couldn't read defenses particularly well. That's why he never became a big-time player.

Vintage Dr. Z, on Redskins Quarterback Joe Theismann

Joe Theismann is Old World. "Give me 50 seconds and two time-outs and I'll put something on the board," he says. Yep, that's him all right. Cocky, brash, likes to ride in limos and wear fur coats and collect a bundle in endorsements. Not well loved by his teammates, but the Jets were divided into pro- and anti-Namath factions, too. And none of it carries over to the field. I took a good look at him up close at the [1984] Pro Bowl workouts last season. He was coming off a downer, the Super Bowl blowout, and a whole season of triumph had been erased by the memory of that one disastrous pass at the end of the first half. But by God he had a hungry predator look to him, broken nose, wrinkles starting to show around the mouth and eyes, raw-looking bruise on the chin. I think that's the kind of face I'd like to look across the huddle and see if I were down by six in the last minute.

– Paul Zimmerman, *The New Thinking Man's Guide to Pro Football*
(Simon & Schuster, 1984)

The Jets hired Lou Holtz from the college ranks after Charley Winner was fired in 1976. The result was a 3-11 season, with Holtz bailing out with a game left on the schedule. Why was his short campaign in New York such a disaster?

PZ: Holtz didn't understand the pro game. The players had no respect for him. One of the problems was that he was little. Big players don't like little coaches, especially the ones who come from college, who were college hotshots. Lou was thin. He couldn't take the wind. He'd be out there shivering in his little jacket, and the players would be laughing at him. He was a comedian. He had his radio show. He didn't understand NFL talent. He was a college coach who was in way over his head.

One team that New York had a pretty good handle on during the late 1970s was the Miami Dolphins. From 1978-81, the Jets were 7-0-1 vs. Miami, despite the Dolphins being a repeat playoff team during those years. What did head coach Walt Michaels, who replaced Holtz, have over Don Shula during that period?

PZ: It wasn't Michaels. It was the players. They seemed to have a hair up their ass when they played Miami. They just didn't like them. They got sky-high against Miami for some reason. Miami wasn't terrible on defense back then, but it was a defense that the Jets liked to go up against. I guess they scored a lot against Miami back then [25 ppg between 1978-81]. Michaels was a defensive coach, so he doesn't get credit for a shoot-out.

Do you think Jets' management gave up on Michaels too soon? He was fired in 1983, just after New York's first AFC Title appearance in nearly 15 years. The team hasn't been back since.

PZ: Let's just say that his personality posed a problem for them. There was more to it than that, but I can't talk about it. I can't discuss it.

Did management give up on him too early?

PZ: It's hard for me to say. Walt was a friend. I knew what his problems were, and they knew what his problems were. He had problems. It was a buyout. They paid him off to get the hell out and keep his mouth shut. Notice he never said anything about it. Walt liked money, and they gave him money.

How about the players? Did they respect Michaels?

PZ: The defensive players did. He knew that side of the football, and they played hard for him. He made the offensive players nervous.

1987 was the first year I covered pro football. San Francisco was in Pittsburgh for the season opener and took a pretty good pounding that day. I went into the 49ers locker room after the game and was basically star struck. I started milling around and getting a few players autographs, like Joe Cribbs, Jerry Rice and...

PZ: [Interrupting] You were getting autographs while you were covering the game?

Well, I asked for a few. It was my first time in a pro lockerroom and I was...

PZ: [Interrupting] Why didn't you go ahead and blow them while you were at it? I hope you were ashamed of that. I hope you don't think it was cute.

C'mon, take it easy. I was only 21 and it was a big deal being there. I was star struck. Anyway, I get over to Joe Montana and I feel this hand on my shoulder. One of their PR guys about threw me into the parking lot for the autograph thing. So my question is, have you experienced any compromising locker room incidents since you've been covering NFL games?

PZ: Well, my first pro football locker room experience was in 1960, the Packers against the Eagles. I was playing semi-pro football myself for the Patterson Pioneers of the Eastern Football Conference. I was a guard, so I was interested in line play. Anyway, I went down to the Packers dressing room to get quotes for Joe King, who was our pro football writer at *The World-Telegram*. I walked into the Packers' locker room and I was scared to death. The first guy I see is Jerry Kramer. He, Fuzzy Thurston and Jim Ringo had done a great job against the Eagles middle three. So I went over to Kramer and introduced myself and said, "Your combination blocks were really great. Your trapping was great…blah, blah, blah."

Kramer lights up. He's ready to talk. Then he says, "Hey, I want you to meet this guy," and he brings Thurston over. Then Ringo comes over. I said to them, "How do you call your audibles? We're having a lot of trouble calling *our* line audibles." So we go through all of that, technically, and I say to myself, "This is great being in a pro locker room."

All of a sudden I see the thing was emptying out and I hadn't talked to anybody about the game. So I go running around. I see Lombardi on the way out, his muffler around his neck, striding towards the door. I said, "Excuse me, coach…." He said, "I've said everything I've had to say," and Boom! – he was gone. Bart Starr was already gone. Paul Hornung had hurt his shoulder and I had to catch him on the way out. I asked him how the shoulder was. He says, "Fine." That was all I got.

So I go upstairs and I see Joe King. He's typing away, cigarette hanging out of his mouth, his hat on. He said, "Alright, whaddaya got?"

I said, "What do you want?"

"How about Starr?"

"I didn't get him."

"Alright. Well, how about Paul Hornung? How is the shoulder?"

"Fine. He said the shoulder was fine."

"*Fine?* What do you mean *fine?*"

"Well, that's all he said."

"How about Lombardi?"

"Didn't get to him."

He put his cigarette down, pushed his hat back, looked at me and said, "Son, what did you get in the locker room?"

"Well, I talked to Kramer and Ringo about how they…"

"Alright, get out of here!" he said. "*Get out of here!*" It took me two years to get back in an NFL locker room.

Is it true that you write up some sort of chart for every game that you watch?

PZ: Every NFL game. I have a little trouble with the colleges because Saturday is kind of a relaxing day for me, and to start getting the college rosters and charting those games would just be too much. But I do chart every bowl game, which is tough because it's hard getting rosters and hard getting lineups.

How did you start that practice?

PZ: I started charting games in 1947 when I was 14. I love football and loved playing football, so I liked the idea of making a chart and having the plays go up and down a gridiron-shaped field. I always liked statistics and messing around with stuff like that. So I did it in '47, then kept refining it and refining it.

I once tried it in a game I played in. Some guy had some paper on the field, so I used it. When I would come out for a series every now and then, I'd sit there on the bench and fill out the chart. It was for some guy who was supposed to be covering the game for *Stars and Stripes*. He was a drunk, a friend of mine. He couldn't make it, and I wanted to help him out. We were kicking the shit out of the other team anyway, so I didn't care.

How many charts are in your collection?

PZ: Well, for the last 20 years I've averaged about 80 games a year. The prior thirty years I averaged 50 a year… I'd say around 4,000.

If you had the chance to chart one game in history that you didn't see, which would it be?

PZ: It would be a game that was never played: Notre Dame vs. Michigan, 1947. First day in heaven, that's what they'll do for me. They'll sit me down and give me some cigars and a chart and I'll watch that entire game.

Why '47 Michigan-Notre Dame?

PZ: They were the two greatest college football teams of all time.

Better than some of the powerhouse teams from the modern era, like Oklahoma or Miami or...

PZ: I *said* they were the best two teams in history.

Vintage Dr. Z, on "Charting" Football Games

A while back, Dave Anderson of the *Times* asked me, "Why don't you do a column about all your charts and all your crazy stuff during a football game?"

And I said, "Because it would seem pretentious and phony," and he said, "So what? Do it anyway."

So this is a column about all the charts and crazy stuff, only it's not crazy to me because I understand it.

I'll try to explain quickly. I keep a chart of the play-by-play, indicating good blocks and good defensive plays and substitutions and different colored ink alongside the play. Naturally, it fills up a page with numbers right away, and it's a little tough to read, and it looks weird, so a casual observer moves his seat away from me in the press box.

Then I'll keep a running statistical chart...so many yards per carry, so many per pass, etc...mainly because I don't trust official statisticians. There are usually about three or four official statistical errors per game.

One might ask, "Why do you care about one carry or a few yards more or less?" and the answer is that I care because I care, that's why I care, and do I tell you how to run your life?

Then I keep a third chart of my own invention, and it's tough to explain. It records all the passes to all the receivers, indicating which defensive backs or linebackers had the coverage, and what happened. I didn't know such a chart had a name until one day the Jets' offensive coach, Clive Rush, happened to see me doing it and he said, "Oh, I see you keep a field chart?"

He understood it immediately, and that scared me. So now when people ask me, "What the hell is that thing?" I say, "It's a field chart."

...There was only one time I got any feedback from my wife about my charts. That was the day before the Jets-Colts Super Bowl, and all the writers had filed their pre-game stories, and we were all sitting around the pool in that hotel in Ft. Lauderdale. All of a sudden I looked at my watch.

"I've got to go chart the Senior Bowl," I told her, and she looked at me kind of funny.

"Why don't you chart me for a change?" she said. (October 30, 1973)

– Copyright, 1973, *New York Post* Holdings, Inc. Reprinted with permission.

And which elusive pro game would you want to chart?

PZ: One game that I was curious about – and I went to NFL Films and got what they had on it – was the 1940 Bears-Redskins NFL Title game. I didn't chart it because they didn't show every single play, but I have all the notes on that game. I would like to see an in-depth version of that game so I could really chart the thing, to really see who was playing well.

In 1984 you wrote, "I'd like to see more stories analyzing the game [of football] itself, leaving the hoop-de-do to the columnists. I'm still waiting, for instance, to read something that will tell me exactly how the American hockey team beat Russia in the 1980 Olympics. Every tear and every proud heart has been duly registered, but I wish someone, somewhere, would have explained, technically, how we won the game."

Why do today's sports editors seem so interested in promoting the hype surrounding these games rather than dissecting the strategy and the tactics being used on the field?

PZ: Nobody knows how to do it.

Nobody knows how, or nobody is really interested?

PZ: Both. They don't care. They get their quotes. They go with the obvious angles. In the case of *Sports Illustrated,* they do some "Yeah, we were there" stuff. You know, the *"Nah, nah, we were there and you weren't. We had a beer with so-and-so the night before the game and he told us what was going to happen,"* and that's a wrap. They don't try to break down what happened on the field. They have no interest. Look at the most popular publication at Time-Life. Do you know what it is? It's *People* magazine. It's all human-interest stuff now, and unfortunately that's the way sportswriting has gone.

But the pendulum swings. *Sports Illustrated* initially hired me because they didn't like the way football was being covered. [Former SI editor] Mark Mulvoy said we needed to get more "nuts and bolts" – that was his fucking term, and if I heard it once I heard it a thousand times and it sets my teeth on edge. But "nuts and bolts" was what they wanted. Then after a while I fell out of fashion. Mulvoy told me my style was passé, to face it. Alright, I'm facing it. Maybe five years from now I'll be back in fashion. Their attention span is short.

What is your favorite piece that you have done for SI?

PZ: The best piece I did for *Sports Illustrated* was the one on the Cowboys-49ers NFC Championship game in 1981. None of the pieces I wrote for *SI* were ever my best because of the heavy editing. The stuff I wrote anywhere else was better because they didn't edit me. The editors fuck up everything. That article was the best of the "B" league.

Why was that your best story?

PZ: Because I did it the way I always wanted to cover a game. I wanted to do a microcosm, isolate one part of the game and get it from all angles. And I did – the famous last drive of the game. I talked to about fifteen different people, and some of them knew what I wanted and really helped. I did that last drive from the inside. That's what I wanted to do, and it worked.

Your first assignment for SI was a story on the L.A. Rams in the summer of 1979. That team went on to win the NFC title later that winter, and gave the Steelers a pretty good battle in Super Bowl XIII. Did you ever project the Rams being as successful as they were in '79?

PZ: That really wasn't my story. It was very clear to me what I was supposed to cover – the shakeup in the Rams' management. And their vision was correct because the story of the feud between Georgia Frontierre and her son broke afterwards. I watched their exhibition game, but I just brushed it off in a paragraph. To answer your question, I had no idea that team would reach the Super Bowl. Absolutely none. Total surprise.

How about their quarterback, Vince Ferragamo? His career seemed to have peaked in that game. Your thoughts on why he never became a more established quarterback in the NFL?

PZ: Ferragamo seemed a little bored. He seemed like he was kinda dead, you know, one of these emotionless guys. Good talent. He could throw. Good player, but it seemed like he had no passion.

What was the best team that didn't win the Super Bowl?

PZ: The Steelers in '76. That was probably the best defensive team I've ever seen, along with the '85 Bears. The '76 Steelers may have been the best Pittsburgh team ever. If not, they're pretty…close…to it. I go back and forth across the '74, '75 and '76 Steelers as to which team was the best.

Another great team that didn't win the whole thing is the 1983 Redskins, which blew through the regular season, then, after an early blocked punt in the Super Bowl against the Raiders, completely unraveled. Your opinion on the '83 Redskins?

PZ: The Raiders were a better team. The Redskins couldn't block Matt Millen. They couldn't block Reggie Kinlaw, the Raiders' nosetackle. What really hurt them was that it was a windy day; the wind kept playing tricks with Theismann's passes. He didn't have enough time to pass anyway.

   Other teams? Let me think about that… Another one that I thought was great was Dallas in 1970. Bob Lilly, Staubach, Duane Thomas. Great team. Very talented. I liked that Rams team from…I think it was '67, the one with one loss. They were a great team that didn't win it either.

You've frequently quoted former San Francisco 49ers coach Bill Walsh in your work as saying, "A pass rush, late in the game, is the key to NFL football." Give me the four best players from the 1970's who'd give you that rush.

PZ: Lyle Alzado, for one. Deacon Jones, although he really wasn't a name in the era we're talking about. His career crested around 1970. Jack Youngblood of the Rams was a great pass rusher. "Tombstone" Jackson from Denver. Harvey Martin from Dallas, another great one. Coy Bacon. Bacon was really one of the unsung players. He bounced around with some different teams – Washington, Cincinnati, San Diego. He was the kind of guy that, once he got on a roll, was a gathering force. The whole trick was to stop him early, then he'd just la-de-da through the rest of the game. But if he got off quickly, he'd just keep picking up steam and getting more powerful through the game. A very underrated player.

Vintage Dr. Z, On Fooling the Pittsburgh Steelers

   The Pittsburgh Steelers are a bunch of roughnecks with money in their pockets. The Dallas Cowboys figured that if you want to take it away from them, you don't use a blackjack. You use three shells and a pea. So, in the great computer room in Dallas, Tom Landry punched the button marked Steelers, the machines whirred and hummed, and the printout came out titled: Finesse. Sub-heading: Trickery.

   Look at what the Cowboys were up against. The Steelers' defensive line has a tackle called Mean Joe and an end called Mad Dog. Their middle linebacker has almost no teeth. Their right linebacker is named Dirt. And their quarterback…man, if Terry Bradshaw ain't limping and bleeding, the argument hasn't even started.

   The computer told the Cowboys what to do, but here's the funny thing about computers. They can't cut down a linebacker or move out a defensive tackle; they can't get down in a four-point stance and fight off a double-team. And when the verdict was in at Three Rivers Stadium in Pittsburgh last Sunday, when the Steelers had stopped every bit of flim-flammery and gimmickry the Cowboys threw at them and had knocked Roger Staubach out of the box while winning by a 14-3 score, Mean Joe Greene, the elder statesman of the defensive line, drew a deep breath and pronounced in that deliberate way of his, "Dallas is a team that tries to fool you. They wait for you to make a mistake. Well, what happens when they don't fool you? Can they blow you out?" And he looked up and paused a moment. "I think not."

– *Sports Illustrated*, November 5, 1979. Reprinted with permission.

Bacon is rarely mentioned in a discussion of all-time great pass rushers.

PZ: Call John Turney and ask him how many lifetime sacks he credits Bacon with. I think he is number three all-time. John Turney is a dedicated amateur from Utah, a guy who has kept all the sack records before the NFL began tracking them as an official statistic. He has a passion for sacks, a passion for football. A lot of the older pros really appreciate what he is doing, and they give him a lot of good information. He's the kind of guy who is always around and people are telling him, "Get lost. Don't bother me because you're not important enough." He does it with a passion, and I've helped him out as much as I could.

I got him a Super Bowl ticket for this last Super Bowl, at cost, when they were going for two grand apiece. He was standing there outside the stadium, looking down in the dumps. I said, "Cheer up, John. I got a ticket for you." I guess you could say he is a professional outsider. It's pretty easy for these PR guys to be shitty to people like him, to turn their noses at him.

The league didn't start keeping individual sack records until the early '80s. How is he able to compile sack information from before then?

PZ: By talking to people, going through every play-by-play sheet. I mean, the guy has worked like nobody else in history. He has every sack recorded that he could find. He has the sacks broken down on the '67 Raiders when they set the record. He's got it all, including stuff from the 1940s.

Give me your take on the rest of your list. Jack Youngblood.

PZ: Great motor. Speed rusher, primarily. Relentless.

Deacon Jones.

PZ: Devastating headslap. They say he'd be hampered today because he couldn't slap, but he'd figure out a way. He was probably the hungriest of them all, the guy who would crawl on his hands and knees to get to the passer. Plus the fact that he had tremendous physical ability, power, speed and that sensational headslap.

Rich "Tombstone" Jackson and Harvey Martin.

PZ: Tombstone was a guy who could split a helmet. He was like an uncorked jar of lightning. I mean, he just exploded. Harvey Martin was a great speed rusher, who was just terrific coming around the corner. He had great technique.

You played in an era when the headslap was a legal defensive maneuver. In terms of competitiveness, do you feel it should have been outlawed?

PZ: The league kept outlawing everything the defense did. I was pissed when they outlawed the bump all the way down the field until I looked at the footage of those games and saw defenses were mugging those guys. The headslap? I didn't really think it was fair when they outlawed it, but I think it would make for a really shitty game today because the quarterbacks would keep going down.

They can't block rushers now, with all the rules they have and all the shit. They can't block them without holding ferociously. There aren't enough good athletes on the offensive line today. You have these 320-lb belly bumpers, and the only way they can get by is to slob all over a guy – you know, this hog technique – and sort of engulf them. So with the headslap, you'd reduce them to blubber.

You once wrote a book about former Denver Broncos DE Lyle Alzado. The story goes that you were given a ridiculously short deadline and you had to write it while you were covering Super Bowl XII in New Orleans. What was that experience like?

PZ: I wrote it in eight days because my wife totaled the car. Berkeley Press gave me $8,500 if I could write it in eight days. I called Dave Anderson, who used to write a lot of quickie books, and asked him if it was physically possible to write a book in eight days if you were covering the event. He said, "Yeah, it's possible, but if you do it you'll wind up in the hospital."

Which is exactly what happened. My back went out. They took me off of the plane on a stretcher to Lenox Hill Hospital. The publisher came up to Lenox Hill when I was lying there and said, "You know, your copy is kinda rough." I said, "No shit. That's what you've got editors for!" He said, "We'll give you another three days. How about if you rewrite it? You're not doing anything anyway." I said all right, and they set up a typewriter right there in the hospital and I rewrote it. For the first five or six days of writing the book, I'd go up to Alzado's room after practice and he'd be lying on his back spinning yarns and I'd be sitting there with my tape recorder. The last two days, he was sitting there spinning yarns and I was lying there with my tape recorder. The back was going. I didn't think I was gonna fucking make it!

Alzado was one of my favorite players, the best. I'll give you a story about Alzado. After the Raiders' Super Bowl against the Redskins, I was in the locker room. It was madness, you know, turmoil. Everybody is flying around, trying to get interviews. He grabs me and says, "I gotta talk to you."

I said, "Now?" He says yes. I figured he got into some kind of trouble at a bar or something. We go in the back, way behind the fucking washing machines and everything, and he says, "How'd I play?"

I said, "Great! *That's* all you wanted?" I wanted to get out of there, so I could get back out and talk to people! But that's what he had to find out. What a character.

Years later Alzado developed terminal brain cancer, which he attributed to his use of steroids. Were you aware that he was using them while he was playing?

PZ: Yeah. He was the only player who confided in me about using them. He laid it all out, told me what it was like. He said he could not function in the NFL without them. Wouldn't be big enough. Maybe that was his security blanket, but he felt that he couldn't compete without making himself bigger.

The brain cancer moved quickly, but there is no way you could tie that to his steroid use. I have yet to see anyone who became seriously ill and died from steroids. They have yet to come up with that information. It's all assumption. Same deal with Pittsburgh's Steve Courson. He had a heart condition and they tried to tie that into steroids. There is no medical evidence that proves steroids cause heart disease either. No one has proved that.

Changing directions again. Former Pittsburgh Steeler Terry Bradshaw was once in a radio show discussion about "big-game" quarterbacks and Dan Fouts, the San Diego Chargers Hall-of-Famer, was brought up. Bradshaw's response was biting.

He said, "I don't mean this in any way to insult Fouts. I think he was an outstanding player but he was not a 'big game' quarterback. Fouts was great in your average Sunday game, but he wasn't the same player in the big ones." Agree or disagree?

PZ: That's exactly right. He wasn't. Fouts was a great everyday quarterback, but when it came to the big ones he came back to earth. Look at his performances in the playoffs. He was a great player, and he was tough. But it seems when he got into the big games, he sorta got himself into a pickle. He didn't chicken-out. He didn't choke. He just got himself into bad situations. That's a very strange way of putting it, I know, but things just seemed to go wrong for him in these high-pressure situations. You can't really call him a choker, but you can't say he elevated his play in the big games.

One of the more intriguing pieces you've written involved the Houston Oilers stealing the offensive signals from the San Diego sidelines in their upset of the Chargers in the '79 playoffs.

PZ: Well, they didn't steal their signs. That was the angle I used in the story, but I found out later what [Oilers LB] Gregg Bingham meant. He said that they were really reading Fouts' feet. When his feet were together, it was a handoff. When one foot was behind the other, it was a pass. That was all there was to it.

So Houston's coaches really hadn't stolen the Chargers' signals?

PZ: No, although that's what I thought at first. That's what [defensive coordinator] Eddie Biles told me after the game. He wanted to make himself look good. And that's what Bingham told me. But I had a drink with Bingham in the off-season, and I said, "What the fuck were you guys doing in that game?" and he told me. "We were reading his feet." That's it? Reading his feet? I wish they had leveled with me before I wrote the damn story, which, by the way, was knocked down by some guy in Cincinnati who accused me of trying to get Biles a head-coaching job. That was silly. Why the hell would I be trying to get Biles a head-coaching job?

Besides reading Fouts' feet, what was the best way to defuse that San Diego offense? Few teams were consistently able to stop "Air Coryell" during those years.

PZ: I remember talking to Rod Rust, who at the time was the defensive coordinator of the New England Patriots, and he gave me the book on how to stop both Fouts and Dan Marino. Those were the days of the 3-4 defense – three down linemen and four linebackers – and Rust said the key was gut pressure, getting to either of those guys with pressure up the middle. Neither one of them could move around very well, so if you could get to them from the inside, they'd either throw it away, get sacked or throw an interception. Rust guaranteed that if your inside linebackers could get two interceptions in a game against Fouts, your team would win the game.

The Raiders always had pretty good success against Fouts during those years.

PZ: Well, that's the way the Raiders have always played defense, ever since 1961 when Al Davis joined the organization. Davis has always emphasized his defense knocking around the quarterback, bloodying his nose, getting 15-yard roughing penalties and softening him up through the game. That was usually good enough to get to Fouts. He couldn't move out of the pocket like Joe Montana or Bradshaw could.

What was the worst way to defend that great Chargers offense?

PZ: For the defense to sit back in a deep zone and let Fouts throw the ball underneath and throw the outs. That whole offense was based on timing patterns, and a soft defensive zone would let Fouts do pretty much whatever he wanted. You couldn't let those receivers like John Jefferson and Charlie Joiner get off the line without bringing the cornerbacks up and giving them a bump at the line of scrimmage. They'd slice you up, and before you knew it you were down by two touchdowns.

Vintage Dr. Z, on the Great Dallas Demolition of 1985

The Chicago Bears turned back the clock in Texas Stadium Sunday, way back, past their old Monsters of the Midway days, past Bulldog Turner and George Musso and Bronko Nagurski, back to an era when men played football on rocky patches of ground and battled with fists and leather helmets. They beat the Cowboys 44-0, the worst defeat Dallas has suffered at Texas Stadium or any other stadium. They clinched their division championship and ran their record to 11-0, and they did it without their regular quarterback, Jim McMahon, who watched the game in civvies, thanks to a sore right shoulder. The Bears defense rushed in wild, frenzied waves and knocked out Dallas quarterback Danny White twice, and held his replacement, Gary Hogeboom, to six completions in 22 heaves. The defense sacked the pair of them six times and scored 14 points of its own and shut down the Dallas running game and, hey, there's no end to it.

– Sports Illustrated, November 25, 1985. Reprinted with permission.

Let's talk about Fouts' rival in Oakland, Kenny Stabler. You once quoted former Raider tight end Dave Casper as saying, "Stabler set coaching back 50 years. He knows everything there is to know on a football field, but when they give him his game plan on Wednesday he probably takes it home and throws it in the wastebasket. No one ever suspected how little he knows about the game plan on a particular week. He's fooled them all his life and he continues to fool them."

Your thoughts on Kenny "The Snake" Stabler and why he isn't in the Hall of Fame?

PZ: Do you know where I got that quote from? A college student from Hofstra University who was covering a Jets-Oilers exhibition game. Houston had brought in Casper to upgrade their tight end position. I had been talking with him just before, then this student got to him as he was leaving the locker room. He just said it like a throwaway line. I overheard it and said, "Holy shit!" Stabler had already been traded to the Saints by then. After the kid had left I went back over to Casper and asked him to explain it a little bit more. He said sure, and repeated it again. I wanted to get it myself and not lean on another guy's quote, especially a college kid. I thought, "Damn, I've never heard anything like *this* before." It was dynamic, an eye-opener.

But weren't Stabler and Casper friends? It's surprising he would make that kind of comment to the press.

PZ: Casper was a real weirdo. I don't know how many friends he had. Strange guy. Stabler was too. He was not a good guy either. When Stabler's name came up for the Hall of Fame, it was one of the few times in my life, during a Hall of Fame committee meeting, that I ever stood up and really dinged a guy. I said, "You *cannot* elect this man to the Hall of Fame." One jackass there had said, "He's always been great with the press."

Well, he wasn't great with the press. Bob Padecki of *The Sacramento Bee* was down in Mobile to interview him once. [Stabler and his friends] planted drugs in his car and he wound up in prison for the night until the police let him go. It was a rigged drug-bust that Stabler had organized. That's the kind of thing he does with those fucking redneck friends of his. As for the Hall of Fame, "Snake" was one of the greatest passers that ever lived. He had that Joe Montana-like timing. But he refused to dedicate himself to the game of football, and because of that he is one notch lower than the quarterbacks that are in the Hall. He doesn't get my vote.

Was Stabler capable of taking that 1980 Raiders team to the Super Bowl – as Jim Plunkett did – had he not been traded to Houston after the '79 season?

PZ: No, because I don't think they would have played as hard for him. The Raiders played really hard for Plunkett. They responded to him. I think the players had had enough of Stabler. That team needed some new direction at quarterback. That's why they went after Pastorini, although that probably wouldn't have worked out real well either. Plunkett kind of fell into their lap and was ready to go after sitting on the bench for a few seasons to clear his head.

Vintage Dr. Z, on Cowboys tailback Duane Thomas

His features bore the look of something ancient, something classical – African, yes, but maybe touched with a Grecian strain. In his running style, you saw traces of Jim Brown, perhaps the greatest runner of all time, the same combination of grace and power, the control, explosive power, but always under control. There was something of the jungle in Thomas' running, the lope of one of the great cats, then the burst as it closed for the kill.

– **Paul Zimmerman,** *Duane Thomas and the Fall of America's Team*
(Warner Books, 1988)

You've written that the decline in the quality of today's quarterback is because many of the better athletes have migrated towards other sports, baseball and basketball in particular. What led you to that conclusion?

PZ: There's more money in other sports now. The position is still as glamorous, but you can make more money and not get the shit beat out of you.

Former Oilers coach Bum Phillips once said, "Two kinds of football players aren't worth a damn: the one that never does what he's told and the other that never does anything except what he's told." Give me a quarterback that fits each of those descriptions. I think I know what one of your answers will be.

PZ: Who do you think I would say?

For "doing only what he was told," my guess is you'll say Dallas' Danny White. You've referred to him in the past as meticulous but mechanical.

PZ: I wouldn't say that about him. I think he was hampered. I don't think he was very adventurous, but I think he was better than people give him credit for. This is a real tough question…Heath Shuler of Washington is one. He just doesn't have a feel for it. He doesn't get the job done. He doesn't know how to work an offense or move the sticks. Same thing with Dave Brown of the Giants.

The ones that don't listen? They're usually the types that have courage and big contracts. Terry Bradshaw was a maverick in his early years. That's why Noll kept benching him. I'll also say the young Joe Namath, especially in his first two years. He didn't give a fuck.

Who have been some of the more interesting NFL coaches that you've interviewed over the years?

PZ: Interesting as far as personality or because of their ideas?

Personality first.

PZ: Abe Gibron, the old Bears coach. He was something else, a real personality. The Bears didn't win much with Abe, but he was good to the writers. Weeb Ewbank was a character, too. He was my number one interview because we were tight.

How about in terms of football insight?

PZ: Bill Walsh, for his clarity and vision. For just talking football and not looking down on you. For not talking to you like you were a fucking moron just because you didn't sit there and watch films with him. I could have good discussions with him. I had good discussions with Chuck Noll, too, but not about football. It was because of our similar interests in wine.

NBC's Curt Gowdy has said that Chuck Noll was one of his toughest interviews, that he never offered any information beyond the typical canned media responses.

PZ: That's because Noll didn't respect him. If Noll thought a guy was a dumb-shit, he'd give him the curled upper lip. He would give guys like that the standard answers. I mean, I never got great football stuff from Noll, but I talked to him about lots of other things. He's very warm now compared to what he used to be. You had to ask him things that make sense, and then you had to stay on him and press him and then he'd eventually say something good. But if you come up to him with those blah-blah, stupid questions, he'd give you one of those sneering answers and walk away.

Or if you'd shove a microphone in his face.

PZ: Well, he hated those [electronic media] guys, and I do too, the ones who are after the sound bites. I think they're an abomination, a bunch of brainless idiots. But I did a two-part series on Noll for *SI* in 1980, and everybody said it couldn't be done. I don't know how good it was, but I did it. Art Rooney, Jr. called me up after it was published and said, "I never thought I'd see that. I never thought it would be possible."

Art Rooney, Jr. had a great quote about Noll. He said, "We get along. I respect him. But talking to Chuck Noll is like talking to the toughest teacher you ever had in college."

Not-So-Vintage Dr. Z, on Miami Drafting Pitt QB Dan Marino

"I don't understand it. Number one, I don't know who is gonna work with [Marino] down there. Where is the great quarterback coaching genius of the Dolphins? I know [Bill] Arnsparger is a great defensive coach. I don't see where he's going to get this great coaching that's gonna overcome the problems he's had. I mean he's strictly a long-range projection down the line, and I think they need help in other directions. Maybe they felt that what they wanted wasn't there and they couldn't get that help. I really don't understand it."

- Paul Zimmerman, during ESPN's NFL Draft coverage (April 26, 1983)

Tell me more about that interview with Chuck Noll. How difficult was it getting him to participate?

PZ: Chuck Noll and I were wine buddies. I was writing a wine column for *The New York Post* and he was interested in wine. He was always interested in people he could learn something from. So when we'd get together, we'd very seldom talk about football. We'd talk about wine. We had gone out to dinner a few times. Then one day I said, "Look, I know you're not gonna like this, but I'm gonna have to do a football story on you."

He said, "Do you have to?"

I answered, "Well, yeah. The magazine is going to want it. You just won four Super Bowls."

Then he said, "Well, ok. I can spare you a couple of hours."

I knew that once we got started a couple of hours would turn into something else. Well, a couple of hours turned into a week. Of course, it was broken up over several different visits. He'd get sick of me if we did it a week straight through. It had to be in pieces.

In the article, there is hardly any direct football talk from Noll. Why his reluctance to discuss the nuances of his own profession?

PZ: Because Noll is a modest guy. He's self-conscious. He doesn't like to toot his own horn.

How awkward were the awkward moments with him, if any?

PZ: There are always going to be your share of awkward moments with Chuck because Chuck is not a comfortable person. He's not somebody that you can take your shoes off and five minutes into the conversation you're telling him your life story and he's telling you his. He's not that kind of a person. There's always a bit of standoffishness there, and you have to be aware of what you're saying.

Were there any moments in which he was surprisingly candid?

PZ: No. I felt that he opened up because he wanted to. I think we got along well, and I think there were things that he wanted me to have in the story that would help me, and so he let me have them intentionally. I don't think anything was ever out of his control or slipped out.

A perfect example is this: One day he brought in a picture of a peewee team that he played for in 1943, and half the team was black. One of the coaches was also black. Now that was really unusual for that era. And he was telling me, "Do you want to know why I am so close to my black players, why I can get a good rapport? Because I grew up in a black neighborhood. I grew up with black kids. I grew up playing with them." He didn't spell it out exactly like that, but he made sure that I understood. That was an example of him spontaneously letting me have a piece of himself that other people didn't know.

Did he ever open up about his players or coaches? Maybe discussing his early problems with Bradshaw or his head-butting with Mel Blount in '77?

PZ: He never talked about his players negatively. He wouldn't give me that, but I wasn't looking for it, either. I could have found that type of thing from his former players. If I had worked Bradshaw a little harder, I could have gotten him to open up about Noll. I would have gotten my share of negatives, but this was going to be the first piece ever done on him. What kind of piece did I want to make it? Did I want to make it a controversial piece, a "Mommy Dearest?" Or did I want to open this guy up and let people see who he is and why the fuck he's won four Super Bowls and why he is a great coach?

I had to come to that decision. What did I want to do? I could have gone that dirty route, digging up the controversy, but I decided not to. Maybe now I'd do it a little differently, but at the time it didn't make any sense to me. The guy had done something that nobody else had done, so let's get a look at him.

But in the article, he never discusses strategy, he never discusses games, he never discusses football as it's played on the field. Was that left out intentionally?

PZ: When I tried to get into that stuff, it kinda closed the whole thing down. I was getting cliché answers to those questions. I was around a lot of postgame interviews with Chuck Noll, and I heard the answers he gave. It was "media" kind of answers. I didn't want to get into that media stuff. I didn't want to be told clichés. I was afraid if I started into stuff like, "Who called the play on the "Immaculate Reception," and all that, I would have gotten the canned media answers. I don't know, maybe I approached the piece the wrong way. I thought I went about it the right way, but that isn't for me to say.

Last question. I was studying the NFL drafts over the past 30 years and...

PZ: [Interrupting] '74 Steelers.

You knew my question. I was going to compare that group with that stellar draft San Francisco put together in 1986 – Larry Roberts, Tom Rathman, Tim McKyer, John Taylor, Charles Haley, Steve Wallace, Kevin Fagan and Don Griffin. That's almost half a 49ers Super Bowl team in one swoop.

PZ: How many of those 49ers are headed to the Hall of Fame? None of them. How many Hall of Famers from the '74 Steelers? Two – Jack Lambert and Mike Webster. Lynn Swann and John Stallworth have a great chance. Donnie Shell, maybe. It's no contest. It's the best draft in history.

— 4 —
Phil Villapiano, Linebacker
Oakland Raiders (1971-79); Buffalo Bills (1980-83)
June 2, 1999

The article took an intriguing angle, an exercise in the football hypothetical. It was a game of "What's My Name?" featured in one of those mind-numbing NFL preview magazines.

Presented with a tedious situation on the football field, the writer's goal was to finger the player best suited for the task. Some typical scenarios:

3rd-and-17, late in the game, and your team is desperate for a completion to keep the drive moving. It's 21 degrees, and a fickle, sneering wind has been playing tricks with the aerial game all afternoon. Which quarterback do you want to make that big throw?

Or...

The league's best outside rushing linebacker has muscled his way past the left tackle and is charging right toward your already ailing quarterback. A blindside shot gets him killed. Which running back do you want set up in pass protection, waiting for the charge?

Things like that. Names like Brett Favre, Jamal Lewis and Randy Moss were coming up as answers. It was a fun read, a good job by the writer.

For some reason, the whole thing got me thinking about linebackers and the rugged, nasty things they're called on to do. What kind of macho linebacking scenarios could I dream up, and which members of history's roll call would best fit the job? Here are a few of those role-plays:

• **Chase down and punish Oilers tailback Earl Campbell, a 225-lb menace who's made an off-tackle charge and is romping toward midfield.**

Big Earl with a head of steam is a scary thought, ripping through arm tackles and out of his tear-away, those 36-inch thighs churning like big riverboat pistons. To track him down requires the skills of a great plains hunter – long bursts of speed and a ferocious kill shot. A saber-toothed cat on the prowl.

The first name that comes to mind is Ray Lewis, the Baltimore Ravens' terrific middle linebacker. Speed? Lewis, even at a solid 245-lbs, leaves a trail of scorched earth when on the move. He once ran down Laveranues Coles, a receiver who whips around on 4.2 speed, after he'd gotten loose in the secondary.

In the punishment department, Lewis can bring the smackdown, a monster hitter in Butkus/Lanier/Nitschke company. You won't see a bigger shot on a thundering runner than the one he laid on 255-lb fullback Jerome Bettis in 2001, Ravens at Steelers. Ray Lewis would be the perfect weapon to take down Campbell on the loose.

• **Provide daylong, blanket coverage against San Diego's deadly receiving corps – Kellen Winslow, John Jefferson and Charlie Joiner – to boost an ailing secondary.**

The vote goes to Tom Jackson from Denver's Orange Crush era. Jackson played outside linebacker with a cornerback's legs and reaction, and could match strides with three-quarters of the league's receivers. His great cutting ability and lateral speed was a perfect complement to the Broncos' maniacal 3-4 scheme. I once spent an afternoon watching him shadow Seahawks' Hall-of-Famer Steve Largent all over the Kingdome, a task few linebackers could ever handle. Largent's tally for the day – one catch, 11 yards.

• The Raiders are in town, it's late, and your defensive line is wilting. There's 1:07 on the clock, 4th down, ball on the goal line, and they're coming at you with a Marcus Allen dive.

Allen was a bloodhound when he caught the scent of a score, the NFL's all-time leader for rushing touchdowns. To counter, you need a linebacker with an equal nose for action at the goal line, and that honor goes to former Chicago Bears' middle backer Mike Singletary. A blistering plugger who could launch his stocky, 6-foot frame into the narrowest of creases, Singletary's signature was broken facemasks and cracked helmets, and…

And then the phone rang. Of all things, an old linebacker was on the line. It was Phil Villapiano, who patrolled the left side of the savage Oakland Raiders defense during the 1970s, returning a call. Perfect timing for a poll question.

"So Phil, under what game conditions were you most effective as a linebacker?"

"I kinda liked it when we were ahead by three touchdowns," he said.

"No, no, what was your forte? In what situations were you the best, like blowing up screen passes or working over a running back on a third-and-short?"

"Ahhh. That would be using the old 'Rake and Can Opener' technique."

"*The what?* The old Rake and what?"

"The 'Rake-and-Can-Opener.' That was my way of taking out a team's best player. The "Rake" part was me coming from behind and slamming my arm under the guy's chin. The 'Can Opener' was jerking up real hard and popping his helmet off. I could knock a guy out cold with it. If done properly, it was a beautiful thing."

Villapiano had done it to O.J. Simpson once, back in '72, his white Bills helmet bouncing across the muddy turf. It sent O.J. into la-la land for a couple of series. Call it what you want, the Rake-and-Can-Opener was a borderline cheap shot.

"So your specialty was the *hack job*? Need a guy on his back, call Phil from Jersey?"

"Nahhh, that was just the roughneck stuff," he said. "My game? I was best at jamming people off the line of scrimmage, knocking the tight end out of his patterns. I was relentless at it. Most linebackers don't do it nowadays. That's why today you see guys like [N.Y. Giants'] Jeremy Shockey and [Kansas City's] Tony Gonzalez running through the secondaries all game.

"Here's a quick story. We went up against New England in the '76 playoffs. Before the game, John Madden made it clear that to win we had to stop their tight end, Russ Francis, keep him from getting off the line. He told me, 'Take this guy out, whatever you gotta do. I don't care how many times they run around your end, take him out.' So Francis and I went at it all afternoon. The refs called four penalties on us that day – two on him for shoving and two for me holding.

"Remember that controversial fourth-down play at the end of the game? The Patriots still bitch about it. Francis gave me a big shove so I grabbed hold of him, but there was no flag. The ref had been watching us all afternoon and just got sick of calling it."

No team lent itself to more twilight zone moments during the 1960s and '70s than Oakland. From being martyrs of The Immaculate Reception to the folly of The Holy Roller, comebacks and bizarre bounces followed the Raiders like the team chaplain or a voodoo curse.

The "Heidi Game" ended in secrecy, as Oakland scored two touchdowns in nine seconds during a sudden television blackout to beat New York. Then the Jets accused owner Al Davis of bugging their locker room.

The Raiders once trailed the Saints by 21 with a quarter and a half left and won by a touchdown. Another year, a quick whistle was blown during a Bears touchdown run that would've iced the game for Chicago. On the next play, Oakland intercepted and the Bears lost by a point.

Season after season, the surprises kept coming at the expense of many, and Oakland became a hated team.

1976 was the year the Raiders finally won it all, that now-fabled team of Atkinson and Stabler, van

Eeghan and Sistrunk. A street gang of a football team built on deep throws and heavy forearms and trouble on every corner. After years of soured glory (AFC runner-up in 1968, '69, '70, '73, '74, '75, Super Bowl losers in '67), good fortune finally stayed the California winter and sent the Raiders a couple of big, beaming winks. Some questionable officiating helped them survive that New England playoff game, then crippling injuries to Pittsburgh's running attack gave the Raiders unimpeded aim at the AFC title. The Raiders fired and the Steelers fell.

Next came the Super Bowl, number XI, a game whose outcome you could sense before halftime. It was a rout – Oakland 32, Minnesota 14, the headgear of Viking receiver Sammy White tumbling across the field like a booted beer can. That one wasn't courtesy of Rake-and-Can-Opener but instead a helmet-to-helmet love letter from safety Jack Tatum. The Raiders finally had their championship.

Then in '77, another AFC title loss, this one to Denver. More soured hopes. Within two years of that January day, Davis would gut the team of many of its core veterans. Villapiano was caught in the purge, traded to Buffalo after nine years with a front row view of the madness.

I once asked him if he felt cheated. Despite all the division titles and glory days, the Raiders were champions only once during his time in Oakland. Was there still an emptiness, a feeling of discontent when looking back?

"You don't know how much it irks me, even still," he said. "We had a championship caliber team in Oakland for years, and all we got was one Super Bowl? All those All-Pros and that great offensive line and that defense? We should've won three Super Bowls. A lot of my teammates feel that way."

It was a heartfelt response and a bitter one, with a tone you'd expect to hear from a man who gave his neighbor a hot stock tip but didn't buy himself. The neighbor then bought two Ferraris and moved to Malibu….

Scenario: Seconds left on the clock, fifty yards to go and the snow is flying. A deep pass is thrown by the visiting team. It falls short, but bounces off the head of a defender. The ball is caught one-handed by a receiver who scores an amazing touchdown. There's an illegal block on the play, but the official misses the call because he's fallen to the ground. His shoes have been tied together.

Give me a team from history that could pull it off. A job for the Raiders of the '70s, right?

Nah, not their style.

They'd have gone with leg shackles on the ref. And Al Davis, well, he would have conned God into calling off the snowstorm.

● ● ●

Former Raiders coach John Madden once made the following observation about linebackers:

"As a coach, I learned that the better the player, the less he knows why he does what he does, especially at linebacker. More than most positions, linebackers demand football instinct. Through the years I asked some average linebackers to analyze what they did. 'My feet and shoulders are lined up together,' one told me. 'My first step is short, only six inches, then my next step is...' The more he talked, the more I realized he was a robot. He was trying to play linebacker the way some dance students try to learn the tango. The more I watched the great linebackers, the more I realized they don't analyze what they do. They just do it."

Based on your old coach's analysis, was Phil Villapiano a great linebacker?

PV: It's funny that John would say that because learning the position was very difficult for me. Actually, when I got out of football, I probably became a better teacher because I began analyzing what I did. But when I was really out there playing, all I knew was to smash in there. Sometimes you'd belt them with your head, sometimes you'd grab them with your arms. You just did it all to stop the other player.

Football is a game of reaction, and you have to react to a million things. After a while, you get pretty good at it. It's like boxing – after a while, a fighter recognizes everything that's coming at him. A good football player at any position plays the game that way. Ask O.J. Simpson or Franco Harris. I don't think they were robots. They just went with the flow.

Funny thing, when I was traded to Buffalo, they coached us like robots up there. It was like a chess game or a checker game. Everybody had to be exactly in the right spot, do exactly the right thing. They would coach every little thing, which was probably one of the reasons I didn't start in Buffalo. I didn't play linebacker the way they wanted it to be played. I played a more instinct type game, and I think John Madden liked that. I fit his mold. Coaches like Tom Landry or Chuck Knox, maybe they liked guys who did it by the numbers. John would rather have guys out there reacting and hitting and enjoying themselves. I think I fit the Madden mold, but I don't think I fit everybody else's mold.

What made you a successful player in the National Football League? How much of your game was robotic versus instinctive?

PV: I was a big studier of the offenses that were coming at me. I had a great football memory and could remember every single thing about them. Watching films, it was almost like having a photographic memory, where I could memorize what offenses were trying to do to me. That was during the week. On Sunday, I made a lot of guesses, but they were educated guesses based on what I'd seen on film. A smarter player does a lot of calculating, but also instinct is huge. You can only calculate so much. Offenses will pick up on that and burn you.

The best thing about me was that you got 100-percent from me, every single down. I think the reason I got the accolades that I did was because I played very, very hard. Anybody that played against me was going to be in for a war. I really used to enjoy playing in the second half of games, when, for instance, somebody's tight end would be quitting. Guys would always come out playing so hard and tough in the first quarter. Then as the game moved on, I'd pretty much have my way with people. I would keep wearing on them, wearing them down. I treated it like a war, and that's the way football is meant to be played. Shit, I did whatever it took on every single play. Luckily, I played for a team that respected that.

If I ever had one goal as a football player, it was to make every single tackle in a game. Naturally, I could never achieve that goal, but I would try. I don't think I was a great pass defender or a great block stopper or a great tackler, but after you put all of my game together, you really had to work to beat me. Over the years there weren't too many Sunday afternoons where somebody got the best of me.

Which teams consistently gave you the biggest problems on Sunday? Who were some of your biggest headaches?

PV: A couple of teams that didn't necessarily have winning records every year but sure came to play were the New England Patriots and the Cincinnati Bengals. Whenever I went against (Cincinnati TE) Bob Trumpy it was a war. Trumpy came to play every time, and we had some great battles. New England had a lot of offensive talent. Steve Grogan, Sam Cunningham, Russ Francis, John Hannah – those guys were good! I don't think they were as talented as the Raiders, but every time I came out of a game with Francis I needed a week off for sure! He was physically so hard to handle.

We were getting ready to play New England one year. Al Davis and Madden kept telling us we gotta stop this Francis guy. So [Raiders safety] George Atkinson and I made a decision that this man was not going to do anything against us today. We got out there and started roughing him up – Bam! Bam! Bam! Then about midway though the first quarter, I grabbed Francis and threw him to my left, and there was Atkinson's big ol' elbow waiting for him. Wham! Right in the nose! Completely smashed it into Francis' face.

Later that year, we go over to Hawaii for the Pro Bowl game. Francis calls me up and says, "Hey Phil, how about I take you out for a plane ride?" He was an experienced pilot, and it sounded like fun. I said, "What a wonderful idea, Russ!" I get there and he's got this little plane with this little door. He says, "Come on, I'll take you out and show you some whales." So we're going over Maui where the whales are. All of a sudden he tilts the plane on its side, then grabs that door and kicks it open and screams, *"Get out! Get out!"* He thought it was funny, but I was scared shitless. That was my payback for the busted nose.

Which other players commanded your respect?

PV: Atlanta's Jim Mitchell was a great player. So was Tom Mitchell who played with Baltimore and the 49ers. When I lined up against those guys I knew what I was in for. Randy Grossman from Pittsburgh? He wasn't a great blocker. He was more of a finesse guy and I could have my way with him, but he was a pretty good pass catcher. If you weren't a great blocker, you probably couldn't get off the line of scrimmage against me because I had my hands all over your face and neck all the time.

Pat Curran from San Diego was pretty good, but he complained about a lot of petty things on the field. I'd play against Ted Kwalick from San Francisco any day. He was a great receiver but not a real nasty guy. I'd rather go up against the great receivers any day than against the real tough guys.

What about weaknesses? How did opposing teams try to attack you and the Raiders' left defensive side?

PV: My biggest weakness was also my biggest strength, and that was aggressiveness. If you wanted to beat me, run a reverse at me because I would always end up on the other side of the field trying to make the play. I couldn't stay at home and play a patient, passive game. I made tons of tackles on the other side of the field, but I also got burnt enough times on reverses or ends-around or play-action passes. That was my weakness and everybody knew it. I had to work very hard at recognizing when they were gonna run that stuff against me.

Once we were playing the 49ers and Kwalick was trying to block me on a reverse. I shoved him and went after the play toward the other side of the field. All of a sudden, [WR] Gene Washington came flying back toward the side I originally had been on. After I recognized the play and tried to get back, Kwalick was waiting for me and blasted me in the face, splitting it wide open. He laughed after the play because he got me so good.

How They Saw Oakland's Fiery #41 From the Booth

"Villapiano? Villapiano? What a name! Where did Al Davis come up with this lad? Why he must have wings like Pegasus for he's making tackles all over the league! Have you ever seen anything like him, Dandy?"

– Howard Cosell on ABC's Monday Night Football,
– Oakland vs. Cleveland, 1972

"Phil is one of the nicest guys we've ever met but he was a killer on the field. I remember doing a Raiders game, and I made a pretty strong comment about him. I said, 'Villapiano is like an assassin. I'd like to have him in my army. I'd send him behind the lines to find the enemy's general and cut his throat.' Pat Summerall and I made these war-like comments all the time. With all that's going on in the world today, we'd probably get in trouble saying something like that today.

"We heard that the Raiders had given him one of those psychiatric tests. After reading the results, the doctor came out and made that exact same comment about Villapiano that we did. And of course, we mentioned that on our broadcast as soon as he came crashing through on the first blitz."

– former CBS football analyst Tom Brookshier

As a linebacker, pass coverage is a big part of your responsibility. You had five regular season interceptions during your first two years in the league, but only six over the next 11 seasons. What can be interpreted from those numbers?

PV: Isn't that something? Only six interceptions in the last 11 years. But remember, I probably had another five or six in the playoffs. I always used to come up with picks in the playoffs and those never counted in my stats.

One factor was the amount of substituting our defense was doing on third down. Around the mid-1970s, coordinators began bringing in the nickel and dime backs and taking out the linebackers on third down. That really cut down on the number of picks I had. And moving me to middle linebacker didn't help either.

The Steelers' Jack Ham and I were once in Florida together at a golf tournament. Ham had 30 or 40 interceptions during his career. He said to me, "Phil, you played all those years and only had 13 or 14 interceptions? *That's terrible.*"

I said, "Yeah, Hammer, whatever. You're the best." I guess the answer is that during my first few years in the league I played all the downs, so naturally I faced more passing situations and was able to get interceptions.

Which was the most meaningful?

PV: It was in a game against Denver. John Madden was upset about something and stormed onto the field, screaming and yelling at the refs. They hit him with his second 15-yard penalty. That really put us in trouble, backing our offense up to around the 15-yardline. We had to punt. Then Denver threw a pass and I picked it off and ran it up their sideline and jumped out of bounds. I never thought twice about the play. I was just doing my job. But on the bus, Madden came over to me and said, "Hey Phil, thanks for bailing me out."

I said, "What are you talking about, coach?"

He said, "Hey, don't think I don't get shit, too, when I screw up."

So I said, "Anytime, coach." I was able to help Madden out, so that interception meant a lot to me.

I had some big ones in playoff games, too, including a big one that helped put Miami away in the '74 playoffs. After Clarence Davis caught that famous touchdown pass in the endzone, Miami still wasn't done. They only needed a field goal to win the game, and Bob Griese brought them back out. I figured they were going to try to hit Paul Warfield deep, so I dropped way back in coverage underneath him and picked it off. That was a pretty big one, too.

Former Bears linebacker Dick Butkus once said, "When I hit a guy, I wanted him to know who hit him without even having to look around and check a number." You have said your fiercest hit came in a 1972 game against the Buffalo Bills, when you drilled O.J. Simpson from behind, ripped his helmet off and pounded him into the turf.

PV: Whenever I played against a player that was better than me, I'd take it personally. I'd say to myself, "O.J. Simpson is supposed to be the best in the league. We'll see who can beat who." That particular play was a fluke. O.J. had that great cutback move. At full speed he could reverse his direction and go back the other way. Their tight end Paul Seymour was trying to block me, but I got rid of him and was flying across the field. Just at that moment, O.J. decided he was gonna do the big cutback.

I had a pretty strong right arm, and I thought I could knock almost anybody out with it by slamming it underneath their jaw and ripping back their helmet. O.J. didn't even see me coming. After I nailed him I knew he'd be out of the game. It felt real good to do that to one of the best players in the league. That was always a goal of our defense. Between Jack Tatum, George Atkinson, Skip Thomas and me, we used to have the "Knockout and Limp-off Competition." It kept us mentally stimulated during the game.

The Raiders' secondary was one of pro football's fiercest during the 1970s. However, because of its aggressiveness it was prone to giving up the big pass play. During the team's playoff run from 1972-77, the Raiders defense allowed nearly 14 yards per completion. Did you feel those players – George Atkinson, Willie Brown, Skip Thomas and Jack Tatum – were more focused on intimidation and head-hunting than on interceptions and solid pass coverage?

PV: Our defensive backs played with the philosophy of instilling fear, that if receivers were afraid to catch the ball or come across the middle because they thought they'd get killed, it would make the secondary's day a whole lot easier. A lot of times, yeah, they'd mark the receivers and try and take them out. I don't think they wanted to hurt anybody, or do what happened to [New England receiver] Darryl Stingley, but they considered receivers as their enemy. If they could take out the starters, it would make their day easier. That's the way they played.

I remember a hit Jack Tatum once put on [Denver TE] Riley Odoms. Tatum caught him under the chin and Odoms landed on his back, and then his eyeballs rolled back into this head. I thought he died! Jack could have hit him low, *but noooo*, he sticks his helmet right under Odoms chin. That's the knockout blow, and Jack was excellent at doing it.

Atkinson was great at clubbing guys in the head to stop the catch. So was Skip Thomas. That's why I'm convinced that the ball never hit Tatum on the Immaculate Reception play. We all know Jack Tatum would never go for the ball if there was a person to hit.

That's just the way those guys played the game, and it was never a problem because we were winning. Receivers didn't want to catch against us. It was great intimidation that helped the Raiders win, and no one was going to stop it.

Al Davis was famous for stressing the importance of pounding the other team's quarterback – kill the head and the body will die. If you had a free blindside shot at any quarterback, who would want you take it against?

PV: To tell the truth, I wanted a clean, broadside shot at everybody. I remember playing against the Jets during my first or second year when Joe Namath was there. This goes back to my philosophy of "the better they are, the more I want to hit them." On one play I sent Art Thoms, our defensive end, up the field and I came blitzing through, figuring I could get a clean shot right at Namath. I got through, and Art ended up going right around their tackle Winston Hill. I took a flying leap at the same time Art did. Well, Namath took just one step backwards and Art and I ended up crashing together and went right to the ground. Namath ended up completing a long one down the middle. He showed us.

There wasn't one quarterback that I ever pulled up on, that I had a shot and didn't try to make it count. I would never cheap shot anybody, but if I got through the line that meant I earned a shot and I took it. One time (Baltimore Colts QB) Bert Jones had broken out of the pocket and was scrambling downfield. Now *that* was one guy that I didn't have much use for. We got to know each other after our careers were over and I ended up liking him, but on this play I meant to take him out. Jones was a tough player, but I ran right through him and that was the end of his day.

Why the dislike for Bert Jones?

PV: Because he was good. He was cocky. He had a good team and we knew the Colts were going to be a thorn in our side. You're out there playing for pride, and you don't want to get beat by anybody. The better the player, the bigger the threat and the more you had to dislike them on the field. I didn't like *anybody* on the field. I couldn't like them because the things you're trying to do to them on the field are vicious.

Even as a veteran, later in your career, you never took it easy on anyone?

PV: Well, I did. The toughest time I had playing against somebody was against Bob Moore, my old roommate with Oakland. He'd been traded to Tampa Bay during the expansion draft. I really couldn't play my game that day because he was my friend. I didn't want to injure him or knock him out of the game. Even when I started going to some Pro Bowls, I started meeting players and becoming friends with them. Then you really don't want to "play your game" because you don't want to hurt those guys.

The "legend" of the 1970s Raiders has been well documented – Pride and Poise, the renegade image, pro football's home for wayward souls. But has part of this legend grown bigger than it really was? What are some of the myths and exaggerations that have become woven into Raiders history over the past thirty years?

PV: Believe it or not, those stories were only scratching the surface. It was beyond belief, the group that Al Davis put together out there. If people knew the things that really happened, it would really shake things up. Nobody would let their mother read about them.

Let this be known – a lot of teams quit against the Raiders. A lot of teams didn't even want to play against us. Had they played hard they might have beaten us, but some teams that were afraid! I couldn't believe it! There were some cases when guys didn't want to block me all afternoon. They'd be out there talking to me, trying to carry on a conversation. If they wanted to talk to me, great, but that didn't mean I wasn't going to smash their running back or smash them.

A lot of teams quit before the game started, and we ended up getting a lot of wins that we shouldn't have gotten. That's just the way it was. A lot of people would be reading the Raiders' PR reports and wouldn't want to tackle us. For example, teams like Denver or San Diego had years when they were horrible. They didn't want to play us at all, so we'd just take the wins and go home.

But the teams that did come out and try to beat us made it fun. Those were the games we liked the most, the tough games. When the Chiefs or the Steelers or the Dolphins were in town, we knew we were in for a war.

As far as all the characters Al put together, I wouldn't call *any* of them misfits. They were just the Raiders' style of people and players. Al Davis liked the instinct players. He didn't like the methodical guys. He wanted guys that were full of instinct and fun, no matter where they came from. Skip Thomas, Atkinson, Tatum – none of these guys were real coachable but they played hard and got the job done. Were they misfits? *Nahhh.* They were just free-spirited, fun-loving, great football players, a whole bunch of them on the same team. And most of the stuff you read about them in these books is probably under-exaggerated, if anything.

Were there individuals who didn't belong on the Raiders, who were out of place playing there?

PV: There certainly were guys that didn't fit, people who joined the team and were more conscious about their own stats. They didn't last too long. For instance, a guy like Mike Siani. He came to the Raiders and bitched all the time. John Madden got rid of him on his first opportunity. Another one was Jeff Queen. I don't know where the hell Queen came from, but they tried to make a Raider out of him and it didn't work. Dave Kopay was another example. He stuck around for just a year or two and was gone. These guys weren't and never could be part of that great Raider tradition because they wouldn't pay the price. They wouldn't "give it up" for their teammates.

One of the guys who Al Davis signed that shocked me was Todd Christensen. He'd been a backup running back with Dallas before joining the Raiders. That guy must have changed a whole lot after I left Oakland because I didn't think he could ever play for the Raiders. He didn't have the personality. He wasn't a very friendly guy, as far as I was concerned. I think he was a little selfish. But he ended up being a tremendous tight end for the team, an All-Pro.

Davis had a wonderful way of bringing the right guys on. He had a way of looking at guys and knowing whether or not they would fit in. And during my nine years in Oakland, most of the guys fit in. Kenny Stabler was a quarterback who could be one of the boys every night of the week, then on Sunday he'd just say, "Keep it close," and get the job done. Guys like John Vella and Dave Dalby would die for the team.

Marv Hubbard and Mark van Eeghan weren't pretty runners but they'd go out and get the job done. John Matuszak and Ted Hendricks didn't care how many tackles they made. Nobody on the Raiders kept stats. Everyone was team oriented. Winning was all we cared about.

I just finished reading a great book called "*D-Day – June 6, 1944*" by Stephen Ambrose. I could see Raiders in that book, guys that would die for each other. Even a guy like Bubba Smith could never be a Raider. They tried to make him one, but he was too selfish. Give me a big guy like Tony Cline, who was 6'4", 235 and wouldn't worry about looking good and getting all the publicity. Or a guy like Otis Sistrunk. Those guys were the true Raiders.

However, some of the worst moves Al Davis ever made involved coaches. He would hire coaches from other teams specifically to hurt the other teams. Well, it would hurt the Raiders just as much. We had a real winning way, and then he started messing around and bringing in guys who probably didn't belong with the Raiders. For example, Myrel Moore was a great linebacker coach. I learned a helluva lot from him, but I think it was a bad move. But hey, it was Al's team and he could do what he wanted with it. He won a couple of more Super Bowls after I left, so I guess he did it right.

Why was it was a bad move for Oakland to have hired Myrel Moore?

PV: Myrel was brought in from Denver where they came up with that Orange Crush defense. We, as Raider players, always said, "Fuck them." At the time the Broncos defense was doing pretty good, but we always thought we were better than them.

Then all of a sudden Al Davis thought Denver was better than us, so he had to go out and get their coach. As much as I learned from Myrel Moore – he might have been one of the best coaches I ever had – they had to fire [linebacker coach] Don Shinnick to make room for him on the staff. We were very loyal to Shinnick. We didn't need that coaching change. We were already good enough.

Then later, Davis brought in Mike Shanahan. It seemed like suddenly he was infatuated with Denver coaches. We were thinking, "What the fuck is going on around here? We don't need them. We have our own good coaches." We didn't like any of the Broncos players and we didn't like any of their coaches either. These guys didn't coach or think Raider football, which was a little different than the rest of the league. No offense against Myrel, but as soon as he arrived he started changing everything. We had already won a Super Bowl, had all these great players, and now all of a sudden everything had to be changed? I don't think so.

Fear and Loathing in the War of the Blackshirts

On behalf of the NFL, [NFL Commissioner Pete] Rozelle could naturally be expected to strongly oppose Nazis, Communists, cocaine, *Hustler* magazine and child molesting, but a couple of weeks ago, with Oakland and Pittsburgh in mind, he added violence. An edict from his office stated: "Violence, as Webster defines it and as the public perceives it, is conduct characterized by extreme and sudden...unjust or improper force. It has no proper place in professional football."

Swell. But not a word about immaculate receptions, mysteriously split tarpaulins, Vaseline on Jerseys, fans attacking tight ends and all of the varying forms of intimidation that have been a part of the Oakland-Pittsburgh series.

Touching briefly on some of the more fascinating incidents in the rivalry, we begin with Franco Harris reception in the 1972 playoff game at Pittsburgh. Bradshaw threw this pass, you see, that was intended for Frenchy Fuqua. It either hit Fuqua or didn't, but officially the ruling was that Oakland's Jack Tatum knocked it down, only Harris caught it and ran for the touchdown that won the game. Films proved to be inconclusive, but Oakland still feels it was an illegal reception.

Next came the great grease scandal at Oakland in 1973. That was when the losing Steelers accused the Raiders of smearing Vaseline on their shirts and pants in order to make themselves harder to tackle. Rot, said Oakland boss Al Davis.

However a couple of Raiders, once they were ex-Raiders, whispered to some newsmen that it was true. And you know how journalists are. They wrote it. At the same time, the Steelers also suggested that the footballs supplied for the Raiders in Oakland – and only the Raiders – were not properly inflated, making them easier for Stabler to throw and for Biletnikoff to catch.

In 1974 Oakland Tight End Bob Moore encountered a hostile mob the night before the game near the Hilton Hotel in downtown Pittsburgh. In their inimitable way, the Steeler fans put a gash in Moore's head, and he was unable to play. Now the Raiders stay at a suburban motel when they are forced to visit Pittsburgh.

The Ice Age playoff took place the following year. As they began the battle for the AFC championship, the Raiders were shocked to discover that Pittsburgh's tarpaulin had mysteriously split the night before, leaving the artificial turf as slippery as a hockey rink, which, in turn, took away Oakland's fanciest pass routes. Pittsburgh won.

And finally, last season there was the [George] Atkinson forearm on [Lynn] Swann's headgear, isolated, slow-motioned and rerun more often than Lucy in the kitchen.

– **Dan Jenkins, *Sports Illustrated*, September 26, 1977.
Reprinted with permission.**

Name an opposing player who was not an Oakland Raider but should have been.

PV: Terry Bradshaw was one. I used to love watching him play. He was so tough. Bradshaw would have been a great Raider because he played every game for keeps. You knew that when you were going up against Bradshaw he was going to play *every single down*. I couldn't believe it when Chuck Noll would get down on that guy. If Noll had to play against Terry Bradshaw, he *never* would have gotten down on him.

You know who else would have been a great Raider? Steve Largent from Seattle. My God, what a great receiver! I would've loved to have had him on the team. He was the next Fred Biletnikoff. Largent played every down, caught all the hard passes and never complained. Larry Csonka, the running back from Miami would've been perfect, too. Man, was he tough! Willie Lanier was another one – a great Raider in a Kansas City uniform [laughing]. I remember he broke Biletnikoff's nose in one game. He just stood there looking at him as Freddie dropped to the ground. I watched in awe, saying, "Oh…my…God… what a player."

A guy that used to call me up all the time, trying to find a way onto the team, was Lyle Alzado. Lyle used to *beg* me to get Al Davis to bring him on board. He said he would do anything to be a Raider. This was while he was still in Denver and Cleveland. Finally, he joined the Raiders in 1980, the same year they traded me to Buffalo. I never got to be Lyle's teammate, but that was one guy I always knew could be a Raider.

You mentioned Larry Csonka, so let's talk about running backs. Envision yourself caught in a one-on-one situation where you are the only person between the runner and the goal line. Who would you not want that running back to be?

PV: Well, there are three types of running backs. The first kind are the quick guys, like Mercury Morris and Clarence Davis and Billy "White Shoes" Johnson. "White Shoes" was nothing to tackle, but forget about getting your hands on him. What made those guys so tough to stop was that you couldn't catch them.

Then there were the all-around backs, like O.J. Simpson and Franco Harris and Earl Campbell, who could run and had speed. They were the ideal running backs who were tough on you all game long.

Then there were the guys I hated the most – the power backs, big horses like Csonka and John Riggins and Boobie Clark. They were guys who could just run you over. Their thighs were so strong and physically hard. When you hit those guys from the side your arms would go numb. You'd almost break your neck because it was like diving full-force into a cement wall. Toward the end of my career, I knew it was nearing my time to leave when I'd hit those guys as hard as I could and it would hurt me more than them. Then you know you're getting over the hill as a linebacker. To answer the question, the one guy that I would have hated to tackle day-in and day-out in front of the goal line was Larry Csonka. He was an absolute monster.

What was the most impressive performance a running back ever gave against the Raiders during your career?

PV: Csonka had one of those games in the '73 AFC Championship in Miami. We couldn't stop him. He was always five or six yards downfield before we could get our hands on him. Their blocking combination was outstanding. They were trapping us all over the field. Every defense we went in, they seemed to have the right play called and that big hog came running right through there. He had over 100 yards and three touchdowns. It was a very impressive game.

In 1973 we played against St. Louis and a guy named Terry Metcalf. It was a really hot day, early in the season. We beat them, but when that game was over we all said, "Wow!" about Metcalf. We didn't get to play against too many NFC teams, but we were really impressed with him. On one play I went down to make a tackle and he jumped right over me. I said, "Hol...leee...shit!" Hey, there were a lot of great players, and when the Raiders came to town these guys wanted to show off. We always seemed to get the best effort from everybody.

Bud Grant, the former Minnesota Vikings coach, once observed, "There are coaches who spend 18 hours a day coaching the perfect game, then lose because the ball is oval and they can't control the bounce." Your former coach John Madden undoubtedly put in the hours making the Raiders a winner, but what was the real key to his success?

PV: John was a great psychologist. He knew how to handle all different types of people very well. He knew when you needed a pat on the back and when you needed to be sat on a little bit. I used to admire John's simplicity and his brain. When he got his announcing job with CBS, I knew that he was going to be great because of his way of communicating. I used to love to listen to him talk because he always made good sense to me. He talked about football in a way I could understand, whether it was complicated stuff or simple stuff.

We were playing the New England Patriots once and I had the worst game of my entire NFL career. I just wasn't prepared to play that day. The next day John said to me, "Phil, I never saw you lose it before, and you lost it last night." He was absolutely right! Out of the hundreds of good games I had played before, I really stunk that night. I started out playing badly in that game, so I tried to make up for it by being more aggressive and playing harder, but I just got worse and worse. John confronted me with that. I didn't say a word because he was absolutely correct.

Madden was a highly demonstrative head coach on gameday, the arms and hair flying as he stomped around the sideline. Was his temper as explosive in the locker room or at practice?

PV: He knew just when to explode, and that was on Sunday afternoon, not during the week. On the practice field, a good head coach always lets his assistants do the work. But almost every summer at training camp, Madden would inevitably go berserk one day and throw everybody off the field, just to get rid of us for a while. That kind of thing goes back to him being a psychologist. Usually he would explode on the rookies and use them as his whipping boys but we all knew he was talking to the veterans.

I was the guy that ran all the social events at camp, like bar room bowling and air hockey tournaments. The guys used to call me "The Commissioner." One day I made a statement to the press during training camp. Somebody asked me about the upcoming preseason game against the 49ers, and I said something dumb like, "Who are we playing this weekend? I'm really just concentrating on the air hockey tournament."

The next morning, I was just about to walk into the dining room to have breakfast when the door flew open. Madden was standing there, screaming in front of the whole team, *"If you aren't ready to play against the 49ers, then get the hell out of here! Who do you think you are?"* He was using me in front of the whole team to make the point that we should straighten up and concentrate on football. Up until that point we hadn't even won a preseason game.

The funny part of that story was the next summer. Madden sent his aide down to my room to get me before our third preseason game. I walk in and Madden looks at me and says, "What the fuck kind of commissioner are you?"

I said, "What are you talking about, coach?"

He said, "How the hell do you expect us to win any games if you aren't having any of those tournaments you used to run?"

So one year he was busting my balls for not focusing on football in camp, then the next year he noticed things weren't the same with the team because we weren't having any of the events we used to enjoy for camaraderie. So by the end of that week we had another tournament to loosen things up.

When was Madden's temper at its worst?

PV: I saw John in so many rages that it was almost expected, and we liked him for that. Remember I said he got two 15-yard penalties in one game? That's a lot of penalties. That game against Denver may have been the worst I'd seen him.

He would get most pissed off at the opposing coaches, including Kansas City's coach, Hank Stram. Kansas City was our big rival. Here's John Madden on one sideline, a big guy, standing out there in a golf shirt looking sloppy. And there is Stram on the other sideline, looking like a little Mussolini or Napoleon in his suit. They were two totally different people with two totally different philosophies. We knew John didn't like Stram. We didn't like their players, and our coaches didn't like their coaches. It was perfect.

The Raiders were consistently one of the NFL's most penalized teams during the 1970s. Why? Lack of discipline?

PV: It seemed that the bigger the game, the fewer penalties we had. We could turn off the penalties just as well as we could turn them on. Take a look at some of the playoff games and the bigger rivalry games. We played pretty good in those games. It was in the lesser games that we had a whole bunch of penalties. We knew what we had to do to win games.

Madden always kept things pretty simple. He thought that we had better players than the rest of the league so if he kept the rules simple – for both on and off the field – we would win. Madden would never get mad at anybody for an aggressive penalty. He'd get mad at stupid penalties. When you got a penalty for being aggressive and tough, nothing was ever said. I was probably thrown out of five or six games for fighting and never had to pay a fine. John or Al Davis would always take care of it. It was never a problem.

I think our coaching staff created as much discipline as any other team in the league, but sometimes the players overdid it. I watch the Raiders today and I see them committing a lot of stupid penalties. To tell the truth, we probably did a lot of the same. The difference is that we always seemed to work our way out of it, and penalties didn't cost the team games. Now they do.

Madden suddenly retired from football after the 1978 season. You must have hated to see him go.

PV: I did, very much so. But he didn't retire on his own. For as much as he contributed to that team, John Madden got fucked by the Raiders. I don't think that will ever be admitted by John or the Raiders organization, but they basically fired him. He said he had an ulcer that contributed to his decision to retire, but I don't believe John Madden was sick. He took a lot of Maalox, but I think he was addicted to it. The Raiders made a very poor decision when they got rid of him, even though they kept him around in some bullshit job for a couple of years. Things turned out great for John eventually, but I don't see any reason why he would have chosen to leave the team. He loved football and coaching the game. The decision was made for him, that's my opinion.

Do you think the team's disappointing 9-7 performance in 1978, which included five divisional losses, had something to do with that?

PV: Yeah, it did. We had a lousy December and lost three of the last four games, which knocked us out of the playoffs. It was the first time we didn't make the playoffs in a long time. Seattle and Denver both swept us. The Raiders hadn't lost twice to the same team in a season since the 1960s, and it happened two times that year.

We were all disgusted after the '78 season. For some reason we got a little bit complacent but it wasn't John Madden's fault. We still had good players. We still could have won the Super Bowl for John. We just weren't sharp, so the Raiders organization thought Madden had lost it. I don't think that was the case. Maybe *his players* had lost it, but not him. I think he could've coached forever.

In Super Bowl XI, Oakland Had 'Em All the Way

On first down Chuck Foreman got a yard to our two, but on second down, Phil Villapiano hit Brent McClanahan, who fumbled. Willie Hall recovered at the 1 for us... In the jubilation of the fumble recovery, Jack Tatum hurried over to me and nodded toward Villapiano.

"You better check out Phil," he said.

"What's the matter with him," I asked.

"I think he's goofy," Jack told me.

"He's always a little goofy," I said.

"No, he's more goofy than usual," Jack said. "When we were in our huddle down there near the goal-line, he was saying, 'Now we got 'em where we want 'em...'"

I walked over to where Phil was sitting on the bench. "You all right," I asked.

"Yeah, I'm fine," he said.

"The guys told me you were saying, 'Now we got 'em where we want 'em.'"

"We did have 'em where we want 'em."

"We did? On our 3... on our two?"

"Yeah. Down there they couldn't throw any deep passes, they weren't going to run any sweeps or reverses, they were just going to run up the middle. I got in there, the ball popped loose, and we got it. We had 'em right where we wanted 'em."

"Yeah, you're right," I said. "We had 'em right where we wanted 'em."

> **– John Madden, from *Hey, Wait a Minute (I Wrote a Book)*
> (Random House, 1984)**

Then why didn't Madden ever get back into coaching? If he still had a desire to coach, don't you think he would have resurfaced somewhere else?

PV: I think John got into broadcasting because he may have had some type of deal cut with the Raiders to stay out of coaching, although I don't know that for sure. He said he was leaving because he was sick. Maybe he really was. I just didn't buy that story. If he really was having all these ulcers from coaching, and if the money was better and the stress was less in TV, then maybe that *was* his real incentive. Maybe that's why he never went to coach anywhere else.

John tried selling real estate for a month or so after retiring. He went in for his first day of work and the guy said to him, "Let's go get a cup of coffee." They came back from having coffee, then pretty soon it was time to go to lunch. They went out and had lunch, and John finally said, "This is bullshit." He probably lasted at that job for a week or two because it wasn't challenging enough for him.

Let's revisit a couple great Raider games from the decade. First, December 24, 1974 – the Miami Dolphins versus Oakland in the AFC playoffs. The last meeting between the two teams was the '73 AFC Championship, where Miami steamrolled the Raiders defense for 266 rushing yards.

"I didn't think they'd be able to do that to us," you said after the game. "We don't get beat that

way. No one runs on us like that." In the rematch, what was the plan to control the Dolphins' potent ground attack?

PV: The Dolphins had some very good line blocking. In that '73 game, they had one great running play that they ran to our weak side. They'd pull one of their guards and smash into Bubba Smith while blocking down on Otis Sistrunk. That play did a lot of damage.

But the play that really killed us was a quarterback draw ran by Bob Griese. The great Miami coaching staff had picked something up in the films. We were in a two-linebacker defense, with me and Gerald Irons playing the running backs man-to-man. On several third-and-long situations they'd flare Mercury Morris and Jim Kiick out to the side, and Irons and I would run out there with them. Then Griese would drop back and run his quarterback draw for eight or 10 or 15 yards. I'll bet he did it five times that game.

In the rematch we took away both of those plays. We took away the weak side play by placing me between Sistrunk and Bubba Smith in what we called the "Under 40-L" defense. Every time they went into that formation I would crash down Bubba and Otis. That stopped any kind of trap play. Then I'd scrape right around the end and the ball carrier would be waiting for me with no blockers. On the quarterback draw, we just played zone instead of man-to-man and Griese had no daylight to run downfield.

Was that contest – a 28-26 thriller won on a desperation pass from Stabler to Clarence Davis – the greatest pro football game ever played?

PV: That was the most *exciting* game I ever played in. And I did something in that game I thought I was going to have to live with forever. There was a long run by Benny Malone that gave Miami the lead with two minutes to go. On that play the Dolphins had brought in their tight end, Marv Fleming. Marv had been in the league 12 or 13 years, and I thought there was no way this guy could hook me. I lined up on his inside because I predicted they were going to run an off-tackle play. They ended up sweeping around my side and Marv hooked me, blocking me out of the play and Malone took it in for a touchdown.

I made a lot of great tackles that day, but that one running play really bugs me. My error ended up being a good thing because it gave us enough time to come back. Had they not scored on that play, Miami probably would have kept chipping away then kicked a field goal to win the game.

You've always been adamant about what happened during the Immaculate Reception. It was the Steelers-Raiders playoff of 1972. You contend that the pass from Terry Bradshaw hit Frenchy Fuqua's back before it was caught by Franco Harris, and according to the rules the play shouldn't have counted. Tell me what you saw as that play developed.

PV: That was one of the greatest all-time plays and I remember it like it was yesterday. I'm not sure of the exact defense we were in. We might have been in that two-linebacker formation I mentioned. On this particular play I was covering Franco man-to-man. Had I been back there in a prevent defense, that play probably never would have happened.

It was Franco's rookie year, and I'll say it to this day: Franco was jogging down the field! Coaches used to jump on young players so badly when they didn't give 100-percent during every second of the game. I said to myself, "Oh, Franco is just running downfield to make himself look good on film."

But God, when that ball ricocheted and he caught it, he put on the jets and he was gone. That whole play was a tremendous credit to Terry Bradshaw, that he was able to scramble around and get the ball downfield. And it was a tremendous effort by Franco, picking the ball up and running with it.

What did you see? Did Fuqua or Tatum touch the ball first?

PV: That ball was definitely hit by Fuqua first. I saw it exactly as it happened. After Bradshaw threw the ball I left Franco and started running towards the play. Then I saw the hit and the bounce of the ball. After Harris caught it, I went after him to make the tackle but Pittsburgh's tight end John McMakin dove right into the back of my legs. It wasn't a vicious clip, but it was just enough to get me stumbling. By that time Franco was gone.

There's no question the ball hit Fuqua first. Jack Tatum never thought twice about hitting anything but Fuqua on that play. He just whammed him, and I remember the way Fuqua's body went into a whiplash. Tatum hit him so hard that Fuqua's shoulder just snapped into the ball. That's why it flew off directly to my right. All Tatum had to do was intercept it or knock it down and we would've won the game, but that wasn't Tatum's style. He always went for the knockout hit.

Some of Oakland's greatest battles came against the Pittsburgh Steelers. Defensively, what were the keys to stopping that powerful attack?

PV: For some reason, we seemed to play Pittsburgh better in the regular season than in the playoffs. I don't know what the problem was. We never seemed to have a great offensive attack in any of those playoff games except the '76 Championship. Defensively, we always played well enough to win. We knew we had to stop their run. If we could force Pittsburgh to pass, we thought Bradshaw could make a mistake, and a lot of times he did. In that kind of situation, we felt pretty good about our chances.

The Steelers were such a good running team with Rocky Bleier and Harris and Fuqua and that big offensive line. They just kept on coming. They could beat you with the pass or the run, and that's the toughest type of team to beat. We beat them in a playoff game in Oakland in 1973 because we stopped their rushing attack and held them to around 100 yards. In the '76 season opener, we clamped down on their running game in the second half and won that one.

It pisses me off that we didn't beat them in the '74 AFC Championship. They scored just enough points to beat us, even though Kenny threw about three or four interceptions that day. Stabler was horrible. We gave them the ball too many times on turnovers, and you can't do that in big games. Fumbles, penalties, mistakes… we just didn't play good Raider football in that one. Joe Greene also did a pretty good job of handling our center, Jim Otto, who was near the end of his career at that time. The Steelers controlled the line of scrimmage that day because their best player [Greene] was going up against somebody who was no longer our best lineman.

Then in '75 Championship they beat us on the ice at Three Rivers. It was something like minus 50 degrees, just a bullshit day. The field was frozen solid, but what really hurt us was that [CB] Neal Colzie wasn't ready to play at a championship level. John Madden used to say that a rookie will cost you a game a year, and it's probably true. The Steelers really exploited him. Willie Brown or Skip Thomas must've been hurt the week before, so we needed Colzie to step up but he didn't.

The Raiders reached the Super Bowl in 1976. The opponent was Minnesota, and before the game you made a bold prediction. You said, "Do yourself and your family a favor and bet the mortgage on us. There's no way we won't cover the 6 ½ points. We're going to kill them."
The Vikings, meanwhile, had lost only two games all season, by a total of five points. Why were you so confident you'd win that Super Bowl?

PV: I couldn't believe that we were favored by only that many points. I knew we could beat them handily, and we did, 32-14. We were the best team in the league, much better than Minnesota. Stu Voigt was their tight end and I knew he couldn't block me. We feared [RB] Chuck Foreman a little bit but nobody else. Fran Tarkenton? We thought he was okay. We weren't worried about him. Their receivers, Sammy White and Ahmad Rashad, were good, but we figured our pass rush would take them out of the game. We knew we weren't going to lose to those guys. We had played teams that were a lot better than the Vikings that year.

You played only two games in 1977 due to a knee injury suffered against Pittsburgh. Tell me about that play, and what changed most about your game after returning to action in 1978?

PV: It happened on a play I'd seen probably a million times. We never practiced on Astroturf, and Pittsburgh had just put in a new surface. During warm-ups that day, our guys were tripping and falling down because their cleats were catching on the stuff.

On the play I got hurt, Pittsburgh faked a toss out to Franco Harris then gave the ball to Bleier, who was following his guard into the line of scrimmage. I stepped out, reacting to the fake, then tried to go back after Bleier. My foot got caught on the Astroturf as Bleier was coming down the line. He kinda tripped and lunged forward. But instead of me just getting knocked out of the way, my knee snapped. It was ridiculous! I tore the ligament on the inside. Back in those days, when you broke a ligament, you had to wear a giant leg cast and go on injured reserve and all that shit. It just ruined the whole season. That play changed my whole career around.

I had to rehabilitate, and I thought I came back 100%. I know I could've still played the left side, but instead they put Ted Hendricks on the left and put me on the right. I was never going to be as good playing there. The next year they moved Rod Martin to the right side and put me in the middle. Rod ended up having a nice career at that position, and I ended up getting traded to Buffalo.

The End of an Era in Oakland

...I was upset with Al Davis, primarily because he'd traded one of my buddies, and partly because I thought he had let a single play influence his decision to trade Phil. A guy will make one lousy play at a critical moment, and it can snowball into the end of his career.

I think Phil's downfall began in the 1978 season against New England. The Patriots were driving for a score and Phil's responsibility was to keep an eye on [QB] Steve Grogan, in case he tried a bootleg. That's exactly what he did, but Phil missed the play. Grogan ran the ball about 30 yards to our four-yard line. They scored and we lost by a touchdown. It was hardly the only time Phil had screwed up, but it was a glaring mistake in a game we really wanted. I don't know if Al and the coaches thought Phil had somehow lost his speed or what, but the next season they tried converting Phil into an outside linebacker. The experiment never really worked and the following season he was traded.

>   – **former Raiders DE John Matuszak**, *Cruisin' With the Tooz*
>   (Franklin Watts, 1987)

Dr. Robert Huzienga, the Raiders' team internist during the 1980s, wrote a controversial book entitled You're Okay, It's Just a Bruise. *He was highly critical of the practices of long-time team doctor Dr. Robert Rosenfeld. Huzienga claims that Rosenfeld, many times at the direction of Al Davis, irresponsibly sent injured players into action before they were properly healed.*

What are your memories of Rosenfeld and the Raiders' attitude toward injuries during the 1970s? Were you ever forced into games, knowing you weren't healthy enough to play?

PV: After your first day of training camp, there is never another day that goes by without something being wrong with you physically. The guys that could play injured were kept around for a long time. I used to go into the training room and ask our head trainer George Anderson to make me better, to make me a special pad for this broken finger or ankle or knee or heel. Anderson was a magician at making special pads to help keep us in the game. Dr. Rosenfeld was a great guy at getting you back on the field with surgery. There were a lot of pills available that helped get us back on the field.

I saw a lot of guys play injured, and I was one of them. But I never saw a guy play injured that didn't want to. This doctor who wrote the book – and I wouldn't even read it – is probably one of these guys that didn't belong in the Raiders organization.

Do you think that Huzienga was exaggerating, or even lying about what he saw?

PV: Hey, the Raiders are no different from the Steelers or Chiefs or Broncos or Chargers. Every team is the same. Pro football is a mean, tough, nasty game. And in order to play it, you gotta play injured. As long as you can run, you can play. I played injured in *every* game. There was *always* something wrong with me. If I was feeling good, it was a rare occasion.

Yes, there are a lot of [medical] practices that average people can't understand because they're not living the life. It's just the way it is. Football is a war, and I'm sure there are practices that the doctors on the beach at D-Day used that a normal doctor here in my lily-white town would never think of using. You do what you gotta do to get the football player or soldier or gladiator back on the field of battle. It may sound ridiculous to some people, but I think any football player that played as long as I did would understand exactly what I'm saying. We laugh about it now, even though we've probably shortened our lives a little bit by playing injured or playing with these medicines in us, but that's the way it was. We all wanted to do it.

Final question: Your career in Oakland lasted nine seasons; it ended with just one championship. Looking back on your career, do you feel any sense of dissatisfaction or underachievement, considering the tremendous collection of talent that was on the Oakland Raiders?

PV: I'm glad you asked that question because I definitely do. We definitely should have more than one ring. We should have four or five of them. We had the players to do that. When I look back, I honestly think some guys left it in the locker room. Some of us weren't ready to play in the bigger games. We could've been more prepared and played a little bit harder in the big games. Some guys weren't as focused as others and when you're tying to win a Super Bowl, everybody has to be focused. Totally focused. Over the years we had some guys who might've been scared or didn't work as hard as the others. It gets you pissed off.

The championship game losses? I don't know how we lost to Denver in '77. I will say they were given a gift when [RB] Rob Lytle fumbled on the 1-yard line and they whistled the play dead. They never should have beaten us. That should have been a Super Bowl trip, too. As far as I'm concerned, '74 and '75 should have been Super Bowl trips as well. Even in 1972, the Immaculate Reception year, we had the talent to reach the Super Bowl. I definitely feel unfulfilled. There's some emptiness inside a lot of us guys who played in the '70s. I'm very happy that I got one ring, but I think our team deserved some more. It just shows you how hard they are to get.

— 5 —
Bert Jones, Quarterback
Baltimore Colts (1973-81); Los Angeles Rams (1982)
July 3, 1998

Pittsburgh quarterback Terry Bradshaw hollered into the losing locker room – to his friend, the Baltimore Colts quarterback – after the Steelers had closed out a lopsided affair at Three River Stadium.

"Bert Jones – I can't figure you out, partner! You dress like a New York stockbroker, but you stand there on the sidelines chewing tobacco! Which one is it?" Jones cracked half a smile as he achingly pulled off his equipment. No answer.

It was the season opener of 1974, and the Steelers had won it, 30-0. Jones, a second-year pro from LSU – "The Ruston Rifle" – was treated roughly in his first visit to Pittsburgh. His numbers for the day: 8 for 17, 100 yards, two interceptions. "My introduction to defensive mayhem," he called it. Pittsburgh had begun its march toward the first of four Super Bowl titles in the decade, while the wobbly Colts were on their way to a disastrous 2-12 season, then the worst in the Horseshoe's history.

Bradshaw, who sometimes dressed like he *grew* tobacco, continued to watch his stock as a Steeler fluctuate between blue chip and de-listed. On this day he was de-listed – coach Chuck Noll had named Joe Gilliam his opening day starter – but Bradshaw could still afford to ride the ups and downs. At 26, time was still an ally, despite the wave of anxiousness that had swept over the fans in Pittsburgh. The city had gotten its first real taste of winning in '72 and '73; there would be no cries for the old days, and there were no Steeler legends to be replaced at quarterback. The first one had yet to come along.

Jones had no such luxury. His job was to replace the 290 touchdown throws and 40,239 passing yards and three world championships left behind by John Unitas. "It was all out there, staring back at me," recalled Jones, "all the records and the big games and the memories…Mr. Quarterback…It was intimidating at times."

"Baltimore still wasn't ready to let go of Unitas," a Colts old-timer once told me, "even though his skills were fading. There'd been too many good times to say goodbye. I was at Memorial Stadium for Johnny U's farewell game in '72. 'Unitas We Stand' Day. All the emotion. Grown men were cheering and crying." Unitas fired a 63-yard touchdown as his final salute back.

But Bert Jones had the talent to create a new distraction for Baltimore, if not to make them forget. A whip-like right arm, plenty of giddyup in his legs, fiery leadership. Yep, the Colts had drafted the right man to fill the void. It's just that they still needed help in other areas, and that would eventually come. Few who observed the evidence displayed that September Sunday in 1974 would have predicted the next two meetings between these teams would occur in the high-stake wars of the '75 and '76 AFC playoffs.

The combination of Jones, head coach Ted Marchibroda and general manager Joe Thomas would lead a sudden Baltimore resurgence to the top of the AFC East in 1975, breaking a four-year Miami Dolphins stronghold that had been well defended. First line of business – get Jones some protection.

"The knock against me was that I bailed out of the pocket too quickly," says Jones, "but there wasn't much of a pocket during my first couple years in the league. You couldn't stay in there and get killed." Jones and sometimes-starter Marty Domres were dropped 81 times between 1973 and '74.

Thomas first looked toward Atlanta for help, shrewdly trading for sturdy All-Pro George Kunz and a

69

swap of first-round draft choices. The trick? Threatening to draft Cal QB Steve Bartkowski, a player the Falcons desperately wanted, with the number one pick and dealing him off to another quarterback-hungry club. The Colts moved down to number three and took an All-America guard Ken Huff of North Carolina. Instant security.

Add in the sudden emergence of a crunching front four known as the "Sack Pack," which would lead the league with 59 sacks (4.2 per game), and the Colts were suddenly back in business. Baltimore finished 10-4 and won the AFC East. Running back Lydell Mitchell became the first Colt to crack the 1,000-yard mark. The offense scored 205 more points than in 1974, and the team's eight-game swing in the win column became, at the time, the greatest single-season turnaround in NFL history. "The Miracle on 33rd Street," they called it.

From 1975 through 1977, the Colts won 31 of 42 regular season games and three division crowns and Baltimore was in a frenzy. There were even secret whispers of "Johnny Who?"

But, boy, did things come crashing down when the playoff door would swing open, especially for Jones. Playoffs meant head-hanging days in Baltimore – three consecutive first-round losses, two of them at home. And John Unitas would not have let that happen.

Jones' playoff numbers reflect the futility:

	Comp-Att-Yds	TD/Int	Result	Notes
1975 at Pittsburgh	6-11-91	0/0	28-10 loss	Left game in first quarter, arm injury
1976 vs. Pittsburgh	11-25-144	1/2	40-14 loss	Sacked five times by Steelers rush
1977 vs. Oakland	12-26-164	0/0	37-31 loss	Six completions going into 4th quarter

Jones' overall quarterback rating in the playoffs? A dismal 59.8. But his teammates supplied him little help in those battles. "To be fair, we gave Bert some lousy protection in the playoffs," said former Colts guard Robert Pratt. "Our line had trouble handling big, rangy defensive ends like L.C. Greenwood and John Matuszak. They gave us a lot of problems. Matuszak tortured Bert in the '77 game. If he wasn't sacking Bert he was swatting down his passes."

Scanning over an entire career, two plays can sum up the way Bert Jones operated on the football field – one represents his sheer toughness, the other a superior, game-commanding arm strength.

December 21, 1975 – Patriots at Colts. Jones was still recovering from painful broken ribs suffered weeks earlier, yet a win would bring Baltimore the AFC East title and a playoff invite. The ball is snapped from New England's 8-yard line, then there goes Jones bootlegging around left end for the Colts' first score. Swarming at the goal line were Patriot linebackers Kent Carter and Steve Nelson, who both levied fierce blasts into his midsection. If their quarterback stays down, Baltimore can kiss its playoff party goodbye. But Jones gets up and finishes the game, and the Colts win it, 34-21.

"The play was there, so you take it, busted ribs or not," Jones said. "Is there any other way to play?"

"I just closed my eyes," said Marchibroda.

The other play came in 1977 under nearly identical circumstances. Patriots are in town late in the season…playoffs at stake…December winds whipping and howling off the Chesapeake… New England has the Colts trapped at their own four-yard line, leading 24-23. Jones drifts back into his endzone, pumps right, then unloads a laser shot to wideout Glenn Doughty, who's running a nifty out-and-up on cornerback Bob Howard. Doughty holds on for a 57-yard gain. I can think of only five or six quarterbacks who could make that throw.

"We needed to get out of the hole," Jones recalls, "so I opened it up. Doughty had the speed to get out there so I didn't have to hold anything back."

"One of the greatest throws I've ever seen, and a back-breaker for New England," said former Baltimore GM Ernie Accorsi. "I'll never forget it." Colts win it, 30-24.

After 1977, injuries became the story for Bert Jones. They plagued him. Shoulder trouble cost him 25 games between 1978 and '79, and, although Jones had healed by the start of the 1980 season, the team around him had been allowed to crumble. Marchibroda, his mentor, was fired along the way. By 1982, Jones had had enough of the Colts dysfunctional team ownership. He demanded a trade and management complied. Jones was shipped west to Los Angeles for what would be his final year in the league, just as Unitas had been exiled to San Diego nine years earlier.

Irony? Not really. Just two big-time quarterbacking careers that started and ended in the same places. The difference was the in-between.

• • •

It was draft day, 1973. The first six teams on the board were already set at the quarterback position:

1st: Houston Oilers – talented youngsters Dan Pastorini and Lynn Dickey battling for the job
2nd: New Orleans Saints – Archie Manning was their future
3rd: Philadelphia Eagles – grooming John Reaves, their first pick in the '72 draft
4th: New England Patriots – secure with strong-armed Jim Plunkett
5th: St. Louis Cardinals – new coach Don Coryell committed to veteran Jim Hart
6th: Philadelphia Eagles – hoping to upgrade the offense with USC tight end Charlie Young

Holding the seventh overall pick were the Buffalo Bills, a team with serious problems at quarterback. Based upon need, it appeared as if you were going to be their man.

BJ: I knew I didn't have any say-so, so I was just hoping to get drafted. I would've liked playing for Cleveland. My father [Dub Jones] played for the Browns and was their offensive coordinator for a number of years, so I had strong ties to the Browns organization. But I didn't do a lot of thinking about it. I wanted to play, hopefully for a good team, and let's go.

Houston selected defensive end John Matuszak from the University of Tampa. Then Baltimore, coming off a punchless 5-9 season behind John Unitas and Marty Domres, trades up for the 2nd pick. Commissioner Pete Rozelle steps to the podium and announces that you are the newest member of the Baltimore Colts. Your initial reaction?

BJ: Joe Thomas, who was the Colts general manager at the time, called me at my house. I just said, "Thanks for taking me. I'm looking forward to coming." I was excited about it. The Colts had a history of great things, and playing where Johnny Unitas had played was certainly an added attraction. He was one of the all-time greats. They had just hired Howard Schnellenberger as their new coach, so it was an exciting time for me.

Was Schnellenberger's intention to start you right away – a baptism by fire?

BJ: The NFL is a great working environment because the best players are the ones who play. I just didn't walk in there and take over. Marty Domres was there, a former number one draft choice. I came along as the heir apparent to John Unitas, who had been traded to San Diego. No job was handed to me. The unfortunate thing for me during my rookie year was the NFL was still playing the College All-Star Game. Instead of going to training camp like every other rookie, I unfortunately went to Chicago to play in that game. When I finally got to camp, I was way behind everybody else.

Target Practice, NFL Style

Bert Jones completed the most passes during any NFL game played in the 1970s, connecting on 36 of his 53 attempts – including a feverish streak of 17 in a row – against the New York Jets on December 15, 1974. When the exhausted Jones was asked if he learned anything by watching the immobile Joe Namath's performance that afternoon, he laughed, "Yes – hit the ground when they're coming at you."

He also learned that completing a whole bunch of passes for gobs of yardage doesn't guarantee a win for the team, as the Jets dumped Baltimore that day in a 45-38 shoot-out.

Here, then, are the NFL's top five individual marks for pass completions in a game, along with a summary of each contest's outcome:

5-tie) 40 of 56 by Ken Anderson, Cincinnati vs. San Diego (12/20/82); 40 of 56 by Brad Johnson, Tampa Bay vs. Chicago (11/18/01) – This rematch of the 1981 AFC title game was nothing like its ice-bound predecessor, and oh, what a show Anderson and Dan Fouts put on for America that Monday night. Fouts had no sooner pulled his arm from the ice bucket after lighting up San Francisco for 450 yards and 5 TDs the previous week when Anderson called him out to the streets for another gunfight.

Bad idea. Anderson did his part in throwing for 397 yards, but his posse – the Bengal defense – headed for the hills as Fouts erupted again, this time for 435 yards and a touchdown. Even Chargers tailback Chuck Muncie got into the aerial action, connecting with Wes Chandler for a 66-yard score. **Chargers 50 Bengals 34**

Brad Johnson holds the record for most completions in a game without a touchdown. That's like setting the all-time record for getting two strikes on a batter. On the Chicago side, three of Jim Miller's 14 throws went for scores. You do the math. **Bears 27 Bucs 24**

4) 41 of 56 by Warren Moon, Houston vs. Dallas (11/10/91) – Sportswriter John Underwood once observed that spectacular football games are almost always settled by the wrong guys – placekickers. "Decided not by heroic, bloodied men who play themselves to exhaustion and perform breathtaking feats," he wrote, "but by men in clean jerseys. With names you cannot spell, and remnants of European accents, and slender bodies and mystical ways." It happened on this day, too. Moon blazed through the Cowboys with his 41 completions (and how many drops?) for 432 yards, but it was Al Del Greco's boot with 29 ticks left in OT that saved the day for Houston. **Oilers 26 Cowboys 23, OT**

3) 42 of 63 by Vinny Testaverde, New York Jets vs. Seattle (12/6/98) – Unfortunately for Vinny, this day won't be remembered for any of his passes but for a short run and a game-ending dose of horrific officiating from the Phil Luckett crew. Testaverde fired 63 times into the AFC's worst pass defense, yet his Jets still trailed by 5 from the five with 20 seconds to play. The call from the sidelines was "quarterback sneak," a gusty gamble usually reserved for fleeter feet than Testaverde's, but he followed orders and charged up the gut. As the stunned Seahawks hauled him down – a full yard from the goal line – the official's arms flew in the air signaling touchdown. Disbelief was everywhere, but the Jets won it on arguably the worst call in NFL history. Instant replay was back the next season. **Jets 32 Seahawks 31**

2) 42 of 60 by Richard Todd, New York Jets vs. San Francisco (9/21/80) – The Great Spacely Sprockets Caper. Niner QB Steve DeBerg fakes a malfunction in his space-age helmet amplifier and heads to the sidelines for repairs. Unknown backup Joe Montana comes in and scoots for an eight-yard TD run on his first play. Later, another phony breakdown is staged by DeBerg; Montana generates another immediate score, whipping a 20-yard TD pass to Dwight Clark. In a desperate display of technological superiority, purple smoke and sparks fly from Todd's mechanical right arm as it fires on 60 of New York's 71 offensive plays. Jets fans are not amused by the Star Trek convention breaking out on the field. **49ers 37 Jets 27**

1) 45 of 70 by Drew Bledsoe, New England vs. Minnesota (11/13/94) – Bledsoe's final completion on this day is a 14-yard toss to FB Kevin Turner that wins it in overtime for the Pats. His 70 attempts broke a 30-year old record (68) set by George Blanda back in untamed AFL days. Did I just write *70 pass attempts*? *From a Bill Parcells-coached team*? Ol' Grind-It-Out Bill? That's an anomaly, like my brother-in-law picking up the tab. But remember, "The Tuna" once had Phil Simms heave it 62 times against Cincinnati back in 1985, a number that's still alive in the Giants' record book. Every decade or so Parcells' Comet whooshes by. It's due again sometime in 2005. **Patriots 26 Vikings 20, OT**

What kind of relationship did you have with John Unitas? Domres once described it as a sour one, saying, "Bert and John did not get along. They were just different personalities. To John, Bert was a wise guy. Bert would kid him, and if there is one thing you don't want to do is try to stick the needle to John."

BJ: First of all, John wasn't even there during my first year in Baltimore. He had already been traded to San Diego. I only saw him during the offseason, and I think my relationship with him was real good. John harbored some animosity towards the Colts organization, but it wasn't towards me. To him I was just another player in the league at the time. His situation didn't have any bearing on me. As a matter of fact, I used to eat at his restaurant once or twice a week, and I had a lot of good times there. I considered us to be good, casual friends.

So Domres was out of line in his remarks?

BJ: No question about it. I always spoke highly of John. Marty may have been thinking of things as they related to him. Marty was the guy that actually took his place. If there were anyone who harbored some hard feelings from John, it would've been Marty. I wasn't there to know that, but I do know that John didn't like the new organization and the way the old Colts team had been dismantled. I don't blame him.

You ended up winning the job from Domres and started the season opener at Cleveland. It was a miserable first day on the job. Six completions in 22 passes for only 56 yards, plus five sacks and an interception. What were your memories of that afternoon?

BJ: I was thinking about playing my first professional game against a team I held in the highest esteem. The Browns were my team. Their defensive coordinator Howard Brinker was my dad's best friend and a dear friend of mine. So it was a lot of fun! If you can't play for them, you want to play against them.

But the Browns beat us like redheaded stepchildren. Defensively they did everything in the world to me. All kinds of blitzes and disguised coverages. Late in the first half I threw an out into double zone, and the defense did what it was supposed to do – pick it off and run it back for a touchdown. It was a rough day for me.

You started four more games that year, losing three of them, and your quarterback rating bottomed out at 28.8. After a 31-13 loss to Buffalo, Domres was back as the starter. How frustrated were you by being sent to the bench?

BJ: I wasn't frustrated at all. I was very willing to sit back and learn and get ready to play some more. There were a lot of new faces on the Colts, and we were getting killed most of the time. It was really a year of transition for the entire team.

1974 was an even more tumultuous season for Baltimore. A mid-summer players strike wiped out training camp and the preseason; one of the Colts' best defensive players, Ted Hendricks, was traded to Green Bay over a salary dispute; then, in late September, Schnellenberger was fired by owner Robert Irsay. The team was off to an 0-3 start and had been outscored 80-23.

BJ: [Laughing] We did that well? 1974 was almost a repeat performance of the previous season. My second year was terrible in terms of trying to learn the game. I was ready to walk into training camp when it opened but the players' strike prevented that. Consequently, all of training camp was aborted. I was ready to go but there was no place to play. I had to play the first game of the season with no preparation.

But the difference from 1973 was that the team was beginning to play competitively under Schnellenberger. The scores might not have indicated it, but we were seeing positive things happen. Players were developing and maturing. The nucleus was forming of what was to become a very good football team.

Schnellenberger's biggest disagreement with Irsay was over who should be playing at quarterback.

He thought the veteran Domres gave the team the best chance to win; Irsay wanted his future star Bert Jones to gain experience.

BJ: I thought all along that I was the best man for the job, but I may not have been ready at that point. Remember, we missed the entire preseason because of the strike. Howard was doing the best job he could as a coach, and that was to field the veterans on the team that knew the plays.

It really came to a head at one point during the game at Philadelphia. Things were not going well. Marty was playing poorly, so Howard had me warming up on the sidelines to go into the game on the next series. At that time Mr. Irsay came down from the press box and told him to put me in the game. Howard wasn't at all happy about it, and he did exactly as any good coach would've done. He said, "Hey buddy, your job is to own the team, my job is to coach." He was going to hold me out just to prove a point to Irsay. Of course, Irsay then fired him, and Joe Thomas took over as head coach for the rest of the season.

What was your opinion of Schnellenberger?

BJ: I think Howard Schnellenberger was a fabulous football coach but he was thrust into a terrible situation. During his first year, it was a terrible team he inherited. The only way you could figure out who the players were was to look at their numbers then check the roster. There was no continuity. Management had cleared the house at the end of the prior season. There wasn't a chance for him to do much that first year.

The team finished in last place with a 2-12 record under Thomas. Then the Colts hired Ted Marchibroda, George Allen's long-time offensive coordinator in Los Angeles and Washington, as head coach. How long into the Marchibroda regime did you realize that he would move the Colts in the right direction?

BJ: Ted really added to the momentum that Howard had started. The team was improving under Howard, but there's no question that Ted put the whole thing together. He did a fabulous job. The first great thing Ted did was bring me up to Baltimore four weeks before training camp. I stayed in a hotel and every day we went through a school session. That's how I learned his system. So when I walked into camp, I had a very good knowledge of what was going on. From that point it was a matter of matching the motor skills to what was going on in the playbook.

The 1975 team started out 1-4, running a gauntlet that consisted of Chicago, Oakland, the L.A. Rams, Buffalo and New England.

BJ: But we were competitive. We almost won all five of those ballgames. We were improving each week. I remember playing Chicago in the opener and getting hit in the head a lot, which was somewhat suspect [laughing]. But we could see that things were starting to come together on both sides of the ball.

Then came game six, a 45-28 blasting of the Jets which marked the beginning of a whirlwind turnaround for the team. Eight consecutive wins followed, and by Christmas the Colts were 10-4 and the surprise champions of the AFC East. Why the sudden turnaround?

BJ: We were maturing the whole time. Probably the most important thing was through all that losing, we learned to win. We figured out what it took to get over the hump, and matured as offensive and defensive units. It was a fabulous rush, that whole winning streak. You don't get the opportunity often to go from last place in the division to first in one year. It was the biggest turnaround in the history of pro football at that time.

I'll never forget this. Ted called us all together after losing those four games and said, "Look, we lost some ballgames, but we were close on every occasion. I'll tell you this: If you win every game, taking them one at time, you'll be in the playoffs." It happened just like he said it would. Every week was building to the crescendo at the end of the year.

Why was Ted Marchibroda the right coach for that football team?

BJ: Ted's greatest strength was that, strategically, he knew where to put the ball on the football field in order to advance it with the players that he had. We didn't have a great team – let's be real candid about this. Even though we had great success, if you stacked up the players on our team against players from other teams in the league, there wouldn't be many of us that were better. But collectively we played as a fantastic unit. The reason was that we did the right thing. We read the blitz, studied the game, and understood opposing teams. We knew what their tendencies and strengths were, and we knew how to attack their weaknesses. It was all because of Ted. The greatest complement to a coach is that he is able to adjust his strategy to fit the players he has on the field, not to fit the players into a system.

> "When I left the Redskins and took the head job in Baltimore, I was leaving behind a man named Sonny Jurgensen, probably the finest passer I'd ever been around. What a quick mind! He could read defenses like cue cards and see things developing on the field very quickly. I was kinda sad to leave him, and I wondered, will I ever get another quarterback with that kind of talent?
>
> "By the time I got to Baltimore, I found out rather quickly that my new quarterback could do those things too. Bert Jones had a lot of the same attributes as Sonny – a fantastic arm and a sharp, quick mind – and I knew right away that he was going to be an outstanding player. I couldn't wait to get to work with that kid."
>
> **– Ted Marchibroda, Baltimore Colts Head Coach (1975-79)**

As a general manager, Joe Thomas had a reputation of being a tremendous talent evaluator, having turned around expansion franchises in Minnesota and Miami. He once said, "There are two things I don't do – draft poor football players or trade good, young football players." Describe his role in the sudden resurrection of the Colts.

BJ: Joe was certainly the instrumental cog in the wheel prior to Ted's joining the team. People can say a lot of things about Joe, but one thing they can't say is that he didn't bring good people to the plate. He was the man who drafted me, Joe Ehrmann, Fred Cook, Mike Barnes, John Dutton, Roger Carr – all the players that ultimately became standouts for the ballclub. He did a good job in assembling players.

If Joe had a shortcoming, it was that he didn't realize the importance of coaching. He thought coaching was a given. Joe thought that having the best coach in the world didn't matter as long as you had the best players. That was a major shortcoming of his. We had a lot of the same players on the team under Howard as we did when Ted took over. It's just that under Ted those players had time to mature and develop.

You and receiver Roger Carr brought the deep ball back to Baltimore's passing game. I was looking through game summaries from the 1975 and '76 season and saw the barrage of big scoring plays the two of you had generated: An 89-yard touchdown against Buffalo; a 90-yard score against the Jets; 68 and 65-yard bombs against Cincinnati; another 79-yarder against the Jets.

Tell me more about Roger Carr, your favorite home run threat, and the Colts' deep passing game.

BJ: Roger was deceptively fast. Early on we caught a lot of people by surprise because they had no idea he could motor like that. He had a tremendous ability to explode and accelerate in catching the ball. Even though the bomb was a low-percentage pass, it functioned very well for us often. Anytime we got single coverage on Roger, we'd exploit it because he was such a talented player.

We ran a different style than what they're doing in professional football now. Back then, everything was basically a seven-step drop and *Let's play ball*. I felt I had the ability that, if you were a receiver and had the defender on your back, I could get the ball in front of you. If the defender was in front of you, I could throw it away from him. I was blessed with a very strong arm, but also a very accurate one. I mean, *I could play some ball*. The truth is, I could designate which side of the chest I was gonna hit that receiver, no matter the distance.

How far could you throw a football on your best day?

BJ: I don't know. Probably 85 or 90 yards without any problem.

Does any specific play by Carr stand out in your memory?

BJ: Oh, there are a number of them. His ability to explode past defensive backs to get to the football was phenomenal. I'll never forget the time he beat that great cornerback from Cincinnati, Ken Riley. Riley had never been beaten deep before and Roger burned him. My old college roommate, Tommy Casanova, who played linebacker for the Bengals, told me, "We couldn't believe he could do that to us."

Another play that stands out was against Miami in 1976. I threw a square-in hook against an "in-and-out" defense. It was a critical third down, and in theory there was no way we should've been able to complete that pass against the coverage. But I had so much confidence in Roger and my throwing ability that I knew we'd make the play. [S] Jake Scott was lying inside, waiting for him, and I'll never forget it. Jake got up screaming at me, "You knew you weren't supposed to throw the ball there, Bert! I had him covered!"

I said, "You're right, man, but I did anyway. First down!"

Former Colts safety Rick Volk had a less flattering opinion of Carr. He once said, "When Carr was the primary receiver, he worked hard running a pattern. When he was not the primary receiver, he dogged it and didn't run out the pattern. I played against him; I saw it. That gave away a lot of the stuff the Colts were trying to do. Carr could run and had great hands, but he didn't have a big heart. He didn't want to come across the middle."
Your thoughts on that statement.

BJ: I think Rick is way off base. You have to put Roger's situation in perspective here. Roger had no intention of playing college or pro football. In fact, he had no intentions of even going to college. His grandmother made him go to school, a little college called Louisiana Tech. He was running intramural track for his dorm, and he ended up broad-jumping 22 or 23 feet or some phenomenal distance, further than anybody on the track team was jumping. So the coaches said, "Hey guy, we'll pay for your books it you come run track for us." Sounded like a good deal to him.

The track field happened to be near the football field, where the football team was having its spring practice. Roger was goofing around with a football and started punting it, kicking it farther than any punter on the team. So the coaches said, "Wow! Come punt the ball for us, and we'll pay for more of your school!" Then they found out that he had soft, gifted hands and could really run, so they said, "Wow! Why don't you come play receiver for us?" It wasn't his desire to play ball, but he ended up doing it anyway.

He played extremely well for Tech, good enough to become a first-round draft pick in 1974. Roger held out of his first Colts training camp because he wanted more money than they wanted to pay him. When he did finally come in, he strained a hamstring, so his first year was kind of a snafu. His second year wasn't much better, and I'm not sure that he really wanted to play the game. But then, all of a sudden in '76, the fire got in him and he turned it on.

I don't think there was a bigger heart on the field than Roger's once he dedicated himself to the game, so I'm scratching my head again as to what Rick is saying. I know that Roger's second year was Rick's last with the team. He used to have to guard Roger in practice and it wasn't a fair matchup. Roger would burn right by him. Maybe that had something to do with his comments.

Introducing Pro Football's 9.0 Club

Since 1970, only eleven NFL quarterbacks have averaged more than 9.0 yards/ passing attempt over an entire season. It's a statistical rarity, and the keys to it are having a fortress of an offensive line, high-octane motors at the wideouts, and a play-caller with a wild hair up his ass. And even then it probably isn't going to happen.

Most of the NFL's best passers haven't been able achieve it. San Diego deepballer Dan Fouts' best average was 8.74/attempt and that came during the strike-shortened season of 1982.

Joe Namath's top year? 8.69.

Brett Favre's? 7.69.

In Randall Cunningham's terrific 1998 campaign he averaged 8.72.

All superb numbers, but not elite ones.

Baltimore Colts quarterback Bert Jones pulled it off in the fall of '76 with a steady combination of deep shots to wide receivers Roger Carr and Glenn Doughty and swings to the shifty Lydell Mitchell, who caught sixty balls that year (9.0 yds/catch). The vital element, though, was Carr, who averaged nearly 26 yards per reception that season, all on big, downfield stuff.

"Carr was always extremely fast and deceptive," says former Patriots DB Dick Conn, "but in '76 he was slicing behind everybody's secondary. I'd watch the films and think, 'Man! How the hell are we gonna stop that?'"

Here's the complete membership of the 9.0 Club since 1970, along with the numbers for each quarterback's top downfield target. I'll also post Greg Cook's amazing 1969 season as an added bonus for suffering Cincinnati Bengals fans. He's the only rookie to make the list:

Year	Player	Yds/att.	Deep Threat	Catches	Yds/catch
1969	Greg Cook, Cincinnati	9.41	Bob Trumpy	37	22.6
1972	Earl Morrall, Miami	9.07	Paul Warfield	29	20.9
1976	Ken Stabler, Oakland	9.41	Cliff Branch	46	24.2
1976	James Harris, Los Angeles	9.24	Ron Jessie	34	22.9
1976	Bert Jones, Baltimore	9.01	Roger Carr	43	25.9
1983	Lynn Dickey, Green Bay	9.21	James Lofton	58	22.4
1984	Dan Marino, Miami	9.01	Mark Clayton	73	19.0
1988	Boomer Esiason, Cincinnati	9.21	Eddie Brown	53	24.0
1989	Joe Montana, San Francisco	9.12	Jerry Rice/John Taylor	82/60	18.1/18.0
1991	Steve Young, San Francisco	9.02	Taylor/ Rice	64/80	15.8/15.0
1998	Chris Chandler, Atlanta	9.65	Tony Martin	66	17.9
2000	Kurt Warner, St. Louis	9.88	Torry Holt	82	19.9

From 1975 through 1977, Baltimore had a scorching 31-11 regular season mark and captured three consecutive AFC East titles, but what people seem to remember most were the team's hasty exits from the playoffs. 1975 was ended with a loss at Pittsburgh; in 1976, it was a 40-14 whipping by the Steelers in your own stadium; then, in 1977, a 37-31 shootout loss to Oakland in overtime.

Why were your Colts teams so ineffective in the playoffs?

BJ: Well, we never really had a dominating defense. We had a competitive defense, especially when we were ahead, because we had really good inside and outside rushers, but we really didn't have great personnel. They played well as a unit and above their ability as a team, but they weren't a dominating force. Because of that, strategically it made us play hand-to-mouth type football to maintain possession of the ball. We scored over 30 points in that Raider game, which should have been enough to win. But it wasn't.

In the '75 playoff in Pittsburgh, I suffered a really weird injury. I was scrambling around in the backfield and jumped over [DB] J.T. Thomas, who was on the ground. His knee hit the back of my right arm and it created quite a hematoma. My arm literally exploded. It almost doubled in size, which knocked me out considering how much blood had coagulated in there. It knocked me out of the game for a while. Marty Domres had to come off the bench. I came back to play in the 4th quarter, but the arm wasn't the same. It was black and blue for a month. Had I not been injured I think we would've had a very good chance to win that game.

However, the Steelers were by far the best football team I had ever seen. When we played them in '76 we were just outmanned. I played in the Pro Bowl one year, and I looked over at our defense and realized that eight or nine of them were the regulars on Pittsburgh's team. Every person on that defense was as good as or better than anybody in the league. They had the NFL's three best linebackers, Jack Lambert, Andy Russell and Jack Ham, who were so talented and fast that they could've been receivers. Thomas and Mel Blount were at the corners. I think Blount was the best player I ever played against. Nobody dominated his position and controlled one half of the football field like he did. So your other choice was to throw to the other side of the field, and there was J.T. Thomas, another All-Pro.

What about the tight end position? Raymond Chester was a tremendous talent for the Colts there. He averaged 33 catches per season in Baltimore, but somehow Chester still seemed out of sync with the rest of the offense.

BJ: You're kinda right, but he had a real chance. Raymond Chester was a good player and a fabulous run blocker. On double-teams he'd block down and just kill guys. He had good speed, but he didn't always seem to be just right. He was more of a runner receiver as opposed to a possession receiver.

I was with Kenny Stabler recently, and we talked in-depth about Raymond. He told me that their system in Oakland was much more suited to Raymond's talents than ours in Baltimore. The Raiders had a luxury that we didn't have, and that was a real large offensive line. Kenny told me, "I would back up 7 to 9 steps, and just wait for things to develop." That wasn't our style of play. We had a good offensive line, but not one you could continuously rely on for five seconds.

When Raymond came to us from Oakland, he was used to running extended, long pass patterns. It was a tough transition in Baltimore, where everything was quick and crisp and in a hurry. We took a 5 or 7-step drop in our pass plays, which didn't accommodate a lot of extended pass patterns from our receivers, and that's where Raymond was at his best. If you split him out wide, he was a very formidable receiver. But we didn't always have the time and the luxury to wait for the play to develop. He caught a lot of balls for us, but probably not as many as we would've liked.

The way we intended to implement the short passing game was by throwing to our backs, not the tight end. We had Don McCauley, who was as fine a possession receiver as I've ever seen. Mitchell was an outstanding receiver. We ended up getting most of our one-on-one situations from our running backs.

Here is another comment from Rick Volk, one that is somewhat critical of Marchibroda's passing game methodology:

"Bert had the best arm I'd ever seen, maybe too much at times. If Unitas had been here, he'd have taught Bert how to go from one receiver to another. But Marchibroda told him, 'If your number one guy is not open, dump it to the backs.' That's why Lydell Mitchell led the league in receptions. Bert did not know how to go from his number one to two to three receivers. Maybe it was because it was a young team and the line couldn't give him enough time to do that. But Marchibroda told him to dump it off."

BJ: In my mind, I know Rick is wrong. If there is one thing that I did, it was to strategically put the ball where it was supposed to be on the field – calling the plays, anticipating the defense, and hopefully hitting my primary receiver. If I completed it to my primary receiver, that meant I anticipated the defense correctly. By no means did I single focus on one guy down the line. I had a progression of reads and went with it all the time.

We threw a good bit to the backs, but we did that for multiple reasons. One of the reasons was because we never ran a basic sweep play, handing the ball to the running back who runs it to the outside. We simply weren't blessed with phenomenal speed at running back. Lydell Mitchell was a fabulous open field and interior runner. The only problem he had was he didn't have the speed to get to the outside on his own. So instead of getting to the outside via the run, we often did it via the pass. It has the same net effect, just a different way to get there.

I consider Rick and I to be friends but I think he is a little off base here. First of all, he didn't play very long with our group. He had peaked out at the time we were starting our run under Ted. Then he went to play for Miami. And I know he has a bone to pick with Ted because that's who released him. Sometimes it's hard to look in the mirror and find fault with ourselves. It's always easier to place the blame somewhere else. I don't blame Rick for that. I'm just giving what possibly was some of the reasoning behind his statement.

The worst defense you faced during the 1970s belonged to which team?

BJ: It was always the Jets, particularly in 1976 when Lou Holtz was their coach. I need to walk on this subject lightly. They had very good players, but trust me – there is a monumental difference between college football strategy and professional football strategy. [Laughing] Playing against a college system was so much fun, simply because you knew what they were going to do, you knew how to attack it, and you knew you were going to beat them.

The Colts always ran up big points in those games. From 1974-77, the Colts offense averaged 35 points per game against New York.

BJ: Always. And it wasn't because they didn't have good players. It was because they were so elementary in their schemes. Lou, in particular, didn't have a very complicated system. We knew what they were going to do, and we took advantage of it. Holtz didn't give his team much of a chance with those simple schemes.

A quarterback always has at least one pass in his career that he wishes he could put back in his pocket. Former Cleveland QB Brian Sipe still has nightmares about his game-ending interception in a 1980 playoff against Oakland. Which throw in your career would you like to take back?

BJ: I remember it. It was also against Oakland, in the '77 playoffs. We were going toward the open end of the stadium, and I was throwing to Raymond Chester on a corner pattern. I released the ball a little bit early, and it went just over his fingertips. Had I waited a second longer I would've gotten it to him. We were near midfield, and he was wide-open down around Oakland's 25-yard line and heading towards our sideline. Had I completed it, the worst-case scenario would have been that we would have kicked a field goal to win the game in overtime. That one corner pattern haunts me frequently, even to this day.

A Looney Crash Landing in Baltimore

Literally minutes after the 1976 Colts-Steelers playoff game had ended, a small airplane piloted by a genius named Donald Kroner slammed into the empty upper deck of Baltimore's Memorial Stadium. Kroner flew into the open end of the horseshoe-shaped structure in an silly attempt to "buzz" the field but failed to clear the upper deck during his exit run. The plane ker-plowed into the seats.

The Colts also crashed that afternoon, losing embarrassingly to the Steelers, 40-14. It proved to be a blessing in disguise for the folks seated in that upper deck.

"I assure you this – if the game hadn't been a blowout," said long-time Colts season ticket holder Ed Remekis, "not a person would have left the stadium. In those days, there would have been a big ol' party in the stands, especially after a win. The diehards would hang around long after the game, having a few drinks, talking football, and enjoying themselves.

> "There's no doubt in my mind that people would have died had the Colts given Pittsburgh a game that day."
>
> Investigators found a secret note in Kroner's cockpit that read: *To Bert Jones, QB, from Blue Max. Good luck, you B-More Colts.*
>
> Good luck, you B-More Colts? Very nice touch. If your idea of a leisurely Sunday outing was to kamikaze a plane into a 50,000-seat NFL stadium, at least do a better job on the farewell missive. Leave a treasure map to a ancient sunken galleon or a good chili recipe or something with value. I tried contacting "Blue Max" several times for this book, but that went nowhere.
>
> (A quick note on Remekis (pronounced 'reh-ME-kiss'): Eddie was a white-haired Lithuanian from Bethlehem Steel who used to wear these noisy, annoyingly white tennis shoes to work every day. You'd hear Ed way before you'd see him, particularly coming around corners. My co-workers started calling him "Ed Reh-SQUEAK-kiss," which he tolerated for about six weeks. Finally, the squeaking stopped. He got rid of the shoes. Now Ed was roaming the building undetected, always lurking. You never knew when he'd roll onto the scene, and that bothered us.
>
> And soon the name became "reh-SNEAK-iss.")

After that playoff loss, the Colts' joyride under Marchibroda ground to an abrupt halt. You started only seven games over the next two seasons and the team managed just ten wins. A dreary time for football in Baltimore.

BJ: It was. I separated my shoulder in the last preseason game against Detroit in '78. Bubba Baker sacked me. But I did something I never should have done. Hindsight is always 20/20, but instead of being smart, stepping back and letting the shoulder heal, I worked to get well as quickly as I possibly could. I came back against the Jets seven games into the year and separated my shoulder again. That compounded the issue.

Then I got real stupid and played against Washington and Seattle with a damaged shoulder and just ripped it beyond comprehension. That put me out for the year, and it took a long time to get well. In '79, I did the same thing all over again. I injured it against Kansas City in the first game, then rushed myself back on the field and did more damage. Stupid.

Was management pressuring you to get back on the field?

BJ: I can't blame anybody but myself. And the truth is I'd probably do it again the same way and hope the outcome would be different. I can't second-guess myself now. But in hindsight I should've just written off the year, then come back and played with a vengeance when I was healthy.

By the time you had completely healed, it was 1980. The team around you was much different than the one that ruled the AFC East years earlier. Marchibroda had been fired after back-to-back 5-11 seasons and was replaced by Mike McCormack. Your arm was back at full strength, but the Baltimore Colts around you had collapsed.

BJ: It really was a different team at that point. The overall object of the owner was to make money, not to win. Key players had left, and the reason was money. John Dutton, Lydell Mitchell, [WR] Freddie Scott had been traded away. Joe Thomas was eventually fired and went to work for the 49ers. We were losing our best players and not replacing them.

How did you perceive the events that led to Marchibroda's dismissal?

BJ: Ted and I both knew it was going to happen. It had been building up over the years. He was actually fired twice. The first time, in the late summer of 1976, was truly unjust, and I basically caused a wildcat strike by the team in protest. Joe Thomas got nervous and Ted was finally reinstated. You want to talk about a wild day! The team was developing, even though there were some philosophical differences between Thomas and Marchibroda. I can't answer what created the friction between those two guys but it was continuous, a constant tension. It basically forced Ted's resignation the week before our opening game against New England.

We were coming off of a season in which we were champions of the AFC East, and to fire Ted was just was not right. I was pretty abrasive over it. I even called up Pete Rozelle and said, *"This can't happen!* We're fixing to hold our team out and we're not gonna play unless you can figure out some way to get Ted his job back!" I got his attention. [Laughing] Ted told me he had never heard of anything like that, but we were prepared to do it. I was the only guy who came out and protested publicly, and I guess it's because I was the most bulletproof one of us.

Joe Thomas ultimately left the team a year later. That's when Bob Irsay began to take a more active role in the day-to-day operations of the team, and that's when it really started going downhill. I think Ted's relationship with ownership remained constant the whole time he was there. Ted is Ted. What you see is what you get. The aspect that changed was Irsay's role with the team. In the beginning, he was just an owner, a spectator. It was a good working relationship. Thomas was the intermediary between the owner and the coach.

But eventually, Irsay became more involved in the day-to-day activities of the ball club. Truthfully, he didn't have a very good idea of what was going on. His ideas were not necessarily right, but he was the owner. As the team deteriorated, he had to place blame somewhere, even though it was a function of his decisions. He placed it on Ted. When he was fired was after the 1979 season, we both knew it was for the best. Neither of us complained too much. He was more fortunate to get out before I did.

Did you ever say to yourself, "This is a sinking ship. Get me the hell out of Baltimore?"

BJ: I never did until the end. I kept thinking that it would get better and I could make it better, even after I had been truly deceived during a negotiation process. There is one thing that's constant in football, and that is everything changes. I was used to the swinging door. I grew up with it. I knew that the door was scheming to hit you in the back if you didn't say, "I want out" first. It was a tough deal, those last years. We were just not together as a team. And we had, really, a very weak coach.

And that was Mike McCormack?

BJ: Yeah. He was probably the weakest coach I've ever experienced throughout the NFL. Not so much strategically but in the way he handled the team. Unfortunately, McCormack didn't have the gumption and ability to take the head coaching position and go with it. He was a coach without a whole lot of backbone.

Why do you feel that way?

BJ: A prime example of him being weak-kneed was what occurred during team meetings. Things were going really bad for the team, and I'll never forget this: We were putting in our offensive game plan one day and I could see four or five people with their heads down on the desk, sound asleep while the projector was running. I just slammed my playbook down on the desk and hollered, "Look gang – we're putting in our offense! Pay attention! Understand what's going on here! This is my livelihood!" I thought McCormack would come forward and agree with me and do something about it, but he didn't say a word. He may as well have told them to put their towels back on their heads and go back to sleep!

During the game that week we had another incident. We were playing the Jets and Curtis Dickey, a running back who was one of the guys sleeping, didn't follow his assignment on the first four plays of the game. Then on the fifth play, we called a short option pass on 3rd-and-4. He was my primary receiver but Dickey didn't go out on the pass pattern. To make it worse, he dodged a linebacker who was charging me instead of throwing a block. The linebacker tackled me for a loss on the play. I jumped up and hollered at him to get out of the football game and not come back until he knew what he was supposed to do. Mike felt the same way at the time, and benched him.

Well, lo and behold, after the game the press came into the locker room. Curtis had a speech impediment, especially when he was nervous. They asked him, "Why did they take you out of the game?" He just stumbled and stammered and didn't say much of anything. Then one guy asked him, "Do you think the decision had racial overtones? Do you think it was because you are black?"

Give me a break! But as bizarre as that might have sounded, one of the reporters wrote it up. The whole following week the story was developed as a racial issue, that I'd been hollering at Curtis because he was black. I couldn't believe it! So I went to Mike and said, "You can't let something absurd like this continue! This had nothing to do with race! Dickey had no idea what he was doing out there! You know that." But Mike never said a damn word to refute that.

Finally I figured it out, Mike was simply allowing the heat to be taken off of him and placed on someone else – me. It was really ridiculous and unfortunate. Anybody who knows me will say that criticizing people because of their race goes against my upbringing, the way I am as a person. Ralph Waldo Emerson Jones, the president of Grambling University and a dear friend of mine, called me on the phone after the incident and said, "Bert, don't say anything, don't do anything. There is nothing you can do to mobilize a defense for yourself. The people who know you understand this whole thing is ridiculous." To this day, McCormack probably still wouldn't return my call because he is either too embarrassed or doesn't have the nuts to handle it.

Tell me more about your final negotiations with Irsay in Baltimore.

BJ: That was really a weird deal. 1981 was the last year of my contract with the team, so my brother and I went to negotiate a new one with Irsay. We sat down and worked out the details. But then he told me, "Bert, I don't want to sign you right now. Let's wait before we actually sign this, but we definitely have an agreement."

In essence, what he was saying was that he didn't want the bank to know about the contract liability, and he wanted to make sure his permanent financing was in order before we signed the deal. He told me he was a man of his word, and this would all eventually be taken care of. I had no problem with that. So I went to discuss this with the assistant general manager, Ernie Accorsi, and McCormack, who was the new head coach. They were both tickled to death to hear about the new contract, and Irsay had even told them later that the deal was wrapped up. Well, time went on and nothing ever got signed. Then the season started, and soon it was October.

All of a sudden, Irsay pulled the contract! I was out there on a limb! The season went on, and things started to get bad with the team. We were losing, and Irsay's response to it all was "Tough luck." Of course, I took the case to arbitration. I had a conversation with Mike McCormack, and he said, "Yeah, I'll testify on your behalf. I know that you and Irsay had a deal."

Well, Mike was fired at the end of the 1981 season, and he ended up telling me he couldn't make the arbitration hearing because of a prior commitment. I said fine, but how about signing a written affidavit that we can use in court? He never followed through on that. I kept calling him but he never returned my calls. When I finally did contact him, he said he wasn't going to testify on my behalf because he was still being paid by the team and was afraid that would put his arrangement in jeopardy. Basically, McCormack just ran and hid. So I just played out the rest of my contract and became a free agent.

The May 10, 1982 cover of Sports Illustrated read, "Madame Ram Gets Her Man," featuring a picture of you and Los Angeles Rams owner Georgia Frontierre. Irsay had traded you to the Rams in exchange for L.A.'s first- and second-round draft picks. That cover is framed, hanging somewhere in your house, isn't it?

BJ: Actually, it is. When it happened I was tickled to death. I knew it was time to leave Baltimore. The Rams had some very good players, and I was really looking forward to playing for them. But then three games into the season I hurt my neck against Kansas City and it was over. I had to have a cervical fusion and spent three and a half months in one of those halo casts. Then I retired and got into the lumber business, which is where I am today. It's not nearly as fun as playing football, but it's a heckuva lot safer!

— 6 —
Lawrence McCutcheon, Running Back

L.A. Rams (1972-79); Denver/Seattle (1980); Buffalo (1981)
April 18, 2002

If you were a dyed-in-the-wool Los Angeles Rams fan during the 1970s, you're probably resting quite comfortably these days. Life is no longer a Sunday version of Edvard Munch's *The Scream*.

Your nurse is a kind soul. She makes things comfortable. The pillows are soft and you're getting three warm meals a day. The night sweats are gone, and you've probably lost the urge to kick those imaginary field goals in your room, the ones that sailed through the goalposts each night to win the Super Bowl for the good guys.

It's okay now. The Rams have long since moved east, far away to St. Louis. The big, old Coliseum now sits empty on Sundays, and life, mercifully, is getting back to normal.

So, are you ready to talk about it?

No, I didn't think so…

In an era of serious deal-closers from Miami, Dallas, Pittsburgh, even Super Bowl-bumbling Minnesota, the L.A. Rams took the role of pro football's biggest tease. Their colors were royal blue and fool's gold. Credit card millionaires who sat with the high rollers but ate from the $4.95 buffet.

The Rams had talent and plenty of it. The '75 Rams put eight players in the Pro Bowl. The '77 and '78 teams had ten. Year after year forecasters would hail them as Super Bowl bound, but come January, pro football's rutting season, the Rams would lower the horns and charge headfirst into the Vikings or Cowboys and knock themselves out cold.

Year after year, their fans stared at the playoff scoreboard with those same hollow looks, then were sent home in an annual procession of disbelief. Or disgust. Or both.

Championship game losses came in '74, '75, '76, and '78. Meek first-round departures in '73 and '77. All of this decorated by a .694 regular season winning percentage and a steady string of NFC West division titles. Call them the gridiron version of today's Atlanta Braves.

The ultimate tease occurred in 1979, when an injured, garage sale-version of the team finally broke through into uncharted waters. The Rams were a plebian 9-7 but managed to earn a last-minute playoff bid. There, in a surprising championship run they jolted archrival Dallas then smothered a wobbly Tampa Bay squad to win the NFC Title, their first championship of any kind since 1951.

In Super Bowl XIV, L.A. swung hard and had the Steelers on the ropes for three quarters until Terry Bradshaw went deep on 'em, twice, to steal back the lead. Then quarterback Vince Ferragamo threw a bad ball that was intercepted and the Rams blew it again. (Remember the clip from the game's highlight film? The forlorn voice from the coaches box calling down to head man Ray Malavasi? "Waddy was wide open, Ray. Waddy was wide open…")

So after more than 25 years, in which direction should the finger pointing finally stop? Which part of the Rams organization wins the blame game for its playoff shortcomings?

The defense? Not with bullies like Jack and Jim Youngblood, Hacksaw Reynolds and Isiah Robertson lurking. "That was one macho group, a defense that could really slam the door," says former CBS analyst Tom Brookshier. It could collapse the sturdiest ground game or disarm big-time throwers. Prior to Super

Bowl XIV, Bradshaw faced the Rams three other times and threw 10 interceptions. Throughout the 1970s, the Rams placed an average of three defenders in the Pro Bowl every year.

"There were no guests on that defense," says Brookshier

The Rams defense rightfully gets a pass. But here are a few supposals that are worth a look:

Poor Playoff Game Plans: Coaches who can't win the big one. Every generation has its El Foldo. The regular season is theirs, but come the playoffs it all unravels. Today Pittsburgh's Bill Cowher wears the crown. In the '80s it was Marty Schottenheimer. Before him it was the Rams' Chuck Knox, who beefed up on the weak sisters of the NFC West but went 3-5 in the postseason, losing to Dallas or Minnesota every time. How does one become playoff-hardened on a steady diet of Saints, Falcons and 49ers?

"In a lot of ways it was a matter of coaching," says former Rams tailback Lawrence McCutcheon. "We changed very little for the playoffs, especially on offense. Establish the run, pound away, stick with what got us there. The Vikings and Cowboys knew exactly what we were going to do and they stopped it."

"Too conservative?" asks the Vikings' national scout Jerry Reichow. "I don't know if I can blame Knox. Wasn't Lombardi the same way? That style of defense and running worked for him. I don't remember the Packers changing too many things around for the playoffs.

"Maybe Minnesota and Dallas were just better than the Rams. Ever think of that?"

California Dreamin': The Hollywood-itis Theory says that football and Tinsletown don't mix, that teams from SoCal couldn't win the big one because they were soft, playing in front of all that celebrity skin. Squads from the rugged northeast and Midwest welcomed the January chill with brush burns, hanging shirttails and short-sleeves, while the Rams attacked with suntans and manicures.

"I know the Rams hated playing in Minnesota," says Reichow. "You could see it on their faces that they didn't want to be there."

"I used to always say about the Rams, look no farther than the stadium parking lot," says Brookshier. "The Steelers and Cowboys were driving pickup trucks and winning Super Bowls. The Rams came in Ferraris and Porsches and took up two spaces."

"That's a garbage theory," says former Steelers scouting director Art Rooney, Jr. "The Hollywood scene has nothing to do with it. Maybe the cold weather did, but then how do you explain the Rams losing home playoff games?"

Next theory.

Dysfunctional Quarterbacking: In all likelihood the true crux of the Rams' problem. Roman Gabriel had given the team stability and some All-Pro efforts at the position from 1963 through '72. Then the revolving door started to whirl. In '73, an aging John Hadl had a nice season but then he went 7 for 23 in a playoff game and they shipped him off to Green Bay.

James Harris was the next project. Although blessed with a shotgun arm, Harris didn't respond well to pressure, particularly at playoff time. He'd come apart. Throws would sail on him. Defenses would get inside his head. His career passer rating was 67.3. In the playoffs it sunk to 39.4. He lasted three years as a starter.

Harris' greatest performance? In '76, I saw him bomb the Dolphins off Miami Beach with 436 yards and 2 touchdowns, all deep stuff. Shula had geared his team up to stop the L.A. running game and Harris went crazy on him. Other than that, no lifetime achievement awards for Big James.

Ron Jaworski? He was young and never really got a fair shake before owner Carol Rosenbloom traded him to the Eagles. The Namath experiment was a disaster from the start. Pat Haden was too short. He probably averaged three batted passes a game and still has never seen the view from behind Dallas' "Too Tall" Jones.

It took Vince Ferragamo, a quarterback from Nebraska, to finally get the Rams to the Super Bowl. Handsome, cool in the pocket, accurate, lots of upside. But then the Rams played hardball at the negotiating table and Ferragamo bolted for Canada.

And since we're counting all the cats in Zanzibar, the 1980s gave us Bert Jones, Dan Pastorini, another run with Ferragamo, Jeff Kemp, Dieter Brock, Steve Bartkowski and Jim Everett. This is a condition psychologists call not being able to make up one's mind.

Lack of a Breakaway Threat: This one was pointed out by Steve Sabol of NFL Films. "The Rams had it all in the '70s, but the one thing they couldn't do was tear off the big run, the big gainer," he says. "They could wear on you all day with four and five-yard runs, but those backs rarely could break it downfield like a Tony Dorsett or Mercury Morris or even Franco Harris could. I think that's what kept them from being a truly great team."

"Hey, we got to the Super Bowl three times with Chuck Foreman," says Reichow, "and he wasn't a breakaway threat either. Productive, yes, but he wasn't a threat to go seventy-five yards."

Which leads us to the focal point of this interview, the Rams' Lawrence McCutcheon. He was L.A.'s feature back for over half of the decade, so essentially Sabol was referring to him. So do the numbers support Sabol's claim? Can they?

Well, the longest run of McCutcheon's career was 48 yards. A nice effort, but over 1521 attempts you'd think there'd be some meatier charges hidden in there somewhere.

On the other hand, in 1974, the year McCutcheon topped the NFC in rushing with 1,109 yards, his longest gainer was only 23. That same year, someone named Alvin Maxson broke one 66 yards for the Saints. Does that mean New Orleans should be held accountable for not winning the Super Bowl, too? Is a breakaway back required to win it all? And what does Alvin Maxson have to do with all of this, anyway?

"Coming out of college, I was timed at 4.4 in the forty," says McCutcheon. "That's straight-ahead speed, which technically is very good for a pro back. But it's not killer speed. Not the speed that can take you 80 yards with a couple of creases and a broken tackle."

Let's put Sabol's theory to the test. We'll run through ten randomly selected Super Bowl winners and post their longest rush of the season. Let's see how many of them beat McCutcheon's 48-yard best.

Super Bowl	**Winner**	**Running Back**	**Longest Reg. Season Run**
III	'68 Jets	Matt Snell	60 yards
V	'70 Colts	Sam Havrilak	26 yards
IX	'74 Steelers	Franco Harris	54 yards
XIV	'79 Steelers	Sydney Thornton	75 yards
XVI	'81 49ers	Ricky Patton	28 yards
XXIII	'88 49ers	Roger Craig	46 yards
XXVII	'92 Cowboys	Emmitt Smith	68 yards
XXXI	'96 Packers	Dorsey Levens	24 yards
XXXII	'97 Broncos	Terrell Davis	50 yards
XXXVII	'02 Buccaneers	Aaron Stecker	59 yards

Six better than McCutcheon, four worse. Which really tells us nothing about the relationship between breakaway threats and championships. So maybe McCutcheon himself can give us a little more insight on those Rams teams of the Ground Chuck era. Why weren't they winning Super Bowls? Why did Dallas and the Vikes have their number? What were the missing pieces? Maybe it will soothe the minds of those who still haven't gotten over the '70s.

After all, if you were one of those guys booting those imaginary field goals way back when, you probably missed most of them anyway.

• • •

Larry Csonka, the Miami Dolphins' bruising Hall of Fame runner, once said, "When you run the ball, your mind is blank. You don't think. You react to what you see. There's no time to think because if you think, you're caught. That's the nice thing about being a running back. You either have the instinct or you don't."

Within that context, how do you describe the difference between a very good runner and a great runner?

LM: Naturally, when you talk about great runners, you talk about Gale Sayers, Jim Brown and O.J. Simpson. Those are guys that did things very effortlessly. When you talked to them and ask them what they did on a certain play, they can't tell you. If somebody says they can stop and think about a play while it's happening, then tell you, "Well, I saw this and that," I don't buy it. Running is instinct, a read-and-react thing. Most of the time – myself included – you aren't even aware of your surroundings. If you don't have the instinct, then you're not going to be very successful. You just read and react to things, and that's what separates the great ones from the very good ones.

Some guys aren't as athletic and have to be a little more patient. They use their blockers better. Those are what I call very good runners. They know how the play is supposed to be run and how the blocking is supposed to formulate. Now it don't always go the way it's supposed to be blocked, and defensive guys aren't going to stand in there and let you make cuts. So there's a lot of bodies flying around, a lot of dervish in the way, a lot of twisting and turning. You can't stop for a moment and say to yourself, "Well, this guy is supposed to go here, so I'll just…" You have to read and react on that stuff all in one motion. That's why on most of my great runs, I can't tell you how or why I did what I did. I'd go back and look at the film and see myself jumping over some guy during a run, and I couldn't recall doing that.

You joined the Rams as a rookie in 1972 but played very sparingly due to a knee injury. What are your memories of that first year in the NFL?

LM: I was on the taxi squad most of that time. You'd practice and play during the preseason, but you didn't travel or play with the team on Sundays. It was a time for me to let my knee heal and learn how to prepare for games, watching film. It was a long season, so you had to learn to pace yourself and train to get ready for it.

During your first year you sat behind tailback Willie Ellison, who in 1971 had just turned in his first 1000-yard season. What were you able to learn about the game from watching him play?

LM: To be honest, not a whole lot. First of all, Ellison was late coming to training camp during my first year with the team. He was a holdout, so he missed most of camp. That was my first indication of how pro life can be, as far as guys negotiating contracts and holding out and stuff like that. That was kind of an eye opener for me. I never envisioned guys coming late to camp.

Willie was a little different runner than I was, so I can't say that I really learned anything about the pro game from watching him run. He was more of a straight line-runner. I think I had quicker feet and more cutting ability than Willie. I did eventually learn how to work and how to approach the game from Willie once he rejoined the team. But in terms of following blockers and reading holes? No. To me, you either have that or you don't have it. You enjoy watching other runners for what they can do, but I like to think I had my own style. Once you reach the pro level, you're still learning things, but if you have to really study the game at that stage of your career, you aren't going to be very productive in this league.

In 1972, the Rams ran off to a 5-2-1 start, then dropped five of their last six games and head coach Tommy Prothro was fired. Considering the talent level on the team, do you feel that owner Carroll Rosenbloom was justified in dismissing Prothro after only his second season with the Rams?

LM: You never like to see a person lose their job. Was Rosenbloom justified in firing Tommy Prothro? Well, he's the owner, which makes him justified. Not to say it's right or wrong, but when new owners come in, they like to hire their own people and put their own organization into place. Rosenbloom kinda sat back and watched how things ran for a year or so. I think he gave the situation a fair assessment. Like it or not, you're judged in this game by wins and losses. To be 5-2-1 with a chance to get into the playoffs then go downhill at a very critical time, well, that probably played a heavy role in Rosenbloom's decision.

Chuck Knox, a tough disciplinarian type from the football mines of western Pennsylvania, replaced Prothro in 1973. What were your initial impressions of him, and what qualities did he bring to the Rams that you thought could turn the team around?

LM: When Knox was appointed coach, he brought everyone in and met with them personally. You knew right away that he was a man who demanded details. He had a goal and a plan for how he wanted to achieve his goals. It would be done by hard work and fundamentals and taking the right approach to the game. If you worked hard, then the results would be realized. That's exactly what happened. Chuck was a very thorough, detailed guy. He was very knowledgeable about the running game, and he made it very clear that is what he wanted to do – run the football. He went to work teaching blocking and all the other details necessary to accomplish that.

When did Knox announce his decision to make you his starting tailback?

LM: Chuck had called me in to see him. Evidently he had looked at some films of preseason games and practices. One of his first questions to me was, "Why didn't you play more last year?" I was honest with him. I said, "I can't answer that for you, coach. The decision was out of my hands. I came to work and practiced hard every day, but the decision was out of my hands." He said, "Well, we're going to give you the ball during the preseason and give you the opportunity to prove yourself." That's the way it went. It also helped when the team traded Willie Ellison to Kansas City. That made the door wide open, and I made the most of the opportunity that was given me. I'm happy that he saw enough in my abilities to give me that opportunity.

As a runner, you must have loved Knox's devotion to the ground game. Suddenly you were expected to carry the football a couple hundred times a season.

LM: Well, that's every runner's dream, but on the other hand, when I look back at how our offense was run and the opportunities that were blown in the playoffs, I kinda wish we had a more balanced offense. We were too one-dimensional with all that running. I think that took its toll on us in the latter part of the season and in the playoffs, kept us from advancing to the Super Bowl.

Took its toll? Why, because of tired legs?

LM: Well, tired legs to a degree, but when you get into the playoffs, teams are able to refine their game plans. Teams knew we were going to run the football and that's what they designed their defenses to stop. If we had opened up and thrown the ball a little bit more, we might have had better results. That's just a guess.

What was your greatest strength as a runner?

LM: I was extremely quick into the hole and had great cutting ability. I was able to cut back against the flow and read things on the run. Those were some of my strongest qualities. But looking back and knowing what I know now, that is something I would have done a little bit differently.

How so?

LM: There were times when I should have paused or hesitated just a second before making my move, just to let things develop in front of me a little more. You're so anxious behind the line when you know the ball is coming to you. All this energy that is ready to explode once the quarterback gives you the ball that sometimes you are too anxious. There were times when I should have let things develop a little more, let the hole open a little wider before trying to shoot through there.

Were there other weaknesses or areas you would like to have improved?

LM: I regret was that I wasn't used more in the passing game during my career. I felt that I had very good hands and was a very good route runner, but we didn't throw the ball very much at that time, especially under Chuck Knox. In terms of my performance on the field, I probably could have been a better blocker. The offenses I ran in high school and college didn't require me to do a lot of blocking, so when I joined the Rams I was a little bit behind in that respect. I became a pretty fair blocker, but not a great one.

Was there a player that you absolutely hated to block?

LM: [Laughing] Most of the linebackers. There was a guy who played with the Green Bay Packers named Fred Carr. Six-foot-five, 250 pounds. He was an All-Pro backer who was so hard to block. He knew how to play the game. If you didn't possess all the leverage and explosion that it took to be an effective blocker, you were going to come up on the short end. I wasn't a guy that used real good technique when it came to blocking, so I usually came up on the short end when I went up against him.

You averaged over four yards per carry during your five seasons under Knox, very solid production. In terms of personal satisfaction, which was your best season?

LM: I'd say 1977. It was my fifth year in the league, and I was still very strong, very agile and feeling good about myself. We were a very solid team, one that probably should've won the Super Bowl that year. Our line was very strong, and I gained over 1200 yards, which was third highest in the league. That was my most satisfying, most productive year.

As for individual games, your 37-carry, 202-yard performance against St. Louis in the '75 playoffs was by far the biggest single workload of your career. What do you remember about that afternoon at the L.A. Coliseum? What aspect of the Cardinals defense were your coaches trying to exploit? St. Louis was a team that rated tenth in the league in rushing defense that year.

LM: It was a very hot, humid day. Buffalo had rushed for almost 300 yards against them a few weeks before, so we expected to have some pretty good success, too. We developed some quick trap plays that we felt would be effective against their defense and they worked. Everything we anticipated them doing defensively happened, so the plays worked almost perfectly. I remember carrying the ball for the first ten or twelve plays, and I was getting pretty tired. I looked over at Chuck Knox, trying to try to tell him, "Hey, let's take a break and throw the ball!" He would just turn his head and look away like he didn't see me. They kept on feeding me the ball.

You operated behind a tremendous group of offensive linemen during your years in Los Angeles – names like Dennis Harrah, Tom Mack, Charlie Cowan, Jackie Slater, Joe Scibelli and Rich Saul. What, in your mind, was the key to that group's long-term excellence?

LM: When I first joined the Rams, the offensive line was a group of veterans who had played together for 8, 9, 10 years. Established guys like Scibelli, Cowan and Ken Iman. They knew how to play the game, and were a very cohesive unit. Well-disciplined and very smart. When Chuck Knox came along, he turned the offensive line into a more aggressive, attacking type unit. He kept things very simple for them, but he took a lot of pride in that unit. That was his pet project. He worked with them every day during training camp, and that's how you have to do it. There are no shortcuts in building a successful running football team.

Pro Football's Greatest Playoff Rushing Days

5) 202 yards by Lawrence McCutcheon, L.A. Rams vs. St. Louis Cardinals (Dec. 27, 1975) & Freeman McNeil, New York Jets vs. Cincinnati Bengals (Jan. 9, 1983) – McCutcheon's playoff eruption startled friend, foe and self. His season high of 114 yards against the toothless Chicago Bears was a footnote, and he had a solid day against the Chargers back in October, but...but where did this come from?

"I have no idea," says McCutcheon. "The Cardinals seemed like a pretty good squad. But [QB Ron] Jaworski kept giving me the ball, and I kept gaining yards."

Ok, what happened was this. The Rams had simplified their attack for their rookie starting quarterback, calling for a heavy dose of drive blocking into the Cardinals' soft left side of DT Charlie Davis, DE Bob Bell and LB Larry Stallings. A high school scheme, for sure, but one that became too effective to ignore.

Working out of the I-formation and with a healing muscle pull, McCutcheon rushed 37 times ("I wasn't all that tired. I could've handled at least four more carries."), including nine bursts on the game's opening drive. The line blocked, McCutcheon ran hard, and the Cardinals were shoved back. Then everyone would huddle and do it all over again. Simple. No need for ruffles and frills on this day at the Coliseum. L.A. won it, 35-23.

Jets at Bengals: In Cincinnati, the Jets offensive line embarrassed a Bengals defense that only a year earlier was playing at Super Bowl level. Their outside linebackers, Reggie Williams and Bo Harris, were no-shows, maybe a handful of stops between them; nosetackle Wilson Whitley played himself out of an '83 roster spot with his flimsy performance in the game; Cincy's injured secondary was too busy grasping at the speedy Jets receivers to lend any real run support.

Meanwhile, Freeman McNeil's production chart looked like this:

Around left end – 4 carries for 73 yards (18.3 avg.)
Around right end – 3 carries for 31 yards (10.3 avg.)
Between the tackles – 14 carries for 98 yards (7.0 avg.)

This all coming from a runner pegged at 4.65 in the 40, the type of speed you usually find on the waiver wire. A new set of wings for the playoffs?

"No, I lost weight," said McNeil, who led the NFL in rushing in strike-shortened 1982. "I started the season at 225. By the playoffs I was down around 212. Gave me that extra burst."

One that blew right through a big Cincinnati sleepwalk. 44-17, Jets.

4) 204 yards by Timmy Smith, Washington Redskins vs. Denver Broncos (Jan. 31, 1988) – The Redskins stayed in character and brought out their heavy equipment for this Super Bowl Sunday, a steady dose of a play called Counter Gap. It was their running game staple in the 1980's, a Joe Gibbs' favorite that relied on extra blockers, misdirection and the concept of big versus bigger. An extra tight end – Don Warren or Clint Didier – often lined up at fullback, putting the brass knuckles on an already imposing fist. Only teams with equal beef were equipped to handle it, so one could smell a mismatch at the line of scrimmage, those big Washington "Hogs" mashing on the smaller Denver front seven.

But then Denver caught a break. Starting tailback George Rogers was scratched from the lineup with a nagging ankle injury, so the 'Skins would be forced to saddle-up Smith, a 216-lb mystery from Texas Tech with just 29 regular season carries. With the Broncos' assortment of stunts and a quickness advantage, maybe they could keep the rookie under four yards/rush, then hope their secondary could hold the thing together. After that, hey, who knows? They did have John Elway on their side.

The strategy worked beautifully on 14 of Smith's 22 carries. He gained just 22 yards. Unfortunately for the Orange Crush, he ripped off 182 on his other eight attempts. (Another 25-yarder was erased by a holding penalty.)

Translation – The Broncos had no answer for Counter Gap. Nor one for 'Skins quarterback Doug Williams, for that matter. Williams fired four second-quarter touchdown passes, and Denver was run out of town, 42-10.

Afterward Redskins line coach Joe Bugel insisted that patience was the only key to Smith's historic performance. "[Counter Gap] wasn't working early on. Denver made some good reads, some good guesses, and maybe our guys were a little anxious up front. But we stuck with it. Then Timmy broke a couple big ones and it all started clicking."

Click...click...click...the Redskins' adding machine whirred until Smith had settled in at 204, a new Super Bowl record.

3) 206 yards by Keith Lincoln, San Diego Chargers vs. Boston Patriots (Jan. 5, 1964) – The Chargers were the league's best team and the Patriots were polite guests in the 1963 AFL title game. Vegas pegged San Diego as modest six-point favorites, but Babe Parilli, the Boston quarterback, envisioned how things easily might break down for his team.

"Our defense lived by the blitz. That's how we attacked all season, and it worked for us. Lots of sacks and interceptions. But if teams can run outside, it puts a lot of pressure on our secondary to make tackles. San Diego has those great backs, Lincoln and Paul Lowe. We have to contain the outside runs."

Parilli's vision became reality on the game's second snap, as Lincoln broke off a 56-yard run. The Chargers scored two plays later. Lincoln's next carry went 67 yards for a touchdown. Then Lowe, the team's leading rusher, hit 'em with a 58-yarder.

By halftime it was 31-10. In the Chargers locker room coach Sid Gillman worried about missing the Grambling band's halftime routine. He spoke quickly then ran out to catch the end of it.

Lincoln would carry 13 more times to reach his 206 yards. He also caught seven passes for another 123. After the game, which ended 51-10, he strangely griped about the weather.

"I didn't feel real good in there early," Lincoln admitted. "The heat got to me after I made those first couple of runs. I didn't seem to have life in my legs."

Man, those rough San Diego winters. Look at the toll it took on the Patriots.

2) 209 yards by Lamar Smith, Miami Dolphins vs. Indianapolis Colts (Dec. 30, 2000) – A landmark you'd expect to have seen erected during the early Shula years, when Miami would clobber teams with Csonka and Kiick then shift gears with the dizzying pace of Mercury Morris. Smash-and-dash was the way in Miami, throw only when needed. The result was three consecutive Super Bowl trips.

Then Dan Marino came along, and the dreamy-eyed Shula never could get his ground game recharged again. Neither could the strong-willed Jimmy Johnson, who took over for Shula in 1996.

It was an unlikely tandem that reached this playoff plateau – Dave Wannstadt, a puzzling head coach who'd previously been run out of Chicago for his losing ways, and Smith, a journeyman back with fragile ankles and just five 100-yard games to his name.

The Colts came to town with a run defense rated 25th in the league, so the Wannstadt strategy was to pound away, make Smith his workhorse. He delivered, carrying 40 times in a game that spilled into overtime. Smith then churned out 40 yards on Miami's game-ending drive, the final score coming on a 17-yard bruiser that won it, 23-17. I remember the phone call that came afterwards.

"He's finished." It was Paul Najjar, a sports radio host from Louisville.

Whaddaya mean? The game just ended!

"Smith is finished. Anytime a back gets more than 33 carries in a game, he's done for the following week. Smith has never had a workload like this. They play the Raiders next week and he'll never recover."

Najjar was right. Smith was a washout in Oakland – only four yards on eight carries.

Matter of fact, we haven't heard from him since.

1) 248 yards by Eric Dickerson, L.A. Rams vs. Dallas Cowboys (Jan. 4, 1986) – The gameplan was to attack the eroding middle of the Dallas defense. All season long the Rams made a living on pitch-left, pitch-right to Dickerson, who gained 1,234 yards despite a two-game holdout, but today they'd be coming straight at the Cowboys.

Two former All-Pros, tackles Randy White and John Dutton, were winding down proud careers in Dallas. Both were creaking and over 33 years old. Behind them was Eugene Lockhart, an aggressive middle linebacker with average talent and a personal bounty on Dickerson. ("He had a big day against my team in college and I didn't like the way he rubbed it in.") Rams coach John Robinson sensed the Dallas' underbelly was vulnerable and softening. Eventually, he thought, it would tear wide open.

Dickerson went right to work. By halftime he had 77 yards. Two nice gainers came on pitchouts, but the real softening was done running straight behind Pro Bowl guards Kent Hill and Dennis Harrah. Then, on the first play after halftime, came the big rip.

Dickerson took the handoff and blazed through the Dallas line, past White and Dutton, past Lockhart who overran the play, and past the gasping Cowboys secondary for a 55-yard score. The Rams were now up 10-zip and Dallas, its offense sputtering, was finished.

"They were overplaying the pitch all day," said reserve center Tony Slaton. "Dallas was scared to death Eric would break one outside. Then I saw his rear end running up field and I knew we'd done something right." From then on, Dickerson was in command, a man against 'Boys.

And that outside-breaker the Cowboys were so worried about? It came in the fourth quarter, a 40-yard gallop down the right sideline that ended in another touchdown.

Aside from Dickerson's whirlwind, the game was historical in another sense. Dallas' 20-0 loss would mark the end of Tom Landry's stretch of glory as the Cowboys head coach. The armor was breaking down, the star peeling off the helmet. Bad times were ahead. Despite the team's 10-6 record in 1985, the signs all pointed to bad times coming.

In '84, the Cowboys missed the playoffs for the first time in ten seasons. The following November they were blitzed 44-0 by Chicago; it was Dallas' second shutout loss ever. At Cincinnati, they gave up 570 yards of offense, the most in team history. Then Dickerson drilled 'em with his 248, the most ever gained against a Dallas defense.

Too many "mosts" and "worsts" and "evers" were happening to Landry's troops, things way out of character. "It was sad to watch," said former safety Cliff Harris. "In the old days, he would've found some way to keep Dickerson under control."

The old days, however symbolic, ended on a record-setting weekend in cloudy Anaheim.

The Rams were consistently among the top running teams in the NFL. Which team consistently did the best job in shutting down that rushing attack?

LM: The team that usually gave us the most trouble, believe it or not, was the New Orleans Saints. We'd go into their place as big favorites and we'd be lucky to come out of there with a two- or three-point win. They always rose to the occasion when we came into town. I don't know what it was. They talked about a jinx or that type of thing, but it was uncanny how they'd find a way to play very well against us. Dallas and Minnesota always had a very good defense, but we could still find a way to move the ball on the ground against them. Against New Orleans, we seemed to consistently have the most trouble.

Despite his impressive 54-15-1 regular season record, the Rams were often sloppy, underachieving and always winless in NFC Title games under Knox. What would you say to someone who insisted that Knox was not a "big game" coach, that his teams were unprepared for playoff competition?

LM: I would say they were full of baloney. But, again, I will also say that coaches are judged on wins and losses. By that standard it would indicate that Chuck wasn't a big game coach.

If Chuck had a shortcoming, it would be that he was very stubborn in trying to accomplish his main goal, and that was to run the football. When you get in playoff games, teams have a week or two to evaluate and study your team. They can put together a defense that will take away your strengths.

If Chuck had been a little more open-minded and opened up the passing game – mixing it up a little bit more – that would've made it a little bit harder for defenses to scheme against us. We had some great receivers during that time, guys like Harold Jackson and Jack Snow and Ron Jessie. Offensively, we never really took advantage of having them. If Chuck was guilty of anything, it would be his stubbornness, his refusal to change the gameplan to help throw off the defense. Teams simply knew what we were going to do.

The 1974 and 1976 NFC Championship games were played in the icebox of Minnesota's Metropolitan Stadium. You repeatedly said in the past that the Rams overall were a better team than the Vikings. Had you played those championships games at home, at the Coliseum, would the outcomes have been different? Did the frigid weather really give Minnesota that much of a home field advantage against you?

LM: Well, I can't really project that. I don't know if the outcomes would have been any different had we played at home. You have to play wherever the game is scheduled, in whatever kind of weather shows up. Whether we played the Vikings in L.A. or Minnesota, I definitely think that during those years we were the better football team. It just made me realize that the best football team doesn't always win. I certainly would rather have played in 75-degree weather rather than 25 below, but I don't want to use the conditions as a crutch as to why we lost those football games. You always like to think you have a little bit more of an advantage playing at home, on familiar turf and in front of your own fans. I'd certainly like to think the outcomes would have been different, but true champions find a way to win. Unfortunately, we didn't get the job done in either of those cases.

To someone who didn't witness the 1975 NFC Championship, a humiliating 37-7 loss to the Dallas Cowboys, how would you describe what happened that afternoon? The odds makers had set the Rams as overwhelming 10-point favorites.

LM: It was very disheartening, especially to lose that way at home. Everything we did wasn't right, and everything Dallas did was right. They stopped our running game, shut it completely down. We had less than 25 yards rushing. We resorted to the pass and that proved to be unfruitful. Dallas played an almost perfect football game that day. We certainly weren't anywhere close to playing what we were capable of. I don't know what else to say about it.

Was the team mentally prepared to play the Cowboys that day?

LM: Evidently not. We *felt* we were. We had played a great game against the Cardinals the week before, then had a great week of practice leading up the Dallas game. We just didn't execute and didn't get any results. It was very disheartening, probably was the worst feeling I ever experienced after a playoff game. I'll never forget that.

The Cowboys Shoot Up L.A. in the '75 NFC Title

Embarrassing, wasn't it? There were 6,555 "no-shows" at the L.A. Coliseum Sunday. Among them were the Los Angeles Rams.

I mean, tell me that was the San Diego Charter. Or the Ace Auto Supply A.C. Or the Clay Hills Men's Club. But not the Rams. Not the team with the best defense in football, the one which gave up only 135 points in 14 games.

Could this be the team that had a record of 12-2 at home? The Rams don't give up 37 points in an afternoon. They don't give up 37 points in a month. Could that be 441 total yards rolled up against the Rams by the Cowboys? You would need tanks for that, wouldn't you?

The Rams, as usual, hit the banana peel on that last step before the Super Bowl. Every year, they keep their fans standing on tiptoe under the mistletoe but they never kiss them. You can always tell a Rams fan. He's the guy who's always looking for a safe to fall on him, or his dog to bite him – or the Rams to lose the Big One. They faint at the site of the Super Bowl...

The game wasn't played on ice or in zero chill-factor temperatures or on unfamiliar surfaces as it had in the other losses. The temperature was in the 60s, the sun was shining, the grass was cut, the wind wasn't blowing. It was the Rams' own deck, table, crowd. So it must have been the stakes that bothered them. When someone says, "I'll fade you for the Super Bowl," the Rams drop the dice or fold the cards or ruin the take. Or they play it for comedy. Either way, they take long showers. (January 5, 1976)

– **Jim Murray, Copyright, 1976,** *Los Angeles Times.*
Reprinted with permission.

You played alongside a revolving door of quarterbacks during your days with the Rams. First it was Roman Gabriel, then John Hadl, James Harris, Ron Jaworski, Pat Haden, Joe Namath and finally Vince Ferragamo. How frustrated were you by management's inability to solidify the game's most critical position?

LM: Don't forget that Bob Lee was there, too. Honestly, we were always pretty confident with the guys we had. Quarterback is probably the most critical part of the offense. If you're constantly changing that position, you lose some of the continuity that you're looking for. Fortunately for us, those guys that played were pretty damn good football players. They just weren't given the opportunity to play more than one or two years. Why so many changes were made? I can't answer that for you. Those decisions are out of the players' hands. You have to roll with the punches and accept the new guy and just continue to play your role in the offense. That's the kind of position all of us took.

In which year was the quarterback instability particularly disruptive to the team?

LM: I can't really point to a specific year. From 1973-79, we were able to win our division and advance into the playoffs, even though we had a lot of different quarterbacks along the way. Going into the '77 season, it looked like Pat Haden was going to be the starter, but then they brought in Joe Namath to run the team. Unfortunately, Joe was at the tail end of his career and he was unable to produce like we'd hoped he could. Then they switched back to Haden. It was a musical chairs kind of thing for the first part of that year, yet we still won ten games and should have won three more. Obviously it wasn't as disruptive as it could have been.

James Harris was the best long ball thrower of the candidates, the best equipped to get the ball to your speedy receivers Harold Jackson and Ron Jessie, and he was given a strong opportunity to keep the position. What were his most obvious shortcomings as a quarterback that kept him from holding the job beyond a handful of seasons?

LM: Again, I can't answer that. When you look back at when James was playing, we won our division three times. He went to the Pro Bowl and was the MVP during his second year. I think he did everything that was asked of him as a quarterback when given the opportunity. Beyond that, I can't answer the question. I'm a little bit biased because he's a very close friend of mine. They traded him down to San Diego, where he had the opportunity to play a couple of years there, but the Chargers also had Dan Fouts, who is now in the Hall of Fame, so James wasn't really in a better position to win the job there either. I think, if given the opportunity to settle in with one team and utilize all of his skills, that James Harris could've been a really good quarterback.

Good enough to win a Super Bowl?

LM: No question in my mind. He had everything that you wanted at the position – big, very strong arm, smart, athletic, good running ability, and a good leader. All the traits that you look for at the quarterback position, he possessed.

Ron Jaworski played sparingly during his three seasons (1974-76) with the Rams before moving to the Philadelphia Eagles and eventually taking that team to a Super Bowl. Of all the young quarterbacks in that group – including Haden, Harris, and Ferragamo – Jaworski enjoyed the most successful career. Why do you feel he was unable to win the job in Los Angeles?

LM: Well, he was playing behind James Harris during his first two years there. Then they drafted Pat Haden, who did a lot of good things when he joined the team, so the competition was really strong. I guess management felt that they could get something for Jaworski and still be pretty strong at the quarterback position. He had started a playoff game against St. Louis and won, so I'm sure he felt he was ready to be a starter. He was a young, brash guy who wanted to play, and he was able to do good things for Philadelphia once he got there.

Joe Namath joined the Rams team in 1977 after his many years in New York. There, he was Mr. Touchdown, the dashing paladin of the American Football League. But things turned out very differently for him as a 34-year old quarterback in Los Angeles. From your perspective, how much did Namath really have left in the tank when he came to L.A.?

LM: From the time I met Joe, he had the attitude that he could still play and be a key part in keeping our offense rolling. I don't think he would have ever agreed to coming to Los Angeles if he didn't feel he could still do it. He was a very calm guy, not what I really expected. I was looking for a brasher guy, more of a cocky guy than the one who showed up. Joe was very down-to-earth and got along with his teammates very well, just a regular guy. That had a very calming effect on everybody on the team. Unfortunately, his skills weren't quite up to par in terms of mobility, so he wasn't able to get the job done.

Do you recall a specific moment on the field that indicated the Namath experiment wasn't going to work?

LM: I don't know if I can pick one play, but obviously after his first two or three games, it was apparent he wasn't going to be the answer. Joe was still very confident, very sure of himself, but once the skills diminish it's very hard to overcome. He was at that point. He couldn't move in the pocket any longer, and teams would just tee off on him. It wasn't too long before we knew another change had to be made.

In 1977 the Rams advanced to the post-season, only to lose another playoff battle with the Vikings – a slopfest at the Coliseum known as The Mud Bowl. The Rams had destroyed Minnesota, 35-3, in a regular season meeting, piling up nearly 400 yards of total offense. What defensive adjustments did the Vikings make that enabled them to shut your team down in the rematch?

LM: They didn't really show us anything different. Again we didn't play good enough to win the football game. Again we lost to a team that wasn't as good as us. The Vikings came out throwing on the opening drive and went all the way in for a touchdown, so we were playing catch-up from the first moment we had the ball, and trying to do it on a terrible field.

There may have been a little bit of a letdown on our part because of the weather. It'd been raining all week. We knew the field was going to be messy, which was going to cause major problems for our offense. We didn't want to have to beat them throwing the football, but unfortunately, that's exactly how it turned out. We couldn't do it.

You had an impressive performance in that Vikings playoff game. On just 16 carries, how were you able to dig out 102 yards in such a quagmire?

LM: I don't know. You have to change your running style to fit the conditions, like running with your feet a little bit closer to the ground than usual. Not being as aggressive in cutting as you normally would. Being a little bit more patient with your blockers. That's the style I used against the Vikings that day. I'm a little bit of a mudder when I have to be.

Chuck Knox was fired after the 1977 season. What were your feelings about that move, considering the overall success the team had enjoyed under him?

LM: By then, I'd been around the league for a while so nothing surprised me anymore. I think Rosenbloom felt it was time for a change. Maybe he felt the team had become a little stagnant, that all the tools were in place but the team couldn't seem to get over it. Maybe a new coach would add some new energy to the staff and that would be the key to get us over the hump. I hated to see Chuck go for a number of reasons. I think the guy was a great coach and an excellent motivator, but I'm sure he knows why he was let go. Chuck may not admit it, but I think if he could go back and do it again he might consider mixing things up on offense a little more.

Coach George Allen was signed for a second tour of duty with the Rams in early 1978. If you blinked you probably missed him, as he was surprisingly fired less than seven months later. "The players didn't like the way I demanded hard work from them," Allen said shortly afterward. Your thoughts?

95

LM: That whole thing happened so fast. When George first joined the Rams he brought each of us in to talk, just like Chuck did. Our meeting was brief. He said he thought I was a great football player and was looking forward to working with me, that we were on to something good in Los Angeles. I told him I admired him as a coach and was looking forward to working with him.

He was only there a short time before they fired him. You certainly wouldn't expect things to happen that quickly but they did. It was like a whirlwind. The guy was in and out so fast that you didn't get the opportunity to really focus in on him, to see what kind of person he was and what direction he was trying to take with the team. Evidently, some things happened that made management uncomfortable, so they went in a different direction really quickly to try and correct the problem. It was a real trying time for us as a team.

Defensive coordinator Ray Malavasi was named as Allen's replacement at the start of the 1978 season. How different was his program from the one that Knox ran?

LM: Completely different. He was nothing like Chuck when it came to running a football team. I loved Ray Malavasi, and I think he was a great defensive coordinator. The thing that he had going for him was that he was already familiar with our players and got along with them. Personally, I never looked at Ray as being head coaching material. He didn't fit what my vision of a head coach was. But the bottom line is that he got some results out of us. We went to the NFC Championship during his first year and to the Super Bowl the next year. The 1979 team he coached was the least talented team I played on during my career in L.A., but we still wound up going to the Super Bowl.

Let's discuss that Super Bowl season of 1979. After a 1-3 start, the team won eight of its next 11 games and captured the NFC West for the seventh straight year. But in the season finale, New Orleans destroyed the Rams, 29-14, in a game that could have squashed any momentum the team had gathered heading into the post-season. What was the team's mental posture as it prepared to face heavily favored Dallas in the NFC playoffs?

LM: We weren't as high as we could've been, considering what happened against New Orleans. But we felt good that we had won the division and made the playoffs. We actually had a good feeling going into that Dallas game. It's hard to describe. When you're playing the Cowboys, America's Team, you always want to play your best. We came close to doing that against Dallas and we were able to beat them.

Then we played Tampa Bay for the NFC championship. We knew we were going to win that game. Tampa Bay was a very talented team on the defensive side and they played well against us. Fortunately for us, they were a little less talented offensively. Tampa Bay didn't present a lot of problems for us in that area. We only kicked three field goals all afternoon, but that was enough to win the game (9-0).

By the time we reached the Super Bowl, we had some very strong momentum on our side. We had just won two playoff games. We had the opportunity to play in front of our fans in the Rose Bowl – a hundred thousand people. We felt very good about ourselves and demonstrated that early in the game. Except for a few plays here and there, we played well enough to win that Super Bowl. Ask the Steelers – they were fighting for their lives. We had an opportunity to win, but they say the game is a matter of inches, and that's the way it turned out.

What was the game plan for cracking the Steelers defense in Super Bowl XIV?

LM: We knew that they were a real solid football team, very aggressive defensively. We felt we really had to mix things up. We did that by establishing the run. Then, as the Steelers began to creep closer to the line, we went to the short and intermediate passing game to keep them honest. Because they were so aggressive, we felt we could throw some play-action things at them and be effective.

Your third-quarter touchdown pass on a halfback option was the Rams' only score in the second half of that game. Tell me how the play was set up.

LM: That play had been in our playbook for years but we never used it. Maybe we used it once against Dallas in 1978. Pittsburgh's safeties and corners were very aggressive on running plays, so we felt it would work perfectly against them. It worked exactly how we had drawn it up. The corners came up to me on the toss, Ron Smith took off on the deep corner post, and it was just a matter of me getting the ball to him on time. It was a tremendous moment for us, scoring that touchdown. Nobody fooled the Pittsburgh Steelers very often.

The Heroic Rams of Super Bowl XIV

The outcome was as predictable as San Diego weather. Pittsburgh Steelers always win Super Bowl games. They're getting monotonous. But they must have thought somebody else showed up in Ram uniforms. These were no Hollywood sissies, no college of profiles, no rhinestone cowboys, no Sunset-and-Vine lilacs waiting for their big break in pictures, no guys bucking for a screen test. The Rams didn't show up with mirrors or makeup men, they were a scratching, scrambling, stubborn, socking team of alley fighters, swarmers spoiling for a scrap…

It wouldn't be fair to say the Steelers were lucky to win but when you need a 73 and 47-yard bomb to pull out the game, you're not exactly steamrolling anybody. They rushed for exactly 84 yards. Steeler teams are accustomed to rolling that up before the anthem dies down. They needed a canary and a lantern in their hats when they disappeared into that Ram line. The line of scrimmage looked like a mine cave-in…

The game was played at long range, like a duel between railroad guns or warships but the Rams returned salvo for salvo. They hardly played nervous football with one touchdown coming on a pass from Lawrence McCutcheon who is not to be compared with John Unitas – or Karl Sweetan, for that matter. It was Lawrence's first pass of the year. In fact, the last pass he made was at a waitress in his second year at Colorado State, but it was just as good as any Bradshaw threw; it was for a touchdown. (January 21, 1980)

– Jim Murray, Copyright 1980, *Los Angeles Times*. Reprinted with permission.

Which was the best Rams team in your mind, the one that should've won the Super Bowl?

LM: I think the 1973 and 1977 teams were our best. But let me put it like this – in the period from 1973 through 1977, we should've had at least two Super Bowl rings. *At least two.* We had the talent to do that. But we didn't get the job done, so we didn't get any.

How should history remember the Los Angeles Rams of the 1970s, a team that won nearly 70-percent of its games but never a world championship? Would you take exception to the label "underachievers?"

LM: I would never label us as underachievers. That wouldn't be fair because I think there were some elements and factors other than just effort that dictated the way things turned out for us. I'd say the Rams of the '70s were very talented teams, very proud teams. For whatever reasons, we never reached the goals that we were capable of.

— 7 —
Steve Sabol, President
NFL Films
July 16, 1998

Moviemaker Spike Lee was once asked why the tension and drama and emotion of big-time sporting events doesn't translate well onto the silver screen, why Hollywood has such difficulty creating its own believable versions of The Big Game. His response was quick and direct.

"It doesn't work because you're trying to recreate something that already exists on its own at the stadiums," Lee said. "The director is trying to replicate all this energy within the structure of another art form and it doesn't translate. Mostly, it comes off as being phony or contrived. Audiences ask, 'Why go to the movies looking for a sports thrill when you can have the real thing?'"

Which posed a problem for Ed Sabol, founder of NFL Films, and his son Steve when they began producing their highlight films for the league back in the early 1960s. Was it possible to translate the excitement and intensity of pro football onto film? Was it possible to create a production that is even more captivating than the game itself? Up until that point in time, it hadn't been done well. Most sports films of the day lacked imagination and were often a step above corny.

But then again, maybe it wasn't a problem for them.

"What saved us was our innocence," says Steve. "We didn't know what we were doing, so we relied purely on our instincts. We were people who loved football and loved to make movies. That kept us going in the right direction. Our goal was to present pro football through different angles and bends and reflections, to give a unique view of the things that make the game great."

Before the days of cable and *SportsCenter* and Direct TV, football fans who craved a stronger dose of NFL action had few places to turn when Sunday afternoons ended. There was no ESPN waiting with its hyperactive summaries and recaps. HBO's *Inside the NFL* didn't come along until 1977, but only a small percentage of subscribers were tuning in. Local TV sportscasts rarely showed more than a handful of clips from the weekend's games.

In the 1970s, the only real fix was *Halftime Highlights* on Monday Night Football and a couple of Sunday morning NFL Films productions sandwiched somewhere between Grambling highlights or *Lamp Unto My Feet* and the network pregame shows. Remember those old staples, NFL *Game of the Week* or *This Is the NFL?* The grand, majestic music? The slow-motion touchdown grabs and splattering tackles? That commanding, drop-what-you're-doing voice that narrated the action? That voice…you didn't know whose it was, but you knew you never wanted that guy mad at you.

So what are the Sabols' magic ingredients, the ones that go into making a great football film? After all, the games have already been played, so the scripts are pre-written before the first ribbon of film drops to the cutting room floor. The coaches and players – the characters, heroes and villains both – have already been cast. And the scores are all final, so there can be no rewritten endings.

Which creative variables were left to explore? To the Sabols, it became evident there were three that could make a difference:

The soundtrack: "For some reason, the rule had always been to use polkas and Sousa marches as the backdrop in football films," says Steve. Beer and pretzel music. 4th of July music. You could close your eyes and see some sweating tuba player marching up the street while Moose Lodge members tossed candy to the crowd.

"The music sounded nothing like football, which is a strong, proud, sometimes violent sport," he says, "so we were compelled to change that." They hired their own composer, Sam Spence, who began to create music fitting for the majestic world of pro football.

The cinematography: "The rule became *Shoot Everything*," says Ed, "including the crowd and the coaches and the referees. We were after angles and sideline shots. We wanted to show players without helmets, so we could show their raw expressions and the sweat and blood. Slow-motion film? It was more expensive, but so what? It gave us the dramatic effect we wanted."

The narration: Network football announcers by default had always been cast as the narrators in these kinds of productions. "Guys like Chris Schenkel, Chuck Thompson and Dick Enberg did most of them," says former NFL Films editor Bob Ryan. "They have great voices for calling live action, but they weren't really very good at reading scripts."

Then they found a man named John Facenda. The Good Lord had smiled at John and said, "I've put dirt and grass on the earth, I've given men the ability to run and throw and catch. Now I will give this game they call football a voice, and it will be yours." And the Sabols cried out, "Alleluia!"

The roots of NFL Films began with a single camera, a 16-mm Bell & Howell (World War II vintage), which was given to Ed as a wedding gift. It quickly became his companion, and making home movies soon developed into a passion for moviemaking. Ed was still trapped in a numbing career of selling overcoats for his father-in-law's business, but during the autumn months he found time to film Steve's grade school and high school football games, often perched atop the roof of the Haverford (Pa.) School's chemistry building recording all the action.

"I had a knack for it," Ed says. "Some of the local high schools even became interested in having me shoot their games." He had grander visions than just recording family Turkey Day dinners or filming Steve in a gang-tackle against Downingtown East. But suddenly it was 1960 and Steve had graduated and gone off to Colorado College. Ed's football subject matter had disappeared. Now what?

[*First, a quick Steve Sabol story from Mike Kearns, an old-timer who worked the Steelers press box for years. He laughs about Sabol being a real self-promoter in the early days.*

"Somebody told me about this guy who put together his own fan club while he was playing football for Colorado College," remembers Kearns. "It was Steve Sabol. So on a whim I signed up to see what this was all about. I sent in my money and ended up getting a fan club membership card and a monthly newsletter that gave updates on the progress of his football career.

"He started out calling himself 'Steve Sabol from Irontown, PA,' which made it sound like he was from some tough, hard-nosed place. Then he became 'The Toddlin' Tot from Possum Trot,' whatever the hell that meant. He used to send all the NFL teams a copy of his newsletter, maybe a way of getting himself noticed by the scouts. The only team that responded was the Minnesota Vikings. They wrote back, 'We're keeping an eye on your progress.'

"I carried that membership card with me for years. I don't know why. I used to show it to people. Then I was out drinking one night and lost the damn thing."

Sabol eventually gave Kearns a cameo in the Super Bowl X highlight film for his undying loyalty.]

The answer came with the slap of a newspaper on the Sabol's doorstep. A local brief noted that Tel Ra Productions, a Philadelphia film company, had paid $1,500 for the rights to film the 1961 NFL Championship game. Ed declared the 1962 matchup would be his, despite the fact that the only formal production he ever completed was a shaky documentary called *To Catch a Whale*.

(Did Ed ever catch that whale? "No," he said, "but I certainly wasn't going to be outbid by Tel Ra.")

Sabol eventually caught the league's attention by offering $3,000 for the rights. Then he met NFL commissioner Pete Rozelle for drinks to chat about a deal. Four martinis later it was done. Sabol and his fledgling company called Blair Motion Pictures (after his daughter) would work the sidelines for the first time on December 30, 1962, Packers at Giants, the NFL title game. The day couldn't arrive soon enough.

"We were so anxious, waiting for our chance," remembers Steve. "But what a terrible, miserable day it turned out to be, maybe worse than The Ice Bowl. It was bitter cold and the wind was blowing the infield dust everywhere. The metal cameras were freezing to the crew's faces. The film began cracking and breaking when we took it out of the cameras."

But the Blair gang survived and headed back to the studio with its canisters. Soon, their film was ready. They called it *Pro Football's Longest Day*. After one viewing, Rozelle called it "the greatest football film ever made." He wanted to have the premiere at Toots Shor's and invite the New York media to have a look.

"They all came out to see it," says Steve, "but the event wasn't planned very well. We ended up using a bed sheet for a screen. Then about halfway through a waiter tripped over the cord, which sent the projector flying along with a tray of shrimp. The film was broken and we had no way to repair it. Somehow, the thing still got good reviews."

By 1965, the NFL had agreed to buy Blair Motion Pictures for $280,000 with the intent to operate it as the league's promotional and historical arm.

"We were actually in competition with Tel Ra and several other outfits that wanted to become NFL Films," says Ed. "So they held a big meeting in Miami and everyone gave their sales pitch. The other guys stood up there with their staid, formal presentations and their "*Next slide, please.*" I didn't like that shit. I just talked to them and made them feel comfortable about the whole thing."

And it's been a terrific success all along. From a worn-out 16mm camera to a freezing day in Yankee Stadium to their brand new 100,000 square-foot facility that houses all the archives (highlights of every game since 1949) NFL Films proudly crowns itself the "Keepers of the Flame."

"I was once asked if I ever got tired of my job," Steve Sabol says, "of constantly being surrounded by football. Aren't all the games starting to look the same? I said, 'Well, Monet painted the same lily pads 300 times. If he could do that....'"

A true labor of love for both artists. Masters of their crafts. Monet there at his easel, lily after lily. For Sabol, the films of ten thousand kickoffs and a million first downs. Possum Trot meets The Blazing Brush of Giverny.

Sound corny? Maybe so. Somehow Facenda would've made it all work.

● ● ●

"If Father Time could put his summary of the 1970s into words, this is what he'd say:

> **'A decade has come, a decade has gone, and so very much has changed**
> **The meek have risen to inherit the earth, the mighty have fallen away**
> **I've ripened a new generation and launched them to courses of fame**
> **I've added some years to glorious careers, and watched men leave the game**
> **I've given men time to look silly, time to feel helpless and lame**
> **It's a chorus of laughs, a choir of fools when men play a little boys game'"**

Those are the words of your great narrator John Facenda, from the end of an NFL Films production called The Super Seventies. *What thoughts come to your mind about pro football in that decade as you hear them again?*

SS: In football, a decade takes its shape from its great teams and great rivalries and the competition between those teams. The 1970s was the Golden Age of pro football, so I think of a time when some of the greatest teams in the history of the sport were playing. The Dolphins of 1972 and '73 come to mind. The 1972 team went undefeated, but many players from that team will say that the '73 Dolphins were even better. Then there were the Pittsburgh Steelers, to me the greatest team in the history of the game. The Raiders were great as well. They were truly the renegades and the cutthroats and the silver and black marauders that people talk about. They're not that way today, but they were back then when the image was created. The phrase "America's Team" for the Dallas Cowboys was coined, which we used for the team's highlight film in 1976. So you have those four teams – the Dolphins, the Steelers, the Cowboys and the Raiders – which gave that whole decade its shape.

But in today's NFL, there are no longer any great teams. Free agency plays an annual game of 52-Pickup and reshuffles the rosters each year.

SS: Especially in the heart and soul of a great team, its offensive line. That's where most of the damage is done. Look at all those teams I mentioned – each of them had a great offensive line. The Dolphins had Larry Little and Jim Langer, who are in the Hall of Fame. The Steelers didn't have many household names except Mike Webster, but they had a really great offensive line. Names like Ray Pinney, Gerry Mullins and Sam Davis. What happens today is not so much the big stars moving around but the offensive linemen that seem to be shifting around.

I remember Mike McCormack, the Hall-of-Fame tackle for the Browns who was once head coach of the Eagles, saying, "A great offensive line operates like the five fingers on your hand, and they all have to work together." The way an offensive line gets to that point is by spending years together maturing, growing up and practicing together. That doesn't happen now. Every offensive line seems to lose at least one starter. To me that is the reason why it's so hard to maintain continuity, let alone a dynasty, in football today. Too many of those guys are shifting around.

Everyday football fans have an appreciation and understanding of the game, but one thing they can't understand or appreciate is that every one of these guys are in pain from November on. Football is a tough sport as it is, but when it becomes November and they're playing on those frozen fields and it's cold and nobody is 100-percent healthy, then the chemistry and emotion really becomes important. That's the only well you have to dip into when you're playing in pain. The emotion, the teamwork, the self-sacrifice that Vince Lombardi used to talk about – it still holds true today.

Most teams play a total of 22 or 23 games a year, including the preseason. To get to the Super Bowl you have to play 23 or 24 games. Shit, that's more than two college seasons in one. The wear and tear that puts on your body is just unfathomable to the average fan.

Let's talk about NFL Films, a company that started out in the 1960s producing what were basically upbeat newsreels of pro games.

SS: That's a pretty accurate point. The first film we ever made was the 1962 NFL Championship game. People think our first film immediately introduced this whole new style of presenting the game, with John Facenda and the triumphant, booming music and the sound. That wasn't the case at all. During the first years of our history, we didn't have a style. No one had really made movies about pro football. The only influences we had were newsreels and those TV highlight shows that aired on Saturday afternoons.

Up to that point, all football films had been produced in a certain way. The music featured lots of upbeat polkas and marches. The scripts sounded something like, "*Milt Plum pegs a peach of a pass to become the apple of coach George Wilson's eye.*" They were written in a clever, cutesy manner, but for several years that was the same basic pattern we used in making our films.

When we were making these films, my dad was the salesman and the figurehead and the president of the company. I was the filmmaker, the little troll under the bridge that would decide how it would sound and look. But at the beginning the company just rode on my father's personality because, until we developed our own style, we weren't really doing anything that was different.

Everything changed for NFL Films in 1966 when we produced a film called *They Call It Pro Football*. That was the first film that John Facenda ever narrated and the first film that Sam Spence wrote the music for. It was also the first film that a coach was miked for sound. It became the *Citizen Kane* of football movies. The script was terse and impressionistic. It really emphasized the drama of the game. Facenda was reading bold lines like "*The face of a tiger,*" or "*The linebacker – search and destroy.*" It was written in those sentence fragments that became the style of NFL Films. That film was absolutely the springboard to the style that everyone recognizes us for today.

They Call It Pro Football *also presented a significant change in the way your films were compiled and edited, correct?*

SS: That's right. We stopped using the typical linear editing, which is showing entire plays from start to finish. We began applying quick-tempo montages, showing bits and pieces of shots, bursts of action. The editor on this film was a guy named Yoshio Kishi, a free-lancer we brought in for the project. He revolutionized the way we thought about film structure and how to organize shots. The funny thing was, he didn't know a thing about football. I had to help him with the fundamentals, explaining to him the difference between a linebacker and a defensive back, or between a fullback and a wide receiver. But while I was teaching "Yoshi" about football, I was also getting an education about editing. We learned from each other.

Describe the underlying influences at work in the development of NFL Films. What were your visions for the company in the early years?

SS: Right from the start, we had two active philosophies that strongly influenced the company. My father wanted to portray pro football the way Hollywood portrayed fiction, with a dramatic flair, original music and a sense of storytelling. I played four years of college football at Colorado College, so I wanted to show the game as I experienced it – with the eyes bulging, the snot spraying, the sweat flying, the passion and the sound. We married those two styles, those two philosophies, and that became the guiding light of our filmmaking. A lot of people have given us credit for creating the image of the game, promoting and helping the growth of pro football. That's very flattering to hear, but to be honest, that was never our purpose.

The one thing that separated us from the other sports – baseball or hockey or the NBA – was our innocence. We never had focus groups or marketing surveys. We never thought of ourselves as packagers or promoters. We were just a bunch of young guys who loved pro football and loved to make movies, and we wanted to convey our love of the game to our audience. I think that's why we've lasted as long as we have and why we have such a following. The fans look at our movies and know those films are being made by people that care about the game, that care about the same things that they do.

Hooray For Hollywood, NFL Style

See Marcus Allen sliding off tackle in super-slow motion and in utter silence. Now hear him fall to earth amid sudden sound and fury. Watch how the camera zooms in on the kickoff and follows the ball end over end until it reaches the return man's arms.

Not enough realism? Then hear Dexter Manley (Unnh! Arrrgh!") get off the line, pound a few helmets and rush the passer. Now listen to the announcers. They always sound like the voices of doom. As has been said, they can make a coin toss sound like Armageddon. And the music! No John Philip Sousa marching bands for this bunch. Long before each session, executive producer Steve Sabol commissions a Munich orchestra to come up with new scores... Ed [Sabol] says, "I wanted closeups. I wanted pictures of faces and hands. I wanted better music. I wanted to be enterprising and exciting. Although the people saw the game on television, I wanted them to have a reason to watch it again on film."

The '62 championship game, in which the Packers beat the Giants 16-7 at frozen Yankee Stadium, set the pattern for every game the Sabols have shot since then. They always plant a stationary cameraman (a Tree in Sabolese) high in the stadium to cover game action. They always assign another man (a Mole) to work from the sidelines. And they always have a mobile cameraman darting all about the stadium to ferret out small details (you guessed it, a Weasel).

The result: a profusion of images that are the signatures of NFL Films. The pass spiraling through the air in slow motion. The mood shot of a hooded lineman sitting on the bench in the snow. (They've made heroes out of guys who wear 73," notes Beano Cook, the ABC football pundit.) The shots of eyes, bandaged fingers, cleats.

**– William Taaffe, *Sports Illustrated*, September 5, 1984.
Reprinted with permission.**

Broadcaster Bob Costas once criticized the league during an NBC pregame show, knocking the NFL for the poor quality of its games. He said that NFL Films productions had become more entertaining than the real thing on Sunday afternoons.

SS: Well, they should be. Alfred Hitchcock once said that, "Drama is really life with the dull parts cut out." A football game requires a full three 3 hours to play but has only 12 minutes of action. We take that 12 minutes and condense and focus and distill it then add music and sound effects to it. What we do *should* be more exciting. Well, maybe not more exciting, because you already know the outcome. But what we do is embellish the game and draw out the story lines, which can be just as emotional to some people as the outcome itself.

The early music of NFL Films, particularly from the late 1960s through the end of the '70s, was brilliant, inspiring work. Often its tone bordered on militaristic. In listening to any number of scores, one can envision General George Patton gathering his troops in a furious charge to relieve Bastogne. What's the story behind this great music you developed?

SS: When we started, all the music was basically the John Philip Sousa, "oom-pah" music. I was a movie buff in college, and I remember seeing *Gone With The Wind*, which was three hours long. All but twenty minutes of that movie had music. I figured if there was any sport that lent itself to music, it was football. You had music before the game and music at halftime, so we decided to develop a certain style of music for our films.

As a kid I used to go camp in the Poconos, and every Friday night we'd sit around a campfire and sing songs like, "*What do you do with a drunken sailor, da da dadum da dadum dum dum dum....*" I always felt that, with great orchestration, this would be great music that would work with football. I met this composer named Sam Spence and I would hum some of these songs to him. He would take some of these melodies and orchestrate them with 60- to 70-piece orchestras. We spent a lot of money on the music in the very beginning because I felt that music was the way to really develop emotion and momentum. Music was not only part of pro football, but it was very much a part of storytelling as well.

How were you introduced to Sam Spence?

SS: Sam Spence worked for a New York composer named Malin Marek, who my father knew. Sam was his arranger, and he'd also been teaching music at USC. My father had been talking to Malin Marek about doing some music for us. He was a Broadway composer and he wasn't really interested in doing football scores, but he said he had an arranger who he thought might be pretty good. My dad and I met Sam and we talked. Then we paid him $50,000 and he did about 15 minutes of music for us. We both liked it, and from then on, he would do an hour's worth of original music for us every year for the next 15 years. Sam had an astonishing range, from brassy band tunes to familiar folk melodies to broad, sweeping symphonic pieces. The rhythms of his music emphasized the rhythms inherent in pro football.

NFL Films has now distanced itself from using those classic arrangements in its productions. Why the switch?

SS: It depends what you're watching. We still use Sam's music in some of our things. There are certain types of music, like Sinatra's, that don't go out of style, and that's true with a lot of Sam's work. It still can be used. That music is so identifiable with the '60s and '70s, but sometimes when people hear it in our newer films, it just doesn't work. It's like taking a score from *The Wizard of Oz* and putting it with *Saturday Night Fever*.

Times change, and the kind of music we listen to changes. In many ways, music reflects our culture. The style and the way the game is played today wouldn't lend itself to that kind of music. The music we use now is a derivative of that original music, but the arrangements are different and the emphasis on the musical instruments is different. But we still try to tell a story with it.

"Writing music is like writing a letter. A lot of people ask me, 'How do you write music?' I tell them, 'How do you write a letter? You get an idea in your head and an image of what you want to say, and then you write it down.' Well, I hear these things and see the image of football and write the music accordingly.

"The most important thing in music, I believe, is melody. A melody has to stick in the ear. They have a wonderful word in German called *ohrwurm*. It literally means 'earworm,' but it's used to signify a catchy tune. A piece of music has to be like a worm that digs into your ear and doesn't give you any peace."

– composer Sam Spence, on writing music for NFL Films

Producing the highlight film for great teams like the 1977 Cowboys or the '89 Niners is likely the easy part of the job. How difficult is it to put together a creative, enthusiastic highlight for some of history's awful teams, like the 1972 Oilers (1-13) or the 1977 Saints (3-11)? Of course, the goal is to emphasize the positive aspects of a team's season, but wouldn't you, just once, like to have the opening script read something like, "In 1989, the Phoenix Cardinals sucked?"

SS: Well, doing lousy teams is certainly not as inspiring as doing 49ers or Cowboys or Packers films, but if you're creative it's a great challenge. Teams that have bad records really just throw up their hands and most of them don't even want to look at the film. The producer of that film, therefore, is left up to his own creative ability to make it interesting.

Actually, a lot of really good ideas have come from the highlight films of the Tampa Bay Bucs, the New Orleans Saints, the Houston Oilers, those bad Giants teams of the '70s. The teams themselves really weren't that interested in it, so it was left up to our producers to make their season seem interesting. So as a producer, in terms of creativity, sometimes it's not that bad to have one of those lousy teams. There's no pressure because nobody is expecting much from you. But if you're doing the highlight film of the '98 Broncos, well shit, everybody is expecting to get goose bumps for the whole 20 minutes of that.

Let's talk about John Facenda, whose voice became the key instrument in the NFL Films soundtracks. What type of void were you trying to fill in your productions by hiring him, and how was he discovered?

SS: John was a broadcaster, a news anchorman here in Philadelphia, and his station was phasing him out. They were bringing in the plastic blowup dolls with the freeze-dried hair to do the news, and John just didn't look like that. He was an old, craggy-faced, weather-beaten guy who had this great, oaken delivery. I had grown up with that voice as a kid, and I remembered him doing the news. Whenever he spoke, anybody that was in the room watching the news just listened.

One of the changes I wanted to make in our films was to write less script. I felt all of the films were overwritten, too much script. I felt the way to build drama was to do it with sound, music and a real sparse usage of words. So who was better to speak those words than a man with the voice like John Facenda?

I was only 22 at the time, a pipsqueak, when my father approached him. We didn't know whether John was even a football fan, but thankfully he said he would do it. I always remember the first line of script that I wrote for him. It became kinda characteristic of the kind of writing I did for him during those first years. It was in the film *They Call It Pro Football*. and it read [imitating Facenda], "*It starts with a whistle, and ends with a gun – sixty minutes of close-in action from kickoff to touchdown.*"

What made Facenda the perfect complement to your work?

SS: He had a certain richness of expression and a great resonance that cut through the music. He made the game seem more important than it was because he read his lines with a dramatic directness. I always felt his voice was distinctive but not distracting. A lot of times today you get a narrator that can be so narcissistic that he calls attention to the way he's speaking, which is a distraction. John wasn't that way at all.

John was a big opera fan. When we'd get to portions of the script that we really wanted to sound dramatic, he'd write the word *profundo* next to it. Or I'd tell him, "This has to be read very briskly," and he would write *allegro*. Or I would say, "This has to be read lightly," and he would write *leggiero*.

So we would have these football scripts with "profundo" and "allegro" written in the margins, and you'd say to yourself, "*What is this? Promuto? Vince Promuto?* He's the guard for the Redskins! What does he have to do with the script?" Well, those were his ways of coaching himself on how to read something. It was the drama in Facenda's voice that enabled us to write much shorter scripts, which is what we wanted to do.

One of my personal favorites is the 1974 NFL season highlight film. It paralleled the entire progression of the football calendar – from the heat of training camp through the playoffs – with the changing of the seasons in nature. The sounds of summer and fall and winter came to life through a voice. That, too, was Facenda.

SS: That film is a classic. It's called *The Championship Chase*. I remember the line, "*The autumn wind is a pirate, rolling in from sea....*" That whole thing has become a part of the culture of the whole NFL. I was always a big fan of Rudyard Kipling and that was my attempt at poetry, with a little assistance from Shakespeare. Whenever I go back and look at the old films that I've done, I always go back and look at that one. It seems that whenever it's shown, on ESPN or wherever, everybody stops and listens.

That film was probably the apogee of that particular style. We've never tried to come back and do it again because I think it would be a little bit clichéd now. But at that time, nobody had ever done a sports film with the music and poetry and kind of Greek chorus that I used in that film. I remember writing those lines of script then hearing Facenda read them and just getting chills and saying, "Boy, this is really great."

November can be cold and gray, November can be surly
With bitter rain upon the world, and winter coming early
Do you fear the force of the wind? The slash of the rain?
Go face them and fight them, Be savage again
The palms of your hands will thicken, the skin of your cheek will tan
You'll grow ragged and weary and wet, but you must do the best that you can

The autumn wind is a pirate, blustering in from sea
With a rollicking song he sweeps along, swaggering boisterously
His face is weather-beaten, he wears a hooded sash
With a silver hat about his head, and a bristling black moustache
He growls as he storms the country, a villain big and bold
And the trees all shake and quiver and quake as he robs them of their gold

– John Facenda, from NFL Films' *The Championship Chase* (1974)

"I discovered John Facenda in a saloon, believe it or not. I knew who he was because he was on local TV, a newscaster in Philadelphia. Every time I went into this saloon, this man John Facenda was there. He loved to talk football. I couldn't believe it! It was all he talked about – football, football, football.

"So I said, John, I really like your voice. How would you like to narrate one of our films? He said, 'Sure! I'll even do it for nothing. Just let me try it!'"

> "John Facenda didn't have the theatrical temperament, the screaming and carrying on that many performers have. He was such a nice man while he was doing narration for us."
>
> **– Ed Sabol, on how John Facenda joined NFL Films**

Facenda's last narration for NFL Films was the Super Bowl XVIII highlight film, as sadly he would succumb to cancer in 1984. Others have held his job since, but that magic voice is now gone. I always envisioned the NFL Films scouts out combing the country, listening to the men sermonizing behind the Sunday lecterns or arguing in smoky neighborhood bars, looking for that next voice of distinction. Did that search ever occur?

SS: It did. We had 300 different audition tapes sent to us over a period of six months. From people like Ed McMahon and Charlton Heston and Robert Stack to guys that were just football fans doing the recording in their basement. You could hear the washing machine in the background going "ka-thump ka-thump ka-thump." People got tapes of our music and would read to it. I even saved some of those tapes. They would all take that piece we did on Lombardi, where Facenda's opening line was, "*Lombardi – a certain magic still lingers in the very name. It speaks of duels in the snow and the cold November mud.*" People would try to read that line like him but it was impossible, like trying to replace a Lawrence Olivier or an Orson Wells. And we never thought we would replace John Facenda.

To tell you the truth, if John was still alive and narrating for us, people now might be saying, "Yeah, NFL Films still uses that old guy with the voice of God, but this is the rap generation." I think Facenda has become legendary because, like many great talents, he was perfect for his time and his place. His talent came at the right place at the right time but I'm not so sure he would be the right voice for the '90s or the new millennium.

In the late 1980s, NFL Films put together The Dream Bowl, *a mythical matchup between the 1978 Steelers and the 1972 Dolphins to determine which was the greatest team in history.*

SS: That was a lot of fun. We ran those two teams through a computer, and it ended up with the Steelers winning, 23-22. But, of course, a lot of that was entertainment based, with a lot of humor and tongue-in-cheek, although it had my true feeling about which were the greatest teams. We tried to put a laugh or two into it. We had Elvis Presley singing the national anthem and tried to do some other funny things with it.

Let's look at it from the other end. Which two teams would be featured in a Futility Bowl, *the battle for the worst team in history? The loser, of course, would get the crown.*

SS: We thought of doing something like this a while back. We were going to call it *The Repus Bowl*, which is "super" spelled backwards. As for the participants, you mentioned one of them earlier, the 1972 Houston Oilers. Of course, the Saints had one stretch in which they were awful, even with Archie Manning there. They were 1-15 in 1980. Tampa had that stretch where they lost 26 in a row. Even Jimmy Johnson's first Cowboys team was terrible and might be one of them. The Steelers of the 1950s had some awful teams. The Packers of '53 and '58 were really horseshit teams. But to me, the worst team of all-time would be the Dallas Texans of 1952. I can't think of one worse. They would have likely lost the Repus Bowl tournament.

Let's go back to the 1970s. It was a decade known for its many great moments, all those miracle plays and fantastic finishes.

SS: Absolutely. I think of the Miracle of the Meadowlands in '78, where the Giants fumbled the game away to the Eagles. I think of The Holy Roller, the play in the Chargers-Raiders game where Ken Stabler fumbled the ball, Pete Banaszak kicked it, and Dave Casper fell on it for a game-winning touchdown. I think of the

Hail Mary – Staubach to Drew Pearson in the playoff at Minnesota. O.J. Simpson's 2,003 yards in 1973. There was The Immaculate Reception, of course.

I think that particular weekend in 1972 was the greatest playoff weekend in NFL history. People forget that right after the Immaculate Reception game, Roger Staubach came into the playoff against the 49ers and led Dallas from two touchdowns behind to win the game. The 1970s had many, many great moments.

What about shooting-star performances by individual teams, ones that rose from nowhere to the tops of their divisions, then fell back out of the sky?

SS: The first team I think of is the Houston Oilers of the late '70s. That was a great story, a terrific wave of emotion. They had Dan Pastorini and Bum Phillips. Their problem was that they had to go through Pittsburgh every year, which meant playing up in the driving sleet and rain and cold. They just couldn't beat the Steelers, especially in that environment. There was no shame in that, since Pittsburgh was the greatest team ever.

After they lost the AFC Championship up there in 1978, the team went back to the Astrodome that night in Houston and the whole city showed up. They had a huge party and parade for them. I remember Bum Phillips saying, "This year we knocked on the door, and next year we're gonna kick the son-of-a-bitch in." The next year, they went up and played the Steelers and were beaten again.

What was that decade's greatest single-season Cinderella story?

SS: The greatest Cinderella story for an individual was Clint Longley, the backup Dallas quarterback on that Thanksgiving Day game in 1974. Staubach was hurt in that game against Washington, and he came in and threw two touchdown passes in the fourth quarter to win the game. Tom Dempsey, the kicker for the Saints, who set the record for the longest field goal in NFL history, was another one. Here was a guy who had been cut from a couple different teams and had half a foot, then goes out and kicks a 63-yarder to beat the Lions. Now, as far as Cinderella teams, you have to say the Pittsburgh Steelers.

A Cinderella team with four Super Bowl trophies? Those Steelers?

SS: Think about it. This was a team that had barely a handful of winning seasons in its entire history, which dated back to the 1930s. As a franchise, they were a joke for decades. Chuck Noll took over the team in 1969, and he only won one game in his first season. Then they got Bradshaw and Joe Greene and Franco Harris. They started having some great drafts, some of the best in NFL history, and then went on to become, in my opinion, not only the team of the '70s, but the team for the ages.

Introducing Steve Sabol's Greatest Hits

5) September 17, 1990 (Kansas City at Denver) – Steve Atwater on Christian Okoye. Okoye (6'1", 253-lbs) was coming off a monstrous 1989 season in which he led the NFL in rushing with his brutish, pounding style, a rhino on the charge. Somehow Denver was spared, as only five carries and 23 yards came in games against the Broncos.

"We hadn't seen much of him in person," said Atwater, the Broncos strong safety, "but based on films I was expecting big collisions. He wrecked a lot of the teams he played."

Atwater, known as "The Hitman," brought a big load himself with his 6'3" 217-lb frame and hellish speed... those big, powerful shoulders which served him well in plugging the run. Okoye took this particular handoff from quarterback Steve DeBerg and thundered toward through line. Atwater dropped him like a bull shot dead between the eyes.

"This was a big moment for us because Atwater was miked for sound," says Sabol. "He actually dented the [microphone] receiver. After the hit, all you heard was static."

4) November 11, 1979 (Oakland at Houston) – Jack Tatum on Earl Campbell. What happens when two heavy booms are lowered in unison. Tatum, a 5'10" free safety, made a career out of going for the knockout, a headhunter in many people's books.

"Jack was always looking to blast somebody," says former teammate Phil Villapiano. "He thought of himself strictly as a punisher, always looking to inflict pain."

On this goal line play in the Astrodome, Tatum didn't have to look far. Houston was going in from the one-yard line, and they were going in with Campbell the NFL's most punishing rusher. Tatum filled the hole off right tackle and slammed the crown of his helmet into Campbell's exposed chin. Most men would have gone straight down. Campbell didn't. Tatum fell aside in disbelief as the running back crossed the goal line, staggering backward like a man who'd just finished his last swig of Wild Turkey.

"An unbelievable collision, says Sabol. "Most people didn't know that Campbell was knocked out cold on the play."

3) January 20, 1991 (NY Giants at San Francisco) – Leonard Marshall on Joe Montana. High drama at Candlestick Park. Ten minutes remained in a rough, warlike NFC Championship bout, typical of the Giant-49er affairs from that era. San Francisco clung tightly to a 13-9 lead, and Montana needed to make a play to stave off the surging New Yorkers, whose defense was going into its typical 4th-quarter python squeeze.

On 3rd-and-ten at the San Francisco 23, Montana found nobody open and was flushed from the pocket to his right. As he surveyed his downfield options, two Giants took aim at him. Lawrence Taylor, who came charging from his linebacker position, had the first shot but Montana made a nifty move and dodged the collision.

Marshall, a defensive end who'd been flipped to the ground on his initial rush, sprung to his feet and refocused on the target. He saw a clear shot at Montana's back, then unleashed a merciless blast that dropped the blindsided quarterback in a heap.

"I looked up and there was nobody between him and me," said Marshall. "You don't get too many clean shots at a guy like Montana, so I hit him as hard as I could."

"It was clean but brutal," says Sabol. "Everyone could see it coming, almost in slow-motion. The only question was whether Montana was going to survive it."

The play changed the course of the game. After Marshall's hit, San Francisco gained only one more first down. Montana left the game with a concussion, a broken pinkie finger, and a bruised sternum.

The Giants, with two late field goals, left Candlestick as NFC champions.

2) December 26, 1964 (Buffalo at San Diego) – Mike Stratton on Keith Lincoln. At stake was the '64 AFL title, so both sides came out growling and snorting flames. The Bills had owned San Diego during the regular season, beating them 30-3 then 27-24, but the Chargers were defending league champs and still packed enough firepower to steal a game in wintry Buffalo.

San Diego struck early, 3:11 into the contest, on a 26-yard TD pass from Tobin Rote to end Dave Kocourek, but the day's emerging story was Chargers tailback Keith Lincoln. The star of the '63 title game (329 total yards versus Boston), Lincoln was now blazing away in Buffalo, gaining 58 yards on four quick touches of the ball. That's when the rugged Bills defense, the AFL's best, decided it had seen enough of that character.

"They were going to [Lincoln] again, this time on a little flare pattern out of the backfield," said Stratton, a 6'3, 230-pounder who operated at right side linebacker. "It was a play they ran pretty often. I hedged on my coverage, and Rote thought he had the right read."

Stratton, Lincoln and the ball all arrived at an ugly, three-way intersection; after the thunderclap, only Stratton and the ball remained in the game. "Stratton hit Lincoln so hard he broke two of his ribs," says Sabol. "His afternoon was over, and at that point Buffalo took control."

Chargers coach Sid Gillman, whose team would eventually lose 20-7, was typically matter-of-fact in his observation of the play. "That was one of the most beautiful tackles I've ever seen."

1) November 20, 1960 (Philadelphia at N.Y. Giants) – Chuck Bednarik on Frank Gifford. The schedule found the Giants and Eagles in a late-season brawl at Yankee Stadium with first place on the line. Philly held a 17-10 lead, but New York quarterback George Shaw had his team on the move, trying to piece together a game-tying drive.

The play called for Gifford to shoot over the middle on a short crossing pattern, but Shaw slightly misfired. The pass sailed a bit behind Gifford, and he had to adjust to make the catch. The distraction was all the fiery Bednarik needed, as he caught the halfback at full force and blasted him into a world of darkness. Lights out.

There's that famous snapshot of Bednarik, a linebacker, gesturing angrily down at his victim, who was splayed on the ground in front of him. "I'll tell you exactly what I was saying to him," says Bednarik. "I yelled, 'This... game... is fucking... over!'"

"That was the greatest hit in the history of pro football," says Sabol. "Gifford fumbled on the play. Philadelphia not only won that game, but went on to win the NFL championship."

Years later, Bednarik popped Gifford again, this time in one of those celebrity roasts. He had the hotel turn the lights down for ten seconds before he started in with his jabs.

"As the lights came back up, I looked at [Gifford] and said, 'Does that ring a bell, Frank?'"

Source: The Sporting News

The Los Angeles Rams captured seven NFC West titles during the decade, yet reached the Super

Bowl only once, losing to the Steelers in 1979. It was an organization loaded with tremendous talent, names like Jack Youngblood, Lawrence McCutcheon, Tom Mack and Nolan Cromwell. What was the missing ingredient that kept the Rams from getting past Dallas and Minnesota in the playoffs and into more Super Bowls?

SS: I think it was the lack of a real breakaway running back. McCutcheon was more of a grinder than a breakaway guy. But when you ask what kept the Rams from getting to the Super Bowl, you've got to look at the teams they had to beat to get there. Dallas and Minnesota were just better teams in most years. And when the Rams finally did make it to the Super Bowl in '79, they ended up playing Tampa Bay to get there, a team they matched up well with.

What was the worst game you ever had the displeasure of filming?

SS: There was a game between Houston and Tampa in 1983, which was a complete disaster. Both teams were really bad, and the game was even worse. There were turnovers and mistakes and the field was all chewed up. It was really an awful game to watch and try to document.

Another really bad game was Super Bowl V between the Colts and the Cowboys. I recently reviewed the footage of that game and, boy, I've never seen so many dropped passes and fumbles and missed tackles. Earl Morrall turns around on a handoff and collides with Tom Nowatzke. Johnny Unitas drops back to pass, loses his balance and throws the ball into the ground. Craig Morton was sailing balls over Duane Thomas' head. That was a really poorly played game.

The NFL decided to put little footballs on top of the endzone markers, and even those were wrong. Instead of saying "Colts" or "Cowboys," they had "Chiefs" written on them for some reason. They didn't even get the teams right. I was researching the game, trying to disprove the notion that it was "The Blunder Bowl," but it really was. It was the worst played championship game I can ever remember, and I've seen them all since 1962.

Here's a bit of trivia – the program from that game is considered the most valuable of all the Super Bowl programs. The truck that was carrying them to Miami got into an accident on the way. A lot of the programs got rained on and were ruined, so there were far fewer of them available for the game.

The use of instant replay has been a heated topic of debate in pro football over the years. Had the league been using it since the AFL-NFL merger in 1970, some of the great plays in league history might have been reversed, including the Immaculate Reception and the Holy Roller play from 1978 San Diego-Oakland. Do feel that instant replay has had a sterilizing effect on the game, one that diminishes the potential for those quirky but fantastic moments?

SS: Well, as for the Holy Roller play, I don't know if that would have been a reviewable play or not. I guess they would have had to decide whether Stabler threw an incomplete pass or if he fumbled. It would be interesting to see how the officials would have ruled once they looked at the replay.

Instant replay certainly would have affected the spontaneity of great plays like the Immaculate Reception, the Miracle at the Meadowlands, or the Holy Roller. During those days, once the referee threw up his hands and signaled *Touchdown!* that was it. Had there been instant replay you would have lost that sense of finality, that when the referee makes the call the play is over.

Of course, look at the lateral at the end of the 1999 playoff game between the Titans and the Bills – the Music City Miracle. You'd think that everybody in the stadium would have relaxed while the officials looked at the replay, figuring it was going to be reversed. Instead, there was an incredible sense of suspense in that stadium because everybody knew that a chance to go to the Super Bowl was riding on this decision. That play had a different element of suspense. It was like being in an isolation booth and the clock is ticking and everyone is waiting for you to give your answer to the big-money question. Instant replay lends its own type of suspense to these kinds of plays.

Which owner raised the biggest stink about quality or content of his team's highlight film?

SS: The first problem we ever had with a team's ownership was back in 1967 or '68. We had just produced a film called *The Football Follies*, which was an incredible success. Everybody loved it. There were a couple of follies that were related to the Raiders, so we added them into their highlight film. They didn't think it was very funny. We felt that, in making a film, it was good to make people cheer and laugh, to cultivate all the emotions. We really didn't know Al Davis at that point, and to him there's no humor in mistakes or losing. To him, it was all about winning. We didn't know that at the time, and he was very upset about it.

But then later, Al Davis became the first owner – and I think this is important – to call and congratulate me on a film. We did the 1976 Super Bowl in which the Raiders defeated the Vikings. After the film was shown, Al Davis got a copy of it and called me at my house to congratulate me. So I don't want to paint Al Davis as a bad guy. I could see why he was upset with those follies. To him, it's *Just win, baby*. Even though they were humorous shots, watching Daryle Lamonica dropping back and falling down or Clem Daniels fumbling the ball was not funny to him. They were funny within the context of *The Football Follies*, but not in a highlight film situation.

We also had an early problem with George Halas when we did montages – cutting from different games and situations throughout the season. He couldn't understand how Rudy Bukich would be throwing a pass at Wrigley Field and Mike Ditka would be catching the ball at the L.A. Coliseum. We told him it was a new film technique called *montage*, but he said to hell with that. He didn't like it. So for ten years, we never had any montages in any of the Bears highlight films. The only plays that were ever shown in a Bears highlight film were from the games that they won. All the other plays, whether it was a terrific Gale Sayers run or a Johnny Morris touchdown catch, didn't appear in the highlight film if the Bears didn't win the game.

Halas also didn't like close-ups. He used to call them "facials." He told me, "I don't want any facials in my film." And I said, "Well, people want to see what Dick Butkus or Gale Sayers look like."

He said, "*Nahhh* – if a player sees his face in those films, he's going to want more money."

They Shoot Imposters, Don't They?

Former Chicago Bears owner George Halas was infuriated after viewing a 1967 NFL Films piece which caught a gun-toting Bears' fan diving for a ball in the stands. Says Sabol, "Halas insisted, 'Those are not Bears fans! We don't have people like that come to our games! We have good fans!'

"Well, Bears fans in the '60s made the Indy 500 infield look like Parliament. They were wild, but Halas didn't want to show that. So the next year, I went to Washington and got close-ups of Redskins fans with their camel's hair coats, pretty sweaters and scarves. Every year I'd splice those shots into the Bears' films.

"Up until the day he died, Halas would say, 'See, those are Bears fans.' He never knew it was one of our running jokes at NFL Films."

Source: *USA Today*

Let's play a final game of word association. I'll give you the description, then you tell me what comes to mind.
"The most underrated running back of the 1970s."

SS: That's a tough one. Tucker Frederickson was a big back with the Giants who had some good years. I thought he was an underrated runner. Tom Woodeshick had some good seasons for the Eagles, but his last good year was in 1969. Dickie Post from San Diego was a very exciting player and a very good receiver. Those three played mostly in the 1960s.

I would have to say that Billy "White Shoes" Johnson of Houston would be my choice for the 1970s, even though he wasn't a running back. He was a wide receiver, but I have to include him because he was a fast, exciting player who probably didn't get as much recognition as he deserved.

"Did the worst job of coaching a very talented team."

SS: The Bears' Jim Dooley had both Dick Butkus and Gale Sayers on his team and won only one game in 1969, so he definitely qualifies. In the '70s, I have to look at Bill "Tiger" Johnson, who had all that talent in Cincinnati but could never get into the playoffs, although having Pittsburgh in the same division didn't help much. Ken Anderson was at quarterback, Pete Johnson and Boobie Clark and Archie Griffin in the backfield, very good wide receivers and defensive talent. I think the Bengals of the mid-to-late '70s could have done more with the team they had.

"If he could only take that one play back."

SS: Roger Staubach's last pass in the 1979 playoffs against the Rams. He threw it to Herb Scott, one of his offensive linemen, which was a sad way to end a great career.

The obvious one was the "Miracle at the Meadowlands," where the Giants' Joe Pisarcik fumbled trying to hand the ball off to Larry Csonka on the last play of the game and Herman Edwards ran it back for the game-winning touchdown for Philadelphia. That game cost assistant coach Bob Gibson, who called the play, his job. Then the Giants ended up firing their coach John McVay after the season. That is definitely one play that a lot of people would like to have back.

"The game no one should have lost."

SS: Miami-Oakland from 1974 was a great one. So was the Miami-San Diego playoff of '81. Another one was the "Ghost to the Post" game between Baltimore and Oakland, where Dave Casper caught the winning touchdown in the second overtime. That was a great one.

"The most brutal, punishing game of the Super '70s."

SS: Any game from the 1978 or '79 seasons between the Steelers and the Oilers. Houston had Earl Campbell and was a very physical offensive team, and the Steelers were a physical defensive team. Those teams just pounded on each other. I remember a 13-3 game played at the Astrodome, which was about as physical and brutal as any game I'd ever seen.

"The greatest job in the world."

SS: Getting paid to make movies about football. I can't think of one better than mine.

— 8 —
Archie Manning, Quarterback

New Orleans Saints (1971-82); Houston (82-83); Minnesota (83-84)
March 25, 2002

I admit it – I didn't want to do it. A friend suggested including a chapter on Archie Manning in this project, and for a brief moment that sounded like a pretty good idea. Manning, a former All-American at Ole Miss and franchise quarterback for the New Orleans Saints, was the NFC West's best passer during the 1970s and one of the league's top athletes.

But after Manning agreed to an interview and I started the whole research dig, it wasn't long before the repressed memories and visions of a horror known as Saints football came back, crawling from the murk like an awful secret from the bayou. It was decades ago, but hey, watching *The Exorcist* is still a nightmare no matter how many times you watch it, right?

The first step was toward the videotapes of his old games, also known as *The Best of Kill the Quarterback*. There stood Manning on the sidelines as his defense gave up the points, game after game looking like a man who'd spent the last three hours watching his house burn down.

Tape #1, the '76 season opener – Vikings 40, Saints 9. Wipeout.

Tape #2, from 1977 – Buccaneers 33, Saints 14. An expansion franchise gets its first-ever win.

Tape #3, from 1979 – Raiders 42, Saints 35. New Orleans blows a big 21-point lead.

No mid-December contests to relive when the stakes were high. No big playoff games to review. No reminiscing over championship seasons and cigars. Just a whole bayou full of losing. Enough with the videotapes.

Next, onto the record books. It had been a while since I exhumed those dismal Saints statistics from that era, but there they were, staring back at me like the evil eye or a shrunken head. All the sacks and penalties and turnovers and dropped passes and blocked kicks and thirds-and fourteen, year after year after year. Here's a sample of the mess that really belongs buried in some forgotten, grown-over crypt:

• **1971 Saints, Manning's rookie year: 4-8-2**. Last place in the NFC West. Their 98 penalties are the most in the league, worth nearly a thousand yards in markoffs. The defense allows the most rushing yards (157.1/gm) in the conference and nearly 25 ppg. All signs of bad things to come.

• **1972 Saints: 2-11-1**. Last place again. The leading rusher for New Orleans? Running back Bob Gresham with 381 yards. You don't want to know the runner-up performance at RB. Okay, it's rookie Bill Butler's 233. Only five rushing touchdowns scored by this offense of ill-repute, then coach J.D. Roberts gets run out of town.

• **1975 Saints: 2-12**. Last place again. Manning throws 20 picks and 7 lonely touchdowns. The offense averages barely 12 ppg and scores over 20 just twice. Saints quarterbacks are sacked 53 times. Coach John North fired with eight games to play, then at season's end the interim coach is blindfolded and given his last Camel.

• **1976 Saints: 4-10**. Fourth but not last in the NFC West, only because of the one-time appearance of the expansion Seattle Seahawks. New coach Hank Stram can conjure up none of his old AFL magic, as Manning is sidelined for the entire season with shoulder tendonitis. The two Bobbys – Scott and Douglass – filling in at quarterback are overwhelmed. Enemy rushers collapse the pocket and ring the bell 51 times.

• **1977 Saints: 3-11**. Seattle has moved to the AFC, so it's back to last place. The Saints lead the league in kickoff returns, which tells you something about their porous defense, one that allows 4.4 yards/carry and 21 rushing touchdowns. In San Francisco, Rich Szaro had a chance to beat the 49ers in overtime, but his field goal attempt whapped the upright and fell back on the field and the Saints lost. Then Stram got canned by an impatient owner when the season was through.

And there's just no end to it. Researching the numbers behind those crummy Saints teams gives an almost sickening feeling, like slowly watching your retirement portfolio erode away each day in the papers. As the decade of the 1970s came to a merciful close, New Orleans' football epithet callously read, "Don't Look Back – There's Nobody Else Behind You."

And as for the interview with Manning, what were the appropriate angles? Do I hit him yet another time with the big cliché, "Did you ever get tired of losing?" Or the probing "Did you ever want to be traded?" How many times over the past 25 years have those dead-fish been flopped in front of him?

Example: *"Uh, Arch, two-part question here – Do you think that throwing to the tight end more would've helped in that 62-7 loss to Atlanta? And how did your coaches tweak the gameplan going into Dallas the following week, which ended in a 40-3 massacre?"* Right.

There had to be a more insightful approach. Manning was a highly skilled quarterback, the right-handed predecessor of Steve Young, not some over-hyped scouting blunder or blown draft choice. The lean had to be positive, with questions that would get him talking – his thoughts on opponents and teammates, the few scattered upsets, gameday stuff. To rehash all that "Aints" business yet another time would probably lead to a very short conversation. The Saints were 45-114-1 during Manning's years with the team, but there must have been some sunshine somewhere.

As the second selection of the 1971 NFL draft, Manning's case was a simple one: great quarterback playing for a broken-down franchise. Think of Steve Carlton and his 1.98 ERA blazing away for the hopeless '72 Phillies. Or James Wilder mashing out 1,300 rushing yards for the 1985 Tampa Bay Bucs, a 2-14 team. Or Stonewall Jackson leading a Weeblo battalion through the Shenandoah Valley.

The NFL draft process intentionally puts great players in the wrong place at the wrong time, and that is the story here. Had fate been kind enough to place Archie Manning in any other NFL city other besides New Orleans, his bio would likely be a much brighter read.

Think Tom Landry could've won with Manning at the controls instead of Roger Staubach? Or what if Manning had wound up with the L.A. Rams, bombing away to speedsters like Ron Jessie and Harold Jackson behind that bedrock offensive line? What about Manning running Don Shula's operation in Miami, feeding the ball to Csonka, Morris and Kiick?

It's stuff for daydreamers, but even today Manning probably still wonders, "Why not me?"

In the world of professional sports, the luck of the draw rules. But sometimes the tough road can end in reward, even more so today with the advent of free agency. Steve Young was a wreck by the time the Tampa Bay traded him to San Francisco, but there he quickly elevated his play to a championship level. Walter Payton was becoming a tired, one-man show in Chicago until the Bears finally brought him some reinforcements. Both Young and Payton's careers ended in storybook style and Super Bowl rings.

Manning? Well, after all that bayou misery he was traded off to Houston in 1982. The bumbling Oilers finished 1-8 in that strike-shortened season. More bad times. Two years later Manning finally hung it up.

Sometimes the black clouds won't go away. Sometimes great talents go to waste. In the bottom-line world of professional sports, sometimes seems to happen way too often.

• • •

Of all your coaches in New Orleans – and that rotating door spun through J.D. Roberts, John North, Hank Stram, Dick Nolan and Bum Phillips – which impressed you as having the best overall football mind?

AM: I'd say Hank Stram. He had more success as a head coach than anyone else. He was very, very involved in the offense and was a great offensive mind. I regret that I didn't get more of an opportunity to play for him. He wasn't there but two years. I missed the whole '76 season with injuries and then missed four games of the '77 season, so I didn't really play but ten games for Hank Stram. I regret that he wasn't given the opportunity to stay longer because he really was a great offensive mind. He really had some good ideas and concepts.

On the other hand, Dick Nolan was a proven defensive coach. He was probably just as responsible for the creation of the Flex Defense as Tom Landry was. Dick had success with it when he was coaching in San Francisco, but we never quite had the players to bring it together in New Orleans. We didn't win a lot of games with any coach, but I had the most success under Dick Nolan.

Stram arguably belongs in the Hall of Fame for his great success with the Kansas City Chiefs, yet he lasted only two years in New Orleans. Why was that cord cut so quickly?

AM: We didn't win. But football was different in those days. Coaches, a lot of times, were given five years to rebuild a team. In the NFL today, if you win seven games in two years you're definitely going to get fired. It wasn't like that back then. Hank wasn't on any speed-dial type of plan. It was more like a five-year plan. He said I was his quarterback and he was going to build the team around me. His whole plan got off to a bad start because I missed so many games while he was there. He was trying to use the draft to build up the team, and he knew that wasn't going to happen overnight. To be honest, Hank thought he had more time to turn the thing around, but [owner] John Mecom obviously wasn't happy with the progress and had a quick hook with him. That caught Hank by surprise. But maybe there were some other things involved. Maybe Mecom just thought the whole Stram thing wasn't working and wasn't ever going to work.

What was your opinion of Hank Stram?

AM: I think Hank could have built the team. He had done it before in Kansas City and there's no doubt in my mind he could have done it in New Orleans. He drafted some players like Tony Galbreath and Chuck Muncie, who wound up being good players for the Saints. I was sad to see Hank go. Actually, I was sad to see all my coaches leave. I had close, personal relationships with every coach we had there. I still call them all friends today.

Which head coach do you feel may have been in over his head, unqualified for the job?

AM: I can honestly say that we had some coaches who got really ridiculed by the New Orleans and national media, and that wasn't fair. For example, they said J.D. Roberts wasn't qualified to be a head coach. Well, to be honest with you, J.D. had some really good leadership abilities. There are players other than myself who will admit that. But when he was the head coach of the Saints, he had no help.

Aside from the man's personal head coaching ability, you've got to have somebody making those drafts and trades. All of our trades slapped us in the face, and whose fault was that? J.D. Roberts didn't make those trades, but he certainly did pay for them. Jim Otis, a very fine running back, was traded to Kansas City for a 7th round pick. We got Margene Adkins from Dallas *for a second-round pick*. We traded away great players like Kenny Burrough and Chuck Muncie and Wes Chandler and got what?

What you need in the NFL to win is talent and, as a general rule, our coaches did not have enough on the roster to really be successful. We did not have great management during my years in New Orleans. There were always a lot of changes. Maybe the management would've been better had the coaching been better, but the opposite was also true. There never was a time when the management and the coaching were *both* great at the same time. That's what really killed the franchise.

What percentage of the Saints' ineptitude do you contribute directly to team ownership?

AM: Looking back, it wasn't that John Mecom didn't hire some capable people. It's just that the chemistry never worked. John was not a cheapo. He spent money and he wanted to win. We did everything first class. I've never asked him this, but I'll bet that today John regrets not finding the best football man available to manage his team and turning it over to him. He had the money to do that. Things might have been a lot different had he done that.

What about drug abuse? Did you perceive that as being a major problem on the Saints?

AM: No. Our problems in the '70s were mostly due to poor management and having too many changes, starting over too many times. But I think I was kind of naïve. There may have been signs that drugs were becoming a problem. I just didn't notice them. I didn't know what to look for. In talking to people years later and reflecting back, I can now see what the problems were. We all know what happened in 1980, with the Don Reese cocaine story in *Sports Illustrated* after our 1-15 season. I honestly didn't know that stuff was going on, but I should have. After reading that article I said, "I must have been blind!" By the time I was traded to Houston, I was a little bit wiser. I knew the kind of things to look for and, believe me, in Houston the signs were there. Drugs were all over the place with that team. It was a major problem for the Oilers.

The Saints' drafts of the 1970s were nothing short of abysmal. Some memorable high-round busts include players like guard Royce Smith (8th pick overall in '72), receiver Larry Burton (7th in '75) and kicker Russell Erxleben (11th in '79). Who, in your mind, was the Saints' most disappointing draft pick?

AM: Royce was a big, good-lookin' guy from Georgia who didn't work out, just didn't turn out to be a good pro player. Larry Burton was drafted as a project, on potential. He finished fourth in the Olympics and was one of the fastest people in the world. With anybody that fast – he ran about a 4.2 or 4.3 – you're hoping for a Bob Hayes, a track guy who was going to turn into a football player. I think he got caught up in some coaching changes and just never developed any confidence.

I don't know if I can say who was the *most* disappointing. But I can remember a couple of days before the 1974 draft I was working out on the West Coast. I saw one of our scouts out there and asked him who he thought we were going to take. We had a pretty high pick that year, in the top ten or so. He said, "There's a receiver from Southern Cal who I think will be available, and I think he can really help us. His name is Lynn Swann."

I said, "Yeah, I've seen him on TV. I think he'll be good."

Then he said, "But the coach wants a linebacker."

Well, Swann was available but instead we picked a linebacker from Ohio State named Rick Middleton. He wasn't very big or very strong. Rick wasn't even the best linebacker at Ohio State. We picked him over Randy Gradishar, who was an All-American. To me, that was one of our most disappointing draft picks.

Let's talk about some of your biggest games in New Orleans. There weren't many, but do any in particular bring back a smile for you?

AM: Playing in big games is what I missed most in my pro career. I've always told my kids that, of course, you want to win championships, but first you want to get into big games and play well in the big games. We didn't get to play in many with the Saints. We had some big upsets. During my rookie year we beat the Rams, who were a very good team. Then we beat the Cowboys, who went on to win the Super Bowl that year. We played Kansas City real tough on a Monday night in 1972. Of course, it was years later before we got back on Monday night again. We didn't have any playoff games at all. It wasn't until 1978 that we made a move and started competing better. We were in the hunt for a while that season. In '79, too. But there weren't many big games in my career, and that's kinda what you miss.

I'll tell you one game that sticks out in my mind. It was 1981. Bum Phillips was here. We went over to Houston and played the Oilers, his old team. *That* was a big game. You wouldn't believe the attention given to that game during the week. It was like Super Bowl Sunday. Every TV station in Houston spent the week in New Orleans covering the Saints. Bum was still a real favorite in Houston. The Oilers weren't doing very well, but they still had some talent, and we went over there and beat them. I'm sure I didn't have a great statistical game but I held us together and made some plays and got us a win in a hostile environment. I always felt that Bum should have been indebted to me for that. Instead, he traded me the next year.

Which was your favorite victory as a Saint?

AM: I would have to say it was opening day of my rookie year against the L.A. It was my first start, and we upset a very good Rams team that was heavily favored. They still had Roman Gabriel and the Fearsome Foursome and a whole lot of talent. I scored a touchdown on the last play of the game to beat 'em. I thought that was a great way to start my pro career.

That final play was controversial. You had fumbled the ball and Jack Youngblood of the Rams recovered at the two-yard line, but the officials ruled that you had crossed the goal and awarded the touchdown. What really happened?

AM: Oh, I fumbled, there's no question about that. But I felt I fumbled after I crossed the goal line. I know the Rams thought it was a turnover and they should've won the game, but I think I was definitely in the endzone before the ball came out.

A few weeks later in Tulane Stadium you stunned the eventual Super Bowl champion Cowboys, 26-14. You were 6 of 15 for 49 yards throwing the football, while your backs averaged only 2.3 yards on 24 carries. How does any quarterback beat Dallas by going 6 of 15?

AM: That Cowboys team was at least three touchdowns better than we were. I don't know how we beat them because we were clearly outmanned. We were coming off a [35-14] whipping by the Bears, so maybe the Cowboys took us lightly. I know as a team we were sky-high going into that game. I remember I ran for a couple of scores and threw for another, and Dallas turned the ball over a bunch of times. Our defense did a tremendous job that day, but I would bet that if we played Dallas ten times that season, we'd only beat them once. And that was the one.

Another stunning upset came in 1973 against defending NFC champion Washington. The Redskins were 5-1 and headed towards the playoffs, while the Saints were 2-4, had been outscored 185-61, and were coming off a 40-0 massacre at San Francisco. For the Redskins, it was one of those contests that former Giants coach Bill Parcells used to call "trap games." A 19-3 Saints victory.

AM: That was the old "Over the Hill Gang." Sometimes we had an advantage over a veteran group like that coming into New Orleans. They probably didn't take us very seriously, and probably didn't train real well the night before. It'd be hot and muggy in Tulane Stadium, and that would work against teams. Honestly, we had a pretty good run defense. We had the capability of shutting people down on occasion, and we shut down the Redskins ground game that day. I think they had less than 25 yards rushing. Hey, when we played Buffalo that year, we even held O.J. Simpson to his lowest yardage of the season.

Archie Manning's Five Greatest Victories (unauthorized)

5) October 14, 1979 – Saints 42, Buccaneers 14: A controversial choice. Arguably could have gone with a win over a Super Bowl team – the 1979 Rams – or even Manning's favorite upset over the '71 Rams in this spot. But a quick retort has been prepared:

    a) The '79 Rams had already clinched the NFC West and were resting starters when they lost to the Saints on season's final week.

b) The 1971 Rams were also-rans, limping along on the dying reputation of the Fearsome Foursome. (Besides, as you'll soon see, too many Rams-Saints summaries make for a dull sidebar.)

So the choice here is a win over a Buccaneers team that reached the NFC title game with a proud, hammering defense.

This game was actually scoreless at halftime, a testament to the powder-keg explosiveness that the '79 Saints possessed. Tampa Bay even led 7-0 early in the third before the Saints went off. New Orleans rushers pounded out 234 big yards, while Manning was efficiently sharp, going 11 of 14 for 141 yards and a TD. All of this came against a Buccaneer defense that allowed the fewest points in the NFL.

"Things just started clicking in that second half," says Manning. "Our line began blowing open holes, and once we got the running game going, I could get *my* act going. I think it was the most points we ever scored while I was in New Orleans. Well, we did score 51 against Seattle once, but I didn't play that day."

4) October 28, 1973 – Saints 19, Redskins 3: "We tried to get ready," said Washington head coach George Allen, "but it's hard to do when your upcoming opponent had just lost 40-0." And 62-7. And 40-3.

The Saints were off to a blundering start in 1973, having been outscored 185-61 in their first six games. The Redskins, meanwhile, were defending NFC champions, a solid 5-1 outfit that was gearing up for another run at the playoffs. But on this day, they were never in the game.

"To come down here and play the way we did, it was shameful," said Redskins QB Billy Kilmer afterwards, "embarrassing." Like being knocked out in a pillow fight with Mariah Carey.

The Saints hammered the league's stingiest rushing defense for 203 yards and sacked Redskin quarterbacks four times. It was an unexpected loss that ultimately cost Washington the NFC East title.

"We could tell pretty early in the game that the Redskins weren't ready to play," says Manning, who hit Bill Butler with a 9-yard pass for the game's only touchdown. "Sometimes that Bourbon Street mischief would work to our advantage."

3) November 17, 1974 – Saints 20, Rams 7: Their previous meeting found the Saints at the Los Angeles goal line, trying to avoid a shutout with only seconds left on the clock. They lost three yards, and the game ended 24-0.

The rematch opened with a wrinkle, a three-receiver set that New Orleans hoped would confound an aggressive Rams secondary enough to get some early points on the board. It worked.

Manning threw for 175 yards and two scores out of the formation. Rams were blowing their coverages. Assignments were missed. Some defenders stood around scratching their heads, looking to the sideline for answers.

"Nonsense," Rams coach Chuck Knox shot back to the press afterward. "Running three receivers had nothing to do with us losing the game. Our defense made adjustments. We were just outplayed."

"I don't remember much about that three-receiver stuff," Manning said years later, "but I do remember the one pass [WR] Bobby Newland caught from me that day – a 79-yard touchdown. The Rams probably remember it too."

L.A. had hit an unlikely speed bump on its way to the '74 NFC title game. The Rams were a team that would field the NFC's second-rated defense that year; New Orleans put up over 300 yards of offense. L.A.'s top rusher, Lawrence McCutcheon, would lead the NFC with 1,109 yards; the Saints allowed him just 28, his lowest total of the season. Overall, the Rams committed four turnovers and were an out-of-sync bunch.

By the end of the third quarter New Orleans was ahead 20-0 and the damage was done. The Rams weren't coming back. As the clock wound down, the Saints were smiling, congratulating themselves on the sidelines. It was an unusual sight.

2) October 22, 1978 – Saints 10, Rams 3: "A rare kinda game for us," remembers Manning. "We didn't win too many of those low-scoring, defensive struggles with the big boys." Or against anyone else, for that matter. Only 13 times in Saints history (147 games played) had the team held an opponent to 10 or fewer points, and it wasn't likely to happen on this afternoon in the L.A. Coliseum.

The Rams were a crisp 7-0 coming into the game, fresh off their emotional victory at Minnesota. "I had a very good feeling about our '78 team," coach Ray Malavasi said years later. "Things were clicking for us. We'd beaten both our key conference rivals [Dallas and Minnesota] by double-digits. Then, for whatever reason, we went sleepwalking against the Saints."

It was a listless effort that included six turnovers and thirteen penalties worth 138 yards. The Rams offense sputtered and wheezed and coughed. Pat Haden's passes hit everything but their target, while the Saints rose up to swallow L.A.'s typically potent ground game.

Three minutes remained on the clock. The game was tied, 3-3, and New Orleans had worked itself down to the Rams' 19-yard line. A nervous Coliseum crowd looked on, begging for a turnover or a defensive stop. Manning would have none of it. Despite his own mediocre afternoon (11 of 22, 130 yards), he read a blown assignment by L.A.'s right outside linebacker and hit running back Tony Galbreath with a short pass. Galbreath ripped down the sideline for the game winner.

"Credit our defense for that win," says Manning. "We didn't give them a whole lot to work with."

Just enough to tiptoe past the daydreaming Rams.

1) October 17, 1971 – Saints 24, Cowboys 14: What was significant about New Orleans' defeat of Tampa Bay in 2002? It marked only the second time in history that the Saints had beaten the eventual Super Bowl champion in the same season. Dallas at New Orleans, 1971, was the first.

The final stat sheets from that day had a quirky look to them. They seemed jumbled, lots of oddball items. For example:

• The '71 Saints allowed the most rushing yards in the NFC (157/game), but held Duane Thomas and Cowboys' powerful attack to 96.

• New Orleans managed only ten first downs but scored 24 points, the second most allowed by Dallas all season.

• Dallas' return specialists averaged 124 return yards/game against the rest of its schedule, but got only 18 against New Orleans.

• The Cowboys committed six turnovers…Manning completed only six passes… indeed, a strange afternoon.

The Saints took a 7-0 lead on a Manning aerial to running back Tony Baker and never trailed. Dallas coach Tom Landry continued his QB switcheroo between Craig Morton and Roger Staubach, which kept the Cowboys offense out of whack. Staubach's second-half effort produced two touchdowns and made things respectable.

"It was one of those days," Manning said. "Emotionally, we were wired. We couldn't have been any more ready to play. And the Cowboys seemed flat." They also had long memories.

"Yeah, the next time we played them, they whipped us by 37."

Which was the most impressive team you faced during your NFL career?

AM: The best team defense I ever played against was the 1984 Bears. I was playing with the Vikings then. I got the start and they sacked me eleven times. With Chicago's scheme, they really brought the pressure. Their whole philosophy was to destroy the pass pocket and force the quarterback to make mistakes. You'd get a good number of man-to-man situations downfield, but the trouble was finding the time to complete the pass. You really had to be concerned with trying to block them all. I can honestly say I had never been under that kind of constant defensive pressure any other time. They were awesome.

The '78 Steelers were also very, very good. They were a better overall team than the '84 Bears, for obvious reasons. Pittsburgh was never a team that relied heavily on the blitz, but by the late '70s, they were becoming more of a high-pressure defense. The rule changes for pass blocking kinda forced them in that direction, where before they could rely on their front four to put steady pressure the quarterback.

Let's talk about some of your teammates in New Orleans. Chuck Muncie was probably the most talented running back ever to wear a Saints uniform. The first pick in the '76 draft, he was built for the position, with raw power and speed and superb hands – a real RoboBack. You must have been thrilled to have that kind of weapon at your disposal.

AM: Chuck was super talented. He was one of these backs that had the ability, the size and the speed. I mean, we're talking Jimmy Brown/Walter Payton type of stuff. This guy was the real deal. He was real fast for a big man and made some tremendous runs. He had some really good games for us. But Chuck wasn't able to get his personal life together. He played on one engine.

Often Chuck played a lot like Earl Campbell. It was great to watch the films on Monday and see the cornerbacks trying to avoid tackling those two guys. On pitchouts you'd see these 185-lb. cornerbacks trying to stay out of the way without looking like they were trying to stay out of the way.

When Chuck was in college at Cal I caught a few of his games on TV, but after we drafted him, at that first mini-camp, you could tell right away that he was something else. He had a real fast first step. I can still see him standing there in that I-formation, the kinda funny way he'd position himself, and then the explosion. Man, he was so quick. After his first step, he was at full speed. He also caught the ball well, and even threw the ball well. On option passes, Chuck was terrific.

Muncie's had some great moments in his career with the Saints, but he was an erratic player. Drugs were evidently a serious problem in his life. When did you first get the feelings that Muncie wasn't going to last in New Orleans?

AM: Well, to be honest, I really didn't know what was going on with him. You know, I'm from Mississippi and conservative and I guess I was pretty naïve. I didn't do drugs, and nobody did drugs around me. I didn't really know what signs to look for. Chuck had his problems from almost the moment he came to the Saints. He didn't practice hard. He didn't have a strong work ethic. He didn't pay attention in meetings. A lot of times I had to tell him what to do on the field while we were running the play. I saw other rookies not make a real quick transition from college life to pro ball, suddenly having all that money in your pocket. I had seen that behavior before, so I was always hopeful Chuck could somehow turn it around. We all thought he had in '78. He had about eleven or twelve-hundred yards that season, and we thought maybe he had turned the corner.

About four or five of us went to the Pro Bowl in 1978, including Chuck. I talked the coaches into letting me play while he was playing, and we got him into some good positions. He was the game's MVP. While we were at the Pro Bowl, we'd been around good guys like Walter Payton and Tony Dorsett and Wilbert Montgomery. We hoped that maybe a little of that would rub off on Chuck, maybe that would help him reach his potential. Unfortunately, that didn't work. But you know, a lot of guys involved in drugs might be distant or have a bad attitude. That was never the case with Chuck. He was always smiling, always in a good mood. He was my kids' favorite player. He played ball with them all time. They really liked Chuck.

After four seasons, Muncie was shipped off to San Diego for a second-round draft pick. Was that a decision that you supported, considering all of his troubles?

AM: Personally, I didn't want him to leave. I kinda liked having Chuck on the team. Now, I knew that he wasn't always prepared, that you couldn't always count on him. He'd play great one week then have some type of injury or ailment the next week. It was hard, but I still liked having him around. I was hoping eventually the light would come on and he would shape up. We had another very good running back named Tony Galbreath. Tony was a super talent and did a lot of good things for us, but he was no Chuck Muncie.

Can you compare Muncie's up-and-down career in New Orleans to the erratic years that running back Ricky Williams gave the team?

AM: I don't think the situations are the same. Chuck's problem was much more personal, not a question of talent. For Chuck, it was about choices. Chuck could have been one of the greatest running backs in the history of the NFL, but his decisions off the field prevented that from happening.

I don't think Ricky Williams has half the ability that Chuck Muncie had. I don't think Ricky Williams is that great of a player. He's a good player but not great. He really does give you a lot of effort and runs hard, but in this league he's not going to break long runs *and* take a big pounding.

I think the Saints felt that Ricky was going to depreciate and be gone pretty fast. That's why they traded him, to get some value for him while they still could. They really weren't unhappy with his play. Now I understand he was late a lot. That was one of Chuck's problems, too.

Bert Jones had Roger Carr; Roger Staubach had Drew Pearson; Ron Jaworski had Harold Carmichael. With which receiver did you have the best on-field chemistry?

AM: The first receiver I really connected with was Danny Abramowicz, who was a really outstanding player. He came to New Orleans a few years before I did. He led the league in receiving in 1969, catching passes from Billy Kilmer. Excellent route runner…not very fast…super determination and toughness…very cagey. Danny and I really clicked. He used all kind of tricks to get open and get behind faster cornerbacks. He was as tough as they came and loved catching passes. He didn't want even one ball to get away.

By 1973, Abramowicz had moved on to San Francisco and the Saints' passing game was without a star receiver for several seasons. Then in 1978, a flashy rookie from Florida joined the team and began lighting up the Superdome with his speed and moves. What are your memories of number 89, Wes Chandler?

AM: Wes was the most athletic receiver that I ever played with. He wasn't as fast as people thought, but he could jump, catch and run great routes. He was everything a quarterback could want. I really enjoyed playing with Wes. To this day, I still can't figure out why Bum traded him to San Diego. Bum said he didn't like his attitude, but Wes wasn't the first receiver to pout a little bit when he doesn't catch a couple balls. That's kinda the nature of receivers, you know? When you don't throw to them for a quarter or a half, well, they get moody. With all the talent we had on offense, I guess we just didn't have enough footballs to keep Wes happy.

For many years the Saints operated with a leaky offensive line. In which season do you feel you had your best offensive line combination?

AM: Probably in 1979. We had traded for Conrad Dobler, who had been with St. Louis. Conrad was pretty beat up by the time he came to us. St. Louis felt he was over the hill, but his presence made a difference right away. Unfortunately, he blew out his knee in '78, but he came back and played in '79.

Conrad was a physical wreck, but he made everybody else around him play good. He had a "No Sack" philosophy, that they should never be allowed. He played on some great lines in St. Louis that didn't give up sacks. That '75 Cardinals team gave up only six. Hell, I'd get that in a single half! Conrad really did make an impact on our young linemen with his leadership and presence. We went from around 40 sacks in 1978 to 17 the next year.

I already had some good backs and receivers, but in '79 the line did its part and we were a very productive offense that year. We got some respect that year. We were getting people open. We were staying on schedule, not coming up on 3rd-and-twelve as much.

In terms of opponents, was there a pass rusher who was particularly rough on you?

AM: When you play a long time on one team, you tend to remember your division opponents because you play them so much. In my first year, Deacon Jones and Merlin Olsen were still with the Rams. Deacon was everything they said he was. He might have been a little older and rested a few plays, but when he wanted to bring it, he could bring it. He was a *faa-ast* man, and that headslap was the real deal. Merlin was a little older, too, but you still saw the greatness there…the consistency…taking on blockers…stopping the run….

Of course, the guy I played against the most, who came into the league the same time I did, was Jack Youngblood. I told Jack that when he got into the Hall of Fame I really should be his presenter. He wouldn't have gotten in without having me to sack.

San Francisco also had a great defense in my early years. They had two ends named Tommy Hart and Cedric Hardman – outstanding rushers, both of them. That was Dick Nolan's Flex defense. Another guy who caused a lot of problems for us was Tommy Nobis of the Falcons. I have no idea why he isn't in the Hall of Fame.

Who was the toughest cornerback you had to throw against?

AM: Two of them come to mind. There was a great cornerback in Atlanta named Kenny Reaves - big, strong and mean, a very good player. But I'd have to say that Jimmy Johnson of the 49ers was the best. He was so clever and so experienced. I was a young player and had to be really careful going up against him. He'd bait you a little bit, play off the receiver and get you looking his way. He was a real pro. Mel Renfro was like that, too. If you complete one on those kind of guys, you'd better start working on somebody else. Don't come back to them again, at least not right away.

Notify The Vatican! A Miracle in New Orleans!

"Good afternoon," said the stewardess over the intercom last Saturday as the New Orleans Saints' charter prepared to take off for Denver. "We'd like to welcome aboard the leaders of the NFC West." At this unexpected greeting, a gasp was heard from the back of the plane – the sort of amazed, self-congratulatory noise one makes when he manages to balance his checkbook for the first time. Small wonder. For the first time in history, the Saints were sole leaders of the NFC West.

That's right folks, the New Orleans Saints, Pete Rozelle's entry in *Ted Mack's Original Amateur Hour*, a team that until a few weeks ago hadn't led the NFL in anything except squandered first draft choices, fired head coaches and consecutive losing seasons, 12. Looking at it another way, the Saints had a perfect record – 12 losing seasons in their 12 NFL seasons. Now, as they flew to Denver, the Saints sported a 5-4 record and a surprising one-game lead over the once-mighty Los Angeles Rams.

This state of affairs seemed highly unlikely a month ago. At that time, the Saints were 2-4 and had just been shellacked 35-17 by the Rams in the Superdome. Rumors surfaced that Coach Dick Nolan's job was in jeopardy. Critics were lambasting Nolan's flex defense, which was allowing more than 27 points a game. One candidate for Louisiana state representative promised that, if elected, he would ban the Flex [defense]. Yes, it was business as usual in New Orleans.

Then, abruptly, the Saints did an about-face. Yielding a total of just four touchdowns, they rattled off three straight victories, equaling their longest winning streak ever. Meanwhile, the Rams lost three straight. New Orleans took sole possession of first place two weeks ago in Washington, when it upset the Redskins 14-10 by stopping them 18 times without a score in goal-to-go situations. That night 3,000 people showed up at Moissant Airport to welcome the Saints home. "They were chanting, 'Dee-fense, Dee-fense,'" says safety Tommy Myers. "A few weeks earlier they could have dropped us all in the Mississippi without a lick of remorse."

And so, suddenly, New Orleans was faced Sunday with a Big Game, a showdown between the NFC West leader and the AFC West co-leader. As quarterback Archie Manning put it, "The only big games we used to have was when your grandmother came to see you play."

– Joe Marshall, *Sports Illustrated*, November 12, 1979. **Reprinted with permission.**

Under Dick Nolan, the Saints had two respectable seasons, going 7-9 then 8-8, the best two-year stretch in team history. 1980 was full of expectations but then the team collapsed to 1-15. What were the main reasons for that embarrassing slide?

AM: I think *that* may have been drugs. Expectations were high for us going into that season. During the first part of the season we were losing but we weren't getting killed. We were getting beat in overtime. We blocked a punt against Miami that set us up to score on the last play of the game, and they called offensive interference on the touchdown pass. All of a sudden, we couldn't win a game and the rats jumped ship. We had some talent but we didn't have much character. That's when the Don Reese thing started and cocaine was prevalent. You're losing, going 0-5…then 0-6…0-7. Then the rats jumped ship. It was just a total meltdown.

Your last coach in New Orleans was Bum Phillips, who came to the Saints after six successful years with the Houston Oilers. What were your initial thoughts about his taking over the team?

AM: Bum was a really hot coach in Houston for some time. But in his last year there he really fell off. They kinda mortgaged that team to win a Super Bowl – bringing over Kenny Stabler and Jack Tatum, those kind of things. When they didn't, the team suddenly got real old and they didn't have any more draft choices. It had become a mess and he got fired. He probably wanted to get fired because he knew he could come over to New Orleans and coach the Saints. I had heard good things about Bum, that all his players liked him.

Did you feel that Phillips was the right coach for the Saints at the time?

AM: In those days, Bum had a pretty good approach to the game, and it really worked in Houston for a number of years. It was a little looser atmosphere, probably more fun on a day-to-day basis.

Basically, Bum's approach was, "Look, I don't have a lot of rules and regulations, but I expect you to practice hard and I expect you to play real hard. Otherwise, just behave yourself and go on about your business." In that era, a lot of players responded to that style in a real positive way. Look no further than what the Oilers did under Bum. You know, if the Steelers hadn't been so good, Houston would have gone to a couple of Super Bowls.

But I think what happens is that you get about five or six players who will take advantage of that looseness. They don't even have to be your best players. Then the whole thing becomes contagious, especially among some of the younger guys. When that happens it can tear the team down, and I think that's what happened in Houston.

I got traded to the Oilers two years after Bum left there and that team was a mess. Drugs were more prevalent in the league then, and there was a lot of that in Houston. You get a few bad apples and they can tear the whole thing down.

Did Phillips promote that type of loose atmosphere when he came to New Orleans?

AM: Ol' Bum was kinda cagey. He was a good, common sense guy…clever…funny. But I think Bum felt he had some pretty good job security in New Orleans, that he knew it was going to be his last coaching job. Like I said before, it was different back then. Not many coaches got fired after one or two years on the job. I honestly believe that Bum wanted to get things started in the right direction, win some games and build some momentum, then move into the general manager's job and let his son, Wade, become the head coach.

We had a decent team during Bum's first year with the Saints (1981). At midseason we were close to .500 and playing pretty decent football, a good start. But then things appeared to change over the second half of the season. I'm not saying that we tried to lose, but basically we just shut it down for the rest of the year. There wasn't any pressure on us to win games. It seemed like there was no pressure on us to make the playoffs. The attitude was more like, "We're building something here. We can take our time." I think Bum wanted to wait until the next year before making a run. Bring in some new players, get rid of some old players – namely me.

Were his training camps run on the loose side as well?

AM: [Laughing] Well, they weren't nearly as tough as some of the ones I had been through before. It was almost like a country club atmosphere in some respects. Things were pretty loose. I don't think Bum thought very much about training camps, probably because he didn't want to wear his team out before the season started.

A lot of folks used to stop by our camp at the end of the day. We'd finish up our 9:00 meeting, and people we used to refer to as FOB – Friends of Bum – would show up. Most of them were country music stars. He'd hand out the t-shirts and shorts and jerseys and such, and then by 9:30 they'd get to *pickin' and a grinnin'*. It was almost like a nightly hoedown. There weren't too many camps that didn't finished up each day with the *pickin' and a grinnin'*.

When did you first get the impression that Phillips wanted to go in a different direction at quarterback?

AM: I knew early on that Bum really didn't want me to be his quarterback, that he wanted somebody else. I don't know why. I worked hard for him, but he just didn't take to me as a player. We never had a cross word or any kind of controversy. I didn't want to get traded. I had been here twelve years and I didn't want to leave. New Orleans was my home. I think I had become part of New Orleans and New Orleans part of me.

But some guys I knew told me, "Bum came to town, and you were the guy that was doing all the commercials. He didn't like that. Bum wanted to do all the commercials." I don't know if that was the reason why he traded me. Years later I told him, "I forgive you for trading me, but I'll never forgive you for trading me to Houston." He knew how bad things were over there. The Oilers were a mess.

How did you find out you had been traded to Houston, and what was your initial reaction?

AM: Officially Bum told me, but I knew before that. Some people in Houston who were involved in the trade told me about it. My reaction was mixed. As a player you don't want to be somewhere where you're not wanted. That's one side of it. The other side is that I had been here twelve years and I didn't want to leave. I always had a vision of playing my entire career in one place. We were coming off an opening day loss to St. Louis and that Monday the rumors started. I heard things all week. Then on Friday morning Bum told me I was gone.

Is it possible a change of scenery was good for you by that time in your career?

AM: Well, a change of scenery is not bad, but I had put in so many years here during the tough times that I wanted to be there when things got better. I really didn't want to leave, but I could see what was happening. Bum had brought Kenny Stabler over from Houston, so the Oilers were a little thin at that position. Their remaining quarterbacks were Gifford Nielsen and a rookie from West Virginia named Oliver Luck, so they needed some help. I knew their coach Eddie Biles, so I could see how sending me to Houston made sense.

To be honest, in Bum's offense the quarterback really wasn't the key guy. He wanted somebody who was willing to hand off the ball on first and second down, then try to complete a pass if it got to be third down.

Archie Manning's Five Worst Defeats (also unauthorized)

5) November 9, 1975 – Raiders 48, Saints 10: "We'd done a pretty good number on Atlanta the week before," says Manning. "That was Ernie Hefferle's first game as coach and he'd given us a pep talk that gave everybody chills. [DT] Derland Moore had tears in his eyes," and the Saints won, 23-7.

After their disastrous, first-ever visit to Oakland, the whole New Orleans team was welling up. The Raiders, headed toward a third consecutive AFC title game, set a club record for first downs (34) and piled on 523 yards of heavy-duty offense in this wipeout. Nine different Raiders carried the ball on the day; nine different had catches.

The Saints operated in Oakland territory only twice, their lone highlight coming on a nifty 32-yard touchdown catch by 6'5" wide receiver Joel Parker.

"Call it what it was," said Raiders coach John Madden afterwards. "An easy game."

4) October 21, 1973 – 49ers 40, Saints 0: First, a reminder this was still a 0-0 struggle with three minutes to play in the half. The Saints were screwing with 49ers quarterback Steve Spurrier's reads and had the whole 'Frisco operation out of whack. Spurrier, who'd thrown for 320 yards a week earlier against Minnesota, was now a measly 5 of 13 for 23 yards. Coach Dick Nolan then turned to his 17-year vet, John Brodie, who wasted no time pulling out the zips.

Zip! a sideline strike to Danny Abramowicz goes for 54 yards...Zip! Another to Abramowicz becomes a 23-yard score...Zip! Vic Washington's catch moves Frisco down to the one...zip...zip...zip.

Nine Brodie zips in all, only one misfire. By the end of the third quarter it was 31-0.

Even third-stringer Joe Reed found the zip code, firing a 34-yard touchdown to his big tight end, Ted Kwalick.

The Saints? Their offense earned one first down. They got another after a 49ers personal foul. Manning went to the bench as hope faded, then his backup Bobby Scott got tackled for a safety. They did, however, manage one zip of their own on the day.

The one posted on the scoreboard.

3) December 3, 1979 – Raiders 42, Saints 35: A strong qualifier because the stakes going into this one were higher than they'd ever been in New Orleans. The Saints were 7-6 and in their first December playoff hunt. The assignment was easily understood – win their final three games and capture the NFC West title. The remaining schedule bared vicious teeth, with home games against Oakland and San Diego and a season-ender at division rival Los Angeles. Only smart, cracking football would get them through it.

First up, the Raiders. "And we were rolling that night," says Manning. "Muncie was running wild (128 yards on 21 carries), and I was finding my receivers. The line was doing its job." Four second-quarter touchdowns had the Raiders reeling and behind, 28-14.

The Saints padded their lead when linebacker Ken Bordelon snagged a floater from Oakland QB Ken Stabler and ran it back for the score. 35-14, with less than nine minutes remained in the third quarter. Phase One of the gauntlet seemed to be behind them.

"What were you thinking at that point, Snake?" Stabler was asked.

"I was thinking it was time to get something going," he said.

So the Saints kicked it back to Oakland, and nightmarish things began to happen for the home team. Defenders suddenly couldn't cover and Raiders were getting open. Tackles were missed. Children began crying.

Stabler *was* getting something going, and the result was a flurry of Raider touchdowns. With 3:19 to play, a short pass to Cliff Branch covered 66 spectacular yards and tied the game.

"We played five different defensive coverages against that guy," said Saints free safety Tommy Myers. "Stabler finds the second receiver like nobody I've ever seen...the best quarterback in the game."

Then Chuck Muncie fumbled the ball back to the Raiders. Another Stabler-to-Branch connection went to the endzone and it was over for New Orleans. So much for running the table and the playoffs.

"Even at 35-14 I never felt comfortable," said Manning afterwards. "Oakland is a real capable bunch."

And in a Monday night meltdown at the Superdome, with their season on the line, the Saints were a bunch of incapables.

2) December 11, 1977 – Buccaneers 33, Saints 14: Prior to the game, Manning flipped a comment to the press that "it would be a disgrace" to lose Tampa Bay. It was an honest remark.

The Buccaneers were a floundering crew. They'd scored just 63 points all season and were still looking for their first victory as a franchise; the record books showed a history of zero and 26. Their only bright spot was an overachieving defense that would eventually finish 13th in the league. Still, Manning's remark pissed off many of the Bucs.

"He's no winner," snapped linebacker David Lewis. "Manning's been hurt most of his career. Who's he to pop off like that?"

"A cheap shot," coach John McKay called it.

The Saints of '77, meanwhile, were masters of blowing the tight game. Among their nine losses were 4-pointers to Green Bay and Detroit, a 7-pointer to the Rams, and a pair of 3-pointers against San Francisco. But the Saints were expected to handle Tampa Bay. Jimmy "The Greek" pegged them as 11-point favorites. Vegas was begging for Buccaneer money.

When it was over, however, the Bucs defense had roared. It scored three touchdowns and allowed only two. It forced seven turnovers and boasted five sacks. Only 40,000 Saints fans came out to see the humiliation.

Tampa Bay quarterback Gary Huff had a meager but efficient day (7 of 9 for 96 yards) and got the win. He wore a big smile. In the winner's lockerroom the journeyman lit up a petrified victory cigar. "I've been carrying these so long," he said, "they're stale."

New Orleans coach Hank Stram had an interesting quote afterwards: "We were strangled by the trauma," he said. I'm still not sure what he meant by that.

1) September 16, 1973 – Falcons 62, Saints 7: An event foretold centuries before in the writings of an ancient Trappist mystic:

> *'Tween Fleur de Lis and fowl of prey, a struggle one shall rue*
> *Tho' without vice, a sinner's price of seven and sixty-two*

In France, the Court of Louis XIV shuddered. A chilling prediction of the monarchy's collapse? 762 years of pestilence? A sudden attack by a large bird?

For years theologians and scholars were puzzled by its hidden message. Then, after the gun sounded at Tulane Stadium on this day, the world finally understood the true meaning – it was the Trappists' "Five-Star Play of the Week," the world's first attempt at long-range pro football handicapping. (Actually, I thought that verse up during church. But wasn't it a better story than going into all the ugly details behind this massacre?)

124

The *New Orleans Times-Picayune* called them the "Sandlot Saints" and "alleged pros." Coach John North called his team's eight turnovers – five of them Manning interceptions – an "embarrassment," then slammed his shirt into his locker. The refs should've called the whole thing off and sent everyone home.

The first fifteen minutes were scoreless, uneventful, except for a scuffle between receiver Jubilee Dunbar and Atlanta's Clarence Ellis. ("He tried to poke inside my helmet with his finger," explained Jubilee, "so I bit it.") Both were ejected.

Then the Atlanta attack erupted and the Saints offered no resistance. QB Dick Shiner went 13 of 15 with three scores, a career day. The Falcons gathered 32 first downs. Their 62 points is still the team record, and they left 17 more on the table (a TD pass to Ken Burrow was called back on a penalty; Shiner fumbled at the Saints' 1-yard line; and Nick Mike-Mayer blew a short field goal).

The few die-hards that puzzlingly stayed booed when it was over. Then they cheered when Tulane came on the field to practice.

"Needless to say, a game I've tried very hard to forget," says Manning.

The German philosopher Nietzsche once said, "That which doesn't kill me can only make me stronger." Were you in any way a stronger person after your difficult career in New Orleans?

AM: Most people who have a life in sports learn to deal with adversity and low times, and in New Orleans we definitely had a lot of experience with that. More than anything, the whole experience taught me a lot about people. I dealt with so many of them. Just watching them – how they react to tough times or adversity or losing games – I was able to learn things about human character. Some people are quitters or complainers or become discouraged and lose their focus. Others keep plugging away, trying to find ways to overcome obstacles, encouraging and motivating people around them. I saw all types during my days with the Saints.

There were four of us that went through it together. Tommy Myers, a safety who joined the team a year after I did, was one. Joe Federspiel, our middle linebacker, was another. And then there was my backup quarterback and roommate, Bobby Scott, who I spent more time with than anyone during my professional career. There was some sort of bond between the four of us because we were on the team for a long time and shared a lot of the same experiences.

There is a different kind of bond that's created during losing times, which I believe is just as strong as one that's forged while you're winning. I was on a successful team in college, so I can make that comparison. In New Orleans, we didn't experience a lot of the happy times or good times, maybe a lot of the things we wanted to forget. A lot of your postgames aren't celebrations. They're more like mournings – wakes, if you will. But you go through them together. You depend on one another, and there's still a bond there.

— 9 —
Larry Little, Guard
San Diego Chargers (1967-68); Miami Dolphins (1969-80)
May 8, 2000

Remember the big-headline defections of running backs Larry Csonka and Jim Kiick and WR Paul Warfield to the WFL, the ones that blindsided the Miami Dolphins in March of 1974? Coach Don Shula's team was only two months removed from its second straight Super Bowl title when an impending "dead end" sign was pounded into the path of his gathering Miami dynasty. Their teammates felt mixed emotions.

"Looking back, their leaving was more of a disappointment than anything else," recalled linebacker Nick Buoniconti. "We were happy for them, but at the same time we knew that without those guys there was no way we were going back to a Super Bowl."

Yet by September of that year, the Dolphins were back to winning games and it was business as usual at the Orange Bowl. An 11-3 record earned Miami its fourth straight AFC East crown and a chance for a last-hurrah championship before Shula & Co. had to begin their offensive rebuild. On came the anxious Oakland Raiders and the AFC Playoffs. An awkward, shot-put heave by quarterback Kenny Stabler to tailback Clarence Davis in the final moments of that game became the kill shot that toppled the Miami empire.

"If we played them ten times, we'd have beaten them seven or eight," QB Bob Griese said years later, a lingering sadness still present in his voice. "Look what it took for them to stop us… on their home field… in front of their home fans. We might well have won a third straight championship had it not been for that fluke play."

The clock on the Oakland Coliseum scoreboard read zero, then Csonka and Kiick – a tandem that, despite nagging injuries, had combined for 1023 yards and 10 touchdowns in '74 – were gone. Gone was Warfield, whose 20 yds/catch average helped clear the deep seams and dissuaded defenses from overloading the line. Warfield, an eleven-year vet, would be the easiest to replace, as talented youngsters Freddie Solomon and Nat Moore were being primed to fill that void.

Csonka and Kiick, however, were a very different matter.

As a team, Miami had rushed for 2,191 yards in 1974 – fourth best in the league. But as the '75 preseason finally approached, it was more than unclear from where those steady ground gains were going to come.

"We had some good running backs in camp that year, but nobody close to what Zonk could do for us," said guard Larry Little. "There was no longer that hammer in the backfield. But Shula told us we were going to run the ball with the players we had, and it was up to the offensive line to get it done. So we just put our pads back on and went to work."

As the players were sorted out and camp drew to a close, these are the names that Shula, with fingers tightly crossed, plugged into his patchwork backfield:

Mercury Morris – A high-traction speedster with 1000-yard potential, Morris was coming off an injury-plagued '74 and was no longer a Shula favorite. Issues with attitude, but still the purest talent of the lot.

Don Nottingham – The "Human Bowling Ball" came to Miami in a '73 trade with Baltimore for backup runner Hubert Ginn. Averaged over 4.1 yds/carry in his first two seasons with the Dolphins,

126

mainly in spot duty for Csonka. Dependable, low center of gravity. Most of his work found between the tackles.

Benny Malone – Shula hoped this injury-prone, bow-legged racer from Arizona State would supplant Morris as the speed portion of his ground attack. Excellent moves and balance, but not the most trustworthy hands when on pass patterns. Second leading gainer in '74 behind Csonka with 479 yards.

Norm Bulaich – A new face in Dolphins camp. A bigger version of Nottingham, his best season came with the '71 Colts (741 yards, 4.9/carry, 10 TDs). Underused in previous two years with Eagles. Worth Shula's gamble for only a future middle-round draft pick.

Hubert Ginn – Former Dolphin who returned as a free agent after a failed stint with Colts. Limited skills at RB, but special teams prowess kept him in the league for nine years.

Stan Winfrey – Second-round draft pick from Arkansas State. Along with WR Freddie Solomon, the only skill position rookies to win spots on the Miami offense. Projected as special teamer with some return duties.

By season's end, what resulted was something close to a minor miracle in the football annals. Shula prodded and coaxed and squeezed his ugly duckling backfield until 2,500 yards worth of tread had worn off – the third highest total in franchise history. Morris led the charge with 875 yards on 219 carries, his biggest workload since joining the team five years earlier. The Bulaich/Nottingham fullback tandem was good for another 1,027 yards and 17 rushing touchdowns. Ginn, Malone and a few others added the rest. And so the '75 Dolphins, minus three of their top offensive weapons, somehow scratched back to the top of the AFC East that year, tying Baltimore at 10-4. The playoffs were missed because of two losses to the Colts, but overall the season was very much a thumbs-up success.

However, the real story behind this ground effort was the rampaging Miami offensive line, which displayed perhaps the most dominating campaign in team history. Remember the names? Bob Kuechenberg, Wayne Moore, Jim Langer, Norm Evans, Larry Little – former castoffs and free agents to the man. The Frankenstein monster in a chinstrap. But by the mid-1970s, they had become the best in the business under offensive line coach Monte Clark.

"Just get the snap count right and make a clean exchange," Clark told his men. "It's all about precision. Then we'll move the pile and clear the debris."

Some opposing coaches weren't watching the '75 Dolphins' ground campaign in silent disbelief. "What else would you expect from a Don Shula team?" said former New England Patriots head coach Chuck Fairbanks, whose club had surrendered 409 rushing yards in two meetings with Miami that year. "Csonka or Nottingham, Morris or Malone? I don't think it really matters who carries the ball for Miami considering the way that line performs. Such a controlled force…they're strong, they're very quick, and their execution is almost perfect."

Little and Kuechenberg, feeling underpaid, had also flirted with WFL money, but this time team owner Joe Robbie opened up the checkbook and made sure no other Dolphins swam away. "It's one thing having to replace a running back who relies mainly on instincts and speed," explained Shula. "There are enough good runners available that you at least stay productive. But once you start pulling parts out of the offensive line, shifting the chemistry, it's not long before the whole thing can come apart."

• •

Watching Larry Little pull from his right guard position to lead the Miami sweep was like watching the eruption of a crazed rodeo bull during its first few seconds of fury. The snap to the quarterback and the gate is flung open. Then witness all hell breaking loose. In either case, the typical result was an adversary flattened on the ground.

As an undrafted free agent out of tiny Bethune-Cookman College, Little's first pro exposure came in supporting the wide-open downfield attack of Sid Gillman's San Diego Chargers, where lockdown pass protection was the order of the day. Give quarterback John Hadl time to find those wideouts, Lance

Alworth and Gary Garrison, streaking downfield, or big TE Willie Frazier knifing behind the linebackers. Retreating, defensive footwork. Buying time for the passer.

"Sid wanted to throw the ball every down," says Little, "and he wasn't going to stand for a leaky offensive line, one that allowed a lot of pressure." A trade to Miami in 1969 eventually and Shula's arrival a year later quickly rearranged this mindset for Little.

"When Shula came to the Dolphins," he says, "he made it very clear we were going to be a heavy running team. 'Get the weight off. I want quick linemen who can pull and trap and sweep,' he told me. That turned my career around. I was an average player at that point. I'm not sure I would have developed much further playing at a heavier weight in a pass-oriented offense."

Instead of keeping Hadl off his back, Little was now clearing the way for an offense that, from 1972 to '75, was running the ball an arrogant 68-percent of the time. "You could see it in Larry's eyes, especially on a sweep, that nobody was going to stop him," said Kiick, "that he was in control of the line of scrimmage. Our whole line was. It got to the point, particularly during the '72 season, that we knew nobody could stop our running game. During those years we ran over Pittsburgh, Minnesota, Dallas, Oakland, Washington. There was nobody left. Maybe a concrete wall."

Shula and his drill sergeant coaching staff transformed Little from a pudgy pass blocker into a fiery, repeat Pro Bowler and the Dolphins into two-time world champions. Years drifted by, then the names began lining up for the Hall of Fame. First came Warfield in '83, then Csonka four years later. Langer and Griese soon followed. Finally, in 1993, Miami's number 66 was summoned.

For the first time since those old days in San Diego, Larry Little didn't have to lead the way.

• • •

Dave Anderson of Sport *magazine wrote in 1974, "The best scout in the NFL is a guy named Nobody; against all odds, Nobody drafted Larry Little and Manny Fernandez."*

Fernandez anchored a sturdy defensive front wall on three Miami Super Bowl teams, while you were named All-Pro six times and played your way into the Pro Football Hall of Fame. What was it that these AFL and NFL scouts failed to see in young Larry Little out of Bethune-Cookman College?

LL: I think it was because the type of school I went to. Bethune-Cookman was a small, all-black school in Daytona Beach, Florida. Only two other guys before me ever played in the NFL from that school. A lot of people talked about my lack of height. But before the draft, I received a telegraph from the Raiders and the Rams, both saying they were going to draft me.

On the day of the draft, I stayed around in the school dormitory, not letting anybody use the phone in the hallway, waiting for a phone call that never came. It was disappointing. I didn't eat all day. I don't think I even went to class that day. At that time the draft was going like twenty-some rounds. I was very upset that nobody picked me, but I said to myself, "If I have the opportunity to play as a free agent, I'm going to prove a lot of people wrong."

After being courted by Baltimore, Miami and San Diego, you signed with the Chargers in 1967. Why San Diego?

LL: The reason I signed with the Chargers was because of a guy named Bud Asher, who hung around the school a lot and was a part-time scout for the Chargers. He was right there with the contract that day. The Colts, when they called, didn't offer me any kind of a bonus. I was trying to milk whoever I could for as much as I could get. San Diego had the best offer that day, so I thought I had better sign now because I wasn't getting a whole lot of other phone calls as a free agent. The best I could get was that $750 up front.

The next day [Miami GM] Joe Thomas from the Dolphins called me and asked me how I would like to play in my hometown. I said, "Joe, I would've loved to play in Miami, but I signed with the Chargers yesterday. But by the way, how much of a bonus were you going to give me anyway?" He said five hundred dollars. I said, "Well, I already beat that by $250."

After sizing up the other rookies, veterans and free agents on the team, did you recognize that you had the ability to be a successful player in the AFL?

LL: Sid Gillman, the Chargers' head coach, would bring in all free agents a week before the drafted rookies were scheduled to report. I thought that all the rookies were going to come in together. Then I read a newspaper article that said something like, "Sid Gillman has brought in a bunch of free agents again. Maybe only one or two will be around when the drafted rookies come in." I took it as an insult that I wasn't considered to be good enough to come in with the other rookies.

I signed as a defensive lineman and was expecting to play defense. But during that first week we didn't even have enough linemen to scrimmage. We were out there in shorts and shoulder pads running our "forties," and I ran a 4.9 forty. I was weighing 273-lbs at the time, and they were impressed with my speed. I had really worked out hard before coming to camp. I had never worked out so hard in my life, but I was determined not to come back home. I had taken everything I owned with me because I wasn't planning on coming back home. I had talked so much trash before I left – saying I was going to make the team – that I probably wouldn't have come back home had I not made it [laughing]."

We were in camp going half line because we didn't have that many linemen. One time we would be on offense, the next time on defense. The next week the rookies came in. What helped me was that I had gotten some good early coaching before the drafted guys came in. That gave me a leg-up on them.

A former college teammate of mine went with me out to San Diego because the team had also signed him. His name was John Knight, a running back. We had never flown on an airplane before, and we were both scared of that. We got out there and introduced ourselves to the rest of the players. I would say, "Hi. I'm Larry Little from Bethune-Cookman College." Guys would snicker at that, saying, "Where's that? What kind of school is that?" That ticked me off! When we finally put the pads on, we would run one-on-one blocking drills and after I finished blocking my man I would jump on him and start fighting him. I wanted the coaches to say, "This guy is a wildman! We've got to look at him twice."

Well, during camp they came up with the brilliant idea that I was fast enough to be a fullback. I was up to about 280 pounds by then. I thought they moved me there so they had a reason to cut me. But then Joe Madreaux, who was the offensive line coach at the time, asked Sid Gillman if he could have me for the offensive line. I didn't know how good I would be on the offensive line. I had practiced it in college but hadn't played there in over a year.

What also helped me was that I played in a pro-style system at Bethune-Cookman. My college coach, Jack McClairen, had played with the Pittsburgh Steelers. He was the first player from Bethune-Cookman to play in the NFL. So all the things we were now doing in the pros, I had done in college. Since I came from a small school, the level of competition may not have been as good, but I had experience at doing pro-style things. We threw the ball a lot, so I was experienced at pass blocking. When the drafted rookies came in, they moved me to guard and things started going pretty good for me. I didn't make the team at first. They put me on the cab squad.

A lot of my college teammates had gone off to play minor league football with a team called the Wheeling Ironmen. Sid called and told me he was going to give me $250 a week to be on the cab squad. He was known for being cheap. I said, "I can't stay here for that. I could go to Wheeling and make more money playing semi-pro!" I told him I would stay for three-fourths of my contract. Joe talked Sid into giving it to me because Joe liked me.

I stayed on the cab squad for four games then a guy who was playing ahead of me, Ed Mitchell, was cut. He'd gotten heavy during the off-season and wasn't the same player anymore. It was a shame because he really helped me out that first year. He was my mentor. Anyway, they cut him and activated me because I could play special teams. But I only played in about four games that first year.

The next season I started six games. But then they started fooling with my contract, which called for a bonus if I started seven out of the 14 games. They would start somebody else then quickly bring me into the game afterwards, just to keep from giving me that bonus. I did play a lot that second year, mostly at left guard because Walt Sweeney was a stalwart on the right side.

In describing the offensive line, one of the best analogies I've ever heard came from the Raiders' Gene Upshaw. "I've compared offensive linemen to the story of Paul Revere," he said. "After Paul Revere rode through town, everybody said what a great job he did. But no one ever talked about the horse. I know how Paul Revere's horse felt." What was it like becoming one of the horses?

LL: It wasn't that different because I had played both ways in college until my senior year. That was the year the new ruling came out saying you could only play one way so I moved to defense. We only had about 45 or 50 guys on the team, so sometimes I had to practice on offense if the starters had any injuries. I was quick. I could run and I had pretty good strength, too, although I'd never lifted weights. So the transition back to offense wasn't that difficult for me.

What about the footwork necessary to play offensive line? Were you initially quick enough?

LL: Yes, I was. Joe Madreaux really worked with me in learning to pull to the left. I could pull to the right okay, but I had difficulty pulling to the left. Joe would get me before practice and keep me after practice. I used to hide from him in the sauna. I'd hear him calling, "*Lar-ree! Lar-ree! Lar-ree!*" and I would hide. The players always told him where I was. He'd yell, "Get your ass outta there!" Joe was a real comical guy. He was about 5'4". His neck was always going back because he had to look up at all the big linemen he was coaching.

You once said, "I demanded respect on the football field." How?

LL: By trying to hit my opponent as hard as I could. I used to think some of those defensive backs were crazy. When I was leading the sweep, a lot of these guys would try to take me on, instead of trying to avoid me and make the play. I would hit them, then I'd tell their coaches to come get them out of the game. Especially a guy who played for the Jets named Steve Tannen. I think I knocked him out about three or four times every game we played them. He'd keep coming at me and I'd knock him out and say to his teammates, "Come and get him! Don't keep bringing that crap in here on me!"

Did you have had mixed emotions about your trade to Miami in the summer of 1969? Your playing time with the Chargers had been steadily increasing, then suddenly you were sent to a team that was two years out of expansion and struggling under head coach George Wilson.

LL: What I think really initiated that trade – and a lot of people don't know this – was that I met Larry Csonka at a Buick dealership one day. I had taken my car down there for service. A guy introduced him to me. "I need some linemen with your size down here in Miami with me," he said. I didn't think much of it, but then the next thing you know I was traded to Miami. Csonka likes to say that he was the one that made the trade.

I really didn't want to play for the Dolphins because they were a losing team. I thought we had a shot at a championship with the Chargers they really had a lot of talented football players – Lance Alworth, Gary Garrison, Paul Lowe, Ron Mix, Walt Sweeney. We had some talent! But I didn't really know that much about the Miami Dolphins. Although they were from my hometown, I didn't pay that much attention to them.

My family was happy I was traded because they could see me a lot more on television. Almost immediately I was competing for a starting position. My first game with the Dolphins was a preseason game against the Bears, and Dick Butkus and I got into a fight. We both got thrown out of that game. I had said to myself, "I know this is the great Dick Butkus but I'm not going to let him beat me, especially here with all my buddies in the stands." I hurt my knee the next week against Philadelphia and missed the rest of the preseason. But then Freddie Woodson, their starting guard, ruptured his spleen in the first game of the year and that put me in the starting lineup for good.

> When Csonka, Kiick or Mercury Morris runs inside, 28-year old Larry [Big Man] Little is often lost in the pileup, as all guards are. But when they run outside, he is obvious. He is also frightening. He is out there in front of them, his legs churning, his eyes peering through his facemask at a linebacker or a cornerback who wishes he were anywhere else.
>
> Once an agile 195-pound cornerback, Charley Ford of the Chicago Bears, tried to pile up a sweep. Big Man came down on Ford as if Little were a 265-pound flatiron. Csonka rumbled for a first down. "You can't get lower than me," Big Man told the flattened cornerback.
>
> **– Dave Anderson, *Sport* magazine, January 1974**
>
> The refinements [to Little's technique] were added by Monte Clark. Little had a habit of looking around as he pulled on a sweep, worrying about blitzing linebackers or crashing safetymen. All Clark wanted Little to be concerned with was blasting the cornerback. Other people would take care of the crashers. One day, Clark yelled at him, "Larry, you look around again and you'll turn into a pillar of salt!" This got his attention. Clark spent five minutes explaining about Lot's wife, and Little never looked around again.
>
> **- Steve Perkins and Bill Braucher, *The Miami Dolphins: Winning Them All***
> **Grosset & Dunlap (1973)**

Your first season in Miami was also George Wilson's last, as the team finished a disastrous 3-10-1. He was fired after the season.

LL: Things were not going well. There were no crowds in the stands. I think the biggest crowd we had in the Orange Bowl that year was a game they were calling "Victory Sunday." We were playing Buffalo, and neither team had won a game all season. A big crowd showed up, about 28,000, and we won the game. That was probably the highlight of the season because we just weren't very good. We did have a lot of young talent on that team, and the talent was getting ready to blossom. We had Csonka, Mercury Morris, Jim Kiick, Bob Griese, Manny Fernandez, and Dick Anderson. They had traded for Nick Buoniconti from New England. Then in 1970, Joe Thomas made the deal that brought Jake Scott out of Canada and wide receiver Paul Warfield from Cleveland. All of this occurred before they fired George and hired Don Shula as coach.

Do you feel that Wilson got a bad deal, considering how Miami's talent level had been improving?

LL: I wouldn't say that. I think that George did the best he could with what he had at that particular time. But when we heard Don Shula was coming, all of us were happy knowing we were getting a coach of his caliber. A lot of the ingredients for a winning team were already there. Shula's job was to refine it.

What was the most dramatic change that occurred when Shula took over the Dolphins in 1970?

LL: Hard work. We worked three times as hard with Shula. With George, training camp was almost like a country club. On a hot day, Wilson would come out on the field and say, "What the hell – it's too hot. Go get in the pool." We'd miss a day of practice. But with Shula? No way we'd ever think of missing a day of practice because it was too hot! When Shula got there, we didn't have any time to spend sitting in a swimming pool.

In 1970 the players were on strike. We didn't come to camp until a week before our first preseason game. I was happy about that. I hated training camp. I hated two-a-days. We finally came into camp on a Sunday and had a preseason game scheduled against Pittsburgh for the following Sunday in Jacksonville. Shula came in here and worked us four times a day. *Four times a day!* I had never been through anything like that in my life! I got through it, but in the process I pulled one of the biggest acting jobs in the history of professional football.

What happened?

LL: I passed out during practice, but it was all staged. The night before I'd told my roommate that I was going to do it. I said, "There is no way I'm going to let this man kill me on that field!" I pretended I had passed out, and then they took me off the field in a station wagon to the air-conditioned lockerroom. I had one eye open, peeking the whole time to see what they were going to do with me. They started packing me down in ice and I got way too cold. Then I had to think up a Plan B. So I jumped off the table, pretending I was having hallucinations just so I could knock the ice off of me. The whole time I knew everything that was going on around me. To this day, Don still doesn't know. I broke down and told him at a banquet once but he thought I was kidding.

Were there distinct differences in the way Sid Gillman's staff coached offensive line play versus the way it was taught under Shula?

LL: There wasn't a whole lot of difference. I learned a great deal from Joe Madreaux in San Diego. I think Joe really had a lot to do with me getting to where I got in my career. Shula brought in a young offensive line coach named Monte Clark, who had just retired from the Browns. Monte was the first one to get the most out of me in Miami. He was such a technician, a guy who was hung up on technique. He stressed the importance of repetition. Clark and Shula were sticklers for details. We would be in practice working on drills and Shula would be on the other side of the field. You didn't think he was watching you, but he was. He would holler out your name from one end of the field to another – "Hey, you're not doing that right!" The man was a perfectionist, and he embedded in our minds that we ought to strive for perfection.

When did you first realize that Shula was going to lift Miami to among the elite of the NFL?

LL: When he got to Miami. We all knew his reputation as a coach. We all listened to everything Shula had to say because we knew the man knew how to get it done. During our first meeting, Shula stressed all the positives, not the negatives. He didn't discuss what we had done before but what we were going to do now and in the future. What set him apart from other coaches was that he could get the most out of his football players. Bum Phillips once said about him, "He can take his'n and beat your'n, and take your'n and beat his'n." Shula could take anybody's team and be successful.

What did Shula contribute to your career that you couldn't have gotten from any other coach?

LL: I met him at his first press conference in Miami. He asked me my name and how much I weighed. I told him 285 pounds. I had gotten a little pudgy during the offseason and hadn't been working out as much. He looked at me and said, "Yeah? Okay." Well, when I got the letter telling me to report to training camp, it said he wanted me down to 265 pounds. He made me lose twenty pounds because it would make me quicker, more effective at what he wanted me to do.

Losing that weight really helped my career to blossom. I was in better condition. It allowed me to make positive contributions to our team, like pulling on sweeps and getting in front of speedy guys like Mercury Morris. He helped me believe in myself because he was always stressing that he was going to feature a lot of the offense behind me. It really helped my confidence, to the point where I said, "Hey, I must be pretty good!" By watching films, he could see I had a lot of talent and could be a good football player if I lost weight.

Let's talk about the first Shula year in Miami, the 1970 season. The Dolphins stormed out to four wins in five games. Then came a three-game losing streak, which included consecutive shutout defeats by Cleveland and Baltimore and a 24-17 loss to the pitiful Eagles. What was the team's mindset during that tailspin, and how was Shula able to prevent a complete breakdown?

LL: That losing streak was more the result of growing pains than anything else. Cleveland and Baltimore were more ready to play than we were and it showed. They were experienced playoff teams and had a lot of talent. We were still looking for our first winning season as an organization.

The Philadelphia game was really the low point of the season. They even had us shut out for the first three quarters of the game. Shula really came down hard on us, but not to the point where he broke our confidence. We scored 17 points in the fourth quarter, trying to come back against the Eagles. Then we went on a roll and won the last six games of the year and made the playoffs. Nobody shut out the Dolphins again until a decade later.

Your former teammate, linebacker Nick Buoniconti, has pointed to a defining moment for the Dolphins franchise. "The turning point of the Miami Dolphins – when they grew up – was 1971 when we played the Los Angeles Rams out in Los Angeles," he said. "The Rams had a heckuva good football team, and we were still 'part of the old AFL.' When we beat the Rams out there, every player, to a man, turned around to another one and said, 'You know something? I think we've arrived.'" Do you share that same memory?

LL: I remember Jim Murray of *The Los Angeles Times* wrote in his column before the game, *"Who are these Dolphins? Where are they coming from? What kind of fish are these?"* We knew we were going up against a good football team in the Rams, who had Deacon Jones and Merlin Olsen and the rest of the Fearsome Foursome, but we knew we had a good football team as well. Going into that game at the Coliseum, we had lost only once ourselves.

Yes, I think winning in L.A. was important, but I think the real turning point for our football team was the longest game in history – our playoff game against Kansas City. They had won the Super Bowl two years before and were still a very good football team. We went up there and knocked them off (27-24) and went on to our first Super Bowl. That was when we really arrived. Although the Rams game was a catalyst and added momentum to our season, in beating the Chiefs we knew we were a true contender.

The Top Five Rushing Seasons of the 1970s

5) 1976 New England Patriots (210.6 yards/game) – The only squad listed here without a Hall of Fame running back leading the charge. Big-bodied pounders, nobody under 6-feet, 200-lbs. FB Sam Cunningham (824 yds) had the closest resemblance to a feature back. Andy Johnson, a converted college quarterback, was the first coming of Craig James. But the surprise payoffs came from big Don Calhoun, whose 5.6 yds/carry led the entire NFL, and dashing, darting QB Steve Grogan (397 yds, 12 touchdowns).

"They're as deep in the running game as any team I've seen in football," said Raiders coach John Madden after watching his team bleed away 296 ground yards one humbling afternoon. "And there's all that horsepower clearing the way. They have five offensive linemen who can block, a fullback who can block, and a tight end who can block. It's like playing against a 7-man line all day."

4) 1972 Miami Dolphins (211.4) – The March of the Undefeated. Everybody knew about the back alley punch that "Butch and Sundance" could pack after watching Miami's surprise run to Super Bowl VI. But what elevated this team into history was the unleashing of tailback Mercury Morris, a 4th-year slasher from West Texas State, who, prior to the '72 season, never had more than 60 carries in a season. "My change of pace," Shula called him. "We pound inside with Csonka and Kiick, then we'll give it to Merc and test the sidelines."

That "change of pace" became a change of heart in '72, as Shula fed the ball to Morris 190 times for 1000 yards and 12 touchdowns, and the Dolphins whitewashed their entire schedule, 17-0. Morris and Csonka became the first teammates in NFL history ever to gain 1000 yards each in one season, while Kiick threw in another half a grand for good measure. It was Operation Devastation.

3) 1976 Pittsburgh Steelers (212.2) – Chuck Noll wasn't taking any chances with his starting QB Terry Bradshaw on the sidelines for six midseason games. The plan for backup Mike Kruczek was a simple one – hand the ball to backs Franco Harris (1,128 yds) and Rocky Bleier (1,036 yds) and get out of the way. What resulted was an intense, concentrated display of ball-control. Keep-away football, driven by a precise, bear-trapping offensive line and subsidized by the greatest defense in pro football history. Someday I'll dig up the time-of-possession numbers and see what kind of work the Steelers did on the clock that year. It must have been ridiculous.

Two games of note from that season: First, hats off to Chuck Fairbanks' New England team, which limited a sloppy Steelers effort to 119 yards on 37 carries at rainy Three Rivers. The quickness of that Patriots' defensive line probably would have given Pittsburgh problems on any surface.

Second: I remember that second-half snowstorm that ambushed Cincinnati on Thanksgiving weekend. Four o'clock game, darkness settled in for the night, clumps of snow flying through Riverfront Stadium and Bradshaw's still on the bench. A Pittsburgh loss means no playoffs, but Franco, Rocky and Kruczek combine for 204 ground yards and a touchdown, and the Steelers stormed on.

2) 1975 Buffalo Bills (212.4) – The Bills hold the top two positions of this elite rushing assemblage, yet they're the only team without a Hall of Fame offensive lineman on the roster. Hammering right guard Joe DeLamielleure, a six-time Pro Bowler, has the best remaining shot at it, but there's been no clanging PR machine working to sway a vote his way. As usual, not enough media eyes watching those guards and centers at work. [*Editor's note: DeLamielleure was elected to the Hall of Fame in 2003.*]

Fullback Jim Braxton pounded out an unexpected 823 yards and scored nine TDs, both career bests. And then there was O.J. Simpson, whose ground blitzkrieg was one of the most spectacular shows in NFL history. How dominating was O.J.? He ran the entire table in 1975, leading the league in all seven major rushing categories: yardage (1,817), carries (329), yards/carry (5.5), touchdowns (16), longest run from scrimmage (88 yds), hundred-yard games (8), and single game yardage (227 vs. Pittsburgh). In history, only Jimmy Brown can make that same boast.

1) 1973 Buffalo Bills (220.6) – 2,003 yards and a trail of vapor, that was O.J. in 1973. He started out the season by ripping the Patriots for 250 yards and two touchdowns. ("Funny thing," he said afterwards, "I was supposed to be the decoy today.") The momentum carried over an entire season, one in which "The Juice" averaged an amazing six yards per rush.

Braxton and Larry Watkins each added over 400 yards to the Bills' effort, while Buffalo quarterbacks threw only 213 passes all season, still the lowest number in AFL/AFC history.

The only team that successfully stopped this charge all season was Miami, on October 21st. The Dolphins allowed Buffalo only 75 yards on 32 attempts. "We took away Simpson's cutbacks, the real key to controlling that attack," said Dolphins' DE Vern den Herder. Apparently, nobody else was paying attention to those cutbacks, as the Bills averaged over 230 rushing yards/game in their other thirteen outings. But with just a 9-5 record, the greatest rushing show of the 1970s was sent to the sidelines for the playoffs.

The Dolphins went on to blank the Colts, 21-0, in the 1971 AFC Championship, but Dallas was clearly the better team in Super Bowl VI. Despite your team's youth and inexperience, could the Dolphins have beaten Dallas that afternoon had some things been done a little differently?

LL: I believe so. I think the mistake that was made was that, although we had three excellent backs in Csonka, Kiick and Morris, we didn't utilize Mercury as much as we could have in that game. All Dallas did was pile up the inside, knowing we wouldn't be able to run to the outside with Kiick. Although Jim was a good outside runner, he didn't have the speed like Mercury did to open up the offense.

Had we used Morris to stretch the width of the field and keep Dallas from bottling up the inside, things could have been different. Not to take anything away from Dallas. The Cowboys were an excellent football team. They had been to the Super Bowl before and lost, so they knew that feeling. We were a young team and, in a lot of ways, we were just happy to be there. But I don't think Dallas was that much better than we were. Not 24 to 3.

Which single game epitomized the historic undefeated season of 1972 for you?

LL: Actually, it started after we lost to Dallas in the Super Bowl the previous year. Shula stood in the locker room and said, "Remember this feeling. I don't ever want to have this feeling again. We're going to come back and we're never going to have this feeling of defeat again." We all took that in. We knew we were a good football team, and we knew we were good enough to get back to the Super Bowl.

Then came the season opener in '72 against Kansas City. We went up there and played them in 115-degree weather, a rematch from that great playoff game the year before. We thought the Chiefs would be out for revenge. We were leading 20-3 at the end of the third quarter and I saw those guys from Kansas City really sucking it up. They were really wilting. However, we were used to that kind of heat in practice. When the gun sounded to end the quarter, I just took off and sprinted to the other end of the field, just to get even more of a psychological advantage. It was just a gut reaction. We were in shape, and I wanted the Chiefs to know it.

Bob Griese, as well as many other former Dolphins, has said he feels the 1973 Super Bowl team, which had two regular season losses, was a more powerful unit than the unbeaten '72 team. Agree or disagree?

LL: Actually, I was one of the first people to make that statement. In '72, we won games but we weren't dominating teams. People were also making comments about our schedule, how we really didn't play anybody that year. So in '73, everybody wanted to be the team that knocked off the Miami Dolphins.

I remember a game during the preseason that year. We played the Vikings in Minnesota and they beat us. Coming off the field, [Vikings coach] Bud Grant was so happy that he was tipping his hat to the screaming crowd. *It was a preseason game!* We were thinking, "What is *this* all about?" Then when the Raiders beat us in the second game of the year, John Madden and his players and their fans were acting like they had just won the Super Bowl!

We made it a point to dominate every team we played that season, to show that we really were a superior, powerhouse football team. Neither playoff game that year – against Cincinnati and Oakland – was even close. Neither was the Super Bowl against Minnesota. We scored the first time we had the ball in each of those games. We never felt threatened that we could lose.

Who was the best defensive linemen you ever faced, and why?

LL: I would have to say that Pittsburgh's Joe Greene was the best I ever played against. He was a combination of strength, speed and quickness. And he was nasty. Curley Culp was probably the strongest guy I ever played against, and Mike Reid from Cincinnati was probably the quickest. But Joe Greene had everything. I could never take a play off against that man.

At Super Time, Miami Was Rough and Ready

Call it Grant's Tomb. Re-title it Shula's Shrine. Or Csonka's Causeway.

Or let 'em keep the name Rice Stadium. No matter. Henceforth this fog-bound battleground will be known as the one where the Dolphins settled themselves by any reasonable measure as football's all time kings.

Forget the final score of Miami 24, Minnesota 7. It was no more a reflection of Dolphin superiority than that 14-7 victory over Washington in Super Bowl VII indicated the one-sidedness there.

Do remember that both Washington then and Minnesota now were and are excellent football clubs. And that the Dolphins did much more than win by 17 this soggy Sunday.

This was murder. It made the St. Valentine's Day massacre look like a draw. The world finally learned why Don Shula had been grinning all week. He knew what he had. Now everybody knows what he's got, which is something nobody had before, the Kohinoor Diamond of football teams. A 32-2 record over two seasons, back-to-back Super Bowl champs.

The Dolphins buried once and for all the myth that other teams have better material. That Miami wins on unity rather than speed or muscle.

Jim Langer and Bob Kuechenberg and Larry Little and Wayne Moore and Norm Evans picked up Bud Grant's fabled Front Four from the Northland and shook them like a gang of King Kongs dangling a cluster of Fay Wray's from the Empire State Building.

Scorning audible check-offs at the line of scrimmage and throwing a Super Bowl-low seven passes, Bob Griese aimed Larry Csonka through the debris and Csonka flung it aside like confetti in his Super Bowl record (145 yards) running show. (January 14, 1974)

- Edwin Pope, Copyright, 1974, *Miami Herald*.
Reproduced with permission via Copyright Clearance Center.

You made your reputation by leading the powerful, churning Miami sweep. Which opposing cornerbacks were the most fearless at challenging you on those plays?

LL: I remember Robert James being one of the toughest guys I had to block. He was a Buffalo cornerback who didn't think twice about coming up and taking me on. He was a very quiet, unassuming guy who wore glasses and looked like a professor. But on Sundays, boy, he was tough. I knew I had to take something to the parlor to get him out of the way. James attacked that play with absolutely no fear.

Bob Griese was known as the "Thinking Man's Quarterback" during the 1970s. Give me your best example of how he earned that title.

LL: Bob always seemed to call the right plays at the right time. I never saw him get rattled. I never saw him get emotional. He never raised his voice in the huddle. I remember in that '72 championship game against Pittsburgh, he came off the bench and immediately hit Paul Warfield for a big gain. He must have seen something from the sidelines during the first half and knew he could get the ball downfield against their defense. Bob always seemed to be thinking one or two plays ahead, trying to envision the upcoming situation and set the defense up.

It took another league, the WFL, to finally stop the surging Dolphins dynasty. What effect did the impending defection of Csonka, Kiick and Warfield to that league have on the team's psyche going into the 1974 season? Did it take the heart out of the team?

LL: No, we weren't disheartened. We were happy that those guys were getting all that money! What it actually did was open up [owner] Joe Robbie's pocketbook to keep the rest of us in Miami. A lot of us went back and renegotiated our contracts after those three defected. I was happy for them, to be honest. Csonka called me and told me he was leaving. I wished him good luck and asked him to take me with him [laughing].

After a season-opening loss at New England, it was business as usual for the Dolphins in 1974. The team won 11 of its next 13 games and captured its fourth straight AFC East title. That meant a playoff trip to Oakland to face the Raiders.

LL: Honestly, we felt we were going for our fourth straight Super Bowl. Make no mistake – despite the distraction of those three guys leaving, we were a confident football team. We ended up losing to the Raiders, but there were some things that happened in that game which were tough to overcome: Cliff Branch catches a pass, falls down, then gets up and runs it all the way…Stabler almost gets sacked and tosses the ball up for grabs into the endzone for the winning touchdown….all the injuries we had on defense. Yet we still had a chance to win it at the end, but it just didn't happen.

Had we beaten Oakland we would've played the Steelers for the AFC Championship. I felt we had Pittsburgh's number. We matched up good against them and probably would've won that game. Up to that point, the Steelers hadn't beaten us. They were an excellent football team, but we had guys just matched up well with them. It would have been a helluva game.

Memories from the '74 Playoffs, Miami at Oakland

"Trying to get back to that 4th consecutive Super Bowl just wore us out. We were physically out of it by the time we reached the '74 playoffs against Oakland. Bill Stanfill, our right defensive end, had a terrible neck problem. I played with ripped and shredded cartilage in my left knee. Bob Matheson was out with a broken arm. Doug Swift had a bad knee. Our starting cornerback Lloyd Mumphord was out. Jake Scott was injured in the game and had to leave…

"I'll never forget it. As Vern den Herder was trying to take Stabler down, the ball fluttered out of his hands. It was a lousy pass. Clarence Davis couldn't catch a cold, but he makes the big catch to win it in the last 30 seconds. It was probably the only catch he ever made in his career. The Raiders were lucky to win against a team that had no defense. We were really decimated that day with injuries. Had we been healthy, it would have been no contest. We would have waltzed through that game, and we would have gotten back to a fourth straight Super Bowl."

– Miami Dolphins defensive tackle Manny Fernandez

"It was a dumb play. It was 1st down and we had plenty of time – 35 seconds and two timeouts. Every play was going into the endzone anyway. So we had three more chances coming up and things were probably going to set up better than this time. I saw Clarence. He had come back, but there were an awful lot of people around him and it didn't look like he was going to be able to catch the ball. He did. It was a great catch but a dumb play."

– Oakland QB Ken Stabler, on his frantic, game-winning touchdown pass

After the departures of Csonka, Kiick and eventually Mercury Morris, the Dolphins' running attack was placed in the hands of players like Norm Bulaich, Don Nottingham, Benny Malone, Gary Davis and Leroy Harris. Your thoughts on that blue collar, yards-by-committee attack.

LL: They were all good, tough running backs, but they couldn't contribute what Csonka, Kiick and Morris could. We definitely were not as good a running team without them. Benny Malone was as hard as a rock, an excellent blocker who had no fear. Gary Davis was a solid running back. Bulaich and Nottingham was our two-headed fullback that replaced Csonka. These guys all contributed but they couldn't dominate, couldn't take over a game. Teams could handle our ground game if they really focused on it.

After six straight years of ten or more wins, the 1976 season was a 6-8 disaster. What was it like being a member of Shula's first losing team?

LL: It wasn't a good feeling, but you know what was ironic about that year? In the 1972 preseason, we were 3-3; in the '76 preseason, we were 6-0. We felt very good about the 1976 team until injuries started hitting us. We were an injury-riddled team that year. We were playing backups at nearly every position. Had we been at full strength that year, we might have won 10 games.

What traits did that losing season bring out in Shula that you hadn't seen from him before?

LL: I don't really think that season changed him. He knew that the reason we were struggling was because of all our injuries. He was being the same Don – raising hell with us like he always did.

But, you know, our last game of the year was different. We played Minnesota at home and a win would have given us 7-7 record for the year. But we stunk the joint out and they beat us 29-7. Don was very upset. After that game I knew a lot of guys wouldn't be back the next year. We had some players who already had one foot in the parking lot during that game, knowing it was the end of the season and we wouldn't be going to the playoffs. That kind of attitude is not tolerated on a Shula-coached team, and some big changes were made during the off-season.

After the Dolphins' Super Bowl victory in January 1974, Miami failed to win another playoff game until the strike season of 1982, a span of nine years. What do you feel was the main reason for that long drought?

LL: Well, let's go through it. We came very close to making the playoffs in 1975, but we lost to Baltimore twice and that kept us out. In 1977, we bounced back to 10-4. To get into the playoffs, though, we needed some help. The Patriots had to beat the Colts for us to qualify. New England jumped out to a big lead in that game, so I called up Wayne Moore and told him, "Get ready to wake up for practice in the morning, buddy!" Then Bert Jones brought the Colts back and Baltimore won the football game. No playoffs for us. That one really hurt!

In '78, we had a great year and played Houston in a wild-card game at the Orange Bowl. This was the same Oilers team that had scored 35 points against us earlier in the season. In the playoffs we held them to 17. But our offense was completely out of sync that day. We couldn't run the ball. We had four turnovers. Griese was playing with bruised ribs and had trouble throwing the football. It was not a good day and we lost. We made the playoffs again in 1979 against Pittsburgh, but we weren't as good as the Steelers. They beat us pretty easily.

But, hey, looking back we played in three straight Super Bowls and had an undefeated season. Those years with Csonka, Morris and Kiick running the ball were some of the greatest in NFL history, and many times I was out there in front, leading the way. Sounds like a pretty good career to me, don't you think?

— 10 —
Cliff Harris, Safety
Dallas Cowboys (1970-79)
April 29, 2002

John Holland was enjoying the benefits of a hot hand when Cowboys safety Cliff Harris had seen enough and ran the big spear through him.

Minnesota at Dallas, 1974, and Fran Tarkenton, the Vikings' passer, was shooting up Texas Stadium. Each of his completions averaged 17 yards and he was taking things deep again, this time from midfield. Holland, a rookie receiver, was his target on a split-post route as the pass settled in at the goal line.

From there, it was your basic hit-and-run; Harris delivered the hit, then everyone ran to see if the target was still breathing.

"I wasn't even supposed to be in the game!" laughs Holland today. "Jim Lash got hurt and I looked around and they were pointing at me to go in. My first catch was an 18-yard out. Then Tarkenton said he wanted to put a dagger in 'em and sent me deep. The ball was there, then the next thing I know it was lights out."

Lights out, that was Cliff Harris all right. A kamikaze defender who always traveled with a knock-out punch. Darrell Royal, the old Texas coach, called him a "rolling ball of butcher knives," as serious a football compliment as they come, however it is that butcher knives manage to roll.

"Probably the best hit of my career," Harris says of his Holland blast. "As close to perfect as it gets. He was looking up and thought he had a sure touchdown, then I put my helmet right through him." (Was it Holland's worst collision? "It should've been, but then a year later Lyle Blackwood threw a cheap shot at me in Baltimore and broke my jaw. At least Harris' hit was clean.")

"That was one world I didn't need to live in, the cheap shots," says Harris, a four-time All-Pro who guarded Tom Landry's defensive backfield for ten seasons. "I didn't need the cheap stuff to be effective. But I didn't wait for the game to come to me like a lot of safeties do. I launched myself into the game. My style was one of disruption, either by confusing the quarterback's reads or blowing up a pass play. Cleanly, but as hard as the rules allowed…always looking for the knockout. Sometimes I'd knock *myself* out."

His nickname was "Captain Crash" and he teamed with Clemson's Charlie Waters to make arguably the best pro safety combo of the 1970s. The Dolphins would throw Dick Anderson and Jake Scott into the argument, and Pittsburgh would raise a fist and shout about the Mike Wagner and Glen Edwards/Donnie Shell years. But for my money the duo from Dallas was cream of the cream.

Harris emerged from one of those never-heard-of-'em places, a school called Ouachita Baptist in Arkadelphia, AR. His college coach Buddy Benson first remembers him as a 17-year old freshman, "a 170-lb fireball who could hit big and run and took well to coaching. By the time he left me, I felt he'd be a pro."

"We discovered Harris watching film," says former Cowboys personnel director Gil Brandt. "He ran back two punts for touchdowns in a game and that got our attention. He played hard but still, the chances of making the NFL from a school that small are pretty slim."

Dallas took 17 turns in the 1970 draft and their final pick would be Glenn Patterson, the center on Nebraska's Sun Bowl team. The last player taken overall, by Kansas City, was Rayford Jenkins of Alcorn State. Harris' name was never called. And so it was that all fiery defensive backs from the land of Ouachita would have to take their chances as free agents. He signed on with the Cowboys despite the team's hollow promises to put him in their draft.

NFL veterans pitched a three-week strike that July, so clubs filled their camps with rookies and no-names and all of them got long looks. "The strike is what saved Cliff," says Benson. "The coaches couldn't help but notice him. I don't know how much true attention he'd have gotten had all the Dallas regulars been around.

"The day before their final pre-season game, Brandt told me Cliff wouldn't see any action but would likely make the final cut and I wasn't supposed to say anything. After the game, Cliff was so upset. We were at dinner and he said, 'I'd do anything, even sweep the floors to make it. But they didn't play me and it's not gonna happen.' I told him, 'Don't be so sure. Just get some sleep tonight.'"

Harris awoke as the Cowboys' starting free safety. The team had switched future Hall of Famer Mel Renfro to his natural position at cornerback, allowing Harris to become a fixture through five Super Bowls and a decade of Dallas swagger.

He roamed the secondary as the wildcard in the Cowboys defense, a gambler who made his money in bluffs and aces but could come across the table with a fierce wallop. His game was a blend of concussions and confusion, of forcing misreads and miscues.

And *those* types would typically drive staid, conservative types like Landry batty. Coaches of that ilk take delight in watching their schemes unfold; gamblers generally bring them nothing but stomach knots.

But maybe Landry saw a little bit of himself in Harris. Their styles as players were surprisingly similar. Both were great anticipators that played with fire.

"Everyone thinks of Landry as a coach, this cold, cerebral icon," says *Sports Illustrated*'s Paul Zimmerman, "But as a player, a Giants defensive halfback, he played a pretty rough game. Lots of emotion and a hard-hitter."

In rehearsal or live action, Harris drew no distinction in bringing his level of punishment.

"He was as intense in practice as he was during games," says Waters. "People used to tease him about that. Our own receivers paid serious attention to where Cliff was on the field. They didn't want to get belted. One time Golden Richards brought him a red fireman's hat, complete with the light and a siren, to keep track of him. Cliff put it on then took some laps. Landry just stood there watching him.

"My favorite Cliff Harris story was probably another incident from practice, from the early days. Craig Morton was the quarterback. On one particular play Cliff was keying on Morton, watching his eyes instead of the receiver. So Morton just fired the ball right over the middle. Cliff jumped on the pass then he slammed right into the goal post…staggered the whole thing.

"It was so funny. Craig will deny it, but I know he threw at the post on purpose. He knew Cliff would chase it."

A decade went by, then nagging injuries, ones that took longer and longer to heal, finally forced Harris to retire after the '79 season. His body had taken enough abuse. His speed and explosion were fading. And the NFL had liberalized its passing rules. Receivers now had to be shadowed instead of banging them down the field, which put even greater pressure on any tired veteran legs that were roaming the secondary.

"It was time to go," Harris admits. "I could have stayed another year or two, but I wouldn't have been the same player. Young guys were coming in. I was on two Super Bowl winners. It was somebody else's turn to bring the Cowboys a championship."

But, oh, how those celebrations flowed in Dallas during the 1970s. Big trophies. NFC titles. Accolades and honors.

Good times in Texas, and the champagne corks popped. "Come quickly! I'm tasting stars!" said the friar Dom Perignon after sampling his sparkling discovery.

And after a decade full of dangerous encounters with Cliff Harris and the Dallas secondary, receivers like John Holland would shout, *"Come quickly! I'm seeing them!"*

● ● ●

Let's begin with your introduction into professional football. How does one get from a place called Ouachita Baptist College in a place called Arkadelphia, Arkansas to the big-time Dallas Cowboys? Sounds like a long, rough ride on the wagon train.

CH: I had a very successful career in college, so I was pretty confident that I'd be drafted. The Rams and Saints had talked to me, but Dallas showed the most interest. The Cowboys at that time had really attempted to develop the small school market where no other pro teams had any interest. The BLESTO syndicate would send a representative scout to the small schools to check things out, but the Cowboys were the only ones in the '70s that really pursued them on their own. They were looking for the best athletes in the south, regardless of what school they played for. That idea was really the brainchild of Gil Brandt, the Cowboys' director of player personnel at that time. The Cowboys scouted me and actually flew me to Dallas with around thirty other guys they supposedly were going to draft. [S] Charlie Waters from Clemson was in that group. We stayed in Dallas for a few days and they ran us through a bunch of tests. Finally, the Cowboys told me they were going to draft me in the sixth round.

Well, the first draft day came and went and no phone call. No phone call on the second day, either. Then after the draft ended, around midnight, I got a call from the Cowboys telling me they were going to fly me to Dallas to sign me as a free agent. Initially I said no, but later that week I changed my mind and signed a contract with them. That was the year of the preseason strike [1970]. The veterans were out, but the Cowboys were well prepared and had 120 rookies – most of them free agents – on the field at Thousand Oaks trying out for the team. I started out playing right defensive cornerback as a backup, but they moved me over to free safety. Rich Flowers, Charlie Waters and I were all vying for the free safety job. I finally won it.

What set you apart from Flowers and Waters?

CH: Mel Renfro had that job for the Cowboys the year before but he wasn't really an aggressive player. He didn't attack the run, and that was a component the Cowboys needed in their defense, so they moved Mel to cornerback. On the other hand, I was a very aggressive player who attacked the run and made plays at the line of scrimmage, but I could also cover downfield for the deep pass. That's what won the job for me. I don't think anyone before me had played the position like me other than Larry Wilson of the Cardinals. At that time in the NFL, the typical role of the free safety was to play center field, to stop the deep pass and not let anyone get behind him. A perfect example of someone who played that way was Minnesota's Paul Krause.

Was there a specific play you made in camp that convinced the coaches that you were the best candidate at free safety?

CH: I can't point to one play, but I can point to a single game that did it for me. I really had a great training camp that year. I would hit guys so hard in practice that I'd knock them out, and that gave me an advantage over Rich and Charlie. I would rather knock out a team's best receiver than get an interception. It was simply the way I played. I wasn't a headhunter, someone who was trying to hurt another player, but I played a rough, physical game. I could also play corner when needed, which gave me another edge.

After it was announced that I had made the starting lineup as a rookie, there was still some doubt among the coaches as to whether I could actually perform under game conditions. The first home game we played in 1970 was against the New York Giants, and Tom Landry did not want to lose to the Giants. He wanted to beat them more than any other team in pro football because he had played for them and coached them. He told us that New York was the media capital of the world and that if we wanted to create some publicity for ourselves, just play good against the Giants, in front of the New York media, and it would happen.

Well, we were losing 10-0 at halftime, which caused Landry to make one of the toughest speeches I ever heard him make in my career. He said we were playing terribly, that we were nothing more than amateurs drawing pay. He wasn't complementary at all. Hearing all the emotion in that speech really inspired me, and

I went out and intercepted two passes with long returns and recovered two fumbles. It was probably my greatest 30 minutes of football. I was all over the field. I think my play during the second half of that game secured my position as a member of the Cowboys. The coaches saw what I could do when it counted.

The Headline Read: "Pokes Win A Cliff-Hanger"

You pronounce it Watch-ee-taw if the word ever comes up in conversation, which is doubtful. Watch-ee-taw Baptist College, named after the Ouachita Indian tribe and located in Arkadelphia, Arkansas, a well-known metropolis somewhat smaller than Chicago. Ouachita Baptists, enrollment 855 men, 794 women. Nickname: Tigers. Colors: purple and gold. Wooden stadium, capacity 5,000.

Ouachita Baptist has not exactly flooded the professional ranks with football graduates. Odds on a Ouachita product getting a pro contract are roughly the same as Rocky Graziano playing Hamlet in par. Odds on a Ouachita graduate winning a starting job in his rookie year are equal to George Wallace winning Man of the Year on Lennox Avenue. And the price on a Ouachita rookie taking personal charge of a football game and turning it inside out in a space of 7 minutes and 35 seconds, well, you could get a better shake entering Totie Fields in the Boston Marathon.

Cliff Harris, however, has been bucking the house for months now. What he did yesterday in the Cowboys' 28-10 thump of the Giants was just continuation of a pattern. The young safetyman might have been the most surprised man on the field, but his teammates weren't.

"He's been doing such a good job for us as a rookie," said secondary coach Bobby Franklin. "I had been wondering when things were going to start happening."

The things that happened at the Cotton Bowl involved two Harris pass interceptions and a fumble recovery, all crammed within a short span in the third quarter, that shook Your Heroes from a limp lethargy into a quick winning effort. From a 0-10 nap to a 14-10 lead and momentum for a fast finish.

Harris is the only rookie to win a Cowboy starting job. He is one of only 40 freshmen to win regular roles throughout pro football. Ouachita Baptist can say that. The University of Texas can't. Neither can Ohio State. (September 28, 1970)

— **Blackie Sherrod, Copyright, 1970, *Dallas Times Herald*.
Reprinted with permission.**

Former Texas Longhorns head coach Darrell Royal once referred to you as being a "rolling ball of butcher knives" on the field, an aggressive, destructive, damaging player. Can a defensive player actually learn to become a ferocious hitter, or does it come from an inner appetite for destruction that not everyone possesses?

CH: It's something instinctive, something I always knew was there. My father played football and had that ability to hit real hard. He always told me to hit through someone, to explode. During a game I was able to focus and concentrate all the energy within me into one place, then release it all in one split second. Every time that I hit I prepared myself for an explosion. I put everything that I had into the impact and released it into the most vulnerable spot of the person I was tackling.

My degree in college was in mathematics and physics and I think, subconsciously, I was applying those principles of angles, movement and force to the game of football. People might laugh and joke about that, but I really think it subconsciously helped me to know the spot where I could deliver the greatest amount of force to the other person's body. Think of it in the way a martial arts expert is able to concentrate and focus all his energy, eliminating the outside world for that split second before delivering a crippling blow. That's

142

what I knew how to do. I don't know where else you can apply that skill in life other than in martial arts or in football.

How did you mentally prepare yourself for combat on the football field? What kind of thoughts went through your head as you were getting ready to play?

CH: Before the game I would always relax myself by listening to classical music, like Rachmaninoff and Bach. I still listen to it today. Going into a game you're looking for a peaceful mind, not a cluttered, frenzied mind. What does a golfer do right before the moment of impact in hitting the ball? He relaxes. He clears his mind and thinks of nothing. He's prepared himself for the shot, then he allows the body to take over. The kind of focus I had in preparing to play free safety was similar to that of a pro golfer. My mind needed to be cleared of all distractions. I had to be relaxed.

Only from the spectator's standpoint is the game of football a violent one. But from the player's standpoint, it's only violent at the moment of impact. Football is mostly a mental game, a game played in the mind where decisions are made very quickly. If you're tense or angry or upset or mad, you can't think clearly. What I tried to do was relax my mind so I could think calmly in a very hectic environment. You can't go out there as a wild man and expect to make clear, good decisions. I don't think people, the fans, understand that. All the crowd sees is the reckless abandon.

In what other ways would you prepare for a game?

CH: I'd watch film. I'd study computerized printouts that would show our opponent's tendencies by down and distance and formation. Football is a study of probability and statistics. "From this formation, Pittsburgh passes 70-percent of the time," or "Philadelphia only runs out this formation on second-and-short." As the play develops, you're quickly analyzing what the potential outcomes could be.

If the quarterback rolls one way, it eliminates all the receivers running on the other side. If you cover their top receiver, you have the ability to take care of other receivers who aren't as critical. As the play develops, you can eliminate more and more options. You do this instantaneously in your mind until you've analyzed the play and you know exactly where it's going. Each play is a series of progressions you've prepared for that allows you to make decisions quickly.

You describe the process as if there's time to go through a mental flow chart; yet the average play only lasts a few seconds.

CH: It's not about thinking. Thinking takes too much time. It's recognizing and reacting, then your instincts take over. You have to make more right decisions than wrong decisions or you'll lose the game. Then someone else will take your position.

You went from Ouachita – two doors down from nowhere – into the defense of the powerful Dallas Cowboys, playing in a secondary with two future Hall-of-Famers, Herb Adderly and Mel Renfro. How did those two players change the way you operated in the defensive backfield?

CH: Those guys were truly pros and were fantastic players. The main thing that Herb and Mel both taught me was to be a professional, to play like a champion, to play at level 10 all the time. Can you imagine being a rookie free agent in the defensive huddle with stars like Adderly and Renfro, Chuck Howley and Lee Roy Jordan and Bob Lilly? I was so impressed.

But one of the beautiful, wonderful things about pro football is that once the ball is snapped, it doesn't matter who you are. All you have to do is your job. In the real world, people can lie and cheat and exaggerate, but you can't do those things in pro football. In pro football there's a 230-lb running back coming right at you, and you can't come off the field with a bunch of *couldas, shouldas, wouldas.* You either make the play or you don't. That's something I learned from those veterans. I remember the first time I came into the huddle with the starting team. Bob Lilly simply looked at me and said, "We're going to the Super Bowl this year, rookie, and I don't want you to do anything to screw it up." I said, "*Yes, sir.*"

Was there ever a moment where you had a clear shot at an opponent – one where you could've easily knocked him out of the game – but instead held back and didn't hit with full force?

CH: Let me tell you something that pro football players understood about me. My opponents wanted to beat me, but they didn't dislike me. I would get quite a few votes for the Pro Bowl because I never took a cheap shot. I never went after a guy's knees. I never tried to hurt anyone maliciously. I tried to hit people as hard as I could every time, to create an explosion. If I knocked them out, I knocked them out. And if I didn't, it wasn't because I didn't try. But the longer I played in the league, the more I got to know my opponents. I wouldn't take that attack shot on some of them, not try to crush them like I did when I was younger. I guess you could say I mellowed somewhat. But I always hit hard enough to try to make them want to go somewhere else on the field.

My attitude was, "Look, if you come into my area, you're going to pay a price." I think receivers responded to that mentality and teams were forced to adjust their gameplans, which defensively played right into our hands. We started seeing more and more outside routes from opponents. Before I became the team's free safety, the Cowboys' biggest vulnerability was the inside route, down-and-in-and-up – the split route. Receivers used to catch the ball and run up the middle or for a touchdown or big yardage against the Cowboys. With me back there patrolling, when a player ran an inside route he paid a price every time. That middle was no safe haven.

The Cowboys' defense made heavy use of the safety blitz, a kamikaze charge at the quarterback. What kinds of things were racing through your mind as you crept towards the line of scrimmage, anticipating the snap of the ball?

CH: You've got to get to the quarterback because if you don't the corners are vulnerable. They have no help back there and the middle is wide open for the deep post route. Our safety blitz was designed for [LB] Lee Roy Jordan to charge on one side of the center and me to blitz from the other. You had to time the snap right and break through the line of scrimmage to force the quarterback to throw the ball sooner, before the post route could develop downfield.

The first thing that comes to mind when you mention "safety blitz" are those Super Bowls against Pittsburgh. Terry Bradshaw and the Steelers analyzed the defensive scheme of our safety blitz pretty well. Bradshaw would set up and throw the ball deep, even before Lynn Swann would make his cut. Bradshaw would just throw it up there and take the hit from me or somebody else. The corner's responsibility was to not get beaten deep on the post, but it happened several times. We were beaten in an area we definitely should've covered in those Pittsburgh Super Bowls.

What was the worst mistake you ever made in a game?

CH: First, let me tell you something about the mentality of the defensive player versus the offensive player. Defensive players can tell you every bad play they ever made. I can tell you from almost every game the big mistakes I made on the football field that ended up hurting the Dallas Cowboys. On the other hand, if you ask me about the great plays I've made, I can't really remember them. The reason for that is that you are being paid to make the big plays, and you're expected to make them. You're not expected to make mistakes. When you make one, it really sinks into your brain because you want to make sure it doesn't happen again.

One bad play that stands out in my mind was during a punt-block attempt in Super Bowl X against the Steelers. Mike Ditka, our special teams coach, designed a punt-block in which I was designated to break through the line. 99-percent of the time it doesn't work anyway. Well, the Steelers were backed up to their 10-yard line. I lined up in my punt block formation and I broke through. I was bumped once but I still made it through the line and got back on the punter, and that's when I made my mistake.

In high school and college, they train you to cross your arms and try to get them in front of the punter. In the pros, if you're a good enough athlete, they teach you to knock it off his foot with your hands. Well, I did kind of a combination of those two techniques. I crossed my wrists and also went for the ball with my hands, but [P] Bobby Walden somehow was able to kick the ball through my arms – right past my facemask – and downfield. It was during a real critical time of the game, and it's one of those plays a big-time player should make. It was my time to make a play, and I've been so mad at myself all these years because I didn't. I blew it.

Memories of the Cowboys' First Championship

The ghosts are now buried and quiet, the closets have been swept clean of skeletons. The Cowboy complexion is now clear of pimples and they may walk down the street on the day after their biggest challenge without yard dogs barking and small boys pelting them with stones. The cold brands of Choke City U.S.A. and the El Foldo Kids and Next Year's Champion must now fall on other brows. The Cowboys have met the big one and he is finally theirs.

Six times they have swung at the big pitch. Before Sunday they had lost more times than Eddie Fisher. They had a stigma that defied brillo but that all went down the drain, hee hee, when they rapped the Miami Dolphins, 24-3, as coldly and calmly as a surgeon removing a benign wart. You'd thought the Cowboys had been winning championships all their borned days.

"What can they say about us now?" said Bob Hayes. "We've done it all. Nobody can take that away from us."

"They can't say we don't win the big one anymore," said president Tex Schramm, dripping from an impromptu shower bath hosted by his players. "And we'll be back. This is just a start. We'll be stronger in the next six years."

This was a day of compliments where the Cowboys have previously felt brickbats.

"They completely dominated us," said Don Shula, leader of the lost Miami cause. "We never really challenged in the big game." It could have been Tom Landry talking after the Cleveland playoff game a couple years ago. Or the year before that...

The Cowboys won this game in exact opposite fashion they had lost others. Where once they fumbled and stumbled and jumped offside in crucial moments, where they had thrown interceptions and dropped passes, now they were methodically sure. The clock told the story. Dallas controlled the ball 40 minutes and 58 seconds of the game. This left 19 minutes and two seconds for the young Dolphins and this was like trying to vault the Eiffel Tower with a broomstick. The Cowboys broke the Miami back with two magnificent long drives, 76 and 71 yards in length, for touchdowns in the second and third quarters. Some shadetree experts called it a dull game because of Dallas' grinding movements, but it is like putting a bad rap on a no-hitter because there were no home runs. (January 17, 1972)

– **Blackie Sherrod, Copyright, 1972, *Dallas Times Herald*. Reprinted with permission.**

There were very few dark seasons for the Dallas Cowboys during the 1970s. To you, which was the team's most disappointing year in your mind?

CH: Without question, it was the 1974 season. That was the year I hurt my knee during a preseason game in Oakland. It was the only time in my ten-year career that we didn't make the playoffs. We were home for Christmas. We ended up with an 8-6 record, which was crummy for our standards. There was dissension on that team. You know, it's amazing what success will do to a team. It breeds camaraderie and friendships. But losing creates animosity. You begin to point out people's weaknesses instead of their strengths.

Which was your favorite season?

CH: It was the very next year, to be honest, 1975. We were the wildcard team and we went all the way to the Super Bowl. We had a very poor preseason and a really slow start, in my mind. Although we won our first four games we went through a bad stretch where we lost to Green Bay, the Redskins, the Chiefs and barely squeaked by Philadelphia, which finished 4-10 that year. The town, the media, sportscasters, fans, even the coaches, all started to count us out early in the season.

But we believed in each other. The team unified and ended up almost beating Pittsburgh in the Super Bowl. I was named the losing team's MVP, which nobody will ever remember. I think the overall challenge that season presented to us was what really excited me. I enjoy winning, but I also enjoy getting there, the challenge of the contest.

You played with quarterback Roger Staubach, one of the deadliest of the two-minute assassins. As a defensive player, which opposing quarterbacks made you shudder with the clock melting and the lead shrinking?

CH: That's an interesting question. Jim Hart was one of the best comeback quarterbacks in football. He had so many late comebacks with those Cardiac Cards. I never wanted to face Hart in the last two minutes of a game. Ken Stabler from Oakland is another one, although we rarely played against the Raiders. Both he and Hart had similar personalities. They seemed lackadaisical at times, almost uninterested. Neither got rattled by bad things or excited about good things as the game was going on. They did their thing and the game drifted by, then they'd look up at the clock and see they were down by 6 points with a minute thirty left. Then the feathers would start flying.

One of the things that made Hart so effective was the potent offense that surrounded him. With a potent offense, there's always the danger of it erupting. It was just like Magic Johnson and the Lakers – don't get too comfortable because they can come back on you in a second. Well, Hart had Terry Metcalf, J.V. Cain, Jackie Smith and Mel Gray on his offense. All were very, very fast. Their coach, Don Coryell, designed a multiple offense that really put pressure on you. The Cardinals tried to finesse me and trick me all the time. Many times Hart would run play-action and send both a shallow and a deep guy on me. They'd send someone at me they knew I liked to hit – Mel Gray, for instance – hoping I'd bite on it. Then they'd run J.V. Cain behind me. Mental games.

But you couldn't make a mistake and guess wrong against that offense because it would lead to a score, not just a long run or pass. Many of the Cardinals plays were designed to score, and they had the speed to do that. As a free safety, you're playing a mental game against a potent offense like that. You're right on the edge of making a major mistake all the time. Other offenses in the '70s were designed to control the football, to control the clock. For instance, Fran Tarkenton's offenses at Minnesota and New York were designed to march down the field – four yards, six yards, eight yards, two yards, then he'd try to hit you with a bomb. They were much easier to manage than the Cardinals.

Why have the ball-handling and faking skills disappeared from today's quarterbacks?

CH: I've thought about that before. I don't know if that skill is as important in today's game as it was in my era. When I played, offenses leaned toward a more balanced attack, a more run-oriented attack. The hash marks were farther apart. Defenses were more dominant. There was less scoring and less passing. Today, the offensive variance comes in the multiple sets and formations, constantly changing the matchups between receivers and defensive backs and linebackers. That means a lot more guessing, a lot more interchanging of roles for the defense.

In my era, there was really one standard offensive formation. Things were much more defined on both sides of the ball. Each team had two running backs, two receivers and a tight end going up against four linemen, three linebackers and four defensive backs. You matched up and tried to beat them, man-on-man, one-on-one. You'd pass on a red formation, run on a brown formation. Deceptive passes, play-action stuff, would come from the brown formation. Consequently, ball faking and play-action was much more necessary in those days.

Landry's theory was always to stop the run and force the pass. That's why his Flex defense was created. A 4-3 is more effective in stopping the run, particularly in our case, where we never really had linebackers who were extremely mobile, who were involved in pass defense. Those linebackers would go a whole year and only intercept one or two passes.

The NFC was full of great receivers during the 1970s – Harold Carmichael of Philadelphia, Charley Taylor and Frank Grant in Washington, the Vikings' Ahmad Rashad and Sammy White. Was there one particular player who gave you the most trouble?

CH: Without a doubt, Charley Taylor was the most intimidating receiver I faced during my whole career. He would attack you in trying to block you. He broke [Cardinals DB] Jerry Stovall's jaw once. He blasted [Cardinals DB] Larry Wilson in the jaw. He knocked me down and almost out after popping me in the jaw. When Taylor would catch the ball, it hurt to tackle him. You really had to gear up for him, differently than against other receivers. Charley was fast and strong. He would talk to you. He'd tell Charlie Waters, "You're no good. I'm gonna beat your ass all day." Typically, it's the defensive back that does the talking, but Taylor was giving it to us.

You mentioned Harold Carmichael. He was a different kind of receiver. You always had to keep a real good position on him because he was so big [6'8"]. You had to have the right angle to hit him or knock the ball down because he towered over you.

In defending receivers, speed was always the real challenge for me because you can't make mental mistakes with speed. You can't attack the run or the short pass because a fast guy is simply going to blow right past you. That made Mel Gray a big nemesis of mine. Harold Jackson of the Rams fits that mold too. Cliff Branch of Oakland was another one. Those speed guys always made me really focus during the game.

Sure, as a free safety you can sit back there 15 yards deep and backpedal and take off for deep middle every time and never get beat. Maybe intercept a few passes. But that wasn't my style. I liked to play on the edge. A guy like Paul Krause would sit back there all day. He'd go against Mel Gray, line up 15 yards deep then sprint downfield. Gray would never get behind him. It's the safe way of doing things. I, however, tried to attack and hit guys at the line of scrimmage and still cover them deep.

Charley Taylor – One Man's Little Big Horn

No matter how hard Cliff alone, or Cliff and I, hit Charley Taylor, we never felt like it did any damage. He never showed it, and he never let it affect his concentration. Even worse, Charley sometimes would go on the attack. Receivers just don't do that.

At RFK one afternoon, it was a classic, low-scoring battle versus the evil Washington Redskins. The first five plays of Washington's drive were running plays...Cliff and Charley Taylor collided head on five straight times. Cliff had to first secure his run responsibility on each play before he could direct his attention to Taylor. Likewise, Taylor, from the wideout position, would execute his blocking responsibility before directing his energy to Harris.

The sixth play was a trap that Lee Roy Jordan successfully stopped. As I was closing in from the side for mop-up, I saw a blur that was Charley Taylor. He was on a mission, just like the last five plays. I was pleased that his target wasn't me – it was Cliff...

The result of the collision seemed like more than what their 190-pound frames could generate. The noise was deafening, and I remember thinking that with that much concentric force, something has to break, right? Wham! Helmet to helmet, body to body, both Cliff and Charley recoiled to the ground. Cliff scrambled up first, always trying to project the most aggression, and stood over Charley as he rolled over and slowly rose to his feet. Cliff was in his face the entire time.

"That's right! Get used to it, punk! It's gonna be like that all day long!" Cliff attacked verbally, pointing his finger for emphasis. Charley quietly gathered himself and retreated to his huddle, passing me on the way. He showed no ill signs from the attack.

> "All day! All day!" Cliff repeated, following Taylor, attempting to hold a position of dominance. "Get used to it!"
>
> The instant Charley jogged across the line of scrimmage into his territory, out of our sight, Cliff fell forward into my arms, clinging desperately to keep from collapsing to the ground. He was completely limp and exhausted as he melted to his knees, managing a low-volume plea, "Please, Charlie, help. He's killing me!"
>
> **– from** *Tales from the Dallas Cowboys* **by** *Cliff Harris* **and** *Charlie Waters*
> **(Sports Publishing L.L.C., 2003)**

Dallas faced the Steelers four times between 1975 and 1979 – including two great collisions in the Super Bowl – and lost every game. Where did Pittsburgh present the biggest matchup problems for the Cowboys?

CH: I do have a definite opinion about that, but after all these years I'm still reluctant to burn any bridges. [Pausing] Let me answer the question in a real general sense. I think that we over-prepared for the Pittsburgh Steelers. We overanalyzed them. The Steelers had a very basic, fundamental offensive attack. Smart, but fundamental and basic, and that's a real tribute to their coaching staff. On the other hand, we had very complicated offensive and defensive schemes. There were lots of reads and shifts. We out-thought ourselves, and as a result we weren't as physically aggressive as we needed to be to beat that team. If we'd played the defenses that worked for us the best, we would've had better success against them. You had to match the Steelers blow-for-blow, man-for-man. You couldn't stand there and take their roundhouses all day and expect to knock them out with a sucker punch.

I will tell you very openly that in preparing for Super Bowl XIII, we overdid it. I was very discouraged by the complexity of the schemes our coaches were presenting to us. They overloaded us. Jack Lambert once said, "When you play the Cowboys, you feel like they're trying to trick you." There may have been some truth to that statement. Preparation can be a good thing, and it was definitely one of the strengths of the Cowboys of the '70s. We prepared well and knew teams' tendencies and went out and demolished them. Three years earlier, in Super Bowl X, our scheme wasn't nearly as complex and we played Pittsburgh much closer and could've won the ballgame.

Had you been making the defensive calls from the sidelines during those Steeler games, what would you have done differently?

CH: I would've run different defenses. I would've run much more fundamental defenses. Things would have been simplified, and that would have worked well against that very basic Steelers attack.

The story goes that you were so baffled by how Terry Bradshaw was able to slice up the Cowboys' defense in those Super Bowls that sometimes you couldn't sleep. Finally, you called Bradshaw in the middle of the night and asked him what he saw, what were his downfield reads.

His reply was, "Well, I'd look for Swann, and if he was covered I'd look for Stallworth, and if he was covered I'd look for Franco." Does the simplicity of that answer still bother you?

CH: Terry was such a great enough athlete that the details sometimes didn't matter to him. He'd throw it into double-coverages because his arm was strong enough to get it there. He was able to overcome a safety blitz because he was strong and mobile and could maneuver around the pocket to buy some time. He understood the real elementary parts of winning football. Guys like Bradshaw know how to win a football game with really basic components. The opposite is someone like Steve Spurrier, the [former] Redskins coach, with his elaborate, complex passing offense. Or Don Coryell, who ran a very complex system in St. Louis.

But Terry Bradshaw relied on a more rudimentary understanding of the game. He kept things simple and let the defenses overcomplicate themselves. He openly told me that. I asked him one time, "Were you keying me or our middle linebacker Lee Roy Jordan on that deep pass to Swann?" He said, "Neither. I just looked over at Stallworth and if he was covered I threw it to Swann." I just shook my head and thought, *"Why the hell did we go through all that game planning then?"*

What was your most bitter loss as a Dallas Cowboy?

CH: Surprisingly, it wasn't any of the Super Bowls. It was the last game I ever played, against the Rams in the 1979 playoffs at Texas Stadium. Had we won that game we would've likely went on to face the Steelers for one last Super Bowl. But we lost in the last the few minutes. The Rams had 1st-and-10 at midfield, trailing 19-14. We normally ran a nickel defense in those situations, but there was some concern that the Rams were going to run on us, so we took a defensive back out and put in a linebacker. The Rams responded by throwing a deep crossing route to Billy Waddy that beat the linebacker for a touchdown. It was a typical Dallas Cowboys play, the way *we* pulled games out in the last few seconds. Only this time Vince Ferragamo and the Rams did it to us. And just like that, on one pass, my career was over. I didn't want to go out that way.

You played behind a line that featured a pair of monster defensive ends in "Too Tall" Jones and Harvey Martin. How did those two affect the way you were able to play free safety?

CH: Any time a Landry-run defense was called, Ed Jones was down in a four-point frog stance and Harvey was off the ball, so they were both in a real poor position to rush the passer. Many times we'd argue on 3rd-and-4 or 2nd-and-6, "Hey, let's run a pass defense!" Most times the coaches wouldn't listen, so in those situations we didn't get any pass rush at all. But when those guys charged, they went hard and they were awesome.

If you put a poor defensive line in front of me, one with a crummy pass rush, I probably wouldn't have been as good a free safety. Harvey and Ed allowed me and Charlie Waters to play more aggressively at times. The whole thing played off itself. We could cover our guys tighter for a shorter period of time because there was going to be a good pass rush. In the meantime, we'd disguise our coverages to put that little bit of hesitation in the quarterback's mind. That caused him to hold the ball a bit longer and gave the defensive line time to trap him. You're at least hoping for a trap or an incompletion, but if they don't get there, eventually a receiver will break free and you're gonna get beat. But when the Cowboys pass rush was firing on all cylinders, that didn't happen very often.

After the retirements of Adderly (in 1972) and Renfro (1977), the cornerback duties were split mostly between three players – Aaron Kyle, Mark Washington and Benny Barnes. How much of a drop-off do you feel the Cowboys secondary experienced with those three players, and should the team have looked to upgrade those cornerback positions even further?

CH: Well, look at who was being replaced at the corners – two Hall of Fame performers. So it wasn't going to be easy. Let's start with Benny Barnes. If I could have my son play like any player, it would be like Benny Barnes. He had the biggest heart and tried extremely hard and made plays despite not having great ability. I could always count on Benny Barnes to make a play. He was a real winner and helped us win a lot of games.

Mark Washington was a corner who came up with me in 1970. When I first joined the Cowboys, he was absolutely the best athlete I'd ever seen. He had the perfect physique, ran a 4.5 forty. He was 6'1" 185-lbs and had incredible coordination. Mark would always cover his man perfectly, but sometimes he would miss the ball. It'd be right there in front of him and he wouldn't knock it down. Benny Barnes was the other extreme. Benny would look terrible but would somehow always knock the ball down.

You started alongside strong safety Charlie Waters for almost your entire career. Talk about how you made each other better players while patrolling the Dallas secondary.

CH: Charlie and I are different in a lot of ways, but we're very similar in our football thinking. We both started out in football playing quarterback. By the time we got to the Cowboys, we were both competing for the free safety position, which I won. He took my spot when I was called off to the army during the middle of the 1970 season, so he developed some experience that way. I came back and took my starting position, so Charlie didn't really get much playing time until he moved to left cornerback in his third year. He was really out of position playing corner, so he had to rely heavily on me for help. I knew that I had to take care of him because, although he was a smart cornerback, he wasn't a particularly strong one. It was during that time we began our teamwork process.

Playing together helped us both to recognize how to work the Landry system, which meant allowing the strengths of the defense to work for you. The whole key was to not let the opposing offense know where your defensive weaknesses were, so as a free safety I would really try to disguise things. If I was double-covering on the inside routes, I'd line up on the weak side and pretend I was gonna blitz, then run all the way over to cover Charlie's receivers on the inside. From my experience at cornerback, I knew how lonely a position cornerback was, so I knew how and when to disguise things to help Charlie out. He and I worked that corner position almost as a tandem, and it helped us confuse the other team's quarterback. That one extra half-second that he held the ball would sometimes give our defensive ends extra time to trap the quarterback.

Let me give you an opposite example. Randy Hughes also played safety for us. Hughes personally would grade out at 100-percent every time. Problem was, the corners were getting beat when he was on the field. He played his position by the book, but the quarterbacks could read what he was doing and would just eat our corners alive.

It was never that way with me and Charlie. We always knew where each other would be. It was on a different level, a metaphysical level that I can't describe. Maybe our friendship had something to do with it. One time we were playing in Seattle and I intercepted a pass and was headed down the sidelines. Just when I was about to be hit, I cut back inside, spun around and tossed the ball in the air. Charlie Waters was running right behind me, caught the ball and ran it in for a touchdown. How I knew he was back there, I don't know. I just knew he was there. That was an example of how we worked together.

Dexter Demystifies the Doomsday "Flex"

What opponents didn't understand with the Flex was that it was stupidly simple. Growing up as a huge Cowboy fan, I always read how complicated the Flex was, but all it really had was a lot of fancy names and terms. If you just looked at the playbook, it was intimidating. It was like taking advanced placement English and having the teacher assign you this 450-page book by some guy named Dickerson or Dickens. You say, "Damn, this big book?"...

The Flex is probably the simplest defense in the world because unless you're the middle linebacker, you have only one thing to do. You just have one gap to control. Of the front seven, the middle linebacker is the only one with two gaps. The object is to control every gap. There are only so many gaps an offensive line can create for a ball carrier, so by their initial movements, the center and two guards tell the middle linebacker where to go. They are his keys...

You see, it was necessary to set two of our four defensive linemen a yard off scrimmage in a frog stance because this allowed them to sit back and see what was going on. They could read the actions of the offensive line, which would tell them which specific area they would control. You didn't control a man, you controlled an area. In the regular 4-3, you tried to control a man, but the Flex took away your natural instincts of pursuit. In effect, you held your ground and waited for the ball to come to you...

In the '60s and '70s this was an absolutely brilliant concept. Lee Roy Jordan was a student of the game and very quick and agile at around 200 pounds. Then came Bob Breunig in 1976, who was very smart and had some jets on him so he could get outside. He wasn't big (maybe 220) or strong, but he at least could pull down a ball carrier.

When [Breunig] retired, all Landry had was Eugene Lockhart, a poor middle linebacker for the Flex. Eugene doesn't have the speed or agility to get outside, and he isn't a thinker like Breunig and Lee Roy. The Flex might have been more dominant in the '80s if the Cowboys hadn't passed over [Baylor's] Mike Singletary. Gil Brandt, as I recall, decided Singletary was too short.

— **former Cowboys DB Dexter Clinkscales, as told to Skip Bayless in *"God's Coach"***
(Simon & Schuster, 1990)

You witnessed the disruptive quarterback controversy in the early 1970s as Landry flipped between Roger Staubach and Craig Morton. The two sometimes alternated plays during a game. What are your thoughts on that quarterback situation, and who did you feel was the best man for the job?

CH: It really was a genuine quarterback controversy. Landry was having a very difficult time with it. He liked a lot of things about Roger Staubach – his demeanor, his presence, his attitude, his character, his grittiness. But in his early years, Roger didn't have the system down. He'd get happy feet and scramble around and couldn't find a receiver because he was a young, inexperienced quarterback.

Craig, on the other hand, was a guy that could read defenses very well. He was a smart guy who understood the Landry system. He would find and throw it to the right guy, but he was not mobile. Craig lived a wilder lifestyle than Roger but, hey, everybody in the world lived a wilder lifestyle than Roger. I think Landry liked Roger better. Both were great quarterbacks. Craig had the advantage over Roger because of his experience, but he didn't have those intrinsic quarterback instincts that lead to winning.

Roger Staubach was a guy that bred confidence. I said this many times in fourth-quarter defensive huddles – *"Hey, we've got to get the ball back so Roger can win this for us."* We had confidence in him. That component alone is something invaluable to a coach and a team. You can't teach a guy that. You either have it or you don't. Craig Morton was a great quarterback who led his team to the Super Bowl, but there are things about Roger Staubach you can't define. He's a winner, that's the best way to describe it. There are quarterbacks with incredible talent and ability that would lose Super Bowl after Super Bowl because they didn't have that one ingredient that Roger had. It was that little drop of extra it took to win the game.

Morton eventually moved on to play for Denver, a team the Cowboys faced twice in 1977 – once during the regular season and again in Super Bowl XII. What did you learn from that first meeting with the Broncos that you used to your advantage in the Super Bowl rematch?

CH: The premise of Landry's flex defense was to stop the run first and force the other team to pass. Well, we already knew that we could stop Denver's running game. The Broncos did not have a great rushing attack. I don't think they had one back with over 500 yards. That fact alone played right into the teeth of the Flex. We knew that to be successful we had to get pressure on Craig so we blitzed a lot.

The game began and we made it clear they wouldn't be running against us, so what do you do next? You go after the quarterback, and that's exactly what we did in Super Bowl XII. If the Broncos were going to score points, they were going to have to do it by getting the ball to their wide receivers, Haven Moses and Rick Upchurch, and their tight end Riley Odoms. I helped disrupt that by knocking Upchurch out. He ran a down-and-in route and I knocked him out in the third quarter. To be honest, it knocked me a little fuzzy too. Haven Moses was a great receiver but it didn't matter. We matched up perfectly with those guys on defense. The strengths of our defense were exactly what was needed to defeat the Broncos offense. We were a machine in Super Bowl XII.

What did you do defensively to disrupt Morton, considering how well the Cowboys knew his tendencies?

CH: Well, that's a real touchy area. Craig Morton has been a good friend of mine for a long time, so I want to be as tactful as possible here. He's a great guy and was an incredible quarterback but I knew we were going to win that Super Bowl.

I did say something in the papers that I came to regret, though. I said, *"We're gonna beat Denver. I know we are. Craig Morton is gonna be knocked out and he won't finish the game."* I didn't say that maliciously but, heck, we were gonna come after him. That was no secret. Craig wasn't very mobile to begin with and I knew he had a big bruise on his leg from the first time we played them. Boy, Coach Landry got upset for me saying that, but sure enough it came true. We did knock him out.

One of the things I always prided myself on was my knowledge of opposing quarterbacks – knowing their strengths, their weaknesses, their tendencies – and I knew Craig's. I had faced him in practice every day from my rookie year until he was traded to the Giants in '74. I had his number. I knew how he thought, what plays he liked to run, what defenses bothered him. And when I've got the quarterback's number, man, we've got things under control. He ended up completing only four passes that day and threw four interceptions. We ran all the right defenses in Super Bowl XII, and that whole Denver operation fell right into our hands.

One of the greatest games never played during the 1970s would have been a Super Bowl matchup between the Cowboys and the Oakland Raiders. Had the dice rolled differently in any of the conference championship games of 1970, '73, '75, '76 or '77, it very well could have happened. Can you describe what an Oakland-Dallas Super Bowl would have looked like in those years?

CH: Oh, that would've been some game. The Raiders were the kind of team that I didn't like to play, and I'll tell you why: The Raiders were old school football, and that just didn't match up well with the precise, prototype, player-of-today Landry attacks. That includes both offense and defense. They were very elementary, a very similar operation to what Pittsburgh ran.

Oakland played on a slow, sluggish turf. They had an offense with a move guy at one wideout [Fred Biletnikoff] and an Olympic sprinter [Cliff Branch] as the other. They had big linemen and big backs that ran a very, very basic attack. Throw left. Run right. Charge all three linemen around the end, with a fullback who weighs 250-lbs as an escort, and try to beat you down.

I'll give you an example using weight-lifting terms. My best lift was a power clean, an explosive lift where you pick the weights right off the ground with one big burst. But the Oakland Raiders were like a bench press, the guy who lies on his back and presses a thousand pounds. I'd rather be involved in a game where the opponent tries to beat you with positioning rather than brute strength, like Don Coryell's teams in St. Louis. I preferred an intellectual battle with spread offenses and fast running backs and quarterbacks making you guess where the ball was going. I thrived in an environment of explosion and movement and quickness and coordination.

Landry's Flex defense was more suited to stop intricate attacks. It relied on disguising coverages and moving strengths from one place to another. On Astroturf you can out-quick people. Put me on a slow Oakland turf, with grass that's three inches thick, and suddenly I'm on the same level as a Marv Hubbard. Hubbard weighed 250 while I was at 195. Who's gonna win that battle after an entire day of pounding? I'm not saying we couldn't have beaten Oakland in a Super Bowl, but I would have preferred to play them on an artificial surface rather than on that wet, marshy stuff they had out in Oakland. We would need any speed or quickness advantages we could get.

How did Dallas' book on Raiders quarterback Ken Stabler read? The Cowboys' scouts must have been preparing for an Oakland matchup in case it ever developed.

CH: Kenny Stabler was a real good quarterback. He had that winning grit. A left-handed quarterback throws everything out of sync for a defense. Your whole defense is geared to stop a right-handed attack, but now that quick out is being fired to the left, so your reaction is slightly different. It's like seeing a left-handed pitcher and you're a right-handed batter. If you've got a weaker cornerback on the left side, you can do a better job of hiding him against a right-handed passer. But against a lefty, the quarterback is looking in his direction all the time and that spells trouble if you don't get him some help.

Let's talk more about Tom Landry. Had he not been a football coach, what would you have envisioned him being?

CH: I think he would have been the CEO of a very successful engineering company. A big bridge-building or aerospace company with lots of employees. He would've been the guy who had the vision and leadership. Tom was an engineer by degree. He would not have been a business entrepreneur. He would have been a methodical businessman that relied on his expertise in a specific field, which allowed him to provide a quality product through a quality organization. He did the same thing with the Cowboys, except the product was football instead of a bridge or a rocket ship.

What was Landry like in person? How different was he from the coach that was portrayed in the media or on America's television sets each Sunday?

CH: There weren't a lot of differences. The ones that did exist were subtle but had a depth to them. You'd sometimes see his feelings about players or games that the press would never see. You'd see an intensity that was incredible and real but subdued. As players, we knew the level of intensity that was inside Tom Landry, but the press and media didn't see it.

Another side they didn't see was the passionate side of Tom Landry, where he would pull you to the side and tell you how to cover and play better. With a few words of wisdom he could clear up a problem or situation like none of the other coaches could. He also had a very strong spiritual side. I often talked to Coach Landry about life and the important things in it. He always said, "You put God first and family second." You knew that he did that privately. He didn't impose his beliefs on the players, but if you asked him he'd tell you his thoughts and feelings about life outside of football.

In describing Tom Landry, words like "coolness" and "preparation" and "meticulous" were often used. But can you ever recall a situation where he acted out of character, where he lost his composure or became rattled or acted purely out of emotion?

CH: The side of him that the press wouldn't see – that I even saw very infrequently – was that expression of intensity. I'll go back to that game against the Giants during my rookie year in 1970. Coaching against the New York Giants twice a season were, without question, the most important games to Coach Landry. I'd like to hear the opinions of other [Dallas] players, but my impression was that he wanted to beat New York more than he wanted to win the Super Bowl. We were behind 10-0 at halftime, and he said, "You're a bunch of amateurs drawing pay," which was about the worst insult Coach Landry could give you. "You're not playing like professionals out there, and I'm embarrassed." I had never seen him talk or act like that before, and very rarely since. He popped that day. Most times he would just give you "The Look" instead.

One time we were playing in Chicago and I was returning punts. We were losing something like 17-14 and the offense was having a terrible day. There was barely any time left on the clock, but we'd stopped Chicago on their own 20 and forced them to punt. We had one last shot at winning the game. Coach Landry pulled me aside, which he rarely did, and said, "Cliff, fair-catch it. I want to stop the clock as soon as possible." The Bears kicked a low punt toward our sideline, and when I saw that I said to myself, "I'm gonna catch this and take off up the sidelines. I'll still run out of bounds to stop the clock, but I'll gain an extra 15 yards in the process. Our offense is going to need it."

I started running when a Bear player came up on me. But instead of heading out of bounds, I juked him and cut toward the middle of the field, trying to gain an extra few yards. Then another guy hit me from behind. As I was falling the ball hit the ground and rolled away. It was within a foot of my hands, but the guy was laying on my legs and I couldn't move. I was scratching into the Astroturf trying to get to the ball that was a foot away. The Bears recovered and the clock ran off. Standing there, six feet away from me on the Dallas sidelines, was Coach Landry. He gave me "The Look," which I'll never forget. Then he just turned away. He never said one thing to me, but I knew exactly what he was thinking and exactly what he thought of me at that time.

Playing for America's Team resulted in playing under America's spotlight when it came to press and media coverage of the Cowboys. How would you describe your overall experience with the Dallas media?

CH: There was constant attention, but for the most part we were treated fairly. For some reason, the incredible PR department of the Dallas Cowboys always seemed to push the offensive players, particularly Roger Staubach, through the media. That may have been because of Roger's overall personality and character and demeanor, and they wanted to project that. The 1970s was a time when guys were a little wilder on the social scene, including myself, and the Cowboys didn't want to project that image to the press. Roger's type of lifestyle was what the Cowboys wanted to project.

Overall, the Dallas media treated the Cowboys with great positive partiality. They did a good job. Bob St. John, Frank Luksa, Andy Anderson – all those guys were my friends and they treated the team fairly. But a writer named Blackie Sherrod was a guy that, for some reason, didn't like me. I don't know why. He was a powerful guy in Dallas and had a lot of influence, but he never seemed to be in my corner.

The one guy that I believe wrote stories for his own good and self-promotion was Skip Bayless. I don't think he was necessarily concerned with being fair or objective. His goal, in my opinion, was to sensationalize, to look for dirt. I was never a Skip Bayless fan. He was a good writer grammatically, and from a literary standpoint he wove a good tale. But a tale is what most of his stories were. I always felt that writers should be unbiased, portraying an accurate picture in a style that readers enjoy reading. They can be critical or positive or just report the news. But don't slant a story or try to dig something up just to create readership, and I think Skip Bayless did that a whole lot. I know there were some stories about me that I didn't like.

Any of those stories still bother you today?

CH: I don't really remember any of them, thank goodness. I didn't read most of them. If you do read them, it shouldn't affect your performance on the field but, hey, it could. I didn't want to be playing the game to appease the writers. I don't have a lot of bitterness in me. I don't have many enemies. You can ask me, "Who are the guys you don't like?" and it would be a very short list. Skip Bayless rubbed me wrong because he was only a "Skip Bayless guy." He wasn't out for the town or the team or even accuracy. He was out for himself, and I don't like those kind of guys. If I miss a tackle or an interception, fine. But don't write junk just to sell papers or to promote your career. Thankfully I didn't pay a whole lot of attention to those stories.

You must be able to think of one incident or story that still irks you.

CH: [DE] Pat Toomay was my roommate at that time, and he was kinda Skip Bayless' mole. He would get Bayless some good dirt, under the table stuff. He and Bayless were both Vanderbilt graduates and were friends and I think Pat was slipping him information about the team. That's all I can really say about it.

A Retort From Pat Toomay and Skip Bayless

"Skip's approach generally is to dig under the image for the reality that's inevitably there and this approach did not endear him to many in the Cowboys organization. If I remember correctly, the first column he did when he came to town was on Tony Dorsett. He went after one of the big guns, and his piece touched on racial issues, which were always an explosive topic in Dallas. Thus, he was viewed as an adversary from the beginning.

"I don't remember the specifics of Cliff's beef with Skip, to be honest. But for me, Skip was a breath of fresh air because he went against the grain and would get at stuff the puff press wouldn't touch. I felt the game needed that kind of sunshine/disinfectant. Had I had more of my identity invested in the organization, I might have felt differently."

– former Cowboys defensive end Pat Toomay

"I really don't understand Cliff Harris' resentment or animosity towards me at all. I don't recall ever writing a critical or negative piece about him in particular, the 'Harris Has Lost a Step' or 'Harris Should Retire' piece.

"I started covering the Cowboys toward the end of Harris' career. The Cowboys were starting to slip as a team but I still didn't see it. They were the defending champs but I was still too young and inexperienced to notice where they were dropping off.

"As far as Cliff Harris, the only incident I can truly think of occurred at the end of their '79 training camp. I'd written an article and mentioned something about Harris' insecurity about his role on the team. It was toward the end of his career and he had lost some of his speed and really wasn't opening up to the press much. When people are feeling insecure about something, they tend not to talk about it and Cliff wasn't talking.

"A few of the Cowboys were having a drink in the parking lot to celebrate the end of camp and I walked by. Then Cliff yelled out, 'Hey Skip, it's not weak safety! *It's free safety*!' I had referred to his position as the weak safety and he didn't like it."

– former *Dallas Morning News* columnist Skip Bayless

Final question. Looking back on your career, would you still go for the knockout rather than the interception?

CH: That's a tough question, one I've debated many times in my mind. I'm a team guy. I tried to make plays for the benefit of the team. The biggest mistake that I made – and it's the reason I'm not in the Hall of Fame – is because I knocked guys out rather than going for the interception. But football isn't boxing, and there are no official statistics for knockouts. But it's also true that knocking out the other team's best receiver helps to win the game.

In every game I played during my career, I'll bet most of the offenses said, "Look, let's not run so many downs-and-in. Let's run an out, let's run some counter things, let's try to finesse Cliff Harris. I think that I was a major factor in our opponents having to change their offensive gameplan, and I was a factor in us winning Super Bowls. I had the respect of my peers, teammates and of the people that knew football, and I still have it today. The Hall of Fame is just an acknowledgment of that. People remember me as the starting free safety for the Dallas Cowboys. If I go into the Hall of Fame, great. If not, I'll still have earned respect.

I guess the answer is that I'd *still* knock the hell out of those guys.

1

Steelers personnel director Art Rooney, Jr. chats with one of his most prized draft picks, linebacker Jack Ham, in the locker room at Three Rivers Stadium. Over a six-year span (1969-74) Rooney's drafts produced an amazing nine future Hall-of-Famers.

2

Bum Phillips stares from the sidelines during the 1979 AFC Championship played in frozen Pittsburgh. "Hammer and tong games" – that's what the former Oilers coach called his team's bitter battles with the Steelers.

Pittsburgh lineman L.C. Greenwood swoops down on quarterback Dan Pastorini during the 1979 AFC Championship game. The Oilers quarterback struggled in his two playoff meetings with the Steelers, throwing six interceptions.

Sportswriter Paul Zimmerman – "Dr. Z," they call him – has covered professional football for over 40 years. No one has done it better.

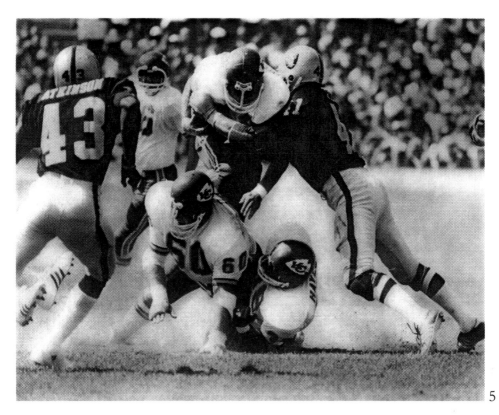

5

Oakland linebacker Phil Villapiano puts the clamps on running back Ed Podolak during an early 1970s clash with Kansas City. The powerful Raiders advanced to six AFC title games during the decade but were victors only once.

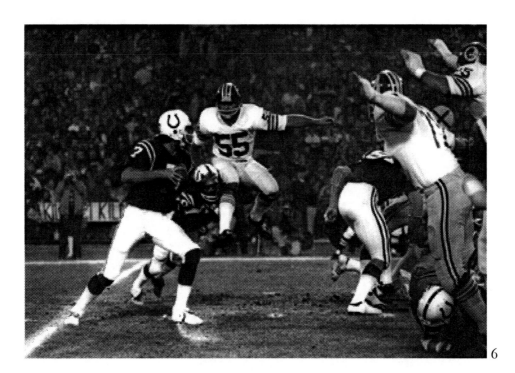

6

The Redskins send an angry mob after Bert Jones on a Monday night contest in Baltimore. The Colts quarterback threw for 191 yards on a damaged shoulder and helped knock Washington out of the 1978 playoff hunt.

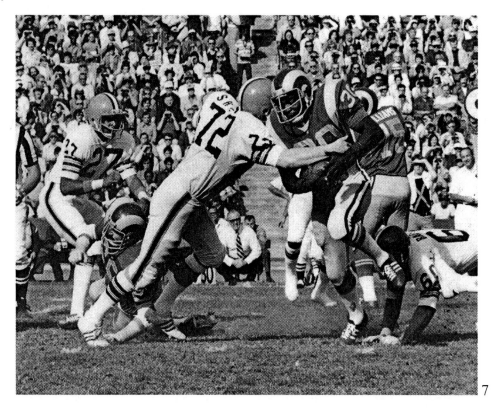

7

Rams tailback Lawrence McCutcheon collides with Pro Bowl DT Jerry Shirk during a December 1973 game at the L.A. Coliseum. On this short burst, McCutcheon set the team's single season rushing record with 1,097 yards.

8

NFL Films' Steve Sabol (center) captures the coin toss before Super Bowl VIII, Miami vs. Minnesota. "The Dolphins were a machine," says Sabol, "cold and methodical in the way they snuffed out the Vikings."

9

Steve Sabol laments the NFL's decision to begin playing its biggest game indoors. "Super Bowl XII – Dallas versus Denver – was held in the Superdome and it just destroyed our lighting. It sterlized everything our cameras were trying to convey."

10

New Orleans quarterback Archie Manning fires a sideline pass against the Bills on November 4, 1973. It was a rare day for the lowly Saints as they punched out Buffalo, 13-0, earning the first shutout in team history.

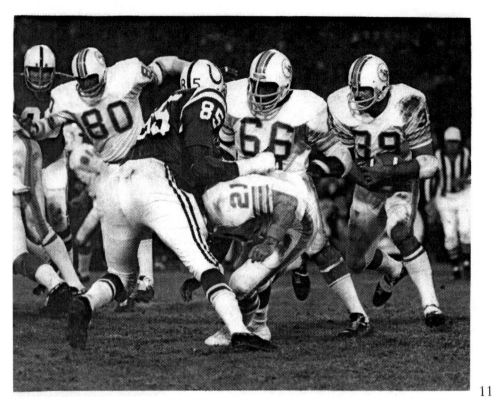

11

Miami Dolphins guard Larry Little (#66) and tailback Jim Kiick (#21) clear the way for hard-charging Larry Csonka in an early '70s game against the Colts.

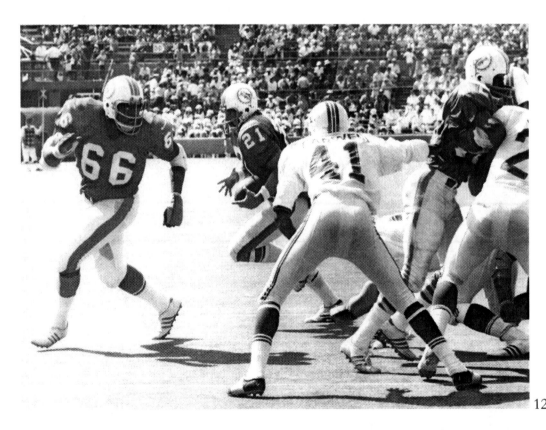

12

"On the sweep, my goal was to drill fear into any defensive back who tried to stop us," says Larry Little. In this contest at the Orange Bowl, Patriots cornerback Larry Carwell draws the unenviable assignment.

13

Larry Little on a search-and-destroy mission against the Packers in 1975. Despite the loss of RBs Larry Csonka and Jim Kiick to the WFL, the '75 Dolphins rushed for 2,500 yards behind one of history's finest offensive line performances.

14

Dallas safety Cliff Harris was known as "Captain Crash," a fierce hitter and special teams dynamo. Here he scores on a dramatic punt return against the Saints in 1971.

15

The Cowboys operated one of the NFL's most destructive blitz packages during the 1970s. Here Cliff Harris lowers the boom on Rams quarterback Pat Haden during a 1978 contest in Los Angeles.

16

Charlie Jones interviews quarterbacks Joe Namath (#12) and John Hadl before the 1965 AFL All-Star Game in New Orleans. "If I was a coach and had one play left to win a Super Bowl," says Jones, "I'd want Namath at quarterback and him calling the play."

17

Inconsistency plagued St. Louis quarterback Jim Hart for years until coach Don Coryell arrived. By 1974, Hart was the NFC Player of the Year and the Cardinals had surged into the playoffs.

18

Both the AFL and NFL mistakenly ignored Jim Hart in the 1966 college draft. Only two undrafted quarterbacks in football history have exceeded his 34,665 career passing yards.

19

49ers DE Cedric Hardman fights through a double team during a 1970 game at Kezar Stadium. San Francisco's vaunted "Gold Rush" collected 381 sacks during the decade; only the Rams, Cowboys, Steelers and Redskins had more.

20

Coach Chuck Fairbanks rescued the New England Patriots after years of ineptitude. Despite a controversial loss to Oakland in the 1976 AFC playoffs, many observers felt his team was the best in pro football that season.

21

A career in transition. The week before this photo was taken, Tom Brookshier was the Philadelphia Eagles' starting cornerback. A broken leg helped put him in the CBS broadcast booth for the next 19 years.

22

Safety Mike Wagner cracked the Pittsburgh starting lineup as a rookie in 1971. "His aggression and smarts gave us the kind of presence we were looking for in our secondary," said Steelers coach Chuck Noll.

23

For years he was the voice of pro football on NBC. From those old AFL duels through the close of the Steel Curtain, Curt Gowdy was one of broadcasting's finest.

24

Before taking over as head coach of the expansion Seattle Seahawks in 1976, Jack Patera coordinated the powerful thrust of Minnesota's famed "Purple People Eaters."

25

Jack Patera's talent-starved Seahawks ran football's most imaginative offense during the late 1970s. Gadget plays, fake kicks, fourth-down gambles – "It was simply a matter of survival," said the coach.

— 11 —
Charlie Jones, Broadcaster
NBC Sports (1965-98)
June 26, 2002

I knew an old steelworker from Baltimore who had it. The voice, one an ear could never forget. Gruff, but golden. Authoritative, yet comforting. The sound of experience, when someone's seen it all and lived to tell. Ed Callahan was miscast in life. He should've been working the broadcast booth on his Sundays rather than trudging through 3-to-11 shifts at the mill. With a voice like that, I would've listened to the man read from a phone book.

He'd sit around that wobbly, carved-up table at the coke ovens of Bethlehem Steel, drinking creosote coffee, talking shop with the crew and bitching about the boss or the kids or his lunch or whatever. Sometimes his stories were funny.

"I'll tell you how dumb my daughter is," I overheard him telling a co-worker. "She goes out to buy a new car...you know, something reasonable...and comes home with a goddamn fully-loaded Escort! Power windows, leather seats, CD player, sunroof, every damn thing. A $7,000 car with seven grand in extras on top of it! That's like putting a dishwasher in your tree house."

I especially liked the days when the subject was football, those tales of the old Baltimore Colts. The mill guys still loved 'em...Marchetti...Unitas...Berry...Lenny Moore...all the names.

"I had an endzone seat in Green Bay the day after Christmas, 1965," Callahan once told me. "Drove the whole way from Baltimore to Wisconsin for that one. 900 miles, straight through, with a guy from the tin mill, right after Christmas dinner. Both Colts quarterbacks were banged up, so Tom Matte is in there with the plays taped to his wrist. Well, they might as well have been taped to his goddamn forehead because he couldn't complete a pass.

"Then the fog came. What it did was hide a missed field goal that the referees called good for the Packers. It flew right over my head, three feet left of the goal post." I listened for a moment and could envision an unsure football tumbling through the Green Bay haze.

"You missed your calling, Eddie," I'd tell him. "With a voice like that you should be broadcasting games like Chuck Thompson. Instead of working in a steel mill, you should be working for the Steelers."

"Aww, the hell with the Steelers," he growled with half a smile. "The hell with the Colts, too," which by 1991 had long since abandoned Baltimore for the Midwest.

But I was always serious when I said that to him. Memorable voices like Callahan's shouldn't be lost in the roars and groans of a steel mill or a shipyard or wherever else they might be found. They should be on the airwaves, somewhere, bringing people the action of the day.

I once asked NFL Films' Steve Sabol about his search to replace his company's legendary voice, the one of John Facenda – Billy Crystal dubbed it "the voice of God" – after he had passed away from cancer in 1984. Did Sabol's hunt take him to the local pool halls or church pulpits or corner saloons? Did he look where real people are found, not in the vapor trail of the pre-fab communication schools, where the *SportsCenter* wannabes practice their standup routine and learn how to apply hair mousse? His response was disappointing.

"At first we did look in those common kind of places, sure we did. We looked everywhere, but eventually we realized it would be a mistake trying to come up with a Facenda clone. People wouldn't buy it, and it probably would've backfired on us. So we just moved on."

Moved on to what? To nothing, obviously, because there is no longer a "Voice of NFL Films." Their voice tracks now rings hollow. Their employees all sound the same. Sabol didn't need to find a Facenda impersonator, just a strong, believable voice with character. It shouldn't have been that difficult.

Hell, it only took me two days to find Ed Callahan.

• •

Charlie Jones thinks he knows where all the great voices have gone. Charlie Jones should know because he is one of them. The long-time veteran of NBC Sports and AFL/AFC football telecasts, Jones shakes his head at the vanilla drone that dampens the action of today's television productions.

"I'll tell you what has happened," he says. "The great ones have all gone by the way of radio. Back in the 1930s and '40s and '50s, radio was by far the number one source of entertainment. Radio days. People were listening, not watching. And to make it as a successful broadcaster, you had to have a strong, distinct voice and delivery and a relative mastery of description. Mel Allen, Vin Scully, Lindsey Nelson, Ray Scott, Curt Gowdy – the Hall of Fame voices – were all radio men before they moved on to television.

"That's no longer true with today's announcers. The requirements have changed because radio has lost a lot of its importance. Television is now king. The picture on the screen tells the story, so you don't need that strong, distinct voice to carry the broadcast, just a competent one to fill in around the action. But as a result, there are really very few distinct voices in sports television today."

Jones' introduction to football came in the form of the wild ramblings of the Southwest Conference during the 1940s. "Arkansas and Texas football – that's all we knew back in Fort Smith [AR]. We tuned in every week. It was great, fun football."

A lawyer by degree, his first job in professional sports came in 1960 with the arrival of the American Football League. "I was hired as director of television and radio for the Dallas Texans during the AFL's first year," says Jones. "ABC had the league's broadcast rights and was looking for announcers because it had no sports department. No producers, no broadcasters, no statisticians – nothing. I called the very first AFL game ever televised. September 10, 1960 – the Texans at the Los Angeles Chargers in the Coliseum. Fred Benners, a former SMU quarterback, was my first colorman. I think it was the only game he ever called."

Jones chuckles at the rudimentary production that was behind the telecast that historic day.

"It was bare-bones. No graphics or replays or anything like that. We basically did a radio broadcast with three black-and-white stationary cameras, one at the fifty and one at each 20-yard line. 19,000 people showed up. The stadium held 106,000. There were occasional pockets of applause during the game. We'd look out from the booth but couldn't see where it was coming from.

"The AFL learned two things that night. One, always sell tickets on the opposite side of the cameras, and two, don't let the cameras follow the football on punts and kickoffs. If you did, all the empty seats are coming right across the TV screen."

His most vivid memory of that historic evening?

"A close game. Jack Kemp was the Chargers quarterback and he threw a long touchdown pass to Ralph Anderson. Each team threw over 40 passes.

"What sticks out most in my mind actually happened *after* the game. We held a short production meeting, and I was talking to [former ABC producer and executive] Roone Arledge. I mentioned to him that it was the first football game I had ever called. He shrieked, 'Thank goodness you didn't tell me that before kickoff! That was the first football game *I ever produced!* We could've had a real disaster on our hands!'"

In 1965, NBC took over the league's TV broadcasts and hired Jones for a stint that lasted 33 years. He knows the network got its money's worth from those vocal chords.

"During the fall, it was AFL or AFC football every Sunday. During the other seasons, my weekends were a real kaleidoscope – golf, swimming, horse racing, basketball, rodeo, bobsled... you name it, I've called it. I've counted my frequent flier miles out in millions. But my true love will always – *always* – be professional football. For me, there's nothing like Sunday afternoons at 1 o'clock."

Sundays once filled with jerseys that read Alworth and Blanda and Lanier and Namath. Coaches known as Stram and Paul Brown and Weeb. AFL names. Hall-of-Fame names.

Jones on the league's merger with the National Football League in 1970: "To me it meant that the AFL had finally arrived. Some purists might've been saddened by it, by the impending loss of identity, but not me. My only criticism was they should've kept the "AFL" name. "AFC" just didn't sound right.

"I watched it grow from a league of castoffs and run-down stadiums and sneering looks to a league of champions, to the Jets and Chiefs winning Super Bowls. There were many great days, and the AFL became part of my life."

For those of us who were watching on all those distant, autumn Sundays, Charlie Jones – and the voice of Charlie Jones – became part of ours.

• • •

How many different football analysts have saddled-up next to you during your years with NBC Sports?

CJ: [Thinking] About 65. When I reached number 51, who was Jimmy Cefalo, I actually gave him a jersey with the number 51 on it. Before him there was George Ratterman, Len Dawson, Jim Otto and Sam DeLuca. DeLuca was the only man I ever worked with who could get excited over a block by an offensive lineman – "[imitating DeLuca] He really nailed him!" I'd look around the field and think, "What the hell is Sam talking about? I must be losing it! What's going on?" It could be a trap block with the play shielded over by four people so you couldn't even see it, but Sam would be going crazy! I can spend all day here going through the list of guys I worked with.

Sixty-five? That's a new partner every six months or so.

CJ: Well, let me explain that a little bit. There were years where I would work with five different people. But they did things different then, entirely different than what the networks do now. Going way back to 1960, tape hadn't been invented yet, so you couldn't have somebody come in and talk against a monitor and look at another ballgame because none of that technology existed. There was no way of testing new announcers except for testing them on the air. And this was the way it was done, even into the 1980s. The other thing you have to remember is that back in the '60s and '70s, the game wasn't big business, like it eventually became in the '80s and the '90s.

I would get three or four different partners during the year, and if it worked they stayed and if it didn't work, they didn't stay. That was a big reason why I've worked with so many people. I developed a reputation of being good with the new kids and getting things out of them, so the network could find out very quickly if this person had some potential.

I always love telling the story about Bob Griese. He retired after the 1980 season and tried out as an announcer with NBC. We sat down and did a broadcast of a preseason game between the 49ers and the Chargers into a tape machine, and he was terrible. Oh, God. When the night was over, I looked at him and thought, "Why does he even want to try this?" He just didn't get it. He didn't understand what was being asked of him, and it was obvious. But NBC signed him anyway, and he did several games when there were some weak matchups. I didn't work with him any during the regular season, but I heard some of his tapes or caught him doing a game on the TV and I'd think, "Oh, man..." He was really struggling.

Then the assignments came out for the next year and I got Bob! I'm thinking, "Holy Cow! Why *me?*" Then we do our first game together and he's dynamite! He had made a quantum leap! I remember going to the airport after the game and saying to him, "What in the hell have you done? What happened? You're there, you're on top of everything."

He told me, "It was exactly like going through my rookie season with the Miami Dolphins. I went through that whole first year and I didn't know what I was doing. I didn't know what anybody expected of me. I couldn't figure it out. I just stumbled and tried and made mistakes, but nothing really worked. But by the end of the year, I got some film and looked at it with the gameplan in front of me. I reviewed it and compared things to the gameplan, then all of a sudden I said, 'Oh, *that's* what it is. *That's* what they want.'" He said, "I did the same thing last summer. I got tapes of every one of my games, and I got out all of my notes and I tried to figure out what the hell it was that the network wanted me to do. And about halfway through the tapes, it came to me. I figured it out." Of course, Bob went on to have a super-successful career, and now he's really very good.

Very Superstitious...Writing's on the Wall

"I would have to say I am a superstitious person, at least about certain things. I had a specific routine that I followed on gameday, and part of that included a breakfast of French toast in my hotel room. Once I was doing a game in Boston and was told that morning that the hotel couldn't give me French toast, so I settled for scrambled eggs.

"Well, right after kickoff NBC lost the audio feed between Boston and New York. I was told that a phone connection had mistakenly been unplugged, but I knew better. *I knew it was those damn scrambled eggs.* They screwed up my routine! Since then, I always made a point to check the room service menu before checking into a hotel."

- Charlie Jones

What kind of problems did Griese initially have in the booth?

CJ: Well, he had no enthusiasm. Bob is a very low-key person anyway, so that was a problem from the start. He didn't know how to talk in twenty-second sound bites. He didn't understand the discipline of knowing that when the teams break out of the huddle, he has to zip up. Once they're out of the huddle, they're mine. When the tackle is made, then he can have them back and do the replay and whatever else he wants. But from the time they come out of the huddle until the tackle is made, they're mine.

If the analyst spills into the play too far, it can be a problem. Once in a while it's okay, especially toward the end of the game when it's been decided. But if it becomes a habit of doing that, then I don't have time to set the skeleton of the down and distance and score. Now they have those little bugs that sit up in the corner of the TV screen. Back then we didn't have that type of technology.

Bob also had a problem – which is a common one for new announcers – of determining what information really fits the scenario. The easiest habit is to simply repeat what you just saw on the screen. Well, the guy at home just saw the same thing, so that type of commentary is no help. Just like with writers or entertainers or stand-up comedians – some just have the timing, the ability to know what fits and when to say it. Bob never had a show biz type of personality while he was playing in the NFL, but he had to become that. And he did. So his first year was very difficult, but he was certainly neat to work with once he got going.

Which analyst, in terms of relaying football knowledge to the audience, was most impressive to you?

CJ: Probably Len Dawson. But you have to realize that the analyst's slot on network television is really only made for two kinds of people. That's either a head coach or a quarterback. They are the only ones who really understand everything that's going on. The quarterback knows the offense and reads the defense, so he sees both things. The head coach does the same.

There are exceptions, however. One of them is Todd Christensen. He is so brilliant. His IQ is out of sight. He has a photographic memory. We'd sit down before a game and interview players for four hours and he would never take a note. Then the next day he could come back and quote verbatim everything that was said. Meanwhile, I've got notes and pieces of paper and Post-Its stuck everywhere, just trying to remember certain subjects, which he would then take off and run with. From that standpoint, he was absolutely brilliant.

Merlin Olsen, a former defensive tackle, had to teach himself the offensive side of the game. He had such a great work ethic and worked so hard at learning it. He'd look at the teams' films on Saturday, setting up a session with an assistant coach. I would only review television films because that's what I knew and that's what I was supposed to talk about – the way that it plays on television. But Merlin wanted to know the details behind what the offense was doing so he learned everything he could. And being an entertainer on television and movies, he understood the show biz side of it, which is something a lot of analysts don't bring to the booth.

What about the opposite side? Were there certain individuals that you clashed with in the booth, where the chemistry was lousy and you didn't enjoy working with them?

CJ: Yeah, Bob Trumpy. I worked with him during my last year with NBC. We just never meshed doing football. It was surprising because we had worked golf together for fifteen years and had really meshed well! When they first told me I would be working with Bob, I was excited about it. I thought we'd really be good. I remembered him from his days as a tight end with the Cincinnati Bengals and I did a lot of his games, covered his entire career. He had been in broadcasting since he retired in the late '70s and had done a great job, especially doing the radio broadcasts with Don Criqui on NBC Radio. But with us it just didn't fit. He would be thinking one thing and I'd be thinking another. If there was an outstanding play I'd want to talk about what the defense just did, and he'd start talking about the offense. The next play it would reverse. It was awkward, like dancing out of step for the entire ball.

So it wasn't a personality issue, just one of chemistry?

CJ: Oh, no! We were good friends and still are. It just didn't mesh. It didn't work.

Last question on analysts: Is there anyone you would have liked to work with but never had the opportunity?

CJ: Oh, I would've liked to work with John Madden, and there are several reasons. The first is that I'd covered him for the whole ten years that he was the head coach of the Oakland Raiders, and I always had a great rapport with him. The second reason is simply because he's good and he's always working to get better. He speaks for the fan. It would also be great fun to travel with him and to have that Thanksgiving turkey dinner with him on that bus. What happens when you work with John Madden as the announcer is you become the supporting actor. Your job is to make him the star. If that works, you both win. And that's very difficult for some announcers to do, especially the younger ones.

I'd like to take this a step further. I've been around so long and have worked with so many people that I have developed my own philosophy about the way you work with your analysts. From the standpoint of television presentation, the greatest NFL play-by-play broadcaster ever is Pat Summerall. He made Madden so great. He did it by setting him up, by allowing him the time, by not letting his own ego get involved. There's an old, old story that goes back to the heyday of radio. When you are conducting a radio interview, you are the supporting actor. The person you are interviewing is the star.

Today, the kids doing interviews on Fox and ESPN and the rest of the networks are not the supporting actors. Their questions go on for fifteen minutes because they want to show everybody how knowledgeable they are. But guess what? The audience doesn't care about them! Their job is to set up the *other* person! Every once in a while I'll lecture college classes and they ask me, "What are we supposed to do?" I'll respond, "All you have to do is say, 'Tell me more, tell me more…'"

You *have* to listen, because if you do your subject will lead you into some wonderful areas. A lot of announcers don't want to do that. They want to talk forever to show the world how much they know, and while their subject is answering, they're not paying attention to what's being said. They're just watching to see when the lips stop moving, thinking about when they're going to fire off the next question.

Is that the most irritating trait today's broadcasters have, not listening to their subjects?

CJ: That bothers me probably more than anything else. Most of them do their homework, and they have the knowledge and the talent. But they also have it in their minds that people are tuning in because they are the star.

Let's talk about how you developed your style and technique of providing a well-announced football game. Can you trace that process back over the years?

CJ: When I was in high school, I sat on the bench as "the other quarterback," which meant I only played in the games where we were either way ahead or way behind. We'd have games on Friday nights, then on Saturdays all the guys would gather at a place we called Ward's Field, which was just this huge side yard of the richest man in town. We'd play touch football, just having fun. Television hadn't been invented yet, so everybody would have their car radios on listening to Bill Stern, who always did the college *Game of the Week*. We'd be playing the game and listening with one ear open to Bill Stern. I specifically remember hearing an SMU-Notre Dame game, when Kyle Rote replaced the great Doak Walker, who was injured. Kyle had this absolutely unbelievable game, and the coverage Stern gave him that day is what set him up to be an All-American. The way Stern broadcast that game really made a big impression on me.

There was a broadcaster from Houston, who also became Vice President of the advertising firm McCann-Erickson, named Kern Tips. At that time, Humble Oil was the sponsor of Southwest Conference football and basketball, and Tips handled that account, so he was close to the Humble people. That enabled him to do the prime SWC game of the week, like Texas-Texas A&M, Texas-Arkansas, SMU-TCU. He had this unique style filled with cowboy references, this real western drawl. That is where I got a lot of the terms I used like, "He lassoed him down," or "He rode him down like a bull rider," or "The shadows of the press box are creeping across the field, as we are coming to the end of the afternoon."

I wrote those things down when I heard them. In fact, at one time I had a big notebook full of expressions that said the same thing twenty different ways. Eventually, I'd scratch out the hokey ones and go back and listen to myself. When you listen to yourself, you begin to broadcast for yourself, in the way you want to hear a game. There are certain things that I like to hear as a listener, so I use them. That process goes on for your entire career. If I were watching a Monday night game and something was said that was really good, I'd figure out a way to incorporate it into my telecast. I'd mention it at the next production meeting and try to work it into our broadcast. Maybe not right away, but somewhere down the road.

Developing your style is an ongoing process of collecting things that sound good. You steal and you borrow and you alter, but you're constantly looking for new things. If it works, great. If it doesn't, then you just throw it away. I tell the young broadcasters, "Broadcast for *yourself*. Don't try to please somebody else. Don't try to sound like me. Don't try to sound like Al Michaels. Broadcast for yourself, because you are unique and what you bring is unique. What you bring is entirely different from what I bring or what Vin Scully or Jack Buck brings.

In doing play-by-play, there are only two things you have to get right – the name pronunciation and the score. If you can get those two things right, then you're half way home. That's the reason why I think basketball is the best of all sports for play by play, because there is always something to talk about. Baseball is the hardest because a lot of times there is nothing to talk about. In basketball, if you follow the person who has the ball, pronounce his name right, say whether the shot is good or not, and give the score, then you've covered it. Then you start adding things like the backdoor trap and the zones and the switches and the strategies and whatever else they're doing. After a while you recognize these things and learn to describe what's going on twenty different ways. It works that way because the same things happen over and over. For example, how many times is there a first down in a ball game?

When you're a young announcer, you go into the booth with this whole list of wonderful sayings, which reminds me of a story. I remember doing a high school football game on a little 250-watt radio station, and I saw a friend of mine the day after my Friday night broadcast. He said, "I listened to the whole ball game, Charlie. It was very interesting."

I said, "Well, what does that mean?"

He said, "Well, was it tackle football?"

"Yes, of course it was."

Then he told me, "You never once said that. You never had anyone making a tackle in the whole ball game. You said, 'They rode him down, they lassoed him, they clotheslined him, they tripped him, they nailed him,' but they never just tackled him." He was just kidding with me, but it's very true that you can trap yourself by trying to be too cute.

Good Time Charlie Loses His Cool

"Good Time" Charlie Jones, we called him. He was always upbeat, fun to be around. Charlie was the ultimate professional in the booth, and he really helped me with my career as a broadcaster. But there was one time during our seven years together that he wasn't the ultimate professional.

We were doing a game down at the Orange Bowl in Miami, the Dolphins versus somebody. Charlie always worked with two spotters for his games, and he relied heavily on them. But on this day, for whatever reason, they didn't show up. Maybe they were stuck in traffic or overslept. It was close to kickoff, and Charlie was getting real nervous… "Where the hell are they? *Where the hell are those guys?*"

Finally, it was game time and we're on the air. No spotters. Charlie was furious. And let me tell you, every chance he got – during commercials or any kind of break - he bitched and pissed and moaned about it. He was beside himself. He was unraveled for the entire first half. I didn't say anything, but his tirade really bothered me. I did not like seeing him lose his cool like that while we were on the air.

Well, the spotters finally showed up at halftime, and things quickly got back to normal. The rest of the broadcast went fine. I kept quiet until we were both inside the limousine leaving the stadium after the game, then I really let him have it.

"Don't you ever…EVER…do that to me again during a broadcast! Do you understand me, Charlie? When we're doing a game, *you're* in charge! *You're* the play-by-play guy! *You're* the quarterback in the booth and I'm looking for you to be the leader, to get us through the broadcast." I was furious.

"When I was a player," I said, "I never came apart in front of my teammates like that, not even in the huddle! No matter if I was getting beat to a pulp because of lousy blocking, or guys were dropping balls on me, or we were getting our asses kicked by the other team – I never came apart like that! I never lost my cool in front of my teammates. They were looking at me as their leader, and I never once acted like I wasn't!"

I think he was stunned at first, but I'm pretty sure Charlie got the message. I'm very sure he remembers that limo ride. He thanked me the next week in Denver.

- Hall of Fame quarterback and former NBC analyst Len Dawson

Who is your favorite announcer?

CJ: I loved listening to Lindsey Nelson. Lindsey worked for the Liberty Broadcasting Network, which used to do the Major League Baseball *Game of the Day*. They used to do re-creation of the games in the basement of KLIF in Dallas. This was at the end of World War II and television was just barely starting. Lindsey was on the radio every day, announcing all the best teams, so I associated him with the national baseball picture. He also did a lot of college football. For some reason, Lindsey's voice always brought me memories of college football. I got a chance to meet him later on and eventually work with him on some NBC golf tournaments. He was an absolutely delightful man. He really had a direct influence on me early in my career.

What about the games themselves? Do you have an all-time favorite football game that you broadcast?

CJ: The Florida State-Notre Dame game from 1993 comes to mind, the battle for number one. It was a great ballgame and you didn't want it to end. Back and forth, all day. I thought to myself, "Don't let this day end! Keep it going! Tie it up and let's play on forever!"

In the pros – and this is a cop-out answer – I did Super Bowl III on NBC radio. It was during the Vietnam War and we were on all over the world on the Armed Forces Radio Network. The Jets, being an 18 ½-point underdog, pulled the upset over the Colts. Namath guaranteed the Jets would win on the Thursday night before the game, and everybody at NBC, including me, went into cardiac arrest. [NBC] Management sighed, "Oh my God….Why did he have to do that?" We just wanted them to stay close. And then they win, and everybody was standing around with smiles on their faces.

In my mind, that game changed the perception of pro football in this country. In reality, it was a giant step for the National Football League. They had already decided upon the merger, and a lot of people thought the league was going to become weaker. But with the Jets victory, the AFL was finally on an even keel with the NFL and people realized that the league was going to become much stronger. It brought parity across the board, which really wasn't present before then.

There's another reason that Super Bowl sticks out for me. About three days after the game, Pete Rozelle called and asked me if I'd go on the NFL tour of the hospitals in the Far East. The Vietnam War was still going on. I agreed, and my roommate turned out to be Joe Namath. We traveled together for twenty-one days and had some great conversations about the game. I had covered Joe since he was a rookie and had done tons of his ball games, so we knew each other and were very comfortable. It was quite memorable, an interesting time.

You broadcast AFL games for NBC and watched that league grow up. Did you honestly feel that the AFL had reached the same competitive level as the NFL prior to the Super Bowl III upset?

CJ: Yes, very much so. But there were not a lot of believers. One of the reasons was a man named Tex Maule, who wrote pro football for *Sports Illustrated*. He thought that the NFL sat on the right hand of God, and the rest of the world were upstarts. He was constantly down on the AFL and in heavy favor of the National Football League. He even wrote a lot of the narration used by NFL Films. There weren't nearly as many national media outlets like there are now, so exposure was very limited. There were three major television networks, *Sporting News*, *Sports Illustrated*, *Sport* magazine, and that was about it.

For those of us affiliated with the AFL from the early days it got to be a running joke. First, the criticism was that the AFL didn't have the premier quarterbacks. Then the next year, it was "Okay, the quarterbacks are better, but the AFL doesn't have any top running backs." And this went on every year, through almost each position. Finally it came down to, "The AFL is as good as the NFL except they just don't have the cornerbacks. The two cornerbacks from the Green Bay Packers can eat the AFL alive." I'm thinking, if they're talking about two cornerbacks as being the only difference, then there is parity between the two leagues and they just won't admit it. We at NBC thought the parity existed but, of course, we were prejudiced.

That's the same opinion that Curt Gowdy, your associate at NBC, had.

CJ: That's funny you mention him. I was thinking about Curt the other day. I think it's sad that there are now two generations that never got to hear Curt and his work. He was so good. I'm not sure there will ever be anybody again who can compile the list of credentials that he did – the World Series, NCAA Finals, Super Bowls, Olympic games. He covered all the top events. He was the man, and justifiably so because he was really good.

Do you remember the atmosphere around NBC back in 1979, the year Gowdy's exile from the network was being planned? Do you remember hearing the rumblings?

CJ: Yes, I do. I know there was a strong push from management for him to retire. The attitude was that Curt had had his day, time to move on. Then Curt went over to CBS and gave them three more good years. Finally he got tired of the traveling and retired. I never really heard the details on how [his firing] happened, but remember I was in California. Actually, I think the reason I lasted 33 years at NBC was because I was three thousand miles away, so they had a tendency to forget about me. They couldn't get pissed at me for coming down the hall or for something I said because they never physically saw me.

The word on the street was that NBC had become too synonymous with Curt Gowdy and that was troublesome to some of the network bigwigs. Similar to what happened with Brent Musberger at CBS.

CJ: That's probably right, but I'm not sure if Musberger is the proper example. The story on Musberger was that he was fired for two reasons. The first is because there was a change at management level. Anytime you have a change at management level, the new person coming in is going to make an announcer change. Somebody is going to get nailed. The reason that happens is because that's the only way they can make a mark that the general public will understand and say, "Oh, *he* did that." If he goes out and hires the best directors and best producers, the public doesn't know. The media doesn't really make a big deal when there is a management change. You might get a little blurb in *USA Today*, but in general, the public doesn't know. The public relates to the talent that is on TV week-in and week-out.

The other thing I heard with Musberger is that – particularly in regards to *The NFL Today* – he became the 800-lb gorilla. He wanted this and he wanted that and he wanted to do this event, and if he didn't get his way then he was raising hell with everybody. Now it's possible Gowdy may have been doing that, even though I don't think that's his personality. But he may have been doing it in his own way.

After all of your great years with NBC, you were never given the opportunity to call an AFC Championship game or a Super Bowl for television. Do you resent not being given that chance?

CJ: Yes and no. Obviously I resented it more then than now, because then it was more part of my daily life. I remember I had a conversation with Arthur Watson when he was the head of NBC. I had been with NBC a while – around 25 years – so I felt comfortable talking to him about that. He knew the caliber of my work, so it wouldn't be a big surprise one way or the other.

We talked, and he said, "Let me explain something to you. Whether you agree or disagree, this is the way you fit into my mind, into my program, and into the way that best works for NBC. You are my all-world sixth man. You are my number one substitute. I know I can put you any place in the world on any event, and you will bring us back as good a show as possible under those circumstances. You're very, very valuable to me, and you'll make a good living here. But you're not going to be my superstar."

He said, "I know that's what you want, and I'm sorry from that standpoint, but this is the way it works right now. Things might change, but this is the way it works now."

Well, things never changed. But I accepted it and got over it. Doing the Super Bowl is good for the ego. I would love to hear myself say that I did the TV broadcasts, but I did work three Super Bowls in other capacities. Super Bowl I, I was on the sideline. Super Bowl III, I did on radio, and Super Bowl IX, I was on the sideline. But that's not the same as being Curt Gowdy or Dick Enberg. So yeah, it is disappointing that I never was able to do play-by-play. But the thing is that, once they kick off, it's the moment. There's just as much adrenaline, just as much fun – assuming the game is pretty good – as any other game. I had some good moments doing football, but I would've loved to have done one Super Bowl. But if I had done one Super Bowl, I would've wanted to do two, then a third and a fourth.

Aside from Super Bowls, was there a classic football game that you wish you could have broadcast?

CJ: Not from that standpoint, but there is one from another standpoint. It was a Fiesta Bowl. I did 13 of 14 Fiesta Bowls. In January of 1987, I did one with Jimmy Cefalo and Bob Griese in which Penn State upset Miami for the National Title. It was moved to prime time and we did a good job and it was a helluva ballgame. Then two or three years later, the same situation came up. Notre Dame and West Virginia were playing for the National Championship, and I just assumed that it was going to be my game again. But they took me off and replaced me with Dick Enberg. That one really hurt because I had done almost all of them before. It was my territory, and then they took it away from me. It was the only one I missed in that 14-year run.

In term of pro games, you want to call the ones that are memorable for circumstances. You want to be there for the Ice Bowl. You want to be there in New England when the guy takes the snowplow out on the field and clears a path for the Patriots kicker. You want to be there when the fog rolls in off Lake Michigan and covers Soldier Field, and you can't see anything so you have to make it all up.

As a side story, I did a college game on radio when I was in the Air Force in California. It was between the Marine Corps Recruit Depot and San Diego State at Aztec Stadium. It was a beautiful, clear Saturday night, and right before the opening kickoff, the fog rolled in and I couldn't see five feet in front of me. It was like talking into a white sheet. The PA announcer went down on the sideline where he could see a little better, and he gave us a skeleton of a play-by-play. We would repeat what he said onto the radio. We were pulling things out of the media guide to make it interesting, and we got into a rhythm where we would angle our bodies in the direction of which way we were told the teams were moving.

So with about two minutes to go in the first half, we were calling the action, saying that the teams were on the two-yard line coming out from what was my left-hand side. Then, all of a sudden, the fog lifted…and there was nobody there. And I'm thinking…Oh…my…this is like *The Twilight Zone*. I'll never forget that feeling. But then I saw that they were at the other end of the field [laughing]. Those are the fun games to do. You've dug yourself a hole, now how do you get out of it?

I would've *loved* to have done the Ice Bowl. I love those kind of weather games, the ones in torrential rains, where everybody is slipping and sliding. In fact, I did a game between the San Diego Chargers and the Denver Broncos about ten years ago that was like that. The snow came into Denver and closed the airport on Saturday night. It kept snowing through the entire game. The city was damn near shut down, and only about five hundred people showed up in the stands. Everyone was freezing and everything kept going wrong, but it was great fun to do.

In the highest corner of Mile High Stadium, there was a couple watching the game from there. [Laughing] I figured that those were their season tickets, but since there were only 500 people at the game they could have moved to anywhere in the stadium! But they sat up there, in the highest, farthest place in the stadium. We spent half of the ballgame talking about it! Those are the kind of broadcasts that are fun, where you have to find things to talk about and play with.

What was NBC's network policy on direct criticism of the NFL during the broadcasts? Was there an unwritten rule on what is "out of bounds," or were things spelled out very clearly on what should not be said?

CJ: I worked at the networks for 38 years, and nobody ever told us what we couldn't say. It wasn't even suggested. The announcers back then weren't critical of players or coaches, but it was part of the times. It was a different generation. The ultra-criticism of the athletes that we have now – good or bad – wasn't part of the landscape. Nobody did it. We grew up listening to Bill Stern and Harry Wismer and Mel Allen. They were our mentors and they didn't do it, so my generation didn't do it either.

I should point out some history here. Originally on televised sporting events there were no color announcers, just the broadcaster. And Gowdy always reminded us of this. He had a difficult time working with somebody because he had spent his entire baseball career working by himself. So working with an analyst was brand new. Videotape hadn't been invented yet, so you couldn't go back and review the replays. Today, probably 80-percent of what the analyst does is off the replays, but back then they didn't have that tool to work with.

None of that had happened until Gowdy started working with Paul Christman. In my opinion, Christman was the first analyst to criticize on the air. It was during an AFL game in 1962, and I will go to my grave remembering that his first criticism was, "What a terrible play! He hit him right in the hands." When he said it, everybody gasped, *"Did you hear what he said?"* This was the beginning.

Paul, in a lot of respects, was the best color announcer there ever was. He had been a player and he knew the details of the game, but he also had a way of saying things. Paul could say, "It's raining," and you'd reach for your raincoat, even though the sun was shining and you're standing in the middle of the desert. He had that great finality in his voice. That's what made him such a good analyst. When he said something, it was like the voice of God saying it, so therefore it must be. For him, being critical was just an extension of his nature.

Of course, the way things are done on telecasts today is drastically different.

CJ: That's because of one man. There is one man who is responsible for the way all of sports are now broadcast, and that was Howard Cosell. Cosell was the first one on a national basis to have harsh criticism, to attack, to say negative things, to go against the grain, to rub people wrong. He was truly the father figure of all sportscasters. Cosell was the one who took all the garbage and all the crap. Roone Arledge, who was the head of ABC Sports, backed him up. They're the ones that opened the doors and won us the freedom of saying everything we wanted to say.

Did you know Howard Cosell well?

CJ: Oh, yes. He was a strange, wonderful, creative, sick man [laughing]. From a sportscaster's standpoint, he was the best thing that ever happened to us. He gained us recognition, more money, and the ability to be honest with the viewers. If somebody screwed up, we could finally say, "They screwed up." He had a brilliant mind, was great fun to be with, and was a tremendous put-down artist. He could hold grudges and be upset at people, but I always found him to be a very fascinating man. He knew his time, he knew who he was, and knew what he was doing. He's the only one out of 240 million people who stood by the side of Muhammad Ali during all his controversy. I couldn't believe it when he first did it. As time went by, I began to understand him more and develop a great admiration for him. Howard put himself on the line.

The networks are not very forgiving, but Howard got lucky because he had Roone Arledge in his corner. He put Howard in the places where he could have the best impact. Somebody once asked Roone why Howard wasn't going to be at the Winter Olympics. [Laughing] Roone answered, "Are you kidding? Do you know what Cosell looks like in a ski outfit?" We all pictured that immediately and thought, "There's no way…!"

Cosell's biggest gripe was always about the invasion of the ex-athlete into the broadcast booth. The "jockocracy," he called it. It drove him crazy and he refused to let it go.

CJ: Oh, very much so. He was like a pit bull from that standpoint. He would get hold of something and shake it forever, never letting it go. He was absolutely right. The people that were coming off the field and into the broadcast booth had no training. They didn't know how to talk on camera or express themselves properly or eloquently. The attitude was, "Sign up last year's All-American! If he's good, we'll keep him. If he's not, well then sign up the second guy." They'd just keep running them through and running them through.

Johnny Unitas was a perfect example. Phenomenal quarterback, but no TV presence whatsoever.

CJ: That's right. Many of them didn't belong on the air in those days. Today many of them do. The athletes now train themselves for broadcasting. They'll go to a speech coach. They'll work at a local television or radio station during the offseason. They listen to other announcers and look for ways to improve themselves. For some time NBC had Marty Glickman working with all of their color analysts. He would get tapes of their games every week, critique them, then call the analysts up and discuss their performance. He was really a big help.

I finally came up with an observation that makes sense to me on this subject. Players came out of the NFL and went into the booth with very little training. However, since they were six years old, they'd always been coached. And after every performance, at every level, they've been critiqued by a coach. For the last 30 years of their life, they've had somebody saying, "Do it this way," or tell them, "Yes! Congratulations! You're doing it the right way."

Suddenly, they're thrown into the television booth. You're sitting next to one of these young announcers who's trying to make a name for himself and you think, "Great...you're wonderful to work with, I really enjoy you, but I could care less about your future. I'm more worried about mine." So everyone is out there struggling. It was very difficult for them. But now, all the background work and coaching and help they receive has become part of the process, which is good. They're getting better.

But hasn't it reached the saturation point? I mean, you're sitting there watching ESPN's pregame show and there are thirteen guys piled around a giant table, climbing all over each other for airtime. Then the next superstar retires and they squeeze the seats even closer. We're beyond the days of three being a crowd. We're into mob scenes now.

CJ: Unfortunately it's the way they're doing it these days. I'll give you a major gripe of mine. The announcers of my generation – Gowdy, Scully, Jack Buck – all started on radio because television had not yet been invented. A big part of our package was our voices. And the voices that we hear now on television, well, I can't tell them apart. And often I can't even distinguish between the color analyst and the play-by-play announcer. There is not enough voice distinction. They're all nice and pleasant, but they all sound alike. I like the announcer to sound like an announcer. The problem is that television management doesn't hold that trait as part of its criteria. They figure people can see what is going on, so there is less for the imagination. But in radio, the voice was the number one criteria – the strength and quality and uniqueness of it. The goal was to bring the picture into focus in the audience's mind.

Going Up in Smoke in Cleveland

Charlie has that great, gravely voice which was perfect for calling a football game. He was a heavy smoker for years, a three-pack-a-day Marlboro guy. I think that actually helped make his voice what it is. There was always a lot of smoke in his booth. When he was working with Bob Griese, Griese would sit there with a hand-held fan trying to blow it away from him. Charlie finally gave up the cigarettes and after a while, like a lot of ex-smokers, couldn't stand the smell of it.

Once he was doing a game in Cleveland and somebody in the box next to him was puffing away on a cigar. Charlie couldn't see who it was. The smoke was billowing in, and it was really bothering him. Finally Charlie got so annoyed that he yelled over, "Hey, will you please put that thing out? The smoke is killing me over here!" The guy with the cigar leaned forward so Charlie could see him. It was Art Modell, the owner of the Browns. I know Charlie wished he could've taken that one back.

- former Miami Dolphins WR and NBC analyst Jimmy Cefalo

Let's talk about pregame preparation. Which NFL coach consistently gave you the best material and insight for that part of your job?

CJ: There were two or three of them. Interestingly enough, when Al Davis became the head coach of the

Oakland Raiders, he was very close to the chest. Nowadays, you can't get near him. But I knew Al when he was an assistant with the Chargers, so I would call him on the Wednesday or Thursday before the game. He would always go through the same routine. "Charlie, I can't tell you what we're going to do. We have a whole new game plan that we're going to use, and I…" and he goes through this whole disclaimer. Then I would always say, "Okay, fine. Now what are you going to do?" And he would tell me everything. Everything! If he said the Raiders were going to do something out of the ordinary, or try something at a particular point of the game, it happened.

I never said a word about that to anybody, not even my color broadcaster. I figured if he is confiding in me this much, I can't take any chances on things leaking out. I figured if they trust you enough to give you information, then take it, keep it quiet, then use it because it will make things more interesting for the viewers. But Al Davis is the first one that comes to my mind. Of all people that I would go to for information, you figured he'd be the last one to talk.

Did your rapport with Davis eventually carry over to John Madden after he took over coaching the Raiders?

CJ: Oh, yes. I remember doing Oakland's season opener against Green Bay in Milwaukee one year, and the Packers beat the hell out of them. I then had the Raiders again the following week in their home opener. It was Saturday morning and the team was going through their walk-through at the Alameda County Coliseum. I came down to watch them. As soon as he saw me, Madden stopped practice. He called all of the security guards over and pointed me out to them, then told them to get me out of the stadium because when I did their ballgames, they lost. He said this loud enough so everybody could hear. I am standing there in front of the stands, and he and the security guards come walking towards me. They get about halfway there, and I yelled out, "John, face it – when you play shitty, you're going to lose!" He stopped, and everybody started laughing. "You're right," he said, "you can stay."

Paul Brown was also very good to me. He always gave me a very good insight to what was going to happen on Sunday. I did Paul's very first game with the Cincinnati Bengals. They were playing the New York Jets at Nippert Stadium. Tom Bass was his defensive coordinator, who I'd known for years, but I had never met Paul Brown. I asked Tom when I saw him on Sunday morning if he would introduce me to Coach Brown. He said, "I will, on one condition. That you call him Paul."

I said, "I can't do that. I would be very uncomfortable calling him by his first name."

He said, "Then I won't introduce you. I won't because Paul will immediately set you at a level in your relationship, and it will always remain that way. If you come in and he's Coach Brown and you're Charlie, in his mind he's going to be up here and you're going to be down there. And it will *never* change. But if you come in and he's Paul and you're Charlie, then you're on the same level. And *that* will never change."

I said, "All right, then let's do it." And I was really uncomfortable. But I called him "Paul," and we went on to become really great friends. We played golf together at the La Jolla Country Club during the off-season.

I'll tell you a story that shows you what kind of man Paul Brown was. I had dinner at his house one night with six other people, and the evening was just like he ran the football team. He announced, "All right, now we're all going to have two drinks." Then after the second drink, he said, "All right, now we're going to have dinner." So we sat down and had a wonderful dinner, then he said, "Okay, now it's time for dessert."

We had the dessert, and he said, "We'll all have a cup of coffee." Everybody had their cup of coffee, then he stood up at the head of the table and said to the seven of us, "All right, that's it. Everybody go home."

Five minutes later, I'm in the car driving home at nine o'clock on Saturday night. [Laughing] It was like you'd been at your grandfather's house. He told you how it was going to be, and that's the way it was.

What about Miami's Don Shula? Was he accommodating?

CJ: Interesting man. It takes years for him to trust you. Once he does, he'll trust you forever. You don't become a buddy immediately. Six years after doing games, maybe then you can become a buddy. It's like a work in progress. He's a very interesting man, and gives very good information. And it was even better when I was working with Bob Griese. With Bob in the room, we would find out all kinds of things from Shula.

I enjoyed Shula, and I have a good relationship with him too. But Don Shula did not suffer fools gladly either. But if you were prepared and you'd studied and done your homework and had good questions for him, he would give you good information. He didn't volunteer anything, but if you were well prepared and had gone to the trouble of finding things out, then he would answer your question. But if you came to him with generic questions, you would get the generic answers.

Which players were your best "insiders?"

CJ: Len Dawson was very good. I had known Len from when the team was known as the Dallas Texans of the AFL, before they became the Kansas City Chiefs. But a lot of them didn't talk. Bob Griese never said anything as a player. Dan Marino? You could get just a little bit sometimes, maybe one item that was usable. Larry Csonka was one who helped you out if you got the chance to talk to him. He'd say something like, "Don't be surprised if they throw long to me." I'd say, "You're out of your fucking mind. They're not going to throw long to you." He's say, "Ohhhh…don't be too sure." So you'd sit there during the game and wait for it, and you could have fun with it when it happened.

The most intense, frightening player you ever interviewed was who?

CJ: Oh, Ray Nitschke from Green Bay. He scared me, even after he was out of the game. I had an idea for a book and was working with a handwriting analyst who knew absolutely nothing about football. The idea was to have him analyze a collection of handwriting samples, thinking that might make a cute book. When the Super Bowl was in California one year, Nitschke was at the NFL hospitality room, along with Deacon Jones and two or three others. I was talking to Nitschke, and I asked him if he would participate and give me a writing sample. He turned to me with a very sudden change of personality. "Nobody is going to read my handwriting," he said. "You'll find out what I'm really like, and I'm not going to let you know." I'm thinking, "Holy shit! What is *this* all about?"

Jerry Kramer of the Packers is another one. I did the pregame interviews in Santa Barbara for Super Bowl I. The network gave me a list of things they wanted covered. They programmed the pregame show to have "these people" saying "these things," so my job was to get Vince Lombardi and half a dozen Packers to say "these things." If they didn't talk about "these things," it didn't fit into the overall theme of the program.

One of the things NBC planned was for me to ask Jerry Kramer how he prepares during the week for the game. So I am standing in front of him with a camera over my shoulder. He starts talking to me and says, "We'll come back to work on the Monday after a game and check with the trainer, maybe do a little light weights, then take the rest of the day off. Then we come in on Tuesday and go over the gameplan. Tuesday is the day you start to put your game face on. Then on Wednesday, this happens and…"

As he progressed through each day of the week, his eyes got bigger and his face more taut, and then he finally growls, "By Saturday, I don't talk to anybody! I don't want to see anybody!" I'm up there saying to myself, "I just hope he doesn't hit me. Please God, don't let him hit me." It turned out to be a dynamite piece of tape, which really played well on the air, but holy cow! It was unreal how intense Kramer became!

Lyle Alzado also comes to mind, but that was because he was so doctored up. I was in the Cleveland locker room before a ballgame, and he was just bouncing all over the place. He would tell me anything, along with the singing and shouting and that crazed look in his eyes. The storage lockers in which they packed the gear were around the room, and he was jumping from one to another with a towel over his head yelling, *"I'm the Ayatollah!"* I'm standing there with Len Dawson, and I looked at him and said, "What the hell is going on?" Len answered, "He just saw the doctor." It was scary.

What is your favorite single-game performance by a quarterback over the years?

CJ: I remember doing a game with Bob Griese in Miami. It was Dan Marino's first start. He was a rookie and had played for the first time the previous Monday night, and now he was making his first NFL start against Buffalo at the Orange Bowl. The Dolphins are on their own 20-yard line, and Marino's first pass is intercepted and returned for a touchdown. Bob and I looked at each other, then talked about the play a little bit, not sure what to think of his performance so far. Then Marino comes back and starts playing a little better… and a little bit better… and a little bit better. By the middle of the third quarter, I looked at Bob and said, "Am I seeing what I think I'm seeing?"

He said, "You are, you truly are."

I said, "Marino is playing like he's a ten-year veteran."

Bob said, "He sure is, and he's going to break every one of my records."

Never before and never since have I seen a rookie that looked like that. It was like he owned the place.

Many people feel that Marino's first season was comparable to Greg Cook's explosive rookie year for Cincinnati in 1969.

CJ: Oh, Cook could have been the greatest. It was all there with him, too. It was such a shame how he got hurt. He was always in control. You know how they talk about Tom Cruise, how he has *It*? Well, Greg Cook had *It*. He was the complete package. He had the leadership. The kids believed in him.

He was the same as John Elway. I've talked to guys who've played with John and asked them, "What's Elway like in the huddle with two minutes to go and you're on your own 2-yard line?" They all answered, "He loves it. *He absolutely loves it*. His eyes get big and he claps his hands and says, 'Let's go.'"

It was the same with Greg. Cook had a great arm and a sharp mind and great running ability, the whole package.

Who was your favorite NFL running back?

CJ: The one that immediately comes to mind is Bo Jackson. I had him for a couple of games in the L.A. Coliseum, and, whew, he had everything. O.J. was another great one, a tremendous player. Earl Campbell was awesome, but the sad thing about Earl was that you knew he wasn't going to have a long career. He was such a physical runner and took such a beating. Back in the late '70s, obviously I was much younger and thinner and had a 32-inch waist. Earl Campbell's thighs were 32 inches. We actually measured them. He was brutal but he took a lot of punishment.

Sum up a great broadcasting career for me.

CJ: First of all, I'm very lucky. I got to do what I wanted to do since my voice changed at age fifteen. I was able to make a nice living at it, too. I traveled the world – something like 5 million frequent flyer miles – and I met some of the nicest men and women in sports, and also some of the other kind. But for me, there's nothing like that adrenaline rush at 1pm on Sunday afternoon, when I said so many times, "Good afternoon, everyone, and welcome to NFL football.…"

— 12 —
Jim Hart, Quarterback
St. Louis Cardinals (1966-83); Washington Redskins (1984)
August 7, 2001

If free agent quarterbacks came in cheery little boxes like donuts, they'd be sardine filled and Limburger glazed and two days old. Nobody would want 'em. Dumpster fill. Even the biggest office mooch wouldn't sneak a bite unless he overslept and missed the morning Krispy Kreme run.

At football's most important position, every pro team would love to have a great quarterback and two really good ones hitched to its roster. Most don't. So when NFL draft day comes and goes and the phone never rings at Joe College's house, the message is a strong one. "Yeah, we saw your workouts, kid, and we sure could use another passer, but you need to start shining up those job interview shoes."

In the old days, when teams had 17 or 20 or even 30 picks on hand, it was considered even more degrading not to be drafted. "Here you are," says former St. Louis Cardinals quarterback Jim Hart, "playing the highest profile position on your college team, getting the most local publicity and attention, everybody in town knows your name, and not one team will take a chance on you, not with even a 16th round pick.

"Instead, they take some backup long-snapper from Ohio Wesleyan. That's pretty tough on the ego."

But many NFL personnel types have a good reason for that.

"Our philosophy on drafting quarterbacks in Pittsburgh was pretty simple," says Art Rooney, Jr., who ran the Steelers scouting department for over twenty years. "If we felt a player wouldn't be competing for the starting job after a few seasons in the league, there was no reason to waste a pick on him. The true talents are generally long gone by the bottom third of the draft. Unless the player can compete at another position like wide receiver or defensive back, all you're doing with these low-round quarterbacks is drafting a body to run drills in training camp. There are plenty of those guys on the street."

From 1960 through 1992 [the final year clubs had at least 12 picks], the Steelers drafted only seven quarterbacks after the 8th round. Only Joe Gilliam, an eleventh-rounder in '72, made the team. "We weren't in the business of procuring career backups," says Rooney.

Sure, a few longshots hang periodically catch on with a team. Just like a few 15-handicappers will drop a hole-in-one on the muni each summer, but none of those guys are getting telegrams from the PGA. Looking at the final 2002 NFL rosters, none of the undrafted quarterbacks were able to hang on, and that's with only a seven-round draft in place.

Few success stories have ever emerged from the free agent quarterback ranks. Jim Zorn found his way onto the Seattle expansion team in 1976 and, after surviving 27 interceptions during his rookie year, led the Seahawks to winning seasons in 1978 and '79. Free agent Dave Krieg replaced Zorn then threw for over 38,000 yards in his 19-year career. Erik Kramer's abilities were obscured as he bounced from Atlanta to the CFL to Detroit before finally taking the Lions to the NFC championship game in 1991. And I'm still shaking my head in disbelief over the amazing Kurt Warner journey from lima bean stocker to the NFL *and* Super Bowl MVP?!

Jim Hart was another one of those unlikely successes, although he came dangerously close to blowing it along the way. Undrafted out of Southern Illinois in 1966, Hart's accurate arm and great field vision won him a spot on Charley Winner's quarterback-thin St. Louis Cardinals. After a year on the bench and some help from the U.S. military, he won the starting job for the '67 season and finished fifth in the league with 3,008 passing yards. Then the rollercoaster kicked into gear.

"I was really an up-and-down player for the first part of my career," says Hart. "Some good games, some not so good. I made some bad decisions. I forced some passes. I had some passes dropped. We didn't have a lot of weapons on offense in the early '70s, so I struggled. By '72, I was really concerned about even having a job in the league any longer, things had deteriorated so badly for me."

By the time coach Don Coryell took over the team in 1973, Hart was a wreck. He owned a soggy quarterback rating of 58.7 and had already thrown 97 interceptions as a pro. He had been benched in favor of journeyman Gary Cuozzo, a shaky 49-percent passer brought over from the Vikings.

"His confidence was way down, but it was obvious to me that Jim Hart was the best quarterbacking talent on the team," remembers Coryell. "The offense St. Louis had been running wasn't suited to his strengths. Jim was a good deep thrower, an accurate one, and that suited me just fine. So we put in the deep timing patterns and worked on his progressions and got the running backs into the passing attack."

"Under Charley Winner and [later] Bob Holloway, we'd throw mainly on passing downs, by-the-book stuff," says Hart. "To Don, every down was a passing down. Teams without a strong pass rush were always backpedaling against us."

By 1974, two mercuric weapons had emerged for the Cardinals in RB Terry Metcalf and WR Mel Gray, while the offensive line, anchored by Tom Banks, Dan Dierdorf and Roger Finnie, became the league's best pass blocking unit, surrendering just 16 sacks all season. Hart was named NFC Offensive Player of the Year and the look-who's-laughing-now Cards made the playoffs for the first time since 1948.

"Don Coryell basically saved my career," Hart acknowledges. "Without him and that great offense of his, I never would've developed into the player I eventually became."

A career highlighted by four Pro Bowl appearances and 34,665 passing yards. Not bad for an undrafted quarterback who showed up at training camp one day and stuck around for 19 years. Not bad for a Mr. Nobody.

● ● ●

It's November 27, 1965, and the names of the rookie quarterbacks selected in the NFL draft began their fade into obscurity almost as soon as they were called. Kentucky's Rick Norton, the consensus top prospect at the position, lasts until the 29th selection. Twenty-nine more names are announced until St. Louis takes Gary Snook of Iowa. Southern Methodist's Ron Meyer is taken off the board at 107.

By the close of the draft, only 10 rookie quarterbacks have been selected. Jim Hart, a 6'2", 195-lb deepballer from Southern Illinois, was not one of them. Your memories of that day?

JH: I'd been led to believe by both the 49ers and Rams that they were going to choose me. They'd been in touch with me by phone, but it never rang on draft day. I never paid attention to who they picked instead of me. I wasn't too bent out of shape about it.

My step-dad was more devastated than I was. He was really hurt that nobody drafted me. That night I went out and baby-sat for my aunt, and he just couldn't believe that I wasn't going to be home in case a team called. My attitude was, "If they call, just tell them to call me at my aunt's house."

Your initial hope was likely to catch on as a free agent, either with the NFL or the burgeoning AFL. How did you finally become a St. Louis Cardinal?

JH: I was hoping to sign with the NFL, which was more prestigious than the new and unproven AFL. My advantage as a free agent was that my coach at Southern Illinois, Don Shroyer, had been an assistant under Wally Lemm with the NFL Cardinals in 1963. Don became head coach at SIU in 1964, but after only two seasons there, he'd been told by the AD – who was kind of a jerk – to hit the road. He hadn't won there in two years, but who can really turn a program around in two years? Don decided to return to the NFL as an assistant and was hired by Charley Winner, the new head coach of the Cardinals.

Don asked if I wanted him to recommend me to the Cardinals. Of course! I would've taken anything! A short time later the Cards sent down their ticket manager to sign me, which shows the amount of importance I had. It wasn't their president or vice-president or a scout or a coach. It was their ticket manager! He offered me a $1,000 check. This was at the time when guys like Joe Namath and Donnie Anderson were signing for something like $600,000.

I said, "A thousand dollars? Is that all you got?"

He said, "That's all I'm authorized to give you. I could try to make a few calls, but it's eight o'clock and I doubt I'll be able to get in touch with anybody." I started thinking that if this ticket manager calls and inconveniences somebody, they might call off the whole thing. "OK, I'll take it."

It was a crowded phone booth for Cardinal quarterbacks that summer, wasn't it?

JH: Oh yes. I was listed as sixth on the depth chart going into camp that year, with little or no chance to make the team. Charley Johnson was the starter; Buddy Humphrey was his backup; Terry Nofsinger was number three; Gary Snook, the high-draft choice was number four; Jack Ankerson, who'd been drafted in '64 out of Ripon College, was five; and me.

But all of a sudden some things broke in my favor. Jack had gained some weight while he was in the service in Vietnam, and so they moved him to tight end. Humphrey had what I call a case of the nerves. His heart wasn't in it. All of a sudden he was gone. Quickly it was between Gary Snook and me. Gary was the high draft choice with a $350,000 contract while mine totaled $12,000, so who were they going to keep? It wasn't going to be me.

The Cardinals then asked Gary to go into St. Louis – we were training in Chicago at that time – and enroll in the Army Reserves so he'd be protected from the [military] draft. I got wind of that and asked them if they wanted me to enroll also. They said quite emphatically, "No." So Gary went to St. Louis, but he never enrolled. The only thing I could surmise was that he hit the sauce pretty hard and chased [women] pretty hard and saw that trip as a night away from training camp and an opportunity to miss 11:00 curfew. He must have gone out that night and never came home. Whatever happened, he missed the army reserve physical scheduled for the next morning, then came back to training camp in Chicago. Ten days later he was drafted by the regular army. Bingo! That left me as the number three guy.

Near the start of the 1967 season, Charley Johnson was called into active military duty, and you suddenly went from a free agent nobody to the Cardinals starting quarterback.

JH: I got unbelievably lucky. Terry Nofsinger, who'd been number two, was traded to Atlanta so I moved into the backup position. I had gone to Stormy Bidwill, Bill's half-brother, during the offseason and asked to negotiate my contract. Their dad had owned the team and the two brothers inherited it from him. Stormy owned 51-percent and Bill the rest. Stormy was a fine man, an honorable man. If he had kept control of the team [instead of Bill] after their fracture in 1972, we would've won some championships. I'm convinced of it.

Anyway, I tried to negotiate my contract, and Stormy said, "Oh, no. It's too early. We don't need to do that." I persisted, and he said, "Wait until training camp. Then we'll see what happens." So I waited until training camp. I went in the first week, and he hemmed and hawed and still wouldn't talk to me. Then he finally said, "Let's wait till we get back to St. Louis." Back then, training camp lasted for six weeks, and I said, "Gosh, anything could happen. I could get hurt and you're not liable if I don't have a contract." He just kept saying, "Trust me." Well, you're always told by veterans not to trust ownership, so I was still very skeptical.

Finally, as I was walking out the door he said, "Who knows? By the time you get to St. Louis, we could be negotiating a first-team quarterback contract with you." I just looked at him and shrugged and walked upstairs to my room. Charley Johnson, who was my roommate at the time, was in there. My head was way down. He looked at me and said, "What's the matter, roomie?"

I said, "Bidwill won't even talk to me. He said something about negotiating a number-one quarterback contract when we get back to St. Louis."

Charley said, "You mean you haven't heard?"

"Heard what?"

"I just got the word. I've been called up for two years of active duty due to my ROTC commitment."

All of a sudden, there it was. It's a week before our first exhibition game, and I was now the starting quarterback. What this proves is that Stormy was really honorable about the whole thing. He could've signed me to a much cheaper deal in the offseason. I was making around $12,000 and was only looking for a raise to about $15,000. He knew Charley was likely going to be activated [into the military], but he wanted to be fair to me.

The Cardinals finished a 6-7-1 campaign in 1967, but your 3,000-yard, 19 touchdown performance grabbed the league's attention that year; only four other passers – John Unitas, Fran Tarkenton, Norm Snead, and Sonny Jurgensen – had more yards. Based on your accomplishments, did you feel you had assumed the role as the team's offensive leader by season's end?

JH: No, I didn't. It was still Charley's team. And that was because it was still Charley's offensive line. The linemen consisted of Bob DeMarco at center, Irv Goode and Ken Gray at guards, and Ernie McMillan and Bob Reynolds at the tackles. They grew up with Charley and were his peers, and to them I was just a necessary evil while he was gone. As soon as Charley came back, they expected him to take over.

But my success in '67 may have opened their eyes a little bit. They thought, "Hey, maybe the kid's got some potential." For so long the school of thought was that it took five years to develop into an effective pro quarterback. I felt it depended simply on how fast one learns and what level of maturity he has. I was a fast learner and pretty mature, so I got off to a fast start. However, I think that early success probably hurt me more than anything else because the expectations of me going into 1968 were much greater. And those expectations didn't materialize.

1968 was a solid year for the Cardinals. You led the team to nine wins and there was lots of optimism in St. Louis. But by 1969 Charley Johnson was back with the team, and throughout the year you two wrangled for the starting position. The result was a 4-9-1 flop of a season. What happened?

JH: Charley and I split time at QB and it was very disconcerting. No question it divided the team. There were loyalists to Charley who wanted him as the starter and those who'd become comfortable with me. We were still able to move the ball and score points, but the defense had big problems, especially with injuries. I think we gave up almost 30 points a game that year. It was really frustrating for both of us.

By the end of the year Charley announced he wanted out of St. Louis. We had played our last game in Green Bay that December, and he passed his helmet around the airplane for everyone to sign, a way of signaling that it was his last go-round with the team. Charley was from Texas and he kept telling me, "I'm out of here. I'm gonna try to go home and play for Houston." Sure enough, in 1970 he was a Houston Oiler.

Let's talk a bit about Charley Winner, your first head coach with the Cardinals. What were your impressions of him?

JH: [Pausing] I'm gonna temper my remarks a little bit. The older players did not really like him. They thought that he wasn't decisive enough, especially with the quarterback position. I don't blame them. I would've probably felt that way if I was one of those veterans. However, it's pretty hard for me to pan Charley because he went out on a limb by making me his starter.

Winner was 35-30-5 during his four seasons in St. Louis. They fired him after a late-season collapse ruined an almost certain playoff spot in 1970. Why didn't the team win more games under Winner?

191

JH: Charley let his coaches coach. He didn't meddle with his assistants over who would play, and that might have hurt him. We were pretty tough defensively and that's what kept us in the games back then. Actually, we had a lot of very good players during my first few years in St. Louis. We should've won more games than we did.

But I think what ultimately cost him his job was that he stuck with Jim Hart, the untested, untried young quarterback. Any time you have a young quarterback, mistakes are going to be made and those mistakes can eventually cost you some ball games.

Through the early 1970s, there was a wildly revolving door at the quarterback position. Out with Charley Johnson, in with Pete Beathard; out with Beathard, in with Gary Cuozzo and Tim Van Galder and Gary Keithley. Although you held the starting job for most of that time, by 1973 you were 29 years old and, in the eyes of Cardinals brass, no longer the future of the team. What do you remember about that span of your career?

JH: Those were some really uncertain years for me. The 1971 and '72 seasons were the most pivotal. In '71, the Bidwills hired Bob Holloway, an assistant under Bud Grant in Minnesota, as our new coach. Bob and I got along personally, but professionally we didn't see eye to eye. Going into the '72 season he benched me. I could just tell he wasn't comfortable with me at quarterback. He was a nice man, but he didn't respect me as a player.

Overall I played in only four games that year, two at the end of the season. We beat Los Angeles, where I completed the longest non-scoring pass in NFL history [98 yards]. The funny thing about that game was that it was really cold and the field was frozen. The grounds crew put down calcium chloride, which is used to thaw roads, trying to melt the frozen Astroturf. That stuff caused a bad reaction on all of us. Les Josephson, who was a running back for the Rams, was actually hospitalized after the game with first-degree burns over all of his body. We first noticed it when we came in at halftime and sat down on our stools. Everybody started hopping around and saying, "Damn! My butt's on fire!" That stuff melted the ice, but it burned us pretty good in the process.

The last game was against Philadelphia, which we also won, and I performed pretty well. Afterwards, Holloway came up to me and did something very uncharacteristic of him. He put his arm around me and said, "Jim, I made a mistake. You're my starting quarterback for next year. I'm through fooling around. You're the starter." I thought, "Great, but we'll see..."

Well, there was an annual fund-raiser for a children's hospital that was always held right after the last game. It was held a few doors down from our football offices, and we were asked to stop by the cocktail party and schmooze with the donors. I stuck around for a couple hours, then a few of us headed across the street toward the parking garage when I happened to notice a locksmith's truck in front of our entrance. We all stopped and thought, "You don't think...do ya? Bidwill wouldn't do it *that way*, would he?"

Sure enough, it came out the next morning that Bob had been fired and he didn't even know it. He was a devout Catholic and was at morning mass, so Billy Bidwill couldn't reach him to tell him before the papers came out. What a tough way to find out you lost your job! Bidwill, subsequently, did that to every coach who came through St. Louis.

Holloway's record in St. Louis was a sour 8-18-2. Why was he a failure as head coach?

JH: Because he tried to be somebody he wasn't. He came across as almost being fake. He tried to be Bud Grant, to do everything the way Grant had done it instead of being Bob Holloway. All along we wanted to tell Bob to just be himself, but the Bidwills didn't give him time to learn that lesson. It also didn't help that he brought along a lot of former Vikings players whose time as players had passed. Those guys were supposed to show us how a winning team should perform. Gary Cuozzo was one of them. It was so blatantly obvious that Gary was finished that we just shook our heads and said, "This isn't going to work."

The early 1970s brought a tremendous influx of young talent the Cardinals franchise. Names like Dan Dierdorf, Conrad Dobler, and Tom Banks helped re-cement the offensive line, while players like Terry Metcalf, Ahmad Rashad, Jim Otis and Mel Gray gave you an arsenal unlike any you had before. Was it obvious to you that these rookies were going to be an outstanding bunch of players?

JH: Yeah, it really was obvious. There was some real amazing talent in those names you mentioned. But what really made it all work was a guy named Don Coryell who became our coach in 1973. That year we ended up with a 4-9-1 season, but by the end of that year things were different. We felt as good about our team as any could with only four victories under our belts. We knew we were going to turn it around. We'd lost some overtime games, some games in the final minutes. But Don Coryell kept saying, "Hang in there, guys. Our time is coming!" You just believed him.

The next year, we started winning the kind of games we'd been losing. We were the ones throwing a late touchdown pass or getting a game-winning field goal. That's how we got the name "Cardiac Cards." We would always seem to be down in the fourth quarter, and Don would go up and down the sidelines, saying things like, "Wehrli – you're gonna intercept a pass and score," or, "Stallings, you're gonna cause a fumble and we're gonna recover it." He'd say to me, "Jimmy, you're gonna throw this great pass and we're gonna get a touchdown out of it!" It was a contagious thing that rubbed off on us. At first we said to ourselves, "Awww, what's this guy doing?" But then those things really started to happen. He made believers out of us.

Coryell was coming off a tremendous collegiate run at San Diego State – a winning percentage of .830 – before he came to St. Louis. What were your initial impressions of him?

JH: I liked him a lot. When he came to town, he gathered all the veterans together at a restaurant to meet him, and we had a blast! I mean, we got zonkered. He started talking about what he was going to do and how much fun we were going to have. No coach had ever done that with us before. He made us feel that we wanted to bust our tails for him. Even though we finished that first year 4-9-1, there wasn't a guy in that lockerroom that didn't think we'd be a success in the near future. He handed me the football and told me I was his quarterback, then he stood behind me year-in and year-out.

What was so innovative about Coryell's offensive approach?

JH: Don's idea was to pass to set up the run. He wanted to attack the defense and move the chains in an era when teams would establish the run to set up the pass. Don actually wanted to throw the ball *even more* than we did. It was only because of [assistant coach] Jim Hanifan that we ever called running plays.

On 3rd-and-short situations, Don would be saying, "Throw it, *throw it!*" Hanifan would just stand there and let Don say his peace, then whisper a running play to me. Don would look over and say, "What do ya got? Are you gonna throw?" Hanifan would just smile. Inevitably we'd pick up the first down and Don would be happy. The few times that we didn't he'd be pretty upset. "*I told you to throw it!*" he'd rant. Don gave both me and Dan Fouts in San Diego free reign to throw the ball. He had some innovations that were fantastic. He was well ahead of his time.

Coryell's NFL offenses always featured a "scat" back – some jittery multi-purpose runner, typically around 5'10" with flashy feet and dependable hands. In San Diego, he had James Brooks and Lionel "Little Train" James. In St. Louis, it was the great Terry Metcalf. What impact did Metcalf make on the Cardinals' offense?

JH: Terry had the great ability to stop and change direction. He would have a linebacker zeroing in on him after catching a pass. Then with one little juke he was gone. The linebacker would be grabbing air. Every time Terry touched the ball I'd take a peek and say, "Boy, I want to watch this." He wasn't a very big guy, but he could really take a hit. Guys would just pummel him and he'd bounce up like a bozo doll with a smile on his face, even though in the huddle he might be hurting like crazy. He always made the opposition feel like they couldn't hurt him.

Coryell designed a play during the '73 season, a screen pass/hook combination that was a killer for us. Our tight end J.V. Cain would shoot into the hook zone while Terry drifted out into the flats. The linebacker would have to decide between covering Metcalf or Cain. It was like shooting fish in a barrel when I was in those situations. If the linebacker covered the tight end, I'd dump it to Metcalf, who'd win most one-on-one matchups in the flats. If he decided to stick with Terry, I'd shoot it to Cain 15 yards up the middle. You don't know how many times we'd see a linebacker looking over to his bench, hands in the air, saying, "*What the hell do I do now?*"

Going into 1974, did you have reason to believe the Cardinals were ready to turn the corner? If so, what did you feel would be the biggest area of improvement?

JH: The difference was attitude, solely. We were a relatively young team and still adding more good players as we went. But Don Coryell was the real reason for the change. We knew things were going to get better if we kept working, and Don convinced us to believe in him.

The "Cardiac Cards" were one of the NFL's great stories of 1974, as the team pulled out 10 wins and won its first division championship since 1948. Nine of those victories were decided in the final two minutes of the game. Instead, wouldn't you liked to have rolled into Philadelphia or New York or Houston and been in cruise control by halftime, with a big, comfortable lead?

JH: No question! That's one of the things the fans would tease us about. They'd say, "You guys are killing us! You keep giving us heart-attacks!" Well, did they think it was any easier on us? It seemed like we were always sending the field goal team on to win the game for us, and I'd be on the sidelines watching like a fan. We always had faith it was going to happen. Most of the time it did, and we could've won a few more.

We lost 17-13 to a poor Kansas City squad in December, and I'll never forget this pass: It was a play called "Zero Eighty-Eight." At the very end of the game, Earl Thomas was coming across the end zone from his split end position and he was wide open! I just threw it too soon. He was running free, and I was trying not to look at him, but my pass sailed right over the top of his fingertips. Whenever I'd see [former Chiefs head coach] Hank Stram after that, he'd always bring that game up to me. "You should have beaten us," he'd say. Yeah, he was right.

Former Pittsburgh Steelers coach Chuck Noll once wrote, "On every team there is a core group that sets the tone for everyone else. If that tone is positive, you have half the battle won. If it's negative, you are beaten before you ever walk on the field." Which players set the tone for the St. Louis Cardinals during the 1970s?

JH: Our leaders were on the offensive line, there's no question about that. The offensive line set the tone for everything we did. Dan Dierdorf, Tom Banks, Conrad Dobler, Bob Young and Roger Finnie – those guys were the anchor for the St. Louis Cardinals. When they were on their "A" game, we usually had a pretty good chance of winning. That group had the respect of everyone on the team. We didn't have a dominating defense like the Cowboys or Minnesota or Washington, so we knew we were going to have to score a lot of points to win games. Our offensive line was the key to that.

Why isn't that Cardinals offensive line given more recognition historically as being one of the NFL's elite units? Only Dierdorf is in the Hall of Fame.

JH: The answer is simple – we never got to "The Big Game." If you don't get to "The Big Game," then you're treated basically like everybody else who never did, which is really unfair. If St. Louis had gotten to the Super Bowl, our line would have become legendary. History would have a whole different view of those guys. The same is true with getting into the Hall of Fame. If you haven't at least played in a Super Bowl, then you're nothing, especially as a quarterback. I don't think that is fair.

Only eight sacks were allowed by the Big Red offensive line during 1975. That's not protection, that's a maximum-security lockdown. It's a record that will likely never be broken.

JH: And of those eight sacks, I was only involved in six of them. Dennis Shaw, our backup that year, was sacked once, and then our kicker, Jim Bakken, got sacked on a field goal that went awry. It's neat to look back and talk about it because in today's game, a quarterback can get sacked five or six times in one afternoon. If I got sacked even three times in a game we would lose. Guaranteed.

I took it upon myself that I wasn't going to take a sack because it would hurt our team. As we got closer to the end of the season, we'd watch the game films and sometimes the offensive linemen would say to me, "You didn't have to throw the ball that soon. You could've held onto it a bit longer." True, but I understood the situation. I knew there was a record there to be broken, and I wanted to help. They would always tell me, "Baloney! Don't worry about that." But I cared. I wanted them to have that record.

Collapsing the Great Wall of St. Louis

Only eight times did enemy pass rushers collapse the St. Louis pass pocket during 1975. Many determined sackers tried their best to topple Jim Hart, but only a few came away with the prize. The names of those facemasked men who did deserve mention here. In order of takedown:

Sack #1 vs. N.Y. Giants (10/25) – Blitzing linebacker Pat Hughes hurdled a mousy, head-down block by Terry Metcalf and tossed Hart to the ground.

Sack #2 vs. N.Y. Giants (10/25) – DE Jack Gregory and DT John Mendenhall combined to collapse the Cardinals' pass pocket, earning ½ sack each.

Sack #3 vs. Washington (11/16) – DE Ron McDole and S Eddie Brown dropped K Jim Bakken on a bungled field goal attempt. Not the classic definition of a sack, but technically it makes the books.

Sack #4 vs. Washington (11/16) – DT Bill Brundige with another Redskins takedown

Sack #5 vs. N.Y. Jets (11/23) – DE Billy Newsome on an ugly, gnarled Shea Stadium field. Hart's passing totals, however, were 11 of 13 for 242 yds. "Other than the sack," he said, "the Jets gave probably the least amount of pressure I faced all season."

Sack #6 vs. Buffalo (11/27) – Bills left DE Walt Patulski charged through a half-assed roll block by Dan Dierdorf, giving him a clear shot at Hart who fumbled on the play.

Sack #7 vs. Buffalo (11/27) – DT Don Croft gave the Bills a deuce on this Thanksgiving Day. A special nod goes to the decimated Buffalo secondary, which showed Hart few creases and swiped four of his passes.

Sack #8 vs. Chicago (12/14) – More of a broken-play tackle than a sack. Dennis Shaw was forced into a wild scramble then Bears LB Doug Buffone hauled him down with one arm. The ball popped loose. Had the game been played in St. Louis, it would have been likely ruled as a rushing attempt.

Source: John Turney

Former Texas head coach Darrell Royal once said of Dobler, "We glamorize hoodlums, the guys who foul and hold. The worst examples of sportsmanship become our heroes. The way Conrad Dobler plays is nothing to emulate." Considering that it was Dobler's job to protect the Cardinals backfield, you probably appreciated his style a little more than Royal did.

JH: Oh, most definitely. I didn't condone it, but I certainly wasn't going to tell Conrad to quit. I was asked about it quite a bit, too. Merlin Olsen had a running battle with Conrad that was legendary. Merlin would ask me many times during the game, "How can you put up with that? You're not like that, Jim! How can you put up with that?"

I'd say, "Merlin, he's protecting me. What do you want me to do, tell him to stop?"

"Hell yeah, tell him to stop! He's doing it illegally!"

The irony here is that Conrad was a devious player when he first started out, but he was cut during his first year with the team. He wasn't good enough. He wasn't an exceptional athlete, and we had better players in training camp that year. When he was cut, I'm sure Hanifan told him, "Conrad, hang around. Don't go away. Things may happen and you might get called back." Well, he got called back pretty quickly. Hanifan would always tell Conrad, "If you listen to me, I can turn you into a good football player." He still pulled all of his shenanigans during his rookie year, but eventually he developed into a good player.

As the '70s went on, I don't think he had to rely on the shenanigans as much, but everyone was still watching him. They were still expecting the leg whips and grabs and bites. To my knowledge, he only bit somebody one time, and that story in itself has become a legend. [Minnesota DT] Doug Sutherland's fingers found their way inside his facemask and Conrad chomped right down on them.

Dierdorf was celebrated for being a cerebral, pounding blocker; Dobler made his name through eye-gouging, ankle-biting diplomacy. What about the rest your offensive line?

JH: Bob Young was unheralded but he did his job time-in and time-out. It was pretty difficult to get by him. Our center, Tom Banks, was another one. He wasn't very big by an offensive lineman's standards, 6'2", but we called him "Squatty Body" because most of his height was from the waist up. All body, no legs. I used to tease him because I had to get down really low to get the snap. When I tried to raise him up a bit, he'd nearly end up on his tiptoes.

Roger Finnie played at left tackle, the most important position to a right-handed quarterback. He'd protect my blind side, and considering some of the people he had to block at right defensive end – Dallas' Harvey Martin and the Giants' Jack Gregory both twice a year – I didn't envy his job. Those guys all did a great job. They were all underrated.

An 11-3 season in 1975 brought the Cardinals an undisputed NFC East title. Yet there were other observers who felt the Cardinals were really an untested bunch, citing a weak schedule (opponents had a collective 56-84 record), the third worst pass defense in football, and a cupcake pass rush that generated only 24 sacks all season. How do you feel history should rate the '75 Cardinals?

JH: That team was the best I played on during my time in St. Louis. That was the year we were going to make a serious run at a championship. We were only run out of town in one game, and that was against Buffalo on Thanksgiving, 32-14. But we also had some very big wins that year. We beat the Cowboys. We beat an improving New England team. Hey, we didn't make the schedule. We just played whoever they put in front of us. I certainly don't apologize for going 11-3. Had we won one more conference game, we would have hosted a playoff game in St. Louis and things might have gone a little differently. We could've made it to the NFC championship.

The '75 playoffs meant a showdown with the Los Angeles Rams, a team St. Louis hadn't faced since 1972. The Rams, at 12-2, finished the season tied with the best record in football and were a Vegas favorite to reach the Super Bowl. By halftime, two of your passes were intercepted for touchdowns and the Cards were in a 28-9 hole. It ended up 35-23. Were the Rams simply a better team that afternoon?

JH: It was just a bad day for us. We couldn't score enough points, and with Lawrence McCutcheon [202 yds] controlling the ball and the clock, it was especially tough for us to generate anything offensively. We were a passing team, but we needed to have the rushing game to win as well. After falling behind, we couldn't afford to grind it out so we threw the ball even more than we normally would.

How often does a team intercept two passes for touchdowns, let alone in the playoffs? Jack Youngblood's interception made it 14-0, then [DB] Bill Simpson's return made the score 21-0. Big comebacks in the playoffs are rare, and we weren't able to make a serious charge. Offensively, their quarterback Ron Jaworski only completed 12 passes, so it was McCutcheon who was the real key to that game. Our defense had no success in stopping him. It's safe to say we had better days.

The 1976 season again ended in heartbreak, as a 10-4 record wasn't good enough for a playoff birth. Wins over Dallas, Los Angeles, and Baltimore were nothing more than window dressing, as two losses to the Redskins gave the wildcard spot to Washington.

JH: It was very disappointing to play as well as we did in '76 and still not make the playoffs. It was all decided on the last weekend of the season. We won an early game against the Giants in New York and had to hope the Redskins would lose at Dallas in a late game. They were trailing 14-13 with around seven minutes to play. Man, we were all Dallas fans on the plane trip home. But in mid-flight, we learned from the pilot that Washington had won and we were staying home for the playoffs.

The Cardinals Win a Stunner at the Coliseum

Jack Youngblood ripped the helmet off his head, slammed it to the turf and cursed the ground he stood on. Tom Dempsey swung his fist at some invisible enemy while screaming out in anguish. And the rest of the Los Angeles Rams slumped collectively on the sideline, mulling over what could have been.

Of all the miracles the football Cardinals have worked in the last three seasons, perhaps none has been as stunning or spectacular as the one created yesterday in the Los Angeles Coliseum.

Confronted by deficits of four points, then eight, then a most-foreboding 15, they clawed their way past the morticians who would bury them and smiled. They defeated the Los Angeles Rams with a bit of voodoo that may someday be known as the Curse of the Cardinal Comeback. And they did it with 4 seconds left, 30-28.

"Sometimes," said Big Red tackle Dan Dierdorf, "I think we amaze ourselves."

What happened yesterday was nothing short of amazing, with no short cast of amazing characters.

There was the field-goal tandem of center Tom Brahaney, holder Roger Wehrli and kicker Jim Bakken – a trio that had botched three field-goal tries only a week earlier – teaming to split the uprights with a you-do-or-you-don't 25-yarder on the Big Red's last play.

There was wide receiver Ike Harris slicing through the L.A. secondary for eight receptions and 130 yards. There was rookie Pat Tilley, filling in for injured Mel Gray, diving and sprawling and clinging to six passes for 120 yards.

There was an offensive line that permitted no sacks, a defensive line that shackled Lawrence McCutcheon and a perseverant Terry Metcalf, whose only net rushing yards for the day (three) accounted for two touchdowns.

And there was quarterback Jim Hart, who bounced back from two first-half interceptions to a second half that read: 16 attempts, 13 completions, 229 yards and one touchdown.

"I'm very proud of these men," said coach Don Coryell. "They never gave up. They kept coming back when to all of you...and me...and probably to them it just looked hopeless." (November 14, 1976)

- Tom Barnidge, Copyright, 1976, *St. Louis Post-Dispatch*.
Reprinted with permission.

St. Louis got off to another meteoric start in 1977, winning seven of the first ten contests. Then Miami came into Busch Stadium on a Thanksgiving afternoon and annihilated the Cardinals, 55-14, your worst defeat since 1969.

JH: That was a brutal one. I remember our practice sessions the week before that game. Our defense was preparing to stop the quick-post patterns that [Miami QB] Bob Griese liked to throw to his receivers, which was a real key in beating Miami. All week long we ran the Dolphins' offense and our defense stopped it every time. But during the game, Miami went up and down the field, throwing those dinky, little quick-posts and tearing our defense up. It wasn't anything they hadn't seen before. Billy Kilmer of the Redskins used to throw it all the time against us. I couldn't understand it. Griese threw six touchdown passes, like our defenders weren't even there.

After that game the team folded down the stretch, losing its final three contests to finish 7-7. Then without much warning, Don Coryell was fired. Rumor was that he was caught in a power struggle with Bill Bidwill over personnel, the draft and other areas of running the team. Is that how you saw the situation?

JH: There's a lot of truth to that. Coryell's attitude towards Bill Bidwill was changing. Billy wasn't allowing Don to do certain things in terms of personnel. For example, he wouldn't negotiate with Terry Metcalf, whose contract was up. He just flat-out refused. Don saw the handwriting on the wall, that nothing good was going to come of staying in St. Louis. Also, Don's family wasn't happy living in St. Louis, so he felt it was time for a change.

    We were very upset when he left. We knew Don was going to be successful wherever he coached and we wanted to be part of it. His tenure with the Cardinals coincided with my best years, so to say I was sorry to see him go was an understatement. Then Metcalf left to play in the CFL, which was a real blow. He was being called "The Franchise" when he joined the team, and only four years later Bidwill was refusing to negotiate with him. It didn't make sense. I can completely understand why Don wanted to move on with his career.

Bud Wilkinson, the long-time coaching legend from the University of Oklahoma, came out of retirement as the surprise choice to replace Coryell. His first NFL campaign in 1978 was a disaster for several reasons: Metcalf was gone; Conrad Dobler and starting wideout Ike Harris had been traded to New Orleans; injuries had wrecked the roster. In all, Wilkinson inherited a deteriorating mess of a team that finished the year 6-10. Was the coach really even given a chance to be successful in St. Louis?

JH: It was a very good move hiring Bud Wilkinson, although I didn't realize it at the time. I didn't know much about Bud before he came, but eventually he became one of my favorites. He tried to do some things that were innovative, things like running the no-huddle, putting the tight end into a full-house backfield to disguise the strong side. But the media attacked him for it. "The game has passed him by," they said. "Look at all the crazy things he's doing." Those were the types of comments you heard or read. But just a few years later, Sam Wyche was doing the same things with Cincinnati, and the media was calling him a great innovator. Weren't they paying attention?

    To be honest, the real problem was we no longer had the great personnel we once had. Metcalf was gone. We had no tight ends, as J.V. Cain had died on the practice field from a congenital heart condition in '79 and Jackie Smith had been released. Bud was trying to operate in a pretty shaky situation.

    Then he got the idea to put together a consortium to buy the team. He made no bones about it, either. He'd tell us players to hang in there, that he was going to buy the Cardinals and really make something of them. Of course, Billy wasn't going to let him do that and he eventually fired Bud.

What did you learn from Wilkinson in his two seasons with the Cardinals?

JH: Bud had such a calming influence about him. He was the only head coach I ever played for who was as calm on gameday as he was during the rest of the week. Most coaches got pretty excited on gameday, all the adrenaline flowing, but Bud always had the same attitude, the same calm in his voice. When things weren't going well, he was like a father to me. After a bad play, instead of yelling, Bud would just look at me and say something like, "Well, you probably wish you had that one back," or "We'll get 'em next time." It made me feel good. I felt like crawling in a hole after making a bad play, and a lot of coaches would want to rip you a new whatever. It wasn't that way with Bud. I think I learned more about life than football from him.

Bidwill fired Wilkinson with three games left in the 1979 season over a dispute over who should play quarterback – you or Steve Pisarkiewicz, the Cardinals' top draft pick from a year earlier.

JH: It was a disturbing situation. Billy said to me on the day Bud was fired, "You know, your friend the coach wanted to trade you." Because of my relationship with Bud, I'd eventually find out the truth. I chatted with Bud about it later, and he told me what had really happened. Bill had called Bud into his office and told him that he wanted Steve Pisarkiewicz to play the rest of the season, to see what he could do. Bud told him, "I know what he can do. He can't play."

Billy insisted, but Bud insisted back, "*Pisarkiewicz can't play! I'm not putting him in there!*"

"If you want to keep your job, you will."

Finally, Bud relented. "Fine, but if you're not going to let Hart play, especially at this point in his career, why don't you trade him? Maybe somebody else can use him."

That's how the whole issue of me being traded came up. Of course, it never did work out with Pisarkiewicz. He had an eye problem, which eventually required surgery. And being the owner, Bidwill won that battle and fired Bud. Think of it – *two* Hall of Fame coaches fired by the Cardinals within two years. Makes a lot of sense, doesn't it?

It had to be discouraging as a player, watching Bidwill run his Mickey Mouse operation?

JH: It's really sad how that whole franchise was run. He doesn't give you the impression that he knows how to build a championship team. Bottom line, it's all about how you treat people. If you treat them well, they're going to respond. If you don't treat people well, the opposite is going to happen. You have to make people want to play for you. He never thought that was necessary. I just hope his sons and daughter, if they continue to own the team, come to that realization someday.

I say those things about a man who paid me for 18 years, and he certainly didn't compensate me the way quarterbacks are being paid today. Year-in and year-out he tested me. He'd bring in those high draft choices at quarterback almost every year. I don't think it was a conscious effort to unseat me because he could've done that anytime he wanted. I just never had a real good personal relationship with him, and I lament that. When you work for someone for 18 years, you would expect to have a decent relationship at the end of that period. I can't say that I did.

One time I went in to negotiate my contract with Billy. He turned over a 3-minute egg timer, looked at me and said, "Talk." As I'm living and dying, that's exactly what he did. I sat there for 30 seconds looking at the timer incredulously. Then he said, "Two and a half minutes."

I said, "You're serious, aren't you?"

"As a heart attack," he said.

That's how the negotiation went. So I said my peace, and he said he'd get back to me. I ended up not getting what I wanted, not even close. Later on in my career, I held out for an extra $10,000 per year over three years, and the answer was again no. I missed the first two days of training camp, and the press just beat me up. They were all over me. *How could this ingrate do this? How could he hurt the team?* Well, today guys hold out for millions and nobody says squat. I think to myself, "*C'mon, where were you people when I needed you?*"

One of the knocks on you as a quarterback was your tendency to throw interceptions. During the decade of the 1970s, you threw 145 of them, second only to Terry Bradshaw's 163. Why so many?

JH: I never thought about things like that. It's all conjecture anyway. I did what I thought I had to do. Maybe I tried to force the ball or thought I was a more talented passer than I really was. Maybe I took some risks that I shouldn't have. I didn't dwell on that then, and I don't dwell on it now.

Which defensive back did you avoid at all costs during your career?

JH: Pat Fisher of the Washington Redskins, no question. He was incredible. That little bugger was able to stay with our receivers like nobody else. He was a teammate of mine for two years, then the Cardinals traded him after the '67 season. They thought he was over the hill, but even into 1973, '74 and '75, he was still a great nemesis for us. Pat was all business. There was no way you were going to crack his visage and get inside his psyche during the day of a game. It was amazing how intense he was.

I had more fun playing against guys like Cliff Harris and Charlie Waters from Dallas. Cliff and Charlie were always trying to reach my psyche as well, but they went about it a little differently than Fisher. Waters would look across the line at me and wink.

One time Harris had crouched way down low behind Lee Roy Jordan, and I stopped the cadence to see what the heck he was doing. He peeked out from behind Jordan, and I peeked out from under center to find him. Then he mouthed the words, "I love you." That threw me right off. He accomplished what he wanted because I totally forgot the play we were supposed to run. Those games against the Cowboys might have seemed to be brutal but we had a lot of fun playing against them.

Which was the best overall secondary you faced during the 1970s?

JH: The Redskins had the best. The Vikings were very talented, but [head coach] Bud Grant believed in playing a safety zone defense, so you always knew where their players were going to be. Their attitude was, "Hey, you know what we're doing. Prove you can beat us."

The Redskins, however, seemed to know what we were going to do before we did it. Of course, Coryell always believed that Redskins coach George Allen was spying on him, but there was never any proof of that. On game days, the Redskins would come up with a defense that was almost perfect for what we had been concocting in practice all week long. There was no way anyone could've known what we'd been planning unless they were watching us do it. We'd get into a formation and you could hear them yelling, "Here it is! Here it is!" We'd be saying to ourselves, "Here *what* is? How do *you* know what's coming?"

Maybe Coryell was onto something. Maybe they were spying. One-on-one, you'd look at the individual talent on their defense and think there wasn't too much to worry about. Well, we had plenty to worry about. For instance, weakside linebacker Chris Hanburger seemed to know everything that was happening on the field. He'd watch our signals from the sideline. I swear he knew our signaling system as well as anybody. Sometimes I'd try to kid with him and throw him off guard a little bit, but no way, he wasn't going to break.

How about Ron McDole, their left defensive end? Ask Dan Dierdorf today who was one of the toughest guys he had to block, and he'll say Ron McDole. Ron looks the same today as he did back then – old! We'd look at him and say, "*No way* he can stop us. Dierdorf can block him and away we'll go." But somehow he'd make the play and we'd say, "Dadgummit! How'd he do that?"

The Spy Wore Burgundy: Football's Cold War Hits St. Louis

The Washington Post article was from March, 1978, and Jim Hart's quote was an intriguing one:

"Coryell had a vendetta against [Redskins coach George] Allen. It was a battle of wits during the week before games. Coryell got so uptight. I found myself fighting that, and it took away from my concentration. Don seemed to get uptight and not do things the way he normally did."

Interesting comment, but that was it. No further insight or clarification from Hart, just a memory of Coach Allen driving Don Coryell nutso and telepathically screwing up St. Louis' prep work the week before the Washington game. So, 23 years after his comment, I called Hart and asked him to expand on what he meant by Coryell "not doing things the way he normally did."

"That was something that went back to the days when both of them were coaching junior college football in the 1950s," Hart told me. "Don's second-string quarterback at Wenatchee Valley J.C. had quit the team one year. A few weeks later they were getting ready to play Whittier College, which was coached by George Allen, and that same kid showed up on Allen's sideline charting plays. That started it all. And Don believed that George Allen carried that kind of chicanery into the pros.

What about the changes in the Cardinals' weekly routine?

"Without fail things were different for us the week before we played Washington. Schedules were rearranged, routines were changed. There'd be extra security around Busch Stadium. Don would have us switch our jersey numbers around, things like that. Anything that could possibly throw off George Allen's spies that were watching us, although we were never able to prove they even existed.

"One day in practice during Redskins week, somebody noticed three guys stationed in the window of a building that overlooked Busch Stadium from the east. One guy had a telescope and the other two were writing on clipboards. We could see them from the field. Don was upset about it, so team management sent security over to see what was going on in that room. For some reason they weren't allowed in. That made Don even more nuts.

"But you know, every time we played the Redskins, they were always unbelievably prepared for us. They always seemed to know what we were gonna do, so maybe there was something to it.

"Maybe Don wasn't paranoid. Maybe he knew what he was talking about."

Here's an observation on aging quarterbacks by former Giants head coach Bill Parcells. I'd like to hear your thoughts on it:

"I think what happens as quarterbacks get older is that they just won't pull the trigger. It's not that they don't know what to do, but they want it to be perfect before they throw it. They're torn between the turnover – which they don't want to make because it's a killer – and throwing the ball when the separation between the receiver and the defender isn't quite enough. They're not the confident throwers like they were when they were younger. That is one of the first signs of a quarterback not being able to do the job well anymore."

JH: I agree with that. I'm a good one to ask because I really overstayed my career. I was 39 during my last year with the Cardinals. I knew I was no longer able to do a 16-game schedule as a starting quarterback. As you get older, the position becomes more and more cerebral than physical. Sure, you have to be able to get the ball downfield and fire it between two defenders, but you pick your spots more carefully. You become much more conscious of throwing the interception, so it's probably fair to say you become less daring. And your arm isn't as strong as it once was. Your legs don't move as quickly. Your reaction time slows a bit. You learn to play smart.

In 1983 you threw your last pass for the Cardinals. Neil Lomax had taken over the starting duties a few seasons earlier, and head coach Jim Hanifan had decided it was time to release his 39-year old backup quarterback. Do you remember how you felt after you were finally let go?

JH: I told Jim I didn't think it was his decision to release me, although he disputed that. Some people didn't think I had enough left to backup Lomax, which was silly because I could still play the position and I wanted to stay in St. Louis. There was some animosity between Neil and me at the time. It had a lot to do with attitudes and the direction the team was going at quarterback, but I would've gotten over that quickly just to stay on with the Cardinals. Hanifan didn't want to hear that, and told me it was already a done deal. Neil and I didn't have the best relationship. Maybe Neil felt he'd constantly be looking over his shoulder if I was still on the team.

You played one final season, as a backup with the Washington Redskins in '84.

JH: At the Super Bowl that year, I was in Tampa doing some work for a local St. Louis TV station. I caught Joe Gibbs, the Redskins coach, in the lobby of the hotel and we did a quick interview. As he turned to leave, I half-jokingly said to him with the camera still running, "Don't forget, Joe – this old rag arm is out of a job.

If you need a backup for next year, I'm your man." At that time, I was pretty sure my playing days were over, but I was willing to listen to any offers. He stopped in his tracks, turned around and said, "[My coaches and I] were just talking about you! We're going to need a backup for Theismann, a seasoned veteran, and you're the guy! Call me this week."

Well, my wife and I ended up leaving for Hawaii the next day for a golf tournament. A few days later we were in bed when the phone rang. It was Joe Gibbs. He had tracked me down at the hotel. "Hey, we'd like for you to come to Washington and be our backup this year."

I answered quickly, "Okay!"

He slowed me down. "Whoa, wait a minute, Jim. We've got to negotiate a contract first."

I said, "No, we don't. Whatever you want to pay me is fine. I'm sure you're going to be fair." The Redskins ended up giving me the same amount of money I'd been making in St. Louis.

It was such a difference between how the St. Louis and Washington organizations were run. I was in the Redskins' training camp in Carlisle, PA the following summer, warming up my arm with Joe Theismann, when [owner] Jack Kent Cooke came by and said, "Come on over here, old timer!" I told him I had to warm up but he said, "Aw, hell, you can warm up anytime. Come over here with me."

We sat on a couple of folding chairs he had placed on the 50-yard line and he asked me, "Is everything going all right?"

"Oh, yes sir. I'm very happy."

"Well, do you need anything?"

"I don't think so," I said.

"Do you need a car or a place to stay?"

I said, "I think I'm okay."

He said, "Well, if you have any trouble, you let me know."

I furled my brow a little bit then said, "You have to remember, I'm not used to this type of treatment from the owner."

He just looked at me and smiled.

"You know, Jim, I'm well aware of that."

• • • •

The Men from Nowhere:
Football's Most Prolific Undrafted Quarterbacks

5) Jim Zorn, Seattle/Green Bay/Tampa Bay (1976-87) – The pride of someplace called Cal Poly-Pomona. Originally signed by Dallas, Zorn lost a tight duel with Cowboys backup Clint Longley for a '75 roster spot, then spent the season hidden on some quirky reserve list. The expansion Seahawks, coached by Jack Patera, received a tip on the 6'2" lefty and brought him into their '76 camp amidst a herd of other culls and drifters – Bob Cason, Neil Graff, Scott Christman, Gary Keithley and other *remember me?* types.

"Watching practice, our quarterback situation was pretty bleak," said former Seattle Scouting Director Dick Mansperger. "We were so lucky that Zorn emerged. Our scouts had no idea who he was, but we had a good relationship with the Dallas people and they pointed him in our direction."

What separated Zorn from the pack were his legs, ones that could dip and dart and create on a quick-revving motor. As a result, the Seattle coaches drew up a dynamic sprint-draw offense for him, which would also help mask the team's porous offensive line. Then luck brought the team another unknown castoff in receiver Steve Largent, and the 'Hawks were in business.

By season's end, Seattle's offense had allowed a respectable 28 sacks ("Emotionally those sacks kill a young team's confidence," says Patera), Largent had snagged 54 catches and Zorn had passed for over 2,500 yards, giving him a strong push for NFC Offensive Rookie of the Year honors.

An 11-year pro, Zorn's best campaign came in 1979 when he threw for 3,661 yards and 20 touchdowns and averaged over six yards a rush. Only a monster season by San Diego quarterback Dan Fouts kept Zorn from grabbing a Pro Bowl spot. "But Jim had my vote," boasts Patera.

From Mr. Nobody to the cusp of greatness, it's a trip very few quarterbacks make. "Jim was never a superstar, but look at it this way," says Mansperger. "Largent's bust is in Canton, so maybe a mold of Jim's left arm should be sitting right next to it."

NFL career: 21,115 yards, 111 touchdowns, 67.3 passer rating

4) Bobby Hebert, New Orleans/Atlanta (1985-96) –

The only member of this group with any height (6'4") and a catchy nickname – The Cajun Cannon. Hebert started his pro career as a USFLer, playing three solid seasons with the Michigan and Oakland franchises – he starred in two of the league's three championship games – before signing on with the NFL's New Orleans Saints.

He logged two years of bench time before Saints head coach Jim Mora, another USFL graduate, named him the starter in 1987. The move paid off big, as Hebert guided New Orleans through a streak of nine consecutive wins that ended in the franchise's first-ever playoff appearance. He led the Saints to the playoffs three more times between 1990 and 1992.

Hebert skipped to Atlanta as a free agent in 1993. He zipped 24 TD passes that year – including a 98-yard highlighter against New Orleans – and was a reserve in the Pro Bowl. But he surrendered the starting job to Jeff George the following year and quietly went away. Retirement came in 1997.

Overall, a good career, not a standout one. The thrilling Hebert memories are few. I remember his sharp, 20-for-23 day in a blowout over Denver in '88... the emotional win over Pittsburgh in '87 that locked up the Saints' first winning season... I'm looking at the press pass from that game right now.

I guess it's Hebert's USFL work that sticks with me most, though. Springtime football...that triple OT affair against Steve Young's L.A. Express in the playoffs...his gutty, 300-yard performance against a roughneck Philly defense in the first USFL title game...a different class of football. Memories for a different day.

NFL career: 21,683 yards, 135 touchdowns, 78.0 passer rating

3) Jim Hart, St. Louis/Washington (1966-84) –

Undrafted by both the NFL and AFL, Hart latched onto the quarterback-challenged Cardinals then roller-coastered along as a below average passer until coach Don Coryell arrived in 1973. By 1974, Hart was MVP of the National Conference and led the Cardinals to their first playoff appearance in 26 years.

His aggressive, downfield instincts often led to interception troubles; Hart ranks sixth all-time with 247. Ahead of him? George Blanda with 277, John Hadl (268), Fran Tarkenton (266), John Unitas (253) and Dan Marino (252). All but Hadl and Hart have busts in the Hall of Fame.

"Hey, my game was going for the quick strike," says Hart, "and I guess the interceptions came with that. I know I'd go crazy trying to run those short, dinking offenses that teams are using today."

NFL career: 34,665 yards, 209 touchdowns, 66.6 passer rating

2) Dave Krieg, Seattle/various (1980-98) –

Krieg looked more like a point guard than a pro quarterback when he arrived at the Seahawks training camp. He stood an unimposing 6'1", 185-lbs, with an arm most scouts have seen a thousand times before.

"Our scout, Ralph Golsteyn, didn't like him at all," says Mansperger. "Dave was a thrower, not a pure passer. He didn't have a real quick arm. But his coach at Milton College, a guy named Rudy Gaddini, wouldn't leave us alone. He kept calling and pestering us. We finally signed him to get Gaddini off our backs."

"I saw two very obvious things in Dave Krieg," says Gaddini. "He was a very good athlete, and the kid didn't get rattled under pressure. Always kept his cool when things were coming apart."

But what separated Krieg from the rest of those nice, 6'1" athletes your find out there?

"He worked his ass off, that's what," Mansperger says. "David's father was a Wisconsin state trooper, a career lawman. They were both tough, self-made guys. All David wanted was a chance in football. He didn't ask for any quarter. He worked and worked with our QB coach, Jerry Rhome, and suddenly the smoke cleared and Dave was still standing."

After three seasons of spot duty, Krieg finally took the Seahawks' reins from a struggling Jim Zorn in a 1983 game with Pittsburgh and never let go. Four weeks later he lit up the Broncos for 420 yards and three touchdowns. Krieg then hit the national spotlight by guiding Seattle to a shocking 27-20 playoff upset over Dan Marino's Miami Dolphins.

"Marino drives to work every morning in a new gold Corvette that matches his hair and arm," wrote *The Washington Post*'s Michael Wilbon before the game. "Krieg, signed as a free agent, comes in a Pinto."

A motor that ran for 19 seasons, with an odometer registering nearly 40,000 worth of yardage.

That Gaddini was one helluva car salesman.

NFL career: 38,147 yards, 261 touchdowns, 81.5 passer rating

1) Warren Moon, 1984-2000 (Houston/various) – Eleven University of Washington quarterbacks are listed ahead of him in the school's career passing yardage. Names like Brock Huard, Sonny Sixkiller and Tom Flick. Moon checks with 3,465 yards, good enough for 12th place.

In NFL yards, however, only Dan Marino and John Elway have surpassed Moon's 49,325 career total.

It began as a disappearing act. America first heard of Moon on New Year's Day, 1978, as he directed the Huskies to a stunning upset of hulking Michigan in the Rose Bowl. NBC announcers Curt Gowdy and John Brodie gushed over his bold, slashing performance that wrecked the Wolverines' trip west. Then the game ended and Moon quietly disappeared off America's football radar.

Typically the term "scouting blunder" refers to some hotshot collegian who the whole world agrees can play at the pro level but can't. The opposite is far less common.

"I wasn't even invited to the league's scouting combine," says Moon. "Nobody would give me a workout to see what I could do, to see if I had the arm strength to play in the NFL."

How does that happen? How does a league full of scouting intelligence miscalculate Moon's potential so badly?

The '78 draft was iffy at best for quarterback prospects. By the sixth round, longshots named Mike Rieker and Dennis Sproul and John Hurtley were being culled by NFL teams. Still, no place for Moon, the Rose Bowl MVP.

"Typical of the way black quarterbacks were graded back then," says Paul Zimmerman of *Sports Illustrated*. "You'd hear things like, 'He's a great athlete, quick, talented and, oh yeah, he happens to play quarterback.' The word given to scouts was that if Moon was projected to be a low-round pick, he was going to Canada. Well, he was projected as a low-round pick."

So it was off to the CFL. As quarterback for the Edmonton Eskimos, Moon filled the Canadian skies with over 20,000 yards of electric bolts and long-distance strikes. He commanded the team to five straight Grey Cup titles before returning to the States in 1984 as a big-ticket member of the Houston Oilers.

By 1988 he was a Pro Bowler. Two years later he was the NFL's offensive MVP, directing coach Jack Pardee's impudent Run-n-Shoot attack. ("A perfect offense for me," says Moon. "All those downfield options.") Moon's teams were frequent playoff participants, although critics cite his soggy 3-7 postseason record when Hall of Fame talk begins to swirl. Another knock was his fumbling; Moon's 161 career drops is the NFL record.

His greatest day came on a dreary December afternoon in Kansas City, 1990. Sid Gillman, the late Hall of Fame offensive guru who'd seen thousands of hours of football, called it the greatest passing exhibition he'd ever seen. Twenty-seven completions yielded 527 yards against a veteran Chiefs secondary that had been the AFC's tightest only a year earlier. His yardage came in giant, thieving chunks. One score to WR Haywood Jeffires covered 87 yards.

All-Pro cornerback Albert Lewis was on the field that day for the Chiefs.

"I played a lot of years, against guys like Elway and Marino and Jim Kelly," said Lewis. "Moon is right there with them. That kind of damage I saw today I've never seen before. What a helpless feeling trying to stop it."

A feeling a lot of defenses had come to know.

NFL career: 49,325 yds, 290 touchdowns, 81.0 passer rating

— 13 —
Cedric Hardman, Defensive End

San Francisco 49ers (1970-79); Oakland Raiders (1980-81)
June 29, 2002

The greatest set of downs I've ever seen unleashed by a pass rusher came back in 1981 – Dallas at San Francisco, early October by the bay. Fred Dean, a 6-3, 230-pound hellcat made his debut at right defensive end for the 49ers that day. He had joined the team just 48 hours earlier, the result of a salary-incited trade with San Diego.

Cowboys' left tackle Pat Donovan was assigned to handle Dean. The season before, in a Monday night meeting with the Chargers, he had contained Dean to just half a sack, but the rusher appeared sluggish at times during that game. He played in spurts, and maybe 10 pounds heavier than his listed weight. Things would be quite different in their rematch.

"A pass rush, late in the game, is the key to NFL football," Niners coach Bill Walsh has been known to say. It comes in rather handy right before halftime, too, as his young football team would find out.

A series of bungling mistakes helped put the Cowboys behind 24-7 with less than two minutes remaining in the first half, but they had moved the ball to their own 40 and were scrambling for the quick score to get back in it. Here's where Dean emerged to cave in any last rays of light from above:

1st and 10 – Cowboys in the shotgun, three-wide, and Tony Dorsett at H-back as either an extra blocker or dump-off receiver. Donovan's lone assignment is to neutralize the well-rested Dean. It never happens. A furious bull rush shoves Donovan ten yards upfield and then, brother, here comes the judge. Donovan gets tossed aside as Dean crashes into quarterback Danny White for the sack.

2nd and 19 – Cowboys again in three-wide, Donovan again draws solo duty on Dean. Donovan lines up a yard behind the ball to minimize his opponent's angle, but this time Dean blows by him with an inside swim move. As Dean and left end Dwaine Board bear down on White, the result is a ruptured screen pass which falls incomplete.

3rd and 19 – Dallas again spreads the field, this time with four wideouts. Dorsett is in the backfield flanking the quarterback. On the snap Dorsett steps up to support Donovan, but Dean instead takes a wide inside loop and finds himself face-to-face with backup center Robert Shaw. He lowers his helmet into Shaw's throat and lifts him off the ground like a bull goring a rodeo clown. Shaw crashes hard on his back, and the one-man stampede resumes his charge on White. *Fourth-and-30.*

The Cowboys offense never reignited after that series and the humiliation ended at 45-14. It was an awesome performance by Dean. "We had no answer for him," said Dallas coach Tom Landry afterwards.

On a side note from that year, right after San Francisco had captured victory in Super Bowl XVI, a local newspaper polled its anxious readers to select the All-Time 49ers team. Fred Dean, a situational pass rusher with only eleven regular season games and three playoffs in SF's red-and-gold, made the team at right defensive end.

Fred Dean? Listed there among 49ers icons like John Brodie and Hugh McElhenny, Gene Washington and Leo Nomellini? Like a mercenary among the Royal Guard.

Several other San Francisco short-timers like Hacksaw Reynolds and Ronnie Lott made that list, too. I question the demographics of the voters… probably a lot of high schoolers and twenty-somethings stuffing multiple ballots. Regardless, the newspaper should have waited six months to run its poll, at least until the fans had cleared their heads of the Super Bowl hysteria, until they were given time to reach back into their memories.

There they would have found Cedric Hardman.

• •

I once asked my best friend, Naje, which NFL player he thought had the most sacks during the 1970s (after already tracking down the answer myself). Naje, who does some radio work in Louisville but traces his football roots back to Sunday morning Grambling highlights, has a way of dancing around questions when he doesn't know the answer. He plays the elimination game. "Well, it wasn't so-and-so, was it?" He did it again this time.

"Well, it wasn't the Steelers' Joe Greene..."

Nope, not Greene. Greene is nowhere close.

"I don't think it was Jack Youngblood…"

No, but Youngblood is high on the list.

"It wasn't Cedric Hardman of the 49ers, was it?"

Hardman – now *there's* a name for ya. Number 86 in your old Forty Niners program.

(The right answer? A journeyman named Coy Bacon, but who would've guessed that? "I thought it would've been Hardman," Naje said. "Helluva player. Don't hear much about him anymore.")

Cedric Hardman *was* a helluva player, and one can easily make a case that he was more deserving of All-Time 49er status than Dean, who played over half his career in San Diego. Hardman, a pass-rush specialist like Dean, collected more total career sacks (121 to 93), but he toiled on some real horseshit 49er teams in the mid-to-late '70s. Dean's arrival, however, coincided with San Fran's first Super Bowl trophy. Hence, the oversight.

Disrupting passing attacks was Hardman's game. During his prime, from 1970 through 1978, he gathered his sacks in bunches, averaging nearly twelve per season, including 18 in 1971.

"When I think of Cedric Hardman, I think of that incredibly quick first step and burst off the ball," says Paul Wiggin, his 49ers line coach in the early '70s. "A great space rusher. Cedric played left end in college but we moved him to the right side to get him away from the tight end. That really opened up his game.

"I once watched him completely destroy Art Shell during a preseason game with Oakland. That in itself was a feat, but what made it more impressive was that Cedric did it shortly after having major knee surgery. He damaged it in the summer and was supposed to miss the entire year, but he came back and completely manhandled Shell. Actually, that whole Gold Rush outfit in San Francisco was one of the best lines I've seen, the complete package."

Ah, the Gold Rush – the NFC's closest rendition of Pittsburgh's Steel Curtain during the 1970s. It was Tommy Hart, Cedric Hardman, Jimmy Webb and Cleveland Elam. One October night in '76 they hauled down Rams quarterback James Harris ten times. ("One of the worst singular beatings I have ever seen administered in professional football," Howard Cosell proclaimed afterward.) That year the Gold Rush crunched enemy passers for 61 sacks, still a distant 49ers record.

"I hated playing against those guys," Saints quarterback Archie Manning once told me. "Most times, before I could even set up to throw, Hardman had already made his way into my blind spot, all that speed coming off the corner. It was like being underwater in some rickety shark cage at night; you didn't know when it was coming, but it was coming."

But Hardman, the big shark, would often swallow the bait, too. For a gung-ho defensive end with quarterback-on-the-brain, teams would anticipate his charge and dart right up Cedric Alley. He couldn't stop the run. Traps and draw plays were sent his way in droves, particularly on third down. The lack of discipline in that area alone will keep Hardman far from the Hall of Fame, despite his lofty sack totals. Hardman himself agreed that it became embarrassing for him after a while. It frustrated his coaches and took years to correct.

"Hardman was incredibly quick, so the key for us was to throw quickly, a lot of three-step drops," said former Cardinals QB Jim Hart. "Those kinds of plays can frustrate any great pass rusher. Then we'd mix in the draw plays, which often worked because he was so aggressive. Then the play-action passes. The whole operation was focused on keeping him off-balance, to keep him thinking. The last thing I wanted to do was sit back there in a seven-step drop and let Hardman make his statement."

And those 121 career sacks are a very loud statement.

"I chased and caught quarterbacks – plain and simple, end of story," Hardman says in that Samuel L. Jackson/*Pulp Fiction* tone of his. "That was my business. That's what I was put on this earth to do. Ask any of those number 12's or 14's what kind of game I brought on Sunday back in the '70s. I can assure you, my friend, their memories mostly aren't pleasant ones."

● ● ●

I'd like to start with a quote from an old teammate of yours from North Texas State, Joe Greene. He once said that, "Playing defensive line is really survival of the fittest, make no mistake about it. They have rule makers but they arbitrarily intervene, so if you are participating you have to be the judge, the jury and the executioner – all rolled into one." After 12 years as an NFL defensive end, you are certainly well equipped to comment on that system of justice.

CH: I concur 110-percent with Mr. Greene. I've always said that the laws meant to protect you in this world, on any given Sunday afternoon in the fall, in any major American city, from one to four o'clock in the PM, do not apply. That was my experience precisely.

A great pass rusher possesses four essential things – strength, speed, desire and instinct. Which of these attributes do you feel contributed most to your success as a defensive lineman?

CH: We're talking over 19 years since I last played, so I now know that pass rushing is a gift you get at the gate. It's not something you order from Sears or Penny's along the way and get in the mail. The skill is not something someone can teach you. A great pass rusher is *born*, not made. All of those other factors you mentioned are important, but you rely on instinct more than any of those others.

And how did you come to this realization?

CH: From watching people that are great pass rushers versus those who aren't. A lot of guys have speed, a lot of guys have intelligence or strength, but they can't get to the quarterback. When talking about my game, I tell people that I *chased* and *caught* quarterbacks. A lot of people chase quarterbacks, but many times it's like the exercise of a dog chasing a car. A dog will bark and cause all kind of commotion and chase that car all the way down the block, but that's where the whole thing ends – in a fruitless chase. And even if the dog were to catch it, he wouldn't know what the hell to do with it. I knew what to do with it.

All great pass rushers come equipped with a secret arsenal, an array of techniques they use to get to the passer. What was in your bag of tricks that enabled you to collect a staggering 121 career sacks?

CH: Most sacks are gotten on the snap count, on the get-off. That's the one thing the rule makers can't take away from you. My main weapon was speed. If I could get off the ball – *I mean, really get off the ball* – there would be no contact until I reached the quarterback. That offensive tackle would not touch me. I lined up way outside, so much that I changed the way that the defensive end position was played. In fact, my style of pass rushing evolved into what eventually became the rush linebacker in the 3-4 defense. Players like Lawrence Taylor and Pat Swilling and Derrick Thomas – they lined up outside the tackle. In a 4-3 defense I lined up that wide as a defensive end. In passing situations, I wanted to be a yard, yard-and-a-half outside the offensive tackle.

I truly believe that if I got off the ball, it didn't matter what you did. I was going to be crashing down on your quarterback. I had an uncanny knack for it, along with a couple secrets here and there. I lined up mostly in a right-handed stance on the right side, my right leg back, and there were certain plays that by the time the ball was snapped and hit into the quarterback's hand, my right leg would already be coming down. If I had a good get-off, it was all academic, my friend. Fourth down, time to punt.

But let me say this: I can never give enough credit to Floyd Peters, who was the best defensive line coach I ever had. He was the greatest specialist at choreographing the movement of a pass rush, four linemen going to the quarterback. The main thing he stressed was the absolute importance of getting off the ball at the snap. Every day when we watched film he was on the clicker checking to see how your timing was in getting off the ball.

Unfortunately, all those sacks you collected aren't recognized by the NFL. The league didn't make the sack an official individual statistic until 1982.

CH: I know it, man. If the league had recorded the things I did, the records would look a lot different. I had quite a few five-sack games, including the '71 NFC championship game against the Cowboys. That effort got minimal recognition since we lost the game, but, hell, if you get five sacks in a game today, you go straight to the Hall of Fame.

I played some games where as many as four people were assigned to me on one play. *Four people*! Heck, I had 16 sacks my rookie year and I wasn't even a starter. That number would easily lead the league today.

I watch the games today to see who is making noise on the defensive lines. Jevon Kearse, the young man who plays for Tennessee [now Philadelphia], is interesting to me. His rookie year he was All-Everything. Everybody was excited about this kid. Since then, I've watched games where his name is never even called. That's just the way it goes.

Your first year in the league? Sure, you can catch 'em by surprise. But if you establish the fact that you're going to get to the quarterback they begin to stop you. Different things begin to happen to you, and you begin to find out just how good you really are. It's the beginning of double-teaming. Then they start doing other interesting things to you, like putting the tight end on your side just to break your concentration. Or they'll pull the center out of the line and hit you from that angle. Now, *can you still* get the quarterback after being double-teamed, triple-teamed and sometimes quadruple-teamed?

The Sacks That Time Forgot

Individual sack statistics have been recognized by the NFL only since 1982, but defensive ends and linebackers had been hauling down quarterbacks way before then. All the names listed in the record books today (*e.g., Most Sacks, Rookie Season – 14.5, Jevon Kearse, 1999; Most Sacks, Game – 7.0, Derrick Thomas, 1990*) are postdated from '82.

"Since when does the 'all-time' clock start ticking in 1982?" says former Rams' rusher Deacon Jones.

And what if you're looking for historical information, the raw numbers? Call up the league office or Elias Sports Bureau asking for L.C. Greenwood's career total and you'll hear, "We don't keep that number, sir. It wasn't an official statistic. He played too long ago."

How about Baltimore's Fred Cook, or the Raiders' Ted Hendricks?

"We don't keep those numbers, sir. It wasn't an official statistic back then. You'll have to somehow find that information on your own." Blah, blah, blah.

One die-hard fan/historian actually went ahead and did that. His name is John Turney, a New Mexican with a passion for pro football and its numbers. I call him "The Sack Man." A lot of older players call him to say "Thank you."

Back in 1992, Turney began a project set on proving that the all-time NFL sack record was actually held by Deacon Jones, not the Giants' Lawrence Taylor, as the league had officially proclaimed.

"I always wondered," says Turney, "why the league refuses to count the 9½ sacks from Taylor's rookie year in his career total, even though they were well-documented in the Giants' statistics. It really bothered me, and I could never get a good answer from anybody.

"Around that time, [Eagles DT] Reggie White had surpassed Taylor's career total. But Jones was loudly proclaiming that Taylor's record was bogus, that *he* actually owned the record. At that point, I decided to begin the long process, to dig through every official play-by-play sheet I could find, to watch every game film I could get my hands on. A lot of doors were slammed at first but the project gained momentum. Now I've reached the point where I have solid sack data on almost every significant player since the 1960s." Turney's findings:

The REAL Rookie Sack Record: "My research show that Oakland's Tony Cline owns the AFC rookie record with 17½ sacks in 1970. Detroit's Bubba Baker had a monster first season in the league with 21½ sacks, which is the NFC and league record. The Lions officially list him with 23 that year, but in a game against Tampa Bay they awarded him three full sacks that should have been partials."

Biggest Surprise: "I assumed that guys like Merlin Olsen, Bob Lilly and Joe Greene each would have been well over 100. But because of the positions they played – mostly as run-stopping tackles – they actually set up more sacks than they got themselves. Then again, Alan Page was able to get a lot of sacks [148½], reaffirming how great a player he really was."

Most Appreciative Player: "There were several. Atlanta's Claude Humphrey was really thankful. He was glad that somebody was doing the work, trying to show that people from his era also had sacks and were great pass rushers. Cedric Hardman was another who was really appreciative and interested. I first called Cedric in the early '90s and told him what I was doing. All he said to me was, "Speak." We got right into it.
"Merlin Olsen, who had 92 sacks himself, was tickled that Youngblood and Deacon Jones were so high on my list. When I showed him their numbers, he looked at me and said, "This tells me I was doing my job.""

Worst Record Keeping: "The Baltimore Colts records from the '60s and '70s were by far the worst. The man in the booth who was typing in the statistics wasn't very specific about who made the sack. One of the big disappointments was that we weren't able to pin down what Gino Marchetti and Big Daddy Lipscomb and Art Donovan had done. I would love to see those numbers, but I'm afraid they're lost."

Biggest Obstacle: "Seymour Siwoff of Elias Sports Bureau, the league's statistical arm, told me he felt that individual sack records shouldn't be kept. I was surprised that Elias wouldn't help me go back and research play-by-plays sheets, even from 1980 or 1981. We could have gotten Lawrence Taylor's whole career stats recognized."

Biggest Help from the NFL: "At the beginning, Rick Smith, the Rams' PR director, was the first to let me in. He was the most helpful. The team that really surprised me by letting me review their records was the Oakland Raiders. I expected to be turned down flat, but obviously they saw the benefit in what I was doing and gave me a lot of help."

How were you able to overcome all that extra attention?

CH: When you get to the point in a game where they're putting three or four people on you, you're just going to the quarterback. You've shut off your mind. The show is on autopilot. And every time somebody shows up in front of you, you just react to it. The first guy is beaten right off the bat. You're already looking at the second guy and by the time you get to him, you see the third guy coming. By the time you get to him, you've already spotted the fourth guy. A lot of time it's just a matter of staying alive. The whole time you're thinking, "I've gotta keep from getting hurt on this play. These boys are trying to hurt me!"

You played defensive end at a weight anywhere from 240 to 258 pounds. Naturally, it contributed to your speed and quickness off the ball, but was being that light ever a disadvantage for you?

CH: By the time Jack Youngblood and I retired, we were two of the smallest defensive ends in the NFL. I played as light as 238. Your only concern about playing at that weight is being able to handle the run. In passing situations, anything over 225 is a liability once the ball is snapped. All that poundage and big heavy weights look good in the program, right until the ball is snapped. Then the weight is a liability because you gotta carry that stuff.

Against the run, we were taught the forearm shiver which, God almighty, is becoming a lost art. They don't have many guys coaching the game today who teach the forearm shiver. When delivered properly, it is quite effective. You use your strength, quickness and body positioning, then you apply the shiver in the right place – like a guy's throat. You can neutralize an elephant if you have to. You had to be quick about it, though. I mean, the second that ball was snapped you wanted that forearm in his throat, just to break his momentum. Then you get both hands on him, lock your body out, then find the ball and go to it.

After the season, I'd take a week or two off to recover. Then I'd go straight into martial arts. A lot of the moves and techniques you use in martial arts coincided with some of the stuff you used in football. That doesn't mean that taking martial arts is going to make you a football player, but it can make a football player a better football player.

Describe how you paced yourself during a game. How could you ensure there'd still be something left in the tank to give an effective pass rush during the fourth quarter?

CH: That's a great, great question. Whenever I speak to young kids, I always tell them this: Any game that you play in which endurance is a factor – football, wrestling, basketball, boxing – it behooves you to be in the very best condition. You have to learn to love to run and run unendingly. You have to run so much that it will make people tired just watching you.

Why? Because the only thing that ever scares a football player is getting tired. When you're in tip-top condition, you don't have to pace yourself. You're coming on every play. You're not ever afraid of getting tired because there is *no such thing.* You can look across the field at your opponent and say, "When we're finished playing this game today, mister, I want you to go home and tell all your friends and neighbors that I WORKED YOUR ASS. Every play. You had *no* room to relax."

When you're in great condition as a defensive end, you come off the ball on a search. I mean, I'm a Great White. I'm on a cruise looking for action. I've come off the snap and taken care of my responsibility, now it's time to giddy-up and find the ball. Because I had real good speed, I thought I could catch anybody.

Most defensive linemen will rest when the play is going away from them. They'll come off the ball, step across the line, then pretend like they're looking for something coming back their way. *There ain't nothing coming back, man!*

Me? I'm looking directly at the tackle in front of me. If he blocks down, I'm cutting right off his butt and heading for the ball carrier. I'm gonna catch that running back because I've already figured out where he and I are going to rendezvous. That's because I'm in great shape. I can run, and I'm gonna do it again on the next play, son.

I wasn't injury prone, but when I got hurt I healed quickly. Being in great shape *keeps* you from getting hurt. When you're in great shape, YOU JUST DON'T GET HURT! Jerry Rice didn't get hurt. Walter Payton didn't get hurt. I mean, somebody's got to go out of their way to hurt a player like Payton. Which, by the way, I actually did one Sunday.

What happened?

CH: We played the '76 home opener against the Bears and they beat us, 19-12. They won by a touchdown but it wasn't that close. They kicked our butt. Payton had 150 yards by the end of the third quarter.

It was the first play of the fourth quarter. I was trailing the play when I saw this solitary foot sticking out of the bottom of the pile, so I stepped on it. *Kiiiiiiinda hard… butnotsohard,* if you know what I mean. I didn't want to maim Payton, but I did want him to be done for the day. He got up and limped off the field, calling me every kind of black name he could think of. I said, "Walter, take your act to the sideline. You'll play again next week. You've got all you need for today."

Former Pittsburgh Steelers assistant George Perles shared a philosophy similar to yours. He said, "All the height, strength and speed in the world can be neutralized if the guy across from you gets a jump on the ball." That is also true for offensive linemen. Name some of the offensive linemen that gave you the most trouble?

CH: The Rams' Charlie Cowan is the first name that comes to mind. He was old and disciplined by the time I started going up against him, but that guy held me sackless more times than I care to think about. Another one is Doug Dieken, who played with Cleveland. But with Dieken it was more of the system he played in. The Cleveland quarterbacks didn't hold onto the ball very long in those days, a lot of shallow drops. I only played against Dieken two or three times, but somehow he knew my best moves and was able to take them away. Same thing with Billy Shields, who played in that old San Diego system.

Who was the dirtiest offensive lineman in your book?

CH: You know, man, I just played the game. There were times when I'd come to the sideline and Paul Wiggin would ask me, "What did you do?" I'd say, "Shit, I don't know. I just went and got the quarterback." He'd go back and look at the film and see that I might have grabbed the lineman's nuts, or I might have stuck my finger up his nose. Any number of things.

A couple of guys may have tried to intimidate me. My attitude in those situations was, "Well, we're gonna take time out on this next play and straighten this out. I'm gonna let you know that I got some of that stuff, too. If you're gonna act the fool, I'll act the fool with you."

When you ran up against those situations where things got a little messy, YOU JUST TOOK CARE OF IT. You had to. You had no choice. If I didn't, then we got no conversation today. There would be no conversation with Cedric Hardman if he didn't handle people who tried to intimidate him.

Here's a story about what you call "dirty" players. The barometer I used to measure myself against was Joe Greene of the Steelers. Joe might be one of the most vicious humans I know. We both made the Pro Bowl after the 1975 season and were down in New Orleans. He had a badly pinched nerve in his right arm and was in bad shape. I said, "Joe, what are you playing for? Why are you even here?"

He said, "Well, I don't get to play against that Conrad Dobler and I've heard so much about him. I came down to grade him."

Towards the end of the game, the NFC scored a touchdown to go ahead. I was on the sideline, looking down toward the endzone. All I could see was this big right leg pumping up and down and a crowd starting to gather. I said to myself, "I'll bet that's Joe." Sure as heck, he was down there stomping on Dobler.

Joe took it to another extreme, obviously. But it's an example of how things were handled in the league. When you ran up against those situations when things got a little dirty, YOU... JUST... TOOK... CARE... OF...IT.

Which opposing quarterbacks would typically come unglued after a few good knockdowns?

CH: That's any quarterback you hit on a regular basis during a game. The offensive line's theme in practice all week long is, "We gotta stop this guy, we gotta keep him off the quarterback." Well, the way to handle that was to either get a sack or hit their quarterback on the very first pass play. If you stomp on him right away, his focus comes back to reality. And the offensive line says, "This is what we thought was going to happen. If this continues, our passing game is in deep doo-doo!"

How about from the opposite side? Which quarterback took everything you could deliver and still kept his cool and control on the field?

CH: Dan Fouts comes to mind first. We loved to hit that son-of-a-bitch because he hated to be hit. I mean, if you hit Fouts and sacked him, he'd squirm and act all perturbed. I never understood that because all it did was make you want to come back and hit him again, then lay on him a little bit longer. Then after the play you'd push off on his helmet, helping yourself to get up. But Fouts was tough and he was arrogant. He never quit. He'd keep on firing the ball, taking just about everything we could throw at him.

Back in the day Roman Gabriel had an attitude like that, too. Roman was the biggest quarterback around in my early years. He was tough. There was no shaking up Roman Gabriel.

Which quarterback was the biggest whiner in the league?

CH: Joe Theismann was. Oh Lord, you wanted to hit him. You really wanted to try and knock him out if you could.

Remember back when you were in school, there was the little girl who thought she knew everything, who was always so prissy and always trying to be the show? And you just wanted to slap the living shit out of her? Joe Theismann was like that on the field. I like him as an announcer, but as a player he was at the top of my list of people I wanted to hit very hard.

Do you remember an afternoon when, after giving a horrific beating to a quarterback, you actually felt sorry for the guy?

CH: God almighty, man, it was Archie Manning. Anytime we played the Saints. In all the years I played against Archie, he never really had a tackle that could block me one-on-one. I remember he told some reporters after one game, "I need to see somebody about this because *I really do believe Cedric Hardman is trying to kill me*." I watch his son Peyton play now. Archie was actually a better quarterback than his son because he had great speed. He just didn't have the blocking or the weapons at receiver that his kid has.

One last question about quarterbacks: There are less than two minutes remaining in the game, your team is up by five points and the opponent has the football with 80 yards to go. Which quarterback do you not want lined up across from you in that situation?

CH: I'd say Joe Namath first, Fouts second, then Roger Staubach. Staubach got us a couple times in big games, and I can't go through this list without mentioning him. But I was more afraid of Namath than anybody. I played against him three times before I finally sacked him. It seemed he had the whole city and state of New York blocking for him when I rushed him. They wouldn't let me get within yelling distance of that guy.

Sacking the Seventies

The Individual Sack Leaders of the 1970s (decade/ career total)

5) Jack Gregory, Cleveland/New York Giants (91/ 103): Nothing fancy here, just muscle and brute upper-body strength storming off the right end. "Jack was tall (6'6") but he had an odd build, those short legs which made him really hard to knock down," said former teammate Jim Kanicki. "All that leverage bulling upfield..."

A dispute with Browns coach Nick Skorich fueled Gregory's trade to the Giants in 1972, where he promptly collected 21 sacks on a run-soft team that surrendered 4.6 yards/rush. "I'll never forget a series he had against Dallas," Kanicki says. "We needed to get the ball back and Jack pressured Roger Staubach into three consecutive bad throws, all by himself. He was like Hercules."

4) Cedric Hardman, San Francisco/Oakland (98/ 121): "Hardman had race car-like acceleration coming out of his stance," says Turney. "He turned in a lot of multi-sack games during the '70s. And he ranks at number four despite missing almost the entire 1979 season. Hardman was built physically perfect for the defensive end position."

Former Cardinals quarterback Jim Hart also remembers those blind-side charges. "You had to not only worry about the sack, but a lot of times Hardman would also hatchet down on your throwing arm, trying to knock the ball loose.

"But I got him on a play in St. Louis once. He came roaring in and tried to chop my arm, but I ducked underneath and flipped a touchdown pass to J.V. Cain."

3) Alan Page, Minnesota/Chicago (101½/ 148½): He gathered his sacks from the right defensive tackle position, which makes him a whole different breed of cat – an interior lineman with monster strength and a big upfield burst. Page benefited from having Carl Eller and Jim Marshall as ends, which flushed a lot of action his way.

"From reviewing films and looking at his sack totals, Page has to be the greatest inside pass rusher of all time," says Turney. "I can't think of anyone better. Maybe John Randle. For his career, Page had 148½, which is unreal for that position."

2) Jack Youngblood, Los Angeles (103½/ 151½): Youngblood likes to tell the story about his lockerroom argument with Rams' orthopedist Clarence Shields during a '79 playoff game in Dallas.

"Clarence told me my leg was broken, but I insisted on going back in, that he should just tape me up. He kept refusing, saying, 'I can't do that, Jack.'

"Finally I exploded. 'This is *my* leg! It's *my* career! I'm willing to put it on the line! Why do you keep saying you can't do that?'

"He looked me in the eye and said, 'Jack, I don't know how to tape.'"

Despite his big sack numbers and Hall of Fame honors, Turney feels Youngblood was actually short-changed by the Rams' defensive schemes. "He played in a Ray Malavasi-coached defense, which meant they used a lot of odd-man fronts on running downs. That didn't always put him in the best position to rush the passer if the offense decided to throw on short yardage. He was still amazingly productive and consistent."

1) Coy Bacon, Los Angeles/San Diego/Cincinnati/Washington (104½/ 130): Not a household name but a terror to those he faced. "Coy was the best rusher I ever saw," said Dave Lapham, Bacon's teammate on the Bengals. "A lot of guys will just stand up and shake and juke at the line, but Coy always gained ground, never wasted any steps."

"What impressed me most about Bacon," says Turney, "was that he played three of his prime years on some terrible San Diego teams (1973-75), surrounded with little help and constant double-teaming. He had the reputation of being somewhat of a bad egg so he bounced around the league quite a bit. But Bacon got to the quarterback, no matter which color uniform he was wearing."

● ● ●

The Best Sacking Teams of the 1970s

	Sacks	Winning %	Notes
1) Los Angeles Rams	444	.694	Feasted on the papier-mâché' offensive lines in the NFC West
2) Dallas Cowboys	432	.729	The mayhem of "Too Tall" Jones & Harvey Martin at defensive end
3) Pittsburgh Steelers	393	.691	The Steel Curtain averaged nearly four sacks per game in 1974
4) Washington Redskins	385	.635	So did George Allen's over-the-hill Redskins of 1973
5) San Francisco 49ers	381	.424	A leaky secondary prevented even bigger things for San Francisco

The Worst Sacking Teams of the 1970s

	Sacks	Winning%	Notes
1) New York Jets	245	.368	Only 16 sacks in 1976, one more than the decade's fewest ('72 Pats)
2) Buffalo Bills	267	.361	1972's top pick DE Walt Patulski was supposed to correct this
3) Philadelphia Eagles	289	.403	Dick Vermeil began to right things in 1977 (47 sacks that season)
4) St. Louis Cardinals	291	.493	Don Coryell's theory was to outscore teams then pray
5) New Orleans Saints	299	.306	Can you name one great Saints pass rusher from the 1970s?

Source: John Turney

Talk about your experience playing for Dick Nolan, your first head coach in San Francisco.

CH: I loved Dick Nolan. If there was no Dick Nolan, there would be no Cedric Hardman. If there is one person responsible for this conversation taking place, it's him. After San Francisco drafted me he told his coaches, "I don't want anybody messing with Hardman! His stance is the most unorthodox I have ever seen. He might not know what the run is, but last year the 49ers had 33 sacks in 14 games. In college, Hardman himself had 38 in 10 games. Leave him alone. I'm gonna turn this guy into a football player, but I'm not going to kill his spirit of rushing the quarterback in the process."

Dick knew what I could do and he didn't try to kill that. He tried to cultivate it. He gave me the freedom to make decisions on how I should line up. If I tried something different but ended up making a mistake, he would pull me aside and say, "Okay, here's what happened. Next time watch for this and react accordingly. Now, I am gonna have to get on you in the meetings about this, so be ready for it."

Later, we'd be watching the film and that mistake would come up on the screen. He'd yell, "Hardman, you can't do that…blah, blah, blah!" I knew it was coming ahead of time, but he did that to reinforce to our defense that we had to stay disciplined.

I see a lot of guys in college or the pros that are great pass rushers. Then they go to another team and the coaches try to fit them into the wrong scheme. Next thing you know, they say the player doesn't have it anymore. But in reality, they've killed his spirit.

I'll never forget this player named Bill Hawkins, a guy from the University of Miami who went to the Rams in the late '80s. Hawkins was a 4-3 defensive end in college but the Rams tried to turn him into a 3-4 guy. They wanted to line him head-up on the tackle but he wasn't that heavy in the butt. His real strength was being on the outside shoulder where he could maneuver and manipulate. The Rams' coaches took that away from him. I remember feeling so sorry for Hawkins and yelling at the television, "This boy can rush the quarterback! They don't know what they're doing!" Then he got hurt and his career went downhill. It's such a shame.

One of the criticisms of your style of play was a lack of discipline against the run. Why was that such a difficult problem for you to correct?

CH: Early on, teams exploited my inability to acknowledge that they would run on third down. I'd line up so wide that I gave them a natural hole to run in. Then on third-and-long they would run that trap and get the first down. That really breaks a defense's back. Nolan would pull me aside and say, "Cedric, I've been telling you over and over – they do the same thing to you! On third-and-long they come out in the Red Formation [split backs], then they put the tight end over there to discourage you. Then you widen out some more and they run the trap *right at you!*"

This went on for three years. Every time, without fail, I'd get caught up in getting to the quarterback on third down, then they'd run it right past me.

Then one day I saw it coming. We were playing Denver. It was a passing situation on third down, and into the red formation they go. Then here comes the tight end. But when they snapped the ball, I blew down inside so fast that I literally broke Paul Howard's back. He was the pulling guard, and I met him behind the center. He didn't even have time to straighten up. After the play I made a mad dash for the sideline, running over to see Dick. I yelled, "Did you see that? Did you see that?" He just looked at me and said, "It's about time," and walked away.

The 49ers were one of the NFL's stronger teams during the early part of your career. The 1970, '71 and '72 seasons all ended with losses to Dallas in the NFC playoffs, yet all three were close, winnable games. During which of those years did San Francisco actually have a better team than the Cowboys?

CH: The 70 and '71 teams. I felt we should have won both of those. And we had a nice lead on Dallas in the '72 game, but I screwed that one up. The ref said I hit Staubach late and that penalty kept the drive alive. We gave up a two-touchdown lead and came apart. That was the beginning of the end for Dick with the 49ers. You know, I really can't say we were better than Dallas. We were even teams. But with their coach, Tom Landry, the Cowboys had the edge.

How so?

CH: Because he outcoached Dick in those games. I'm not saying that in a demeaning fashion. Dick was the defensive backfield coach on Landry's staff for a number of years, so that's where the 49ers got the "Flex" defense from. When Dick came to the 49ers, he began to mold the team in the image of the Cowboys. Nolan was an introvert in those years and Tom was his closest friend. He talked to Landry all of the time except for when we were getting ready to play the Cowboys. During that week Dick didn't have anybody to talk to.

You said the '72 playoff loss was the beginning of the end for Nolan in San Francisco. From 1973-75, the 49ers went 16-26 and were basically non-competitive. What caused the collapse?

CH: Things began to go downhill for a number of reasons. When Dick got fired after the '75 season, I felt really bad. I felt like it was my fault, like I hadn't done enough to help him keep his job. And key people simply got old. Star players like [QB] John Brodie, [LB] Dave Wilcox and [DT] Charlie Krueger all retired.

We also had some high draft picks that didn't pan out. In Nolan's first year, 1969, his top two draft choices were Gene Washington and Ted Kwalick. In 1970, his first two choices were me and Bruce Taylor. All four of us were in the Pro Bowl in '71. That's what first-round draft choices are *supposed* to do.

But then came Terry Beasley, a fast, hard-working guy from Auburn. He didn't really help us. Mike Holmes and Tim Anderson were two other top picks that went bust. For three straight years our first-rounders didn't pan out.

Another thing that helps destroy a ball club is that when you win, other teams start tearing down the fiber of your team. Today they go out and get your free agents. Back in those days they took your coaches, and our coaching staff slowly began to come apart. We lost Paul Wiggin to Kansas City. Ed Hughes, the offensive coordinator, left the team. We lost our offensive line coach Ernie Zwahlen in 1971 to Houston. He was real vital. Nolan was never an offensive guy, so losing those coaches made things all the worse for us.

The common denominator of all great teams, no matter what the sport, is chemistry. A glaring example of that occurred when [Ravens head coach] Brian Billick had the nerve to think his system was so great that he didn't need to invite his own quarterback, Trent Dilfer, back the year after winning the Super Bowl. I don't know what is wrong with these damn people, messing with Dilfer. The boy had won the last 15 or 18 games he started, and Billick wouldn't even invite him back the next season! They talked about what Dilfer couldn't do, but they didn't talk about what he *could* do, and that was *win*, dammit! That's the bottom line! We're talking about chemistry. *Don't mess with chemistry!*

An Observer's View of a 49ers Feeding Frenzy

In the lexicon of pro football, "sack" is the ultimate four-letter word, the consummate catastrophe. A fumble can be recovered, an interception can be 60 yards long and no worse than a good punt. But a "sack" is a net debit, costing the team anywhere from two points to 30 yards. It's unredeemable.

It is an ugly word like its counterparts in other sports – like "shank" in golf, "balk" in baseball. A "sack," i.e., the unceremonious dumping of the quarterback in the act of throwing is demoralizing to a whole team. To the offensive line, it signifies the breakdown of law and order. A criminal element is loose in its society and running amok. You see, an offensive lineman regards the body and person of his quarterback as sacred. For a defensive end to defile it is like taking a hammer to the Pieta.

The quarterback, for his part, once sacked, begins looking for tall intruders instead of swift receivers. He begins to behave like a guy in a haunted house. His neck is on a swivel. His fingers sweat on the ball. His teeth begin to hurt. He begins to worry about his "drop," his "release," his plant foot, his Blue Cross, and finally, his job. It's like being the lead beater in a lion hunt.

One "sack" a game is an embarrassment. Ten is Waterloo, Dunkirk, Little Big Horn. The Sack of Rome. The Visigoths at the gates. Anarchy.

> Prior to Monday night's game in the Coliseum [against San Francisco], the Los Angeles Rams' quarterback had been sacked only twice this season in four games. Ram quarterbacks, ordinarily, get more protection than the Hope diamond. In 1972, they bit the dust only 16 times all year. Last year, the total was only 30… [Tommy] Hart and Co. gained 97 yards for the 49ers through sacks. This was more than the entire Ram running attack got all night and more than any receiver gained all night. (October 13, 1976)
>
> - Jim Murray, Copyright, 1976, *Los Angeles Times*. Reprinted with permission.

I'd like to hear your thoughts on the other defensive linemen who played alongside you during the "Gold Rush" days of the 1970s – Jimmy Webb and Tommy Hart and Cleveland Elam. Historically, it was an underrated unit; yet San Francisco featured one of the best pass-rushing quartets of the decade.

CH: Precisely. Shit, we set the record in '76 with 61 sacks. When the ball was snapped, all four of us were headed north. We were all motorizing.

But when mentioning the Gold Rush, you cannot say any of our names without calling Coach Floyd Peters' name. Floyd was *the man*. He actually made it a joy to come to practice. He would get more excited than any of us. When my intensity and his were matched, most other people didn't find room to participate. When he and I were on the same track, we were a real force. And when we weren't it was just a damn mess [laughing]. Floyd always said I was the catalyst of the group, but he and I would sure go at it. All the guys used to get scared because they thought we were going to come to blows.

Peters was definitely a hands-on coach. When the other groups were in meetings, Floyd would have us in the weight room. And, oh God, we ran. We did these gassers every day after practice. You had to run back and forth across the field, and once you finished you had to stand on the line. No walking around trying to catch your breath. That was part of the discipline. He was a stickler for these things. And the first thing he paid attention to was where everybody was positioned after the play was over. He wasn't so concerned with who made the tackle as much as who was *not* headed toward the football.

What was unique about 1976 was that out of those 61 sacks, our starting front four had 57 of them. Tommy had 18, Cleveland and I had 16 apiece, and Jimmy Webb had 7. Two linebackers, Dave Washington and Willie Harper, split the other four. Today, if a defense were to get 61 sacks, it very well might be divided amongst 15 to 20 people…a guy that got cut early in the year might have had one…a backup defensive end might get one at the end of a blowout. They'd be scattered all over the place. But whoever got the sack never rejoiced. The other three boys rejoiced for you.

Jimmy Webb rated fourth in that group in terms of pass-rushing skills, but it was designed it that way. Jimmy's skill was tying up traffic. We needed him because he always had to occupy the center and the guard. That created one-on-one situations for the rest of us that Floyd wanted. Inevitably one of us was going to break loose.

Things began to look up for the team when Monte Clark took over as head coach in 1976. The Niners went 8-6, putting together their first winning season in four years.

CH: Monte Clark had been the offensive line coach for the Miami Dolphins under Don Shula. He came to San Fran and got things going in the right direction. But the only day of the week we got along was Sunday. We used to get into shouting matches. I didn't care. I was mean. But, boy, was he a great coach.

At one point during the '76 season we were 6-1, but then I broke my ankle and [WR] "Fast Willie" McGee broke his femur and some other bad things happened. We finished 8-6. But, man, we thought we would win the Super Bowl the next year. We were all excited for '77. We knew that if Monte didn't kill us, we would win it. He and Floyd worked us so hard. I thought Monte was the best offensive line coach in football, and I've always been fond of saying that if you don't have an offensive line coach, you can cancel Christmas – it's not coming.

Monte Clark and I had a relationship that dated back to the very first time I showed up in San Francisco. I flew out there to negotiate my rookie contract. Joe Greene and I lived back in the same apartment complex back in Denton. He kept me up all night playing cards and got me real wasted, so I had this terrible hangover.

When I arrived the next day in San Francisco, I was *straight outta Texas*. I mean, I had on some cream-colored boots with some cream-colored polyester pants with a cream-colored shirt that had ballooned sleeves and a cream-colored headband and sunglasses. I was out there, man. They sent this guy Roy Gilbert out to pick me up at the airport. He had a '65 Galaxy. I thought, "Boy, they don't care much about me if they sent this piece of shit car to get me."

So Roy takes me to their complex, and the first person I ever meet from the 49ers is their line coach Paul Wiggin. I had a great reverence for the man. He had played the game. I knew the name, a defensive end with the Cleveland Browns. So in a real smooth, laid-back tone I said, "*Yeahhh, that's cool. Real cool. Nice to meet ya. Let's go to work.*"

Out of the corner of my eye, I saw this guy standing behind me. I didn't pay much attention, since I was dealing with this hangover. But my adrenaline was flowing. I was a little bit excited so I said, "*Yeah, you know what I do, and we're gonna do this together.*"

Then Wiggin says, "Cedric, I got somebody I want you to meet. This is my best friend, Monte Clark. This is the guy you're gonna go against when we play Cleveland." I sobered *all* the way up. I stood straight up and took my glasses off. I looked him up and down. Monte was knock-kneed and in his fifteenth year of pro ball, and I said, "Boy, with a set of knees like that, you'll never block me!" Then I put my glasses back on. He was so pissed! Paul thought Monte and I were gonna fight right there. I said, "No, no, no…we'll settle it later on."

Did you really believe that the 49ers were becoming a Super Bowl caliber team under Clark?

CH: Oh, definitely. He was putting a show together on the 49ers. We had Delvin Williams and Wilbur Jackson in the backfield. I thought Williams was the best running back in football. He had what I call "Can't Catch Me" speed, which all the great ones have. O.J., Tony Dorsett, Delvin Williams, Mercury Morris – they all had it. It wasn't a long list of running backs who could play every down and withstand the punishment and still, if they got out in front, there wasn't anybody on your team or in your city or state that was gonna catch 'em. Delvin was in that class.

We had Gene Washington and Fast Willie McGee at wide receiver. We had Plunkett, and he fit in real well with us. For some reason, everybody seemed to think that Plunkett's career really kick-started with Oakland but, man, when he came to San Francisco he had that offense rolling. He knew how to command a ground attack. Monte had that same Shula philosophy, that you don't throw the football any more than 12 to 22 times a game. If you do that, you're gonna win. And Monte was putting together an offensive line. We were young and excited and fired up, man.

Then the DeBartolos bought the team in 1977 and Joe Thomas became part of the deal. He was the new general manager. Well, Monte declared right away, "If Joe Thomas comes, I go." He knew Thomas from his days in Miami. Joe had distinguished himself as a general manager when he went to Baltimore in '73 and ran all the veterans out of town – Bubba Smith, Johnny Unitas, everybody. Everybody in the league hated this guy. So when I heard Thomas was coming to San Francisco, it was the most crushing day of my career. I just did not believe – I was so naïve – that there was anything that came above winning. Well, my innocence was laid open that day. Monte Clark left the team. And Joe Thomas destroyed it when he came onboard.

Why do you feel Thomas was so disruptive?

CH: There are people, even today, who are involved in the game but actually resent the fact that they couldn't play. They want to prove to the world that they could have played but this, that, or whatever happened somehow they should still belong. Joe Thomas was one of those. He would make a statement like, "On draft day I don't want nobody in that room but me. I don't need those coaches or nobody." It was like he had something to prove to the world. He was on the verge of having a nervous breakdown because of all the stress that he put on himself.

I remember one Monday night some fan had a sign that berated him in front of the entire stadium. It said, "Joe Must Go." He was ranting and raving and sent security guards over to the guy. But I will say this: Joe Thomas liked me. For some reason he just liked me. That was the reason he kept me around after he started cleaning house. But Joe ruined that team.

But is it really necessary to have been a professional player to coach the pro game or manage an NFL franchise?

CH: Well, maybe I'm exaggerating here. But, you know, the game is so sacred. For a man who never played on the NFL level, it's extremely difficult for him to relate, particularly to the players. Now, there are a lot of them that *can*. Hank Stram was one that could. Hank was obnoxious and all that other stuff but nevertheless those boys loved him. George Allen was another. He loved the game so much and put so much of himself into it. Men like that can relate mostly because of their love and respect for the people who play it.

Bill Walsh did it out of resentment that he couldn't play. He didn't have the love that Stram or Allen had, so his players didn't love him that way. He had that arrogance about him. I'll never forget when he first came to the 49ers in 1979. We were 2-14 that year, and we went about seven or eight games into the season before we finally won one. Then came Atlanta on the schedule, and it was a team that Walsh thought we could beat. So he said to us, "If we win this game, the first two guys who carry me off the field on their shoulders get fifty dollars." Then he paused a second and said, "Aww, I was just joking."

But he wasn't. We won the game, and then Ruben Vaughan and Al Cowlings whipped about four people to get to Walsh. Hell, they were just after the fifty bucks, man. Walsh and I didn't really see eye-to-eye on a lot of things, so I'm walking off the field thinking, "Look at this bullshit." Everybody in San Francisco was all excited, and it looked like all the players really loved him. In reality, a lot of folks would've liked to have shot the son of a bitch.

Joe Thomas Shakes Up San Francisco

Ed [DeBartolo] Jr. has changed a lot since he became the president of the 49ers. He came into the situation naïve and starry-eyed, believed everything that [Joe] Thomas told him, but he has lost that naiveté since. He was not at all prepared for the buffeting he would get from the media and fans, but he's accepted it.

He admits he knew nothing about an NFL operation before he got involved, but he has studied other clubs since. He now realizes that Joe Thomas's way is not the only way.

The fact is, Thomas embarrassed the DeBartolos.

He sold them on the fact that it would take a rebuilding job with the 49ers, but I doubt they realized that it would more resemble a demolition. In two years under Thomas, the 49ers have gone from 8-6 to 5-9 to 2-14, the worst in their history.

Thomas hired two head coaches who were mistakes, Ken Meyer and Pete McCulley, before settling on Fred O'Connor, who seems to be a good choice, based on what he has done in the final seven games this season.

Thomas has gotten rid of players who have been of value to the team – one example was linebacker Dave Washington, who played for Detroit against the 49ers Sunday – without getting much in return, in his frenzy to overturn the team.

Worse, he has alienated the fans in the area. He is totally oblivious of public relations, and he has no sense of humor about himself, as became painfully obvious when he ordered the "Joe Thomas is to blame" banner removed during a home game. He believes that winning is the only important thing, but he isn't winning. (December 19, 1978)

- Glenn Dickey, Copyright, 1978, *San Francisco Chronicle*. Reprinted with permission.

Walsh took over as head coach in 1979 after Joe Thomas' departure. What was it about Walsh that you did not like or respect?

CH: Oh, I knew he was an offensive mind that was unparalleled. You couldn't help but admire his cockiness and his approach to the game. Like Dick Nolan knew he could stop anybody, Walsh knew he could score on anybody. He just had that. If he could get our defense turned around, the 49ers were shortly going to become a force to be reckoned with. I could see it coming.

Actually, I had more of a conflict with one of his assistant coaches than anything else. I was going to kill [defensive coordinator] Chuck Studley. After playing under Nolan, Wiggin and Peters, my game was set. I knew how to play defensive end in the National Football League very well. I knew how to rush the passer. With Walsh, I was on my sixth head coach with the 49ers. It's funny how new coaches come in and say, "I want you to forget everything you ever knew about playing defensive end. *This* is how you're going to do it now."

Well, after playing on a whole string of losing teams, I finally had the attitude that, "*The next son of a bitch that walks through this door and tells me to forget everything I ever learned about playing defensive end, I'm gonna lose it.*" And that was precisely the first thing out of Studley's mouth. He had been a second-string offensive guard at the University of Illinois. So when he came in and said that, my attitude went south. I didn't want to hear it, all the new vernacular and lingo.

It's one of the things I love about coaching kids today. Instead of yelling at a kid who can't get a technique down, I roll up my sleeves because there obviously is something that *I am…not…telling… him.* It's not his fault. I know he wants to get it.

I got this attitude from Dick Nolan. There would be times when I couldn't get something right. Instead of him yelling at me and really putting my ass on edge, he'd roll up his sleeve and put his arm around me and say, "Let's start from the beginning." When you've got a willing participant, you can teach him. You can make him see it because you know he wants it.

But with a coach that hasn't played the game, a lot of times his response is, "You've got to suck it up!" Okay, I've sucked it up.

"Well, you gotta want it more." Okay, I want it more.

"Okay, give me the next guy…!"

Coaches like that don't know the answer because they haven't done it. He can't teach you a forearm shiver because to teach it, he's had to have thrown it at least five thousand times and he hasn't. That was Joe Thomas. And that was Chuck Studley.

Which teammate in San Francisco do you feel had the most talent but whose career never progressed the way it should have? For whatever reason – lack of desire, drugs, injuries, etc.

CH: Mike Holmes comes to mind, a defensive back from Texas Southern. Man…man….man. Remember when Deion Sanders was in his prime and the ball was in the air, how he looked like the receiver on the play even though he was on defense? Mike Holmes was the same way. He had great speed and great fire, but not enough chest to back up the fire. He was a real high-strung fella and a great athlete but it didn't happen for him. Muscle pulls are what kept him back, hamstrings. I can remember some times in practice when Gene Washington would run patterns on him. Brodie would put that ball out there and Gene would have Mike beat. All of a sudden Mike would float right by Gene, just like he was the receiver. They tried everything to help his muscle pulls but nothing worked.

Last question – What was the one piece of advice that you never forgot to take onto the field with you?

CH: Get *all* of the ball, then get *off* the ball. By "get all of the ball" I mean, get as close to the line as you can before the refs tell you to get back. Then get off on the snap count. That knowledge, along with my natural abilities, made me the player I was.

You know, there are some retired players who look back and are bitter about the game. They feel they didn't get paid enough or play enough or they carry injuries through the rest of their life. When I look back on my career, they can't take away nothing I got from the game. *Nothing*. I loved every second of it. I wouldn't trade the experience for nothing in the world. But I wouldn't go back. I repeat, *I wouldn't go back for nothing in the world*. Please remember, the two greatest moments of my career were the day I got drafted and the day I quit.

— 14 —
Chuck Fairbanks, Head Coach
New England Patriots (1973-78)
January 22, 2002

I heard one of my favorite pep talk stories back in the '80s when I was a columnist for *The Pitt News*. Scot Ross was the paper's managing editor for a few semesters, a big, bulky guy with messy hair who reminded you of John Candy. Funny…good at impressions…loved the cigarettes.

I'd sometimes see Ross in a bar and he'd go into his routine, lighting up a Marlboro and yanking up the sleeves on his blue windbreaker. He'd take a big drag on his smoke then get into character, imitating an actual speech made by his grade school football coach back in Erie, PA.

"We've got a big game today, men, maybe the biggest game of your lives," he'd say. "Years from now, who knows what kind of life you'll have or where you'll end up." He'd get this serious, squinting look on this face.

"But I'll tell you *one thing* – they can take away your sight or your health; they can take away your arms and legs; they can take your house or your money or your kids. But one thing they can never, ever take away from you…IS THE ST. STANISLAUS PEEWEE FOOTBALL CHAMPIONSHIP! *NOW LET'S GET OUT THERE AND GET IT DONE!*"

I told that story to Chuck Fairbanks, the former New England Patriots and Oklahoma head coach, and asked him if he ever reached for the old "arms and legs" speech to fire up the troops.

"No, I never did. But it sounds like the guy was coaching a bunch of blind, broke, homeless amputees. Did he win the game?"

I don't remember if the Stanislausers won or not, and I'm not sure how funny Chuck Fairbanks thought that story was. But the Patriots team that Fairbanks inherited in the winter of 1973 might have given those amputees a run for their money because, by that time, pro football had long turned sour in New England.

An original AFL franchise, the Patriots put together a string of chin-high efforts in the early 1960s, including Mike Holovak's '63 team that somehow stumbled into the AFL Title game with a wobbly 7-6-1 record. The core consisted of rough, hardened veterans like QB Babe Parilli, end Gino Cappelletti, DE Bob Dee and Jim "Earthquake" Hunt, a 5-11 hard-charger with a mean inside pass rush from his defensive tackle position. The Pats suffered only two losing records in their first seven years of football. You could spot the holes in those lineups, yet Bostonians generally had reason to come out for the show.

But by 1967 the Patriots had crumbled into a 3-10-1 ragtag operation. Shaky management, lopsided trades (All-AFL linebacker Nick Buoniconti to Miami for who?), barren drafts, chronic bad bounces – symptoms you typically see when franchises nosedive then stay submerged.

The quarterbacks of '68 – Mike Taliaferro, Tom Sherman and King Corcoran – completed only 39% of their throws.

The offense of 1970 scored only 11 points per game.

The '72 defense gave up an average of 32 per game and the coach quit before the 3-11 season ended. Second-year quarterback Jim Plunkett – the Heisman Trophy still fresh on his resume – closed out the season with a dismal passer rating of 40.4. Bad news flooded the fall sports pages in New England.

A major reclamation was due, so team ownership turned its eyes toward the colleges for relief. By the time Fairbanks signed on from Oklahoma in 1973, the New England Patriots had won just 22 of their last 84 games.

Actually, Fairbanks wasn't the Patriots' first choice. Owner Billy Sullivan's search consisted of sifting through an entire list of New Year's Day bowl matchups looking to fill the job. Penn State's Joe Paterno, whose team had just dropped the Sugar Bowl to Oklahoma, was first to say no.

Next came the '73 Rose Bowl winner, USC's John McKay. *Move from Southern California to frigid Massachusetts?* No thanks....

Okay, onto the Orange Bowl, where Nebraska has just walloped Notre Dame 40-6. "Whaddaya say, Bob Devaney? No? Then let's check the other sideline.... Ara Parseghian, wanna coach the Patriots?"

No takers from the Orange Bowl.

Darrell Royal had just coached Texas to a shocking upset of top-ranked Alabama in the Cotton Bowl. He turned it down, too.

Finally back to the Sugar Bowl and Chuck Fairbanks, who quickly accepted the well-worn offer. The press asked him if he was offended by being so far down on the Patriots' wish list.

"What difference does that make?" he said. "I'm the choice right now, aren't I?"

Indeed he was. A moody, introverted disciplinarian, Fairbanks saw little hope on his newly inherited roster. "I may have had more talent at Oklahoma," he half-joked. "Listen to the names I had there – Lee Roy and Dewey Selmon, Ray Hamilton, Bob Kelso, Steve Zabol, Ken Mendenhall, Joe Washington, Dexter Bussey, Mike Thomas, Tinker Owens, Steve Owens, Greg Pruitt..." and on and on and on.

Thus began an upheaval of legendary proportions. Patriot lockers were cleared by the dozens. Faces changed by the day. In one week alone New England put in 27 waiver claims, and by the end of the 1973 season a total of 168 different names had appeared on the Patriots' roster. The original Big Dig. Betsy Ross helped stitch names on the jerseys. It took a few years, but Fairbanks would eventually put life back into the team.

I've highlighted two of Fairbanks' six seasons in New England and filed them away in an overflowing folder marked *What If?*

The first was 1974, a study in football extremes. By late October the surprising Patriots – a toothless 5-9 squad only a season earlier – were leering down on the rest of the AFC East. They were 6-1, with victories that included an opening day stunner over defending-champion Miami and wins over NFC powers Los Angeles and Minnesota. They averaged 28 points a game. Plunkett was re-armed with weapons like Darryl Stingley and Reggie Rucker at WR, Sam Cunningham at fullback and Bobby Windsor at tight end. Mighty mite Mack Herron, a 5'5" CFL export tailback, was darting for 4.1 yards/carry. The defense, meanwhile, had switched to a 3-4 base and would allow the fewest rushing yards in the American Conference.

Things changed quickly, however. By early December the season had gone down in flaming wreckage, ruined by injuries to key offensive stars and riddled by a barrage of turnovers. Plunkett had been disarmed, his weapons carted off and replaced with lesser names like Randy Vataha and Ed Hinton, John Tarver and Bob Adams. To paraphrase Bum Phillips, Plunkett found himself caught in a swordfight using a pocketknife.

"Had that 1974 team stayed even remotely healthy on offense," said the late *Boston Globe* columnist Will McDonough, "it might have been the surprise story of the decade, considering where it had been. Hell, they nearly beat [eventual Super Bowl champion] Pittsburgh with a bunch of backups."

And the turnovers? Through the first six weeks of the season the Pats had committed only nine, minor annoyances. But then, beginning in the Minnesota game, the interceptions and fumbles struck from nowhere like lightning bolts on a wedding day and never stopped.

Here's a quickie chart that reflects the number of short fields that Fairbanks' defenders were trying to hold over the second part of the '74 season:

	Turnovers	Yds allowed/gm	Points allowed/gm	Record
Weeks 1-6	9	284.8	15.2	5-1
Weeks 7-14	28	298.3	24.8	2-6

Fairbanks' 1976 team, however, was the real heartbreaker, a force from nowhere (3-11 in '75) that quickly became Super Bowl material but suffered some shady breaks in a playoff loss at Oakland.

"My favorite group," he calls that team. "A lot of young hustlers and veterans who were tired of losing."

Those Patriots slugged their way into the postseason on a macho rushing attack (5.0 yards/carry) and a defense that churned up 50 turnovers, both league bests. When things got stuffy in the pocket their exciting new quarterback, Steve Grogan, had legs that motored along at 6.6 yards a clip. He scored 12 rushing touchdowns, still the NFL record for QBs.

"Grogan changed the whole look of that offense," said former Colts head coach Ted Marchibroda. "The team seemed to rally around him. Plunkett was a good runner, too, but it was mostly out of necessity. Grogan's legs added another weapon to what that offense already had."

By early October New England had whipped Miami, Pittsburgh and Oakland and the league took serious notice. NBC's Curt Gowdy openly called them the best team in football. He also called their playoff game against the Raiders and witnessed the officiating debauchery that kept the Patriots out of the '76 AFC Championship game.

"It was awful, some of those calls," Gowdy said. "It was like somebody had it in for New England. I know there were some league people who were really embarrassed by the officiating in that game."

Yep, I felt the same way. One of the all-time hose jobs. Then two years later it was all over for Fairbanks in New England. Unhappy with escalating meddling from within the Sullivan regime, he wanted out of professional football. After a messy court battle he was back in the college game, coaching at Colorado, and by 1981 the Patriots were back to the pangs of 2-14.

Such is life when you find yourself filed among the *What Ifs?*

Fairbanks and I talked in January of 2002, shortly after his old club had beaten the Oakland Raiders in another controversial playoff game – the infamous Tuck Rule incident.

• • •

The New England Patriots...the Oakland Raiders...the playoffs...a dose of old-fashioned officiating controversy – that combination must bring back some stinging memories for you after seeing the events that unfolded this past weekend in Foxboro.

CF: Absolutely. Obviously, I was partial to the Patriots. I'm glad they won it. But did I look at it as a revenge game for what happened to my team against Oakland in the 1976 playoffs? Not really. That game was over 25 years ago.

I think the controversial ruling on [Patriots quarterback] Tom Brady's fumble was made properly and within the rules. I was very pleased to see him have such an outstanding second half after not doing very much in the first half, to lead the team back and perform well under pressure.

I was also impressed with Adam Vinatieri's performance, how he was able to make those kicks under very difficult kicking conditions. Not only difficult for him, but difficult for the center, the holder and the protection. All those things come into play in a critical situation where ball handling is tricky and the footing is bad for everyone. Those were big time performances by the whole team. And I thought New England's defense played well. They have good personnel on that side of the ball. I think they have a little better defense than people give them credit for.

Vinatieri's game-tying field goal – a 50-yard blast in a heavy snowstorm with seconds remaining – certainly is one of the all-time great kicks in NFL history.

CF: Well, years from now nobody is going to remember what that kick looked like. All they're gonna know is whether it counted or not. But for Vinatieri to knock it through the goalpost under those circumstances was a real accomplishment.

Let's revisit that playoff game with the Raiders, way back in December of 1976. Your 11-3 New England team won the AFC wildcard that year, while powerhouses Baltimore, Oakland and Pittsburgh took the divisions titles. Which of those three potential opponents gave your team the most favorable matchup in the playoffs?

CF: Absolutely, it was Oakland. I thought we were better than the Raiders. We wiped them out earlier in the year and we thought we could beat them again. Pittsburgh was a helluva team and had become dangerous again after a slow start. The Colts could beat us on any given day. But the Raiders? That was a team I knew we could beat.

You are referring to the 48-17 hammering of Oakland earlier that season in Foxboro. That game was unquestionably your most impressive win as coach of the Patriots, as your team erupted for 296 rushing yards and scored the most points on any Raider team since 1963. What cracks did you detect in the Oakland defense that led to the mayhem that afternoon?

CF: Their defensive line – especially a defensive end by the name of Charles Philyaw – wasn't good enough to compete against our offensive line and our tight end, Russ Francis. Francis was a great blocker. People tend to remember him for some of the great catches he made during his career but, believe me, that guy could really block. In Oakland's season opener that year, Pittsburgh had almost 200 yards rushing against them, so we knew with our guys – [G] John Hannah, [C] Bill Lenkaitis, [T] Leon Gray and Francis – we could put some real pressure on the Raiders' defensive line. We came at them with two tight ends, and we specifically attacked Philyaw because we felt he wasn't up for the challenge. It proved out because the guy didn't last very long in the NFL.

We wore Oakland out by running the football. That set up everything else for us. We knew we could get some positive plays out of Steve Grogan's scrambling ability, and he had over 50 yards rushing and scored two touchdowns. We also had a tough guy by the name of Jess Phillips, a reserve running back who had played for the Raiders the year before. Jess was a real leader for us in that game and helped arouse our whole football team. We also learned a few things about the Raiders personnel from him, which helped our gameplan.

When the '76 playoff schedule was set, the Steelers were at Baltimore and your team was headed to Oakland for a rematch with the Raiders. It was the war that everybody expected, but this time Oakland pulled it out, 24-21. John Madden's team was better prepared in the rematch.

CF: They were better prepared, but we played well in that game too. Both teams had a lot of penalties. We trailed by three points at halftime but we dominated the third quarter and had a 21-10 lead. But then in the fourth quarter some things happened – some out of our control, some within our control – that let the game get away from us. I don't feel there was any type of conspiracy or coalition against us, but there were some bad performances by officials made in crucial situations. Some very controversial officiating.

One in particular was a third-down situation late in the game where their linebacker, Phil Villapiano, blatantly held Francis. Grogan was rolling out to his right, looking for Francis, who was running a short drag pattern toward the sidelines. Our right guard, Sam Adams got caught between Grogan and Francis, so Grogan had to throw the ball slightly behind. Before Francis could adjust and make the catch, Villapiano grabbed his left arm and pulled him to the ground. Incomplete pass but no flag.

In terms of officiating assignments, there was one man responsible for the tight end area. For him not being able to see or make the call – considering how obvious Villapiano's hold was – was just not acceptable. We then had to try a 50-yard field goal, which was at the far end of our kicker's range, and it was just short.

You obviously feel, even today, that the game was stolen from you.

CF: I don't want to come out and say that, but the officials sure didn't help us. Then again, our players made some mistakes that didn't help us either. One that really hurt us came right before Villapiano's hold. We were deep in Raiders' territory and needed about six inches for a first down. Grogan had played wonderfully for us all season, but it was only his second year in the league and basically he was still a rookie. Because of his lack of experience, we sent in a play to run Sam Cunningham behind Hannah and Gray – two of the best offensive linemen in the game at that time – using Jess Phillips as the lead blocker.

Grogan, unbeknownst to me, changed the starting count in an attempt to draw Oakland offside, which was not a good decision. So instead of drawing Oakland offside, he caused Phillips to jump. Jess still had the presence of mind to continue in motion to his left, which allowed us to run the play, but the result was that we were one blocker short going into their line. We didn't get the first down.

The Raiders took over at their 32, and their last drive – which used up the final 4:12 of the game – was the slow, taunting kind of death you were hoping to avoid. Then, more questionable officiating.

CF: Well, Stabler started throwing to Casper and Biletnikoff and moving it up the field, but we finally got them into a third-and-18 situation. We knew they had to throw it relatively deep, and we were in the right defense for that type of play. Stabler's pass was incomplete and it should have been fourth down, but they threw a flag on Ray Hamilton for roughing the passer. It was a ridiculous call, absurd. That penalty kept their drive alive and the Raiders went in to score.

Hamilton didn't rough Stabler on that play. Kenny Stabler was a great player, and he had the presence of mind in that situation to fake that hit pretty well. He was trying to do everything he could to win. I don't really blame him for what he did, but the call never should have been made. It still bothers the hell out of me.

Ben Dreith, the official who called the roughing penalty on Hamilton, really did a poor job. My feelings were upheld by the league because he was banned from officiating New England Patriots games for many years after that. The league knew he made the wrong call. If that penalty flag hadn't been thrown, we would've sat on the ball and the game would have been over. Then we would have gone into Pittsburgh and faced a crippled Steelers team – they had lost their top running backs against Baltimore – and probably would've won that game. Then in the Super Bowl it would have been Minnesota. We would have beaten them because we were too good for the Vikings. So there's no doubt in my mind we would've won the Super Bowl in '76 had we gotten past Oakland.

What did the Raiders defense do that hampered your offense in the rematch? You scored 48 against them in the regular season, but only 21 in the playoffs.

CF: The only thing that stood out to me was the increase in aggressiveness from their defensive backs. They were much more aggressive and physical than in our first meeting. They really tried to rough up our receivers. [S] George Atkinson put an aggressive hit on Francis that broke his nose early in the game, which really hampered him.

To be fair, Oakland was having defensive problems the first time we played them, particularly on their line. They weren't getting pressure on the quarterback and therefore their secondary was taking fewer chances. They weren't as hawkish. But by the playoffs those line problems were fixed, so the secondary went back to its attacking style. That was the biggest difference.

A lot of people felt you were coaching the best team in football in 1976.

CF: I think we were one of the best, but you gotta finish. You start the season and you finish it. You don't get many chances in pro football, and that was one game we weren't able to put away.

The 1976 Playoffs – a Nightmare in Stripes

A weary supervisor of officials, Art McNally, answered the phone yesterday. I told him there were eight or 10 or 12 things on my mind after I watched the Oakland-New England game on TV Saturday.

"OK, go ahead, shoot!" he said, sounding very much as if he expected a bullet.

"Villapiano on Russ Francis' arm, on that crucial fourth-quarter pass. No flag by the field judge, Ed Merrifield. How come?"

"You know the answer to that. It's a judgment call, and I can only explain rule interpretations – for the record," McNally said.

"How about off the record?"

"This is also for the record. Every call in a game like this is reviewed. When the case warrants it, the official may be called into our office to explain certain situations, OK?"

Comment – OK, OK, already, we know he blew it, he knows he blew it, McNally knows he blew it, even though he can't say it. But I saw a guy blow a worse one two plays before that, and no one mentioned it on TV, and no one wrote about it. And guess what, it wasn't an official, it was a player – Sam Cunningham, Patriots' fullback.

Second-and-eight on the Raiders' 35. Patriots up, 21-17, four and a half minutes left. Cunningham sweeps left. He has the first down if he puts his head down and drives for it. Instead he pussy foots out of bounds, inside the first-down pole. He looks at the pole and comes up short.

Number one, you don't go out of bounds and stop the clock when you're trying to sit on a lead, and number two, you try to get your first down. Maybe you win the game if you keep the drive alive. Sam Bam was a mouse on that one. I call that a worse play than the one Merrifield blew.

Back to Mr. McNally. How about the roughness play – Ray Hamilton on Stabler? NBC didn't have a replay camera on it, but a highlight film showed Hamilton putting a rush on Stabler, and he was pretty close to him as Stabler released the ball.

"The rule is pretty clear," McNally says. "If you strike the QB with a fist or forearm, it's a penalty. The fact that Hamilton might have deflected the pass had nothing to do with it. I couldn't tell whether he tipped the ball or not, but when you club a guy in the head the referee has to call it."

Comment – I see quarterbacks clubbed in the head all game long. A flag drops maybe once or twice. Consistency is the answer, but if you consistently drop the flag on the defensive linemen, then it's not a game anymore, it's a parade. Still, it was a helluva time for the call. (December 21, 1976)

- Paul Zimmerman, Copyright, 1976, *New York Post* Holdings, Inc.
Reprinted with permission.

Let's go back to the start of your career in the NFL. You were the head coach at Oklahoma in the winter of 1973 when the Patriots approached you about their position. You were not their first choice.

CF: Not being their first choice didn't bother me at all. I really wasn't looking to leave Oklahoma. Becoming a professional coach was really not an early objective of mine. Oklahoma was a wonderful place to be for a young college coach. There is wonderful support from the fans and University, great players. We had more great players on those early '70s teams than the law allows. I had a couple of young coaches on my staff, Jimmy Johnson and Barry Switzer, who turned out pretty well. I had the best line coach anyone could ever have in Buck Nystrom.

The Patriots job just fell into my lap. Frank Leahy, the old Notre Dame coach, had watched my Oklahoma teams and was impressed enough to recommend me to his friend Billy Sullivan, who owned the team. Bill came to me wanting to discuss the New England job.

The key was that it presented a personal challenge for me. I wanted to see if I could be successful at the next level. It wasn't a case of money because I was making more at Oklahoma than what the Patriots had offered. But I wanted the opportunity to compete against the best coaches in the world, with some of the best athletes in the world. In the NFL, you're at the very epitome of the technical side of coaching. So when I left Oklahoma I had no regrets. It was a career objective I wanted to fill.

The team you inherited in New England was a 3-11 train wreck. The 1972 Pats had surrendered 32 points/game while their offense scored only 23 touchdowns all season. Head coach John Mazur said the hell with it and quit with five games to play; a 52-0 loss to Miami had cemented that decision. It was some undertaking, trying to rebuild this franchise.

CF: That's true. We needed better players, that was the bottom line. Talent-wise, the club wasn't far above an expansion team. I didn't have a chance to schedule mini-camps or workouts because back then the draft was much earlier in the year than it is today. The draft was held immediately after I got there, so I had to rely heavily on the scouting information that was prepared by Bucko Kilroy. Bucko was in charge of the scouting department and he had a very good staff already working for him when I got there. Then I brought in people like Hank Bullough, Red Miller, and Charlie Sumner who'd been in the league and understood what was going on.

I was fortunate enough to have a couple of number-one picks in '73, then I traded running back Carl Garrett to the Chicago Bears for another one. Garrett was a good player but a problem guy for the Patriots, not the best attitude. So we ended up with three number one choices, including the first overall pick. We took John Hannah from Alabama with the first pick to shore-up the weakest point of the team, the offensive line. Our quarterback Jim Plunkett had been knocked down fifty-some times in 1972 and we needed to get him some protection. He was getting sacked time after time and was knocked down unmercifully many other times. He had no time to play his game. It was easy to see that the foundation up front wasn't good enough.

Then we took fullback Sam Cunningham out of USC, who was a premier college back, and Darryl Stingley, who was a wonderful pass receiver. Those were the first three guys we picked in starting to rebuild the team. All three of those players – Hannah, Cunningham and Stingley – were able to contribute as rookies and were critical to building the franchise.

We had so many holes to fill. We'd plug a hole in the dike and another would spring somewhere else. So we kept on finding more players. We signed [T] Leon Gray off waivers from Miami. The Dolphins had drafted him, but they were so deep on their offensive line that they had no room for him. Leon was recommended to me by a guy who played for me when I coached high school. He was an Eastern Airlines pilot named Bruce Kostamo. Bruce called me and said, "There's a real good prospect on the Dolphins, but he's not gonna make the team because of all the veterans they have. You *have* to sign him." Well, we did and Leon became another great player for us.

Once I had a conversation with Vince Dooley, the head coach at the University of Georgia. He said, "I got the best running quarterback I've ever had, and I want to learn how to run options. Can you help me?" I said, "Sure, send your coaches out here." So they came out to Oklahoma and learned a lot about what we were doing. Later that year I watched a player named Andy Johnson break all the Southeast Conference rushing records for a quarterback. He was a great athlete and a smart guy. We drafted him in '74 and made him into a running back. Johnson became the best third-down back in pro football during his prime. He was a great receiver, a great blocker and not a bad runner. He understood football perfection from A to Z.

You quickly developed a great deal of confidence in Bucko Kilroy and his scouting department.

CF: We had a great relationship. Bucko reported to directly to me. He provided information and counseling about players. He taught me a lot about pro grading systems and how to grade players properly, how to put everybody on the same page in determining the value of a player. Bucko had a world of experience and I leaned on him.

When it came time to make a decision about a player, I gave everybody an opportunity to express their opinions but the final call had to be mine. I wanted *my* type of players to be there. I didn't want our scouts looking for the prototypical NFL player. They needed to understand what we wanted our players to do for the New England Patriots, so every scout went through training camp with our coaching staff. They'd spend two weeks with our line coaches, two weeks with our offensive backfield coaches and so on. They'd go to every practice and every meeting. When they were on the road, we wanted our scouts to be able to determine which players could do the things we'd be asking them to do. At scouting combines you hear things like, *"This is what a defensive end is supposed to look like."* That's not what I wanted. I wanted a defensive end that could play the schemes we were teaching.

Give me one former Oklahoma player you wished had joined you in New England.

CF: Without question, it would be a running back by the name of Steve Owens. That name may surprise you because he didn't have a real successful pro career. Steve hurt his knee early on with the Detroit Lions so he was never the same player he was in college, but he'd been a great player for me at Oklahoma. So durable...played his heart out for you every game. You could give him 40 or 50 carries in a game, then he'd be like a spring colt the next day in practice.

Another player that comes to mind is Lee Roy Selmon. I left Oklahoma before his sophomore year, but I can say without hesitation that Lee Roy gave the best performance by a college defensive lineman ever. He had all the physical tools, but what separated him from everyone else was that he never took any plays off. Never. Play after play, game after game, Lee Roy Selmon was coming at you 100-percent. Most college linemen play in spurts, whether it's within a single game or over an entire season. Not Lee Roy. I have never seen anything like him, and I'd have taken him in New England in half a heartbeat.

Your first year in New England produced only five wins. Despite the losing record, were there any satisfying moments from that 1973 season?

CF: To be honest, I wasn't very happy until we started winning a lot more games. In pro football, one game is not the mark of a team unless it's a championship game. The margin between the bottom and top of the league is not very great in any given week. Every year you see dramatic upsets where a team with a poor record beats a contending team. That happens in pro football because there's not a lot of difference in the overall talent among teams. There *is* a major difference, however, in the overall quality of people on a team, as well as the depth needed to perform at a high level for the duration of a season.

The toughest parts of a season are two-fold. The first is keeping a mental edge, an even keel, not to get too emotionally high or low. The second part is to play relatively injury-free. That was the biggest hurdle I faced in my first few seasons with the Patriots. There isn't a lot of depth on a pro roster, so when you lose a key player there's no place to get another one just like him. You can't go and open a can of running backs or tackles. When they're gone, they're gone. You get your team together at the end of the preseason by making cuts, which is the equivalent of getting rid of your depth. Then you begin to play the season and, unfortunately, there are injuries. Some teams lose more players than others, but that's the luck of the draw.

Let's talk about Jim Plunkett, the former Stanford All-American who was your first quarterback with the Patriots. How would you describe his psyche when you first met him? He was coming off a miserable '72 season in which he threw 25 interceptions, had the NFL's worst passer rating, and suffered a horrific beating from defenses.

CF: The biggest thing I noticed was that Jim was very nervous in the pocket, very jittery. The sense of self-preservation had him moving around, not getting properly set to deliver the ball. His pass protection just wasn't there. It had nothing to do with Jim's competitive nature. Being jumpy was just a natural reaction to being constantly knocked down. Every time he dropped back it was like a jailbreak. People would be coming from all angles. A team has to be able to protect the passer. If it can't do that the quarterback has no chance. By the end of Jim's time in New England he was being knocked down quite a bit less. That's because we went out and got him some good protection.

Describe your relationship with Plunkett during your three seasons together. There were rumors of a constant friction existing between the two of you.

CF: Jim Plunkett is a friend of mine to this day, but he's not the kind of person who readily accepts people.

He's not the kind of person that would be real "buddy-buddy" close to his coach. And as a coach, I wasn't necessarily going to be chummy with players. There is a distance factor that is healthy to have between the coach and his players. It's necessary to maintain authority.

I had great respect for Jim Plunkett, and I think he learned to have great respect for me and my staff. I don't know how to describe it better than that. We never had an adversarial position. We never had a conflict. There was never any situation, to my knowledge, where we weren't on the same page. We had a solid, respectful coach-player relationship.

In 1974, the Patriots finished the season a surprising 7-7. I see four keynote games from that schedule – a 34-24 shocker over defending champion Miami on opening day; upsets of both Minnesota and Los Angeles, teams that would eventually meet in the NFC championship that season; and a gutsy, hold-the-Alamo loss to Pittsburgh, the eventual Super Bowl champ. You competed with the NFL's best that season.

CF: We started out very strong, considering that rough schedule. No question, our biggest improvement was on rushing defense. In '73 we gave up the most rushing yards in the entire league, but the next year we gave up the fewest in the AFC. Teams were used to running right through the Patriots, and suddenly that wasn't happening anymore. We held Miami under 100 yards both times we played them that year.

What hurt us in 1974 was injuries. We lost both of our starting wide receivers, Darryl Stingley and Reggie Rucker. We lost our tight end, Bobby Windsor. Sam Cunningham was hurt. By December, we were out of weapons on offense. We went into that Steelers game with basically Jim Plunkett, [RB] Mack Herron and [WR] Randy Vataha on offense and still were only a couple of plays away from winning that game. It was frustrating to know that, had we been a healthy team, we could have challenged for the playoffs.

Chuck Fairbanks Leads a Patriot Uprising

From the wonderful land that gave you statesmanship, rusted anchors, America, intellectuals, banking, town houses, landscape painting, Ted Williams, Bill Russell and Bobby Orr, there now comes football. A new kind of madness is sweeping New England. Four weeks deep into the season some guys known as Patriots instead of your basic Celtics or Bruins or Red Sox or Political Activists or Scrods just happen to be undefeated and untied and unafraid, and if this sort of thing continues much longer there is the possibility that someone sitting around Harvard Square discussing Sanskrit poetry as it applies to the works of Joan Didion may even look up from the water pipe and ask who Chuck Fairbanks and Jim Plunkett are.

It all started way back there on Sept. 15 when the Patriots, those funny people who used to play football wherever they could find an empty parking lot, whipped up on the Miami Dolphins. It continued when the Patriots, those hilarious comedians who once played a home game in Birmingham, Ala., defeated the New York Giants. It kept up when the Patriots, those laugh-a-minute clowns who used to view their game films on bed sheets, startled the Los Angeles Rams. And last Sunday, the excitement held at a peak when the Patriots, those howling vaudevillians who once almost had to elect John Quincy Adams their most valuable player, went out and utterly destroyed the Baltimore Colts by 42-3.

Heretofore, the Patriots had been doing what they were not supposed to do. They had been scoring upsets. This time, as heavy favorites, they were confronted with having to look good against a group of mystery folks, the Colts, who were in the midst of a strange emotional trauma. And all the Patriots did was come roaring into their stadium out there in an obscure forest halfway between Boston and Providence and look as though they could pile up about a million points if they needed to.

...What the Patriots did, of course, with all this new confidence and collegiate kind of spirit that has been given to them by Head Coach Chuck Fairbanks, was once again unleash the throwing arm and savvy of Quarterback Jim Plunkett; the unnerving speed and psssst of

Running Back Micro-Mini-Marvy-Mack Herron; the good hands and stimulating antics of Reggie Rucker, the pass catcher; and the swarming gnat-like defense of a bunch of unknown gypsies culled from waiver lists, the 14th round of drafts and the exotic world of free agents. The Patriots were so certain of what they could do against Baltimore that they hopped up and down, clapping their hands, before the pregame introductions. Then, one by one, led by Rucker, they aroused the crowd by trotting out with their fists raised in the air. College kids, right?

- **Dan Jenkins, *Sports Illustrated*, October 14, 1974.**
Reprinted with permission.

Why the sudden turnaround defensively?

CF: Very simple. It was because of my decision to switch to the 3-4 as our full-time base defense. We had very little success playing a 4-3 in 1973. We couldn't stop anybody and we couldn't rush the passer, considering what little talent we had. But the 3-4 created a whole different set of problems for our opponents. They didn't know how to block it.

At that time, everyone in professional football thought of the 3-4 as a prevent defense to be used in passing situations. Well, we had a shortage of quality, prototypical defensive linemen. They just weren't around. 85- to 90-percent of all college teams at that time were using a three-man line. There were far more linebackers available than top quality defensive linemen, so I built a defense that required less of them. I felt it was the only way we were going to have a chance to stop teams.

The 3-4 allows you to use shorter defensive linemen at noseguard because the position requires strength and leverage more than anything else. We had drafted Ray Hamilton in 1973 and he proved to be the perfect nose guard for that defense. He had unbelievable quickness, arm strength and intelligence – dimensions you need to run the 3-4. It also calls for strong defensive ends rather than speed defensive ends, since they line up directly in front of the offensive tackles. Well, we had strong defensive ends in Mel Lunsford and Julius Adams.

Another factor that contributed to our success was that in the 3-4, our linebackers lined up in the same position every single play, from the first day of training camp through the last day of the season. This is crucial because the biggest component of playing defense is simply play recognition. When you start moving linebackers around all the time, they're not as likely to recognize offensive plays from the different angles and positions. Having them line up in the same position, snap after snap, helps to develop play recognition and allowed us to use young, inexperienced linebackers successfully.

Running back Mack Herron was one of the great stories of 1974. A 5'5" free agent out of Kansas State, he led the Patriots in rushing with 824 yards and set an NFL-record with 2,444 combined yards of rushing, receiving and returns. But by the end of the '75 season he was released. What are your memories of the meteoric rise and fall of Mack "The Knife" Herron?

CF: Mack was a great all-around back. He could run and had great acceleration. Everybody looked at him as being small but, in reality, he wasn't as small as he was short. He had very powerful, compact legs and a powerful body, but he was short in stature. He had wonderful hands and would catch anything thrown at him. He had a wonderful feel for the passing game and was also a great kick returner.

I had watched Mack play at Kansas State, where he was very productive. After college, Mack went to the Canadian league and was very successful there before getting into trouble with drugs. Basically, I gave him a second chance. We were totally aware that he had a drug problem, but we thought we could counsel him and maybe he'd put that behind him. He had a marvelous start with us, breaking Gale Sayers' record for all-purpose yardage. I remember telling him, "Mack, you've got yourself out of the ghetto now. All you have to do is behave and take care of yourself and your family." But he didn't do that. He got into drugs again.

One of my former college classmates, who was working for a government drug enforcement agency, called and told me they were watching him, that they were going to do a bust in Boston. Mack was there when they raided. The next day I called him into my office and told him, "Mack, you're done. I'm putting you on waivers today, and I don't think anybody is going to touch you because they know that good players aren't put on waivers unless there's a very legitimate reason. They're going to know there's a problem."

I never told anybody that Mack had a drug problem, but nobody touched him after that. He ended up in a federal penitentiary, which is a shame because he had worked his way out of a bad area in Chicago. He got to the top of the world but he couldn't stay with it. It's one of the biggest disappointments I've had in my career – seeing somebody try to elevate himself but not having the ability to stay away from drugs. I'm not passing judgment on anybody. I'm just disappointed.

The 1975 draft brought you two players that had a major impact on the fortunes of the Patriots – Steve Grogan and Russ Francis. First, Grogan. What did you see in the young player from Kansas State that made you believe he could develop into a solid NFL quarterback?

CF: When I was at Oklahoma, I was lucky enough to witness a talent at Kansas State named Steve Grogan. He had played very little during his senior year because of a neck injury, but prior to that Grogan had been evaluated as the top quarterback prospect in college football by our scouts. I was very impressed by him. I told our guys, "If Grogan is there in the fifth round, we're gonna take him because he's a real athlete. He's smart and a tough competitor."

The fifth round came and he was still available so we drafted him. Some people thought we had picked Grogan to be an eventual replacement to Jim Plunkett, but that really wasn't the case. We did need to improve the depth at that position because we had none. The plan was to give Steve plenty of time to learn the pro game and, more importantly, to get completely healthy. We didn't think he'd be pressed into action so much in his rookie year.

What about Russ Francis, a player many considered to be the most gifted tight end of the 1970s?

CF: He was another player who missed his senior year in college. Russ Francis was the greatest pick I ever made, the guy I was most excited about taking in the draft. I had coached against him when he was playing at Oregon. I saw this kid and said, "Wow! What a helluva young player this guy is!" Dick Enright, the assistant who had recruited him for Oregon, had been named the head coach during his sophomore year. He only coached two years, then they fired him after the '73 season. Russ didn't think the school gave Enright a fair chance, so he decided not to play his senior year.

I sent Red Miller to Oregon to check Francis out. Red looked at the film of him as an underclassman, then called me, very excited, and said, "This guy is really something!" So I said, "Well, *go find out where the hell he is now.*" Turned out Russ was living on a ranch somewhere up in Idaho or Wyoming or some damn place. Red went up to the house and there was Russ, standing barefoot in the kitchen in a pair of Levis. Red asked him to come outside and run a 40-yard dash for him. So they went out in the snow and Russ lined up on this old gravel driveway and ran a 4.6 forty! Red brought the film back for us and we decided to draft this guy.

We had a telephone hookup from our drafting room in Foxboro to New York. When we called in and announced "Russ Francis" as our first-round pick, it brought the house down because nobody had ever heard of him. The big-name All-Americans like Steve Bartkowski, Walter Payton, Larry Burton and Mack Mitchell were coming off the board, then we took some guy named Russ Francis with the 16th pick and the whole place was in an uproar. They thought we were nuts.

Russ was a great athlete. He could catch the ball exceptionally well, anything within a country mile of him, and run with a lot of strength and speed. He was also an outstanding blocker. Sometimes he'd make blocks and cave in the whole side of the defensive line. There wasn't much he couldn't do.

The Legend of Mack Herron (a short story)

Dick Butkus, the one-man violent world, was raising hell as usual – only this time it was during a timeout. The Patriots were driving on the Bears for what would be the winning touchdown in the last minutes and Butkus was raging at his teammates, his opponents, at the sky and the earth, at, for all we know, the energy crisis.

"Butkus," a voice squeaked up, "you're an unmentionable indelicacy."

"Who said that? Who said that?" Butkus demanded, fire shooting out of his nostrils. There was no response. The man who said it had straightened up in the huddle to shout the unthinkable and then had wisely ducked back into anonymity. The man was Mack Herron, who anyway, doesn't have to duck to hide on a football field. Mack Herron stands 5'5".

"I wasn't trying to start trouble," Mack Herron was explaining yesterday after the Patriots became a team the Jets could beat. "I was just trying to keep things level. I was letting Butkus know we were going to keep him honest."

Well, you see, Mack Herron does weigh a chunky 175 pounds.

You might think Dick Butkus, and all the Dick Butkuses in the NFL, would eat Mack Herron for an hors d'oeuvre, or stamp on him as though he were a fat beetle, but there's a trick to it. You have to catch him first. It would be easier to catch Kohoutek, the coming comet…

So far the only people who have caught him were college recruiters and the Royal Canadian Mounties.

Mack Herron broke the great Buddy Young's high school track records in Chicago, where in football he became known as "Scoe" – ghettoese for score. He was recruited by Hutchinson Junior College in Kansas, then by Kansas State, where he teamed up in a dynamite backfield with Lynn Dickey (Oilers), Mike Montgomery (Cowboys) and Larry Brown (Redskins). He was drafted by the Falcons, but declined their no-money-down offer and went to Winnipeg. There, after two big years, he was fined $1000 and put on two years' probation for possession of marijuana and cocaine last May.

The Patriots, so desperate that they claimed 27 players on waivers in one three-day period during the exhibition season, took a shot with him. Rookie coach Chuck Fairbanks, who had announced his intention to build a team of "good citizens" after trading Carl Garrett, took one look at the Patriots and decided that rehabilitation wasn't such a bad idea after all.

"People always look at me and ask, 'What can he do?'" Mack Herron said. "And I show them." Take that, Dick Butkus. (November 12, 1973)

- **Larry Merchant, Copyright, 1973,** *New York Post* **Holdings, Inc.,**
Reprinted with permission.

You've mentioned some of the successes that the Patriots had in the draft. Who was your most disappointing pick?

CF: I would say it was a quarterback from the University of Pittsburgh named Matt Cavanaugh, who we took in the second round of the '78 draft. He was the one for whom I had the greatest expectations but he never reached that level. Cavanaugh had a wonderful college career and looked to be so promising as a pro, but it didn't work out. I would guess that if I asked Matt today if he was happy with his performance as a professional quarterback, he probably would agree with me and say he didn't realize the dreams he had for himself.

How did Cavanaugh fall short of your expectations?

CF: Because he simply wasn't a good enough passer. Despite what we thought we saw in him, Matt never developed into the kind of passer that could be successful in the National Football League. The physical part of throwing the football was his biggest shortcoming. He was very smart, a good leader, but the accuracy and velocity of his throws weren't good enough. He was a backup for quite a few years because he was smart enough to be ready to play without taking all the snaps in practice. That's one thing you need in backup – the ability to be ready to play without physical preparation. But Matt's overall arm strength prevented him from making all the throws and getting the proper spiral on the ball. Those kinds of things you really can't teach past a certain point. That's why he never became a starting quarterback.

Let's continue with your early years in New England. After the great strides he made in 1974, Plunkett injured his shoulder in the '75 preseason and the team started into a downward spiral. By mid-October the Patriots were 0-4. What was going through your mind during that time?

CF: 1975 was probably my most disappointing year in New England. With Jim going down, we had to make a bunch of quick adjustments offensively. We hadn't planned on Steve Grogan playing at all that year. He was greener than a gourd and we hadn't prepared him as well as we would have liked. Had Jim been healthy and played the whole year, I think we could have challenged for division title in '75. He wasn't, and we finished 3-11.

A lot of other things went wrong that year. We lost the second-most fumbles in the league [22]. Mack Herron got himself into trouble and we weren't able to use him – that removed over 2,000 yards from our offense. Defensively, we needed a lot of help in the secondary. It seemed we couldn't cover anybody back there. Teams were completing almost 60-percent of their passes against us, which forced us to load up on defensive backs in the '76 draft.

Plunkett was playing again by early October of that year, but he re-injured his shoulder in a game against the 49ers. Sportswriter Larry Fox, in his book entitled The New England Patriots, criticized you for having the still-fragile Plunkett run the split-T option, a play in which the quarterback is highly exposed to the defense. Your response to that criticism.

CF: We never ran a split-T offense with Jim Plunkett! I never coached a split-T offense in my life, college or pro. I ran the wishbone option in college, so I made a trade for my college quarterback Jack Mildren, who was playing safety at Baltimore. We thought we might use some of the theories of the wishbone with Mildren in goal line and short-yardage situations, but that never materialized for us. We never put it to the test. If you were going to run a full-time option offense in the pros, you'd need a true running quarterback, not somebody like Jim Plunkett.

But the injury to Plunkett's shoulder did occur on an option play.

CF: Well, let me clarify. We had a simple two-step option play that we ran against one certain defensive alignment, the under-shifted defense. Whenever we saw that alignment, we ran an option play that allowed Plunkett or Grogan to pitch the ball. It was a very successful play for us. Defenses couldn't stop it. That was the only situation we ever used that play.

We ran it against Oakland in '74 and Plunkett must have gone for 35 or 40 yards before he pulled a hamstring. In the 49ers game, their linebacker Dave Washington hit Plunkett but what really injured him – what actually knocked the surgical screw out of his shoulder – was the contact he made with the ground afterward. The hit from Washington wasn't all that terrible, so I don't think the play calling had anything to do with the injury. It was just the way he hit the ground.

What circumstances led to Plunkett's trade to San Francisco in the spring of 1976?

CF: We still needed more better players. Despite the progress we'd made, we still weren't talented enough to consistently compete with teams like Oakland, Baltimore, Pittsburgh and Miami for the AFC championship. The most talented player we had was Jim Plunkett; therefore, he had the biggest trade value.

When I drafted Grogan in 1975, I planned on sitting him on the bench to avoid any trauma to the neck injury he had suffered at Kansas State. Unfortunately, when Plunkett re-injured his shoulder against the

49ers, Grogan had to start the next eight games. But he exceeded almost everyone's expectations. So based on Steve's performance, it was now possible to make a trade that would bring multiple talents onto our team.

So we started quietly asking around, and there were only three teams that really wanted Jim. Denver, who had John Ralston as head coach, was one. Ralston had coached Plunkett at Stanford and knew him well. The Los Angeles Rams were also interested. They weren't really happy with their quarterbacks, James Harris or Ron Jaworski. And there was San Francisco, which also needed help at quarterback.

Since Jim was from northern California, he was very popular in that area of the country. The 49ers were the most interested team so we traded Plunkett to San Francisco, despite the objections of their head coach Monte Clark. San Francisco ownership was bound and determined to acquire Plunkett. Monte thought they were giving up too much, which was three number-one picks, a couple of number-twos and a backup quarterback named Tommy Owen. Clark felt the trade was taking too much away from their team.

What if you had been in Monte Clark's position? The 49ers depth chart prior to the trade consisted of Owen, 35-year old Norm Snead and a washed-up Steve Spurrier. And now a talent like Jim Plunkett was made available.

CF: In my opinion, you only make that kind of big trade when the player you are getting is good enough to put your team into the Super Bowl. Well, San Francisco wasn't that good at the time. If I were Clark, I would've probably bitched *louder* than he did.

From 1976-78, the Patriots won 31 games with Steve Grogan at quarterback. Do you feel your team would've enjoyed the same kind of success with Plunkett at the controls during that time?

CF: They were both extraordinary players, although in different ways. Both of those guys went to the Super Bowl and played for a long time. I would have loved to have coached Plunkett with a better team around him. He didn't have the luxury of playing with a good team during his time with the Patriots. Jim had the ability to lead and perform at the highest level of pro football, and he proved that later with Oakland. Plunkett was a marvelous deep passer, better than Steve, and that's why he fit in perfectly with the Raiders. The Raiders had the outside speed, and their passing game was predicated at hitting the long pass.

Grogan, however, was a better all-around athlete who could run fast, was very quick and could jump. We utilized Grogan's running ability much more in our system. During one of those years (1978) we set the all-time rushing record for pro football (3,165 yards), to which Grogan contributed tremendously. I think he had five or six hundred yards. We won a lot of football games with Grogan, and we would've won a lot with Plunkett. However, I still feel that making the trade was the right decision. But if I could start a new franchise tomorrow, I'd take either Plunkett or Grogan in a heartbeat.

Going into 1976, the landscape had dramatically changed for your team. Grogan was an experienced starter, the offensive line was emerging, and the defense had received some much needed help in the draft. How did you feel about your team when camp broke that year?

CF: I was excited. I expected to challenge for the division. That might sound a little crazy, considering we won only three games the year before. But people around the league knew we had talent. We were solid at all positions on offense and defense, although we didn't have a lot of depth. We added rookies Mike Haynes and Tim Fox to our secondary and almost doubled our interceptions from the year before. Our defense was more aggressive and experienced. We caused the most turnovers in the league.

The big turnaround game for us in '76 was beating the Steelers in Pittsburgh. That game really gave us the confidence that we could play against the premier teams in the league. The Steelers had been in the Super Bowl twice before, and they had all of their great players on the field that day. It wasn't like we were going up against their backups. Bradshaw and Franco Harris were out there. Rocky Bleier, Swann, Stallworth, Joe Greene, L.C. Greenwood and Jack Ham – they were all there.

We went into Pittsburgh as an underdog and came away with a victory. It was sloppy, not the most artistic victory in the world, but we performed well in critical situations. That win gave us the confidence to say that we had now arrived and could be successful against the best teams.

Were the '76 Patriots your best team in New England?

CF: Well, we won 11 games that year, and a lot of people will agree we could've won the Super Bowl. My 1978 team was probably the best in terms of seasoned talent, but it wasn't as intense as the '76 team. The '76 team was the young, new kids on the block. They played with great emotion and became a crowd favorite, while the '78 team was a little deeper and more experienced. I don't know if they had as much of that young enthusiasm.

The main thrust of your Patriots offense was always the rushing attack. For example, your 1978 squad carried the football an incredible 671 times, the third most in NFL history. Yet you produced only a single 1,000-yard rusher during your six years in New England – Sam Cunningham in 1976.
Would you have preferred to have had the prototypical "feature" back in your arsenal, one in the John Riggins or Franco Harris or Chuck Foreman mold? Or were you more comfortable with a running back-by-committee, the fresh legs approach?

CF: Cunningham was the closest we came to having the feature back you're talking about, but I could never have too many running backs on my team. Don Calhoun, Andy Johnson, Horace Ivory, Mosi Tatupu – I'd take as many as I could get because their career expectancy in football is the shortest of any position. To me, using more than one running back puts more deception into your offensive attack. It gives you more options. If you're constantly using one "feature" back, everybody knows who's going to get the ball on a given running play.

You know, pro football isn't the same game it was back in the '70s. They're not asking today's backs to do the same things we did 25 years ago. Today teams basically use one-back offenses, where one player carries the ball 90-percent of the time.

There was also a different set of rules back then. Today's rules favor the passing game much more than they did in the 1970s. They're much more lenient in how linemen can pass protect and use their hands. Also, receivers have more freedom to run down the field unmolested. Teams are putting more receivers on the field and getting bigger offensive linemen that can pass protect.

The setback is that these linemen don't have the maneuverability to run block anymore. Vince Lombardi had guys like Fuzzy Thurston and Jerry Kramer who were famous for their run blocking techniques. They were out there leading sweeps and were very well known. They were all agile people who could run and maneuver and employ intricate blocking schemes, which fostered the running game. I don't know if Tom Landry ever had linemen who were over 260 pounds.

Today, that's not the first priority. The first priority for offensive linemen today is pass protection. That's just been the evolution of the game since the rules were changed. I am not saying it's a better game or a worse game, just different.

Tell me more about Sam Cunningham, your keynote runner in New England.

CF: Sam was a wonderful pro football player, an exceptionally talented guy who did the things a fullback has to do in the NFL. I coached against him in college when he was at Southern Cal and I loved they way he worked in short-yardage situations. That's why we drafted him.

But I think he was ill advised. His career never really reached the pinnacle it should have because his agent, Howard Slusher, influenced him to hold out over a contract dispute. Sam lost something during that holdout. He was never the same player again. He played as if he were protecting himself against injury, without the same reckless abandon he had when he first came into the league. He had the ability and he produced on the short term, but his overall career wasn't as productive. It's a shame.

One of the Patriots' greatest assets was the quality of the coaching staff you had assembled, which included names like Sam Rutigliano and Fritz Schurmur, Ray Perkins and Red Miller, Ron Erhardt and Raymond Berry....

CF: They were all great. I was blessed with some fantastic individuals on my staff. Hank Bullough was as good a coach as you could ever hope to have, smart and knowledgeable about the game. He knew the little things to look for in players that help teams win. Hank helped build the foundation of the Buffalo Bills teams of the 1990s. He brought in players like Jim Kelly, Will Woolford and Mark Kelso, who started to turn that franchise around.

Red Miller taught me how to organize and run a pro offense. Raymond Berry had a great grasp of the passing offense. Charlie Sumner was the best guy I ever had in the press box on defense. When game time came around, Charlie was so calm and precise, working the press box like nobody you'd ever seen.

Jim Ringo had coached against me when he was at Buffalo and I thought he'd lost his job prematurely. So I asked him to work for me as an assistant and he did a helluva job. For him to take a step backwards after being at the top, well, I don't know if I could have done that myself. I respected him greatly for it. He taught some of our young lineman, like Shelby Jordan, John Hannah and Pete Brock, who all turned out to be damn good players. Coaches like Fritz Schurmur, Ringo and Rollie Dotsch make your job easy. If I wasn't so damn old, I'd go back into coaching and bring all of those guys back with me.

After all the fireworks and ovations in '76, expectations were high going into 1977. But a highly publicized and disruptive holdout by your All-Pro linemen John Hannah and Leon Gray contributed to a stumbling 1-2 start. The momentum you hoped to carry over from '76 had evaporated. Tell me about the frustration you were feeling during their holdouts.

CF: It was very disruptive. That particular situation was the beginning of why I decided to leave pro football. Hannah and Gray had the same agent representing them and they both chose to hold out. About a week before the start of the season I spent a long session with their agent Howard Slusher. He was a damn good agent and a damn good businessman, a tough negotiator. We negotiated until the wee hours of the morning at my home on a Wednesday night and finally agreed to a contract for both Hannah and Gray. I invited them to my home to celebrate that the deal was done.

Not long afterward, Bill Sullivan's son Chuck convinced his father to renege on the agreement that I'd made with the players. He thought they were getting too much. When that happened I said, "I can't work this way. I cannot have credibility with my team if we're going to do business like this." Then the whole thing went to arbitration and the team ended up being upset for the whole year. It damaged the entire chemistry we'd built. The job was hard enough to then have that kind of interference and meddling. What's ironic is that when arbitration was finally settled, both players ended up with more money than had originally been agreed upon! The Sullivans would've been better off accepting the original offer.

You felt your authority had been undermined in this situation?

CF: Yes, I did. When I first joined the Patriots, it was a publicly held team and there were five board members who I reported to, including Bill Sullivan. Up until he gained control of the team, Bill was basically very good to me. But shortly thereafter his family members wanted prominent roles in managing the Patriots, particularly his son Chuck, who was not a football person. That began the dilution of the authority that had been granted to me by contract. It was my primary reason for leaving the Patriots. I just couldn't mentally cope with that kind of interference. I knew it wasn't in the best interest of the team. That's why I eventually left. I had made up my mind that I wasn't going to stay in New England under those circumstances.

To be honest, I didn't even know if I was going to stay in football, period. I owned a business in Dallas, but I wasn't really ready to commit to that full time either. What I did know was that my experience in New England took a lot out of me. I don't know if the Patriots necessarily got the best out of me during my last few years there. I was so disappointed with what happened. I had worked very hard to make the New England Patriots a real pro football franchise, which I never thought they were before. We became one of the best teams in the league and one of the best organizations. It just wasn't allowed to work right. In '77 we recovered from that slow start and finished 9-5, but I never really felt the same again. After the season ended, I thought about it some more and decided I owed the team at least one more year, so I went back to work.

Fairbanks Gets Scolded for His Messy Departure

Quietly, perhaps facetiously, perhaps not, the password for the New England Patriots had been "Win One for The Quitter." Their coach, Chuck Fairbanks, had announced his intention to desert them in order to take command of football at the University of Colorado following the Patriots' last playoff game – a 31-14 loss to the Houston Oilers yesterday that provoked a few hundred Patriot loyalists, many in red-white-and-blue stocking caps, to gather noisily near the entrance to the Patriot locker room.

"Goodbye, Chuckie, goodbye, Chuckie!" they were chanting. "Goodbye, Chuckie, we hate to see you go!"

Not really. The fans felt betrayed. And as Chuck Fairbanks, with a state trooper in a black leather jacket ushering him along, hurried toward them, the loyalists shouted invective and hurled beer and soda-pop from paper cups at him. Moments later, the coach disappeared inside the green-and-white tented tunnel that led to the locker room...

Whenever a clubowner discharges a coach, it is accepted unequivocally. But when a coach discharges a clubowner – as Chuck Fairbanks has done, as Lou Holtz did to the Jets two years ago – some people moralize too much.

Nobody moralized when Lou Holtz left the Jets because the Jets were a disaster then. And perhaps nobody would have moralized if Chuck Fairbanks had waited until after the playoffs to talk about going to Colorado, but when the controversy flared the afternoon of the Patriots' last regular-season game, he had sabotaged his team's opportunity to win Super Bowl XIII, no matter what his players may say now, at least what they say now for public consumption.

"I don't think we were betrayed," said Russ Francis, the Patriots' tight end. "It's a business. He had a better opportunity. I think Chuck Fairbanks is of the highest moral fiber, that he's taking his family into consideration."

But surely Chuck Fairbanks did not take his players into consideration. In the Patriots' media guide, he is described as promoting "the image of oneness among his charges, strives for solidarity and believes in esprit de corps." And say this for him. Judging by the comments of his players, they appear to be united in their understanding of why he's leaving. Billy Sullivan even mentioned that "it wasn't fair" to blame this loss on the Chuck Fairbanks situation.

In the months to come, however, maybe the Patriots will realize that subconsciously it's impossible to win one for a quitter. (December 31, 1978)

- Dave Anderson, Copyright © 1978 by *The New York Times* Co.
Reprinted with permission.

1978 proved to be your last year in the NFL. The Patriots had played well again and took an 11-4 record into the last game of the season. Then on Monday, December 18, you finally confirmed the rumor to your players and announced you'd be resigning after the playoffs to take the University of Colorado job. Billy Sullivan immediately suspended you and the team lost to Miami by twenty points.

You returned for the playoff game against Houston, but the Patriots were pounded again, 31-14. In all honesty, how much of the team's late collapse do you blame on yourself?

CF: Things were chaotic with the team, I can't deny that. The players were distracted and didn't play well against Miami. I'd called Mr. Sullivan to have a meeting with him before the game and told him I was unhappy with the way things were going for me. I recognized it was his team and he could run it any way he chose, but I was unhappy and was going to resign after the season. He was upset, naturally. Our meeting was cordial but nothing was resolved. So I was suspended for the game and Hank Bullough and Ron Erhardt coached the team against the Dolphins.

The Houston playoff game was a different story. It was agreed that I would coach the team for the playoffs and I had it very well prepared. Let me make this very clear – we lost to Houston for one good reason, and that was because Steve Grogan hurt his knee the week before against Miami. He was not healthy. Houston definitely was a good team and deserved to win but had Grogan been healthy, things might've turned out differently. He didn't take one snap in practice the week before the Houston game, and he only played the first half before he took himself out. That was the biggest factor. How many teams win in the playoffs without their top quarterback? Not very many.

I felt the rest of the team was mentally ready to play. They were professionals. This was their career and they were going to play hard regardless of my decision. How far could we have gone had Grogan been healthy? I don't know. We could've played with anybody in the NFL. We would have met Pittsburgh in the AFC Championship, and that would have been fine. We could've won that game, too. It would have been interesting to see.

Your departure from the Patriots deteriorated into an ugly court battle that tainted both parties by the time it was settled. You became the coach at Colorado and the Patriots promoted Ron Erhardt, but there were still scars. I'm sure you wished things had ended differently.

CF: Absolutely. I tried to do it gently but it didn't work out. I tried to notify Mr. Sullivan that when the season was over I was going to be done. It appeared that it was going to work out fine, but then Chuck Sullivan decided to take a legal position and say, "You can't do this." That's what made it get messy, all the legalities and injunctions and such. It never should have happened that way. If I could do it over again, I would have waited until the playoffs were over and then simply resigned.

What are your regrets?

CF: I still feel badly that my NFL career ended like it did. My staff and I helped build a solid pro franchise in New England and gave the fans in New England a winner. Unfortunately, I think a lot of people still remember all the trouble at the end. It was difficult and probably avoidable.

I found out that I could be successful in pro football. That was satisfying. But I didn't stay long enough to realize the ultimate goal, which is winning the Super Bowl. I probably should have stayed in the game longer to fulfill more of my personal ambitions. My '76 and '78 teams were probably good enough to win it all, but you have to be both good and lucky to do it. If I could do it all over again, sure, there are some things I would do differently. But there are a lot of things I would have done exactly the same. I had a good time in New England. I enjoyed it.

• • • •

Roadbump to Glory: Worst Days of the Champions

Rarely do great teams, those of Super Bowl stock, get blown out during the course of their championship run. A double-digit loss here and there, well, hey, the scoreboard has been known to tilt in ways that give the illusion of a runaway.

But to be *embarrassed* in a game, dynamited clear out of the stadium? That's something different. It's a rarity, and it shouldn't happen to the league's elites, but it has.

Here, then, are recaps of the six worst beatings ever experienced by an eventual Super Bowl champion. Fairbanks' 1976 Patriots were responsible for one of them.

♦♦♦

6) 1979 – Cincinnati 34 Pittsburgh 10: During the Steel Curtain's reign of terror (1972-79), Pittsburgh's record against teams with losing records was a greedy 50-1; this game was the 1, a slippery, sloppy affair in which the Bengals just stood in line as the Steelers handed out footballs.

Cincinnati was winless, 0-6 before kickoff that day, but they grabbed seven fumbles – the most by a Pittsburgh team since 1943 – and returned two of them for touchdowns. Steelers QB Terry Bradshaw served up two interceptions, and it was 27-3 at halftime. Too deep of a hole for even Men of Steel.

After the game a writer asked Bradshaw if he'd dropped the soap in the shower. He said, "Yes, were you watching me?" Everybody laughed.

Fatigue might have been a factor here, as the Steelers were working on their fourth road game in five weeks. And there were indications during practice that week that they were taking the whole thing lightly. "Back to basics," said Steelers coach Chuck Noll afterwards, which is what he always said.

The mighty Steelers empire had revealed its first foreboding crack. Another would surface five weeks later in San Diego. **(24-point loss; Steelers won Super Bowl XIV)**

5) 1992 – Philadelphia 31 Dallas 7: I've always wondered, when does greatness recognize itself? For instance, when did Einstein know he was an Einstein? At what age did Michelangelo realize he wasn't destined to paint Fiorenzian apartments? Is there a flash of enlightenment for these types, or is it a gradual revelation?

Early in 1992, Jimmy Johnson's burgeoning Dallas Cowboys still hadn't figured it out. Johnson's first season was a 1-15 calamity. Dallas made the playoffs in '91 but they couldn't sack anyone and good passers ate them alive. Then the '92 draft brought defenders Kevin Smith, Robert Jones, and Darren Woodson and they traded for DE Charles Haley and boy, it was time to start thinking big.

But on a Monday night the corner bully bloodied Dallas' nose and set its parade back a few steps. Philly clung to a 10-7 third-quarter lead and was coming after Dallas quarterback Troy Aikman. They whacked his arm and out popped a flutterball that was picked off and the Eagles were in business. Eight plays later it was 17-7.

Then the Eagles turned loose the wrecking crew, that big defensive line of Reggie White, Clyde Simmons and Mike Golic, which roughed up Aikman and helped force four turnovers (there's that word again). Philly rolled the rest of the way.

"It's a funny thing, how we always do well against Aikman," said Golic. "Maybe it's a psychological thing, and he thinks he can't ever beat us."

An unsung hero was Eagles punter Jeff Feagles, who put the squeeze on Dallas' field position with four boots averaging more than 52 yards each. The Cowboys returned only one, for 16 meaningless yards. But not long afterwards something clicked in Dallas. A good team became a terrific one. The Cowboys would win three of the next four Super Bowls, probably the last pro football dynasty we'll ever see. **(24-point loss; Cowboys won Super Bowl 27)**

4) 1979 – San Diego 35 Pittsburgh 7: The story of the day was Bradshaw's five interceptions and how they led to 28 San Diego points, and Chargers linebacker Ray Preston claimed his guys saw it all coming.

"We noticed on film that Bradshaw was throwing the ball to spots where there'd be three of four defenders," said Preston, "and his receivers were coming up with great catches. We felt if we could pressure him, we'd come up with some of those throws."

The Chargers' idea of pressure was a steady charge from its massive front four of Fred Dean, Gary Johnson, Wilbur Young and Leroy Jones. They kept Bradshaw from getting his rhythm and sacked him four times. And Dean, an explosive right end who spent the afternoon working on Pittsburgh's proud 11-year left tackle, Jon Kolb, would trigger the turning point of the game.

Trailing 21-7 late in the third quarter, the Steelers had worked their way down to the San Diego 37-yard line. A touchdown gets them back in it with plenty of clock left. But now it was fourth-and-ten, and instead of a pooch punt or something to pin the Chargers deep, Noll kept the offense on the field, hoping to get the ball to one of his receivers and move the chains.

WHOOSH! In came Dean, flashing past Kolb with a move. Bradshaw had no choice but to let it go or take the sack. He had spotted Lynn Swann cutting across the middle and fired. Linebacker Woody Lowe caught a deflection and ran it back 77 yards for a touchdown. That was the dagger.

Both teams would finish the season at 12-4, but this victory would give the Chargers home field advantage for the AFC playoffs. They responded by losing to Houston in the first round. The Steelers then responded like they always did. **(28-point loss; Steelers won Super Bowl XIV)**

3) 2003 – Buffalo 31 New England 0: All the pregame hype centered around safety Lawyer Milloy and the revenge factor. The Patriots had released the popular All-Pro in a salary dispute, and the Bills picked him up in time for an opening day start against his old team. Everyone predicted New England would be a flat club, and they were right. Tom Curran of *The Providence Journal* covered the game in Buffalo.

"Milloy was the last player introduced and the place went bananas," said Curran. "There's a lot of ill will between these teams, dating back to the deal that brought quarterback Drew Bledsoe to Buffalo. It was very obvious that day.

"The Bills knew what was coming. Milloy tipped off his new team on all the Patriots' tendencies, and it was too late in the week for New England to rearrange its gameplan." Pats QB Tom Brady threw four interceptions and looked clueless.

Lasting memory – Sam Adams, the 335-lb defensive lineman stole one of those passes and rumbled down the right sideline for a score. It took forever. *Sports Illustrated* ran a photo of it on the cover, the dance of the hippos.

On the season's final week the teams met again, and New England handed the Bills a carbon copy payback, 31-0. **(31-point loss; Patriots won Super Bowl XXXVIII)**

2) 1976 – New England 48 Oakland 17: I still remember the NBC scoring updates flashing across the Zenith that Sunday afternoon. 7-0, Patriots…14-0…21-zip at halftime…then 35-10…42-0…like the ching-chinging of a pinball machine.

Something was wrong here. This kind of steamrolling didn't happen to the Oakland Raiders, not to Stabler and Tatum and Atkinson and that bunch of roughnecks.

But it did, and two key strategies led to the onslaught. First, New England attacked the center of the Oakland line, namely nosetackle Dave Rowe and linebackers Willie Hall and Monte Johnson. Big men being mashed by bigger men.

"We got two guards that weigh 260-270 pounds," running back Jess Phillips told *The Boston Globe*. "Their inside linebackers weigh 220-230. No way they could stand up." Patriots ground yards came in gushes, 296 for the day.

Secondly, New England centered its passing attack on its running backs. "Oakland likes to shut off the wide receivers," said Phillips, himself a former Raider. "They couldn't handle our backs catching the ball." Patriot runners grabbed seven passes for 119 yards.

"Mentally we weren't ready for them," recalls Oakland linebacker Phil Villapiano. "We'd won our first three games by a total of seven points, just enough to squeak by, then New England just unloaded on us. Their offensive line rolled through our guys like a Panzer division. Long, long drives. That game was more than a wake-up call. It was a sledgehammer to the face."

But the loss provoked a mighty Silver and Black blitzkrieg, one that didn't lose another game until the fall of '77. **(31-point loss, Raiders won Super Bowl XI)**

1) 1994 – Philadelphia 40 San Francisco 8: Ask the Raiders' Al Davis about the key to winning pro football and he'll say something like, "Take out the opponent's quarterback. Kill the head and the body will die." The Eagles slipped that message into their gameplan and turned out the shocker of the '94 season.

San Francisco had put together an all-star team, the offspring of some slick salary cap maneuvers – "One of the greatest teams ever assembled," Don Shula would later say – but it had injury problems and would face Philadelphia with three starters missing from the offensive line. The Philly coaches smelled blood and handed out pictures of quarterback Steve Young and told their players to hunt him down. They came like wolves in a pack.

The Eagles sacked Young twice and knocked him down nine more times. He was getting woozy and losing focus. Meanwhile, the scoreboard read 23-0 before San Francisco got a single first down. Rookie tailback Charlie Garner had ripped off 111 yards in 16 carries and the Niners defense stood around scratching its head because they'd never heard of him.

By the third quarter Frisco coach George Seifert had seen enough and pulled his quarterback in an act of mercy. Young barked at him on the sidelines but it was a hollow one. His afternoon was over. Seifert said bluntly afterwards, "I thought to myself, 'The hell with this. I'm not going to leave him in anymore.'" A wise decision. It's a long season.

Maybe he remembered that line from *The Outlaw Josey Wales*, when the gunfighter warned that "Dyin' ain't much of a living.'" **(32-point loss; 49ers won Super Bowl XXIX)**

— 15 —
Tom Brookshier, Broadcaster
CBS Sports (1964-83)
October 29, 2001

The mystery remains as to what prodded the wise poet Robert Frost to proclaim, "Half the world is composed of people who have something to say and can't, and the other half who have *nothing* to say and keep on saying it."

Was it, as a youth, having to struggle through a sticky July sermon at his Swedenborgian Church? ("The light and heat that angels and spirits have," say the Swedenborgs, "is different than the light and heat that men have.")

Maybe a weary train ride from Nashua to Baltimore, being held in captive audience by a non-stop mouth or perhaps a stutterer with big ideas?

Or was it something even more sinister, a foreshadowing of things to come? A futuristic vision of sports on network television, where blathering and shouting ex-athletes have overrun the sets, trampling over any form of intelligent debate that wanders in their way?

And what does any of this have to do with an interview with Tom Brookshier, the former CBS color analyst and NFL defensive back, who's retired and minding his own business out in Conshohocken, PA these days?

"To be honest," Brookshier laughs, "it sounds like a swipe at the ESPN pregame show."

Former athletes clogging up the airwaves – there are more of them out there today than ever before. It was one of the many things that drew the ire of ABC's on-air elitist Howard Cosell. The announcer despised ex-jocks in his profession. Their perceived simplicity, lack of journalistic insight and aversion to generating criticism was poison to the ears, he felt.

"Generally speaking," Howard told us, "these alleged analysts and colormen serve a limited role. They rarely prove themselves capable of bridging the gap between entertainment and journalism. The bottom line: They are not communicators."

"The Jockocracy," he called them. Cosell loved that term. Brookshier took his portion of the flogging in stride, even after Cosell had smeared him in one of his books.

"Howard had his opinions," says Brookshier, who worked the Eagles defensive secondary for seven years before finding his way onto Sunday NFL telecasts. "But it's funny. Even though I was a player, I kind of agreed with him on the athletes-in-the-booth thing. Back in the 1960s and '70s, there were a number of former players doing games who were very bright but had trouble spitting things out, getting their points across, or were just restating the obvious.

"Today there seems to be an army of them talking non-stop and telling us too much. Sometimes an incomplete pass is just that, but you'll get a three-minute dissertation. It's beyond overkill."

Brookshier unwittingly became a member of these broadcast infidels after a terrible injury suddenly shut down his playing career.

Eagles at Bears, 1961. Brookshier, a seven-year pro, was zeroing in on a Chicago sweep when two blockers put the scissors on him and snapped his right shinbone into pieces. Waiting for the ambulance he sat in the Wrigley Field mud, took a long last look around then lit up a cigarette. Extensive surgery followed.

Then before they even handed him his crutches, they handed him a microphone.

"I was still groggy from the anesthesia when this Philadelphia radio station asked me if I'd consider doing some short segments for them. I'd write five minutes of copy for one minute of airtime, then talk as fast as I could to get it all in.

"I didn't even have time to think about a career after football. It was handed right to me."

By 1964, Brookshier's witty personality earned him a job with CBS Sports as a football colorman. The network was flush with Grade A broadcasting talent during those years, so he would receive his tutoring from big voices like Jack Buck, Lindsey Nelson and Ray Scott. Viewers soon learned to appreciate Brookshier's gameday insight that came spiced with a refreshing lack of solemnity. By 1974, CBS had moved him into its top Sunday slot, working alongside Pat Summerall on Cowboys/Redskins and Vikings/Rams and the rest of the NFL weekend headliners.

"Brookie was very likeable on camera, a quick thinker," says former CBS sports director Charles H. Milton III. "He was clever. There'd be a big hit and Brookshier would say something like, 'Boy, he really put the mustard and onions on that one.' Being a former player, he was very protective of the game but he refused to sugarcoat it."

Long-time CBS producer Bob Stenner saw him the same way: "There was no false sense of football reverence with him. Brookshier became popular with fans because he was believable. He wasn't a performer, doing some routine on the air. People could sense that. They liked his sense of humor, his easy laugh."

I asked Stenner to compare Summerall's two long-time partners, Brookshier and John Madden. Both were charismatic characters, and Stenner had spent years working with both of them.

"You know, after 25 years people still love the way Madden calls a game," he said. "They haven't grown tired of him. But Madden in real life is not the same guy you see on TV. He's not constantly in this world of "Bam!" and "Boom!" and facemasks full of mud. He's a much more complex person than that.

"But the Brookshier you saw on the air each Sunday was the same person you'd meet walking down the street or in a bar. He was approachable. He didn't switch his personality on and off."

Brookshier had his critics, as they all do. Some were turned off by the hang-'em-high attitude he'd frequently inject into the broadcast. A player would get creamed coming across the middle, knocked unconscious, and Brookshier would throw something out like, "Mmm…casualties of war, gang…that Redskins secondary is no place you wanna roam." The macho routine. To some, it wore a little thin, all the blood-and-guts references.

"Hey, football is a rough sport," Brookshier says today. "There are collisions and injuries and real pain. Pat and I both knew what it was like down there, so there was no need for a rehearsal. We both just said what came to our minds. Two guys having a conversation about a football game."

"Brookshier and I got into it one time in Dallas," remembers Milton. "It was early in the season and oppressively hot inside Texas Stadium. By the second half they began carting players off the field from heat exhaustion. Brookshier kept dwelling on the conditions, saying, 'Guys are dying out there. They're dying on the field.' Finally I cut to interrupt and barked in his ear, 'Stop saying these guys are dying! It's too depressing and we're gonna start losing viewers.'

"He snapped back at me, 'Well, dammit, they *are* dying out there!'"

Summerall/Brookshier lasted a little over six seasons at CBS. They called three Super Bowls and ten playoff games together. By 1980, the winds of change had kicked up again. The execs were enamored with their new analyst, former Raiders coach John Madden, who brought a more rudimentary feel to their telecasts. He used easy, regular-guy words like *guys* and *piles* and *Whap!* and *Bam*! The Emeril Lagasse of football.

Soon his ranting Miller Lite commercials followed and Summerall/Brookshier was split up. Their last game was the 1980 NFC Championship game in Philadelphia. Madden & Summerall was the new show in town, and Brookie was back doing regional telecasts.

"I wasn't real happy about it. Pat and I had a good thing going. We had a good following. I was sad they broke us up, but I finally got to do some play-by-play work, which I'd always wanted to do."

You can add a third category to Frost's list of communicators. Brookshier and Madden both fit it.

"Someone who had something to say, and had a helluva good time saying it."

• • •

I'd like to start by reading a rather scathing commentary on professional athletes who make the transition into sports broadcasting.

"Put an ex-jock in the booth, and their cliché-ridden presentation of a game is the least of their sins. As a result of their lack of training, most of them are blessedly lost when trying to establish a story line for a telecast – i.e., detecting trends, keying on the personality and experiences of a player as they relate to his performance on the field, know his strengths and weaknesses, recalling the flow of events from earlier in the game and from games in other years. Thus, they tend to view a game as a series of plays rather than a contest, and often they are ignorant of the human perspective."

Those are the words of the late broadcaster Howard Cosell of ABC. As a former player who successfully made the transition from pro football into network television, how would you respond to that type of criticism?

TB: Howard was jealous of those of us who'd played the game, but I actually agree with his opinion in some ways. In the 1960s and '70s, there really wasn't enough commentary about what the player was thinking while he was playing. Even today, announcers get too tied up in the mechanics of what's happening on each play and avoid much of the human-interest angles. Pat Summerall and I used to get into a lot of that back in the '70s. How was the player feeling as he tried to play hurt? What is the cornerback thinking as he lines up in man-coverage again after being beaten earlier? What were the Cardinals coaches going to do differently with their pass rush in the rematch with Dallas? In many ways we tried to make it seem more humanitarian, if you can even say that about the vicious game of football.

Was Cosell being too hard on these athletes-turned-announcers? He was talking about people like you.

TB: Probably not. I think some ex-players are afraid to be critical from the booth because they still know a lot of the people down on the field. They play it safe and end up using a lot of the fluff talk. When I first starting doing play-by-play, CBS tried several different analysts with me. One of them was Roger Staubach, the old Dallas quarterback, who had recently retired. Roger only did four or five games, but it was obvious that he was really going to be good. But he was so worried about how he was being received by other players because everything he said was being printed out of context by the major newspapers. He couldn't believe the writers would do that.

During a telecast Roger would say something like, "Jim Hart has thrown a better pass," and it would show up in print looking like, "Hart can't throw that pass anymore." He was afraid that the players would take offense to some of the things he said. Halfway through the season, he called me and said, "I'm done. I'm not going to do any more games. It's just not worth it. I had a really good time working with you, and thank you so much. But I'm just going to stick with real estate." It was a shame he quit because he was really becoming good.

What was your motivation to start a career in broadcasting?

TB: Prior to my retirement as a player, I'd never really thought about going into television. What really changed the direction of pro football was the 1958 NFL Championship game. That game was the real birth of pro football on television, and it caught my attention that day. I was still playing for the Eagles and we had just finished a 2-9-1 season. I was living in Colorado during the offseason. [Laughing] It was safer out there because we had such a bad team in Philadelphia. I watched that '58 game between New York and

Baltimore on television, and I'll bet five different Eagles players called me to talk about it. We had never seen an overtime game before, and we were tremendously impressed with it. I have a feeling that a few million people tuned into that game, including many who had never watched pro football before.

Then came 1961, and I had broken my leg in a game against the Chicago Bears. That was pretty much the end for me as a player. In 1962, I had an offer to do some radio work for WCAU in Philadelphia, so I did that for a few years. In '63 I started doing Eagles television and took over hosting a pregame show that had been hosted by Johnny Lujak called *Countdown to Kickoff*. Few people remember that Johnny was the first real "jock" to get into television.

One of my most vivid memories from those early years was the November weekend after Kennedy was assassinated, when Pete Rozelle decided the NFL would play its games. Everybody was still very uptight because of what had happened. I was doing the Eagles-Redskins game at Franklin Field. The night before the game there was a tremendous fight at the Eagles hotel. [Eagles DB] Ben Scott got into it with one of his teammates, a defensive tackle named John Mellekas. He got Mellekas down on a marble floor and beat his head in. It was really a vicious fight.

Later, I headed over to Franklin Field. There was still a lot of confusion with the local station as to whether to broadcast the game or not. We all knew Kennedy liked pro football, but the league really was having second thoughts. Then on the way to Franklin Field, I was listening to the radio when they announced that Jack Ruby had shot Lee Harvey Oswald. I almost wrecked the car! It was such a surreal day.

Then in 1964 CBS requested your services.

TB: That's right. They seemed to like the work I'd been doing, so they hired me. I started out with Lindsey Nelson, then worked with Jack Buck and Ray Scott. CBS would move people around to see who got along with whom, and in the process I got to work with some fantastic people. Jack Buck was a favorite of mine. Jack was someone who would never leave you hanging. Whatever you would say, he would have a way of tying it into the game. He was a remarkable broadcaster.

Were you a fast learner?

TB: I learned as I went along. The play-by-play announcers in those days would let you do your own thing. They'd lead you at times, throw things at you like, "Tom, what do you think Theismann was doing on that play?" Most of us color analysts are generally outspoken by nature, so the reply would be something like, "*He just threw his helmet. He's mad because he had a receiver wide open and he missed him. For a quarterback, that's about the biggest sin there is.*"

We had so many talented people at CBS in those days. I remember the first isolated replay we ever did at CBS. Tony Verna was our director, who was so talented. He probably should have been involved in those early space exploration shots, but at the time he was still just learning how to direct. He said to me one day before a Dallas game, "I've got an isolated camera. Who do you want to focus on?" Jokingly, I said, "Let's watch John Niland, the Cowboys' offensive guard and see what happens when he pulls."

Sure enough, we're doing the game when Tony says in my ear, "Guess what. We're going to do the 'iso' on Niland." I'm watching the play develop, and John Niland pulls, then trips over somebody's feet and falls flat on his stomach. We started laughing in the booth, then we replayed it and laughed some more.

About a week or so later, we were back in Dallas for another Cowboys game. Niland came over to me and said, "You bastards have made me the laughing stock of the team! All the other players have been kidding me, tripping themselves and rolling around on the ground." All of a sudden we realized, "Oh my God! We have a monster here!" We were using this isolated camera and we had no idea the effect it was going to have on our broadcasts. All of those things, like the isolated camera and the endzone shot, sort of happened by accident. Being there involved in it, you didn't realize it was such a big thing that was developing.

What was your greatest shortcoming as a young analyst, the one you worked hardest at correcting?

TB: There were several things I was doing wrong. Enunciating words too quickly…saying things in quick sentences…getting all wound up then not coming to a conclusion…being a little too wordy…talking too much. I'd have to tell myself sometimes, "Don't talk so darn much, Brookshier."

Probably the biggest fear I had was over-hyping the situation. You know, a two-yard gain is a two-yard gain. Sometimes it's a good defensive play and sometimes it's just a lousy offensive play.

Summerall and Brookshier – The Boys in the Booth

Brookshier may be sportscasting's freest spirit, a 48-year-old hybrid of Hunter Thompson and Huck Finn. Around the Tower of Paley, where dignity and reserve rule almost by decree, Brookshier's irrepressible style meshes like neck jewelry with a pinstripe. His on-air asides have overheated so many CBS switchboards that network executives have dubbed them "Brookieisms."

There was the 1972 Dallas game: "The Cowboys aren't taking any prisoners today." That came during one of the U.S. Army's worst weeks in Vietnam. There was the 1976 Washington game, following a touchdown bomb by the Redskin quarterback: "I'd like my son to grow up to be just like Billy Kilmer." That came one day after Kilmer was arrested for driving while intoxicated.

So much for Brookshier's conservative side. Out on the town, he becomes more reckless. One of his favorite amusements is to hail a taxi on a rainy night by lying down in front of it. Sometimes he even lies down in front of passenger cars. "I once tried that trick in Milwaukee," he recalls, and two girls who looked like Laverne and Shirley damn near put tread marks across my chest…"

Brookshier and Summerall were sitting in Giants Stadium wondering how to handle a pre-arranged halftime interview. The guest will be Ted Kennedy. "Can you think of any questions for the senator?" Summerall asked. "No," quipped Brookshier, "but I'm sure not going to ask him for a ride to the airport." Once again, Brookshier got blitzed by fate. How was he supposed to know that his mike, supposedly disconnected, was actually hooked to an open feed into the stadium's VIP boxes? Kennedy, who was considering a run for the Democratic presidential nomination and had been sitting in one of those boxes, showed up for the interview well ahead of schedule.

"All right," he demanded. "Which one's Brookshier?"

- Inside Sports magazine, March 1981

As a player, your era was the gritty 1950s and early '60s. The league was rich with names like Bobby Layne, Marion Motley, Chuck Bednarik and "Night Train" Lane, but the game itself was still evolving. By the 1970s, pro football had matured and was ready to push baseball aside as the country's top sporting draw. Do you feel that pro football had reached its pinnacle during that decade?

TB: I can't think of a better era. There were so many great teams in the 1970s and so many fantastic matchups. You know, great teams are what characterize and elevate a sport, and during those years there were a bunch of them. The 17-0 Dolphins of 1972…George Allen was pumping up his Redskins, who were made up of old guys with only a couple of years left in the tank…Oakland doing all kind of damage in the AFC…the Steelers and Cowboys locking horns in those Super Bowls.

The way the game is played today has changed. The size and speed of the players have increased, but I don't feel that the core mentality of a pro football player has changed. In 1984, CBS sent me to the Super Bowl to do some PR work. I was talking to the press group there, which had people from all over the world. I said, "I'm gonna tell you guys something: These two teams – the Redskins and the Raiders – would meet here and play their butts off for the whole game without any of us being around, without any television or radio or newspaper coverage." The people looked at me like I was crazy.

I said, "You don't understand this, but when the football player gets on to the field for the game, that's all he cares about. They want to go out there and beat their opponent and win the game. These players would do this without anybody covering it, without 120 million people watching."

The media people got up and walked out of the room thinking, "This guy is a crazy man." Even today I go down to watch the Eagles practice. I still talk to some of the players. We look each other in the eye and it's still the same way. If it came down to it, these guys would tee it up and play their last game without anybody watching, and probably for no paycheck. It's a very interesting psychology. The mentality of the player on the field has not changed over the years. They have a lot more exposure and make a lot more money today, but when it comes down to playing the basic football player is still inside that helmet.

Let's discuss your infamous encounter with Duane Thomas during the postgame of Super Bowl VI. The Dallas running back had forced a bizarre silence on the media, refusing to speak to anyone with a press pass. What was your production team's pregame strategy for handling the Thomas situation? If he gains only 39 yards in the game, it's a non-issue. But if Thomas rips the Miami defense and becomes the front-page story, CBS was going to have to deal with him.

TB: Doing postgames were really fun in the 1970s, especially in the winning locker room. The players wanted to be seen, and if they won they'd get up there with me and look the camera right in the eye. But with Thomas it was different. Before that game, [Dallas WR] Bob Hayes had told me that Thomas probably wouldn't come up for an interview with us. [CBS announcer] Irv Cross had tried to get Thomas to talk earlier in the year and he refused.

I knew this situation was still potentially going to be a problem for us, so I wanted to clear the issue with our whole crew, to make sure everybody was on the same page. We were in our production meeting the Saturday night before the game and I asked CBS president Bob Wood, "What if Duane Thomas wants to talk tomorrow? What do I let him say?"

Thomas hadn't spoken to the press for the previous six or seven weeks. Everybody else in the room thought that was a ridiculous question, but Wood paused for a minute then said, "Wait a minute…that's a very good question. If he wants to speak, let him say anything he wants. We'll deal with it." Thank God I'd cleared that up the night before because the whole crew then understood that the possibility was there. I wasn't counting on Thomas spilling his guts to us, but we would at least be ready if he did talk.

Thomas turned in an MVP-caliber performance in Super Bowl VI, then surprisingly agreed to go on camera after the game. You once openly described yourself as being "scared to death" in the moments before the interview.

TB: I was very nervous. I didn't know what to expect. But I did know that I didn't want to be embarrassed on national television if Thomas tried to make things difficult. I'd been interviewing Cowboys cornerback Herb Adderly, then I asked him, "Do you think Duane Thomas would talk to me?" No sooner had I said that when my director said, "Tom, you've got him right behind you."

During the interview, the first thing that flashed through my mind was the play where Thomas had made Miami linebacker Nick Buoniconti miss him at the goal line. I gave him one of those questions about his speed, and he gave me that infamous "Evidently" response. I said to myself, "Oh… my… God. Is he going stand here and give me one-word answers all day?" [Former Browns RB] Jimmy Brown saw I was starting to sweat and tried to break the ice a little bit. He said, "Are you nervous, Brook?" Well, *yeah, I am*! I'm on national TV trying to come up with questions for this guy, but I know he's not going to give me any kind of a real answer no matter what I ask!

After we finished, the press in the locker room asked me what Thomas had said. I told them, "Not much." Then they asked me, "Did you find out why Thomas hasn't been talking to us all year?" I said, "No, I didn't. That was the first time I've ever talked to him. Why don't you go ask him yourself?" I wasn't in a very cooperative mood after all that.

A lot of people in the media were unhappy I didn't get more out of Thomas. A columnist from an Oakland newspaper named Shapiro, who'd always been a pretty good guy to me, really tore me up over that interview. I wasn't real happy about it, so I called him. Surprisingly he said, "I have to be honest with you, Tom. I never even saw the interview."

I was stunned. I asked him, "Then why would you rip me like that?"

He said, "Well, everybody felt that you…" Then he paused.

Finally, he admitted, "My secretary told me about the interview. I never really saw it, but I felt I needed to write about it."

I said, "I can't believe you would do that to me, just to fill a column."

Looking back, I should have been better prepared for Duane. That interview could have gotten me fired. I wasn't sure how the people at CBS were going to react, but when Bob Wood asked me to fly back to New York on the corporate Gulfstream jet with him and the CBS brass, I knew that everything was all right, that it would all eventually blow over.

Did you resent Thomas for putting you in such an awkward, difficult spot on national television?

TB: Absolutely not! I was more perplexed than anything else. I found out later that Duane was having some personal problems, mostly involving drugs. I learned that he was "coked" for that Super Bowl. Jim Brown had become somewhat close to him and was really trying to help. He told me he had lined up a couple of commercials for Duane to make after the game that would have paid him around $70,000. But as the two of them were walking out of the stadium that afternoon to go to the shoots, Duane walked right away from him, got in another car and drove away. He blew off the commercials and never got back to Jim about it. Duane was going through a really strange, tough time in his personal life, which was likely why he acted the way he did. I really don't hold anything against him.

Have you spoken with Thomas since that day?

TB: Yes, I saw him years later. He was sorry, contrite and down on his luck. What a wasted talent, what a wasted career.

Being Duane Thomas and the Silence of '71

… [Thomas] didn't speak to the local media, who dubbed him "The Sphinx."

"See, the media is not the same today as then," Thomas said. "The NFL controlled the media. That's how they kept players in line – through fear, which is an old slave tactic. Pit one against another. I was misunderstood. It [was] not about being misquoted. It [was] about how am I understanding what you are saying? It was all about fear. Tom [Landry] would tell you one thing and tell the media something else."

Frank Luksa, a sports columnist at *The Dallas Morning News* who covered the Cowboys in those days for the Dallas Times Herald, says Thomas wasn't always so angry.

"He was a delight as a rookie, very clever," said Luksa. "Before the first Super Bowl, I asked how it felt to be playing as a rookie in the ultimate game. He said, `If this is the ultimate game, how come they play it every year?' But then money changed everything.

"He had gotten a signing bonus in 1970," Luksa said. "Although he got a raise in '71, it wasn't as much as his combined bonus and salary, so he was making less money." Thomas reportedly brooded.

"He wouldn't come out of his room for practice in training camp in 1971," Luksa said. "He'd climb through a back window to get to the chow hall and wouldn't answer the roll call. He didn't talk to teammates. He wasn't talking to anybody. He just turned sour. I tried to approach him and he'd say, ` [Expletive] off.' He was a pain in the [expletive]. He took five years off my life."

But Thomas said he did talk to his coach and teammates. "I had to talk to them in order to get the plays taken care of," he said.

Other than that, the silence continued until the Cowboys beat the Dolphins in New Orleans in the Super Bowl. Thomas ran for a game-high 95 yards and caught a pass for a touchdown. In the postgame hoopla, Thomas consented to break his silence, with the legendary Brown standing at his side for support (although Dave Anderson wrote in *The New York Times* the next day that Thomas did provide a few short answers to questions in the locker room immediately after the game). The interview, with CBS sportscaster Tom Brookshier, is part of Super Bowl lore.

Brookshier, who acknowledged later that he was nervous, staggered through an awkward exchange that lasted only seconds but seemed like a lifetime.

"Duane, uh, you do things with speed, but you never really hurry a lot like the great Jim Brown," Brookshier said. "Uh, you never hurry into a hole. You take your time, make a spin, yet you still outrun people. Are you that fast? Are you quick, would you say?"

Thomas stared into the camera for what seemed like a very long time before issuing his reply. "Evidently," he said. Brookshier couldn't find his way out; Thomas couldn't think of any other way to respond.

"I wasn't trying to show him up," Thomas says now. "I was camera-shy . . . the lights . . . that's a different world than being on the field. I never heard of Tom Brookshier. That was my very first time meeting Brookshier. That was his first time ever interviewing a black player.

"I couldn't think of anything else based on what he was saying. `Are you really that fast?' The only word I could think of was `evidently.' I thought of `uh-huh,' but then they'd say I'm stupid. If I said `yeah, man,' I'm still stupid. I was not groomed to deal with the media, and players are not groomed in dealing with the media today. Every player based on the amount of money they are making should have their own press agent."

The interview continued.

Brookshier: "Do you like football, Duane?"

Thomas: "Yes, that's why I'm a pro football player."

The last question was about Thomas's difficulty keeping his weight down.

"I weigh what I need to," was Thomas's reply.

Brookshier was teased about the interview for years. Thomas was vilified. (September 10, 2003)

Let's talk about the Summerall and Brookshier team, CBS's dynamic duo throughout most of the 1970s. How did one of the most famous pairs in sports broadcasting get its start?

TB: I was doing games with Jack Buck at that time. Right in the middle of the 1974 season I got a call from CBS Sports president Bob Wussler. He said, "Guess what. You've got a new partner." I said, "Why? Jack and I get along great!" He said, "It has nothing to do with that. Summerall wants to do play-by-play."

I joked, "You mean he didn't choose Frank Gifford?" Turns out, Pat really wanted to work with me. I thought that was really weird. Pat is a man of few words, while I talk in paragraphs, so I thought it would be a strange pairing.

Pat was still doing color at that time and he wanted to try his hand at calling the action himself. That weekend we were at the Vet in Philadelphia doing a Redskins-Eagles game. He was sitting there looking at me. The sweat was pouring off him. It was strange how it all worked out because there never seemed to be an awkward moment between us, no pause in time. We just sat there like two former players talking to each other. The formula was rather simple, to be honest. We just said what we wanted to say. We always felt that the job was never too serious, and I'm not sure if that exists in the booth today. Football is such a simple game, yet announcers act like it's World War III going on in front of them.

That laid back style you described, "like two former players talking to each other," was very popular with the general public. However, it also brought criticism from those who felt there was a lack of seriousness in your broadcasts.

TB: That was ridiculous. We were always very well prepared. I think the source of the criticism really had to do with us being out on the town on Saturday nights more than anything else. For years, Pat and I did a show called *This Week in the NFL,* which we used to call our great scouting reports. We used to do that on Mondays, and we got to see all the action from the other teams in the league. It really helped us prepare for games we were going to call on the following Sunday.

But people would sometimes ask me, "Why don't you stay in on Saturday night and study the teams' players to prepare for your broadcast?" I'd say, "Does a coach change his gameplan on Saturday night? If

I've prepared all week, and the coaches trust me and tell me exactly what they're going to do on Sunday, why would I stay in on Saturday night?" We liked to go out to dinner and meet people from Los Angeles or Dallas or Chicago and have a great time, then we'd go back to the hotel. A lot of reporters took umbrage to that. They didn't like the idea we were out on Saturday night. They thought we were supposed to lock ourselves in a room like we were studying for an exam.

One of Summerall's great instincts as an announcer was knowing when to choose silence over dialogue as a big play was unfolding. For example, Tony Dorsett would shave the corner on a sweep then race off to another long-distance touchdown. You and Summerall would be completely silent until the very end of the play, when he would calmly say something like, "Seventy-three yards… and the Cowboys have put it away." Your thoughts on Pat Summerall's sense of timing and drama.

TB: Pat was the best at it. Too many announcers, especially today, think that they are the show, that people are tuned in to hear them talk. They ramble on and on. Hey, sometimes a three-yard run is just a three-yard run, no further explanation needed. Today announcers walk all over the game. Pat was never like that. To him, the action on the field was what counted, and his job was to fill in the blanks and bring out analysis from his color partner when appropriate.

One of the greatest calls I ever heard him make was nothing more than complete silence. It was a game between the Cowboys and Redskins in 1974, that famous Thanksgiving Day game. The Redskins jumped out to an early lead, then [Redskins LB] Dave Robinson rung Roger Staubach's bell and knocked him out of the game. Dallas clawed its way back behind some no-name quarterback named Clint Longley, but was still trailing with about 30 seconds to play. Then Longley throws this deep pass to Drew Pearson, and while it was taking place, we didn't say a single thing. It was all natural sound. It was the damnedest throw you'd ever seen, and Dallas won the game.

After it was over, we just let all the excitement and fervor in the stadium take over. Our only comment was that George Allen must have been shocked. The audience could see that Dallas had just won the game. They knew that this Longley fellow had just worked a miracle. Everything was right there on the television screen. What more could Pat or I have added? After the game we were told that Allen, as that last pass was flying through the air, looked at his bench and simply said, "*What is a Clint Longley?*"

How did Pat Summerall make you a better football analyst?

TB: He never left you hanging. I remember another game between Dallas and Washington in which Cliff Harris jumped up in a crowded endzone and knocked down a pass. I'd been reading a book on naval aviation called *The Right Stuff*, so the topic was still fresh in my mind. At the moment Harris made that play, I made the comment that "It was like trying to land a plane on an aircraft carrier in a rough sea." Summerall, who was so sharp, picked right up on it and continued with the thought. He was one of those guys who would wrap up your comments and not leave you hanging out there. If you'd say something like that today, some of these guys would just sit there in silence thinking, "Why did Brookshier say that?"

Since Pat was a former player, he wasn't confused about the things I said during a game. He understood where I was coming from. Lindsey Nelson and Jack Buck sometimes wouldn't understand certain innuendoes or remarks I made during a broadcast. For example, one of them might say to me, "I don't understand – you would intentionally *hit* another player on his injury?"

And I would respond, "Of course! If your opponent is playing with a big arm bandage or something on him, you'd hit it!" They would look at me with shock. On the other hand, Pat would somehow temper the remark to make it not seem so vicious.

I got into some trouble one time in Philadelphia. It was during an Eagles-Bears game. Eagles tackle Stan Walters half-missed his block on Chicago's defensive end Mike Hartenstine. Ron Jaworski was Philadelphia's quarterback and he had dropped back in the pocket and was standing there, almost in a Heisman Trophy-like pose. Hartenstine just drilled him, right in the back. Luckily, Jaworski didn't see him coming so he didn't tense up, but the hit knocked him to the ground into a fetal position. He was lying on the ground, sorta sucking his thumb. It wasn't an illegal hit but Hartenstine was fined $2,000 for the hit even though there was no flag on the play. They carried Jaworski off the field, and then Summerall said to me in his real matter-of-fact tone, "What do you think of that?"

I said, "They ought to give him a bonus."

I said that because a guy like Hartenstine waits a whole season for a shot like that – a bad block, the quarterback is looking the other way trying to throw, then Hartenstine hits him and knocks him out of the game. He's not trying to hurt Jaworski or kill him. Well, a writer for the *Chicago Tribune* took great umbrage to that remark, calling me a blood lusting ex-jock. But after such a punishing hit in which the quarterback is carried out of the game, all Summerall had to say was, "What do you think of that." It was such an easy lead for me to follow.

During which game do you feel you gave your most uninspired performance in the booth, and why?

TB: You're going to be surprised at this answer. I'm pretty sure this event still ranks in the top ten TV ratings of all time. It was Super Bowl XIV between the Rams and the Steelers. To be honest, I didn't think it was going to be a very good football game. The excitement just wasn't there for me. Pittsburgh was a powerhouse that had been there three times before, and the Rams had some good players but had only won nine games that year. The game wasn't supposed to be close, but after three quarters the Rams were still in it. That's why people probably kept watching. If it hadn't been for those two great catches by John Stallworth, Los Angeles probably would've won that game. But as a broadcaster, I don't think I did a particularly good job on that game.

"Brookie" Takes a Shot from the *Chicago Tribune*

Sunday's coverage of the Chicago-Philadelphia game showed just how badly [Summerall and Brookshier] have slipped. It was almost as if Brookshier had been suspended in time for the past 10 years or so, the way he kept glorifying most any act of violence his aging eyes detected, the way he kept making cutesy, macho remarks during the honey shots of Philadelphia's cheerleaders, the way he kept giving off those throaty, rumbling laughs whenever one of the players did something extraordinarily bone-shattering on the field...

Brookshier was as quick to defend the violence he saw as he was to glorify it. When Philadelphia quarterback Ron Jaworski was knocked cold by a devastating blindside hit, the announcer was quick to report the hit was neither illegal nor cheap. "A tremendous shot," he called it. "But that's the way game of football's played." Summerall, whose reaction to Brookshier's babble generally was an approving grunt or chuckle, was compelled to chime, "If they legislate things like that out, all the ballparks would be empty."

- Ron Alridge, *Chicago Tribune*, October 31, 1980

That Steelers-Rams matchup was one of the best Super Bowls ever played. Why did you pick the biggest game of the year to go in the tank?

TB: Because I wasn't terribly interested in it. It showed that day in the booth. The game didn't have the same punch as some of the other Super Bowls I'd done. Two weeks before we watched the Steelers play the Oilers in the AFC Championship. That was an exciting football game – big plays, controversial plays, the catch/no-catch play involving Mike Renfro in the back of the endzone. Then Pat and I do the NFC Championship between Tampa Bay and the Rams, and all we get are three field goals. 9-to-nothing, a complete flop. The highlight of that game was watching the sun set over the water that evening. I remember

Pat saying to me, "Well, there goes a beautiful sunset." I said [laughing], *"That was the best shot we've had today."*

As the Super Bowl got closer, the more and more it felt like a big letdown. I thought it was going to be a one-sided game, that the Rams didn't have a chance. My heart wasn't into it so I didn't give my best performance. I let those Super Bowl parties get in the way of my preparation. A few hours before the game, I suddenly realized that I didn't have a single intelligent thing to say about those two teams, and it showed that day in the booth. There was also some politics going on within CBS, and having John Madden on the scene did not help. I actually thought about quitting after that game.

Earlier you discussed your biggest weaknesses as a broadcaster. In what situations were you at your best?

TB: After a while I became very familiar with the teams I was covering, especially their offenses. I could almost call the plays that were about to happen, at least within a play or two. I could even tell you which players they were going to. After it would happen, Summerall would just look at me and roll his eyes. For example, in Super Bowl X I predicted two or three times that Lynn Swann was going to get the ball thrown deep to him. People thought I was stealing the game plans out of the locker room. Actually, I could feel the tension of the moment and what the offense was trying to do. I could almost feel what Bradshaw was going to do during that game. I don't really know if it was some great talent or attribute of mine. It was just fun for me when I was right, even though it probably didn't mean that much to the people watching at home. Well, maybe it did. People still tell me they enjoyed listening to me predict plays during the telecast.

Let's talk about some of the NFC teams you covered in the 1970s. For starters, George Allen's Washington Redskins. Former St. Louis QB Jim Hart called the Redskins secondary of Pat Fisher, Mike Bass, Ken Houston, Joe Lavender the toughest unit he had to crack. Your thoughts?

TB: They were a good bunch, there's no question about that. Then they added the Pro Bowler Jake Scott from Miami in '76. And having that veteran group on the defensive line with their strong pass rush made the secondary even better.

One of the craziest things I ever heard was from Harold Carmichael, the great 6'8" wide receiver for the Eagles. He came over to me once during practice and said, "Is Fisher still playing for the Redskins?"

I said, "You mean you're worried about him? At *your* size?"

He said, "Tom, Fisher gets right on my bellybutton and he fights and battles and gives me more trouble than anybody in the league!"

Fisher was a bow-legged, tough football player. We used to watch those two battle and it was amazing. You talk about athletes at complete different ends of the spectrum. Fisher was the only guy that Harold used to worry about. He was a George Allen-type player.

You heard all the whispers about the covert reconnaissance operation that Allen was allegedly operating out of Redskins Park? The rumors of his great spy network, stealing information from around the league.

TB: I did, and I always wondered about those great Redskins teams under Allen. The 1970s – the Watergate days – was a time when everybody in Washington seemed to be carrying tape recorders in their pockets. I always wondered if the Redskins had tapped their opponent's phones from upstairs. I have no evidence of this, but the Washington defense always seemed to know exactly what their opponents were going to run.

For instance, Roman Gabriel would bring the Eagles offense out of the huddle, and you would see the Washington defense shift over into the hole that they were going to run through. I'd see the quarterback give a puzzled look like, *God almighty! How do they know what we're trying to do?* It was amazing. I don't know how they did it. I always wondered if somebody was tipping something along the line for that team. I don't want to take anything away from George Allen because he was really a good coach. His players really played all out for him. We'd interview Allen while preparing for the broadcast but he'd never open up much. He rarely gave us anything of substance. George was paranoid. He thought we were working for the other side.

What about those "Over-The-Hill" characters that Allen played at quarterback?

TB: Sonny Jurgensen and Billy Kilmer. [Redskins RB] Larry Brown once told me that the best pure passer he ever saw was Sonny Jurgensen. He said, "When I was running swing patterns, I could put my hands up and look for the linebacker at the same time – never had to worry where the ball was. It gave me the greatest feeling in the world because Sonny, without taking any zip off his pass, would put it right in my hands. The pass would be fuzzy but firm. I was able to look and see where the SOB that was trying to hit me was."

Jurgensen never led a championship or Super Bowl team, but that's because he never had a solid team around him. But in terms of purely throwing the ball, he might have been the best.

Kilmer? He never threw a spiral in his life, but his receivers caught every ball he threw at them. One day I was at an affair in Washington, and I was kidding around with [Redskins WR] Charley Taylor and a few other guys about Kilmer not being able to throw a spiral. They got pretty heated about it. They told me, "Don't you say that about Billy!" I was just kidding, but they weren't happy about it. You didn't make fun of Kilmer or Jurgensen in front of their teammates, even though Kilmer and Jurgensen *were* fun to make fun of.

Then there were the Minnesota Vikings. They had Hall-of-Fame quarterbacking with Fran Tarkenton and the "Purple People Eaters" on defense; power running with Foreman and Ed Marinaro and a slew of exciting wide receivers. All of this and zero championships.
What is your analysis of Bud Grant's Vikings of the 1970s and why they were never able to bring a title to Minnesota.

TB: I remember Super Bowl IV in New Orleans between Kansas City of the AFL and Minnesota. I was still doing CBS pregame and postgame at that time, and everybody in the world was picking the Vikings to win. They had only lost two games and had just taken apart Cleveland to win the NFL title. About seven or eight members of our crew went out in the French Quarter one night, and we saw a bunch of good-looking gals over in the corner. We went over and started talking to them, and it turned out to be the wives of the Minnesota players. I said to [Vikings QB] Joe Kapp's wife, "You're gonna be with the Super Bowl champions this time tomorrow night."

She said, "Oh, no we're not!" I was shocked, and I asked why not.

She said, "Joe doesn't think his offensive line can block these guys. They're very worried. They think Kansas City is really tough."

I almost fell through the floor, but women are honest as hell and they'll tell you the truth. Well, we went ahead and did the game, and as I watched I kept thinking, *Kapp was right. The Vikings can't block these guys.* Bobby Bell and the rest of the Kansas City defense were all over them.

If you look at how Grant's teams performed in the Super Bowls that followed – against Miami, Pittsburgh and Oakland – their offensive lines couldn't handle what was coming at them. Their offense scored a total of 28 points in four Super Bowl games, and a big part of the reason was because their offensive line was overmatched. They couldn't get the job done. But I do give them some credit. For the Vikings to get to the Super Bowl four times was amazing. Bud Grant was such an underrated coach. And because of his public demeanor, he was an underrated person.

Another team that bullied the NFC in the 1970s was the Los Angeles Rams. Year after year, L.A. fielded powerful, exciting teams with championship talent, yet only the 1979 version – a 9-7 squad that barely won its division title – reached the Super Bowl. Why couldn't the Rams win the big one during those years?

TB: To me, it was simple. We used to always look at teams' parking lots on Sundays to see which guys were driving the pickups and station wagons and four-wheel drives, and who was driving Porsches and Ferraris. The Rams were driving the Porsches and Ferraris. We always felt the Rams were Brentwood, while Pittsburgh was the Bessemer furnace. It wasn't necessarily indicative of the truth, but maybe there was something to it. The Rams were very good, but I think other teams – Dallas, Pittsburgh, Oakland – were tougher. Mentally tougher.

I was doing a Rams game once, and I was told by my producer to go down into the stands and interview Jonathan Winters for a short pregame segment. So I go down to the section where Winters always sat and he wasn't there. Somebody from his section told me "Jonathan isn't here, and he might not make it. Sometimes he crashes on his way to the stadium." I thought, *Great... Now what?*

Then I looked down and I happened to see Roy Rogers there. He saw me and said, "Tom, do you need an interview? I'll do it. I've been watching Rams quarterbacks since Bob Waterfield." So he gets up wearing this red polyester sport coat and we get in position to do the interview. Then through my earpiece my producer Bob Stenner says to me, "Tom, he's got dandruff on his coat. Put your arm over Roy's shoulders so the audience can't see it." I thought, *Oh, God...What a helluva thing to say in my ear.*

He ended up doing the cutest interview, talking about all the Rams quarterbacks over the years. He loved Bob Waterfield and "The Dutchman," Norm van Brocklin. I never knew he was such a huge Rams fan. I thought we were about finished, then Stenner said in my ear, "We need another 30 seconds, Brook. Give me 30 more seconds!"

So I asked Roy, "Where's Trigger?"

Roy said, "I'm glad you asked that question. He's stuffed and right in my living room!"

Then I heard somebody in the production truck say, "*Holy Shit!* Okay, time to say goodbye, Tom."

It seemed that you and Summerall were perched atop Texas Stadium nearly every Sunday, calling Dallas Cowboys games. Did you ever get bored pounding the Cowboys beat for CBS?

TB: It seemed like we were always doing something involving the Cowboys. Since we were the number one broadcasting team at CBS, they'd send us to where the best NFC teams were playing. In the 1970s, that usually meant something involving Dallas, the Rams, the Vikings or the Redskins. We'd hit St. Louis once in a while. That was about all that was happening in the NFC back then. San Francisco was down. Chicago didn't have anything except Walter Payton. The Giants were not a good team.

Pat and I got to know Landry and the Cowboys pretty well from doing all those games. Dallas did make it to five Super Bowls during those years. The first Pittsburgh-Dallas Super Bowl was one of the best games I ever called. It was absolutely fascinating that the Cowboys could be that different from the Steelers, in terms of both personality and the way they approached the game. Those teams were total contrasts of one another and yet they played like hell. Staubach and Bradshaw had nothing in common – never have and never will. It was some of the best, most interesting football ever played.

The thing I remember about Super Bowl X was the producers cutting my microphone with two minutes to go in the game. They told me to go down to the Steelers' lockerroom and get ready to do the postgame show. At that time, the score was 21-10 in favor of Pittsburgh. So I went out and found a couple of state troopers to escort me down to where I needed to be. Sonny Jurgensen, who was going to help me do the postgame, had been out someplace before the game doing cocktails with Brigitte Bardot.

We go into the locker room, and then they tell us we can't be visible when the Steelers first comes in because they are going to be doing a team prayer. So they lock me, a cameraman and Jurgensen – who is half in the bag – in this closet. But we can still hear the radio broadcast being played, and all of a sudden we hear, "*Staubach goes back, back...here's the pass...touchdown!*" Then everybody else in the locker room ran back out onto the field to see the end of the game, and we're locked in a closet! Great. We're probably now in the losing locker room because it looks like Dallas is going to come back. How are we going to do a postgame show from here? Well, Pittsburgh hung on and we ended up in the right place.

I have another funny story about the Cowboys. During a Dallas-L.A. Rams playoff game one year, they told me to get "Too Tall" Jones to stand next to the Rams quarterback, Pat Haden. I wasn't sure it was going to work, but I asked "Too Tall" to do it and he reluctantly agreed. Then I asked Haden, who is smart as hell and really a good guy, "Will you come out on to the field a little early so I can do a little interview with you?"

He looked at me and looked at me, then finally said, "What are you going to do?"

I said, "Well, I want you to come out and stand…" and before I could get the words out he said, "Too Tall Jones, right?"

I said, "Yeah, we'd like you, at 6-foot and a half inches, to stand next to 'Too Tall,'" who was about 6-foot-nine.

Pat wouldn't do it. He said, "No way am I going to come out there and stand next to him in front of all the fans."

At his height, Pat was a good little quarterback but I don't know how he ever threw the ball over some of those players. "Too Tall" Jones was like a basketball player out there, like Dikembe Mutombo running around. But in those days, your offensive linemen could cut block, and you could get the defensive linemen to keep their hands down by cutting their knees out from under them a few times.

An Ex-Eagle Swipes at the Cowboys' Mystique

"Dallas fans never feel the Cowboys have lost a game. It's always that the referees screwed them or the Good Lord looked the other way or something. It's the toughest place to broadcast a game. Sagebrush, USA. The fans don't know football. They just know something's wrong if the Cowboys aren't winning by two TDs.

"A few years ago their highlight film was called *Like a Mighty River*. Boy, that's Texas all right. And John Wayne is the quarterback. You do a game in Detroit, say. The people there have seen a little football. You can't BS them. But try to tell the truth in Dallas and you'll find some frozen hemlock in your nachos."

- Tom Brookshier, *Sports Illustrated*'s "College & Pro Football Spectacular" (1982)

Being a former Eagles player, you obviously had an interest in Philadelphia's resurgence in the late 1970s under Dick Vermeil. The Eagles hadn't put together a winning campaign since 1966, but after taking over the team in 1976 Vermeil had turned the team into NFC champions within five years. What were your impressions of Dick Vermeil?

TB: Coaching had been a problem in Philadelphia for some time. Vermeil came in from UCLA, but he previously had been with George Allen's Los Angeles Rams so he knew the pro game. Allen made him the first special teams coach in the history of football. Dick was the hot candidate at that time because UCLA had just upset a great Ohio State team in the Rose Bowl. Eagles owner Leonard Tose desperately wanted a winner, so he hired Dick.

Vermeil went right to work. The first thing he did was find people in town who would support him. He got Chuck Bednarik and a few other old timers back in the fold. If I was in town broadcasting an Eagles game, he'd come over to the sidelines at a practice and spend a few minutes with me. He cultivated that whole operation, even to the point where he'd be sleeping at the office. He just flat burned himself out. He didn't know when to quit, but he did take a team with average talent all the way to a Super Bowl.

In 1980, the Eagles had beaten Oakland during the regular season and were getting ready to play them again in Super Bowl XV. NBC was broadcasting the game that year, so CBS told us to go down to New Orleans for some PR work. We were all over the French Quarter having a good time, but we never saw any Eagles around town. Around midnight on the night before the game, we were sitting in the Absinthe House. John Matuszak, the starting defensive tackle for the Raiders, was sitting next to me. I asked him, "What the hell are you doing here? You have a big day tomorrow." He said, "Aww, hell. The Eagles are probably going to beat us. They've already beaten us once." He laughed and laughed. Then he finished his drink, slapped me on the back and left.

The Raiders came out and absolutely killed Philadelphia in that game, took them apart. It was the only really bad game I ever saw Ron Jaworski have. The Eagles must have been really tight. Dick kept a close watch on them, but to be honest I'm not sure if that really mattered. Oakland was a more talented team, a more aggressive team. I didn't think the Eagles could beat them twice in a row, especially the way Jim Plunkett was playing.

What was your perception of the level of drug usage among NFL players in the 1970s?

TB: I didn't really see it, but I don't think I was really ever in a position to do so. We had Dexedrine back in the 1950's when I played. One of my teammates on the Eagles gave me a speckled pill before a game once and I ended up in three fights, two of them with my own teammates. It was crazy! I said to myself, *Damn! I have to be rational and reasonable when I'm out here playing. I can't be that when I'm taking these things.* So I just never did it again.

During the 1970s, we had always heard that some teams were doing drugs more than others. Some players used to joke about Deacon Jones, saying he would take a pill in the lockerroom before kickoff on Sunday then say, "See you on Tuesday!" But I don't think there were a lot of players using drugs. The ones that were using them took things that would pep you up, sorta like what truckers and cab drivers take to stay awake. But it really wasn't perceived as being illegal back then. It wasn't like the police were going to show up and arrest you. In fact, Rozelle used to say, "The NFL does not have a drug problem." Of course, the San Diego Chargers of that era probably changed that opinion for most people, but Glorietta Bay will do that to you.

Give me the one game that you didn't broadcast but always wished you had?

TB: I would've loved to have called the Ice Bowl between Dallas and Green Bay. I did work the pregame and postgame segments of that game but I would've loved to have been in the booth. It was the coldest day I ever experienced, just amazing. Frank Gifford told me he got a black cup of coffee then set it down for a moment. When he went to pick it back up, he accidentally knocked the cup over but it didn't spill because the coffee had already frozen. We had to cancel the halftime interviews because everybody who'd been on the field had frozen voices, which made them sound funny when they started to warm up. I was supposed to interview Paul Hornung, who was on suspension for gambling. Paul had been outside by the Packers bench during the first half, so when I tried to interview him his voice started resonating so the producers just told me to cancel it.

Lambeau Field was an ice rink that day. Flanker Bobby Hayes spent the whole day with his hands in his pants. He couldn't have caught a pass if Don Meredith had hit him in the back of his head. We walked down on the field to check out the underground heating system that the Packers had just installed to keep the field thawed, and the damned thing was frozen solid. When Lombardi heard that he smiled and said, "Perfect! It's just right."

[Packers WR] Carol Dale looked at me and said, "*Perfect?* It's like a skating rink!"

There were some plays made on that field that day which I don't know how were ever made. Green Bay's Chuck Mercein, who was a good player not a great one, made a couple of plays on that last drive that nobody in America could've made. It was amazing. I don't think Dallas got over losing that game for a long time.

On January 11, 1981, Dallas was at Philadelphia for the NFC Championship. Did you know that was going to be your last broadcast with Pat Summerall?

TB: Neither one of us realized it, although we had heard the rumors about pairing Pat with John Madden and me with Vin Scully. Neither of us hoped they were true but, unfortunately, it was. The one good thing that did come from it was that I was able to start doing some play-by-play work, which I enjoyed quite a bit. But it was nothing compared to the great fun and friendship that Pat and I enjoyed while we had the top billing at CBS. It was a magical time.

Final question: You interviewed hundreds of players during your career with CBS. In terms of intensity and seriousness off the field, which player most stands out in your mind?

TB: Oh, without a doubt, Ray Nitschke from Green Bay. He was so intense, so into the game that even during an interview it was sometimes scary. I can't think of anyone who was as intense as him. After the Ice Bowl, I was in the Packers' dressing room doing interviews. Nitschke came by, so I said to the camera, "Here's the madman of the Packers." I thought he was going to belt me. But I had meant it as a compliment! To me, a madman meant you were a really fierce guy, a tremendous player, but he didn't like that. He didn't like the idea that anyone would think of him as being uncivilized or a Neanderthal. Later I heard that one of our directors in the truck said, "If he punches Brookshier, we're going to commercial!"

— 16 —
Mike Wagner, Safety
Pittsburgh Steelers (1971-1980)
June 16, 1999

A modern military adage warns that the army which control the sky will ultimately control the war. For the American forces battling in World War II that was certainly true.

"Hitler built a fortress around Europe," FDR winked, "but he forgot to put a roof on it."

In football it doesn't always work that way. If those forces controlling the sky also own a run defense that leaks like the *C.S.S. Hunley*, then it's not long before Operation Shutdown becomes Operation Touchdown – none if by air, six if by feet.

But it does prompt us to ask the question, What is the definition of a great pass defense?

Many coaches and players will tell you the key is heavy pressure, constant, raging heat on the quarterback. Makes sense. Give any old pro time to throw and he'll eventually find his target; therefore, the goal should be to minimize his free time in the pocket.

But if a strong pass rush is the only factor, then explain how a team like the '84 Redskins generated 66 sacks but still gave up an embarrassing 4,300 passing yards. Or, in contrast, how did the 1979 Bills gather only 23 sacks yet still allow the fewest passing yards (2,713) in the AFC? The contradictions are already lining up.

A quick conclusion – it's not just about pass rush.

How about interceptions, swiping enemy passes from the sky? Definitely a big part of it, but then explain some of these anomalies:

1967 Dolphins –28 interceptions, but Ouch! those 31 touchdown passes they let sail by
1977 Colts – AFC leader with 30 INTs but allowing the third-most passing yards in the NFL
1983 Seahawks – AFC-leading 33 interceptions but gave up over 260 yards/game through the air
1983 Redskins – 34 interceptions while surrendering the most passing yards (4,377) in the league

Larcenists, all of those teams, but none are considered to be among the history's elite at stopping the pass. Call them pirates with leaky ships.

The NFL takes a cop-out approach in rating its pass defenses. It simply ranks clubs by passing yards-allowed then calls it a day. The team with the fewest is the best, the most is the worst. It's a quick but thoughtless method that, again, measures only a portion of a team's effectiveness. More half-truths at work.

In reality, a combination of variables is required to define the great ones. A premier pass defense not only smothers, it sabotages. It wrecks two-minute drills. It creates hideous things like tipped passes and fourth-downs and holding penalties. It destroys hope.

So how are the truly great ones identified?

Let's start by polling the pros, gathering feedback from the men who played the game. It's a good way of introducing the intangibles to the equation – intimidation, reaction to pressure, coverage instinct, etc. Some stories from the front:

John Hadl, QB, San Diego Chargers: "Oakland was the toughest team for me to pass on during those years, and a lot of it hinged on one man – Willie Brown. Willie was by far the best cornerback I ever had to play against. Unbelievably fast and instinctive. He'd lock onto [Chargers WR] Lance Alworth and they'd have some real battles. Oakland's other defensive backs, Kent McLoughlin and Warren Powers, were very good. They also had some pretty talented linebackers. But Brown was the real key. Part of the reason Sid Gillman developed his so-called 'West Coast' offense was to neutralize that Oakland pass defense. A lot of creativity went into getting guys open against the Raiders."

Boyd Dowler, WR, Green Bay Packers: "The Detroit Lions from about 1960 through '63 get my vote. Dick Lebeau and 'Night Train' Lane at the corners…Yale Lary and Gary Lowe at the safeties. 'Night Train' was more like 'Night Mare,' the single-most disruptive force in football. He played a lot like Deion Sanders, gambling a lot and lining up all over the place. Lane watched the quarterback a lot and jumped a lot of routes, which technically you're not supposed to do. But Lane got away with it because he was so quick and reactive. And if you did catch a ball on him, he'd take your head off.

"Lebeau should probably be in the Hall of Fame. He never let anybody get behind him, and neither did their safeties. Detroit's linebackers – Wayne Walker, Joe Schmidt and Carl Brettschneider – were very good at coverage and excellent blitzers. I could talk about the '63 Bears, too, but over a longer period of time the Lions were the best."

Len Dawson, QB, Kansas City Chiefs: "Without question, it was the Pittsburgh Steelers. [CB] Mel Blount was so physically intimidating and could cover extremely well. Their linebackers – particularly Jack Ham and Jack Lambert – could lock onto almost any running back or tight end and shut them down. But I won't answer the question without mentioning the awesome strength of Pittsburgh's front four. Those guys placed so much pressure on the passer that the Steelers could easily drop seven into coverage and shut everything down. If a quarterback has all kinda time, he'll eventually find a receiver. That didn't happen against the Steelers."

Joe Ferguson, QB, Buffalo Bills: "The Miami Dolphins of the early to mid-1970s. They didn't have the best talent or the best athletes, but they were the best-coached group. Shula's schemes were fantastic. They were great at disguising coverages. The best at it were [S] Jake Scott and [LB] Nick Buoniconti. Both of them were very smart. Scott covered a lot of ground, while Buoniconti often knew where our play was going before we even ran it."

Jimmy Cefalo, WR, Miami Dolphins: "The Raiders, with Mike Haynes and Lester Hayes at the corners, were the best of their era. Haynes was a long-strider, a Hall-of-Famer with good speed and instinct. Hayes was a bump-and-run madman. He belongs in the Hall, too. A corner with sprinter's speed, so much that he waited on every move then reacted and recovered. Hayes loved to talk to receivers across the line from him before the ball was snapped. But the problem was, he stuttered. He couldn't put two words together. He'd talk his smack but all you heard was a lot of muttering. After a while I'd say, 'C'mon Lester, spit it out, will ya?'"

Louis Lipps, WR, Pittsburgh Steelers: "A tie between the Kansas City Chiefs and Cleveland. I rate them equally because of the great corners both teams had. The Chiefs had Kevin Ross and Albert Lewis, the Browns with Hanford Dixon and Frank Minniefield. They were in your face every down, so close they could sniff the oxygen you were breathing. Serious bump-and-run guys. They played so close to the line that a lot of times the ref would have to tell them to back off. The only way to beat them off the line was to sell them hard in one direction, then make a clean break the other way."

Another way of rating history's premier pass defenses is by crunching the raw statistics, letting the gameday numbers create the profile. The quickest method of doing this is to borrow the NFL's quarterback rating formula, which the league uses to measure the efficiency of its passers.

For quarterbacks, the higher the score means the better the passer. San Francisco's Steve Young holds the highest single-season rating at 112.8, while Kurt Warner currently owns the NFL's best career mark at 98.2.

For pass defenses, however, generating low scores is the goal. The ultimate pass defense would destroy everything and rate a 0.0. On the opposite end of the scale, a team like the 1969 Saints defended the skies like canaries and gave up 17 yards per completion. Their rating was 108.0, one of the worst in history. The average pass defense in today's game rates around 75.0.

The pass defense rating is determined by the following factors:

1) Completion percentage allowed
2) Yards/completion allowed
3) Touchdown passes allowed
4) Interceptions

I ran those numbers through the formula for every defensive team from the modern era (1960-2002) and a picture of the game's true dominators began to emerge.

Two separate groups, however, had to be created because of significant rule changes that had occurred in the game over time. The years 1960-1977 represent pro football's bump-and-run era, when defenses could bang on receivers until the moment the ball was thrown. The headslap was also legal and blockers couldn't extend their arms while pass protecting.

1978-2002 reflects the game's current environment, where the five-yard chuck rule and liberalized blocking rules have given offenses a significant advantage. It's the era of the open skies.

So here are the results, the teams of the Air-Traffic Control Hall of Fame. At the end of this chapter I provide a quick write-up on each of them.

The NFL's Greatest Pass Defenses (pass defense rating)

1960-1977	1978-2002
1) 1970 Vikings (35.5)	1) 1988 Vikings (46.8)
2) 1973 Steelers (36.7)	2) 2002 Buccaneers (47.5)
3) 1963 Bears (36.8)	3) 1978 Broncos (49.3)
4) 1969 Vikings (38.3)	4) 1978 Buccaneers (52.4)
5) 1961 Chargers (39.96)	5) 1981 Buccaneers (52.9)

(**Note**: The 1982 Dolphins rated 43.4 but are disqualified due to the strike-abbreviated schedule played that year.)

• •

When the talk is about the Steelers defense that rampaged through the 1970s, it generally centers around Pittsburgh's front seven, that swirling, suffocating black hole where running games and the five-step drop went to die – Joe Greene, L.C. Greenwood, Dwight White, Jack Ham, Jack Lambert, Andy Russell, those names. The Steel Curtain, hung from thick stakes driven into the line of scrimmage.

The secondary? That was the Steelers' special ops unit. It came to life when The Curtain was trespassed. Its job was to ground enemy aerials and punish crafty runners who had slipped through the barbed wire and the dragon's teeth up front. Here are its members:

• **Mel Blount** – 6'3, 205 lbs of solid muscle and cornerback out of Southern University. His physical, smothering style was often blamed for the eventual illegalization of the bump-and-run. A five-time Pro Bowler, Blount was named the NFL's Defensive MVP in 1975. He took revenge for Oakland's habitually rough treatment of Lynn Swann by pile-driving Raiders receiver Cliff Branch headfirst into the ground in the '76 opener. A Hall of Fame inductee.

• **J.T. Thomas** – Another big, rangy corner – 6'2," 196 lbs. Steelers coach Chuck Noll loved intelligent, fiery players and Thomas, a first-round pick out of Florida State, fit the bill. Not the abuser Blount was but a roughneck with good feet and technique. Stole key passes in '74 AFC Championship and Super Bowl X that helped clinch Pittsburgh victories. Switched to safety after Steelers drafted cornerback Ron Johnson in 1978.

• **Donnie Shell and Glen Edwards** – Both worked the free safety and nickel back positions. Shell joined the Steelers as a nobody free agent from S.C. State and retired with 57 interceptions, third-most in Steelers history. A linebacker in college, he relied on smarts and aggressiveness rather than speed and guesswork. "What made Donnie great was ability to hit and his sharp reaction time," says former Steelers scout Bill Nunn. "Some fast guys run a 4.5 but they react in 4.7; Shell was timed at 4.6, but reacted in 4.4."

"Pine" Edwards came to the Steelers as an undrafted tailback with little chance of making the team. But Chuck Noll saw his great athleticism and rattler-like mean streak which prompted his move to defense. "Edwards was small and wiry, only 175 pounds, but he would light you up," says Nunn. "He had what Shell didn't – speed and quickness." A famous Edwards' highlight features a wicked forearm blast into wideout John Gilliam, which ended a deep Vikings drive in Super Bowl IX.

• **Mike Wagner** – a 6'3" tomahawk who roamed Pittsburgh's secondary for ten solid seasons. An eleventh-round pick out of Western Illinois, Wagner hit rookie training camp with fists flying and by the season opener was named Pittsburgh's starting safety. "We needed a fast, aggressive player, a sure tackler that would help stop the run," said Noll. "Mike came in as a long-shot, but fairly early in camp we saw that he was our man."

Wagner led the NFL with eight interceptions in 1973 and earned Pro Bowl honors in '75 and '76.

"Our quarterback on the defense, a real thinker," Steelers defensive coordinator Woody Widenhofer called him. "But Mike didn't have to think about knocking the hell out of you."

Which is a good lead-in to a conversation with Mr. Wagner. Let's hear about his view from behind the Steel Curtain.

● ● ●

Shakespeare once wrote – evidently after spending a Sunday at Three Rivers Stadium – "Some men are born great, some men acquire greatness, and some men have greatness thrust upon them." Can you apply that observation to your teammates on those awesome Steelers teams of the 1970s?

MW: I don't know if I can identify specific people in that manner. When you define players as being inherently great, particularly at the professional level, you'd have to name the All-Pros and the Hall-of-Famers. They were inherently great football players. Players who were drafted in the top four rounds were great athletes who were expected to be great players. When people like Joe Greene or [Terry Bradshaw were drafted, you knew they were going to be stars. It's a matter of giving them a chance to develop. A lot of those players from the high rounds who didn't make it failed for two reasons – either they didn't have the desire or they got hurt. Chuck Noll had a saying, that "Everybody was a prospect." Training camp was for finding out who the real players were.

Which players had to work hard at becoming great? I'd say anyone drafted from the middle rounds down to the free agents. The person I respected most in terms of working hard to become great was Donnie Shell. He joined the Steelers as a free agent and just kept working at it. He was a linebacker in college then learned the safety position with the Steelers. Donnie had a great attitude and was willing to do anything to contribute to the team.

What about players that had greatness forced upon them?

MW: Well, you'll always have support players. One thing the Steelers coaches and organization didn't do was force players into roles they couldn't perform. They didn't push them. They built the team by letting the players do what they did best. Look at a guy like [TE] Randy Grossman, who was undersized but blocked adequately and had great hands. He was a tough kid, the "go-to" guy sometimes when teams would double-up our receivers. Randy ended up having a wonderful career for the Steelers. He didn't get the acclaim that some other people did. No one ever thinks of Grossman as a key component but the team was sure proud of him.

We had other tight ends that were bigger and stronger than Randy, but it's more than athleticism. It's heart. Who will play when he's hurt, or when things get really tough? Or when he doesn't feel like practicing, or is having a bad day? That's what makes a champion.

You joined the team as an eleventh-round draft pick out of Western Illinois and a long shot to make the roster. Were you even expecting to be drafted into the NFL?

MW: Yeah, I expected to be drafted. Problem was, I had played injured during my whole senior year and it really hurt me in the draft. I'd been clipped during a scrimmage and sprained both ankles. I also had a hip problem that was really acting up. But I felt for a number of reasons that I had a good shot at being drafted. Whether it was high or low didn't matter. If I could stay healthy I knew I could play the pro game. I was very fortunate that in high school and college we played pro defenses. Although the pro game is much more sophisticated and the players are faster and bigger, that wasn't intimidating to me. All I wanted to do was stay healthy and get a chance to show the Steelers what I could do.

Pittsburgh wasn't a powerhouse at that time. The Steelers had a long tradition of losing, so I wasn't enthusiastic about going there. But I viewed it as a tremendous opportunity. Chuck Noll was still cleaning house and making big changes. He was willing to play his young players. If I had been trying to win a spot on of the league's top defenses or secondaries, the odds were good that I would've been traded or cut. But the Steelers' incumbent safety, Chuck Beatty, blew his knee out four plays into the first preseason game so I was thrown in there. That was the beginning of my career. From then on, I got a lot of playing time. Sometimes I played well and sometimes I played like a small-college rookie.

Then in 1972 Chuck brought in some new coaches. Bud Carson, in particular, was one who really created an ideal situation for our defense. He put in the 4-3 and two-zone defense that we played 89-percent of the time. That allowed us to be very successful.

Defense Rules in the Battle of Three Rivers

Outlined against a ghastly gray January sky, the Four Horsemen rode again. You remember them. Lambert, Wagner, Russell and Holmes. Al Davis will remember them. They will be in the nightmares of the Oakland Raiders' owner forevermore. The resilient inner core of the Steeler defense played so well that you knew up there on some heavenly vista, Vince and Knute and Granny and the boys were smiling, nodding and nudging one another in the short ribs.

Defense? No, Deee-fense. Like the Stalingrad winter. The stuff that cut Oakland's rushing average in half and made Ken Stabler a 42-percent passer....

Defense. The primary reason the Steelers put it on Oakland, 16-10, yesterday to win the AFC championship in the wildest, gut-wrenchingest, slam-bangingest football game that you, or I, or the 49,103 cases of frostbite at Three Rivers Stadium ever saw.

A suck-it-up, shut 'em down Valley Forge of a defense that zapped the Raiders nine of the 11 times they crossed midfield to win a long-running, playoff war in which the combatants have met four successive times, the Steelers taking three....

And most pertinently, a defense that broke the heart of Al Davis and anyone else who thought Pride and Poise was a letterhead slogan and not what you had to have when it was late, and the wind was in your face, and the other guys were howling back from the dead.... Which lets Mike Wagner say without a trace of cockiness, "It was a playoff game and we're a playoff team, and we just got together and did a number on them." (January 4, 1976)

- Phil Musick, Copyright 2005, *Pittsburgh Post-Gazette*, all rights reserved.
Reprinted with permission.

What impressed you most about Bud Carson?

MW: He was the most influential coach I ever had with the Steelers. I had a series of tough, strong-minded secondary coaches in high school and college. They were very demanding and I didn't always like that. Bud was demanding too, but he was also willing to teach a little bit. He could adjust his style to whomever his players were, but he was able to convince everybody that his way of playing defense was going to be successful.

Bud Carson was willing to let his players improvise and change his schemes. He had such confidence in our secondary and linebackers. It was really exciting to see the packages he would come up with each weekend. Although the Steelers played a basic defense, Bud was always adding little tweaks to it. He was willing to work with players, but Bud wouldn't back down from anyone. He'd go after a player if he had to. He had many run-ins with Mel Blount. Of course, you worry about that type of tension and conflict within the team, but somehow it brought the best out of us.

A lot of us never showed Carson our appreciation, probably because his temperament sometimes didn't blend well with our personalities. He wasn't the type of guy who said "great job" or "good effort" to the players. We had a couple of other assistant coaches who were always praising their players, and some of us were jealous of that. We sometimes wished that Bud was that way. But I know that all the defensive players have tremendous respect for what Bud Carson did for the team.

Joe Greene, in discussing the Steelers' rise to power, once said, "There was a point, late in 1974, we were in what they call a 'zone.' We could just look at each other out there on the practice field, and everybody knew it. We weren't going to lose. There wasn't a chance." Your thoughts on Greene's statement?

MW: If we were invincible, well, I still remember some real bruising battles. I think Joe was speaking in the right context but back then he always seemed to be in a different spiritual plane. He always had the biggest grin in the toughest matches. He just loved those games. Some of us would be getting bloodied and beaten and be digging down deep, and Joe would be saying, "This is the greatest."

I think defensive linemen look at the game differently than defensive backs. Linemen are always in search-and-destroy mode, trying to hammer on quarterbacks or running backs. Defensive backs are sitting back there in prevent mode, saying, "Gee, I can't give up the big play." I agree with him that we played with a lot of confidence, but I can't say I had the feeling we were invincible, that things were always going to go our way.

There was a period of time – probably from that '74 period through the next four or five years – that no one could really beat us when we were on. Much to our coaches' frustration, a lot of players only played half games. It seemed that some of them had a switch and would turn it on when they had to, many times in the fourth quarter. If you look at all the victories during that time period you'll see a lot of comebacks, where the defense had to play tough late in the game and the offense had to put some points on the board. That's probably where Joe could sense it.

As an offensive coordinator, how would you attack the Steel Curtain? Did that defense have any hidden soft spots?

MW: I was at this football clinic one time, listening to younger quarterbacks debate this very point. They had all the perfect solutions [laughing]. I never saw anybody really clean house on us during that period of time. It was a difficult defense to attack because it was so simple. It was hard for us to make mistakes. To our coaches' credit, they put in a system here that we all loved, that two-zone defense.

I talked to [former Redskins QB] Billy Kilmer once about this. Kilmer told me, "The problem with playing against the Steelers defense was that we knew exactly what you guys were going to do. We would call the perfect play to attack you but you guys would just out-execute us."

The teams that were the most successful probably attacked us by passing because our run defense was smothering, especially the way our big, physical cornerbacks played. You had to have a tight end who was big and fast and could get downfield. The receivers had to be the same way. If you didn't have three players penetrating the secondary, you just couldn't get it done. That was the type of defense we played in the mid'70s. So the simple solution was to change the rules, which the NFL did. After the rule changes of 1978, there were finally ways for teams to attack our defense and have some success.

Do you really believe that the NFL changed its passing rules because of the Steelers defense, or was it simply an effort to improve the overall offensive quality of the game?

MW: Because of our defense! It's been confirmed! Our coaches told us that. The Cowboys' general manager Tex Schramm said they changed the rules because of our corners and linebackers. No longer could you touch the receivers after five yards. We used to jam the receivers and hold onto them, push them into the middle. That kept them from getting deep and allowed more time for the pass rush to get to the quarterback. Our rush was fast anyway, but the routes wouldn't develop and the quarterback would have no place to throw the ball. So they changed the bump rule, as well as some of the pass-blocking rules. Of course, that had a major effect on how we played defense from then on.

Offenses are much more open in today's NFL than they were in the 1970s, particularly in the diversity of the passing game. How do you feel the Pittsburgh defense would have matched up against today's offensive firepower?

MW: That's a tough one to answer, and a lot of it has to do with how the philosophy of defense has changed. We would've probably done things differently than the way teams are playing now. Mel Blount and J.T. Thomas and Ron Johnson would've still jammed the heck out of the receivers then covered them downfield. I think our 225-lb linebackers Ham and Lambert, who both could run, would've done the same thing. One of the reasons why Ham is in the Hall of Fame is because he could cover someone like [Bengals WR] Isaac Curtis all over the field. That would allow the safeties to cover other people or bunch up the middle.

The talent in today's game has changed. Because of the smaller receivers, the defensive backs have gotten smaller too. They're quicker and can stay with them. Then all of sudden a big receiver like the Vikings' Randy Moss comes along. We played against big receivers like him before. You know what we would have done against Randy Moss? We would've fucked him up. *We would have absolutely fucked him up!* We would have hit him on every possible play. But I'm not sure that kind of defensive philosophy exists today. I'm not sure if the rules would permit it.

Quarterbacks? You can't touch them anymore. There weren't too many quarterbacks that finished the game against the Steelers, but there are different rules now. You have to be really careful when you get near the quarterback. So it's really hard to say how our defense would've stacked up. But if you look at some of the athletes that we had, we would've matched up pretty well.

The 100-Yard Badge of Courage

Just how well-tempered was the celebrated Pittsburgh Steelers defense of the 1970s? During the Iron Age - from the fall of 1972 through the winter of 1980 - the Steelers held opponents to ten points or less in 49 of 116 regular season games played; enemy quarterbacks threw for over 200 yards only 24 times; 100-yard rushing days? Forget about it - only twelve were ever conceded.

Here are the top seven rushing performances against that angry Pittsburgh defense. These names should be preserved forever, etched proudly in stone...or steel.

1) September 28, 1975   O.J. Simpson, Buffalo Bills - 28 carries for 227 yards (8.1 avg.)
2) October 19, 1972   O.J. Simpson, Buffalo Bills - 22 carries for 189 yards (8.6)

3) October 4, 1976	Chuck Foreman, Minnesota Vikings – 27 carries for 148 yards (5.5)
4) September 22, 1974	Otis Armstrong, Denver Broncos – 19 carries for 131 yards (6.9)
5) October 14, 1973	Boobie Clark, Cincinnati Bengals – 28 carries for 112 yards (4.0)
6) October 19, 1975	Mike Adamle, Chicago Bears – 17 carries for 110 yards (6.5)
7) December 10, 1979	Earl Campbell, Houston Oilers – 33 carries for 109 yards (3.3)

The AFC Central division had its share of offensive firepower that you faced twice a year – names like Isaac Curtis and Bob Trumpy in Cincinnati, Kenny Burrough and "White Shoes" Johnson in Houston, Reggie Rucker, Dave Logan and Ozzie Newsome in Cleveland. Were any of those receivers visibly intimidated by your defense?

MW: I can't say if we intimidated anyone into getting "gator-arms," where their arms would get real short while looking for the hit. I have more memories of guys we beat on all day who'd still come over the middle to make a tough catch. It wasn't fun for them to come over the middle against us. They knew they were going to take a pounding from us, but most of them hung in there. I have tremendous respect for those receivers because I know that Blount and our corners really pounded them. Bob Trumpy had his helmet twisted around his head a few times but he kept on coming downfield. It wasn't easy for tight ends to run down the middle because they'd get the shit kicked out of them. I question how many of today's receivers could have played during our era.

Most guys in the NFL back then loved to play the game. They loved to challenge us and be tested. Not that they wanted to get knocked around all the time, but the attitude generally was, "Is that the best you can dish out?" There was a tremendous sense of competition. The difference would be if you hurt somebody. That's not intimidation. Physically hurting somebody is not the goal. But if somebody gets their bell rung, sure, they're not going to play as well.

Which receiver did you fear the most?

MW: There was only one that made me nervous – Paul Warfield. Consistently he was the guy that would cause sleeplessness for me. It didn't matter where he lined up. Very rarely did I have to cover him one-on-one because the Steelers were basically a zone team. However, the way to attack the two-deep zone is to run a lot of quick posts. The quarterback would try to pop it in just past the linebackers, then the receiver would head upfield before the safeties could latch onto him. Miami was more than willing to run any of their receivers at those safeties. And Warfield, with his size and talent, was one of the few receivers in the league who could do that effectively.

I always felt totally mismatched against Warfield. He was able to come downfield and make his moves at high speeds. His breakaway speed could easily get him past all of our defensive backs, especially me. On top of that, he was willing to make the tough inside post catches, both short and long, and was willing to come over the middle and take a hit. He was the best I played against by far. When he went over to the WFL for that one season I was really happy. But then he showed again up in Cleveland at the end of his career, so I had to go against him again.

Which offenses were the most difficult for the Steelers to handle?

MW: In terms of schemes, the most difficult for us was the Cincinnati Bengals, especially when Bill Walsh was there...the quick passing attack...the three- and four-receiver sets. Their defensive coordinator went ballistic one year after we beat them in Cincinnati because their quarterback Kenny Anderson went 20 for 22 and they still lost. Anderson set an NFL record but only got 140 yards passing out of it. His longest completion was for about 8 yards.

The other big challenge was the Dallas Cowboys, with all their talent and the way they attacked a defense. They always tried to shake us up, but our coaches insisted we wouldn't let any offense dictate what our defense did. The purpose of Dallas' shifting was to determine whether a defense was in man or zone coverage, and a lot of times defenses would show their hand. But we refused to let that happen. Every time the Cowboys would shift, we would shift our defense into an attack defense and try to screw up [Roger] Staubach's reads. It involved a tremendous amount of effort and preparation – probably more mental than physical – to get ready for those Dallas teams.

Obviously you can think about the other big games we had during that time, against teams like the Raiders or Oilers. Those were all intense, physical games. The Dolphins, during their championship run, were a tough team for us to play. Not a complicated attack but clever, a real test. Bob Griese and Don Shula were as shrewd as can be. They had the threat of Warfield deep, the speed of Mercury Morris around end or off tackle, and Larry Csonka running like an absolute bull. I got to play against Earl Campbell a number of times. He and Csonka were the hardest running backs I ever had to drag down. Once in a while Campbell would try to run around you, but Larry would just try to run over you every time.

Let's discuss the controversy generated by Chuck Noll after the 1976 season opener at Oakland. Referring to a violent, cheap-shot forearm by Raider DB George Atkinson on Lynn Swann, Noll said, "There is a criminal element in every aspect of society. Apparently we have it in the NFL too. People like that should be kicked out of football. It was a criminal act." What were your initial thoughts about that situation?

MW: I thought the whole thing was just a big joke. Football players only care about what happens on the field. The finger pointing, the hoopla, the derogatory comments are fine before and after the game. That's all emotion or frustration, and it has to be viewed in that light. Emotions get high and players have egos. Atkinson and Tatum and the Raiders just wanted to distract our team and to put Noll through some aggravation. That's what it all came down to.

A lot is made about how much hatred and animosity existed between the Steelers and the Raiders. But listen, I went to two Pro Bowls, and what I saw there was Jack Tatum, Dave Casper, Ken Stabler and the rest of those guys were sitting around the bar drinking with the Steeler players, laughing it up like we were best friends! It's a different world that the fans and media don't see. Most of that on-the-field business doesn't continue outside the stadiums.

But Atkinson eventually sued Noll and the Steelers for slander. During the trial, Noll reluctantly admitted that several of his own players – including Mel Blount, Joe Greene and Glen Edwards – fit his definition of "criminal element" in their style of play. What effect did that have on the team?

MW: That whole incident was like an on-going circus. Again, we have to keep this whole thing in perspective. I played pro football, and there's something in me that makes me want to go out and beat on people. I don't know if that is a "criminal" instinct or not. Chuck was probably trying to make light of it. I don't think it was said viciously. It was more of a gut response in a football context. We had very aggressive people on our defense, but Chuck didn't like aggression that involved openly blindsiding someone.

Yet Blount was so offended that he, oddly enough, also filed a slander lawsuit against Noll.

MW: Mel was going through some tough times during that period. He'd been benched a couple of times. He was facing some performance and discipline issues with the team. At some points Mel was reluctant to play within the system, within the defense that was called, and Chuck wasn't happy with that.

We all sometimes think we are smarter than some of the coaches. And sometimes that warrants the coaches having a talk with you, or giving you a seat to see if somebody else can do a better job. Maybe that lawsuit was some retaliation on Mel's side. But he eventually dropped it. The bottom line is that the whole thing ended up blowing over. If you talk to Mel about it now he would just laugh. He loves Chuck.

Most pro football observers acknowledge that the 1976 Steelers turned in the greatest defensive campaign in NFL history. The team started out poorly at 1-4, but over the final nine games the defense turned into Godzilla. Only 28 total points were allowed during that stretch, and there were five shutouts. What are your memories of that incredible effort?

MW: Earlier you mentioned Joe Greene's remark about being in a "zone." *That* was really the time that I felt we were invincible on defense. Not the '74 era. We had our backs against the wall because of a poor start. Then Bradshaw got hurt and our offense was struggling with his backup, Mike Kruczek. As the season went on, it became clearer and clearer that we were going to have to play shutout football and score on defense, to do whatever we could to help our offense.

It became a serious challenge for us. How many games could we go without giving up a point? Can we score on defense? I was always amazed by how well the players in front of me performed. Because of where I was positioned on the field, I always used to tell people I had the best seat in the house. That season we turned the switch on and left it on. We just ran out of steam in the playoffs.

Is there a single play or moment that summarizes the 1976 season for you?

MW: My personal memory of that streak involves the first touchdown we gave up after all those shutouts. It had become a source of pride for the team. We had held five teams in a row without a touchdown, and now Houston was coming into town. They weren't having much of a season, but John Hadl ended up hitting Kenny Burrough with a long bomb for a score. I don't remember if it was my fault or Blount's, but after that play we both felt so bad. No one wanted to give up the first touchdown. But once we did, the whole thing started over again. We rode that feeling through the rest of the season and into the playoffs. We knew that if our offense could give us any kind of scoring punch, we were going to be unbeatable.

It Was Hadl's Comet...then The Streak Was Over

"Playing the Steelers, with that overwhelming defense, was not any fun. They had, in my opinion, the greatest defense that's ever been assembled. As a quarterback you go into those games being concerned about your own people. It was a physical mismatch most of the time. Pittsburgh's front seven played with a lot of reckless abandon because their two corners out there handled one-on-one situations really good. You didn't have a lot of time to get rid of the ball. Their pass rush was ferocious for a good percentage of the game, and that created a timing problem for all quarterbacks who faced them.

"On the touchdown pass I threw at Three Rivers – the one that broke their shutout streak – it was a short-yardage, play-action pass. The defense really came up on the play, figuring we'd give it to Ronnie Coleman or Fred Willis, but Kenny Burrough got behind his man and was wide open when I hit him for the long touchdown. We had to trick 'em. It wasn't like it was 3rd-and-10 and the Steelers were waiting for us to throw it. If that were the case, it wouldn't have happened."

- John Hadl, Houston Oilers QB, 1976-77

Bob Trumpy, the former Bengals tight end, once said, "I've always thought the key to the Steelers' success was coaching. Everyone has built them up over the years to be these monsters who just overpowered people. Hell, they hardly had anybody over 225 [lbs]. I remember how great they were at making adjustments."

MW: Every once in a while some of us, myself included, like to talk about how great we were. We had tremendous talent, and some people think that anybody could have coached that team. That's not true. As I said earlier, Noll built a program that put the right coaches into place, the players in the best positions, and employed the best schemes to take advantage of their abilities. At the same time, he was able to get his players motivated and disciplined enough to perform.

I thought the greatest thing about Chuck Noll was his halftime stuff. There was never any rah-rah. It was more like, "Okay, let's see what we need to do. Let's see what works and what's not working. Let's make the changes and get back out there." It was always very analytical, very low key. He didn't want any "highs and lows" during practice or during the games. He wanted the emotional makeup of the team to be like a straight line. The assistant coaches played their subtle games and handled all the outside forces. Noll was more concerned with discipline through repetition and maintaining a high intensity level on the team. He wanted none of those peaks and valleys. And I think he was absolutely great at achieving it.

How did Noll typically react after a loss?

MW: He would get angry, but there was never any name-calling or screaming or derision. It was more like, "Okay, let's get on the bus and get ready for practice on Tuesday. We'll look at the films and see what we did wrong." It was always very analytical. He'd point out the mistakes and instruct on what should be done the next time. On the sidelines, he might be screaming and yelling, ranting and raving. No one likes that, but that's just the emotion of the game.

I'll also say Chuck was very determined, almost to the point of being stubborn or bullheaded at times. His attitude – which drove all of the fans crazy, and probably some of the players, too – was that if a play was perfectly executed, it would work. He was convinced that execution was the key. It didn't have to be a great play. It didn't matter if the defense knew the play was coming. His attitude was that if you execute, the play will be successful and you'll win. If the play called for a 230-lb guard knocking down a 280-lb defensive end, then that's what had to be done. And our players did it. Grossman knocked down players bigger than him. Jack Ham stood up 280-lb tackles. It was amazing to see what these guys were able to do.

Throughout all of those great victories and championship seasons, Noll was never voted NFL Coach of the Year. When the legendary coaches are discussed you hear names like Bill Walsh and Don Shula, Paul Brown and Tom Landry, Sid Gillman and Vince Lombardi. Rarely is Chuck Noll mentioned. Why not?

MW: From an insider's standpoint, the media doesn't know everything that goes on. They get their information third-hand. They're not the ones in the locker rooms and the trenches, so a lot of what they report is speculation. Chuck Noll was a great coach, one of the best. How can you win four championships and not be? I don't care if you have all the talent in the world; you still have to be able to coordinate it.

A lot of people still second-guess Chuck. They say the Steelers could have been better. Well, we were pretty damn good. He created a defense that is well known in the annals of football. He produced Hall of Fame players on both offense and defense. He's even in the Hall of Fame himself! What more does this guy have to do? On the football field he wasn't the most jovial person. That's why it's so nice to see him in retirement because now he's Mr. Happy Smiley Face. He's enjoying himself. He's a real pleasant guy now, like Santa Claus.

Noll was a different type of coach than Lombardi, but he's on the Lombardi level. I don't know if I could have played for Vince Lombardi. The guy would be screaming at you all the time and I wouldn't have liked that. And I would definitely put Noll ahead of Walsh, who liked to emphasize the importance of his system. Chuck would always make you feel like it was your system, your program.

I have a theory that if you're a professional athlete or coach in a big media market, you've got to schmooze and be responsive to the media. Then, if you're a great coach, you'll be categorized as the greatest. An average player will be known as a better player. And the reverse will also be true. Instead, Chuck held the media respectfully at a distance. He never wanted to go out drinking or golfing with them.

He used the media to basically make his team play better, not to promote himself or the team.

Noll once said that, "Discipline means no guessing." How was he effective in drilling that trait into his football team?

MW: [Laughing] He wasn't talking to me when he said that. Of course, it's really bad when the guys in the secondary become undisciplined because things break down pretty quickly. But Noll's attitude was, "This is how we're going to do it. If you don't want to do it, we'll find somebody who will." He brought people in who would respond to that.

It's hard to play the game of football and be disciplined all the time. What is the definition of a non-disciplined football player, anyway? What coaches would call "guessing," the players would call reacting to a situation that develops on the field. Chuck just wanted consistency.

What drives coaches crazy are players that don't do what they're instructed to do. Behind the so-called "Theory of Discipline" is the fact that coaches simply don't like surprises. However, the players are out there flying around like fighter pilots, zooming around at a thousand miles an hour, thinking, "Yeah, discipline is important, but what I'm doing is going to work." Well, a 190-pound safety might be disciplined enough to try to plug up a tackle trap, but he's going to get killed on every play.

What were some of Noll's shortcomings as a coach? How could Noll have done a better job?

MW: I'm not going to touch that one. I'm not going to go there. I will say, however, that Chuck was a taskmaster. Even though he was a great teacher, I was always intimidated by him. I felt it was better to have him out of our defensive meetings. Our whole defense played better without him being directly involved. Chuck's strength was being a head coach and a motivator. It was difficult when he would step in and start coaching the linebackers or secondary. We were more relaxed, better able to concentrate, when he wasn't directly involved.

One of the few controversial moments of your career involved a hit you made on Houston tight end Mike Barber in the 1978 AFC Championship. Barber angrily accused you of trying to destroy his knees while he stretched for an uncatchable pass that sailed over his head. What are your memories of that incident?

MW: Did you see the play?

Yes, several times.

MW: Well, what are your memories?

I saw Dan Pastorini throw a deep pass that sailed high over Barber's outstretched arms. You came from Barber's left and slammed into his thigh, just above the knee. Basically, you wiped him out on what was basically an uncatchable ball. Then some time later, while you were hospitalized for an injury, Barber came looking for you.

MW: It's just an incident from my past that people most remember about me. We beat the Oilers pretty badly in that game, and the Houston media didn't have much to talk about so they made a big deal of it. I don't believe I hit Barber above the knee. I think I hit him around the ankle with my shoulder pad, but I was hoping he'd jump over me. There was no flag thrown on the play. I went over to Barber to apologize and see if he was all right, but he wasn't satisfied with that. He continued to make a big deal about it.

If you really want to know what happened, you should talk to Mike Barber. That story about him coming to the hospital was nothing more than him coming to apologize for some things he said after the incident. I talked to him about it later. I wasn't happy with all the accusations he made about me intentionally trying to hurt him.

Could I have missed him, gotten out of his way? Like I told you before, in our defense tight ends over the middle were fair game. If the ball is coming down the field and the tight end is flying down the middle, then it's time to buckle up. It's football we're playing here, son, not volleyball.

Between 1974 and 1979, Pittsburgh was NFL champion four times. But by 1980 the team had slipped to 8-8 and some serious cracks began to emerge in its foundation. That year the Steelers missed the playoffs for the first time since 1971. Here's a quote from running back Rocky Bleier on the end of the Pittsburgh dynasty:

"If you asked everybody on that team, 'Do you want to win?' they all would have said, 'Yes, we want to win.'
"If you asked them, 'Would you like to win?' they would have said, 'Yes, we'd like to win.'
"But if you asked, 'Do you want to commit yourself, to go the extra mile?' the answer probably would have been 'Well, I don't know. We've already done that.' That's when you knew the edge was gone."

When did your instincts tell you that the great Steelers run had ended?

MW: Our defense had been struggling. We were getting a little long in the tooth, and some players were playing with chronic injuries, including me. Personally, I didn't feel I could play championship football for the Steelers anymore. I had come into the '80 season with some hip problems and I never really got up to full strength or speed. In the opener against Houston, I cracked two ribs. By the end of 1980 I was pretty beat up. I was thinking, *If I can't play a full season at an All-Pro level, then maybe it's time to get out.* Some of the other players probably had similar thoughts. As a group, we didn't play with the same level of intensity that we had a couple of years earlier. The armor was starting to fall off.

Sports Illustrated's *Paul Zimmerman once wrote, "Age ended [the dynasty] in Pittsburgh...Noll was loyal to his old vets and perhaps he held onto them just a year or two too long, a tribute to him as a human being but not as a member of the corporate world of coaching." Do you agree with that perspective?*

MW: I don't think that's an accurate analysis. I've heard that before and it surprises me that someone would think that way. That wasn't the way Chuck Noll ran a football team. Noll always put the best players he could find at the position. He could make tough decisions. For some of the players, it was just the opposite. They thought they could still play a few more seasons, but Chuck kinda opened the door before they wanted to leave.

In terms of replacing the old veterans, I don't think there was a lot of great talent waiting in the wings, so in certain circumstances Noll may not have had any choice. One time late in my career I was hurt, limping around the field with a hip problem. I said, "I gotta get out of the game." Joe Greene said to me, "No, I want you out here. You playing hurt is better than what would come on the field to replace you."

The thing that the public didn't really recognize, that no one talked about, was the number of coaching defections we had during those years. Assistants like George Perles, Bud Carson, Lionel Taylor and Dan Radakovich all left at some point. I think that really affected the team. When we played Los Angeles in the '79 Super Bowl, two or three Steeler coaches from the previous year were on the Rams' side of the field. That kind of thing doesn't get any play with the public or the media. Assimilating new assistant coaches into our system was probably harder for Noll than for the team itself, but it was another major factor that contributed to the eventual downfall. Anyway, they say all good things come to an end, don't they?

• • • •

The Air-Traffic Control Hall of Fame

The lower a team's pass defense rating, the more difficulty you have throwing against it. For instance, in 2004 the NFL's toughest team to pass on was the Buffalo Bills, which compiled a stingy rating of 58.9. The worst belonged to Kansas City, where air travel went essentially unimpeded; the Chiefs' rating was 95.2.

(For comparison purposes, the league average that year was 79.2.)

Here then, as promised, is a recap of the teams with the best pass defense ratings over the past 45 seasons.

The Bump-and-Run Era (1960-1977)

1) 1970 Minnesota Vikings (35.5 pass defense rating): The champion of the ratings game. Their cornerbacks were Bobby Bryant and Ed Sharockman, the safeties Karl Kassulke and Paul Krause. No team made a living throwing the ball against Bud Grant's Vikings, which featured a big secondary – not a member under 6-feet – and rangy, efficient linebackers.

Minnesota's defense created a thick purple shadow in 1970 and watched the efforts of the NFL's best disappear into it...Len Dawson, 18 of 27, 164 yds...Bart Starr, 8 of 16, 32 yds...Roger Staubach, 9 of 16, 109 yds...Roman Gabriel, 10 of 21, 61 yds. The Vikes allowed only 9.2 yards/catch that season (the league average was 13.2), still the fewest in modern football history.

One Hall of Fame QB, however, doesn't buy into this pass-rating business, and has a drastically different opinion of the Vikings defenders. "Minnesota had one of football's worst secondaries, and I don't care what the statistics say," barks Dawson. "Their cornerbacks were average at best. The key to that defense, by far, was their great defensive line, with Alan Page, Carl Eller and Jim Marshall. *Those* were the guys that created all the problems for quarterbacks, not their secondary."

The Vikings' pass defense rating against Dawson? In three meetings, it was 62.6. Dawson lit up Minnesota when it mattered most – 12 for 17, 142 yards in Super Bowl IV – but the purple guys worked him over pretty good in the other two games. The truth about these misunderstood Vikings is probably hidden in a deep cave somewhere in Norway. Right next to those Super Bowl rings which never came.

2) 1973 Pittsburgh Steelers (36.7): Most people would expect to see the legendary '75 or '76 versions of their defense in this spot instead, but '73 wins it. The booster shot was Pittsburgh's league-leading 37 interceptions that it collected that year, still the team record. Over 10% of all passes thrown against them were stolen.

"Our success was derived mainly from our pass rush," says Chuck Noll. "We still didn't have the exact personnel we wanted in our defensive backfield (forgettables like John Dockery, Dennis Meyer and John Rowser still held roster spots), but by shutting down the run and pressuring the quarterback we created opportunities for our secondary."

That's Noll's typical press-release version of the story. Here are the bloody details:

Week 1 vs. Detroit: Greg Landry's first look at the Steel Curtain ends in 11 of 27 with 3 interceptions.
Weeks 2 and 11 vs. Cleveland*:* Mike Phipps gets picked off six times in two games with much frustration.
Weeks 3 and 13 vs. Houston: Dan Pastorini and Lynn Dickey are squeezed for 7 INTs in two ugly losses.
Week 6 vs. NY Jets: A rookie named Bill Demory is sacrificed to the Steel gods (6 of 15 with 3 INTs).
Week 9 at Oakland: Humiliation comes to Daryle Lamonica in the form of five sacks, four interceptions and two intentional groundings into the Oakland mud.
Week 14 at San Francisco: The Brodie/Reed/Spurrier QB trio combines for five interceptions.

This version of the Steelers didn't win the Super Bowl, but during the fall of 1973 the skies over Pittsburgh were shut down and all runways closed for landing.

3) 1963 Chicago Bears (36.8): The splintering gang of marauders that Boyd Dowler nodded to earlier. Statistically, an effort almost identical to the '73 Steelers' – bunches of interceptions (36), scattered TD passes (10) and only 146 yards/game allowed through the air. Chicago benefited from assistant coach George Allen's crafty man/zone/nickel combination coverages brought over from his years directing the Rams. The cornerbacks were Dave Whitsell and Bennie McCrae. Both Bears safeties, Rosey Taylor and Richie Petitbon, played at a Pro Bowl level, as did aging linebacker Joe Fortunato.

"What a job it was in practice, trying to get open against that wrecking crew," said former tight end Mike Ditka. Former Lions and Steelers coach Buddy Parker once called Chicago's secondary the best he had ever seen.

Their efforts peaked in the NFL title game, as Chicago smothered the vaunted Giants air attack, forcing quarterback Y.A. Tittle (60.2% completions, 36 TD passes in 1963) into a miserable 11 for 29, five-interception afternoon. Remember the famous snapshot of the bloodied Tittle kneeling in the frozen mud of Wrigley Field? That one was taken after a 12-yard *completion!* (Just fooling.)

4) 1969 Minnesota Vikings (38.3): Close your eyes and think of the '69 Vikes, Minnesota's first Super Bowl team. What do you see? Quarterback Joe Kapp's fluttering knuckleballs somehow finding their mark? A raging defensive line crumbling passers with brutal charges and lunging forearms? 168-lb safety Bobby Bryant springing into the air like Peter Pan, snatching one of his eight interceptions?

I think of the Vikings' capricious twelfth man from late that season – the soggy, sloppy weather – and the havoc it lent to an already great defensive team. Snow and mud in Detroit on Thanksgiving; whiteout conditions against the 49ers, with those wacky flaming lawnmowers the stadium crew used to thaw the field; the giant mud bog in Atlanta that nearly swallowed both teams. Opposing passers threw just one touchdown pass against Minnesota in those three games, a one-yard flip from SF's Steve Spurrier to Ted Kwalick.

In '69, the Vikings built themselves a fortress with a roof on it. Opposing quarterbacks were sacked 49 times. Only eight passes went for touchdowns against them, while 30 were intercepted. The average completion gained less than 10 yards. It was a tremendous, inspired effort. Then Mother Nature blustered in wearing her shoulder pads.

5) 1961 San Diego Chargers (39.96): A lonely, old AFL antique that's been begging to be dusted off. Everyone thinks of that scorching offensive attack when the talk is of coach Sid Gillman's early 'Bolts, but the Powder Blue could play some defense, too. Gillman lauded the play of three star rookies – defensive linemen Earl Faison and Ernie Ladd and linebacker Chuck Allen – for ratcheting up big pressure at the line of scrimmage. Quarterbacks were roused and tumbled, routes were snipped short, and the big payoff came in the form of 49 dizzying interceptions, nine which were returned for scores. Both marks still stand as NFL records.

"One of the benefits from developing a strong passing attack," said Gillman years later, "is that you also develop a pretty good idea of how to shut one down."

Honorable mention: '73 Dolphins (40.6), '67 Packers (42.4), '62 Packers (42.5), '71 Vikings (42.9)

◆◆◆

The Run-and-Gun Era (1978-2002)

1) 1988 Minnesota Vikings (46.8): So *this* is the NFL's stingiest pass defense over the last twenty-five years? A Vikings team that lost to 4-12 Green Bay – twice! – and at 6-10 Miami? The same defense that, at the end of their NFC playoff game in San Francisco, lay in shredded ribbons at the feet of Joe Montana, 34 to 9 losers? Those Vikings?

The numbers say so. It's a situation, however, that calls for further dissection.

Scanning over the Vikings' schedule from that year, one can quickly see where this is all heading. It was the soft-serve special. Seven of Minnesota's 16 games came against punching bags like Green Bay, Tampa Bay, Detroit and Dallas, a padded gauntlet with a combined record of 16-48.

A look at the quality of quarterbacks that challenged them is even more revealing. Minnesota spent nine weekends – over half its games – defending against the likes of Vinny Testaverde (1988's interception king), Don Majikowski, Randy Wright, Rusty Hilger, Chuck Long, Kevin Sweeney, Dave Wilson and the remains of Steve Grogan (age 35). That passel of passers ended the season with a combined QB rating of 56.4; against the Vikings, it was a sickly 24.5.

This is quickly turning into a diatribe, a knock against a valid 11-5 playoff team, and it shouldn't be. Make no mistake, the Vikings could bring some heat on defense. They could destroy pass pockets and erase passing lanes, most notably through linemen Chris Doleman and Keith Millard and SS Joey Browner, a six-time Pro Bowler. Corner Carl Lee had his moments, too. The Vikes picked off Dan Marino three times in Miami that year, and greedy deep-ballers like Jim Kelly and Randall Cunningham were allowed only rations of bread and water.

But in '88 the schedulers fell asleep, so it's easy to be skeptical about the Vikings' lofty place in history. But...sigh...the numbers say it's so. Lies and damned lies.

2) 2002 Tampa Bay Buccaneers (47.5): "Give us a ball-control offense and we'll rule the world," frustrated Buccaneer defenders cried over and over. Tony Dungy constructed a monster of a defense during his years coaching the team (1996-2001), one spiked with seven growling Pro Bowlers and feet of lightning. It roamed in packs, constantly near the crest of the NFL's rankings.

But Dungy's offenses were often his team's downfall, punchless, erratic units that averaged more than 20 points/game only twice. His defense often grew weary trying to protect the shallow leads handed over to it.

Then new head coach John Gruden arrived and righted things in one season. His quarterback, Brad Johnson, became the NFC's most efficient passer almost overnight. His offense averaged 22 points/game, outscoring opponents 124-41 in the fourth quarter. It controlled the football and committed only 21 turnovers, a franchise record. And so the defensive beast, with names like Brooks and Sapp and Barber and Lynch, could finally close out games on rested legs. The result was a season of tyranny.

"Gruden was the difference," said offensive line coach Bill Muir. "He's the consummate salesman, and his enthusiasm was infectious. He's like the carnival barker, selling his $1.25 bottle of snake oil that cures everything."

In 2002, Tampa Bay's defense allowed the league's fewest points, first downs, passing yards and TD throws. It intercepted the most passes (31) while hoarding 43 sacks. It surrendered a single touchdown in the NFC playoffs, then in the Super Bowl shattered Oakland's top-rated passing attack like an angry fist through a windshield.

Their new captain stood and grinned as the Buccaneer flag was raised over the battlefield. It was, as the Super Bowl bounty was carried off, a promise kept.

3) 1978 Denver Broncos (49.3): "Speed is what I remember about that team," says former Bengals receiver Isaac Curtis. "Most great defenses have it, and so did the Broncos."

The key was a quartet of versatile linebackers that wreaked havoc on the designs of opposing offenses. Inside territory was patrolled by fiery Joe Rizzo and Randy Gradishar, a 6'3" jackhammer who was named the NFL's defensive MVP in '78. "What made Gradishar great was his uncanny sense of anticipation," says former 49ers quarterback John Brodie, "a sixth sense that helped him disrupt a heckuva lot of plays."

The outside linebackers, Bob Swenson and Tom Jackson, were the wildcards in coordinator Joe Collier's dynamic 3-4 system. It wasn't uncommon to see Swenson blitzing off the corner or stunting inside while Jackson sped downfield covering a wideout like a third cornerback. As a whole, the Orange Crush stole 31 interceptions and allowed just nine touchdown passes all season. Only 12.4 points/game were scored against them.

"Three guys come to mind from that Denver team," says former Bengals WR Isaac Curtis. "Tommy Jackson is the first. I can see him flying from sideline to sideline, hitting everything in sight. He wasn't a big guy (5-11, 228) but he was smart. He knew the game, spent a lot of time in the classroom. He was fast enough to cover the outs and hooks and crosses.

"Then there was Louis Wright, a big corner who could push you around, disrupt your routes. Smart, too. You really had to work hard getting open against him. That whole Denver defense was just full of athletes."

Weren't there *three* Broncos that you specifically remember?

"Oh, yeah. Steve Foley, another big defensive back. I shouldn't forget him. One time he blasted me coming across the middle and broke my face in three different places."

4) 1978 Tampa Bay Bucs (52.4): Now things take a big turn for the weird. Our fourth spot is held by a motley bunch, a 5-11 outfit that was two years removed from expansion status. The '78 Bucs finished last in the NFC Central, lost to the 2-14 49ers and.... Hey, wait a minute...*another* NFC Central team? What's going on here? And look – *so is the next one on the list!*

As a matter of fact, seven of the ten teams profiled in this section have roots to or from the old NFC Central division, something way beyond coincidental. Here I am, trying to line up phone calls to former defenders Cecil Johnson and Jeris White, to see what kind of magic the ol' Bucs were using, and instead have stumbled into some kind of statistical anomaly. One should wonder – did they always play great defense in that division, or was bad quarterbacking in on it, too?

A quick roll call of the passers Tampa faced in '78: Jerry Golsteyn, Joe Pisarcik, Tony Adams, Bob Avellini, Gary Danielson, Bill Munson, Scott Bull, Steve DeBerg, David Whitehurst...you get the picture.

This isn't a story about a great, oppressive defense. It's more like a menu, a list of all-you-can-eat quarterback hors d'oeuvres. And Tampa Bay's plate was full of them.

Lies and more lies, Part II.

5) 1981 Tampa Bay Bucs (52.9): The tone was set on opening day. Minnesota trailed the Bucs 14-13 with 35 seconds left. They needed a half dozen more yards to set up a chippie, game-winning field goal. The play called for a short sideliner to Terry LeCount, who hoped to slip out of bounds and stop the clock.

"They'd been running that dinky down-and-out all night," said Bucs cornerback Neal Colzie. "A smart defensive player would have seen what was coming." Colzie jumped the route and it was a one-man race to the endzone, 82 yards for the clincher.

Tampa Bay would intercept 32 passes that season, a surprisingly high number for a team that could only generate marginal pressure on the quarterback.

An even more impressive footnote – the average return on all those Buccaneer interceptions was 20.3 yards. CB Cedric Brown took one back 81 yards for a touchdown versus Green Bay... rookie Hugh Green had a 50-yard return in a game....

The Buccaneers became Central Division winners on the strength of their gambling, knock-'em-out pass defense. They allowed barely over 10 yards/catch, stingiest in the league. Only one quarterback threw for over 300 yards against them (San Diego's Dan Fouts).

But all weaknesses are exposed in the playoffs, and it became true for Tampa. Offensively, the Bucs couldn't run the football. They couldn't stop it either, and their playoff opponent, the Dallas Cowboys, knew it. The last number we need to mention here is the score from that game – Dallas 38, Tampa Bay 0.

Honorable Mention: '80 Redskins (54.1), '79 Chargers (54.3), '78 Steelers (54.9), '86 49ers (55.4)

— 17 —
Curt Gowdy, Broadcaster
NBC Sports (1966-79)
February 11, 1998

The first football game that Curt Gowdy ever broadcast wasn't kicked off at the Rose Bowl or Yankee Stadium or any other grand old venue that suited a voice of such esteem. It was played in a vacant lot, a place where you'd expect to find tumbleweeds or a rusty can or a limping stray dog with a sad face.

There were no fancy bleachers or concession stands. No stripes marked off the yardage or sidelines. No pumped-up crowds (only fifteen people watched). Not even enough players to fill out two complete teams.

"They played six-man football in zero degree weather," remembers Gowdy. "St. Mary's High versus Pine Bluffs. Both teams showed up on the same bus. They still have to play the game that way in some parts of the West. There aren't enough people around."

It was Cheyenne, Wyoming, 1943, a place once settled as a train stop for the Union Pacific railroad. And Gowdy, the man we came to know as the legendary voice of NBC Sports, was coming off painful back surgery and wondering what to do with a life that had been granted a reprieve from duty in World War II.

"I'd been in the ROTC at the University of Wyoming, a second lieutenant," says Gowdy. "It was an infantry unit they eventually trained for assault landings. After graduation I changed direction and enlisted to become a fighter pilot.

"I'd injured my back playing basketball in college but really didn't know the severity of it. Then the day before I was to leave for the service, I was cutting my parents' lawn when I felt something pop. Then I hurt it again during calisthenics at Camp Edwards in Cape Cod. Down I went. Spent six months in the hospital with a ruptured disc. They eventually gave me a medical discharge."

It was a lucky piece of paper. About half the boys in his unit died on the beaches in Italy.

Doctor's orders were to stay at home, no work or stress for another six months. It became a lonely, depressing time for Gowdy. "I felt kinda lost. I had no idea what I was going to do with my life. Maybe try to get into business."

Then one afternoon a strange phone call came. It was Bill Grove, the manager of KFBC, the Cheyenne radio station, with an out-of-the-blue proposal. He offered Gowdy five dollars to broadcast a high school football game for him. ("I remembered him from the Wyoming basketball team," Grove had said. "Curt was one of the few sports guys still left around town. Everyone else was off fighting the war.")

Gowdy was hesitant. "I didn't know a damn thing about broadcasting. Grove told me, 'Look, either you do it or my wife and I will, and neither of us has ever seen a football game before.' My mother finally talked me into it. She drove me down to the game the next day, about nine blocks from our house."

Down to that vacant lot. The setup was sparse, almost pathetic – two goal posts stuck in the ground and two soap boxes on an alleged sideline. One box was for a microphone, the other for Gowdy.

A stranger was standing there waiting for him. His name was Dick Lane. "I'm here to do the commercials," he said. Ten sponsors had paid $5 apiece for the privilege.

Gowdy asked the coaches for their rosters but there were none. The players wore no numbers, either. Time for panic? "Not really. I just started making up names, guys I knew from college and the Air Force... McCarthy...Hancock...Volker.... I guess they liked what they heard. Grove later told me I was a natural and hired me to do Cheyenne High basketball games. Eventually it turned into a salary of $30 a week."

Three years later Oklahoma came calling. "The general manager from KOMA in Oklahoma City was driving to Denver one night and he picked me up on the radio. Then he called me at home at 11:00 at night, wanting to meet with me. We met for breakfast. Eventually he offered me the radio play-by-play job for Oklahoma football that upcoming fall."

Oklahoma football was a big-time gig back in 1946. ("Bud Wilkinson was still an unknown assistant when I got there.") So was New York Yankees baseball in 1949, Gowdy's next stop, followed by the Boston Red Sox in '51. His Boston stint lasted 15 years.

"Fenway was always my favorite park to broadcast in," he says. "You felt like you were part of the game. The booth was low and to the left of home plate. You could almost reach down and touch the guy on deck."

Gowdy's Wyoming roots and western ways earned him the nickname "Cowboy," and his career carried him across all three major networks, through nine Super Bowls, 13 World Series, 14 Rose Bowls, 24 Final Fours and eight Olympics. But if there's one call from that rustic, corduroy voice which still echoes in my head, it was the one he made on the afternoon of December 21, 1974, the one that declared my beloved Miami Dolphins officially dead for the season. It was a crime scene, and Gowdy may as well have wrapped the Oakland-Alameda County Coliseum in yellow tape.

"Here he is, fading, looking... looking... looking...he's under the gun...he's caught.... he throwwwws! Touchdown!! Un-believable!!"

Yeah, it was unbelievable, all right. Kenny Stabler, the Raiders' Houdini of a quarterback, had squeezed off an eight-yard shot-put fling of a pass with 35 seconds to play. It should've been intercepted or knocked away. Instead, Clarence Davis, a running back with feet for hands, caught it for a touchdown between two crunching Miami defenders.

"A dumb play," Stabler admitted in the locker room. "I never should've thrown it."

"A miracle," says Gowdy. "Stabler was full of 'em."

"Under the gun" was one of Gowdy's signature gameday expressions. He'd use it when things were getting tight and the pressure was starting to break in one team's favor. Joe Namath was under the gun while he led his underdog Jets against Baltimore in Super Bowl III. ("The greatest upset ever," Gowdy proclaims.)

The Steelers' Terry Bradshaw was under the gun as he let fly that desperate heave that bloomed into The Immaculate Reception.

Miami's Garo Yepremian was under the gun as he concentrated before a kick on Christmas Day, 1971, trying to beat the Chiefs in pro football's longest game. So was Oakland's Dave Casper in the '77 playoffs, with his over-the-shoulder, do-drop-in touchdown that stunned the Colts.

Old games. Historic games. Gowdy was there, behind a shiny NBC microphone, for all of them.

And everyone watched and listened as this Cowboy, once under the gun himself in that empty Cheyenne lot years ago, called out the action through sights which rarely wavered.

• • •

Like most broadcasters from your era, your roots began in radio. Baseball and basketball were your early mainstays. When did you begin doing football games on television?

CG: Paul Christman and I started out doing the college football *Game of the Week* for ABC in 1960 and '61. ABC had outbid NBC for the right to broadcast these college games, even though they didn't even have a sports department at the time. It was a huge upset, almost like the way Fox took away pro football from CBS. Everybody was shocked, including the NCAA. Roone Arledge, who was about 31 years old then, was the producer. We did a helluva job on those games. In fact, Bill McPhail, the former president of CBS Sports, later told me, "I used to have my people watch you and take notes because you were revolutionizing how to cover football." Our theory at ABC was, "Don't take the game to the fans, but bring the fans into the game." We wanted to bring them into the locker room, onto the field. Take them places they've never been before.

Then in 1962, ABC lost college football to CBS. CBS liked my work and offered me the job to do the play-by-play for them, but I still had another year to go on my ABC contract. So I asked ABC, "What kind of work am I going to do if I stay?" Their response was that they were going to put me and Paul on the American Football League. Well, Christman was very unhappy about that. He took it almost as an insult, like he'd be taking a step backwards in his career. The AFL was struggling and not very well respected by the public.

Finally I talked Paul into doing the games with me, and we had a lot of fun. It was a challenge at first, but it was also a very exciting time, watching that young league come on. Every year you could see the AFL getting better and better. We covered the games from '62 through '65, but then ABC gave up the AFL rights. So NBC jumped in and grabbed it.

Joe Foss, the AFL commissioner, and couple of owners asked us if we were interested in moving over to NBC. I said, "Yeah, I like doing the AFL." I went back to Roone to talk about things and he said, "Stay put, Curt. We'll eventually get pro football back at ABC." I said, "You probably will, but I'd like to do football now." So they let us go. That's how Paul and I wound up at NBC, right after they picked up the AFL package in 1966.

Casey at the Bat? No, He's at the Bar

I've met a lot of characters over the years, but I'd have to say that [former NY Yankees/Mets manager] Casey Stengel was probably the funniest guy I ever met. I'll tell you a story. It was 1949, his first year as manager for the team and my first year broadcasting Yankees games. We were in Cleveland playing the Indians for a series and we went out for a drink after a game. Stengel ordered a draft beer and knocked it down in one big gulp. I looked at him and said, "Holy hell, Casey! You really drink fast!"

He said, "I've been drinking that way ever since the accident."

I never heard about Casey being in an accident. I said, "You were in an accident?"

Casey said, "Yeah, somebody knocked over my beer."

- **Curt Gowdy**

During the developmental stages of ABC's Monday Night Football, you were offered a chance to return to the network as the show's first play-by-play man. Why didn't that come to fruition?

CG: It was 1970 and Arledge called me up, asking me to come to New York for an important meeting. He said, "Curt, we just got this Monday Night package. It's going to be the biggest thing in sports, and we want you to do the play-by-play." I said, "But I have two more years to go on my contract with NBC. And besides, they hate you guys over there. NBC isn't going to let me go." Arledge said, "Well, ask them anyway. Tell them you're unhappy and maybe you can work something out. We'd really like to have you back."

So I called Carl Lindemann, who was the vice-president of NBC Sports at the time. I went over to his office and told him I was interested in leaving for Monday Night Football. God, he really kicked up a storm. He threatened to sue me. He could have, too, since I was still under contract. At that point I just said forget it. I could see I wasn't going to be able to get out of the contract. I called Arledge back and said, "It's not going to happen. NBC is dead set on me finishing my contract here." I would've loved to have worked on Monday Night Football, but it just wasn't meant to be.

The three-man team has been in vogue for sports broadcasting over the past few years. In the mid-1970s, you had shared the booth with Al DeRogatis and Don Meredith at NBC. What was it like in that booth? Was three a crowd?

CG: No, I enjoyed that experience very much, but more because of my colleagues than the arrangement itself. Al was very knowledgeable, one of the best analysts I've ever worked with. He had great insight about football. And I got along great with Meredith, too. He was a fun guy and we became very good friends. I had a lot of fun working with both of them.

But I'm of the belief that the broadcast booth is really a two-man place. When you're doing play-by-play with three men in the booth, you're really nothing more than a traffic cop. You sit there thinking, "Should I lay out? Should I come in?" There's a lot of talk going on in the booth. The networks say that sports is show business now and having three guys is necessary, but the broadcast is still most effective when you have just a good play-by-play man and a good analyst. Look at how successful Madden and Summerall are. Why do you need a third guy? If anything, he should be down on the field reporting, not up in the booth.

You worked with Meredith at NBC from 1974 through the '76 season. But, during his years on Monday Night Football he was a frequent target of Howard Cosell. He trashed Meredith's work ethic, once saying that he was "worth his weight in irreverence." Did you have the same impressions of Dandy Don?

CG: Don Meredith was a fun guy with a great personality. It's true, however, that he wasn't a very well-prepared broadcaster. He didn't study game films or read everything about the teams that he could get his hands on. He didn't do any of that stuff. He was just a free spirit who called the game as it came along. His personality carried him during the broadcast. I was the one who eventually talked him into at least buying a briefcase. But I do know that he worked harder with us at NBC than he did on Monday Night Football.

NBC fired your partner DeRogatis after the 1975 season. What were the circumstances surrounding his dismissal?

CG: I don't know why they let Al go. I was very unhappy when I found out he wasn't going to be teamed up with me anymore. However, Al was having a lot of problems with his eyes at that time. He had glaucoma and a detached retina, and it got to the point that he couldn't see very well, so maybe that had something to do with it.

As a partner I thought Al was very good. He was very astute on football. He was a good analyst and had a lot of guts. But as a fan, you either liked him or you didn't. He had a voice that a lot of people didn't like. Al made a great call on Super Bowl III. Just before the kickoff I asked him, "How do you see this game turning out?"

He responded, "If the Jets gain over 100 yards on the ground, they will beat Baltimore." Well, Matt Snell made over 100 yards himself, and the Jets ended up winning the game.

Our last game together was the 1975 AFC Championship game, Oakland at Pittsburgh. Probably some executive high up there decided it was time for a change and got rid of him. In those days, the networks kept changing faces, bringing in new people and new faces. Nowadays, the old guys seem to stay around longer. They're allowed to hang on and on.

Several teams carved out great legacies during the decade of the 1970s – Don Shula's Dolphins, Chuck Noll's Steelers, Tom Landry's Cowboys. Did you have a favorite team from that era, one that you enjoyed covering most?

CG: The best team I ever broadcast, and still the best team I've ever seen in pro football, was the Pittsburgh Steelers of the 1970s. They intimidated other teams. They were dominant. Not only were they the best defensive team in the game, but they had a great offense as well. They were superbly coached and well-balanced. I enjoyed doing Steelers games as much as any team in the NFL. I enjoyed going to the Orange Bowl for Miami games, too. Don Shula was always fair to me. None of those coaches ever tell you any inside stuff, but Shula always answered my questions.

The 1972 Dolphins were undefeated and untied, yet they're rarely recognized as being the greatest team in NFL history. You covered a number of Miami games during their great run in that decade. How would you rate that '72 team?

CG: Miami had a great team, but I don't think they were as good as the Steelers. They had a smart quarterback in Bob Griese. They had Jim Kiick coming off the bench on third down. They had a wild bull at fullback in Larry Csonka. They'd put in Mercury Morris, who was a dazzling runner with great speed, to get to the outside. They had that good offensive line, and that No-Name defense. Shula put together an excellent team, probably one of the three or four best that ever played the game. But I still don't think they were as good as the Steelers teams.

DeRogatis made another amazing statement that I'll never forget. It was real early in the '70s, before the Dolphins became really good. We were doing a game in the middle of the season and he said, "Curt, right here is the next great team in pro football." He was talking about the Dolphins.

I asked, "Why do you say that?"

He said, "Because they're building an excellent offensive line. You can see it developing."

An offensive line takes time to build, whereas on defense you just pin your ears back and go after people. But he predicted their greatness just by recognizing the development of their offensive line...Jim Langer...Kuechenberg...Larry Little....

You spent a lot of Sunday afternoons in the Oakland-Alameda County Coliseum, covering the Raiders with their Silver and Black war paint.

CG: Well, the Raiders were sort of special in those days, a very colorful, exciting bunch. They pulled more games out of the fire and had more dramatic wins than any other team, especially when they were playing at home. I became very friendly with their owner Al Davis. That didn't make me get on the air and favor the Raiders – I always tried to call games down the middle – but Oakland was a great team to broadcast.

The Raiders were a bunch of renegades. They picked up a lot of guys that other people didn't want and made them into great players. The people out in the Bay Area loved 'em. A lot of their games they pulled out in the last minute, with Stabler taking them 80 yards to win it. They had great wide receivers in Biletnikoff and Branch, a good running game, and a terrific offensive line with Upshaw and Shell. The left side of that Raider line was the best in pro football. If you don't have an offensive line in the pros, you can forget it. The Raiders had one of the best.

You must remember the furor surrounding Chuck Noll's remarks after the '76 season opener, Pittsburgh at Oakland. It was a game you covered with Meredith, and there were some vicious, unnecessary hits on Pittsburgh's receivers that day, particularly Lynn Swann.

After the game, Noll was quoted as saying, "You have a criminal element in all aspects of society. Apparently we have it in the NFL, too." Do you feel there was a criminal element on those Raider teams, considering their aggressive, roughneck style of play?

CG: No, I just think they played the game hard and to the hilt. I don't think they really set out to murder anybody or hurt them. They had Jack Tatum and George Atkinson back there, both who were tough guys. They had that defensive end, Ben Davidson, and one of the most underrated players in the game in Ted Hendricks. I know Hendricks is in the Hall of Fame but I say he was *still* underrated. "The Mad Stork" blocked more kicks than anybody in the history of the game. He was a helluva linebacker.

What was your favorite rivalry in the AFC during the 1970s?

CG: There were two: Oakland-Pittsburgh and Oakland-Kansas City. Oakland and Pittsburgh met mostly in the playoffs, at least that's where their most memorable games were played. The Steelers beat them in that Immaculate Reception game. Oakland beat them twice in '76, the first year they won the Super Bowl. The

Steelers' top two running backs, Franco Harris and Rocky Bleier, were injured and didn't even play in the '76 championship game. Without them, Pittsburgh was really weakened. But all those Steeler-Raider games were brutal. Big games. Tough and intimidating. That's the best way to describe them.

Oakland and Kansas City? They both had good ball clubs and they met twice a year, which really added to the rivalry. The best way to say it is that they hated each other. That's not an exaggeration, either. That rivalry really hit its peak in the late '60s. I know we're talking about the 1970s, but I still can't leave that one out of the conversation.

Another team you've always held in high regard was the '76 New England Patriots, a club that went 11-3 that year and beat Pittsburgh, Oakland, Miami and Baltimore along the way. You broadcast their last game of the season, a playoff in Oakland in which the Patriots lost with the help of some questionable officiating.

CG: I remember that game! That game was lost by the Patriots, *not* by the referees! I thought New England had the best team in football that year, a Super Bowl caliber team. They beat the Raiders badly in Boston during the regular season, 48-17. I covered that game, also. They should have beaten Oakland in the playoffs, too, but they gave it away.

New England had the ball around the 35-yard line of Oakland late in the game. Sam "The Bam" Cunningham was their fullback and he had a bad shoulder. They pitched out to him for a sweep around left end and he gained about seven or eight yards. Just as he was about to get hit, Cunningham stepped out of bounds so the defense wouldn't hit his shoulder. It was a yard short of a first down. If he had dived forward, New England would have had a first down and could've easily killed the clock or at least prolonged the drive enough that Oakland wouldn't have had time to come back.

Then the Patriots lined up for the next play and had a motion penalty. That sent them back five yards. Now it was third-and-six. They threw a pass to Russ Francis, their big tight end, and I'll never forget this: As Francis went to catch the ball, a linebacker of the Raiders pinned back Francis' arms and the pass hit him in the chest. None of the officials saw it. After the game, the head of the officiating crew came by to see me. I said to him, "Jesus! Wait till you see this play on Monday. *Boy, was there holding!*" He called me on Monday and said, "You're right, by God. I don't know how we missed it."

Had the officials called that penalty the Patriots would've had a first down. But New England was forced to try a field goal, which failed. Then the Raiders got the ball and went right down the field. There was a controversial roughing penalty in which Stabler threw the ball and was hit as he let it go. The officials threw a late flag. Then Stabler ended up running it in for a touchdown with a few seconds to go. The Patriots argued that it wasn't a late hit, but on the very same play their defensive backs ran one of the Oakland receivers into the grandstand.

Please, Al, Don't Believe the Hype

NBC football analyst Al DeRogatis was astute enough to predict the New York Jets' upset in Super Bowl III and the emerging greatness of the Miami Dolphins, but the comment he made during the early stages of the Super Bowl IX telecast was a laugher. It was Pittsburgh versus Minnesota, January 12, 1975, on NBC Sports:

Gowdy: *"Back deep is Steve Davis, 35, for the Steelers. Flanking him are [Reggie] Harrison, 46, and Preston Pearson, 26. The field is in pretty good shape. It has been vacuumed off. [Vikings kicker Fred] Cox will be kicking against the wind."*

DeRogatis: *"A tense football game, Curt. This could be one of the really important plays – the opening kickoff. You'll see where the tension's at."*

The opening kickoff? One of the game's most important plays? I never heard a statement like that before or since. It's obvious the real tension was up there in the booth.

After the Jets broke the ice by winning Super Bowl III in 1969, the AFC went on to dominate pro football throughout most of the 1970s. Were you surprised at the conference's overwhelming success against the NFC, considering its lowly AFL roots?

CG: In the late '60s, I kept telling everybody that the AFL was better than people think. They had three teams – the Raiders, the Jets and the Chiefs – that could play with anybody. Those three teams were as good as the top three or four teams in the NFL. After the Jets beat the Colts, everyone started saying that the AFL was now as good as the NFL. Well, that wasn't true. From top to bottom, the AFL wasn't as good. The NFL still had more depth. I don't think the AFL's lesser teams could have beaten the NFL's lesser teams.

Super Bowl III was my most memorable broadcast. It wasn't the best game I ever saw or the most exciting, but it was a tremendous upset. The next year Kansas City beat Minnesota rather handily. From then on, the AFC simply dominated. I think the AFC won eight or nine of the Super Bowls played in the 1970s.

Were you shocked by the outcome of Super Bowl III, or could you see the Jets' upset coming?

CG: I wouldn't use the word "shocked." To be honest, I thought the Jets would play the Colts a pretty good game but I didn't think they'd beat them. That year the Colts won 15 games and lost only one. Obviously they had a great team, but they sorta had a bad day in that Super Bowl.

Maybe the Jets made them have a bad day. Joe Namath was a superb quarterback. He had two great receivers in Don Maynard and George Sauer. Matt Snell was a terrific fullback, both a runner and a blocker. They had a very quick defensive team. Their defensive line wasn't too big, but they were quick as cats.

I remember coming down to the lobby of the Americana Hotel in Miami before heading over to the Orange Bowl for the game. Howard Cosell was sitting there. This was before he latched onto Muhammad Ali and was doing Monday Night Football. He was well-known in New York at the time but not nationally. I'm standing there and I hear someone yelling, *"Cowboy! Cowboy!"* I stopped and he came over to me and said, "You know, Cowboy, I hate to see it today. The Colts will break Joe Willie Namath's legs."

I said, "Well, nobody has broken them yet. He has bad knees, but what the hell? These other teams the Jets have played were after him, too."

"They'll kill him," he said. "It's a disgrace, matching these two teams up."

That started getting me mad. I said, "C'mon, Howard. I think the Jets will give them a helluva game today."

He said, "Cowboy, you're a shill for the Commissioner."

I turned away and got in the car and said to DeRogatis, "That bitch really got me mad." DeRogatis had said all along he thought the Jets might win.

What do you remember most about that broadcast at the Orange Bowl?

CG: It was something I said. The Jets had led the whole way, and the score was 16-0 with about three or four minutes to go. It was obvious they were going to win the game, so I said on the air, *"You are looking at one of the greatest upsets of all time in pro football!"* Jeezus, the writers all got on me, saying I was prejudiced towards the AFL, which wasn't true. I went right down the middle broadcasting that game.

I also said on the air that this was a game that will change the future of pro football. Boy, did I get blasted for that, too. But it *did* change the future of the game. The AFL now had the championship team in all of football. Their ratings went up. The AFL was able to raise their television rights and command a lot of money. I once took [NFL commissioner] Pete Rozelle up to Alaska with me on an *American Sportsman* show, and we sat down one night after fishing all day. He got a pad out and started writing things down. Then he said, "You know, Curt, financially that was probably the single most important game ever played in America, considering the money that changed hands after that game." The attitude of the American sports fan completely changed, too. They thought, "Hey, the AFL is good! They're not a bunch of guys from Upper Slobovia like we used to think."

The outcome of that game also affected the structure of pro football. At the winter meetings that year, the AFL wanted the same amount of teams as the NFL had. Paul Brown had led the charge for that. Vince Lombardi got up during the meetings and said Brown was right, that the AFL had won the Super Bowl and deserved it. For three days they fought about it up in those smoke-filled rooms. When they came back down, the Colts, the Steelers and the Browns left the National Football League and joined what is now called the AFC.

Many people in Baltimore still think that Super Bowl III was fixed, that the Colts intentionally weren't playing as well as they were capable. They cite all the dropped passes, missed tackles, etc.

CG: You mean they think the Baltimore players took money to fix the game?

Let's say that many of them feel the outcome was prearranged.

CG: [Sternly] The Colts had a bad day! There's nothing else to say about it!

Joe Namath's career peaked that afternoon in the Orange Bowl. He never enjoyed the same level of success again and, by the time he retired in 1977, he was a physical wreck.

CG: Namath was a great athlete but unfortunately he had bad knees. You'd go in the locker room and look at him and say "My God!" It looked like a mummy stuffed on both knees. He had a lot of trouble. Look at Bret Favre or John Elway. They had the great ability to be elusive back there, to be able to get out of the pocket and break down the defense with the threat to run. Steve Young was fantastic at it. But Namath couldn't do any of those things. He had a great release, a gutsy guy, but he was just a sitting duck.

I did the Orange Bowl game one year when Oklahoma played Alabama, 1965. Namath was a sophomore. I think he made 97 or 98 yards rushing in that game. He'd take the ball, sprint out from center and cock his arm. If the defense didn't come up to take him he'd run. If they'd pick him up, he'd throw.

[Alabama coach] Bear Bryant and I became real good friends later on and he used to tell me that Namath was one of the best athletes he'd ever coached. He said, "This kid has an instinct for football. If we had a problem on the blackboard in a coaches' meeting, we'd call Joe in and see if he could solve it for us." If Namath had the same knees in the pros that he had during his sophomore year in college, hell, I don't know what he would've become. He did great with what he had, but with those knees he was a sitting duck back there in the pocket. He just couldn't move.

How well did you get to know Namath?

CG: Not very well. He knew who I was, I knew who he was. But I could never get close to him.

What about Terry Bradshaw and his great years as the Steelers quarterback? You also watched his career blossom from the broadcast booth.

CG: Bradshaw was great. He won four Super Bowls. When he first got to the pros, everybody thought he was dumb. He was so strong. Many times on third-and-9 or third-and-12, he'd get a first down himself by running with the ball. He could've played running back in the NFL. He had a strong arm, a good touch and the confidence of his teammates. He was a helluva quarterback, one of the best.

Bradshaw also had excellent receivers. I did one of Lynn Swann's games in the Rose Bowl when he played for USC. Al Davis called me after the game in my hotel in Pasadena. I'll never forget it – he came right out and asked me who I liked out on the field that day. I didn't hesitate. I said, "That wide receiver for Southern Cal, Swann. He could jump like a kangaroo, very acrobatic."

You could see from watching Swann play that he had it. He had great hands and was a great jumper. He could take the ball away from the defender. Davis didn't say a word, though. Oakland had a chance to draft him but didn't. Maybe he felt the Raiders were already set at wide receiver. Bradshaw's other target, John Stallworth, was more of a glider than Swann. He was a possession receiver who eventually became a deep threat. I think they both belong in the Hall of Fame.

Speaking of the Hall of Fame, it's a good time to mention a player who's not been enshrined – Oakland's Kenny Stabler. He's a quarterback known for his great comebacks and fantastic finishes but rarely mentioned as a serious candidate for the Hall.

CG: Oh, I believe he belongs. I'll tell you a funny, true story. I went down to do a hunting show in Alabama for *The American Sportsman*, on a plantation down there. It was the early '70s. Bear Bryant and I were sitting in this motel one night. Ol' Bear is drinking something and he asked me, "Why isn't Kenny playing with the Raiders?"

I said, "I don't know. Let's call Al Davis up and find out."

I picked up the phone and called Al out in Oakland. I said, "Al, there's somebody here that wants to talk to you." I handed the phone to Bryant and told him to ask Davis himself.

The Bear sort of had a rumbling voice. He said [imitating Bryant], "Hi, Mr. Davis. How are you? Why in the hell isn't Stabler your quarterback?"

I didn't hear what Al said, but then Bear said, "*Goddamn, if you play him, you'll win!*"

Stabler was a very accurate passer, and his teams really believed in him. I think I'd put him in the Hall of Fame, too.

Did you have any favorite backs or receivers that you enjoyed watching play?

CG: Jim Brown, the greatest runner who ever lived. I also used to like Billy "White Shoes" Johnson of Houston. He was a great punt returner, a real threat. Those two come to mind first.

What about coaches? Were you particularly close to anyone? Did any give you a consistently good interview and good insight before a broadcast?

CG: I never had any of them give me inside information, but I never really wanted it. What are they gonna tell you? They're not gonna tell you their game plan. One guy who was good to me was Bill Walsh, when he was the quarterback coach at Cincinnati. But I never said to any of them, "Hey, c'mon, what are you gonna do today? Give me your plan."

Could you envision Walsh's future success as a head coach, knowing him from his time with the Bengals?

CG: I'd say so. I thought the Bengals made a mistake not giving him the head job after Paul Brown retired. The story was that Brown promised his assistant coach, "Tiger" Johnson, the head coaching position after Brown retired. He kept his promise, so Walsh left and went to San Diego.

Walsh was a very bright guy. You could tell. I used to talk to him a lot. I'd go to the stadium a couple hours before the game and we'd walk the field together. I didn't necessarily ask him for his thoughts about this team or that team, but he'd give a bright, quick answer to what I did ask. Cincinnati should have hired him as a head coach. It would have been interesting to see what would have happened with him there.

You covered nine Super Bowls for NBC. Which was your favorite?

CG: I would elect Super Bowl XIII, the Steelers' 35-31 win over Dallas. There were so many Hall-of-Famers in that game – Bradshaw and Roger Staubach and Franco Harris, so many names. Both teams had such great players. They just opened the throttle and went all out that day. It was one helluva game.

As far as the greatest football game ever played, you've always maintained that the Miami-Kansas City playoff of 1971 is at the top of your list.

CG: That's right. That game was extraordinary for a lot of reasons. First of all, it was the longest game ever played. It went deep into the sixth period. Secondly, it was played almost perfectly. I think there were only a couple of turnovers in the whole game. Thirdly, it was very, very exciting. One team would drive 80 yards for a touchdown, then the other would drive back for one. Ed Podolak made over 300 yards combined that day in kickoff returns, receptions and running. Jan Stenerud missed a chip shot field goal for Kansas City by about a foot that would have won it. Instead, it went into overtime. A lot of people were able to watch that game on TV since it was played on Christmas Day. I know my wife was unhappy that I had to go out and do it. But that was the best game I had ever seen, and a lot of people that saw it agree with me.

Do you have a second favorite?

CG: I think the Oakland-Patriot game we talked about was good. So was Oakland-Miami, 1974. In fact, that one might have been a little better. Miami scored with about a minute and a half to play when Benny Malone ran in for a touchdown, but they scored too early. They gave ol' Stabler just enough time to drive the length of the field. But overall, I'd have to say the Oakland-New England playoff was my second choice.

You were in Pittsburgh on December 23, 1972, for the Immaculate Reception game, Raiders versus Steelers in the AFC playoffs. You saw that famous play unfold live, and you've seen the NBC replays. What, in your mind, actually happened on that play?

CG: John Madden still argues to this day that the ball hit Frenchy Fuqua in the shoulder. He was the intended receiver, and the ball had caromed to Franco Harris. In those days, it was an incomplete pass if two people from the receiving team touched the ball. As I recall, Tatum reached over Fuqua's shoulder and the ball deflected to Franco, who was running down the field. He was the most surprised guy in the stadium when it came to him. I'd have to take that play, inch by inch, and really break it down, which I haven't done. It was one of the miracle plays of all time. What are the odds on that happening? A million to one.

There's a funny story on that game. It was third-and-27 for Pittsburgh, end of the game, and Art Rooney, the owner of the Steelers, came by my booth. He opened the door and flipped a cigar on the table. He knew I smoked cigars now and then. Then he gave me a little salute and started for the elevators to go down and congratulate his boys. By now it was fourth down and Bradshaw was running around back there. He threw the ball and the Immaculate Reception happened. At the same time, Rooney was getting off the elevator downstairs when a couple of ushers ran up to him. They were hugging him and congratulating him. He said, *"What the hell do you mean we won? We had fourth down and a mile to go! What is this, a riot going on here?"* He had no idea the Steelers had won the game.

You were the voice of AFC football for 13 years. What were the circumstances surrounding your sudden departure from NBC in 1979? I was watching your last two NBC telecasts – the 1978 AFC Title game and Super Bowl XIII – and your broadcast partner, John Brodie, seemed to hint that you were nearing the end of your time there.

CG: Well, really nothing happened. They didn't fire me. I didn't do anything wrong or make anyone mad at me. They didn't call me and say, "Hey, we don't want you back anymore." The only thing you could say was that it ran its course. I could've stayed, but I had been talking to CBS some. It was the last year of my contract at NBC, and my wife wanted me to cut back. CBS was offering me the opportunity to do pro football along with a program that was basically their version of *Wide World of Sports*. I was only interested in doing 20-25 events a year, so that workload was good enough for me and I took CBS's offer.

I would've liked to have stayed with NBC. They had the rights to the 1980 Olympics, so I met with Don Ohlmeyer, the president of NBC television, during the '79 Rose Bowl game to talk about working that. He told me that I could have my pick of any events I wanted. I said, "Great! Let me decide after I look at the schedule." I was probably going to do track and field and basketball. But then the Olympics were canceled, so I never got to do it.

Many people were under the impression that your departure from NBC was under unpleasant terms, that it was a disagreeable parting. That wasn't the case?

CG: No, they all remained friends of mine. My contract had run out with NBC, and they did want to talk to me about the future. But then CBS had a meeting with me and offered more money than I was making at NBC. I'd be doing fewer events, too. That pleased my wife, so I took it. That's the real story.

Kicking A Fallen Cowboy

Gowdy's sudden departure from NBC in 1979 was hidden in shadows, a hushed sweep under a peacock rug. Most major newspapers chose to ignore the story.

Television sports critics, the Rudy Martzke's of the world, the types who'd normally give the inside scoop on a shakeup like this, weren't yet in newspaper vogue, so the story went largely unreported. As a result, after 13 years of fine broadcasting, the sporting world's attitude toward Gowdy had curdled into a great big, sour "Curt Who?"

But there was one particular columnist, Gary Deeb of the *Chicago Tribune*, who was paying attention to the change. When word leaked in early 1978 that NBC was stripping Gowdy of all his major play-by-play assignments, the writer proceeded to add insult to injury with a pair of angry blasts in his weekly TV-radio column. It was a vicious, out-of-the-blue attack on the broadcaster. Here are excerpts from the work of a ripper:

"Putting Gowdy out to pasture is a terribly unpleasant chore to NBC. But it's difficult to conjure up any sympathy for him. Here's a guy who spent the last decade chloroforming millions of viewers, frequently miscalling plays, and immortalizing such clichés as "He is a fine athlete with most of his future ahead of him." For this, he never was paid less than $200,000 a year. Gowdy's flat, nasal voice was perfect for making the most sensational achievement sound like the dullest routine. On the other hand, whenever he tried to act excited, he appeared to be reciting off a Teleprompter." ('A Curt Goodbye' – March 31, 1978)

Here's another:

"With just three weeks remaining till Super Bowl weekend, the bosses of NBC Sports are both ecstatic and miserable. They're happy because this year it's NBC's turn to telecast the Super Bowl, the pro football championship that normally attracts a nation-wide television audience of more than 75 million. But they're feeling uncomfortable because they want to be nice to Curt Gowdy, the slumber-inducing announcer who has become the most inanimate object in sports since the Goodyear Blimp arrived on the scene.

"As previously reported in this column, NBC has been systematically stripping Gowdy of his top assignments for the last few years. In 1976, he was deposed as NBC's main baseball voice by Joe Garagiola; last winter, he was toppled by Dick Enberg as play-by-play man for the NCAA basketball championship game; and for the last few months, he generally has been superseded by Enberg as NBC's No. 1 broadcaster on the Sunday afternoon football games...Barring any last minutes obstacles, it looks like Gowdy's final big moment will take place at the Super Bowl. It's unfortunate that we viewers will be the ones who pay for it." ('One Last Fling' – December 29, 1978)

A real hatchet job. And some of Deeb's roughest shots aren't included here.

Like Gowdy's performance as an announcer or not, Deeb's words went beyond the scope of a professional critique. You sensed it was something personal, a strike aimed at the heart. His comments were unexpectedly harsh and biting, especially when considering they were directed toward someone with as prestigious resume as Gowdy's.

In his defense, Deeb wasn't imagining things. Others at the network had privately grumbled about Gowdy's increasing errors and decreasing fervor. Maybe Cowboy Curt was beginning to slip. Maybe he was losing some of his sharpness. Maybe his overall interest in sports, with its swelling level of commercialism, was waning.

Or maybe Curt Gowdy was simply getting tired, finally wearing down after many long years on the road. After all, his career had become one continuous cycle that went from pro football to college basketball to major league baseball, season after season, year after year, with few breaks in between.

Whatever the circumstances, he didn't deserve that kind of abuse.

After a brief hiatus, Gowdy went on to work for several more years, calling games for CBS then the University of Miami. They seemed happy enough with his work. So did HBO, which hired him to work on its respected *Inside the NFL* program.

NBC even brought him and Al DeRogatis back for a four-game NFL stint in 1988. Gowdy sounded great, his voice carrying a refreshed enthusiasm. Then a few summers ago, ESPN gave him, at age 83, play-by-play duty for a Yankees-Red Sox game and he was marvelous.

I once asked Gowdy to comment on that dark part of his career, his departure from NBC in the late '70s, but he declined. There was an awkwardness in his voice, as he opted to simply complement his former employers and leave it at that. Water under a dignified, old bridge.

They say Matisse continued painting even after he went blind. Maybe that's what the great artists do; they can never abandon their craft.

And Curt Gowdy carried on as well, even after NBC and a spite-filled writer from Chicago tried to wish his voice away.

Did you have any idea that the Dallas-Pittsburgh Super Bowl was going to be your last game at NBC?

CG: No, I had no idea. Not at the time. I knew I my exposure was being cut back, the number of events I would cover, but I didn't know it would be my last NBC telecast.

I once read a newspaper column describing CBS's reasons for dismissing Brent Musberger. One of the comments made was that the network didn't want its sports department to be overshadowed or identified by one single personality. Is that a fair comparison to your situation at NBC, considering your almost omnipresent role at the network?

CG: I don't think so. My situation wasn't the same as Musberger's. I had a great relationship at NBC. I think NBC just wanted to jazz things up a bit in their broadcasts. One thing that happened is Monday Night Football had hit big for ABC. They had Don Meredith and Howard Cosell, so NBC decided they needed to get some colorful personalities in their broadcasts, more entertainment features, things like that. I think that was somewhat in the background of them letting me go. They were very jealous of Monday Night Football and the success it was having. Also, I had a few problems with some executives up there. That probably had something to do with it, as well. But those same executives remained good friends of mine.

Do you ever miss your view from up in the broadcast booth?

CG: No. I had 50 years of it and that was enough. The traveling got to be very tiring to me. I traveled about a quarter of a million miles a year. I used to go from baseball to football to basketball, year round. Then sandwiched in between were all those *American Sportsman* shows for ABC, which required traveling around the world.

By the time I retired my children were grown and gone, so we had an empty nest. My wife, Jerre, had stayed home alone all those years and raised them. After I retired I still had other opportunities in front of me but finally she said, "I've stayed home for you all of those years; now you stay home for me." That sort of hit a target for me. I just wasn't interested in going out on the road anymore. I had a long run, but it was time to say goodbye.

— 18 —
Jack Patera, Head Coach
Seattle Seahawks (1976-82)
September 17, 2002

They don't make expansion teams like they used to.

The new franchises that joined the NFL in the 1990s – Jacksonville, Carolina and Cleveland – were treated like guests at the royal table, a walk on the big, red welcome mat. Two years of extra draft choices… major salary cap exemptions…access to prime free agents….

"I remember thinking," says John Thompson, the first general manager of the Seattle Seahawks, which joined the league back in 1976, "My Lord, what if they had given that to *us*?"

Back in the old days, before the chaotic churnings of open free agency were introduced to the league, the process of filling expansion rosters was far less generous. First, there was the veteran draft. Existing teams would expose the bottom tiers of their depth charts – "The Shame of the Unprotected," I heard a player once call it – then the new clubs would rummage through the bodies for salvageable talent.

Next came the regular college draft. After that, the only other source of bodies for expansion clubs was to round up a whole mob of street free agents, give 'em a workout, and hope to find a few prizes in the cracker jack box. Thanks and good luck.

"We held a tryout at Civic Stadium in Seattle and invited everybody we could think of," remembers Thompson, "and if somebody showed up who wasn't invited, well, that was okay, too. The first guy we signed was a wide receiver named Dave Williams, basically a PR move because he'd been a start at the University of Washington."

You scraped for an edge wherever it could be found.

"That first year," says Thompson, "we hired a bunch of local business men and trained them how to sign free agents. Then on draft day we stationed them at the airport, ready to fly out as soon as it was over and sign undrafted players around the country. We had our incentive clauses printed on stickers, so they could just peel them off and stick them on the contracts."

The man chosen to coach the original Seahawks was Jack Patera, a longtime NFL assistant who found his craft in molding some of history's great pass rushes…the Fearsome Foursome charge of the L.A. Rams… the Purple People Eaters of Minnesota. Proud defensive football, that was Patera's game.

But when he landed in Seattle there was no Lamar Lundy or Deacon Jones or Carl Eller waiting on the tarmac. Instead, a sea of nameless faces and faceless names. "I'd been around so much defensive talent as an assistant that I was spoiled," recalls Patera. "Smart, rugged veterans…Hall of Fame types…coaches on the field. Then as we moved through that first camp in Seattle I remember thinking, "Will we be able to stop anybody? This could really get ugly…."

"For an expansion team, Jack had a pretty well-run operation," says Lyle Blackwood, a Seahawks safety who'd been plucked from the Cincinnati Bengals roster. "His coaching staff did a good job putting together a team even though he had a roster full of players nobody wanted. The only gripe I had was being given one pair of socks to use in training camp."

But Patera was right. The Seahawks couldn't stop anybody. They gave up 31 points/game during that first season and got murdered, only two wins. The following year they allowed 27 ppg and finished fourth in the division. Defensive help, it seemed, wasn't coming any time soon.

So Patera, that old-school defensive hardliner, turned to offensive razzmatazz and rigmarole in trying to squeeze a few more wins out of his young, overmatched club. What followed was an array of trick-play delights – fake punts and quarterback draws, flea-flickers and reverses from Tight-I. One time against Atlanta they went for it on 4th-and-12 at their own 32-yard line. In the third quarter. With a ten point lead.

The Seahawks of the late '70s came at you from all directions. They were masters of surprise. The Pink Panther routine, with Cato pouncing out of the linen closet at Clouseau and his raincoat.

"We needed to do something," says Patera. "We needed some kind of extra spark to stay competitive. Since we couldn't stop anybody on defense, we had to outscore 'em. Hey, a touchdown is a touchdown, whether it's a two-yard run or your wide receiver throws it to the kicker off a double reverse."

For a short while they were the most exciting team in pro football. Two major stars emerged in quarterback Jim Zorn and receiver Steve Largent, and the wins started to come. The team was 9-7 in both 1978 and '79 and sniffed at the playoffs.

But over the next two seasons the razzle-dazzle was wearing off. Opponents were ready for it. Seattle won only ten of its next 32 games and the boos came thundering down. The Seahawks were regressing, while the Tampa Bay Buccaneers – the other expansion team of 1976 – had already played in a conference championship game.

Then came another slow start in 1982 and ownership had seen enough wheel spinning. Patera was fired that October and never came back. He left the game of football for good.

"I've often wondered what it would have been like coaching an established team," he says. "You know, in many ways it took a lot out of us. We put so much effort into building something out of nothing." There's hint of sadness in Patera's voice, even after all these years.

But in many ways Patera did his job. The Seahawks became a playoff team the following year under his replacement, Chuck Knox. The cupboard wasn't bare, not at all. Knox was able to take something and make it into something better. For that, give Patera credit for building the "something" part.

• • •

Your Seattle teams were always known for their offensive fireworks, but your true roots lie on the defensive side of the ball, correct?

JP: That's right. As a player I was drafted by Baltimore as an offensive guard in 1955. That was when there were only 33-man squads and people often played both ways. The middle linebacker position was just developing, as the 4-3 defense had only been in use for a year or so. Eventually I became the backup middle linebacker for the Colts. The defensive linemen there were Gino Marchetti, Art Donovan, Don Joyce and Tom Finnin. They were important in establishing my attitude on how that position should be played. They were very good players, but they weren't in very good condition.

I really hadn't considered coaching as a profession. My degree was in education. Don Kellett, Baltimore's general manager, asked me if I planned to coach. I said, "No, I have way too many memories of coaches being in the office right after games, working ridiculous hours. They never have any time off!" He said, "That's good, because coaching is the hardest way to make an easy living." That stuck with me.

During my second or third year at Baltimore I got a call from Len Casanova, my college coach at Oregon, asking me to come back there. He said, "You just can't play all your life. You gotta get into your life's work eventually." Well, I didn't want to quit playing just to go into coaching. I never would have done that. In my mind, I was never going to be a coach.

Don Heinrich , who was my teammate on the Cowboys for a few years, was hired as the offensive coach for the Los Angeles Rams in 1963. He called me and said, "I know you don't want to get into coaching, but [Rams head coach Harland] Svare can't find a good defensive line coach. Why don't you come down and talk to him?" I did, and ended up taking the job. I had never coached before but I did understand a lot about football. The concept of the game came easy to me. I knew all of the assignments on both defense and offense. In the two years that I was in Dallas under Tom Landry (1960-61), I learned his defensive philosophy. That gave me the defensive background that Harland Svare wanted. So the combination of understanding football and having a background with Landry was how I developed my basis for teaching defensive line play.

Who was the greatest defensive lineman you'd ever seen?

JP: I played with two of the best in Baltimore: Marchetti and Donovan. Donovan was a player who never took conditioning seriously. When he warmed up, he shook his left leg and then his right leg and he was ready to go. [Cowboys QB] Eddie LeBaron used to say that, while Donovan was down in his three-point stance, he'd make the snap count extra long so that Artie would have to get up to catch his breath. Then he'd snap the ball. [Laughing] That really wasn't true, but it could've been.

In my playing days, I'd say that Marchetti was the best in the business. Phenomenal. He made play after play, always rose to the occasion. But Marchetti, as great as he was, was never in shape either. He always looked like the next play was going to be his last, with all the huffing and puffing. That didn't keep him from playing well but he was always gasping for breath. That influenced me when I became a defensive line coach. I wanted my players to be in great shape so they could continue to pressure the quarterback and play the run throughout the entire game.

By the time I started coaching, players had changed physically. They became bigger and stronger and faster almost overnight. I coached some great talents like Deacon Jones and Merlin Olsen and Carl Eller. Deacon was bigger and faster than anyone I had ever seen. Carl Eller could do whatever he wanted to do on the field, but he didn't play as good as he could have throughout his whole career. Olsen was a great player, a solid defensive tackle. I would've loved to have taken him in the expansion draft for Seattle, but he said he would rather retire than play for an expansion team. If I had to pick the two best players I ever coached, they would be Deacon Jones and Alan Page. They could do it all.

But the greatest defensive lineman in history that you're looking for never existed. That player would have been an "in-shape" Gino Marchetti. Had he gone through the weight training and offseason workouts that players dedicate themselves to today, the list of the all-time greatest linemen would have one name on it – Gino Marchetti. I would've loved to have seen it.

You eventually moved to the Vikings, where you directed the famous Purple People Eaters outfit from 1969 through 1975 – Page and Eller and Larsen and Marshall – that helped the Vikings reach three Super Bowls. Individual awards, honors and accolades decorated that defense for years. Who was the most underrated player on the team, the quiet contributor that rarely made the headlines?

JP: If there was an under publicized player on the team, it was Jim Marshall. Eller and Page were widely regarded because they were so dominant, but Jim was our captain and a very good athlete. If we had to enter one Viking in a decathlon, it would have been Jim. He had an amazing sense of leverage and was so quick. He didn't dominate his position because he wasn't overly strong and weighed around 250 pounds. But he did a great job for our defensive line for a lot of years.

Which of your Vikings defenses was the most dominant?

JP: Without question, the 1970 and '71 defenses were tops. We were really at our highest level during those two years and set a lot of records. We had a great pass rush and played the run well. Our defensive backs were all good enough to seal off the secondary, particularly safety Paul Krause. Our linebackers – Roy Winston, Lonnie Warwick and Wally Hilgenberg – might not have been all-stars, but they were solid. We weren't weak in any place. They were wild kind of guys but still reacted to discipline, that raised hell within the scheme of things. But they practiced as hard as any group I have ever been around.

You coached under the great Bud Grant at Minnesota, who obviously was an influence on you as a coach. What were some of his strengths, and why was he successful at creating winning football teams?

JP: Bud didn't talk to his assistants very much. I don't think he was in my office more than two or three times during the entire seven years I was there. Bud just demanded a lot without being emotional. He certainly wasn't like Vince Lombardi, who chewed on everybody all the time and drove them into the ground. Bud ran the team and everybody knew he was in charge. To maintain control without being a taskmaster is really a hard thing to do as a head coach.

I went crow hunting with him once, and when I got home my wife asked me, "Well, did you and Bud have a conversation today?" I said, "Yeah, he told me to set up the phonograph over there and sit down and wait for the crows. That was about it." There weren't many great conversations. When I was hired by the Vikings, I had never met Bud before so I didn't really know what to expect. Our first conversation went something like this:

"Do you like to hunt?"

"Yes, I do." Then silence. Finally I asked him, "Do you?"

"Yes." More silence. Then he asked me, "Do you have dogs?"

I said, "Yes." More silence.

"What kind?"

"Shorthairs." More silence. "Do you have dogs?"

"Yes, labs." More silence.

It was the strangest conversation, a strange interview, but it really wasn't uncomfortable. Evidently things went well because I was hired. Later on he said to me, "Everybody can draw X's and O's. I wasn't interested in a coach's conversation. I wanted to find out some things about you." I guess he wanted to see if I'd fit in with the other types of people he had brought onto the staff, and dogs and hunting were obviously part of that.

We had a 20-year reunion of the 1969 Super Bowl team, and all the players and coaches came to Minneapolis. We had been there a few days, attending dinners and parties. Then about 30 minutes before game time that Sunday, Bud and I were standing underneath the goal post. Of course, there was no real conversation, but finally Bud says, "Jack, I'd like to give you a compliment. It's quite a bit overdue. Would that be all right?"

I said, "Sure, I'm always up for a good compliment."

Then he said, "I want to tell you how much you meant to the team and what a good job you did for us back then. I know it's twenty years late, but...."

I said, "That's all right, Bud, I'm glad you got it off your chest [laughing]."

That's the type of guy he was. He never told me once while I was there that I was doing a good job. I just understood that I was, since he never told me otherwise. It's strange, but that's one of the things I like about Bud.

Grant was always the stone face on the sidelines – no emotion, no carrying on. What was the most animated you ever saw Grant behind the scenes, away from the cameras?

JP: I've *never* seen it. I was upstairs in the booth during the games, so I was never there when the team was first coming off the sidelines. I do remember one game that we had lost, and I had made my way down to the dressing room afterwards. Two or three people remarked that they had never seen Bud so emotional, but that was just a rumor. Bud really never had to get emotional. He wouldn't scowl or get the steely look in his eye. It was more body language with him. He was able to get his intentions across very easily without verbally expressing it.

Grant's teams had often been criticized for their poor showings in championship games. Paul Zimmerman of* Sports Illustrated *once wrote, "I didn't like the Vikings of the '70s because I feel they were poorly prepared in each of their Super Bowls. Their game plan stunk and they got killed as a result." Can you comment on that remark based on your first-hand experiences in Minnesota? Were the Vikings not prepared for those championship contests?

JP: I had never heard that quote before. I was never a big fan of Paul's analysis anyway, but he was probably right. I don't feel we really were well prepared for those games, and that's something that stuck with me as I began my career as a head coach. If I could ever run a football team like Bud did, that would be fine. But if I was ever fortunate enough to take a team to the playoffs or the championship, I would do things a little differently.

When we got to those Super Bowls, it was like we were going back to training camp – meetings all the time, curfews, bed checks every night. It seemed like we were always going to some kind of meeting or practice or team meal. Lots of tension and strict routines, always having to be somewhere. There was no time to relax, to clear your mind, particularly for the coaches. It was like we were more focused on the routine than winning the game itself.

The basic philosophy toward winning in the National Football League is this: If you beat the teams you're supposed to beat, and split with the teams that are your equal, then you'll be in the playoffs. Once you get to the playoffs, I've always felt that you have to do some things different to get past the teams that are as good as or better than you. With Bud, we treated those playoff games just like any regular season game. I don't want to be critical of Bud because he won a lot of football games and won championships in the CFL and beat some very good teams to get into those Super Bowls. But we were too predictable.

I never felt we were unprepared except for that first Super Bowl against Kansas City. Defensively, we did a very poor job against the Chiefs. That's all I want to say about that game. We didn't play the kind of defense we were capable of playing because the coaches didn't prepare well enough. The next year we played the Chiefs in the regular season and beat them handily because we switched things up a little bit. Now, we lost to Miami and Pittsburgh because they were better teams. I don't think it was preparation issue in those games. We didn't play as well as we could have, but the Dolphins and the Steelers both did.

The Vikings reached their third Super Bowl in January of 1975. Going into that game with Pittsburgh, was the pressure of "finally winning the big one" starting to have a negative effect on the team's psyche? Was there a snake-bitten mentality present?

JP: No, I don't think that was a factor. We had a good gameplan for the Pittsburgh game, and had it been executed properly we could have won it. But there was something different happening on the team. We had been a good team for the past six or seven years, but some of the players were actually starting to lose focus. The discipline had begun to break down for some of them. They were thinking, "Hey, we're here again. We're better than the Steelers. We can win this game without all this [coaching and preparation]."

That '74 Vikings team wasn't as tightly knit, either. That great feeling of camaraderie had really faded over the last few seasons. Some of the players were displeased with each other. There was definitely a sense of resentment on the team. Some players were all business and very committed to winning the game. Others were just going through the motions. I'd rather not name names.

That's fine. Being a defensive line coach, which of the opposing offensive lines impressed you most in those Super Bowls – Miami's or Pittsburgh's?

JP: Pittsburgh's did. Maybe it was their running game. Their scheme was very simple and their backs weren't as good as Miami's, but the Steelers just did the basic things very, very well. The Dolphins line could run better, run sweeps better. They pulled well and were very athletic looking. But the real grind-em-out, smash-mouth type of football was played in Pittsburgh. Overall I was more impressed with Steelers' offense than Miami's.

Your last game with the Vikings came in December of 1975, the infamous "Hail Mary" contest against Dallas. Statistically, the Cowboys dominated the game, but Minnesota held the lead with just 24 seconds left. How did the Vikings let that game get away?

JP: In the fourth quarter, I don't think our defensive line rushed the passer nearly as well as it could have.

That was probably the most disappointing performance by the defensive line that I had seen during my entire time in Minnesota. It was almost like being in high school for those guys, thinking, "Well, I'm tired now. Maybe somebody else can get the quarterback." That was exactly my feeling while I was watching that game. I never watched it on film because I went to an interview with the Seahawks right after the game. But that was the only time in Minnesota that I was really disappointed in everybody. I didn't think that anybody gave as big an effort in the fourth quarter as they should have.

A 'Hail Mary' Meltdown in Minnesota

Former Vikings' defensive line coach Jack Patera called his team's pass rush during the fourth quarter of the 1975 playoff against Dallas "the worst I had ever seen during my time in Minnesota." But after reviewing each play of that period, I'm not so sure.

Although the Cowboys won 17-14 on that legendary "Hail Mary" heave – Roger Staubach to Drew Pearson down the right sideline – Minnesota's hard-charging front four of Marshall, Lurtsema, Page and Eller had a pretty good handle on things during that fateful quarter. They rushed the passer well. They stirred the pocket. And on the two big completions of Dallas' final drive, well, Staubach got his passes away in three seconds, not nearly enough time for the Vikes to generate serious pressure.

Here is the rundown on Dallas' fourth-quarter drives for that game. Staubach operated almost exclusively out of the shotgun, while the Vikings countered with their standard four-man defensive front. Next to each significant passing play, I show the amount of time that Staubach had in the pocket before releasing his throw.

1st Dallas Drive, 4th Quarter (13:15 remaining)
1-10-D20: Trap to RB Robert Newhouse, gain of 1
2-09-D21: Swing pass to RB Doug Dennison, gain of 4. Staubach hurried by LB Fred McNeil (2 sec)
3-05-D25: Illegal procedure, Dallas. 5-yard penalty
3-10-D20: 48-yard pass to WR Golden Richards, dropped. Blitz by McNeil, LB Jeff Seimon (3 sec)
4-10-D20: Punt
Net result: 3 plays, 0 yards

2nd Dallas Drive, 4th Quarter (5:07 remaining)
1-10-D26: WR screen to Drew Pearson, incomplete. Pressure by DE Jim Marshall via poor block by Ralph Neely
2-10-D26: Coverage sack of Staubach by Marshall, DT Alan Page, loss of 8 (6 sec)
3-18-D18: Delay of game, Dallas. 5-yard penalty
3-23-D13: Low snap out of shotgun formation, Staubach scramble gains 9 yards.
4-14-D22: Punt
Net result: 3 plays, -4 yards

3rd Dallas Drive, 4th Quarter (1:51 remaining)
1-10-D14: Swing pass to RB Preston Pearson, gain of 9 yards. No pressure from defensive line (3 sec)
2-01-D23: Pass to Richards, incomplete. Pressure from DE Carl Eller (4 sec)
3-01-D23: Pass to Richards, gain of 8 yards. Late pressure from Eller (6 sec)

1-10-D31: Low snap out of shotgun, fumble recovered by Staubach.
2-17-D24: Pass to TE Jean Fugett, incomplete. Staubach pressured, hit by Page (4 sec)
3-17-D24: Scramble, pass to TE Jean Fugett, incomplete. Pressure from DT D. Sutherland, Eller (5 sec)
4-17-D24: Deep out complete to Drew Pearson, gain of 26 yards. Pressure from Page, Eller (3 sec)

1-10-D50: Pass to RB Preston Pearson, incomplete. Pass rush no factor (3 sec)
2-10-D50: Fly pattern to Drew Pearson, touchdown. Pass rush no factor (3 sec)
Net result: 9 plays, 76 yards, touchdown

Let's discuss how you became involved with the expansion team from Seattle, the Seahawks. How did you become a candidate for that job, and what led to your eventual hiring?

JP: When I first came to the Vikings, John Thompson was the assistant GM for the team. During the short time we were there together we became good acquaintances. After a year, John received an offer from the league office to work for George Halas, who was the president of the National Conference. We stayed somewhat in touch. Then Seattle was awarded an expansion franchise in 1974, and John was given a five-year contract as general manager for the Seahawks. I wrote a letter to John and applied for the head-coaching job. I tried to impress on him that Seattle really needed to have a head coach in 1975, even though the team wasn't yet playing. He said no, they'd begin their search after the '75 season. So that forced me back to being a Vikings assistant one more year.

Near the end of the '75 season, John wanted to interview me for the job, which I did. During the interview, Herman Sarkowsky, who was the General Managing Partner of the team, shook my hand and said, "I think you'd make a very fine head coach." I was wondering if that meant I had gotten the job. Within a day or so, I learned they had picked me.

Did you have any reservations about your first head-coaching job being with an expansion team?

JP: Oh, yes. I remember meeting with Don Shula in Minneapolis while I was still with the Vikings. We had been teammates on the Colts and I had known him for a long time. I asked for his advice about taking a job with an expansion team. He said, "Take the job with the first guy that offers you one because it may never happen again." That was basically all I needed to hear.

I felt that the Seattle job was very similar to the situation that Tom Landry had in Dallas. The Nordstrom family was the team's ownership group, and Lloyd Nordstrom was their spokesman. Lloyd really admired the way the Dallas Cowboys had built their organization. He knew that Tom Landry was given a ten-year time span to create a winner, and he wanted the Seahawks' coach to operate under the same conditions – no pressure to win immediately, but a plan to build gradually and solidly.

If you could have stolen one player from Minnesota and taken him to Seattle with you, who would it have been?

JP: There weren't really any members of the Vikings defensive line that I would've taken at that point. All those guys were well over 30. Same with other players like Wally Hilgenberg, Roy Winston and [C] Mick Tinglehoff. I would've likely taken a younger player, someone who would have given me seven or eight good years on the Seahawks.

Chuck Foreman would've been near the top of that list. Linebacker Matt Blair would have fit in very well, also. But in hindsight I guess Ed White would have been my choice. He was an offensive lineman for the Vikings and, at 29, still had a lot of good years left. But you know what? I probably would've moved White to defensive tackle. I *guarantee* you Ed would've been great at that position. He had the skills to easily make the transition over to defense. And a solid, two-way player like that would've been invaluable to an expansion team.

Your first draft choice in Seattle – the number two overall pick of the 1976 draft – was Steve Niehaus, a 270-pound defensive tackle from Notre Dame. Big things were expected from him, but by 1979 Niehaus had been released and was out of pro football. Not a great first step in building an expansion team, was it?

JP: No, it wasn't. As a college lineman, Steve Niehaus was very good because he had size and extreme quickness. But he wasn't a very strong person, at least not strong enough to be an NFL lineman. He had amazingly small hands. Whatever the scouts saw in Steve, none of it ever showed up in training camp that summer.

Did you have a strong influence in the selection of Niehaus, considering it was your first draft as a head coach? Did you feel he was the player who would help the Seahawks the most?

JP: Yes, but I really had to lean heavily on our scouting department and trust their judgment. That was their function and it wasn't like they were brand new to the profession. We had veteran scouts and we trusted them. The real "can't miss" player from the '76 draft was Lee Roy Selmon from Oklahoma. Selmon was clearly the better player, but there was supposedly nothing wrong with taking Steve Niehaus either.

Niehaus was a first-team All-American in college. There's no question that a team drafting behind us like San Diego, Cleveland or Chicago would have grabbed him. But after Niehaus joined the team I was just amazed at his lack of physical strength and his small hands. And for being 270, he played kinda light and got banged around in there. It didn't seem like this was the same guy that was described in the scouting reports. I was disappointed in how Niehaus turned out. Had he been drafted by a team with a solid defensive line like Minnesota, he probably wouldn't have made it through that first training camp.

Another player who showed up at your first training camp was cornerback Dave Brown, the Steelers' top draft pick in 1975. Brown turned out to be one of your great success stories in Seattle.

JP: Dave was probably our best defensive back during my years there. The Steelers had left him unprotected in the expansion draft, simply because he was inexperienced. When he came to us he certainly didn't look like a first-round talent. In comparison, when we drafted Kenny Easley out of UCLA, you could watch him in training camp and immediately tell why he was a first-rounder. It was obvious. That wasn't true with Dave Brown. He had enough talent to make our ballclub, but it wasn't until three or four years later that he became a great player. That came simply through gaining experience.

Jack Patera Meets the Press

"Jack's greatest attribute as a coach was his innovation. What made the Seahawks successful relatively early was that Jack realized our shortcomings on talent and created ways to help us win – trick plays, fake field goals and punts, onside kicks in the second quarter, anything to catch our opponent off guard. We didn't get to nine wins by our third season of existence by simply running off-tackle and throwing to the tight end. It was exciting football, and we sold a lot of tickets in Seattle because of it.

"On the other hand, Jack's biggest failure was his inability to get along with the local media. I'm not talking behind Jack's back when I say this because he knows it's true. He didn't like the media and, as a result, the press was very, very tough on him. I felt it was a problem and from time to time we'd talk about it. I thought he was just making his job tougher by not cooperating with them. I guess he had good reasons for it, but I always felt he could have made life easier for himself as a new coach who was having a tough time winning football games.

"I remember one incident back in 1979 after a game against the Rams. We had only 48 yards of total offense that day. Jack walked into the press conference and sat down. The first question came out and he must not have liked it, so he said, "That's it," and got up and left. Georg Meyers, who was the sports editor for *The Seattle Times*, wrote a very funny column about it. He had his tape recorder running that day and timed the entire press conference at seven seconds."

- John Thompson, Seattle Seahawks general manager (1975-82)

How did Jim Zorn, an undrafted free agent from Cal Poly-Pomona, become the first starting quarterback of the Seattle Seahawks?

JP: Jim was a free agent when he came to us. He had been on some type of injured reserved list with the Cowboys in 1975, but they waived him after the season. The Rams wanted to sign him to add some depth to their quarterback situation. They were trying to hide Jim, stash him away so nobody else could sign him. Some of these "transactions" bordered right on the legal line. Our personnel man, Dick Mansperger, had previously been with Dallas and was aware of Jim's background and ability. Somehow our scouting department snuck in there and signed him. I guess we were able to convince him that his chances of playing in Seattle were much better than with the Rams. And they probably were.

Jim was the victim of a lot of coaching instability. He had two different coaches during his last two years in college. Then he went to Dallas and had a different coach. Then the Rams were working with him in their system. When he finally got to Seattle and worked with Jerry Rhome, it was the first time he had been with the same coach for more than a year. That really helped him develop.

Let me tell you a quick story about Jim. After he signed with us I took him out to dinner with my kids, who were teenagers at the time. He fit right in with them. I mean, clowning around, blowing bubbles in their drinks, acting silly. He even looked like a teenager. Sure, he was fun to have around but I thought, "Holy mackerel! *This* guy is going to quarterback my football team?" I never thought he was going to end up playing as well as he did. But once we got Jim out on the field, there was no doubt that he had talent.

To say that you were nervous about your quarterback situation going into 1976 must be a real understatement.

JP: We had twelve of them in camp that year. Zorn, Gary Keithley, Neil Graff, Steve Myer…there were so many of them. I thought that Graff was going to be the guy who'd eventually starting for us. Mechanically, he looked like the best. Myer had talent, too, and he knew the game very well. The competition was pretty tight and no one really stood out. But Zorn was the best athlete. He moved better than the other quarterbacks. He was also a very enthusiastic person. I guess it was Jim's ability to move around the pocket and create exciting plays that helped him eventually win the job.

Did you feel it was initially important to have a scrambler at quarterback, someone who could create with his feet as things began to break down?

JP: When selecting your quarterback, you don't think, "We'll choose this guy because he can get away." If the rest of the offense is doing things right, he shouldn't have to be scrambling all the time. We certainly wanted someone who could escape from trouble on his own, but we weren't interested in having our offense rely on random, schoolyard maneuverings when things fell apart.

Jerry Rhome, our offensive coordinator, put in designed rollouts and scrambles that would prevent our quarterbacks from sitting back there as pocket passers. We didn't have a real strong offensive line so we wanted to change things up regularly. On the other hand, leaving the pocket too early generally doesn't help a quarterback. There are patterns that take three or four seconds to develop and a discipline is required for that. If he finds himself concentrating on the rush, then he's probably not concentrating on reading the defense and throwing the ball accurately. So having a scrambler is both a blessing and a problem.

When Jim became our starter, we watched his style develop and sometimes we'd cringe on the sidelines. We felt that he'd become a better quarterback if he would just stand in there and throw rather than allowing himself to be flushed out at the first sign of perceived pressure. It was fun to watch but it wasn't the kind of effectiveness we were looking for. Jim's completion percentage was well under 50-percent in his early years. He threw more interceptions. He just did things that rookies did. Of course, as he matured and gained more experience, he learned to sit in the pocket. His completion percentage went up, his interceptions went down, and he had much more control of the football team.

Do you have a favorite Jim Zorn performance?

JP: I don't think Jim was ever more exciting than in our very first regular season game in 1976. We were playing at home against the Cardinals and Jim had the Kingdome in a frenzy. We were behind 23-3 in the third quarter and Jim started to bring us back. He threw for almost 300 yards and two touchdown passes, then ran one in himself. The game finally ended with Jim getting tackled on their 1-yard line, just short of the game-tying score. What a way to start the season! We thought, *Hey, we're a pretty good football team. We were just a little unlucky today.*

Another player who showed up at your first training camp eventually left Seattle as a Hall-of-Famer, and that was wide receiver Steve Largent.

JP: Steve was just fantastic. He'd been released by the Oilers and we picked him up. The first day he came to camp, he was head and shoulders above anybody we had. He ran excellent routes. Talk about a guy looking the ball into his hands! Steve never took his eye off the ball until he caught it. And he *never* dropped it. The way Steve could turn a defender around and get open was just amazing. I couldn't believe Houston would let him go. And with Largent joining the team, it also allowed us to get rid of a guy who was a potential troublemaker.

Who was that?

JP: Ahmad Rashad, an extremely talented receiver we had signed from the Bills as a free agent. But soon it became clear he wasn't going to work out for us in Seattle. He had shortcomings we weren't too happy with, so we ended up trading him to Minnesota.

What kind of shortcomings?

JP: Well, Rashad was coming off a knee injury when we signed him. I guess that was causing him to break all of his patterns short. If it was supposed to be a 17-yard comeback, he'd turn around at 14. A 10-yard pattern he'd break off at 7. Now this was an expansion group of players we had, so it was tremendously important that we had discipline on the squad. We couldn't afford to have internal strife and divisions on the team. But "Ahk-mahd," as I call him, would get into arguments with Jerry Rhome over how things should be done. We just couldn't have that, so we made the decision to trade him.

When you finally wrapped up that first training camp in the summer of '76, did the regular season bring a sense of impending doom or did you expect to field a competitive team?

JP: As a coach you have to be an optimist. I thought we might be able to win quite a few games. But I often joked with our general manager after that first season. I'd tell him, "I thought we'd be 12-2 instead of 2-12. I just got the numbers turned around." Maybe if I'd been a head coach before I took the Seattle job, I might have looked at things with more of a jaundiced eye and not been so enthusiastic. But I always felt if you tried hard and did all the right things, you probably have more than just a chance. But, realistically, as an expansion team you have to get lucky and surprise some folks.

Your Seahawks of the late 1970s were into the wacky stuff on offense – option plays and double reverses and passes out of field goal formation. It generated a kind of excitement that we really haven't seen in the NFL since. Did that offensive mentality evolve from a survival mentality due to your overall lack of overall talent on the team?

JP: As a player in Baltimore I was always fooling around with trick plays, scratching down things on paper to show my coaches, looking ways to be creative on special teams. When I was playing for the Colts, I used to return kickoffs in practice against our coverage team. One day Lenny Moore and I were back waiting to return a kick. I told him, "Lenny, you sneak up the opposite side of the field that I return it to, but stay behind me. I'll throw the ball back to you." Well, the play worked perfectly for a touchdown. Everyone was laughing and having a good time with it. [Coach] Weeb Ewbank liked the play so much that we ran it against the Rams and it worked. After the game, the writers asked Weeb where the play came from. He said, "Well, I was sitting on the toilet and it came to me, so I decided to put it in." I said, "Weeb, give me a little credit, will ya?"

My football philosophy was simple – to be solid both offensively and defensively. In Seattle I ended up with a team that could move the ball pretty well but couldn't stop anybody. We would put the ball in the endzone, but it was a matter of time before the other team scored on us. So I figured that to win more ball games we would simply have to gamble more.

If we ran any kind of trick play on offense – a reverse or a statue-of-liberty play – that was Jerry Rhome's call. The ones we ran on special teams were called by me. All those crazy calls you saw out there on kickoffs and punts and field goals were my idea. But they were well scouted, believe me. We didn't call them on a whim. If we threw out of a field goal formation, it was only when the other team lined up a certain way and rushed the same people. If we tried an onside kick, normally it was because one of their front line tackles was turning and leaving too quickly.

It was a lot of fun to run those plays, but we weren't doing them for kicks. We were trying to win. I didn't want to run the same basic plays over and over and lose 14 times. Of course, after five years on the job we still found ourselves having to run them, which meant we weren't as solid as we should've been.

A little bad blood once developed between you and former New York Jets coach Walt Michaels over one of your trick plays. What happened?

JP: I don't know what caused it. Maybe he just didn't like me personally or was frustrated because we had beaten them five straight times. But I'll tell ya, Michaels sure was grumpy whenever I was around him. We were playing the Jets in 1981 and we had put in a play where our punter, Jeff West, was going to throw to Ken Easley, who was on our punt coverage team. We noted on film that New York had a bad habit of letting their cover men get downfield too far on punts, so we wanted to take advantage of that. Normally, I would punt the ball early in the game, just to see if the Jets were still doing what we saw on film. We had a 4th-and-seven on our first series so I said, "Hell, let's just go for it. Take 'em by surprise."

Well, it didn't work. The Jets covered Easley and the pass was incomplete. As the players were coming off the field, I looked over at Walt and he was shaking his fist or giving me the finger or something, like he was saying, *This is gonna be it, buddy*! He was really hot. Well, we ended up beating New York anyway, with our second-string quarterback. [Laughing] I never did lose a game to Walt Michaels.

Very few NFL teams could say they had the Oakland Raiders' number in the 1970s but your team certainly did. Seattle beat the Raiders four straight times between 1978 and '79. What was your secret to stopping that veteran Oakland team?

JP: I don't think anyone can answer that question. We got 'em a couple of times on fake field goals. We beat them once on a long field goal from Efren Herrera. We just seemed to rise to the occasion whenever we played Oakland. The same was true when we played the Jets. I really don't have a good, logical answer to that question.

A Wild Monday Night in Atlanta

The public is not going to be denied the type of entertainment witnessed last night by the national television audience hunkered in front of their lobotomy boxes for the first-ever Monday Night Football appearance by Patera's Pigeons.

...[Seattle] came from 14 points down to win it with some of the most audacious football strategy ever... They saw blocked punts, faked field goals, fourth-down gambles that produced incredible joy and instant despair.

- John Owen, *Seattle Post-Intelligencer*, October 30, 1979

One team that presented major problems for you in the AFC West was San Diego, with its vaunted "Air Coryell" attack. From 1978-81, you beat them only once in eight tries.

JP: The Chargers offense was very simple, actually, but we couldn't stop it. Going against all the offensive firepower on that team, you had to counter with some serious talent on defense and we didn't have that kind of personnel. Blitzing put us into one-on-one matchups that we weren't going to win.

There was no doubt about what San Diego was going to do – throw it into a double zone and keep sending Kellen Winslow downfield to wear out your linebackers. We'd try to take away their wide receivers, but Dan Fouts was no dummy. He read the defenses very well. We tried every kind of coverage and rush scheme imaginable, but nothing really ever worked. It got so desperate that I resorted to complaining to the officials all game long, trying to squeeze a break out of them. It came down to that.

Is there one player that you regret not selecting in the draft, somebody that you still pinch yourself over not having on your team?

JP: Oh yes. It was back in 1981, and the player was Lawrence Taylor from North Carolina. We had the fourth pick in the draft that year, and almost to a man our staff wanted Kenny Easley, a defensive back from UCLA. They all agreed that Taylor was a tremendous talent, but there were some other things they had some reservations about. They wanted a solid person, the cleanest guy available, so Easley had jumped to the top of our list.

I had gone down to San Francisco to watch practice for the annual East-West game, and I was standing on the sideline with [Vikings' Director of Football Operations] Jerry Reichow, waiting for the teams to come out. We were talking and all of a sudden this Lawrence Taylor comes out and starts doing his thing on the field. I said, "Holy Mackerel! This guy looks better live than he does on film. *I love him already!*" He was truly the greatest player I had ever seen. Jerry looked at me and said, "Yeah, but you'll be lucky to get him."

Well, draft day came and New York picked Taylor at number two. I guess the Giants prevented me from making the biggest mistake of my career. I say that because had Taylor still been available, my staff still would have talked me into taking Easley. And I would have regretted that forever.

Who was your most difficult roster cut?

JP: There's no one that stands out for me. Cutting a player is the hardest job for a coach to do, and I don't know a coach who will disagree with me. You like many of the players that have to let go. You're telling them their careers are over, that they're not good enough anymore.

If I had to pick one guy who was the hardest for me to cut, I would say Nick Bebout. Nick was a big offensive tackle from Wyoming who was with me from that first expansion season. He was a guy that you just liked to have around the team. Great enthusiasm, worked as hard as he could, gave his best effort. All the players liked him. He just didn't quite have the talent that we were looking for to build a real good offensive line. After we released him going into the 1980 season, I knew we had made a mistake. We should have kept Nick around for one more year instead of going with a rookie [OT Andre Hines], who we thought had more talent and would eventually develop for us.

I remember during our first season we had the team autograph a bunch of footballs that were going to be donated to charities and auctioned off. And every club that I was ever with, there was always some smart guy that would write "Batman and Robin" or "Tarzan" or "Harry Houdini" or something. So I gave the team my little talk and said, "Hey, these footballs are going to a good cause. I don't want to see any goofy names on these balls. If you can't write your name or don't know how to spell it, just put an X."

Later I was up in my office and there was a knock at the door. It was Nick, and he was standing there with his hand behind his back. He said, "Coach, can I come in and see you?"

I said, "Sure, come on in."

He said, "The players really appreciate what you've done for us as a coach, and we'd like to give you a little something as a token of our appreciation." Then he hands me this football with 47 X's on it!

During the 1980 and '81 seasons the Seahawks went 4-12 and 6-10, respectively. Then in '82 the team started out 0-2 before the league was hit by a players strike. It was during that strike period that you were fired as head coach. What are your feelings today about your departure from Seattle?

JP: We had a slow start and ownership thought it was best to fire both me and John Thompson. Based on our record, it was one of those things you could have seen coming. But I never dreamed I would be fired during the season. I kept thinking, *Why now? Why do it during a strike? Give me a chance to turn things around.*

I was so disenchanted. And I was absolutely floored they let Thompson go. I can understand them wanting to change coaches, but firing John Thompson? He had done a tremendous job for the Seahawks. He had made the team very profitable in a short period of time, paid off all the debt, and did all the things a general manager was supposed to do. The whole time I thought, *What a mistake they're making.*

But by that point I needed a break from football. I didn't want to take another coaching job unless I had complete control of the football side. Something like, "Jack, we know you're another Mike Holmgren. Here is all you need to be successful. Go run the team." I would've taken that kind of job. But that didn't happen, so I decided to step back and see what else I could do.

Of course, I found out that I couldn't do anything else. If I wanted to be gainfully employed, I would have to get back into coaching. I wasn't ready to do that. I'm still not. And I haven't coached a day since.

Index

Esiason: Boomer, 77
Evans: Norm, 127, 135
Everett: Jim, 86
Ewbank: Weeb, 38, 295
Facenda: John, 99, 100, 101, 104, 105, 106, 173, 174
Fagan: Kevin, 51
Fairbanks: Chuck, 127, 134, 221, 222, 223, 229, 232, 237, 238
Faison: Earl, 271
Favre: Brett, 52, 77, 281
Feagles: Jeff, 239
Federspiel: Joe, 125
Ferguson: Bob, 3; Joe, 258
Fernandez: Manny, 128, 131, 137
Ferragamo: Vince, 43, 84, 85, 86, 93, 94, 149
Fields: Totie, 142
Finnie: Roger, 189, 194, 196
Finnin: Tom, 287
Fisher: Eddie, 145; Pat, 200, 251
Fleming: Marv, 65
Flick: Tom, 204
Flowers: Rich, 141
Flutie: Doug, 14
Foley: Steve, 272
Ford: Charley, 131
Foreman: Chuck, 64, 66, 86, 235, 252, 264, 292
Fortunato: Joe, 270
Foss: Joe, 19, 20, 276
Fouts: Dan, 23, 46, 47, 48, 72, 77, 94, 193, 203, 211, 212, 273, 297
Fox: Larry, 233; Tim, 234
Francis: Russ, 53, 55, 224, 225, 226, 231, 237, 279
Franklin: Bobby, 142
Frazier: Willie, 128
Frederickson: Tucker, 110
Fritsch: Toni, 31
Frontierre: Georgia, 43, 82
Frost: Robert, 241, 242
Fry: Willie, 15
Fugett: Jean, 291
Fuqua: Frenchy, 12, 60, 65, 66, 283
Gabriel: Roman, 85, 93, 116, 212, 251, 270
Gaddini: Rudy, 203, 204
Galbreath: Tony, 114, 118, 119
Garagiola: Joe, 284
Garner: Charlie, 240
Garrett: Carl, 227, 232
Garrison: Gary, 128, 130
Gary: Keith, 16

George: Jeff, 203
Gibbs: Joe, 90, 201, 202
Gibron: Abe, 49
Gibson: Bob, 111
Gifford: Frank, 108, 248, 255
Gilbert: Roy, 217
Gilliam: Joe, 9, 13, 69, 188, 260
Gillman: Sid, 21, 24, 25, 91, 108, 127, 129, 132, 204, 258, 267, 271
Ginn: Hubert, 126, 127
Glanville: Jerry, 21
Glickman: Marty, 184
Golic: Mike, 239
Golsteyn: Jerry, 272; Ralph, 203
Gonzalez: Tony, 53
Goode: Irv, 191
Gowdy: Curt, 49, 174, 180, 181, 182, 183, 184, 204, 223, 274, 275, 276, 279, 284, 285; Jerre, 285
Gradishar: Randy, 115, 272
Graff: Neil, 202, 294
Grant: Bud, 62, 135, 192, 200, 252, 270, 288, 289; Frank, 147
Gray: Ken, 191; Leon, 224, 225, 227, 236; Mel, 119, 146, 147, 189, 193, 197
Graziano: Rocky, 142
Green: Hugh, 273
Greene: Joe, 2, 8, 11, 19, 44, 66, 107, 135, 206, 207, 209, 211, 217, 234, 259, 260, 262, 265, 266, 269
Greenwood: L.C., 2, 5, 16, 70, 208, 234, 259
Gregory: Jack, 195, 196, 212
Gresham: Bob, 112
Griese: Bob, 57, 65, 126, 128, 131, 135, 136, 138, 175, 176, 182, 184, 186, 187, 197, 198, 265, 278
Griffin: Archie, 111; Don, 51
Grogan: Steve, 55, 67, 133, 223, 224, 225, 231, 233, 234, 238, 271
Grossfeld: Stan, 248
Grossman: Randy, 13, 16, 17, 56, 261, 267
Grove: Bill, 274
Gruden: John, 272
Haden: Pat, 85, 93, 94, 117, 253
Hadl: John, 26, 31, 85, 93, 127, 128, 203, 258, 266
Halas: George, 110, 292

Haley: Charles, 51, 239; Dick, 6, 14, 15
Hall: Willie, 64, 240
Ham: Jack, 2, 10, 11, 16, 57, 78, 234, 258, 259, 263, 267
Hamilton: Ray, 222, 225, 226, 230
Hanburger: Chris, 200
Hanifan: Jim, 193, 196, 201
Hannah: John, 55, 224, 225, 227, 236
Hanratty: Terry, 9, 13
Hardman: Cedric, 120, 206, 207, 209, 211, 212, 213, 214
Harper: Willie, 216
Harrah: Dennis, 89, 91
Harris: Bo, 90; Cliff, 92, 139, 140, 142, 147, 148, 155, 200, 249; Franco, 2, 12, 13, 16, 17, 55, 60, 61, 65, 66, 67, 86, 107, 133, 155, 234, 235, 279, 282, 283; Ike, 197, 198; James, 77, 85, 93, 94, 206, 234; Leroy, 137
Harrison: Reggie, 279
Hart: Jim, 71, 119, 146, 188, 189, 192, 195, 197, 199, 200, 203, 206, 212, 216, 243, 251; Tommy, 120, 206, 216
Hartenstine: Mike, 249, 250
Havrilak: Sam, 86
Hawkins: Bill, 214
Hawthorne: Greg, 15, 16
Hayes: Bob, 115, 145, 246, 255; Lester, 258; Woody, 8
Haynes: Mike, 234, 258
Hebert: Bobby, 203
Hefferle: Ernie, 123
Heinrich: Don, 287
Hendricks: Ted, 60, 67, 73, 208, 278
Henning: Dan, 39
Herrera: Efren, 296
Herron: Mack, 222, 229, 230, 232, 233
Herzeg: Ladd, 22
Heston: Charlton, 106
Hilgenberg: Wally, 288, 292
Hilger: Rusty, 271
Hill: Kent, 91
Hines: Andre, 297
Hinton: Ed, 222
Hitchcock: Alfred, 103
Hogeboom: Gary, 47
Holland: John, 139, 140
Holloway: Bob, 189, 192

Photo Credits

About the Author

Tom Danyluk is a freelance writer with a passion for pro football and its history. He is a graduate of the University of Pittsburgh and Loyola College of Maryland. His weekly column, "The Pro Game," can be found at *ProFootballWeekly.com*.

Tom and his wife Melinda currently reside in downtown Chicago. This is his first book.

CPSIA information can be obtained at www.ICGtesting.com
Printed in the USA
LVOW10s1233190215

427543LV00002B/6/P